SPECIAL CATEGORY

The IRA in English Prisons
Vol.2: 1978–1985

Ruán O'Donnell
University of Limerick

IRISH ACADEMIC PRESS

First published in 2015 by Irish Academic Press
8 Chapel Lane
Sallins
Co. Kildare
Ireland

www.iap.ie

© 2015 Ruán O'Donnell

British Library Cataloguing-in-Publication Data
An entry can be found on request

978 0 7165 3301 6 (paper)
978 0 7165 3302 3 (cloth)
978 07165 3303 0 (PDF)
978 0 7165 3316 0 (epub)
978 0 7165 3317 7 (mobi)

Library of Congress Cataloging-in-Publication Data
An entry can be found on request

All rights reserved. Without limiting the rights under copyright reserved alone, no part of this publication may be reproduced, stored in or introduced into a retrieval system, or transmitted, in any form or by any means (electronic, mechanical, photocopying, recording or otherwise), without the prior written permission of both the copyright owner and the above publisher of this book.

Printed in Ireland by Sprintprint Ltd.

Contents

Acknowledgements

I acknowledge and greatly appreciate the generous assistance of Eddie O'Neill, Ann O'Sullivan, Siobhan Maguire, Mairin Shiels, Eila Moloney, Liam McCotter, John McComb, Jimmy Ashe and Con McFadden. Documentation and support was received from Eileen Shiels, Jackie Kaye, Maureen Maguire, Mairin Higgins, Billy Armstrong, Leo Wilson (RIP), *An tAthair* Piaras O Duill, Colm Moore, Gerry Cunningham, Seamus Ó Mathuna, Tomas O'Malley, Gerry Kelly, Mary Pearson, Aly Renwick, Jim McDonald, Kevin Dunphy, Pat Magee, Ronnie McCartney, Ella O'Dwyer, John McCluskey, Pat Hackett, John McCann, Deirdre O'Shea, Eddie and Rose Caughey, Tony Clarke, Eamon Nolan, Gerry McDonnell, Eddie Butler, Damian McComb, Labhras O Donnghaille, Jim Monaghan, Rose Dugdale, Deasun O Longain, Charlie Cunningham, John Fogarty (RIP), Paddy Ryan (RIP), Sean Smyth, Kathleen Horne (nee Doyle), Wally Heaton, Roy Walsh, Mary Walsh (RIP), Eoin Dougan, Irene McDonnell Cahill, Jack Cahill, Tony Coughlan, Muriel Sadlear, Anne Marie Whitaker and the staffs of the Linen Hall Library (Belfast), Cardinal Tomas O Fiaich Library (Armagh), Sinn Féin/Coiste na Iarchimini Archive (Dublin), National Archives of Ireland (Dublin), National Archives (London), Public Record Office of Northern Ireland (Belfast), Tamiment Library, (New York University), Glucksman University of Limerick Library, University of Villanova Library (Special Collections) and Hesburgh Library (University of Notre Dame, Indiana).

This series was otherwise aided by Criostoir de Baroid (Ciste Ceant Dunlaoi Teoranta, Corcaigh), Lisa Hyde, Jonathan Scherbel-Ball, Jim and Geraldine Donnelly, Fionntan McCotter, Jim Smyth, Marcas McCionnaigh, Sonja Tiernan, Glenn Rosswurm, Muiris O'Meara (RIP), Chris Fox, Seamus Ashe, Micheal O hAodha, Padraig Óg O Ruairc, John O'Callaghan, Adrian Cormican, Paul Hayes, John Mulqueen, Finbar Cullen, Brian McNally, Gay Clery, Shay Courtney (RIP), Mary Courtney, Geraldine Crawford, Leo Cooper (RIP), Rab Hunter, Charlie Cunningham, Geraldine Bailey, Paul Holmes, Gerry Mac Lochlainn, Ann Rossiter, Joe McKenny (RIP), Paul Norney, Hugh and Winnie Doherty, Joe and Mary Jamison, Rab Fryers, Gerry Mac Lochlainn, Francie Broderick, Aodh O'Lunney, Jack Kilroy, Mike Carty, Owen Rodgers, Jim Panaro, Norman Breslin, Charlie Rice (RIP), Jeff Leddin, Sean McKillen, Ger Maher, Gearoid Phelan, Sean O

Murchada, Joe O'Hara, John Logan, John O'Brennan, Charles Caulfield, John O'Connor, Seamus Ashe, Nicky Cuddihy, Briona Nic Dhiarmada, Maire Durack, Jim Cullen, Mick Nolan, Conor Duffy, Catherine Kelly, Lorcan Collins, Rita O'Hare, Pat Doherty, David Yaffe, Bruce Sillner, Tam Brawley, Kathleen Dowley, Patrick Miller, David Granville, Gary O'Reilly, Charlene Vizzacherro, Joe Lennon, Lorcan Collins and Mary Elizebeth Bartholomew. Special thanks to all those who agreed to be interviewed and who entered into correspondence. As always, thanks to Maeve, Ruairi, Fiachra, Cormac and Saoirse O'Donnell.

Ruán O'Donnell
May 2015

Glossary

Activist: Person who directly engages in political campaigns

Active Service Unit: Cadre of IRA personnel

Adjudication: Disciplinary process in the Dispersal System

Adjutant-General: Second in command of the IRA

Allocation: Induction period following sentencing ahead of dispatch to main Dispersal System prison in England and Wales

An Cumann Cabhrach: Republican prisoners charity organization

Angry Brigade: Term applied to coterie of English, Irish, Scottish and Welsh anarchists in 1970s' Britain

Anti-Internment League: Coalition of non-violent political organizations opposed to internment without trial in Ireland from August 1971

Ard Chomhairle: Ruling body of Sinn Féin

Ard Fheis: Convention of Sinn Féin

Armley: Prison in Leeds

Army Council: Seven-person ruling body of the IRA

Army Executive: Twelve-person committee of the IRA under the Army Council

Association: Time permitted daily to prisoners for social and educational purposes

Association for Legal Justice: Civilian watchdog organization focussing on abuses of civil liberties in Ireland and the UK

Banged Up: Locked in a cell

Belfast Ten: Persons tried for March 1973 IRA attacks in London. Supported by the Belfast Ten Defence Committee, a legal and non-violent group with links to the Republican Movement

Birmingham Six: Persons wrongly convicted of November 1974 IRA attacks in Birmingham

Blanked: A prisoner ostracized by others

Blanket Protest: Wearing blankets or towels instead of prison uniform

Block: Section of a prison

Board of Visitors (BV): Prison committee dealing with disciplinary and general matters (aka Visiting Committee)

Bomb Squad: Police section dealing with subversive offences

Cabhair: Republican prisoners charity

Category A: Prisoners bearing the highest level of security rating in England and Wales.

CCDC: Central Citizens Defence Committee

Chief of Staff: Head of the IRA

Chiv: Improvised bladed or pointed weapon

Circle: Part of prison offering access between wings

Circuit: Frequent prison moves

Citizen Defence Committee: Unaligned civilian grouping in Belfast and Derry which organized local defence of nationalist communities from 1969

Clann na hÉireann: Legal political organization representing the official republican movement in Britain

Clan na Gael: North American pro-republican organization

Closed Visit: A prison meeting in which family and friends are denied physical contact with the prisoner

Colour Party: Organized flag-carrying element of a republican march

Comm/ Communication: Slang for smuggled written information passed between republicans

Con/ Convict: Sentenced prisoner

Control Unit: Experimental segregation wings in Wakefield and Wormwood Scrubs

Connolly Association: Legal, non-violent, left wing, political organization of the Irish in Britain and their local allies

Cooler: Twenty-eight day period in segregation, generally involving prison shift

Coventry Six: Persons charged in connection with IRA activities in the British Midlands

CPGB: Communist Party of Great Britain

CPI: Communist Party of Ireland

Cumann/ Cumainn: Organized unit/s of Sinn Féin

Cumann na mBan: Illegal female IRA auxiliary organization

Dáil Éireann: Irish parliament in Dublin; the Dáil/Seanad (Leinster House)

Democratic Unionist Party: A unionist political party in the Six Counties from 1971

Department of Foreign Affairs: Irish civil service department dealing with Anglo-Irish relations et al

Diplock Court: Jury-less court in Belfast used to try political offences

Director of Engineering: IRA GHQ position responsible for explosives and heavy weaponry

Director of Intelligence: IRA GHQ position regarding intelligence and counter-intelligence

'Dirty Protest': Pejorative British term for an IRA/ INLA prisoner's non-cooperation with maintenance of cell sanitation, termed 'no wash protest' by republicans

Dispersal System: Network of maximum-security prisons in England where Category A inmates were accommodated under the Mountbatten Report recommendations

DPP: Director of Public Prosecutions

ECHR: European Convention on Human Rights (Strasbourg)

E(scape) List: Term for prisoners subjected to additional security practices owing to their perceived potential for success

Fenian: Member of Irish Republican Brotherhood (Ireland, United Kingdom, France, Australasia) or Fenian Brotherhood (aka Clan na Gael: United States of America/ Canada); illegal, republican, revolutionary organization superseded by the IRA

Fianna Fáil: Political party in the Republic of Ireland

Fitted up: Framed

FCA: Forsa Cosanta Áitiúil, part time and reserve element of Irish Defence Forces (Army); later 'Reserves'

FCO: Foreign and Commonwealth Office (United Kingdom)

Fine Gael: Political party in the Republic of Ireland

Free State: Pejorative term for post-partition Republic of Ireland

F Wing: Former Control Unit of Wakefield prison

Gardaí: An Garda Síochana; Irish police

GHQ: IRA term for General Headquarters (Dublin) comprising various specialised Departments of the Republican Movement

Ghosting: Unexpected prison move; also 'ghosted', 'Shanghaied'

Going behind the door: Voluntary segregation under Rule 43

Good Order and Discipline: Rationale for a governor imposing Rule 43

Governor: Chief administrator of a prison

Grass: Informer

Green Cross: Republican prisoners charity

Guildford Four: Persons wrongly convicted of IRA attacks in England

H-Blocks: Modular prison complex built at Long Kesh, County Antrim (aka Maze prison)

HMP: Her Majesty's Prison

Hooch: Homemade alcohol

Home Office: Administrative body comprising the Prison Department and other state agencies in England and Wales

International Marxist Group: Trotskyite political grouping in Britain

International Socialists: Left wing political grouping in Britain linked

Irish National Caucus: Washington DC-based Irish lobbying group

Irish National Liberation Army: Illegal, republican, socialist, paramilitary organization linked to the IRSP

IPHC: Irish Political Hostages Campaign

Irish Republican Army: Illegal, republican, paramilitary organization (proscribed in Britain in November 1974); armed element of the Republican Movement (aka Óglaigh na hÉireann)

Irish Republican Socialist Party: Legal, left wing, socialist, republican party linked to the INLA

ITGWU: Irish Transport and General Workers' Union

Joint Action Committee: Coalition of prisoners rights' groupings

Lie-down: See 'Cooler'

Lifer: Prisoner serving a life sentence

Liquid Cosh: Dosing of prisoners with tranquilizing pharmaceuticals

Long Kesh: County Antrim site of internment and prison camp

Long War: Conflict in Ireland, c. 1968-98

Loyalist: Term for pro-British paramilitaries, specifically members of the generally illegal Ulster Volunteer Force, Ulster Defence Association and Red Hand Commandoes; may denote persons who support maintaining legislative union with Great Britain by non-violent methods

Maguire Seven: Persons wrongly convicted of assisting the IRA in England

MO: Medical Officer

MOD: Ministry of Defence

MP: Member of Parliament (Westminster)

MI5: British intelligence organization

MI6: British intelligence organization

MUFTI: Minimum Use of Force (and) Tactical Intervention, squad of staff officers deployed to counter perceived incidents of prisoner indiscipline

Mutiny: Term for participation in a prison riot and lesser infractions

Na Fianna Éireann: Republican scouting organization

Nationalist: Supporter of non-violent achievement of Irish reunification

NCCL: National Council for Civil Liberties (United Kingdom)

National Graves Association: Voluntary organization tasked with building and maintaining republican memorials

National Front: Right wing political organization in Britain

NICRA: Northern Ireland Civil Rights Association, non-violent civil liberties organization founded in 1967

NIO: Northern Ireland Office

NORAID: Term applied to the pro-Republican Movement Irish Northern Aid organization in the USA

No Wash: See 'Dirty Protest' [sic]

Nutted off: See 'Sectioned'

O/C: Term for IRA leader (Officer Commanding) of a unit or grouping

Official IRA: Illegal, left wing, republican, paramilitary organization linked to Official Sinn Féin (later The Workers Party)

Official Republican Movement: Collective term for the Official IRA, Official Sinn Féin, Official Na Fianna Éireann and allied republican groups following the 1969/1970 split. Does not denote automatic support for specific or illegal elements

Old Bailey: Central Criminal Court, London

Open Visit: A prison meeting in which family and friends are permitted limited physical contact with the prisoner

People's Democracy: Left wing political grouping founded in Ireland in 1968 which supported non-violent civil rights agitation

Placed on report: A prisoner accused of an infraction of regulations

POW: Prisoner of War

Prevention of Terrorism Act: UK special powers legislation introduced in November 1974

PRINDUS: Prison industrial schemes employing inmates

Principal Officer: Senior prison staff officer

Prisoners Aid Committee: Legal body which supported republican prisoners

Prison Department: Constituent of the Home Office responsible for administration of prisons in England and Wales (aka Prison Service)

Preservation of the Rights of Prisoners: The National Prisoners Movement (Britain)

Provisionals: See Irish Republican Army (aka 'Provos')

Provisional Category A: Prison Department term for remand prisoners expected to be classified Category A if convicted

Quartermaster General: IRA GHQ position regarding armaments and munitions

Reception: Area of prison from which newly arrived inmates are processed

Recess: Area of prison with running water facilities

Remand: Term for prisoners who have been charged but untried whether released on bail or held in custody

Republican: Person who supports the establishment of a democratic unitary republic but not necessarily violent or illegal methods to achieve the objective

Republican Clubs: Pre-split Sinn Féin in the North of Ireland and post-split Official Sinn Féin in North America

Republican Movement: Collective term for the IRA, Cumann na mBan, Sinn Féin, National Graves Association, republican youth and marching bands which emerged from the 1969/1970 split. Does not denote automatic support for specific or illegal elements

Royal Ulster Constabulary: Armed police force in the Six Counties in 1970s

Rule 43: Regulation regarding segregation of a prisoner from general population

Saor Eire: Historic name used by separate Dublin and Cork ultra left revolutionary organizations in 1970s

Sectioned: Slang term for committal to a psychiatric prison wing or institution under the Mental Health Act

Security Officer: Prison officer with security specialization

Segregation Unit: Area of prison used for solitary confinement

Scéal: Irish for 'story', i.e. news.

Scotland Yard: Headquarters of the London Metropolitan Police

Screw: Slang for prison officer

Shank: See 'Chiv'

Sinn Féin: Legal republican political party supporting the objectives of the IRA. 'Official' prefix denotes affiliation with pre-December 1969 Republican Movement. 'Provisional' prefix indicates association with breakaway Republican Movement. Generally used in relation to the non 'Official' party from the mid-1970s

Six Counties: Northern Ireland (aka the 'North'/ 'Ulster'/ the 'Province' [sic])

Slopping Out: Emptying portable toilet receptacles

Social Democratic and Labour Party: Moderate nationalist party in the Six Counties from 1970

Special Branch: Detective units dealing with political offences

Special Category A: Unofficial term for IRA prisoner in England (aka 'Irish Category A')

Special Criminal Court: Juryless court in Dublin used to try political offences

Special Secure Unit/ Block: A small cellblock area or building for long-term segregation of prisoners

Split: Schism within the IRA in December 1969 and Sinn Féin in January 1970 creating rival Provisional and Official Republican Movements

Spring: External assistance in a prison escape

Spin: Cell search

Spur: A small section of a wing

Stiff: Written message or letter smuggled out of prison

Stormont: Devolved regional assembly outside Belfast administering the Six Counties (prorogued in 1972)

Strangeways: Manchester prison

Strip cells: Spartan cells for temporary confinement of prisoners

Strongbox: Double-gated small cells used for punishment

Submarine: Leicester Special Unit

Sunningdale: Failed power-sharing initiative in the Six Counties which excluded the Republican Movement and Loyalists in 1973-4

Supergrass: Person who gives evidence in court against multiple former associates

Swapping: Replacement of an IRA prisoner with another in a wing or prison

Sympathizer: Person supportive of the general aims of a political organization

Tanáiste: Irish Deputy Prime Minister

Taoiseach: Irish Prime Minister

Tariff: The minimum number of years to be served of a sentence

Tossed: See 'spin'

Tout: Slang for informer

Troops Out Movement: British non-violent, pro-republican campaigning organization

Twenty-Six Counties: Republic of Ireland (aka the 'South' [sic])

Ulster Defence Association: Loyalist paramilitary organization (aka Ulster Freedom Fighters)

Unaligned: Activist who endeavours to support the objectives of a political organization or grouping to which they do not belong

Uninvolved: Person of no political connection

UK: United Kingdom of Great Britain (England, Scotland and Wales) and Northern Ireland

Ulster Volunteer Force: Illegal Loyalist paramilitary organization

Uxbridge Eight: An IRA unit in London

Verbals: Interview notes concocted by police (aka 'verballed' and 'verballing')

Visiting Order: Document authorizing prison visits

Volunteer: Member of the IRA or INLA

Walton: Liverpool prison

Westminster: British imperial parliament in London; House of Commons/House of Lords

Wing: Section of a prison

Winson Green: Birmingham prison

Young Prisoner: Prisoner under 21 years of age

Introduction

By the late 1970s it was evident that Irish Republican Army members would continue to accumulate in the prisons of Ireland and England. This was a direct result of the violent conflict in the North of Ireland which displayed no signs of short-term abatement. The most deadly, extensive and persistent insurgency in Western Europe after the Second World War seemed interminable. Neither the IRA nor the British Government credibly reaffirmed rival and incompatible predictions of imminent military victory. The leading Belfast republican Gerry Adams used the prescient phrase 'long war' to describe ongoing events in September 1976, when his pamphlet, *Peace in Ireland? A broad analysis of the present situation* was released into what State censorship rendered a select group of avid supporters within Sinn Féin's private distribution net, mortal enemies who monitored such communications, and persons capable of vicarious access. Written in the penal compounds of Long Kesh, County Antrim, under author-noted 'prison restrictions', Adams argued that the underlying causes of the late-twentieth century variant of the perennial Anglo-Irish crisis encompassed a British imperialist interest in Ireland as well as an untenable reactionary mentality in the Twenty-Six County Establishment in Dublin.[1]

Covert British strategists, meanwhile, manoeuvred night and day to defeat the IRA using a combination of greatly enhanced intelligence gathered since the 'ceasefire' of 1974–75 and focused responses to the republican challenge. Tactics included assassination of known opposing activists by Special Forces supplemented by malleable pro-Unionist 'death squads', who aimed to intimidate prospective republican supporters by seemingly random killings of socially ambitious nationalists. Others were simultaneously and indiscriminately shot and bombed in an apparent bid to induce paranoia, inertia and communal distress, in tandem with generally unsuccessful efforts to provoke republicans into diverting their scant resources towards politically compromising acts of retaliation. Severe interrogation of detained IRA suspects complemented the utility of 'special legislation' which not only generated greater numbers of confession-predicted convictions in the total absence of physical evidence, but also imposed maximal psychological pressure on those held for up to seven days. Republicans referred to this crudely effective process as the 'conveyor belt'. Persons convicted by juryless 'Diplock' courts in Belfast were pitched into the ultra-modern 'H-Blocks' where, from March 1976, former benefits of 'political status' were not extended.[2]

Armed IRA activity in Britain was confined by tradition and *modus operandi* to the territory of England where analogous forms of counter-insurgency were rarely, if ever, applicable. Explosions and shootings in England provided greater publicity and international reportage than the far more frequent and deadly attacks in the North of Ireland. This incentivised the Republican Movement to provide the logistics necessary to underwrite hazardous activity in England. If the highly trained British Military reinforcements deployed to the North of Ireland in August 1969 could not defeat the IRA, it was equally clear in 1978 that republicans waging unilateral and illegal 'armed struggle' would not triumph by the intensity of their insurgency alone. 'Operation Banner' proved to be the longest and one of the least decisive campaigns in the history of the British Army, a professional North Atlantic Treaty Organization constituent that had waged wars across the globe. In seeking to widen the political discussion, Adams addressed the fluctuating republican campaign in England from various perspectives:

> IRA violence has spilled over into England … many people have died or been seriously injured as a result. This recent overspill fits the pattern which has evolved over the decades. English people should be interested in what their country's army is doing in Ireland. Sadly, this interest has only come when the problem has involved them directly … British soldiers are dying on Irish streets and there are periodic bombings in England itself. Two Irishmen, Michael Gaughan and Frank Stagg, have died on hunger strike within the last two years, in English gaols, and Irishmen and women are still being brutalized in prisons in England.[3]

He claimed that 'revolutionary violence' should be 'controlled and disciplined'; a strategic caution which, he implied, included an IRA front in England alongside far-sighted ambitions to mobilize progressive allies in Britain.[4] The mid-term objective of evolving a variant of 'armed struggle' in England, however, was complicated by the Prevention of Terrorism Act (PTA), which simplified the harassment of legal pro-republicans, as well as anti-war advocates in Britain. During the heyday of the PTA, the most tenuous UK-located population were Irish-born permanent residents and migrants who comprised Britain's main 'foreign' population. Entitled by birth to 'British' passports if born on the island of Ireland prior to the declaration of the Republic of Ireland in 1949, all who eschewed this option still availed of reciprocal rights to free travel between the neighbouring islands. Introduced by the Labour Government in November 1974 amid the furore ignited by the IRA's unintentional infliction of heavy civilian casualties in Birmingham, the draconian PTA had been prepared by the previous Conservative administration and was primed for promulgation whenever the republican campaign in England attained momentum.[5] At this crucial and parliamentary moment, following the October 1974 casualties sustained in bomb attacks on 'soldiers pubs' in Guildford and Woolwich, the British public were not advised that the PTA contingency was inherently discriminatory and of limited value in apprehending IRA ASUs.

Upper echelons of the British Military, contrary to vacuous assertions of imminent victory over the IRA by Roy Mason, knew the Republican Movement was too embedded in Irish communities to be readily destroyed. This was the assessment of a secret dossier entitled 'Northern Ireland: Future Terrorist Trends' complied by Brigadier James Glover of the Ministry of Defence's Intelligence Staff on 2 November 1978. Under unusual circumstances, the IRA obtained a copy from an unoccupied vehicle and published it in full in *An Phoblacht* on 10 May 1979. Brigadier Glover claimed that having adopted a more functional cellular structure in the course of 1977, 'The Provisional IRA (PIRA) has the dedication and the sinews of war to raise violence intermittently to at least the level of early 1978, certainly for the foreseeable future'.[6] While Glover's possibly disingenuous overview expressly excluded consideration of IRA attacks in Britain, which had garnered disproportionate media attention since the 1920s, it was implicit that such operations would continue. Further prison losses in England were consequently assured, even though it was obvious that many IRA Volunteers temporarily active in the country were never arrested. The MOD document recognized that the IRA leadership intended to maintain attacks until Britain made a 'declaration of intent ... to withdraw from Northern Ireland' and had instituted 'an amnesty for all "political" prisoners, including the release of all PIRA prisoners in goal on the mainland [sic]'.[7]

The Dispersal System

Sentenced and remanded prisoners in the common jurisdiction of England and Wales were held in accordance with policies developed by the Mountbatten Committee in 1966, and revised by an expert panel headed by Sir Leon Radzinowicz in 1968. This entailed the segregation of prisoners deemed a danger to the public within the 'Dispersal System' of maximum-security prisons. From 1970, the network included Gartree, Long Lartin, Wakefield, Hull, Parkhurst, Albany and D Wing of Wormwood Scrubs. Prisoners were also allocated to the Special Security Units (aka 'Blocks') of Leicester and Parkhurst and, if undergoing punitive segregation, F Wing of Wakefield. H-Wing in Durham was used for actual and presumed female IRA prisoners, the only facility deemed suitable for sentenced Category A women in England. Most Irish republicans had previously been remanded in custody ahead of trial in Brixton and Wandsworth in London or, if detained in the Midlands or North of England, Walton in Liverpool and Winson

Green in Birmingham.[8] Whereas the notorious Control Unit in Wakefield was remodelled following a liberal backlash in 1974 as 'F Wing', the retention of 'Special Wings' repudiated the humane dimension to the *Mountbatten Report* and resulted in the use of the two modern SSUs in Parkhurst and Leicester. Maximum-security detached 'prisons within prisons' were largely preserved owing to the presence of IRA personnel in England. Penologists Roy D. King and Sandra Resondihardjo, following insights from Home Office specialist Roy Walmsley, noted that SSUs were 'used primarily for the custody of Irish terrorist prisoners'.[9]

Mountbatten categorized prisoners in England and Wales on a scale of A, B, C and D. Persons accorded the most restrictive rating, Category A, could in theory progress to lower levels as their sentence elapsed and parole loomed.[10] Security classifications of sentenced prisoners were determined by the Home Office after trial and prior to allocation to a Dispersal Prison. A 'special Home Office committee' met every three weeks in St. Anne's Gate and was understood in 1987 to solely administer those presumed to be Category A men and women. According to Tim Owen, 'classification into the other categories is made in the various regional administrations of the Prison Department'.[11] Decisions of the 'Category A Committee' were communicated to prisoners via relevant prison authorities in the late 1980s.[12] Suspected Irish Republican Army and Irish National Liberation Army members were generally rated 'Provisional Category A' prior to sentencing and were evidently earmarked for assessment by the 'special' Home Office committee in consequence. Ratings of Category A prisoners were annually reviewed in a process reputedly informed by governors and 'other staff at the establishment'.[13] Yet, the vast majority of IRA prisoners commenced and ended their sentences at the top security tier, contrary to the concept of incremental reclassification. In 1983, the Inspector of Prisons admitted there were 'no standard procedures' for changing a prisoner's category, by which time Irish republicans demonstrably fell within the discretionary area.[14] Until 1992, the specific criteria used to reach such decisions remained classified, even from governors made responsible for managing their long-term detention. It transpired that persons convicted of 'murder (except of a family member), armed robbery, rape and terrorism', as well as 'any offence under the Official Secrets Act' were liable to be allocated as Category A.[15] They were accompanied when moving within prisons by teams of staff members, including dog-handlers and officers required to update journals which logged prisoner location and activities in considerable detail. Cell searches and moves were far more frequent for Category A prisoners. They were obliged to receive visits from a limited pool of vetted family members under close observation. The Approved Visitors Scheme operated in an exceptionally strict fashion for the relatives of IRA prisoners, with the effect that only immediate family had any real prospect of occasional access following in-depth probing by the Special Branch.[16]

The 1964 edition of *Prison Rules*, an amended Home Office codex setting down general administrative practices in the jails of England and Wales, provided multiple means of sanctioning those deemed recalcitrant. The most commonly employed regulation, Rule 43, permitted governors to segregate a prisoner if it was believed the 'good order and discipline' of the prison had been threatened or was likely to be disturbed.[17] A variant known as 'Rule 43 own protection' enabled prisoners who believed themselves to be under threat to be housed in isolation, a resort referred to as 'going behind the door'.[18] The pre-emptive form was widely applied to the IRA in English prisons who were additionally subjected to exceptionally frequent jail shifts referred to as 'ghosting' and twenty-eight day periods of 'lie-downs' in 'local' prisons. Temporary accommodation outside the Dispersal System entailed solitary confinement in 'local' prisons that were invariably ill-equipped to hold maximum-security men. Irish republicans in England were involved in numerous breaches of *Prison Rules* throughout the 1970s in their efforts to assert political status. Those who did not feature prominently in protest actions were still liable to be denied optimum parole conditions and, therefore, served high proportions of their sentences. The cumulative effect of such treatment resulted in the IRA being referred to as 'Special Category A', a term with no formal legitimacy under the 1966 *Mountbatten Report*. Deprivation of liberty, if an occupational inconvenience for career criminals, challenged ideologically motivated political prisoners to redirect their energies towards confronting the Dispersal System.

NOTES

1. Gerry Adams, *Peace in Ireland? A broad analysis of the present situation* (Belfast, 1976), p. 14. Repetition of the phrase 'long war' and 'broad' signaled the continuation of a military campaign until a wider alliance or acceptance of the position of the Republican Movement achieved meaningful negotiations.

2. See Laura K Donoghue, *Counter-Terrorist Law and Emergency Powers in the United Kingdom, 1922–2000* (Dublin, 2001) and Kevin Boyle, Tom Hadden and Paddy Hillyard, *Law and State, The case of Northern Ireland* (London, 1975).

3. Adams, *Peace in Ireland?*, p. 11.

4. Adams, *Peace in Ireland?*, p. 13.

5. See Ruan O'Donnell, *Special Category, The IRA in English Prisons* (Dublin, 2012), Volume I, pp. 267–70.

6. J[ames] M G[lover], 2 November 1978, 'Northern Ireland: Future Terrorist Trends' in Sean Cronin, *Irish Nationalism, A history of its roots and ideology* (New York, 1980), p. 339. See also Ibid., pp. 339–57. The dictated IRA Army Council statement read by Jimmy Drumm at Bodenstown in June 1977 stated that the organization was committed to a 'long haul' campaign against the British Government. *Irish Times*, 29 December 1993.

7. G[lover], 'Terrorist Trends' in Cronin, *Irish Nationalism*, p. 340.

8. O'Donnell, *Special Category*, I, pp. 7–11.

9. Roy D King and Sandra L Resondihardjo, 'To max or not to max: Dealing with high risk prisoners in the Netherlands and England and Wales', *Punishment and Society*, 2010, Vol. 12, p. 69. See also *New Society*, 30 January 1975, pp. 254–5.

10.   *Report of Her Majesty's Chief Inspector of Prisons, 1983* (London, 1984), p. 18.

11.   Tim Owen, 'Prison Law: 1' in *Legal Action*, January 1987, pp. 10–11. See also 'Working Party on conveyance of Provisional Category "A" prisoners', 11 July 1974, National Archives (England), Home Office 391/ 53.

12.   RJ Hardiman to Robert R [Roy] Walsh, 3 March 1987, Private Collection (Walsh).

13.   Roy Walmsley, *Special Security Units, Home Office Research Study 109* (London, 1989), p. 29. See also *HC Deb 21 June 1984, vol. 62, cc. 216.* A founding member of the IRSP, Belfast man Sean McGourgan, was sentenced to four years in Lancaster Court on 5 September 1975 for stealing three Coptic crosses and possession of detonators. Sr. Clarke, 'Sean McGourgan', Clarke Papers (COFLA). McGourgan was not claimed by the organization, despite having apparently survived an attempt on his life in Lancaster by a rival Official IRA/ Clann na hÉireann member. The non-political aspect of his trial lessened his public profile. Sean McGourgan, 12 March 2012.

14.   *Report of Her Majesty's Chief Inspector of Prisons, 1983*, p. 18.

15.   *Guardian*, 11 March 1992.

16.   'Letter to persons wishing to be submitted for Approved Visitors List' to Eddie Caughey, 2 August 1996, Private Collection (Eddie Caughey).

17.   See Joyce Plotnikoff, *Prison Rules, A working guide*, Revised Edition (London, 1988), pp. 81–3.

CHAPTER 1

Year of Crisis

In a radio interview broadcast on 8 January 1978, Irish Taoiseach Jack Lynch called on the British Government to state its intention to withdraw from the North of Ireland and claimed that in such an environment, outstanding prisoner issues would be resolved.[1] This pragmatic and domestically shrewd declaration angered Britain's Secretary of State for Northern Ireland, Roy Mason. At a meeting with Senior Department of Foreign Affairs (DFA) officials in Dublin on 5 May 1978, Mason noted somewhat illogically that 'references to a possible amnesty had sown seeds of doubt which have now been removed' by assurances on cross border security.[2] Various British agencies knew that the Irish Government was unwilling to formally confer political status on IRA prisoners concentrated in Portlaoise Prison. On 29 April 1977, they had been one of eighteen powers who abstained when the Diplomatic Conference on Humanitarian Law, Geneva, recognized guerrillas as meriting prisoner-of-war status. Ending the bitter conflict, however, required *de facto* acceptance of captured and sentenced IRA and INLA members, as well as pro-British 'Loyalists', as political prisoners. Thus, their treatment pending a negotiated settlement was a highly sensitive matter.[3]

Negative trends within the Dispersal System fully warranted the retrospective characterization of 1978 by the London *Times* as a year of 'crisis'.[4] Acknowledgement of a trying period by Britain's paper of record stemmed from the undeniable and diverse pressure points being exerted on the establishment. The Prison Officer Association (POA), an innate bastion of conservatism, had instigated a muscular campaign of industrial action to assert the rights of its beleaguered union membership. Understaffing, demoralization and a stressful labour environment exacerbated loss of paid overtime and sundry workplace entitlements. Overtime in the late 1970s 'local' prisons could be compulsory and obliged junior staff to present themselves for thirteen days' duty in a fourteen day period.[5] Extra pay for longer, and budgeted hours in uniform, was otherwise lucrative. The resultant ferment was described by the taciturn Home Office as 'unprecedented', and far in excess of the disturbances of 1972, when generally passive resistance from prisoners coincided with POA members working to rule.[6] In the course of 1978, senior prison officers stood trial for alleged criminal offences arising from the violent suppression of the

Hull riot in August 1976. The illusion of omnipotence and immunity was permanently shattered. Overcrowding all but ensured that physical confrontations with inmates increased in frequency and seriousness. The range of countermeasures developed to maintain control, not least common usage of tranquilizing drugs, draconian punishment 'F Wings', and secretly trained riot units served to discomfort moderates. By early 1979, when Justice May conducted a root and branch inquiry into the prison service, 42,000 prisoners were held inside a system with a Certified Normal Accommodation (CNA) of 37,735. Only 31,656 had been jailed in the jurisdiction in 1969, when both recorded crimes and convictions were considerably lower than 1978.[7]

As the unpopular conflict in Ireland entered its tenth year, the presence in English jails of militant republicans fostered a distinct range of challenges. The British Government received an embarrassing check on 18 January 1978 when the European Court of Human Rights (ECHR) in Strasbourg found it had breached Article 3 of the European Human Rights Convention (1953) by its administration of interned persons in the Six Counties from August 1971. This revelation was palliated by the Court's careful description of pertinent unlawful seizures and interrogations as constituting 'degrading treatment', despite the Commission's prior use of the politically loaded yet applicable term 'torture'.[8] The extraordinary delay in official deliberations permitted equivocation and disavowal. Britain's NATO allies were circumspect with regard to formalizing allegations of human rights' violations on the western side of the mutually militarized 'Iron Curtain'. UK Attorney General Sam Silkin dutifully assured the European Court in February 1977 that such controversial practices had been discontinued, but he could not defend the fact that the conveniently mild verdict from Strasbourg came in the midst of numerous claims of gross excesses in the treatment of detainees in the North of Ireland. This reality, coupled with developments in England's Dispersal System, indicated that further recriminatory judgements in higher Continental courts were in the offing.[9]

Right wing and predominately Europhobic British Conservatives were appalled by the ECHR decision and Airey Neave, Shadow Northern Secretary, decried Silkin's 'unprecedented incompetence' in failing to vindicate the UK.[10] Neave, a former British Intelligence operative during the Second World War, had received milder handling by German captors in 1940s' Colditz than many Irishmen interned by Britain did in the early 1970s.[11] Numerous men detained without trial and with little or no connection to the IRA had aside from been badly maltreated in Gough Barracks, Ballykelly and Long Kesh as well as the advanced interrogation techniques inflicted on the selected 'hooded men'. Irish republicans Noel Jenkinson, Sean O'Conaill, Michael Gaughan and Frank Stagg had all perished in custody by February 1976 as a direct result of their imprisonment in England.[12]

The announcement in Strasbourg coincided with a significant statement by Taoiseach Jack Lynch. On 18 January 1978, Lynch called upon the British Government, headed by Labour Prime Minister James Callaghan, to state its intention to withdraw from the Six Counties. This bid to break the stalemate in the North of Ireland was supported by Cardinal Tomas Ó Fiaich who would have inferred from Lynch's overall comments that the Taoiseach was prepared to grant an amnesty to IRA prisoners in the southern jurisdiction. Open political commentary of this kind rarely emanated from Dublin and was underpinned in this instance by the prior public engagement of US President Jimmy Carter. The mild-mannered Democratic Party leader had expressed a willingness to offer political and economic sponsorship to an Irish peace process in late 1977. Callaghan, however, failed to respond with the requisite degree of commitment for which he incurred the criticism of powerful Irish-Americans, such as Senator Ted Kennedy. If high-level negotiations had commenced in the course of 1978, the immediate or phased release of IRA prisoners would have featured on the agenda. The Strasbourg censure remained to agitate both poles of political opinion in the interim.[13]

Celebrity intellectuals Jean Paul Sartre, Angela Davis and Herbert Marcuse were amongst those who backed leftist calls for an international tribunal on British crimes in Ireland to be convened in London. Davis had a deep interest in the maltreatment of black American prisoners and spent eighteen months in jail prior to her June 1972 acquittal of aiding a bloody courthouse escape bid in August 1970.[14] Sartre had condemned the conditions imposed on Red Army Faction (RAF) members in West Germany's Stammheim Prison in 1974.[15] Despite evoking the scorn of the politically 'sectarian' revolutionary left, British MPs Joan Maynard, Tom Litterick, Dick Kelly, Arthur Latham and Maureen Colquohon declared their support, as did Irish-based moderates, media, trade unionists, socialists and constitutional republicans Dr Noel Browne, Eddie McAteer, Bernadette McAliskey (nee Devlin), Matt Merrigan, John Mulcahy and Michael Mullen. Numerous additional public figures promised solidarity. Among the litany of essentially rhetorical questions posed were requests for information from the authorities in London concerning 'allegations of abuse and assault on Irish prisoners in British, including English, jails'.[16] Sinn Féin correctly interpreted this development as one of the salient 'issues for 1978' and expected the England dimension to be raised in Strasbourg.[17]

In Britain, the Government's legal position appeared, superficially, to have been rendered more secure. Recent domestic court cases, primarily *Becker v The Home Office*, had confirmed that the *Prison Rules* were 'regulatory' and not subject to 'civil claim', even if found to have been breached.[18] Prisoners effectively had no rights, merely privileges, which governors were entitled to either suspend or modify without external consultation and statutory oversight. Moreover, the High Court in London had ruled in 1977 that the adjudications of Board of Visitors were 'separate and immune from ordinary judicial procedure and review'.[19] BOVs were fundamental to the adjudication of discipline within the jails where they operated on an individual basis. They exercised responsibility for administering often significant penalties for infractions of locally observed rules. The disparity between their function and actual legal capacity was found to be in breach of Article 13 in March 1983.[20]

An important and unexpected development arose in the Court of Appeal in London in October 1978 relating to the suppression of the Hull Riot of 31 August–2 September 1976. Lord Justice Shaw, in *R v Hull Prison Board of Visitors, ex parte St. Germain,* found that BOVs performed a quasi 'judicial role', contrary to the sense of an earlier judgment in the High Court. As such, while BOV rulings were not subject to standard external appeal mechanisms, they were open to 'judicial review', during which the integrity of decision-making processes could be reassessed and outcomes potentially 'set aside'.[21] Prisoners could contest BOV punishment. The Home Secretary retrospectively, in October 1983, described the *St. Germain* ruling as strategically significant in that it initiated a novel process whereby 'the [Queen's Bench] Divisional Court [of Appeal] began, in 1978, to exercise its supervisory jurisdiction over the [prison] system'. This inspired inconveniently imaginative implications for 'what kind of adjudications' could reconcile 'effective determination' of disciplinary cases with 'safeguards for the prisoner'. This perennial conundrum of insecure political elites informed the agenda of the *Prior Report* which the Home Office commissioned from the Committee on the Prison Disciplinary System. Personnel were selected in the emergency environment of May 1984. Eventual publication of the *Prior Report* in October 1985 followed serial acts of subversion by numerous IRA prisoners in England, as well as non-republican militants, which profoundly altered the tenor of life in the Dispersal System.[22]

The well-informed Home Office evidently anticipated a spate of tactical reverses. In November 1983, the Divisional Court ruled in *R v Secretary of State for the Home Department and Board of Visitors of Albany Prison, ex parte Tarrant and others,* that BOVs must properly consider a prisoner's request for legal representation if they were facing serious charges. This progressive reform gravely weakened the virulent potency of both in-house Governor dictations and BOV prescribed adjudications.[23] It did not go unanswered by the Prison Department of the Home Office in St. Anne's Gate, London. Justice Webster accurately predicted in late 1983 that 'charges of mutiny', amongst the most detrimental to any prisoner proved guilty of the offence, could be 'referred to the criminal courts'.[24] Webster, in fact, advised that any BOV proceedings involving possibly severe repercussions for transgressors should be tried within 'the normal criminal justice system with all the rights and protections which automatically go with such [a]process'.[25]

The 1985 *Prior Report* also recognised the complaint taken to the European Court of Human Rights (ECHR) in Strasbourg by IRA prisoners Sean Campbell and Fr Patrick Fell which was 'adopted' on 12 May 1982.[26] Campbell and Fell had initiated their historic action in 1978, arising from the illegal manner in which they were treated during and following their assault by prison staff in Albany in September 1976.[27] From January 1984, the cumulative effect of *Tarrant* and *Campbell and Fell* was that prisoners not alone received legal advice from outside lawyers but enjoyed their actual representation at adjudications if basic reasonable criteria applied. The 'implication' of this breakthrough for the Home Office, according to the *Prior Report*, encompassed nothing less than 'the whole question of the proper limits of the disciplinary system'.[28] Unwelcome judicial attention into the often secretive affairs of the Prison Department occurred in tandem with extraneous political developments which altered the physical structure of the Dispersal System during years of Conservative Party governance. The IRA inside and outside the prisons in England played a notable part in stimulating this far-reaching reconsideration between 1978 and 1985. Indeed, the *Prior Report* claimed: 'In the context of the prison disciplinary system, the most important [ECHR] case ... is that of Campbell and Fell'.[29]

The IRA had featured prominently in the strategic planning of the Prison Department since the early 1970s. Home Office writer Roy Walmsley highlighted the importance of the 8 March 1973 London explosions for contemporary prison policy-makers. The first car bomb attacks in Britain had raised the prospect of 'future similar incidents' and a generation of 'new candidates for [special security] unit places' in England. The IRA had inadvertently disrupted Home Office projections at a critical juncture and halted the abolition of the SSUs, which the influential *Mountbatten Report* had regarded as uncivilized in 1966.[30] According to Walmsley:

> It was immediately clear that Irish republican bombers, once detained and convicted, would pose a serious new threat to security, and there was real doubt as to whether they could be held safely within the dispersal system. This perception removed the impetus behind the policy of progressively phasing out the security units... By the beginning of 1978 there were already five bombers among the total of fourteen unit occupants [in Leicester and Parkhurst], and it was strongly felt that nowhere but the security units could safely contain such men... The case for the retention of two units and the construction of a third thus rested on the arrival of the Irish republican dimension, the dangers of increased terrorism from a variety of sources, and the increasing number of robbers with resources to finance their rescue.[31]

The British Government and subordinate Home Office was understandably anxious to prevent public sympathy accruing to their Irish republican opponents in English jails. In January 1978, Merlyn Rees responded to a question on the numbers of IRA members either convicted or beaten in custody by denying any such subcategory existed. Rees sidestepped Sheffield MP Joan Maynard's query in the Commons, as well as the declared *raison d'etre* of the Prevention of Terrorism Act (PTA), by claiming that 'there is no separate offence of terrorism in our criminal law', and it was therefore impossible to collate the desired data.[32] Despite this disavowal of any form of tailored protocols adopted in relation to republicans, the IRA intuited that the Home Office was devising a fresh approach to pressurize its most vulnerable imprisoned comrades. It was alleged that Wakefield had retained an anomalous place in the Dispersal System after the official closure of the Control Unit in late 1974. Trainee Assistant Governors reportedly received courses in Wakefield in the psychological dimension of long-term maximum-security detention. This reputedly encompassed the controversial theories of Fields Medal recipient Rene Thom, whose 'Catastrophe Theory' straddled mathematics, singularity theory, philosophy and biology with a penological application in the 1960s.[33] 'Sociobiology', another alleged Prison Service area of interest which republicans found sinister, was defined in a 1975 American publication by Edward O Wilson. Insights into biological determinants of social behaviour and adaptation also offered potentially pertinent guidelines for those running penal institutions.[34] Despite parliamentary privilege, Rees declined to comment on whether he believed Prison Regulations met European Convention standards on the distinctly evasive grounds that the question was then 'under consideration' in Strasbourg.[35]

Persons connected with republican prisoners held in England require neither Home Office admissions nor Strasbourg rulings to confirm the routine discrimination meted out to Irish republicans within the Category A population. Civil Rights advocate Fr. Denis Faul enlisted the aid of Sr. Sarah Clarke in January 1978 to answer queries posed to him on the subject by Lord John Kilbracken (John Godley). The republican nun was attached to the La Sainte Union Convent in Highgate Road, London, and worked with the city's Irish Chaplaincy. Her primary endeavour was at the hub of a discrete circuit of contacts that extended welfare assistance and legal liaison to Irish prisoners in England. Prior to going to England the Galwegian had taught at the prestigious Our Lady's Bower in Athlone, County Westmeath. Fr. Faul learned that often-fraught family visits provided the clearest evidence of policy differentiation of prisoners assigned an identical security rating by the Home Office. In her briefing to Kilbracken Sr. Clarke explained:

> The visits esp[ecially] in Albany are limited. The Irish prisoners have visits in a special area. Three small rooms are set aside for them. One of these rooms is for closed visits, i.e. behind glass & wire etc. Two rooms have a large table and there

are two screws behind the prisoner & two screws & a police woman or security woman in civilian dress behind the visitors. A large table is between the prisoner & the family. All other than Irish Cat[egory] A prisoners have visits in open rooms, well heated [and] comfortable at coffee tables with free access to canteen facilities. There are approx 12 Irish prisoners in Albany ... The Irish visitors however cannot visit when it is convenient for them, they must come when one of the two rooms mentioned above is not being used by other prisoner's visitors. Nobody wants a visit in the 'closed' room.[36]

The basic situation outlined by Sr. Clarke, who had assisted prisoners' dependents from the early 1970s, described the unacknowledged existence of a 'special' Category A cohort of Irish republicans.[37] She also ascertained that visitors to IRA prisoners in Albany in late 1977 and early 1978, who frequently arrived at the complex at the same time as others calling to see criminal inmates, were not permitted to use the Waiting Room. Being required to stand outside the main gate imposed hardship on the elderly and the young during winter months, some of whom travelled to the remote Isle of Wight from as far as Donegal. It was obvious to all but the most hardened cynics that this physical dislocation inflicted, possibly intentionally, psychological harm on the families of the imprisoned. This, in turn, discomforted the prisoners. However, scenes of this nature were replicated across the Dispersal System, as Sr. Clarke knew well on the basis of constant interaction with the families her network conveyed to and from England's many prisons and airports.[38] The Prisoners Aid Committee (PAC) astutely regarded such aggravating policies as 'a kind of "political status" within the Brit prison system'.[39]

Kilbracken had sought precise information from Longford in the light of reading Faul's disturbing *In prison in England* pamphlet, circulated in December 1977.[40] This consultation was intended to assist him in framing a parliamentary question for the House of Lords which was aired on 7 February 1978. Writing from his home address in Killegar, Cavan, Kilbracken claimed to be 'personally in favour of Irish prisoners being transferred to Ireland', but felt that the objective could not be fruitfully addressed as the 'UK Gov[ernmen]t have clearly set their minds against this'. His well-intentioned intervention did not enlist support from republicans as it envisaged a proposal to concentrate Irish Category A prisoners in a 'convenient' location for family visits. Wormwood Scrubs in London was posited as the best option for this purpose; it was a prison designated the Lifer Assessment Centre for southeast England in January 1975.[41] This resembled a superseded line of argument in the *Mountbatten Report*, albeit one substituting humane visiting conditions *in lieu* of security considerations as the underlying justification.[42] The Ministry of Defence appreciated the importance of family contact and made elaborate arrangements *vis à vis* accommodation, allowances and communications for dependents of soldiers serving in the North of Ireland under 'Operation Banner'.[43]

Sr. Clarke, who furnished much of the original data drawn upon by the campaigning Ulster priests, reviewed the Kilbracken letter on behalf of Fr. Faul. In her draft response she wrote: 'Rees, when I spoke to him … said something about [why he] could not return them [to Ireland. It was] because they would have to enjoy political status'.[44] If this viewpoint was accurately recalled, Rees admitted that the key reason for opposing the repatriation of IRA prisoners was their subsequent entitlement to political status in Long Kesh, site of the H-Blocks. His own Labour Government, however, was moving purposefully to eliminate the last vestiges of this much-resented vestige of internment in Belfast, Derry and Armagh, a process that led to an uncompromising republican reaction in 1976–81. This historic policy shift may well have been a critical element in shaping Home Office attitudes towards the republicans it retained in England. On 7 February 1978 Lord Harris deflected the central thrust of Kilbracken's representation by claiming 'there simply are not enough facilities in any one dispersal prison to take up to 100 IRA prisoners who at the moment are serving sentences in this country'.[45] The prisoners in question, meanwhile, persevered in their efforts to use the courts to expose injustices within the Dispersal System and exact a financial toll from their captors. 'Uxbridge Eight' prisoner Gerry Cunningham reflected:

> It was attack …a way of getting back … The system was there, why not use it? … Numerous cases [mounted by other IRA prisoners] as well, not because they believed in British justice, not because they believed they were going to win, but because they were going to court. And because they'd get legal aid and because it was costing the state … for those cases to be defended. They had to defend them.[46]

Legal initiatives mounted by Irish republicans, and their willingness to make common cause with British prisoners, raised the status of the IRA among those confined in the Dispersal System. Derry republican Brian McLaughlin noted: 'They more and more came to respect us because they witnessed that on different occasions we had protested not only for ourselves but for better conditions for them also'.[47] The solidarity demonstrated between the IRA, British gangsters and others during the 1976 Hull Riot, and the court proceedings that ensued, had accelerated the process, and Irish republicans in English prisons believed that the system 'changed' in consequence.[48] More generally, the basic approach of staff towards Category A prisoners fell, in the late 1970s, within the theoretical definition of 'coercive power' coined in the 1990s. This was the most severe of several available modes of interaction and was characterized by 'increased use of segregation, transfer, privilege removal, disciplinary punishments and lock-downs'.[49]

The Prison Department maintained its remit of estranging the IRA from the general Dispersal System community at a time when they were, as evidently suspected, utterly determined to disrupt jail administration. According to Eddie O'Neill: '[Hull] put fire into a lot of prisoners. It empowered a lot of prisoners who previously felt impotent'. The attack by staff on the IRA men in Albany, furthermore, enraged their comrades: 'That finished us with any idea that there was some course of diplomacy to deal with things like minor protests. It was all out war at that stage ... [and] the Hull riot empowered a lot of guys ... The fear that had been generated by repression before that suddenly dissipated ... for a long period of time the place was just a tinderbox'.[50]

Broadening the front

A Bloody Sunday commemoration parade from London's Hyde Park on 24 January 1978 attracted around 500 persons, while another 500 marched from Shepherds Bush to Hammersmith. The scale of the events was a decrease on the numbers that had attended Irish demonstrations prior to the implementation of the PTA in 1974, and a pale shadow of those that had protested internment in Trafalgar Square in 1971.[51] The highly emotive Derry anniversary, however, served to promote joint political activities of pro-republican bodies based in Britain in 1978. Twenty members of the United Troops Out Movement (UTOM) from Leeds, Sheffield, Bradford and Doncaster picketed Wakefield prison four days later as part of a week of interlinked events.[52] This linked to a notorious and specifically English concern for the wider Irish struggle, albeit from a numerically small subsection of the British population.[53] Statements of support from the PAC and the IRA prisoners in Wakefield were as appreciative as ever, even if opportunities to reach receptive audiences were steadily diminishing.[54]

An Cumann Cabhrach, the charity that assisted with the welfare of prisoner's dependents, continued to receive funds from its international associates, which in February 1978 included the Celtic Club of Melbourne, Australia, and Na Fianna Éireann (NFE) in San Francisco, California. Income of the level that had preceded the Birmingham bombs of 1974 was no longer available from UK sources, although newspaper sales and discreet donations continued.[55] The international pro-prisoner networks contained elements with multiple lines of communication to the Republican Movement. The Cathal Brugha Slua of NFE, San Francisco, did not come under the umbrella of the Dublin HQ, yet produced republican activist Christina Reid, one of the IRA linked 'Boston Three' in 1990. She was an acquaintance of San Francisco-born IRA member Liam Quinn, who was jailed in Ireland and extradited from America to England in 1986.[56]

The task facing Sinn Féin and An Cumann Cabhrach was complicated by unanticipated developments in England and Ireland. The closure of Leicester

Special Unit on 28 February 1978 created a new challenge in that two prominent Irish prisoners, Hugh 'Hughie' Doherty and Eddie Butler, were sent on a protracted tour of 'local' jails, where they were held in solitary confinement pending the refurbishment in Leicester. In February 1977 the men had received multiple life sentences with a thirty-year minimum, which the trial judge retrospectively wished to amend to 'natural life'.[57] Doherty ultimately spent two years in solitary confinement in Durham, where he was initially denied access to his personal books owing to the theoretically temporary nature of his stay.[58] Leicester SSU did not reopen until 26 February 1980. Parkhurst Special Unit, the only other structure in England deemed suitable for the men, was not only full but contained Harry Duggan, Brendan Dowd and Joe O'Connell, all of whom the Home Office wished to separate from their former associates.[59] The Clareman noted: 'They obviously didn't want the four of us [IRA co-defendants] together. It would be too political ... too much of a statement'.[60] Following a very rare escape, Parkhurst SSU had undergone a security upgrade between 26 November 1976 and 12 April 1977, which included the construction of an additional wall as well as an electrified inner fence. Whereas Harry Roberts had once planned an escape using bolt cutters smuggled into the prison by his Irish mother, a much greater degree of preparation was necessary following the additional security investment.[61]

Sinn Féin and the UTOM attempted to keep such matters in the news by picketing Winson Green (Birmingham), Leicester and Gartree in the months ahead, but made little headway in the context of other events.[62] The POW Department of Sinn Féin claimed in 1980 that Doherty and Butler were 'outstanding cases of victimisation' in the English SSUs.[63] Dowd was equally meritorious. Between August 1976 and June 1980 the Kerryman was in Bristol, Albany, Wandsworth, Armley, Strangeways, Parkhurst and Winchester for periods of two to three months. Frequent movement between solitary confinement cells induced disorientation, weight loss, hair loss and impaired vision. Republicans attributed the unusually harsh treatment to Dowd's centrality to the appeals of the 'Guildford Four' and 'Maguire Seven', who were unjustly jailed for the actions of his London ASU. He was moved into the Leicester SSU in June 1980.[64] Dowd was known to be a prominent IRA member, a former O/C in London and, from 1975, as 'Dennis Power', a disguise he used while living in Manchester.[65]

Prison Department scrutiny of Doherty and Butler in Leicester prior to its renovation probably derived from their knowledge that the men had explored various means of escape, which evidently inspired the improvement of the complex. The 'Balcombe Street' group, when on remand in Brixton following their televised arrest in December 1975, had been moved to Wandsworth when a criminal informer betrayed their plan to use smuggled explosives to blast through a toilet block wall to access a point where they could escape to freedom.[66] Ironically, Brixton and Wormwood Scrubs were listed on targeting documentation found in a safe house used by the IRA and ASU at the time of their arrest.[67] On arriving into Leicester's cramped unit following sentencing and allocation, Butler, closely followed by Doherty, encountered tensions with several English occupants, and one in particular. High-profile prisoners such as John McVicar, Johnny Joyce and Freddie Sewell did not welcome the new arrivals, and Butler had 'a bit of an altercation' with an Englishman. This did not flare into a violent confrontation, however, a critical factor, as the IRA men had discussed 'doing' the main protagonist under such circumstances, regardless of consequences.[68] The practise devised by Martin Coughlan, Martin Brady, Roy Walsh, Vince Donnelly, Billy Armstrong and other life-sentenced IRA men in 1970s' England was to consistently retaliate with great force in order to deter opportunist attacks on isolated comrades.

On receiving an unsubtle warning from the two IRA men in the small TV room, the irritable Englishmen gradually adapted to their presence. Scope for assertion was boosted by the knowledge that their associates in Parkhurst were not facing significant threat and that the IRA throughout the Dispersal System were forming *ad hoc* alliances.[69] Following McVicar's release, two of the remaining Englishmen in the Leicester Unit were invited to participate in an escape for which one subsequently offered to furnish firearms. This was declined by Doherty, who knew that 'dummy runs' were being conducted nearby in preparation for moving a hoist adjacent to the wall. The specialised equipment was capable of lifting four men over an inner wall and the forty-foot perimeter boundary. There seemed to be no justification for intimidating unarmed staff with weaponry. However, the two Irishmen were 'ghosted' within days of involving others and they divined from the sudden decision to construct a roof over the small yard attached to the 'Submarine' that they had once again been thwarted by human agency.[70]

Doherty was held in a large but freezing cell in Durham where he jogged and slept in his clothes to keep warm during the cold Yorkshire winter. Beatings were common in the Segregation Block, and Doherty received his first of many in England when he refused to leave the yard when the stipulated daily period of one hour was abruptly cut short:

> I seen the screw hitting the bell and I thought, "oh fuck, they're going to come to get me". I just grabbed the screw and let him have it and then he just collapsed. The next thing they just came in ... all I could hear was Winney [McGee] shouting they're killing me. No one seen it like, there were that many of them. I was down and they were all on top of me and they were punching and kicking each other but Winney got over the fence to help me. I got dragged into the strip cell and you'd be bollock naked for a few days and then up on adjudication and the usual ... You'd be asked for your name and number. You'd just look at them. The Governor says,

"I was in the RAF and I remember my number" and I says to him, "what is it?"
He was absolutely rabid and then the penny dropped ... I was dragged out again.[71]

After months of tedious application, Doherty was permitted access to the
main prison library accompanied by eight staff and a guard dog. Deprived
of any face-to-face contact with other prisoners, he snatched momentary
shouted exchanges with Ray McLaughlin, Tony Clark and Stevie Blake
whenever they appeared within earshot. Doherty had moved in different
IRA circles in Ireland and Britain but shared bonds of republican politics.
The Dispersal System also fostered a sense of comradeship. Occasional brief
conversations were possible with Ann and Eileen Gillespie, who spent most
of their sentence after 1 March 1975 in Durham's H Wing. The all - female
facility was located in the vicinity of the 'cage' compound where prisoners
being held in solitary confinement received exercise and fresh air.[72] Such
modest and unguarded acts of solidarity were invariably seized: 'They would
shout to you ... and you would shout back'.[73] All three possessed strong
County Donegal connections, as did Stevie Blake. Winnie Coyle, an Irish-
Glaswegian who later married Hugh Doherty, travelled from Annagrey,
Donegal to visit him in Durham on 28 August 1978. She found that her
fiancée had 'got thin and small but he was in good spirits'.[74] Doherty had
hitherto declined visits in Durham to spare his family hardship and was
involved in an altercation during his reunion with Coyle arising from the
oppressive conditions imposed on ostensible security grounds. Having
made his point he promptly 'disappeared' on a lie-down to Winson Green,
obliging Harry Duggan and Joe O'Connell to seek his whereabouts through
the prison grapevine.[75]

    Eddie Butler was moved via Strangeways in Manchester to Winson Green
in Birmingham, where unsuitable security facilities entailed a protracted stay
in solitary confinement. On being returned to Leicester SSU with Brendan
Dowd, the IRA men were initially joined by just two other life sentenced
prisoners: Harry Roberts and Donald 'Black Panther' Neilson. Roberts
fatally shot two plainclothes detectives in August 1966; the detectives had
incorrectly believed he and his associates may have been involved in an
escape attempt from Wormwood Scrubs. The men in the van were actually
professional criminals preparing to commit an armed robbery. Roberts used
skills obtained in the British Army in Malaysia to avoid capture for three
months and claimed at trial that the military had also taught him how to
kill in the course of a brutal counterinsurgency. A third policeman was shot
dead during the same incident by John Duddy. Whereas Roberts, who had
an Irish mother, was well disposed towards republicans, Neilson was far
more guarded.[76] Neilson had also belonged to the British Military and did
National Service in Aden, Kenya and Cyprus. He received four life sentences
in 1976 for a lethal criminal rampage.[77] Proximity to exceptionally violent

men, however, was not a bone of contention for IRA members, many of whom were viewed with equal opprobrium and accepted the reality of their imprisonment in England. Friction was inevitable in the close confines of a sealed area within an otherwise non-maximum security complex.[78]

It was immediately suspected that the Prison Department were testing tolerances of newly restrictive administration under which hobbies and facilities were withdrawn. All four promptly cooperated in 'decorating' the main office with several days' worth of human waste for which they were locked down. The next step was a planned assault on the Governor and Chief Security Officer during their daily inspection. Neilson declined to take part and physically removed himself from the equation by using the Rule 43 'own protection' protocol to 'go behind the door'. The remaining three were surprised to be unlocked the following morning as it was patently obvious they intended to escalate their protest, even if Neilson had maintained silence. Instead, the Principal Officer approached them in the kitchenette and requested a one-hour postponement of any action to which they assented. Ultimately, the Governor and Chief Security Officer arrived with a reinforced but non-threatening complement of staff and offered to meet most of the demands which had been previously presented in the form of a list petition. Mutual self-interest enabled such acts of compromise and accommodation in SSUs, which would have been all but impossible on standard prison wings where numbers, crowd dynamics and regulations impinged.[79]

Ennui was a major threat to the psychological health of O'Connell, Duggan, *et al* in Parkhurst SSU, a detached two-storey building developed from the former 'punishment block'.[80] Irregular communications with republicans in England and Ireland were generally possible over time but insufficiently frequent to counteract the limitations stemming from spatial isolation. Maintaining morale was a constant battle at times when the 'Long War', as reported in the mass media, was failing to deliver the strategic dividends hoped for by armed republicans: 'What kept you going was what was happening on the outside. For the first few years it was very quiet. It looked like the IRA campaign had been driven into the dust. The Roy Mason ['conveyor belt'] situation and all that – that the IRA were being defeated. Then gradually the IRA reorganised, especially in the North leading up to Warrenpoint [in August 1979]'.[81] By the early 1980s the IRA in English prisons had perfected local organization and communications to the point that they were formulating policy documents for consideration by the Army Council and Ard Comhairle.

Parkhurst escape attempt, 24 February 1978

An IRA escape attempt from Parkhurst's A Wing at 7.15 p.m. on 24 February 1978 revealed the strengths and weaknesses of the grouping at the time. In this instance, friendly relations built up over time between the republicans and black prisoners proved instrumental. Whereas the IRA cells were searched once or twice daily, Category B prisoners received far fewer checks for contraband.[82] Compton Finnlader, a black South African, allowed the Irishmen to cut a hole through the planking of his cell floor and then breach the outer wall over a period of almost six months.[83] While the IRA and Sinn Féin had close connections to the armed MK (Umkhonto we Sizwe) established by Nelson Mandela and the broader African National Congress to the extent of providing weapons training, direct assistance and specialist equipment, Finnlader was not imprisoned for political offences in England.[84] Stanley knives were used to cut through the wooden floor of Finnlader's cell, A4/ 30, where a cavity separated the bottom of the top-landing tier from the arched ceiling of the accommodation below. Andy Mulryan and Noel Gibson then worked on dislodging the brickwork of the wall. This painstaking methodology ensured that much less effort had to be made to conceal the progressive damage once the floor entryway was adequately disguised.[85]

Gibson was an exceptionally militant prisoner from the outset. Following arrest after the shooting of a plain-clothed policeman in Manchester on 1 July 1975, he was plunged into what he recalled as a 'very emotive and charged atmosphere', during which 'everyone got a hiding. It was all part of the hysteria and excitement, and probably fear on their part as well'. His detention was not without incident: 'When I was arrested I had two teeth knocked out, my nose was broken, I was hospitalized afterwards'.[86] Walsh had been punished for attacking a staff member in Wormwood Scrubs on 26 June 1975, and then for joining two other IRA prisoners, Martin Coughlan and Stevie Blake, in a highly destructive roof-top protest on 14–15 November 1975. His BOV adjudication recorded the men had damaged '90 per cent of the roof tile on the east side of 'D' Hall and 100 per cent of the glass in the roof of the same wall', in addition to considerable ancillary acts of sabotage. This entailed contravention of Rule 47 (11) as well as Rule 47 (7), (18) and (20).[87] The London incidents pertained to the assertion of political status, whereas Walsh and his comrades intended to escape from Parkhurst.

Andy Mulryan, Sean Kinsella, Noel Gibson, John Higgins, Gerry Small and Roy Walsh were aided by Tony Madigan prior to his move to Albany.[88] Madigan never set foot in Finnlader's cell but assisted in the sewing of small bags from curtain material which were used to distribute the 'rubbish and the rubble'.[89] Other discrete preparations went undetected. Walsh persuaded an unconvinced UVF prisoner of the merits of doing him a 'right favour' by exchanging his A Wing cell for that of his own on B Wing.[90] He otherwise could not participate. Gibson and Mulyran did much of the physical work on the basis that their known friendships with black prisoners provided cover for an otherwise suspicious presence on the top landing. Mulryan was compromised one day when an unexpected check of 'bars, bolts and locks' by prison staff trapped him in the cell. Although shirtless and sweating profusely from the labour, no comment was made.[91] Gibson recalled: 'Every night I went up there and chiselled out, worked on the things. Played music [to cover the noise]. After about two months, I got through to the last brick and we could see a little chink out. That was it'.[92] Dirt and minor debris was scattered in the yard from the workshop-produced bags and the damage covered nightly by Finnlader's numerous reggae music posters.[93]

The IRA men gathered in Finnlader's cell on the evening of the bid with parts to assemble a twenty-foot ladder made from bolted Formica tabletops. It had been donated by a respected English gangster formerly associated with the Kray twins.[94] The men also possessed ropes made from sheets and various items of useful paraphernalia. When the last few bricks were prised away, Walsh and Gibson descended the precarious thirty-foot drop to the ground. They were in the act of receiving the equipment needed to scale the walls from Mulryan when they were noticed by two alert warders who had braved heavy rain to mount a night patrol.[95] A prisoner lookout positioned at the far end of the wing had not seen the staff members return towards the busy exit point.[96] Walsh, a renowned fighter, spotted the prison officers radioing for assistance while staring transfixed at the extended knotted sheet rope, realised that physical resistance was futile. Within seconds 'alarms [were] ringing everywhere. We were outside the building and the [inner] fence was about twenty yards away'. The plan had been to climb the two fences, and lacking outside harbourers and transport away from the island, to simply 'hope for the best'. The men believed the fence line was not properly alarmed and that external help could have made the high-risk effort a viable prospect. As matters stood, 'bad luck' doomed it to failure.[97]

All aspirant escapers still inside the building managed to get away from the scene of the wall breach and avoided detection. They were surprised to be neither punished nor moved, a strong indication that informers on the wing had remained silent if not oblivious. Speculation that men were waiting to assist the group if they got over the exterior wall was not confirmed.[98] Walsh and Gibson were seized in the open and punished with eighty-six days in solitary and were placed on the 'E[scape] List'. Finnlader's selfless aid to the republicans resulted in fifty-six days in solitary confinement and the loss of six months, remission.[99] The Prison Department was undoubtedly relieved that the IRA men had been contained, not least in that it maintained its impressive record of just three Category A absconders between 1975 and 1978.[100] Walsh was held in Wormwood Scrubs until 6 September 1979, followed by a month in solitary in Wandsworth before being shifted to Hull where deleterious 'conditions' induced him to refuse family visitors.[101]

Shane Paul O'Doherty

Shane Paul O'Doherty had been regarded as vulnerable prior to his transfer until he ended his blanket protest in solitary and was moved into D Wing of Wormwood Scrubs in November 1977. D Wing was the maximum-security part of the large London complex, parts of which dated from 1874. By February 1978, the Derryman, a close friend of Martin McGuinness, was a potentially problematic prisoner due to his public distancing from the Republican Movement. His refusal to wear prison uniform had been intended to secure repatriation to the Six Counties and succeeded in attracting the notice of concerned liberals.[102] This evinced militancy. Contact with John Hume, MP for Derry and a leader of the SDLP, proved encouraging, although he was one of very few Irish politicians closely involved in backing O'Doherty. Bishop Edward Daly of Derry and Lord Longford supported his position, as did British Labour MPs Andrew Bennett and Philip Whitehead.[103] He was persuaded that the Home Office would not relent on repatriation if it appeared that they had acceded to pressure exerted by the 'blanket' protest. Accordingly, O'Doherty abandoned his campaign in November 1977 'after fourteen months naked in solitary' to give his influential supporters room to manoeuvre.[104] This resulted in his relocation to D Wing of Wormwood Scrubs where, for the first time, he was in a position to interact regularly with other IRA prisoners such as Belfast gunrunner Jimmy Kelly.[105]

O'Doherty's major break from the IRA ranks dated from 17 February 1978 when a letter originally intended for *Republican News* appeared on the front page of the *Derry Journal*. The smuggled communication had been passed by a family member to a senior republican in Derry and elicited a message that the Belfast-produced republican organ required deletions. The prospect of censorship aggrieved O'Doherty, who turned to Derry's main newspaper in the hope that an unexpurgated version would be published in the letters column. He was taken aback when it received the prominence of a lead story, although he must have realized that life-sentenced IRA prisoners in any jurisdiction rarely aired such controversial issues in public.[106] The letter caused a minor sensation and its contents were widely reported in the Irish and British media.[107] His basic argument was that revolutionary socialism was incompatible with Christian morality on the grounds that it tended to create a totalitarian political environment. This view would have been contested by contemporary republicans, but any critical analysis attributed to an IRA 'lifer' could not be dismissed out of hand. Editorial comment added by the *Derry Journal* presented the communication as a repudiation of the argument that the conflict was a 'just war' under theological definitions devised by the Christian and specifically Catholic tradition. O'Doherty's experience was cited in order to assert that political violence was 'not justifiable'.[108] As an avowedly pluralist and secular organization with numerous non-Catholic members, the IRA was uninterested in the moral status of its campaign within the Vatican, but published commentaries, which strengthened the analysis of the SDLP at the expense of Sinn Féin, were clearly unwelcome. The Derryman would have been viewed in some quarters as undermining comrades by disseminating such an important unilateral statement. This would have been a more daunting prospect in Portlaoise and the H-Blocks, where republican command structures would have militated against a solo run.

In the short term, O'Doherty faced the possibility of a backlash from fellow IRA prisoners in England. He claimed that some ostracized and 'verged on wanting to beat me up for speaking my mind', although other 'more broadminded' individuals offered unconditional support.[109] The unsympathetic Prisoners Aid Committee (PAC) speculated that O'Doherty acted when 'suffering from the psychological effects which inevitably follow upon prolonged isolation' and had been adversely influenced by 'pacifist Lord Longford'.[110] In retrospect, the Derryman believed that the negative response from Irish comrades was a by-product of the enhanced importance and perception of 'solidarity' among the political prisoners in England.[111] When moved to Maghaberry, County Antrim, in September 1985, he perceived a greater degree of tolerance for his perspective, albeit within a prison regime designed to undermine paramilitary authority. However, it is extremely unlikely that he would have been allowed to remain on a republican landing of Portlaoise or an IRA-controlled prison environment in Crumlin Road and Long Kesh in 1978. Prisoners in England generally had far more freedom of association and routine than under the formal O/C arrangements maintained in Ireland. Among those he may have presumed to be hostile were men who believed that he had refused to enter into dialogue.[112]

The 'Blanket Protest'

The shifting context of the Irish situation changed the relative significance of the prison struggle in England. The mounting severity of the Blanket Protest in the H-Blocks in the early months of 1978 competed for the limited resources available to pro-republican advocates in Ireland and Britain. A case in point was the London meeting convened in Conway Hall on 3 March 1978 which highlighted the demand for 'Prisoner of War Status'. The focus was very much on Belfast as opposed to Parkhurst, and the gathering was similar to those held by the new Relatives Action Committee in Limerick and elsewhere. The Irish bias was logical given that 'special category' had been expressly removed to undermine republican cohesion in the Six Counties. This had resulted in a gruelling, widespread protest. Prisoner groups organized by Sinn Féin Headquarters in Dublin, not least the RAC of Belfast, sought publicity in England for the parallel protests in the

North of Ireland.[113] Belfast RAC drew strength from precursor and kindred groupings, and Andersonstown founding member Leo Wilson had belonged at various times to the Citizen Defence Committees, the Association for Legal Justice and later the National H-Block/ Armagh Committee.[114] Linked events included the picketing of newspaper offices on Fleet Street, London, by twelve blanket-clad women on 1 March and a public meeting in the House of Commons. Many London-based personalities of the prisoner campaign participated in the Conway Hall evening, including Sr. Sarah Clarke, Jim Reilly, Jackie Kaye and progressive Labour politician Ken Livingstone.[115] The International Marxist Group and Socialist Workers Party were prominent in the London gathering yet were criticized by Kaye and Reilly for their 'failure ... to support Republican prisoners in England'.[116] Generally, the strategy of the PAC Central Committee was to 'maintain friendly relations with all anti-imperialist groups and to co-operate with them wherever possible in the mutual struggle against repression'.[117] The lack of rigid alliances provided room for criticism of policies and tactics within the groupings.

Tensions between the PAC and elements of Sinn Féin in London, partly due to uncoordinated fundraising arrangements, had calmed since a flare up in the early months of 1977. 'Official' Sinn Féin, which had recently added the suffix 'The Workers' Party' to its title as part of an ambitious process of reinvention, commented on the matter in their *Eolas* newsletter. The Official Republican Movement had a vestigial interest in the fortunes of the PAC given that the group had emerged from its Clann na hÉireann affiliate in England. 'Official' Sinn Féin claimed that An Cumann Cabhrach in London had complained that *An Phoblacht* editor Gerry O'Hare and 'Provisional' Sinn Féin in general was overly supportive of Kaye and the PAC.[118] O'Hare, a man with a Peoples Democracy background, was described as an 'ultra-left' activist in the same edition of *Eolas,* which promoted the impression that the Provisionals were politically incoherent and riven with dissension.[119] While there were indeed divergences on strategic direction between the PAC and Sinn Féin in England, the key bone of contention in London in 1977–78 centred on money-raising for prisoners in a small pool of city locations. An Cumann Cabhrach relied upon such venues to fulfil its obligations of providing welfare support to the families of imprisoned republicans. The Official Republican Movement, which retained an armed existence for fundraising and feuding into the 1980s despite its nominal 1972 'ceasefire', underplayed its commitment to imprisoned adherents compared to Sinn Féin and the IRSP.[120]

Sinn Féin in England was increasingly preoccupied with the political status campaign in Ireland. A planning meeting in London on 19 February 1978 preceded the 26 March Easter Sunday parade from Marble Arch to Kilburn Square. Advance publicity stated: 'This year ... the commemoration will have added significance. There is a growing campaign in Ireland demanding Prisoner of War status for all Republican prisoners and an end to the torture of prisoners in Long Kesh, Crumlin Road and Armagh prisons'.[121] Sinn Féin (Britain) recognized that it would have to take the lead and that its role in the UK was to harness, as far as possible, 'the revolutionary left and Irish prisoners groups'.[122] Given the fractured nature of UK jurisdictions and its weak constitutional framework, Sinn Féin was essentially lobbying for reforms which, if granted by Westminster, would not automatically apply to imprisoned IRA personnel in England and Scotland.

There were limits to what could be achieved by an overstretched Sinn Féin, and the party's efforts to build support in Britain were subject to well-orchestrated state obstruction. On 5 April republican strategist Jim Gibney was held in Manchester for the full seven days permitted by the PTA on travelling to address a National Union of Students conference. He was duly issued with an Exclusion Order which effectively nullified his contribution to any England-centred campaign.[123] When the United Troops Out Movement conference met in Leeds on 22 April, Kaye's speech on Irish prisoners in England competed for attention with an ultimately successful attempt to move a resolution pledging support for 'the Republican Movement in the Irish Freedom Struggle'.[124] UTOM comprised a breakaway from the original TOM with whom it differed in July 1977 on the primacy of 'armed struggle' *vis à vis* mobilizing the British public on the Irish question. British radicals in the late 1970s were stressed by the dilemma of urging an immediate, unilateral military withdrawal rather than pressing first for a Bill of Rights and other forms of legislation designed to promote parity between the two political traditions in the Six Counties.[125] TOM had raised consciousness in Britain regarding the human price being paid by the military in the early-to-mid 1970s. Founder member Aly Renwick believed this informed the 'Ulsterization' strategy: 'There was a period when they were at their wits end about what they were going to do about the North. They were quite close to going for withdrawal'.[126]

The 1978 Easter Sunday rally in Kilburn had created a platform for the PAC and Sinn Féin to canvas allied left wing groups. This was followed up by a 5 May PAC meeting in the NUFTO Hall, London, to address a two point agenda: 'Prisoner of War status for all Irish political prisoners within the terms of the Geneva Convention and amnesty within the context of British withdrawal from Ireland'. Kaye chaired on behalf of the PAC and Jim Reilly of Sinn Féin (Britain) gave the main oration. The date selected for the event, the birthday of Karl Marx, was intended to honour his role, along with Friedrich Engels, in campaigning on behalf of Fenian prisoners imprisoned in Britain from the 1860s. The PAC had previously commemorated Marx, and the gesture was an example of the anti-imperialist dimension of the prisoner controversy in England.[127] Dozens of organizations and individuals had been invited to send messages of support and the meeting received statements from the IRA PROs of Parkhurst, Long Lartin, Gartree and Albany.[128] The message from Albany had been smuggled out of the Punishment Block where several IRA prisoners had been confined since 25 April 1978 when, according to the Prison Department, 'a group of Republican prisoners refused to go to work when ordered to do so' in order to protest visiting arrangements.[129] The statement, with input from Eddie O'Neill and Ray McLaughlin, was substantial and militant in its rhetoric:

> Revolutionary greeting to all Comrades gathered here to expose the crimes of British imperialism in Ireland. We urge all socialist comrades in Britain to show solidarity with the Irish revolution and to wake up to the fact that a victory for socialism in Ireland is a victory for socialism everywhere ... From our attempts to politicize British prisoners we realise the difficulty of your task. We have made progress through our examples of solidarity and undying hatred of the prison system. The prison regime attempts to make psychological cabbages out of Republican and socialist prisoners but it will never succeed. The carrot of parole holds no attractions for Republican socialists. They cannot buy us so they will never control us. This message comes from the block in Albany prison. We are down here as a protest over the apartheid-style visits given to Republican socialists and to innocent Irish framed for Republican operations. We are not only [Category] 'A' prisoners but we are segregated from other prisoners. We are unable to embrace our wives or girlfriends, our mothers and fathers ... Victory will come through solidarity combined with positive action.[130]

While Amnesty International did not regard the IRA as 'prisoners of conscience', the organization had been critical of Britain for its harsh interrogation of prisoners in the Castlereagh Centre, and this lent credence to similar and well-founded allegations in respect of the H-Blocks and England.[131] The 5 May event in London, and another in Manchester on 26 May, fostered common ground between the Revolutionary Communist Group (RCG) and PAC on the wider question of political status.[132] From December 1976, the RCG paper *Hands off Ireland!* was one of the most focused publications emanating from the British left on the conflict and a strong proponent of the contentious 'troops out now' position.[133] TOM was divided on absolute demands for an immediate British military withdrawal from Ireland for fear of unleashing uncontrollable forces, a proposal vigorously opposed by Gerry Fitt of the SDLP, Garret FitzGerald of Fine Gael, and other anti-republican moderates.[134] Two promising joint meetings held in May 1978 were interspersed by a third in London in which the Roger Casement Cumann of Sinn Féin unfurled its 'first H-Block banner'. This debut, and the significance ascribed to it by its creators, illustrated the mounting preoccupation of the party structures in England with Long Kesh.[135] In a telling development, the numerically small PAC formed a 'Prisoners in Ireland' sub-committee to concentrate on campaigning for republicans in the two Irish jurisdictions.[136]

As before, the most powerful and well-resourced organization of the British Left, the CPGB, refused to be drawn into a declaration of solidarity. The Stalinist CPGB remained wedded to a *de facto* policy of following the lead of communist affiliates in the North of Ireland, a body with disproportionate input from persons drawn from the Unionist as well as sectarian Loyalist community. This produced a glaring paradox whereby the CPGB voiced support for international leftist revolutionary organizations in Continental Europe, Africa and Asia, while condemning the closest equivalent within the UK and Ireland. Moreover, the stance of British communists necessitated ignoring Moscow's general opposition to allied front groups backing sub-national elements. Irish communists were by no means immune to such tensions, and the far left was badly factionalised in the 1970s, not least by the 'Two Nations' tendency promoted by British Irish Communist Organization (BICO), which critics contended had conferred a degree of political legitimacy on a hardline Unionist position.[137] Individual communists and far left trade unionists, however, were sympathetic towards Irish republicans. Although a well-known Spanish Civil War veteran turned his back on Eddie Caughey at a funeral in Burton-On-Trent, he obtained legal assistance for his imprisoned republican son from a CPGB union official.[138]

The studied and damaging detachment of the CPGB from the 'Irish Question' resulted in the PAC picketing their offices in King Street, London, on 16 June 1978.[139] The SWP, NCCL and Connolly Association were also criticized for their perceived failure to rally behind the PAC/ Sinn Féin driven campaign on political status and amnesty.[140] The Labour Party, similarly, was generally indisposed to back radical proposals from its TOM membership. This reflected sensitivity on the block votes cast by several craft and engineering unions which supported the minority opinion of their Unionist membership in Ireland. This position shifted towards a more pro-Irish Labour Party stance in late 1981 in the aftermath of the H-Block hunger strike.[141] Amnesty International, frequently criticized by Irish republicans for their silence on the maltreatment of political prisoners in England, published findings on torture in the North of Ireland in June 1978 after a seven-month investigation.[142] Shocking reports of the 'blanket protest' in the H-Blocks, and the severity of interrogations in Castlereagh distracted English radicals from the local brutalities of the Dispersal System, but even this sense of exigency failed to stimulate left wing unity in Ireland. New 'H-Block Committees' in Oxford and elsewhere in Britain, and a dedicated TOM demonstration in London against the Castlereagh abuses represented further, if logical, redirection of English political energy towards problems in Ireland.[143]

British counter-insurgents, meanwhile, gradually substituted the crude psychological and physical methods used in Castlereagh to extract 'confessions' with 'supergrasses' whose unsupported testimony was used to convict scores in the juryless Diplock Courts.[144] The Brehon Law Society of New York, an organization comprising Irish-American and humanitarian practitioners of the legal profession on the East Coast of the USA, described the new Diplock proceedings that matured in the early 1980s as 'show trials'.[145] The allusion to Stalinist-era extremity in the Soviet Union's legal system was intentional and geared towards aggravating socially conservative Irish-Americans. The tactical use of informers and agents in court, surprisingly, was never utilized against the IRA in Britain, possibly owing to attention it would have brought to bear on the conduct of certain jury trials and the statutory requirement to air 'accomplice evidence' in front of a civilian panel. Commitment to the jury tradition, as the numerous miscarriage of justice cases affirmed in the 1990s, provided no guarantee of fair or appropriate verdicts in trials where forensic evidence was vitiated. There were, moreover, no IRA prisoners in England willing to compromise in such a manner in the 1980s.[146]

The Campbell case at Strasbourg

The European Commission of Human Rights on 9 May 1978 decided to admit the test case taken by Sean Campbell alleging breaches of the European Convention by the British authorities in relation to Irish prisoners in England. The breakthrough signalled that the Commission in Strasbourg believed there was a *prima facie* breach of Article Six arising from the refusal of the Home Office to permit Campbell to consult with his lawyers between October 1976 and March 1977. This essentially reasserted the *Golder v UK (1975: 1 ECHR, 524)* judgement of February 1975. Another element of the complaint focused on the conduct of the Board of Visitors who had punished the Tyrone man with solitary confinement and loss of remission. However, this potentially significant advance was tempered by the failure of the Commission to accept claims from Campbell and others that Article Three had been breached by the violence inflicted by staff on the Albany prisoners.[147] The case was still under consideration in March 1982 when Campbell was released and deported, having served all but a few months of his full sentence.[148] Prisoners could petition the Home Secretary for restoration of forfeited remission under Prison Rule 56 (2), but IRA members rarely pursued this theoretical option. Campbell evidently did not elicit the support of the various adjudicating bodies who had imposed sanctions and who enjoyed in doing so the capacity to make restoration under Order 42 (a) of *Prison Standing Orders* (1977). This directed: 'Where a prisoner's institutional behaviour has shown a significant improvement, indicative of a genuine change of attitude (as opposed to staying out of trouble), and the improvement is likely to be maintained, a governor or Board of Visitors, depending upon which adjudicating authority originally awarded the forfeiture of remission, may restore part of the remission a prisoner is forfeited if restoration will bring forward the earliest date of release'.[149]

Movement in Strasbourg revived the waning issue of Irish prisoners in England. The *Times* of London observed that the presence of over 100 persons regarded as IRA personnel in the Dispersal System had exacerbated pressures arising from overcrowding.[150] In January 1978, the official tally of those 'connected with the IRA' was ninety, of whom seventy-eight were Category A. There were fifteen Loyalists of whom six were Category A.[151] The Home Office acknowledged the general problem when pressed by the *Irish Times,* and a spokesman honestly conceded that the IRA 'obviously caused additional strain on prisons and prison officers'.[152] Given the comparatively small numbers involved, the real difficulty was posed by the perceived necessity of applying labour intensive restrictions which collaterally stressed long-term prisoners accommodated in England's maximum security wings by virtue of disproportionate resource allocation. Such men were on occasion discommoded by being obliged to share the lot of the Irish militants in their midst or, more typically, granted more consideration than IRA members sharing the Category A designation. The presence of republican women in H-Wing, Durham, warped the experience of all those contained in the annexe and it could not be concealed from informed parties that the administration of IRA prisoners had displaced many of the most dangerous men in Britain from the SSUs. This unusual admission of Irish exceptionalism in London came very close to conceding the consistently denied existence of political prisoners. Relating republican 'behaviour' to their typically long sentences, and supposed enmity with other prisoners, obscured the characteristic dynamic of political assertion and culture of resistance fostered in the IRA cadres. The airing of such matters, however guardedly, coincided with a bid by Hull prison officers, articulated by Kenneth Daniel of the POA, to register their objection with the Home Office to suspension of members due for trial arising from the 1976 riot.[153]

An Anti-Repression Conference convened by Capuchin Fr. Piaras Ó Duill in Dublin on 19–21 May 1978 attracted numerous activists engaged with the political prisoner question in Ireland. Belgian, French and Basque legal experts formed part of a panel of inquiry which convened in Liberty Hall, Dublin.[154] They received reports from various expert contributors, including solicitor Alastair Logan and Jackie Kaye of the PAC, who addressed the situation in England. It was claimed that the panel 'found the plight of Irish political prisoners in England most disturbing ... they are discriminated against in a racist fashion, beatings and solitary confinement being the usual punitive measures'.[155] Young Derry republican Micheal MacLochlainn, who had been held in four English prisons prior to 23 December 1977, contributed a statement in which he described the collusion between criminals and Brixton staff in the potentially fatal attack on Eddie O'Neill with boiling water in November 1974.[156] The conference was informed that there were eighty-five such prisoners, of whom all but three were classified as Category A. This number compared to the 300 republicans involved in protests in Crumlin Road, Armagh and Long Kesh.[157]

Government-level interest in the management of imprisonment in the EEC was manifested by the publication in 1978 of *Treatment of Long Term Prisoners* by the European Committee on Crime Problems. Penological research commissioned by a subcommittee of the Council of Europe examined six countries. The study incorporated Home Office-aided research on 215 inmates within English prisons and included a seminar hosted in Wakefield. When reviewing the publication for the *Prison Service Journal*, J Williams, Governor of Long Lartin, concluded that it contained 'no startling new theories or propositions'.[158] Project psychiatrist, Dr. Sluga, concluded that men who had served four to six years of long sentences under conditions of isolation were prone to 'functional psycho-syndrome'. Symptoms included emotional and cognitive disturbance, infantile regression and difficulties in social interaction. Williams, however, noted the findings of psychologist Professor Smith in the English Dispersal System, where 'general deterioration' was not as strongly in evidence as might have been expected, although hostility towards the self was a major issue. The reviewer emphasised the positive conclusion that severe mental health threats were neither inevitable nor irreversible. Williams, moreover, stressed that 'Resolution 76 (2) on the treatment of long term prisoners', endorsed by the Council of Ministers in February 1976, recognized the practical difficulties of implementing certain reforms and the rights of individual prison regimes to reject recommendations they deemed inappropriate. The tone and content of the Williams review would have reassured his Home Office employers in that it downplayed the relevance of many potentially disturbing factors. It also indicated that the Dispersal System was in no danger of being exposed to serious criticism.[159] Other international physiatrists differed on this key mental health point and reiterated contrary findings well into the 1980s and 1990s.[160]

Re-organization and resistance, February-July 1978

IRA prisoners in England appreciated in 1978 that their perspective on the armed struggle and specific interests were in danger of being occluded by the extremity of the conflict in Ireland and the mounting seriousness of the crisis in Long Kesh. Many had friends, associates and relatives enduring the grim and deteriorating 'blanket protest'.[161] April had witnessed the escalation to a 'no wash' protest in Long Kesh, during which prisoners incapable of removing bodily waste from their cells in the conventional manner of 'slopping out' began spreading it on the walls.[162] Billy Armstrong communicated from Wakefield: 'All my comrades both in this prison and the other prisons [in England] … are right behind them all the way, no matter what the consequences that might befall us'. This hinted that actions would follow, a threat which the IRA were more capable of delivering in 1978 than at any time since 1969.[163] Martin Brady claimed:

> We worked as a group – if one went down to the block we all went down to the block. We made sure they had company … They wouldn't drive you crazy in solitary when you were downstairs … As our prisoners were coming in they were becoming more educated. Looking at our rights in jail, our human rights, fellows sat down over the years, passed tests … They seen we were educated and we were using the system for our own advantage … So we started building friendships with the gangsters and the robbers. We got on with them. Ninety per cent of them got on with us. They were good towards us … You got the odd screws that upped the tempo, to stir up trouble.[164]

His co-accused, Armstrong, noted: 'There were two sorts of screws: the ones who were frightened of you, and the ones that pretended to like you. But at the end of the day they bottled out from fear that you would kill one of them before they got to you. The screws often set us up for other prisoners, but at the end of the day they hadn't really the bottle for it'.[165] Leading IRA member Brian Keenan reflected:

> The screws were in no doubt that the IRA people, if it was necessary, wouldn't hesitate to kill them, and I think that that type of common position had been created over a long period of time with IRA prisoners. And the screws knew how far they could go with this and by and large we just got on with our time and the only priorities we ever had were our families and escape attempts. Outside of that you just done time in the best you could.'[166]

Increasingly, prisoners utilized their growing numbers in English jails to form loose groupings represented by a PRO. Isolation in the Dispersal System, a comparatively minor numerical presence on the wings, and detachment from command structures in Ireland negated the functionality of an appointed O/C. Moreover, the very factors that militated against the selection of O/Cs ensured that the Governors could readily deny prospective leaders the mobility they needed to adequately function. Republicans in English prisons devised more reliable means of communication between each other and the outside world. This enabled the men to marshal their new strengths and experience towards significant, co-ordinated action.

The first major statement highlighted by the Republican Movement in 1978 originated in Wakefield in February. Irish prisoners alleged a 'high level conspiracy by the Governor and his goons to ill-treat and intimidate the POWs' and named 'Big' Mick Murray, Jimmy Ashe, Paul Norney and Billy

Armstrong as having been 'placed in the control unit for various periods of time'. The claim that the Control Unit remained in operation contradicted Government assertions that it had been closed in 1974. The IRA insisted 'the only thing that had changed was its name, as they use the control unit as the [punishment] block and it is regarded by the screws as a place in which prisoners are broken ... using sensory deprivation methods'.[167] Immediate concerns were expressed for Norney who was then spending twenty-three hours a day in his cell and isolated during the remaining hour from other prisoners.[168] His stay in the wing was extended by seven days when he defied his captors by running rather than walking around the small outside enclosure where he was permitted fresh air for up to one hour a day.[169] The message contained an allusion to what had happened in Albany in 1976 and communicated the view that 'all this harassment is to provoke us into taking some form of action'. Needling by the authorities placed the IRA in a quandary in that a mistimed unilateral protest could incite further repression and demoralization. Failing to act, however, risked giving the impression of conformity and weakness. Consequently, the February statement insisted: 'We will take our stand when we are ready, not when the screws want to set us up'.[170] Having outlined the short term issues in play at Wakefield, the prisoners solicited support for the 'war for national liberation' as 'the best way' to support political prisoners.[171]

The IRA PRO in Parkhurst published a greeting in *Republican News* in March 1978 which praised 'revolutionary ... and all those other prisoners at Parkhurst ... without whose wonderful help the recent escape attempt would not have been possible'.[172] This sincere, if somewhat inflammatory, statement testified to the existence of a small political cadre in the prison which claimed a role for itself within and without the Dispersal System. The propaganda potential of reaching a republican readership was clearly evident. Similarly, the Albany PRO drafted a letter in April which analysed the recent Workers' Party/ Republican Clubs Ard Fheis. The 'Officials' were taken to task for claiming the mantle of 1916 Irish Citizen Army icon James Connolly whilst 'feuding with progressive socialist groups and taking part in colonial run elections'.[173] This referenced the violent struggle between the Official IRA and emergent INLA and IRSP which had claimed the life of Seamus Costello on 5 October 1977.[174] Costello had been shot dead in Dublin by ex-England Official IRA prisoner Jim Flynn. Collective action permitted individual assertion and Fr. Pat Fell published a personal tribute to the assassinated Marie Drumm, shot in the Mater Hospital, Belfast by British-backed Loyalists on 28 October 1976.[175] Criticizing opponents and praising comrades was very much the standard discourse of Sinn Féin cummain in Britain and Ireland. While such communications regularly emerged from Long Kesh, Portlaoise and Armagh, the input from England represented a bid for inclusion in the totality of prisoner affairs. Politically minded IRA men such as Eddie O'Neill, Ray McLaughlin, Gerry Cunningham, Paul Holmes, Ronnie McCartney, Joe O'Connell, Vince Donnelly, Tony Cunningham, Sean Campbell, Kevin Dunphy, Tony Madigan and Busty Cunningham were not easily excluded.[176]

Visits to Albany were disrupted in February 1978 when staff contacted Irish families at short notice to cancel their pre-booked Visiting Orders. Only two Irish prisoners were permitted to have simultaneous visits, and staff employed what Sr. Clarke termed 'a new trick' in which they interrupted sessions, claiming that the space was required for another family who would otherwise forfeit their slot.[177] The IRA men conferred in mid-February when the Board of Visitors refused to compromise on the running of 'closed' visits, but could not decide on a specific plan of action. Three voted for a roof top occupation and four for non-cooperation. IRA prisoners in Ireland generally followed the direction of an O/C who was advised by an Adjutant and Intelligence Officer and, at times, the external leadership. Republicans in Albany commenced a policy of 'non-cooperation' with prison staff in early April when 'visiting and other conditions seriously worsened'.[178] This was unusual in that April 1978 witnessed the announcement of a Civil Service Pay Settlement that ended staff protests.[179]

Recourse to a more concerted protest followed the failure of a formal overture by Ray McLaughlin, via his solicitor Alastair Logan and Joan Maynard MP, to the House of Commons. Maynard's question on visits at Albany and the Dispersal System elicited the disingenuous claim from the Home Office that the IRA were not subject to discrimination. Home Office denials and Board of Visitor intransigence set the scene for a confrontation.[180] Indeed, Maynard's methodical probing of the Home Office in June 1978 had revealed that Category A IRA prisoners were obliged to accept untypical visiting conditions explained in vague terms of 'security reasons'.[181] Logan revealed that the main proposal by Governor Lister to defuse the situation in April was to remove one of the two wall-to-wall tables from the unsuitable space provided to enable visitors to embrace their relatives. The result was the repositioning of two staff members who usually sat in the corridor inside the small room when in use.[182] McLaughlin apprised Logan that in addition to a loitering female 'matron' or WPC, 'there are still at least four security employees listening in on every visit, two of these sit about three feet behind the prisoner and the other two behind the visitor'.[183]

This supposedly irenic-minded adjustment was deemed unsatisfactory by prisoners, especially when it was balanced by a new policy of strip-searching before and after sessions. According to Logan:

> It is making it impossible for visits to take place. The Governor knows full well that the individuals concerned will not voluntarily submit to a strip search. Strip

searching is normally only carried out accompanied by what is known as a "spin" when the prisoner's cell is thoroughly searched by a team of Officers to find out if he have any unlawful material … If he is right and the prisoners decide not to accept visits under these conditions, he will have got over the problem which the visits have been causing by constant complaints.[184]

Lord Harris insisted on 11 July 1978 that this reform was 'purely a security precaution and not, as the [George E Baker & Co] solicitors appear to be suggesting, a control or punishment measure'. Harris rejected calls to investigate what he believed to be baseless 'allegations … that Irish Republican prisoners are discriminated against'.[185] The FCO, which preferred questions on prison policy originating in the Irish Embassy to be redirected to the Home Office, viewed Maynard as 'an active supporter of the "Troops Out Movement"' and Logan as a solicitor who had 'close connections with IRA prisoners in this country, and an active propagandist for them'.[186]

Refusing work in Albany entailed confinement in the Segregation Block for terms of fourteen to fifty-six days. All the republicans, baring the abstaining Fr. Pat Fell, and innocent ex-Official IRA man Sean Smyth, were confined in the Block by 25 April. On rejecting an invitation from the Governor to resume their 'duties' as normal after a twenty-four hour period of enforced reflection, the recalcitrant men were returned to cells set aside for the obdurate and disobedient.[187] Tony Madigan favoured the option of taking to the roof, but the discovery of rope ladders in his cell, along with paint he intended to use to daub slogans once *in situ*, negated the plan: 'The visits again were a bone of contention. The lads then said we'd all refuse work and again I disagreed … I thought you caused them more problems being up in the general population than you can be isolated in the Block. If you let them isolate you, you are not threatening them … We were down there for ten months'.[188] Every effort was made to frustrate the efficient running of the unit by such means as banging doors, shouting, singing and making noise in contravention of regulations. This inspired English prisoners to join in and offer a united front of defiance to staff.[189]

Two focused bouts of agitation won a Derry criminal a light bulb in his cell and Busty Cunningham access to the weekly bath he was nominally permitted. Success, however, entailed repercussions from an establishment that could not be seen to weaken in the face of protesting prisoners. Beatings during future 'lie downs' were promised, and the core of the IRA group was disrupted by swopping Eddie O'Neill for Tipp Guilfoyle in Gartree, and Ray McLaughlin for Stephen Blake in Wakefield.[190] Once delivered, Guilfoyle declined to wear prison uniform in Albany and spent fifteen months in segregation in consequence.[191] Blake was initially located on a standard wing but became embroiled in a 'fracas' when he refused the demeaning job of sewing uniforms.[192] Madigan did not believe much had been achieved in the Block by what he termed the 'Terence MacSwiney Syndrome', whereby republicans sought moral victory by endurance and self-sacrifice rather than mere infliction. The question of stepping up resistance by means of sabotage, however, had been raised as an alternate strategy.[193]

The May 1978 statement released by the Albany men to the Sinn Féin/ PAC Karl Marx commemoration in London evidenced their appreciation of the utility of political propaganda. A constant stream of publicity from the jails was necessary to ensure the refreshment and wide dissemination of the republican message. Rallies, commemorations and marches organized by their allies in England created regular audiences for communications addressing a wide range of topics. Latitude from Headquarters was in evidence given that General Order No 2 (c) of the IRA Constitution prohibited Volunteers from 'promoting communist or capitalist literature', and open identification with Marxist figureheads met with disapproval in traditional republican heartlands.[194] GHQ and Sinn Féin Head Office understood that the political dynamic in England warranted a more ecumenical approach to republican assertion. Accordingly, 'comrades' at liberty in Britain were exhorted by the Albany prisoners to combine street agitation with educational work in order to advance the universal socialist agenda. Contemporary matters of specific and urgent concern within the Dispersal System were generally raised in such expansive addresses.[195]

Gartree's IRA PRO published a notice in June 1978 which alleged that privileges were being extended to Loyalist prisoners beyond those normally available to Category A men. The Leicestershire prison had a strong cohort of republicans in the summer of 1978 which included Phil Sheridan, Eddie O'Neill, Martin Brady, Peter Short, Brian (aka Donal) McLaughlin, Paul Holmes, Jerry Mealy, Ronnie McCartney, John McCluskey and Paul Hill. Whereas the innocent Hill was included in the 'Republican POW' company due to his many acts of solidarity, IRA member Michael Sheehan was listed as simply an 'other Irish political prisoner' along with the wrongly convicted Pat Maguire and Gerry Hunter.[196] Rolls were often inaccurate due to the constant shifting of Category A men and were open to misinterpretation. Although present in the jail, Brady had spent virtually all his time in segregation due to punishments imposed for the Hull Riot.[197] Hill had also been subjected to lie-downs in Armley and a fractious induction to Gartree, where he spent three days in the 'strong box' for insisting that a razor found in his cell was not his own property.[198]

Brian McLaughlin hailed from the Claudy area of north County Derry and was jailed in October 1976 for conspiracy to cause explosions in Birmingham with the Pat Christie-led grouping of Peter Toal, David Owen and Mick Reilly.[199] The men were among those who assumed prime responsibility for the Midlands sector following the arrest of the experienced IRA cluster headed by Dublin's Martin Coughlan in November 1974. Republicans were reserved in detailing McLaughlin's political background, which, according to printed sources after his release on 7 July 1982, stemmed from the experience of being attacked by the Parachute Regiment in Derry city on 30 January 1972. He had ran past Rossville flats on 'Bloody Sunday' when an unarmed man at his side was one of fourteen mortally wounded by British soldiers. According to McLaughlin: 'That was the turning point for me … From that moment on I realised there was only one answer to British violence and occupation-unconditional British withdrawal'. A year on remand in Winson Green, Birmingham, was followed by temporary incarceration in Liverpool ahead of allocation to Gartree where other Irish republicans were held.[200]

The Gartree spokesman highlighted the fact that two of the four Loyalists were given assignments as trustees despite being Category A prisoners. One, John Gadd, worked as an assistant to a Church of England chaplain and was accused of having viewed files pertaining to the IRA prisoners. Another, Harry James, cleaned the special visiting area set aside for the republicans and was deemed to pose a risk to the well-being of their relatives by virtue of being present when they arrived. Sammy Carson, serving fifteen years for attempting a no - warning bomb attack on 'Biddy Mulligan's' pub in Kilburn on 20 December 1975 received the prized job of wing orderly and, according to the PRO, was permitted to take Open University classes and receive normal 'open' visits. The fourth Loyalist, Norman Skinner, was evidently not as well situated as his comrades but his relative lack of patronage, consideration or progression within the complex was typical of all republicans.[201]

The thrust of the republican argument was that Loyalists were treated as if they were classified as Category B and by virtue of receiving enviable conditions of employment in the jail, were seen as gifted opportunities to jeopardize the personal security of the IRA prisoners and their families. The IRA did not, however, advance specific allegations, and relations with Loyalists were far better than would have been the case in contemporary Crumlin Road prison. The disparity of work allocation substantiated republican allegations of being persecuted. The PRO was highly explicit when citing unfavourable comparisons between the privileges bestowed on Loyalists and their concurrent denial to republicans serving similar sentences for similar offences. Sheridan and Short were named as men who had been, for all intents and purposes, wronged by the Governor for failing to take account of their relatively short sentences.[202] For most prisoners, the ongoing IRA campaigns in Ireland and England ensured that they were unlikely to be reclassified as Category B in the foreseeable future. The process of re-categorization, moreover, was secret, as a test case taken against the Home Office confirmed in May 1977.[203] Justice Cantley, who presided at several major IRA trials, including that of Brendan Dowd, had made the negative ruling arising from a challenge by a man classified as Category A in 1968.

Cantley upheld the right of the Home Office to prevent prisoners making 'representations against their classification' and the authority of staff to withhold pertinent information on file. The general lack of standardized policy regarding security classification was tackled by a Prison Department working party in 1981 without immediate impact.[204]

Questions posed by Joan Maynard in the Commons on 21 June 1978 revealed that two unidentified Loyalist prisoners had benefited from special, temporary and permanent transfer arrangements between 1974 and 1976.[205] Home Secretary Merlyn Rees also divulged an extraordinary statistic when he confirmed that of eighty-four prisoners in England subject to having 'visits in closely supervised conditions in the interests of security', no less than seventy-one were 'thought to have Republican links'. This represented a vast over-representation of IRA prisoners within the population, a fact played down by referencing 'security' fears to mask outright discrimination.[206] Rees also detailed the manner in which furniture, partitions and staff positioning was used to create a 'closely supervised' visit in Wakefield. In June 1978, a mere thirteen non-IRA Category A prisoners were obliged to endure 'closed' visits in the entire maximum security network. This offered strong evidence that republicans were genuine in describing their real position in the Dispersal System as 'Special Category A', a term with no official Home Office recognition.[207]

It was also clearly relevant that no IRA prisoner qualified for short-term relocation in order to receive accumulated visits. The criteria for temporary transfers within the UK consisted of the agreement of the Home Secretary and Secretary of State for Northern Ireland. In Whitehall, the NIO assumed full responsibility for 'permanent' transfers.[208] Only those born in the Six Counties or those who had spent 'a very long time' living there could be considered, and only then if the authorities were satisfied that suitable and secure accommodation was available. Those regarded as 'badly behaved' by a prison governor or persons deemed 'likely' to misbehave during transfer were ineligible. All applicants had to have served two years since allocation following sentence.[209] The case of Billy Armstrong was specifically considered following private high-level representations from Joan Maynard and Martin Wright, who had attempted to enlist the aid of veteran progressive Lord Fenner Brockway. Lord Harris was 'not persuaded' that the Belfastman should be facilitated, 'having regard to all the factors'.[210] Wright's commendation of the 'adoption of Christian pacifism' by Shane Paul O'Doherty, which he evidently interpreted as a positive sign of personal reformation, did not alter the equation.[211] Wright, Director of the Howard League for Penal Reform, acknowledged the multiple negative provisos, as well as NIO claims of overcrowding, in his 16 May 1978 overture to Brockway. Wright assured Brockway that the 'Howard League has no wish to become involved in the complexities of the Northern Ireland situation' while urging that the five remaining 'Belfast Ten' prisoners in England should be repatriated. Sensing official objections, Wright argued that 'humanitarian grounds' pertained and implied the Home Office was being 'unfair'.[212] He later advised Sr. Clarke to consider legal proceedings in cases where IRA prisoners in England were being held 'for long periods in special "cooling off" local cells' for more than the maximum twenty-eight days.[213]

The Gartree statement also referenced the halt in the repatriation of IRA prisoners following the April 1975 movement of Hugh Feeney and Gerry Kelly and, in the context of more frequent facilitation of Loyalist prisoners, suggested that the special negotiated circumstances arising from the 1973–4 hunger strike had lapsed.[214] It appeared as if the renewed fight for political status in Long Kesh encouraged pro-activity in England where, despite William Whitelaw's misleading statement on 'special category' in the Commons in 1972, no comparable privileges had ever existed. The Home Office could be forgiven for viewing the airing of such points in Gartree as the mere reflexive and obvious declamations of Irish republicans. However, the newly assertive and aggressive tone of the message was soon manifested in terms that demanded attention, if not also redress. Those monitoring expressions of discontent by the IRA in Gartree knew that Tipp Guilfoyle and Martin Coughlan had been at the centre of controversies in 1977–8.[215]

Significantly, the Gartree protest was the most dramatic manifestation of an unprecedented and concerted effort to highlight grievances in English prisons. IRA prisoners in Albany, Long Lartin, Parkhurst, Wormwood Scrubs and Wakefield all participated in planned actions on 5–7 July 1978.[216] Ironically, prison shifts authorised by the Home Office and implemented in the name of security assisted IRA strategizing in the advent of the protests. While no great motivation was required to spur the active engagement of republicans, the ghosting of particular prisoners spread and accentuated their sense of persecution. Lifer Vince Donnelly had been fasting in Long Lartin from 19 May to press his claim a line of work pursued by a number of his Tyrone-born siblings. His move to Wakefield on 4 June, however, reprised a trajectory which had fatal consequences for Frank Stagg in February 1976. This was viewed as a virtual death threat and served to harden rather than weaken resolve in the spatially fractured republican jail complement.[217]

The timing of the new strategy placed the Wakefield IRA men in a quandary as they were assembling a cache of escape equipment that was neither readily utilisable nor, in all probability, securable from discovery if major protests commenced. IRA comrades asked Donnelly upon arrival to abandon his hunger strike owing to such 'other developments'. The jail contained Ray McLaughlin, Tony Clarke, Michael Reilly, Sean Hayes and the innocent Paddy Armstrong on C Wing. Paul Norney, Jimmy Ashe and Mick Murray were on D Wing while Joe Duffy (aka Michael/ Joe Mooney) and Billy Armstrong were on A Wing. Murray had just emerged from sixty days in F Wing for allegedly assaulting a prison officer whom he deemed had been unacceptably confrontational. The Dubliner had difficulty speaking after spending two months in silence.[218] F Wing windows comprised eighteen three-inch square blocks of semi-opaque glass set two feet into the wall at a height of seven feet. Two sets of bars covered the interior of the window and a wire mesh its exterior.[219]

Much of the escape kit, including two 'shank' knives and lengths of roping made from cloth material, was discovered in the jail on 2 July. Six of the ten IRA prisoners were punished with one month's loss of privileges and loss of pay. The search was inspired by the discovery of wax traces on a 'pass key' belonging to a Prison Officer who had been on holiday, a find of enormous significance in that the bearer of a complete key could move between different parts of the complex.[220] On 3 July, Armstrong and Donnelly were ghosted to Strangeways and Reilly and Hayes to Armley, Leeds. Reilly's wife and family had travelled that day from Birmingham to see him in Wakefield. Donnelly had recently been prevented from receiving a visit from Frank Maguire MP and thereby lost an opportunity to confer on the wider situation.[221] McLaughlin and Clarke were sent to Durham. The other IRA men did what they could to participate in events they knew to be imminent, but their contribution was necessarily minimal due to close confinement. Murray was returned to F Wing where, despite an initial sentence of fifty-six days' segregation, he was still held seventeen months later.[222] Ashe and Norney, who was already in 'patches' due to his escape attempt from Wormwood Scrubs, remained in solitary.[223] Donnelly, Hayes and Armstrong received their own E List designations arising from the incident.[224] Visitors to republican prisoners in several jails on 5 July were informed that a co-ordinated protest was planned in support of political status, repatriation and improved visiting conditions. The demands were restated in a statement from the Gartree PRO in the aftermath of the protest.[225] News from the prisons prompted the creation of an ad hoc Irish Political Prisoners Support Group to spearhead demonstrations in London. The anticipated incidents commenced that night in Albany when republicans vandalized cell furniture.[226]

On 6 July, IRA prisoners in Long Lartin, Wakefield, Wormwood Scrubs and Parkhurst refused meals, although it was evident despite this impressive co-ordination that no major hunger strike had been initiated.[227] Seven prisoners in Albany, who were already being held in the Segregation Unit, aka 'Punishment Block', were charged with 'smashing their cells'.[228] This entailed throwing chamber pots into the corridor, breaking furniture and, in some cases, gouging plaster from the walls. Loyalist Alex Brown, one of the group who attempted to bomb 'Biddy Mulligan's' pub, joined the IRA - led strike and was beaten by staff for this courageous act of identification.[229]

Subjected to further restrictions on access to sanitation, attendance at religious services and visits, the republicans progressed along a path of confrontation that resulted in a full blown 'blanket protest' in October.[230] The Prison Department disdained the 'demonstration', which was officially regarded in a cold, decontextualized manner as a refusal 'to use the normal sanitary facilities' resulting in the fouling of the landing floor and several staff members. Those responsible were reported as 'choosing not to wear prison clothes for part of the time'.[231]

While there was ongoing concern for those subjected to the F Wing regime, it was the 'no wash' of Long Kesh which inspired the selected mode and rhetoric of the 6 July fracas in the House of Commons. Two Socialist Worker's Party activists threw bags of horse manure from the public gallery onto the MPs sitting below whilst shouting questions about conditions in Long Kesh. The business of Parliament halted while the benches were hastily cleaned and the splattered MPs refreshed.[232] One of the protesters was Yana Mintoff, daughter of Maltese Prime Minister Dom Mintoff. The second was Irishman John MacSherry, who lived in London.[233] Long Kesh and 'solidarity with the H-Blocks' was also the declared primary spur of IRA prisoner action in Gartee the following day.[234]

Gartree, 7 July 1978

The most serious Dispersal System incident occurred in Gartree where, on the morning of 7 July, Eddie O'Neill, Paul Holmes, Jerry Mealy, Ronnie McCartney, Phil Sheridan, Martin Brady, Brian McLaughlin and Paul Hill made it to the rooftop by the unconventional means of using John McCluskey as a human ladder.[235] Aware that the staff expected something to occur, the chance to congregate in the yard and seize the initiative was not passed up. McCartney recalled: 'We thought about the boys on the blanket and the women in Armagh ... So the next day out on the yard we said: "Right, let's hit the roof"'.[236] Brady recalled: 'McCluskey, a big giant ... says, "I'll push you up"' and shoved the impressed Belfastman upwards 'about twelve feet'.[237] McCluskey, tall and powerfully built, boosted the others onto a low roof but could not follow before guard dogs approached at speed. O'Neill regretted that his 'Uxbridge Eight' co-accused had been 'sacrificed', but realised there was no other way of getting so many IRA men into position in the time available. McCluskey knew in theory how to neutralize trained guard dogs and was aware that a minor error in his unpractised technique would lead to a savaging. However, against all expectations, the trained dogs loosed on him were wary of approaching aggressively and he was not seriously hurt before being hauled off to segregation.[238] Access to the upper roof of the prison services block was quickly gained from the lower level reached from the yard. Loyalist prisoner Sammy Carson, another 'Mulligan's Bar' attempted pub bomber, tossed the republicans useful materials from his cell window.[239] Banners and painted graffiti were displayed which referenced IRA demands for repatriation and political status, as well as affinity with the H-Block campaign.[240] Slogans visible from the street stated 'End H-BLOCK TORTURE', 'P.O.W. STATUS', 'SOLIDARITY', 'REPATRIATION' and 'H-BLOCK'.[241] O'Neill had stitched a large Irish Tricolour together from three pieces of sheeting. This was held aloft by one of the protesters whilst showing the leftist revolutionary clenched fist. It was intended, from the outset, to remain on the roof until the London rally planned for 9 July had taken place. Two of the men donned blankets to visually bolster the connection with Long Kesh.[242]

Improved communications between the prisons and supporters ensured that the protests were backed up by the largest pro-Irish street demonstrations in several years. A sit down by a small group outside Buckingham Palace on 6 July led to four arrests when the women involved disrupted the ceremonies of the Household Cavalry.[243] Other actions briefly impeded the first day of the hyped summer sales in Oxford Street, London while students protested in Edinburgh. The appearance of the four women in Bow Street Court on 7 July on charges relating to the Household Cavalry incident preceded an evening press conference in the House of Commons, convened by the new Irish Political Prisoners Support Group. Joan Maynard MP explained that the men were protesting their right to humane visiting conditions, political status and repatriation. She was assisted by Tom Litterick, MP for Birmingham (Selly Oak), one of several British parliamentarians refused permission to visit the H-Blocks.[244] Alastair Logan supported Maynard's accusation of the ill-treatment of Irish prisoners by reminding the audience that forty cases were pending at the European Commission on Human Rights. He specified the harassment endured by relatives of prisoners who travelled to England.[245] Pro-Irish republicans in the US avidly followed such developments.[246]

The Gartree incident and subsequent discussion in the Commons attracted rare front page coverage from the *Times*. It was accepted that the complaints of the 'Irish republican prisoners' extended to 'assault and prolonged solitary confinement', although the published account did not allude to the MPs who had advocated redress. Instead, the conservative orientated daily restated the position Home Secretary Rees had outlined the previous year which they summarized as meaning: 'There would be neither an amnesty nor the granting of political status for Irish prisoners'.[247] Rees was in much closer contact with republicans than was desirable for a prime IRA target, and on one occasion unwittingly procured the plastering services of Cork man Tom Goodchild, mainstay of Harrow Sinn Féin and An Cumann Cabhrach.[248]

When a major PAC - sponsored rally met at Marble Arch on 9 July, it did so under the banner of 'End silence on torture of Irish Prisoners of

War'. This was boosted in terms of credibility by an Amnesty International report which accused the British authorities of standing over numerous acts of maltreatment in the North of Ireland. The damning text was read in its entirety into the *Congressional Record* in Washington DC.[249] The PAC echoed what Maynard and Logan had asserted in the House of Commons in relation to excesses taking place within England's Dispersal System.[250] Around 5,000 marched in London, including contingents of the RCG, IMG, Big Flame, Workers Revolutionary Party, UTOM and IRSP, as well as leading elements of Sinn Féin and the PAC. Several trade unions were represented, notably branches of the ASTMS and TGWU.[251] Deep ideological divisions within various far left organizations remained, but the display of unity on the prison question produced the largest republican march in London since 1972.[252]

Most of the Hyde Park speakers addressed the deepening H-Block crisis, although the English dimension to the wider prison struggle was well noted, and many of the placards listed the names of those held in the Dispersal System.[253] Kaye claimed in an interview with *Republican News* that the 'courageous stand taken by the prisoners' in Ireland had been critical to the success of the London rally.[254] Sinn Féin (Britain) was represented by Jim Reilly, who addressed the crowd.[255] Vanessa Redgrave, a famous actress and leading WRP member, was widely quoted as saying on the occasion: 'victory for the IRA in their struggle against imperialism'.[256] Her comments exemplified the type of vigorous left cooperation sought by many inside Sinn Féin and the PAC in England. However, no platform was extended to the SWP in Hyde Park, owing to their visceral protest in the Commons three days earlier, which was regarded as undignified and potentially harmful.[257] Despite the minor factional quibbling, Kaye was credited by sympathetic republicans with 'unifying the fragmented left on this issue'.[258] Orchestration favoured the requirements of republican propaganda. Photographers got within sufficient range of Gartree to acquire dramatic images of the prisoners on the roof. The ephemeral SWP sponsored Irish Political Prisoner Support Group noted that they had 'cut through the media censorship for the first time since the Price Sisters nearly died' in June 1974.[259] The general public outside Gartree were sufficiently close to hear the shouted comments and rebel songs from the men on the roof. They were not well provisioned, however, and were unfortunate to be exposed to unseasonable high winds and heavy rainfall.[260]

Rainwater, at least, provided essential liquid which had been lightly contaminated by lead cladding. A more serious concern arose from news that the staff had acquired additional 'E-List' uniforms for the protesters, which indicated that those involved were to be regarded as attempted escapers with resultant diminution of privileges. It was negotiated that Ronnie McCartney, already 'in patches', would climb down and meet as planned with visitor Una Caughey, to whom this message could be relayed. This duly occurred, and having registered their position in very clear terms, the IRA men descended around 3.30 p.m. on 9 July.[261] Numerous prisoners on exercise refused to return to their cells 'until they knew the Irish prisoners were safe and well'.[262] All eight received forty-two days solitary confinement from the Board of Visitors on 21 July. John McCluskey was given fourteen days solitary for his less obvious but still critical role in getting them into position.[263] Jerry Mealy, who was moved to Wormwood Scrubs, lost thirteen months of remission, which was subsequently restored by legal action.[264] The IRA in Parkhurst was reported to have continued their hunger strike until 9 July.[265]

Armstrong was returned to Wakefield when his punishment elapsed and found that Ray McLaughlin, who had been teaching him Irish, was 'on the blanket' after his stint in Durham.[266] McLaughlin had started a unilateral protest in early August to strengthen his demand for repatriation and was immediately sent to F Wing.[267] His refusal to wear prison uniform led to the withdrawal of exercise time and incarceration for twenty-four hours a day in a barren, drab cell.[268] Albany prisoners were deprived of cell furniture following their recent destruction of prison property, and Tipp Guilfoyle invited extra punishment under Rule 43 by throwing the contents of his chamber pot over a warder. Strangely, no immediate repercussions were imposed in Long Lartin following the forty-eight hour fast of IRA prisoners.[269]

All such incidents were scrutinised by the Prison Department. Recommendations advanced by Chief Inspector of Prisons Gordon Fowler in the wake of the Hull Riot were addressed in July 1978 by the creation of a Dispersal Prisons Steering Committee, chaired by the Controller (Operational Administration). This restructuring was designed to extend scrutiny of the network by a Prison Department tasked with additional responsibilities for lower grade institutions without interposing itself between Headquarters and the Regional Offices. The Controller (OA), M Gale MC, convened monthly meetings to make 'joint oversight more effective' in the sector in which Category A prisoners were routinely held. It was acknowledged by the Home Office in July 1979 that the body was provided with information from the Adult Offender Psychology Unit, which monitored the Dispersal System population 'as a whole and in relation to particular establishments'.[270] By then it was reported that: 'Attempts are also being made to devise a system for forecasting the growth of a dangerous climate in an establishment by recording in detail certain aspects of prisoner behaviour thought to act as indicators of tension and alienation in the prison'.[271]

The annual anti-interment rally in London attracted approximately 2,000 to Hyde Park on 13 August. Niall O'hAogan of Sinn Féin's Ard Comhairle in Dublin joined the familiar voices of Jackie Kaye, Michael

Holden, Jim Reilly and Kevin Colfer, Chair of London Sinn Féin. Support from Scottish republican bands, UTOM and An Cumann Cabhrach was in evidence, although the leftist organizations were not as well represented in what was viewed as an inherently Irish republican occasion.[272] Brendan Gallagher of Strabane, Tyrone, was held for several days in Lancashire under the PTA when he travelled to preview a BBC TV play regarding the case of his son in the H-Blocks. William Gallagher was then nearing the end of a forty-eight day hunger strike to protest what he claimed was a wrongly imposed conviction for an IRA bomb attack in the west Tyrone town.[273] The tenth anniversary of the historic Dungannon to Coalisland Civil Rights march was marked in Tyrone on 27 August 1978 by a major demonstration against the Blanket Protest in the H-Blocks. The original Coalisland march had united politically assertive Nationalists, radical students and republicans in a publicity seeking venture intended to highlight institutionalized discrimination by Stormont towards non-Unionists. The commemoration, however, was organized under the auspices of the RAC and drew in supporters of Sinn Féin and the IRSP, as well as the allied PAC and many others. This reflected the significant change in political emphasis in the course of the proceeding decade during which the more moderate Nationalists had combined within and around the non-violent SDLP. With the focus firmly on the prison struggle in the North of Ireland in 1978, Kaye stressed the PAC view that 'the political status issue is to do with the struggle going on outside the goal'. Only concerted action in the form of 'revolutionary struggle', she averred, would resolve the anomalies of the Irish prisoners in England and the North of Ireland.[274]

From 8 August 1978, Sinn Féin was engaged with applications from four H-Block prisoners at the European Commission on Human Rights, claiming 'multiple breaches' of the European Convention.[275] This initiative followed the damning indictment of Long Kesh by Archbishop Tomas O Fiaich who famously described the cell conditions he observed on 1 August 1978 as being reminiscent of 'the sewer pipes in [the] slums of Calcutta'.[276] The high-profile denunciation and the imbalance of prisoner numbers ensured that significant legal developments in Strasbourg on the English dimension were overshadowed by the Long Kesh controversy.[277] Among the main public responses of English Catholics to O Fiaich's comments were criticism of his viewpoint in the *Tablet*, which allegedly complimented private overtures by the British Delegation to the Holy See to oppose his meteoric advancement from Archbishop to Cardinal.[278] Sr. Clarke defended O Fiaich, and implicitly, the validity of his stinging 'Calcutta' allusion in the letters page of the *Catholic Herald*.[279] Roy Mason, one of the most fervent political promoters of the H-Block regime, rejected the Cardinal's pronouncement as 'a disaster'.[280] The NIO claimed 'these criminals are totally responsible for the situation in which they find themselves … These facilities are better than those available in most prisons in the rest of the United Kingdom'.[281] In hindsight, it became clear that mutually destabilizing prison issues on both sides of the Irish Sea were teetering on the precipice of intensifying the Long War.

NOTES

1. *United Irishman*, February 1978.
2. Minutes of Anglo-Irish Meeting, Iveagh House, Dublin, 5 May 1978, Public Record Office of Northern Ireland (Belfast), CENT/1/7/6.
3. *Irish World*, 30 April 1977.
4. See *Times*, 8 and 14 November 1978.
5. See John Sutton, 'PFF–the breakaway trade union' in Nicki Jameson and Eric Allison, *Strangeways, 1990, A serious disturbance* (London, 1995), pp. 86–7. Sutton was a founder member of the putative Prison Force Federation (PFF) which was 'born out of anger at the lack of representation for non-supervisory grade prison officers' in 1979. The PFF's attempt to split from the POA was obviated in 1980 by the parent union and conservative vested interests. *Ibid.*
6. *Report of the work of the Prison Department, 1978* (London, 1979), p. 11.
7. *Daily Telegraph*, 21 February 1979. The 'average daily [prison] population' in England and Wales in 1978 was an unprecedented 41,796. *Report of the work of the Prison Department, 1978*, p. 3. 11,016 shared cells and 5,082 were held three to a cell. *Ibid.*, p. 4.
8. See *The Listener*, 26 January 1978. See also *Republican News*, 11 March 1978 and *Irish World*, 28 January 1978.
9. *Irish World*, 21 January 1978.
10. *Irish World*, 28 January 1978.
11. See Airey Neave, *They have their exits* (London, 1953) and *Saturday at MI9, The inside story of the underground escape lines in Europe in World War II* (London, 1969).
12. Fr. Denis Faul and Fr. Raymond Murray, *Ballykelly, RUC Special Branch Interrogation Centre*, pamphlet ([1973]).
13. Dermot Keogh, *Jack Lynch, A Biography* (Dublin, 2008), p. 414. See also Pat Walsh, *Irish Republicanism and Socialism, The politics of the Republican Movement 1905 to 1994* (Belfast, 1994), pp. 178–9.
14. See Angela Davis, *If they come in the morning: Voices of resistance* (New York, 1971) and http://www.biography.com/people/angela-davis-9267589.
15. See Ronald Hayman, *Sartre: A biography* (London, 1987).
16. *Socialist Challenge*, 2 March 1978.
17. *Republican News*, 11 March 1978. Litterick suffered a heart attack in March 1977 at a time when his comments on the Irish community of Birmingham being harassed under the PTA and description of Prince Phillip as a 'useless, arrogant parasite' was deemed to warrant police protection. *Irish World*, 26 March 1977.
18. See Alastair Logan to the Editor, *Guardian*, 25 March 1978.
19. *Guardian*, 27 July 1978.
20. *Times*, 26 March 1983.
21. *Prior Report*, I, p. 3. See also *Prior Report*, II, pp. 129–30.
22. Cited in *Prior Report*, I, p. 2.
23. Cited in *Prior Report*, I, p. 2.
24. Cited in *Prior Report*, II, p. 19.
25. *Prior Report*, I, p. 3.
26. *Prior Report*, II, p. 35. See also *Prior Report*, I, p. 3.
27. *Irish Times*, 10 May 1978.
28. *Prior Report*, I, p. 14.
29. *Prior Report*, II, p. 132.
30. Walmsley, *Special Security Units*, pp. 22–23.
31. Walmsley, *Special Security Units*, pp. 22–23.
32. Cited in *Republican News*, 11 February 1978.
33. *Republican News*, 11 February 1978 and EC Zeeman, 'Catastrophe Theory' in *Scientific American*, April 1976, pp. 65–83. Ray Mitchell of the Prison Service College and Dai Curtis of the Officers' Training School were Wakefield-based members of the *Prison Service Journal's* Review Committee. See *PSJ*, No. 33, New Series, January 1979, p. 17. University of Southampton sociologist Roy King, a member of the Parole Board for England and Wales, noted 'it is no accident that the worst prison

troubles in living memory have occurred in the dispersal prisons ... extreme security actually provokes trouble'. *Times*, 14 March 1978.

34. See Edward O Wilson, *Sociobiology: The New Synthesis* (New York, 1975) and Catherine Driscoll, 'Sociobiology' in *The Standford Encylopedia of Philosophy*, http://plato.standford.edu/archives/win2013/entries/sociobiology.

35. *HC Deb 8 June 1978 vol 951 c207W.*

36. Clarke to Kilbracken, 28 January 1978, MS draft letter, Clarke Papers (COFLA). Kilbracken renounced his British citizenship after Bloody Sunday in 1972. He was later in direct contact with leading Provisionals John Joe McGirl in Leitrim and Ruairi O'Bradaigh in Roscommon. Kilbracken condemned the death of Frank Stagg on hunger strike in 1976 and was persuaded by republicans to maintain his opposition to the PTA rather than resigning from the House of Lords. *Saoirse*, February 2012, p. 15. See also *Irish Times*, 25 November 1977.

37. *Sunday Tribune*, 27 May 1984.

38. Clarke to Kilbracken, 28 January 1978, MS draft letter, Clarke Papers (COFLA). Sr. Clarke had recently received news from visitors to Sean Smyth and from Wally Heaton. *Ibid.*

39. *PAC News*, August/ September 1977

40. *Hibernia*, 16 December 1977.

41. John Kilbracken to Fr. [Denis] Faul, 23 January 1978 Clarke Papers (COFLA). See also *Disturbance in D Wing*, p. 15.

42. Kilbracken to Faul, 23 January 1978 Clarke Papers (COFLA). Longford had been disconcerted by the IRA attempt on the life of his son-in-law, Hugh Fraser MP on 22 October 1975. Fraser supported the death penalty and narrowly missed being killed on the day that the Guildford Four were wrongly convicted. See Clarke, *No faith*, pp. 93–4 and Moysey, *Balcombe Street*, pp. 108–9.

43. See Lieutenant-Colonel HEC Willoughby, 'Family life in Northern Ireland', Typescript (Victoria Barracks, Windsor, 12 November 1975). The document was endorsed: 'This leaflet contains information on various aspects of family life in Northern Ireland as it is expected to apply to the 2nd B[attalio]n Coldstream Guards which will start an 18 month tour in September 1976 at Ebrington Barracks, London[d]erry [sic]'. *Ibid.*

44. Clarke to Kilbracken, 28 January 1978, MS draft letter Clarke Papers (COFLA). See also Merlyn Rees, *Northern Ireland, A Personal perspective* (London, 1985).

45. *HL Deb 7 February 1978, cc922–3.*

46. Gerry Cunningham, 25 September 2007.

47. *AP/RN*, 29 July 1982. McLaughlin commented: 'When we explained to the English prisoners the nature of British imperialism in Ireland and that we were not-as the British gutter press daubed us- "mindless terrorists" out to kill innocent British civilians, they were able to see for themselves the victimization of republican prisoners by the prison administration'. *Ibid.*

48. Hugh Doherty, 23 June 2006.

49. Alison Liebling, 'Prison Officers, Policing and the Use of Discretion' in *Theoretical Criminology*, 2000, Vol. 4, p. 341.

50. Eddie O'Neill, 23 June 2006.

51. *Republican News*, 28 January and 4 February 1978. Niall Fagan, who had been present on Bloody Sunday, addressed the Sinn Féin parade at Hyde Park. *Ibid.* For an analysis of ideological 'sectarian' divisions between elements of the British left on Ireland, including differences between the allied PAC/ RCG and IMG/ SWP/ UTOM, see *Hands off Ireland!*, No. 6, January 1979, pp. 3–4.

52. *An Phoblacht*, 18 February 1978. UTOM split from TOM on 2 July 1977. *Fight Racism! / Fight Imperialism!*, September 1982, p. 11. For an RCG account see Diane Fox, 'Building an anti-imperialist movement, resonant declarations v revolutionary propaganda' in *Hands off Ireland!*, No. 3, November 1977, pp. 13–15.

53. *An Phoblacht*, 15 February 1978.

54. *Republican News*, 4 February 1978.

55. *An Phoblacht*, 8 February 1978.

56. Karen McElrath, *Unsafe haven, The United States, The IRA and Political Prisoners* (London, 2000), pp. 70–1 and Francie Broderick, Gerry Coleman, Peter Hegarty and Jack Kilroy (eds.) *Where is Liberty?, The prosecution of Irish Republicans in the United States*, Pamphlet (Ohio, 1995), p. 30.

57. Sr. Sarah Clarke, 'Hugh Doherty', Sr. Sarah Clarke Papers O Fiaich Library, Armagh (COFLA). Twenty-five charges against the Balcombe Street group were rejected by the jury and a murder charge in relation to the bombing of the Hilton Hotel was reduced to manslaughter when it was accepted that 'police had failed to clear the hotel after 20 min[ute]s warning'. *Ibid.*

58. See Jackie Kaye, 'Irish political prisoners in England' in *AP/RN*, 26 May 1979 and John Higgins et al, *Irish political prisoners in England, Special Category 'A', An account of prison life in England based on the experiences of Irish Republican John Higgins imprisoned between 1976 and 1979*

(Dublin, 1980), pp. 70–1 and *AP/RN*, 13 May 1980. Hugh Doherty was in Leicester in January 1978 when solidarity notices were published in Belfast. *Republican News*, 7 January 1978. He had his books in Durham by July 1978 when Ray McLaughlin was sent in on a 'lie down' from Wakefield. Doherty left reading material in the recess area for McLaughlin to collect, including Vladimir Lenin's *Imperialism, the highest stage of capitalism*. Ray McLaughlin, *Inside an English jail, The prison diary of the IRA Volunteer Raymond McLaughlin* (Dublin, 1987), p. 44. Eddie Butler was moved to solitary confinement in Manchester prison in February 1978. *IRIS*, 12 January 1979.

59. *Irish political prisoners*, p. 71. Scotland's only Special Unit at Barlinnie, Glasgow, was generally not used for the few IRA prisoners held in the separate jurisdiction during the Troubles. *Ibid.* Belfast republican Matthew 'Gerry' Ward, who received five years for IRA activities in Scotland, was released on 24 October 1975 having passed through Peterhead and Perth. Sr. Clarke, 'Mathew 'Gerry' Ward', Clarke Papers (COFLA).

60. Joe O'Connell, 7 June 2008.

61. Joe O'Connell, 7 June 2008.

62. *Republican News*, 24 March 1979 and *AP/RN*, 26 May 1979.

63. *Irish political prisoners*, p. 71.

64. Sr. Clarke, 'Brendan Dowd', Clarke Papers (COFLA). See also Jackie Kaye, 'Irish political trials in England' in *Hands off Ireland!*, No. 2, June 1977, pp. 2–4.

65. Michael Herbert, *The wearing of the green, A political history of the Irish in Manchester* (London, 2001), p. 164.

66. Hugh Doherty, 23 June 2006.

67. See 'List of names found after IRA terrorist siege at Balcom[b]e Street', December 1975, NAE, PREM 16/ 676. The Prison Department headquarters at 89 Eccleston Square was also listed. *Ibid.*

68. Eddie Butler, 21 December 2007.

69. Hugh Doherty, 23 June 2006. In Parkhurst SSU Joe O'Connell claimed: 'You were in with the same people day after day, year after year. You were sort of fed up looking at each other. But we did get on fine. There were very few [problems] even with the English prisoners here was the odd falling out. Not too serious. There was the few serious falling out among the English prisoners that were in there. The pressure would get to them different ones'. Joe O'Connell, 7 June 2008.

70. Hugh Doherty, 23 June 2006.

71. Hugh Doherty, 23 June 2006.

72. Hugh Doherty, 23 June 2006. For H-Wing see Elaim Genders and Elaine Player, 'Women Lifers: Assessing the experience', *The Prison Journal*, 1990, Vol. 70, pp. 46–57.

73. Hugh Doherty, 23 June 2006.

74. Sr. Clarke, 'Hugh Doherty', Clarke Papers (COFLA).

75. Winnie Doherty, 7 June 2008. Doherty was assisted on her trips to prisons in the North of England by members of TOM. She was initially 'a bit nervous of them because they were so English' but later mused: 'would we be so good to them?' *Ibid.*

76. *Guardian*, 27 October 2014.

77. Shari-Jayne Boda, *Real crime: four crimes that shocked a nation* (London, 2003).

78. Pat Magee, 'Comments on Leicester SSU', MS, 19 December 1989, Private Collection (Pat Magee).

79. Eddie Butler, 21 December 2007.

80. Walmsley, *Special Security Units*, p. 34.

81. Joe O'Connell, 8 June 2008.

82. Tony Madigan, 7 March 2008.

83. *Irish political prisoners*, p. 82.

84. Leading republican Gerry Kelly stated: 'We are as one with the ANC'. Gerry Kelly to the Editor, *FRFI*, May 1987.

85. *AP/RN*, 20 January 1983.

86. Noel Gibson quoted in *AP/RN*, April 1998.

87. 'Walsh-BOV Adjudications' in A Aylett [For the Treasury Solicitor] to BM Birnberg & Co, 28 September 1990, Private Collection (Walsh).

88. Roy Walsh, 9 March 2008 and Andy Mulryan, 17 November 2008. Communication difficulties ensured that *AP/RN* claimed that the attempt occurred in 1978 'several months' before the March 1979 roof top protest. *AP/RN*, 20 January 1985. Sr. Clarke noted 'around March [19]78 Roy Walsh & Noel Gibson tried to escape from Parkhurst'. Sr. Clarke, 'Roy Walsh', Clarke Papers (COFLA). Sean Kinsella was the centre of a black joke when a London prisoner learned he had been a barber in Monaghan at the outset of the Long War. With reference to a heavy caliber revolver he quipped: 'What does he part your hair with then, a forty-five?' McLaughlin, *Inside an English jail*, p. 33.

89. Tony Madigan, 7 March 2008.

90. Roy Walsh, 9 March 2008.
91. Roy Walsh, 9 March 2008.
92. Noel Gibson, 24 August 2008.
93. Sean Kinsella, 3 August 2007.
94. Noel Gibson, 24 August 2008.
95. *Irish political prisoners*, p. 84.
96. Andy Mulryan, 17 November 2008.
97. Roy Walsh, 9 March 2008.
98. Sean Kinsella, 3 August 2007.
99. *Irish political prisoners*, p. 84 and 'Walsh-BOV Adjudications' in A Aylett [For the Treasury Solicitor] to BM Birnberg & Co, 28 September 1990, Private Collection (Walsh).
100. *Report of the work of the Prison Department, 1978*, p. 25.
101. Sr. Clarke, 'Roy Walsh', Clarke Papers (COFLA).
102. Shane Paul O'Doherty, *The Volunteer, A former IRA man's true story* (London, 1993), p. 207. Jack Duggan, a Tipperary IRA man settled in Manchester, was held in solitary in Dartmoor for over two years in the 1940s 'with nothing in the cell but a compressed paper pot and a bible'. He and other republicans on protest were forcibly dressed by guards once a week when obliged to appear before the Governor. *United Irishman*, February 1968.
103. O'Doherty, *Volunteer*, p. 207 and 'An Irish prisoner and Home Office lies' in *The Irish Prisoner*, No. 11 [1987], pp. 10–11. See also Conlon, *Proved Innocent*, p. 185. Whitehead also assisted Gerry Conlon of the Guildford Four. Gerry Conlon, University of Limerick, 18 March 2014.
104. O'Doherty, *Volunteer*, p. 209.
105. Jimmy Kelly, a West Belfast republican and occasional resident of Southampton, England, received a five-year sentence on 27 January 1976 for contravening the Firearms and Explosives Act. He progressed from Winchester to Long Lartin and Wormwood Scrubs by January 1977 and was present when O'Doherty was transferred. See Sr. Clarke, 'James Kelly', Clarke Papers (COFLA). In 1975 Derry republican socialist and former MP Bernadette Devlin contacted progressive London solicitor Mike Fisher to assist Kelly's defence. Fisher, an innate liberal of Catholic and Jewish parentage and educated in Mount St Mary's Jesuit boarding school in Sheffield, became one of the most important lawyers willing to take 'Irish cases'. *Guardian*, 28 January 2015.
106. O'Doherty, *Volunteer*, pp. 209–10.
107. O'Doherty, *Volunteer*, p. 210.
108. *Derry Journal*, 17 February 1978. For overview of 'just war' concept and theology see Charles E Rice, *Divided Ireland, A cause for American concern* (Notre Dame, 1985), Chapter IX.
109. O'Doherty, *Volunteer*, p. 211.
110. *PAC News*, February 1978, p. 1.
111. O'Doherty, *Volunteer*, p. 211.
112. Eddie O'Neill, 1 February 2008. O'Neill was held with O'Doherty in Wakefield but not close enough for the pair to converse. He gained that impression that the Derryman 'wouldn't talk to any of us … He wouldn't talk to anyone'. See also *Irish Post*, 14 September 1985 and O'Doherty, *Volunteer*, p. 228.
113. *Republican News*, 4 February 1978. Sid 'Seanna' Walsh had already spent a year on the blanket in H5. Walsh spent over twenty years in prison and was selected to read the IRA's standing down statement on 28 July 1995. *Ibid*. See also *An Phoblacht*, 1 March 1978.
114. See *An Phoblacht*, January 2014, p. 4 and *Prison Struggle, Paper of the Relatives Action Committee*, March [1980].
115. See *Republican News*, 11 March 1978.
116. See Jim Reilly and Jacqueline Kaye to Editor, *Republican News*, 18 March 1978. London Sinn Féin leader Jim Reilly addressed the Workers Revolutionary Party conference in Wembley on 26 February. *Ibid.*, 11 March 1978. His socialist inclinations and trade union work appealed to several left wing groupings with which Sinn Féin interacted on prisoner issues. See RCG tributes in *AP/RN*, 4 October 1980 and *FRFI*, November/ December 1980, p. 16. For Livingstone and Ireland see Curtis, *Ireland and the propaganda war*, pp. 207–11. Kaye, an English leftist who had met Eamon Smullen on a work camp in 1960s Cuba, became drawn into prisoner support when he was jailed on arms charges in England in 1969. See Jackie Kaye, 'What price peace?' in *FRFI*, October/ November 1999, p. 6.
117. PAC Statement in *PAC News*, July 1977.
118. *Eolas*, April/ May 1977, p. 12.
119. *Eolas*, April/ May 1977, p.11.
120. See Des O'Hagan, *Letters from Long Kesh* (Dublin, 2012). O'Hagan's twenty-two short articles were published by the *Irish Times* in 1972, arising from an agreement with its liberal editor Douglas Gageby. The collected edition did not appear until 2012. See Ultan Gillen, 'Introduction' in *Ibid.*, pp. xi-xii. Earlier feuding between the Official IRA and the nascent INLA/ IRSP disturbed Belfast IRA men in

England: 'Is there not enough Irishmen being killed without them knocking each other off?' Billy Armstrong to Leo Wilson, 10 March 1975, Private Collection (Wilson). Armstrong understood the tensions were caused by Official IRA inaction *vis à vis* 'religious assassinations' by British backed Loyalists. *Ibid.* Wilson had polled 4,000 votes in the South Antrim constituency of the October 1964 general election at which time Sinn Féin was banned in the Six Counties. Involved in the Civil Rights movement, he was a leading member with Clara Reilly and Fr. Brian Brady of the Association for Legal Justice in Belfast. See *An Phoblacht*, January 2014, p. 4.

121. *Republican News*, 3 March 1978.
122. *Republican News*, 3 March 1978.
123. *Republican News*, 22 April 1978 and *IRIS*, 17 February 1979. Forty-seven exclusion orders were issued between March 1978 and March 1979. *HC Deb 21 March 1979 vol 964 cc1505–6*. Dominic Behan, brother of Brendan and writer of 'The Patriot Game' rebel ballad, was among the more socially prominent people detained under the PTA in Liverpool. *Irish World*, 10 November 1979.
124. *Republican News*, 27 May 1978. Jim Reilly of the Sinn Féin Ard Comhairle represented the party in Leeds. Kaye and Alastair Logan participated in the Independent Public Enquiry into the abuse and torture of prisoners in Ireland, which convened in Dublin in May 1978. They described the workings of the PTA and the Irish prisoner experience in England. *Ibid.* Peoples Democracy claimed that by early 1978 Sinn Féin 'remained ambiguous about the value of united work' on prisoners and tended to recognize only groupings which supported the armed struggle. The RAC, closely linked to Sinn Féin, gradually excluded ultra-leftist political parities such as the Irish Workers Group which had demanded speaking rights at rallies without investing sufficient effort in the campaign. Ultimately, the PDs also 'lost any formal position in the campaign'. See *Prisoners of Partition, H-Block/ Armagh, A Peoples Democracy pamphlet*, New edition, p. 12. See also *IRIS*, 24 March 1978.
125. See Jim Johnson, 'Lessons of TOM' in *Hands off Ireland!*, No. 1, December 1976, pp. 13–15. See also Workers Power, *The British Left and the Irish War* (London, 1983), p. 38. UTOM reverted to the TOM designation in 1979. *Ibid.*
126. Aly Renwick, 16 November 2007.
127. *PAC News*, June 1978. For the 1977 Marx commemoration in Highgate Cemetery see *PAC News*, June 1977.
128. *PAC News*, June 1978. Messages of support were received from Sean Mac Stiofain, Michael Mullen (General Secretary of the ITGWU), Frank McManus, Frank Maguire MP, Joan Maynard MP, Maureen Colquhoun MP, Eddie McAteer, Phil Flynn, Women and Ireland, Black Aid, UTOM, IRSP (Dublin), PROP, ICRA, RCG, IMG and Revolutionary Communist Tendency. Members of the Stagg, Gaughan, Dowd, Donnelly, McCaffrey, Fox, Nordone, Madigan, Butler, Campbell, Hackett, Mulryan, Armstrong, Kinsella, Norney, McLaughlin, Byrne, Coughlan, Gibson and Kelly families registered their approval. Republicans John Joe McGirl, Joe O'Neill (Bundoran Urban District Council), Vincent Conlon and Frank Glynn (Galway City Council) were also listed. Nancy Jenkinson, widow of Noel, and Mary Stagg, mother of Frank, joined members of Michael Gaughan's family in expressing approval. *Ibid.*
129. BR Grange to DG Blunt, 21 November 1978, NAE, FCO 87/ 763.
130. 'Irish POWs Albany' in *PAC News*, June 1978. Fr. Pat Fell and Hugh Callaghan remained on the wings in Albany. *Ibid.*
131. *An Phoblacht*, 22 April and 10 June 1978. See also *IRIS*, 31 March 1978, p. 3. Amnesty International refused to support repatriation and its view that convicted IRA personnel did not quality as 'prisoners of conscience' ensured very little attention was paid to their situation. *IRIS*, 28 April 1978, p. 4.
132. *Republican News*, 13 May 1978. London Sinn Féin activists Kevin Colfer and Tony Kearns highlighted the H-Block situation at a Kilburn meeting. The Michael Gaughan Cumman of Glasgow Sinn Féin also co-operated with RCG in Scotland. See *Ibid.*, 1 July 1978. *Ibid.*
133. See *Hands off Ireland!*, No. 1, December 1976. Jim Reilly contributed and article to the May 1978 edition. David Yaffe, Frank Richards, Sheila Marston and Brian Mitchell were leading RCG members. See also *Revolutionary Communist, Theoretical Journal of the Revolutionary Communist Group*, No. 2, May 1975.
134. *Times*, 24 August 1978.
135. *IRIS*, 18 May 1978, p. 9.
136. *PAC News*, June 1978.
137. See Geoff Bell, *British Labour and Ireland: 1969–97*, Pamphlet, (London, 1979), pp. 29–35. Bell wrote from the perspective of the rival IMG.
138. Eddie Caughey, 16 September 2008.
139. *Republican News*, 10 June 1978.
140. *PAC News*, June 1978. See Anthony Coughlan, *C. Desmond Greaves, 1913–1988: An obituary essay*, Pamphlet (Dublin, 1991).
141. *Irish Times*, 12 October 1981.

142. Ciaran De Baroid, *Ballymurphy and the Irish War,* Revised Edition (London, 2000), p. 200.

143. *Republican News*, 17 June 1978. See also Bell, *British Labour and Ireland*, pp. 20–21.

144. See Fr. Desmond Wilson to the Editor, *Irish People*, 5 February 1983. See also Andrew Boyd, *The informers, A chilling account of the Supergrasses in Northern Ireland* (Dublin, 1984).

145. Keara O'Dempsey (President) and Albert Doyle (Vice President), Brehon Law Society, to Chief Justice Lord Lowry in *Irish People*, 19 September 1983.

146. Peter Grimes, a Westmeath native resident in London, claimed in October 1976 to have been induced and threatened into becoming an informer by the Special Branch when in custody following a raid on his east London apartment. *Irish World*, 9 October 1976. He was rearrested on 1 September 1977 on charges of 'withholding information' relating to 'terrorist' crime. Although bailed on surety of £5,000, he was required to have no contact with the IRSP. His associate, Harry Driver, was arrested in Kent and remanded in Maidstone Prison ahead of trial for possession of explosives. In early December 1977 Grimes was sentenced to three months imprisonment. Sr. Clarke, 'Peter Grimes', Clarke Papers (COFLA). He was rearrested in Golders Green under the PTA in May 1979 during investigations into the assassination of Airey Neave MP. Although released without charge, the NCCL provided the press with a 22 November 1978 statement made by Grimes in the presence of solicitor Harriet Harman in which he claimed to have been pressed to act as an informer. *Guardian*, 3 May 1979.

147. *Irish Times*, 10 May 1978. For the case of Fr. Pat Fell see *Irish Times*, 21 March 1981. See also *PAC News*, August/ September 1977 and *Daily Telegraph*, 30 April 1979.

148. *Irish Post*, 3 September 1983.

149. *Prison Standing Orders* (1977). See also *Prior Report*, II, p. 33.

150. *Times*, 15 May 1978.

151. HC Deb 25 January 1978 vol 942 c593W.

152. *Irish Times*, 16 May 1978.

153. *Irish Times*, 16 May 1978.

154. *Report of the Independent Public Inquiry into Abuse and Torture of Irish Prisoners*, Pamphlet, (Dublin, 1978). Judge E Bloch and lawyers Paul Bjkaerk and Juan Maria Bandres headed a panel which also comprised Yann Goulet, Uinseann Mac Eoin, Ken Quinn, Brendan O Cathaoir, Breandan O Cearbhaill and Dr. Donal McDermott. *Ibid*. In a 1980 interview ex-IRA Chief of Staff Sean Mac Stiofain claimed: 'I regard our struggle in Ireland, the struggle of the Basque people, the struggle in Zimbabwe, in Southern Africa, in Southern America-anywhere in the world-as one struggle'. Quoted in *FRFI*, March/ April 1980.

155. *IRIS*, 26 May 1978, p. 2.

156. Deposition of Micheal MacLochlainn in *Independent Public Inquiry*, p. 10.

157. *IRIS*, 26 May 1978, p. 2.

158. J Williams review in *Prison Service Journal*, No. 3, New Series, January 1979, p. 17. Continental European oversight may have been more compelling had the IRA succeeded in assassinating Christopher Tugendhat, Britain's EEC Commissioner, in December 1980. *Irish World*, 17 January 1981.

159. Williams review in *Prison Service Journal*, No. 3, New Series, January 1979, p. 17. See also Joe Sim, *Medical power in prisons–The Prison Medical Service in England* (London, 1990).

160. GD Scott and Paul Gendreau, 'Psychiatric implications of sensory deprivation in a maximum security prison' in *Canadian Psychiatric Association Journal*, Vol. 14, No. 4, pp. 337–341.

161. See Armstrong to Wilson, 6 March 1979, Private Collection (Wilson). Best wishes were imparted 'to your son Padraic [Wilson] and comrades on the Blanket. Let them know they are not forgotten'. *Ibid*.

162. *IRIS*, 28 April 1978, p. 3.

163. Armstrong to Wilson, 28 February 1978, Private Collection (Wilson). Visits of Cardinal O Fiaich to the H-Blocks were keenly followed. Armstrong to Wilson, 3 March 1980, Private Collection (Wilson).

164. Martin Brady, 10 April 2008. Paul Hill's memoir included a blackly comic account of a viewing of 'The Long Good Friday' film in Parkhurst in which a fictional IRA unit in England is portrayed as taking on and ultimately besting a leading East End London gangster played by Bob Hoskins. This evidently 'created a lot of tension between the IRA prisoners and the armed robbers and Cockneys'. Hill, *Stolen years*, p. 137. Hoskins was socially familiar with a number of London gangsters and attested to the good character of hitman John Bindon during his murder trial. Bindon, ironically, was reputed to have 'contacts in the IRA' and had gone on the run in Ireland when wanted for a gangland killing. 'Starring John Bindon', Granada TV, UTV, 15 February 2007. Bindon had a cameo role as an amphetamine dealing London gangster in the 1979 film 'Quadrophenia' based on the 1973 audio recording by 'The Who' rock band.

165. Billy Armstrong, 'Fighting all the way' in *AP/RN*, 22 February 2001.

166. Brian Keenan, 26 May 2007.

167. 'Wakefield letter' in *IRIS*, 24 February 1978. Murray was charged with assaulting two prison officers and in addition to fifty-six days in F Wing lost five months remission of sentence. Ashe received

fourteen days in the block after an attack by an English prisoner. Stevie Blake was returned to F Wing from a 'lie-down' in Durham before being moved on to Albany. *PAC News*, June 1978.

168. 'Wakefield letter' in *IRIS*, 24 February 1978.
169. Sr. Clarke, 'Paul Norney', Clarke Papers (COFLA).
170. 'Wakefield letter' in *IRIS*, 24 February 1978.
171. 'Wakefield letter' in *IRIS*, 24 February 1978.
172. *Republican News*, 25 March 1978.
173. Albany PRO to Editor, *Republican News*, 22 April 1978. They claimed that the Worker's Party 'have in fact rejected revolutionary politics and have gone up the blind alley of pragmatism in taking part in elections in both the Six Counties and the Free State. This must ultimately lead to further splits in their movement'. Although both harsh and prophetic, this condemnation was accompanied by an acknowledgement that the Officials contained 'good individual socialists', a rare accolade from Provisional prisoners. See *Irish Voices*, p. 152.
174. *Lost Lives*, p. 736.
175. Fr. Padraig Fell to Marie Drumm Memorial Committee in *Republican News*, 20 May 1978. See also *Ibid.*, 10 June 1978. The establishment of the IRSP and INLA in Lucan, County Dublin, on 8 December 1974 ensured that TOM received briefings on their political outlook. INLA Chief of Staff Seamus Costello addressed the TOM convention in the Mansion House, Dublin, on 18 September 1976. See *Seamus Costello, 1939–1977, Irish Republican Socialist* (Dublin, [1979]), pp. 65–9. For Drumm see Maire Drumm Commemoration Committee, *A rebel heart, Maire Bn. Ui Dhroma*, pamphlet, October 2001. On 8 August 1980 leading IRSP and INLA member Ronnie Bunting was arrested in Belfast with TOM member Francis Barry. Both were released without charge. Holland and McDonald, *INLA, Deadly Divisions* (Dublin, 1994) p. 157.
176. See McLaughlin, *Inside an English jail*, pp. 34–8. Other IRA prisoners moving in and out of Albany in late 1977 and early 1978 included Liam Baker, Paddy Mulryan, Fr. Pat Fell, Pat Christie and Sean Kinsella. Hugh Callaghan of the 'Birmingham Six' was also in the prison but did not participate in the IRA protests. *Ibid.* See also Sr. Clarke, 'Anthony Cunningham', Clarke Papers (COFLA).
177. Sr. Clarke, 'Albany', Clarke Papers (COFLA).
178. *IRIS*, 12 January 1979.
179. *Report of the work of the Prison Department, 1978*, p. 12.
180. McLaughlin, *Inside an English jail*, pp. 38–9. The Chairman of the Albany Board of Visitors was a retired Royal Navy Admiral whom the IRA believed to be a member of the Conservative 'Monday Club'. *Ibid.*, p. 39.
181. See *HC Deb 21 June 1978 vol 952 cc205–6W*.
182. Alastair Logan to Joan Maynard, 5 May 1978, NAE, FCO 87/ 763.
183. Ray McLaughlin to Alastair Logan, 28 April 1978, NAE, FCO 87/ 763.
184. Logan to Maynard, 5 May 1978, NAE, FCO 87/ 763.
185. Lord Harris to Joan Maynard, 11 July 1978, NAE, FCO 87/ 763. The republicans claimed that their visitors were also required to undergo strip-searching and as this was untypical of Category A men such policies constituted 'discrimination'. [David] Blunt to [Brian] Gange, 10 October 1978, *Ibid.* Maynard was also in contact with the NIO regarding IRA prisoners in the H-Blocks. See Joan Maynard to Don Concannon, 22 February 1979 in Faul and Murray, *H Block*, p. 93.
186. PLV Mallet (RID, FCO), 'Letter from Miss Joan Maynard MP', Memo, 2 June 1978, NAE, FCO 87/ 763.
187. *PAC News*, August/ September 1978.
188. Tony Madigan, 7 March 2008.
189. McLaughlin, *Inside an English jail*, p. 40.
190. McLaughlin, *Inside an English jail*, pp. 40–41. McLaughlin arrived in Wakefield in May 1978. *Irish News*, 13 November 1979.
191. *AP/RN*, 17 October 1985.
192. Sr. Clarke, 'Albany Notes', Clarke Papers (COFLA).
193. Tony Madigan, 7 March 2008. Terence MacSwiney, a senior member of the Irish Republican Brotherhood, Irish Republican Army and Sinn Féin, died on hunger strike in Brixton on 25 October 1920 when asserting his status as a political prisoner. He famously declared on taking office as Lord Mayor of Cork: 'It is not they who can inflict most but they who can suffer most will conquer'. Quoted in Dave Hannigan, *Terence MacSwiney, The Hunger Strike that rocked an Empire* (Dublin, 2010), p. 11.
194. See Brendan O'Brien, *The Long War, The IRA and Sinn Féin, 1985 to today* (Dublin, 1993), p. 294.
195. 'Albany POW Statement', *Hands off Ireland!*, No. 5, September 1978, p. 24 and *PAC News*, June 1978.
196. Gartree PRO in *Republican News*, 10 June 1978.
197. *Republican News*, 21 January 1979.

198. Hill, *Stolen years*, pp. 195–7. Hill, following the privations of Hull, regarded Gartree as 'a liberal establishment. I wear a sweat shirt and trainers. The screws are not so aggressive. But it's no good. I can't settle in. I should not be in prison, I am innocent. I argue and demonstrate'. *Ibid.*, p. 197.

199. *AP/RN*, 29 July 1982. See also O'Donnell, *Special Category*, I, p. 428.

200. *AP/RN*, 29 July 1982.

201. *Republican News*, 10 June 1978 and *Irish political prisoners*, p. 13. Noel Moore Boyd was also named in connection to the Kilburn attack while associates Alexander Brown and Archibald Brown were charged with related offences. Boyd and Carson appeared in court on 4 March 1976. They were convicted on 12 October 1976, receiving terms of between ten and fifteen years. Sr. Clarke, 'Biddy Mulligan's Explosion', Clarke Papers (COFLA). Boyd was on good terms with Gerry Conlon and several IRA prisoners in Long Lartin. Conlon, *Proved Innocent*, p. 199. Three members of the 'Manchester Loyalist Association' were charged with possession of firearms on 26 February; David Anderton, Robert Watson and Malcolm Rough. *PAC Bulletin*, March 1976.

202. *Republican News*, 10 June 1978. The person referred to as 'Gudd' in the published account was convicted English Loyalist John Gadd. Sr. Clarke received information that Tommy Thompson, regarded as a leading Loyalist in England, was one of the very few on the Category A list yet even then received 'preferential treatment' when in Hull. See Clarke to Kilbracken, 26 January 1978, MS letter draft, Clarke Papers (COFLA).

203. Cohen and Taylor, *Prison secrets*, p. 56.

204. *Report of Her Majesty's Chief Inspector of Prisons, 1983*, p. 17.

205. In 1974 two Loyalists jailed in England were granted temporary transfers to the North of Ireland 'to receive visits' over a period of twenty-three to twenty-seven days. One was granted a permanent transfer in 1975 and the second was downgraded to Category B in 1976. The Category B Loyalist received a second temporary transfer of twenty-nine days in 1978. See *HC Deb 21 June 1978 vol 952 c205W*.

206. *HC Deb 21 June 1978 vol 952 cc205–6W*.

207. *HC Deb 21 June 1978 vol 952 cc205–6W*. Rees noted: 'Prisoners and their visitors [in Wakefield] are allowed to embrace at the beginning and end of visits held under these conditions'. *Ibid.*

208. *Irish News*, 5 July 1995.

209. *HC Deb 11 July 1978 vol 953 cc494–5W*.

210. Lord Harris to Joan Maynard, 22 June 1978, Clarke Papers (COFLA).

211. Martin Wright to Fenner Brockway, 16 May 1978, Clarke Papers (COFLA).

212. Wright to Brockway, 16 May 1978, Clarke Papers (COFLA). See also Lord Harris to Fenner Brockway, 12 July 1978, Clarke Papers (COFLA). Brockway had a long history of intercession for political prisoners in England. At the height of the IRA 'Border Campaign' of 1956–62 he sought compassionate parole for EOKA prisoner George Ioannou, a comrade of republican prisoners in Wakefield who planned a joint escape. See Fenner Brockway to RA Butler, 25 July 1958 in Vias Livadas, *Cypriot and Irish political prisoners held in British prisons, 1956–1959* (Nicosia, 2008), p. 219.

213. Martin Wright to Sr. Sarah Clarke, 27 February 1980, Clarke Papers (COFLA). Wright recommended the services of Offenbach & Co; George E Baker & Co (Alastair Logan) and BM Birnberg & Co (Gareth Pierce). Wright reminded Sr. Clarke that prisoners were obliged to use all 'internal procedures' before contacting a private solicitor. *Ibid.*

214. For Kelly and Feeney see *Andersonstown News*, 14 April 1975.

215. *Republican News*, 10 June 1978.

216. *Republican News*, 22 July 1978 and *Irish World*, 15 July 1978.

217. *Republican News*, 22 July 1978. Donnelly began fasting in Long Lartin due to the refusal of the staff to authorize an exploratory x-ray. This rebuff, and simultaneous axing of a milk supplement he needed for his health provoked the hunger strike. The move to Wakefield aroused suspicions that the 'same regime' which 'murdered' Stagg was threatening Donnelly. *Ibid.* Stagg and Gaughan were commemorated in Leigue Cemetery, Mayo, on 16 July 1978. Daithi O Conaill gave the oration. *Irish Times*, 17 July 1978.

218. McLaughlin, *Inside an English jail*, pp. 42–3. Duffy was sent on a 'lie down' from Wormwood Scrubs to Wandsworth on 29 December. On completion of the twenty-eight days he was moved to Wakefield and a further 'lie down' in Bristol. *Republican News*, 22 March 1978. When in Wormwood Scrubs Duffy attacked a prison officer who had assaulted him previously. Sr. Clarke, 'Joe Duffy/ Mooney', Clarke Papers (COFLA). 'Joe Duffy' was the name used by Dubliner Michael J Mooney when convicted in England. *Irish People*, 5 February 1983. See *PAC News*, February 1978, p. 1.

219. *FRFI*, March 1984, p. 12.

220. *Irish Times*, 4 August 1978.

221. *Republican News*, 5 August 1978. Armstrong met Eddie Butler in Manchester. Butler had been in the block for seventeen weeks. They were denied normal outdoor exercise rights as the authorities

had commenced building a 'wire cage' to prevent helicopter escapes. Armstrong to Wilson, 25 July 1978, Private Collection (Wilson). Butler received just an hour long 'closed' visit from his mother and a sister who had traveled from America. *Republican News*, 5 August and 30 September 1978. Armstrong claimed that the Wakefield move occurred on 3 July, although McLaughlin indicted 5 July. McLaughlin, *Inside an English jail*, p. 43.

222. *Republican News*, 29 July 1978. In 1978 F Wing retained its Control Unit style regime of cold meals, a rule of silence, minimum communication with staff, isolation from other prisoners and dim lighting. *Ibid*. Ray McLaughlin recalled: 'When you're let out, you're unable to speak. All your reactions slow down and it takes a little while to understand what anybody says to you. It probably takes at least a month to be able to cope again with a conversation and all the normal prison things'. Cited in *AP/RN*, 13 December 1984.

223. *Republican News*, 5 August 1978.

224. McLaughlin, *Inside an English jail*, p. 44.

225. See PRO Gartree in *Republican News*, 5 August 1978.

226. *Republican News*, 29 July 1978.

227. *Irish Times*, 7 July 1978. See also Sr. Clarke, 'JJ Coughlan', Clarke Papers (COFLA).

228. *Times*, 8 July 1978.

229. *The Irish Prisoner*, No. 5, June 1979, p. 3 and Sr. Clarke, 'Albany', Clarke Papers (COFLA).

230. Sr. Clarke, 'Albany', Clarke Papers (COFLA).

231. Gange to Blunt, 21 November 1978, NAE, FCO 87/ 763.

232. *Republican News*, 22 July 1978.

233. *IRIS*, 7 July 1978, p. 5. See also *Times*, 21 October 1978.

234. Ronnie McCartney, 12 April 2008.

235. *Republican News*, 22 July 1978. For Brian McLaughlin see *AP/RN*, 29 July 1982.

236. Ronnie McCartney, 12 April 2008.

237. Martin Brady, 10 April 2008.

238. John McCluskey, 2 August 2007. McCluskey claimed: 'When you're in solitary, the Screws have got total control over almost every aspect of your life, your food, books. For reading material they give you comic books. They're supposed to give you an hour's exercise but most times they cut it down to half an hour. You always lose weight in solitary'. Quoted in *AP/RN*, 13 December 1984. Gartree's dog handlers were apparently more successful on 2 March 1978 when they apprehended a man using a grappling hook to scale the inner fence. Dick Callan, *Gartree, The story of a prison* (Leyhill, 2005), p. 44.

239. Ronnie McCartney, 12 April 2008.

240. *Irish political prisoners*, p. 92.

241. *Irish political prisoners*, p. 92 and *Times*, 8 July 1978.

242. *Republican News*, 5 August 1978.

243. *Irish Times*, 7 July 1978. Dianah Jeffrey, Stacey Charlesworth, Sandra Lester and Stephanie Pugsley were arrested. *Ibid*.

244. Faul and Murray, *H Block*, p. 114.

245. *Republican News*, 22 July 1978. In late 1978 Logan was National Convener of the International Tribunal on Britain's Presence in Ireland. See Faul and Murray, *H Blocks*, pp. 117–18 and *Irish Times*, 7 December 1978. Logan delivered a minibus acquired by Luton area Sinn Féin for the use of prisoners' families in Ireland. The vehicle had been repaired having been badly vandalized by police 'looking for something'. Michael Holden, 23 June 2008. The history of Gartree prison recorded many minor incidents in 1978 but not the IRA protest that rated discussion in the Commons. See Callan, *Gartree*, pp. 44–5.

246. *Irish World*, 12 March 1977. See also *Irish Press*, 28 February 1977.

247. *Times*, 8 July 1978.

248. Michael Holden, 23 June 2008. See also *Irish World*, 24 April 1976.

249. *Irish Post*, 2 September 1978.

250. *Republican News*, 24 June 1978.

251. *Republican News*, 24 June 1978. Other marching delegations included Harringey Trades Council and the NUJ Book Branch. *Ibid*. See also *Hands off Ireland!*, No. 5, September 1978, p. 3.

252. *FRFI*, September 1982, p. 11.

253. *Republican News*, 22 July 1978. Kaye of the PAC, Jim Reilly of Sinn Féin spoke at Hyde Park, as did representatives of the RCG and UTOM. A message from Daithi O'Connell was read. *Ibid*.

254. *Republican News*, 30 September 1978. The issue advertised the first edition of the re-formatted *PAC News*. *Ibid*. See also *PAC News*, No. 1, August/ September 1978.

255. *Irish World*, 15 July 1978.

256. *Irish Times*, 10 July 1978.

257. *Irish Times*, 10 July 1978. Redgrave, narrator of the film 'The Palestinian', attended its Belfast premier in Turf Lodge on 30 July. *Republican News*, 29 July 1978.

258. McLaughlin, *Inside an English jail*, p. 45. See also *IRIS*, 13 July 1978, p. 6.

259. *Republican News*, 29 July 1978. See also *FRFI*, September 1982, p. 11.

260. *Republican News*, 22 July 1978.

261. Ronnie McCartney, 12 April 2008, *Irish political prisoners*, p. 92 and Martin Brady, 10 April 2008. A busload of supporters was en route to Gartree when they learned the roof protest had finished. *Republican News*, 29 July 1978.

262. Sr. Clarke, 'Gartree', Clarke Papers (COFLA).

263. *Irish political prisoners*, p. 94. Mick Sheehan, the only other IRA prisoner in Gartree in July 1978, was too physically ill to participate in the roof top demonstration. By escaping punishment he was in a position to smuggle tobacco, matches and newspapers to his comrades in the Punishment Block. See Hayes (ed.) *In prison in England*, p. 23.

264. Sr. Clarke, 'Jerry Mealy', Clarke Papers (COFLA). Mealy had received 'open' visits in Gartree. Sr. Clarke, 'Albany', Clarke Papers (COFLA).

265. *Irish Times* and *Times*, 10 July 1978.

266. Armstrong to Wilson, 27 September 1978, Private Collection (Wilson).

267. McLaughlin, *Inside an English jail*, p. 45. McLaughlin recalled: 'I was given a towel to wrap around me but no blanket. My bed was removed from the cell between 6.00 a.m. and 8.00 p.m. The only time that I was allowed out of the cell was at 7.00 a.m. to slop out. During the weeks that I spent on the blanket, I never talked to another prisoner and only very infrequently to the screw. When my wife visited me in October she informed me that there was no support among the other POWs throughout England for a sustained blanket protest. So I decided to come off the protest'. *Ibid.*, pp. 45–6.

268. Wakefield IRA PRO to editor, *Irish News*, 13 November 1978. See also *Irish News*, 8 September 1978.

269. *Republican News*, 5 August 1978.

270. *Report of the work of the Prison Department, 1978*, p. 26.

271. *Report of the work of the Prison Department, 1978*, p. 26.

272. *Republican News*, 26 August 1978.

273. *Irish World*, 26 August 1978. See also *Ibid.*, 2 and 30 September 1978.

274. *IRIS*, 1 September 1978, p. 2.

275. Faul and Murray, *H Blocks*, p. 44. Nine Articles of the Convention were identified as having been transgressed (3, 6, 8, 9, 10, 11, 13, 14 and 18). These included breaches on 'degrading treatment', 'impartial tribunals', 'freedom of association' and utilization of solitary confinement. *Ibid.*

276. Statement of Archbishop Tomas O Fiaich, 1 August 1978 in Faul and Murray, *H Blocks*, p. 28.

277. For reaction to O Fiaich's comments see *Hibernia*, 3 August 1978, *Irish Times*, 5 August 1978 and *Irish Press*, 2 August 1978. In January 1978 O Fiaich, in his first major interview after becoming Primate, stated his opinion that the British 'should leave' Ireland. *Irish World*, 21 January 1978. He regarded Cork IRA leader Tom Barry, an acquaintance, as a man devoted to 'freedom for the Irish people to be themselves and to be masters of their own country'. O Fiaich cited in Meda Ryan, *Tom Barry, IRA Freedom Fighter* (Cork, 2005), p. 14.

278. See *Irish World*, 26 August 1978.

279. Sr. Sarah Clarke to the Editor, *Catholic Herald*, 1 September 1978.

280. Mason, *Paying the price*, p. 210.

281. NIO, 1 August 1978, 'Comment by Northern Ireland Office spokesman on Archbishop O' Fiaich's statement', PRONI, NIO/12/68.

CHAPTER 2

Gartree, Wormwood Scrubs and the Blanket Protest in England

The Gartree Riot of 5–6 October 1978 was a non-political and essentially spontaneous upheaval in which IRA men played a part. As with Hull in 1976, the trigger for what mushroomed into a major protest was a belief amongst the prison population that one of their associates had been maltreated. In this instance, the bone of contention revolved around the alleged involuntary drugging or tranquilization of a black prisoner.[1] Complaints on such practices had been smuggled out of Gartree to the prisoner's organization PROP for two years before the matter sparked a riot.[2] Martin Brady noted the general deterioration of conditions, with reductions in association time, during which 'exercise yards only opened if the sun shone'. He identified the 'abuse of drugs from the medical side' as the primary cause of the violence which ensued. In Gartree, Brady claimed, ordinary prisoners received 'whatever ... [they] wanted – Mogadon, any kind of sleeping tablets ... Nothing recorded'.[3] Ronnie McCartney likened the surreal atmosphere at times to the disturbing chaos and alternating chemically induced conformity depicted in Stanley Kubrick's feature film *One Flew Over The Cuckoo's Nest*.[4]

Allegations persisted that inappropriate dosages of dangerous drugs were being administered in English prisons in pursuit of an agenda to either conduct experiments in a controlled environment or simply render prisoners more subject to control. Establishing the truth proved extremely difficult in the face of the numerous defence mechanisms devised by the Home Office. The BBC was successfully sued in the High Court in July 1978 for alleging improper practices in Albany on the part of Dr. Brian Cooper and Dr. Andrew Todd.[5] Dr. Cooper was a familiar name to IRA prisoners, and despite his public and private disavowals, was widely regarded as the man who force-fed Michael Gaughan to death in June 1974. His professional position had been consolidated in Parkhurst by the October 1969 riot from which he emerged with a modicum of credit. From 1970, he and Mr. Anthony Pearson supervised an experimental unit in Parkhurst's C Wing for mentally disturbed prisoners. Inmates were given small financial inducements to work and to behave well during leisure periods. Payment was calculated on a sliding scale from zero to ninety pence a week and overall conduct was linked to other forms of amelioration. Cooper and Pearson administered a 'progression' path in C Wing 'from the ground floor living area to a top floor pre-release area'. They were, in consequence, influential figures on the Isle of Wight in 1972 prior to the return of significant numbers of IRA men to the prison.[6] The operation of C Wing in this mode ceased abruptly in March 1979 when the destruction of the roofs of two other wings by the IRA inspired the relocation of its inhabitants into the ill-appointed Hospital Wing.[7]

A BBC documentary entitled *South Today* alleged in February 1978 that men were being drugged in Albany to render them docile. This tangentially implicated Dr. Cooper and Dr. Todd, who both had overall responsibility for issuing prescriptions on the island. Cooper, moreover, was meaningfully described by the BBC as being 'principal medical officer and psychiatrist to the prisons on the Isle of Wight'. Such charges were serious in that Dr. John Whitehead, consultant psychiatrist of the Brighton health district, and Peter McCann of the BBC, claimed that up to 70 per cent of Albany's inmates were being dosed with drugs harmful to liver function. The High Court found on 28 July 1978 that this dire accusation could not be sustained in law while awarding damages to both practitioners. If the most actionable malpractice charges had been rejected amid the decorum and dignity of the elitist forum, both doctors admitted prescribing drugs for undefined 'therapeutic reasons'. Details of exact dosages and prevalence of individual treatments remained unspecified in published trial press reports.[8] Many English prisoners, nonetheless, genuinely feared 'Dr. Cooper's wing for dangerous and insane inmates … the "Psycho Wing"'.[9] Sedated men were unflatteringly dubbed 'Cooper's Troopers' by those who watched, transfixed, as they were obliged to bear witness. Scottish militant Jimmy McCaig claimed his instinctive wariness of 'Doctor Death [Cooper] … nutting [him] off' to the much - feared Rampton inspired the seizure of Parkhurst Assistant Governor Gerry Schofield as a hostage on 4–5 January 1983.[10]

Regardless of legal processes, a substantial element of the prison population believed that they were vulnerable to the consequences of irresponsible drug administration. A combination of unhealthy drug dosages and bad diet presumably lay at the heart of the Blood Transfusion Service policy of rejecting donations offered by inmates of Wormwood Scrubs.[11] The Gartree allegation touched a raw nerve on 5 October 1978, and Dr. Whitehead restated his opinion that the prison was a location where Largactil and other powerful drugs were routinely used to pacify inmates. Former prisoner George Coggan of PROP averred that the concerns raised related to the 'use [of drugs] that cannot be countenanced as medical'.[12] Paul Hill was shocked at the sight of 'mad' prisoners under Dr. Cooper's care in Parkhurst:

> They can have Largactyl, Mogadon, Triptosal – as much of it as they want. The
> screws take a little plastic cup and mix up the drugs like a cocktail. They ask you

if there is anything else you want. They will not let you have tobacco, fresh fruit, vegetables, but you can have as many of their drugs as you like. The men on F2 stagger about all day out of their heads. Cooper's Troopers have knives and shifts [i.e. 'chivs'] and there is violence. The screws are happy to let it continue – it gives them an excuse for the wing's existence.[13]

The Home Office insisted that normal National Health Service 'conditions' pertained in all prisons, although the lack of independent oversight rendered this defence incredible to informed observers.[14] Dr. C H McCleery, ex-Medical Officer in Parkhurst, created a sensation in October 1978 when his 'Treatment of psychopaths with Dexipol' appeared in the restricted publication *Prison Medical Journal*. Dr. McCleery admitted that persons 'regarded purely as Albany discipline failures' were given combinations of Mogadon, Tranxene, Lentizol and Valium. Numbers were transferred to the Parkhurst Prison Hospital where six medically fit persons were injected after 'a lot of persuasion' with the anti-schizophrenia drug Dexipol.[15] The precise purpose of this procedure was open to question and it was noted that the Danish pharmaceutical was 'not a tranquiliser'.[16] The Home Office was exceptionally well situated to shield itself from unwanted investigation, it was not until October 1983 that Dr. John L Kilgour, formerly of the Royal Army Medical Corps, Parachute Field Ambulance and World Health Organization, became the first Director of Prison Medical Services appointed from outside the body.[17]

Although more general prisoner concerns were clearly in play, the Gartree riot was sparked by fears for the welfare of 22-year-old Michael Blake who, on 5 October 1978, was forcibly given tranquilizing drugs before being taken to the prison infirmary. Three prisoners were granted access to check on his condition and it was later claimed that trouble flared 'during or shortly after that visit'.[18] When Martin Brady saw Blake: 'He was bouncing off the walls ... he was full of drugs and he was only a young kid – doing six years or something. That was what the riot was over – the abuse of drugs'.[19] Ronnie McCartney concurred that Blake had been 'drugged up by the doctor'.[20] John McCluskey was approached just after being unlocked by a prisoner who claimed his friend had been 'taken to the hospital and he's been drugged'. Several concerned prisoners then congregated outside the ground floor office on A Wing to request a meeting with the Governor. The Principal Officer made repeated phone contact with the Governor at ten to fifteen minute intervals and inaccurately reported his imminent arrival at least twice. An exasperated black prisoner intervened with a threat: 'We'll give you another ten minutes and then if something doesn't happen we've got to take some action'.[21] Republicans regarded what happened next in hindsight as 'a good bit of solidarity with the blacks'.[22] McCluskey noted:

The ten minutes passed by and the riot just started and the prisoners started smashing up. Of course there was nothing else they could do. Everything was smashed up. The screws in the office ran out and left all their mates behind. So the screws on the landing were barricaded in. They were very frightened. Some time later we decided that as the protest wasn't against the screws we'd have to take part of the barricade down and get the screws out, which we did. None of them were harmed in any way. The funny thing was that while the riot was going on they released Blake out of the hospital. If only the screws had done this at 6 p.m. or even at 7 p.m. there wouldn't have been a riot. We held the wing and kept the screws out.[23]

Official accounts were less explicit. A and D wings were seized by prisoners at 7.30 p.m. who then blocked the entranceways to the sector with makeshift barricades to hinder their reoccupation by the staff. Rioters gained control of B wing where the audible commotion and word of its causation had been relayed. Heavy cell doors were levered off their hinges, plumbing mangled and the expensive heating system totally destroyed.[24] By 9.25 only C Wing was under staff control and the future of Gartree within the Dispersal System was in doubt.[25] Eddie O'Neill, heavily guarded due to his 'E List' classification, lamented: 'We could only get five people that would do anything on that wing'.[26] Records seized from offices, including the 'Incident Book', furnished prisoners with information that aggravated the situation. Notes regarding the importance of destroying his relationship with his fiancée incensed McCartney. He found it necessary to protect a Loyalist prisoner from retribution from Liverpool men who disapproved of incriminating details which came to light.[27]

Serious fighting between approximately eighty-six prisoners and a reinforced complement of staff were brought in. It proved impossible to access the roof where structural levels of damage could have been achieved. Yet, prison officers wearing protective riot gear were attacked with hot water and petrol bombs. Their visible garb probably encouraged attacks by volatile cliques who did not seriously intend to main or kill. Paul Hill recalled: 'We toss the petrol bombs at them. Their shields catch fire and they flee in panic. They bring armed men into the prison. I see one of them carrying a pistol'.[28] Staff claimed, in a bid to explain their embarrassingly unsuccessful counterattack, that 'rioting prisoners fended off prison officers with the aid of homemade spears, cans of boiling water and hot-plates used as barriers'.[29] IRA prisoners demonstrated how to make effective incendiaries using turpentine and showed the best techniques for prising heavy cell doors from their mountings.[30]

Surprisingly, given the potential lethality of such improvised defences, only one prison officer was hurt. His misfortune probably owed much to the actual failure of the specially trained and equipped counterattacking riot squad to penetrate the obstacles being fiercely defended by prisoners.[31] In retrospect it was revealed that the men deployed comprised one of the new and still officially secret Prison Department 'Minimum Use of Force Tactical Intervention' (MUFTI) squads formed on 20 February 1978 to address problems of riot control exposed in Hull in August/ September 1976.[32] Their performance in Gartree was less than impressive; a factor which may have had bearing on the extremity of their actions during the subsequent Wormwood Scrubs 'riot' in August 1979.[33] The Home Office account of the 'serious disturbance in Gartree', published as required by statute in July 1979, omitted reference to the MUFTI and misleadingly attributed counter-riot efforts to 'off duty staff' being called in to augment those already at work.[34] This account, although required by law in England and Wales, was patently untrue. McCluskey *et al*, however, were well aware that their opponents were strangers:

> These weren't just the Gartree screws. These were specially selected riot squads from other prisons. We didn't recognise them because of the uniforms they were wearing. They had all the protective gear on worn by any riot squad, and over that they had brown overalls, and they carried long sticks which looked more than anything like a pickaxe handle. We could see them coming in, in bunches of ten or fifteen. They kept coming in. They would run from the gate to the back of the wing. This kept going for about an hour … From my experience at Albany I knew how serious this was … I told them that we had to defend the barricade because if these people came in on top of us they'd probably kill some of us. They tried twice to come through the barricade of tables, chairs, any furniture we could find. They couldn't pass the barricade.[35]

Believing that the protest had 'achieved our objective', prisoners told staff via a cell window that they would dismantle the barrier at 10.00 a.m. on 6 October 1978. This was achieved by 11.00 a.m. Armed police were sighted moving inside the prison buildings and in the garden outside, but no attempt was made to overpower the prisoners.[36] They did not resist the re-entry of prison officers. Bob Booth, Deputy Regional Director of the Prison Service, claimed that no concessions had been made, but his insistence that nothing improper had occurred with Blake was simply discounted.[37] Hill, a veteran of the brutal post riot assaults in Hull, had an unnerving 'sense of *déjà vu*'. Letters of assured good conduct distributed by the Assistant Governor were on this occasion honoured in full.[38] Although the Board of Visitors gave promises that personal possessions would be forwarded to those moved to other locations, it transpired that many, including McCluskey, did not receive belongings listed in Gartree.[39]

The direct agency of Dr. Peter Smith in treating Blake troubled ordinary prisoners in Gartree. Smith was an ex-employee of Broadmoor and was reputed to have 'sectioned' or 'nutted-off' more inmates than any other to secure psychiatric institutions.[40] The term derived from the authority of Section 72 of the Mental Health Act (1959), which enabled doctors to commit persons they regarded as violent or potentially so to a mental institution such as Rampton Special Hospital.[41] Prisoners referred to Smith as 'Doctor Death', as was highlighted in a *Leveller* special, although the alliterative sobriquet was otherwise used in relation to Dr. Cooper on the Isle of Wight. According to Ray McLaughlin, 'the prisoners felt they had to make a protest to protect themselves from being subjected to a similar fate' to that of Blake in Gartree. It was alleged that militant prisoners had been drugged against their will in Gartree to demonstrate the capacity of the medical staff to apply pressure.[42] The Home Office insisted that drugs were 'only' administered on the basis of 'clinical judgement' by qualified persons 'for the restoration of health or the relief of symptoms'.[43] Largactil, one of the most potent and feared pharmaceuticals dispensed in England, had been widely consumed in the prisons since 1958.[44] Prisoners placed no reliance in official statements averring appropriate dispensation. The concern of Gartree's wider jail population was by no means allayed by the refusal of Rees to publish the relevant report furnished to the Home Office by the governor.[45]

Dr. Smith went on record in May 1979 in opposition to the key strategic Dispersal System concept of 'human containment within secure perimeters'. He severely criticized the supposedly liberal approach, delineated by Tory icon Lord Mountbatten in 1966, as lacking 'commonsense'. When recalling events of Gartree's 'long night', a term redolent of deep negative subjectivity, Dr. Smith deflected plausible accusations of administrative culpability within his office for what had transpired with references to prison staff grappling with 'the explosive psychopathic mixture which we have watched and listened to'. His trenchant views elicited praise from the POA and their leader, Bob Brown, who claimed during their annual conference in Margate on 24 May 1979 that 'the people who are being punished are the staff and their families'. Brown, following Dr. Smith, implied that the psychiatric rehabilitative function of the English prisons, insofar as it really existed, was unimportant. He claimed, in order to counter allegations of inappropriate dosages being supplied to prisoners, that many fellow officers were taking proscribed medication 'simply to get them into work the next day'.[46] Access to subsidized alcohol by staff was a perk of the prison service noted by their singularly deprived captives. Owing to denial of eyewitness status, they could form no cogent opinion as to whether the palpable frisson within their locked-down wing community, arising from heavy drug utilization, was in any way mirrored in the ranks of those paid to keep them under lock and key.

On 1 November 1978 the POA branch in Gartree circulated its own fifteen-page document which, in addition to promoting service demands, 'urged the removal of mentally ill prisoners'.[47] They were reported as claiming that at least twenty of seventy-five disturbed and psychopathic prisoners in Gartree at the time of the riot 'should have been in Rampton or Broadmoor'.[48] Inmate behaviour and treatment were clearly major issues for staff in the Leicestershire prison, although Home Office Minister Lord Harris had declared himself to be 'totally satisfied with the medical regime at Gartree and throughout the prison service' on 6 October. This indicated confidence in the colourful Dr. Smith, who when questioned that day by journalists as he left the prison held aloft a green customs sticker while saying 'nothing to declare'.[49] Requests from Birmingham - based psychiatrist Dr. Maire 'Betty' O'Shea to examine Blake were reputedly ignored. Leftist Dr. O'Shea had been prominent in the campaign against the force-feeding of IRA prisoners in 1974–5 and a vocal supporter of prisoners' rights to humane treatment and, in the case of the republicans, political status. She was acting in 1978 on behalf of the Medical Committee against the Abuse of Prisoners by Drugging.[50]

The Board of Visitors imposed punishments on those deemed to be culpable, and did so with the confidence imbued by the recent High Court judgement that they had full legal authority, albeit subject to legal review. In October 1978 the Court of Appeal accepted that a prisoner had 'residuary rights appertaining to the nature and conduct of his imprisonment' and that decisions taken by a Board of Visitors were subject to re-examination. Outside courts had hitherto declined to rule on internal prison procedures on the grounds of jurisdiction.[51] Those accused of rioting in Gartree, moreover, had communicated with London-based solicitors who would have been in a position to assist with their defence had the option of hearing criminal cases in an outside court been green lighted. PROP had welcomed this prospect as the 'first test case' of the post-Appeal Court decision, although the Board of Visitor process was followed in the event.[52] Gartree rioters were ultimately sentenced to eighty-six days in solitary confinement, and those not serving life sentences forfeited a year's remission of sentence. Time spent awaiting adjudication was not deducted and the net effect of the Board's deliberations was that Jerry Mealy lost 440 days remission.[53] Republicans alleged that IRA members, British anarchists and other political prisoners were singled out from the main body of those responsible. It could not be denied, however, that the IRA had been deeply involved in the disturbances, and their agency was noted in the *Times*.[54] Many life-sentenced prisoners were moved due to the loss of accommodation which compounded the reduction in places occasioned by the Chelmsford prison fire in March.[55] Being shifted after a hiatus in receiving visits ensured that the families of those 'ghosted' around England were uncertain where to re-establish contact.[56]

Paul Holmes was one of the few IRA men initially retained in Gartree where he received a sentence of 186 days in solitary despite having played no part in the riot due to his enforced isolation from events.[57] He was then moved to Long Lartin where he served the additional sentence. Brian McLaughlin, who had only just been returned to Gartree from a 'lie-down' in Bristol, was also retained in the prison. After repeated requests for medical examination in the aftermath of the riot, McLaughlin was diagnosed with TB.[58] Martin Brady was regarded as a 'ringleader' and was sent to Wakefield where he was promised a 'hard time' from staff. This threat was easily delivered within the hermetic confines of F-Wing.[59] Paul Hill and Phil Sheridan arrived into Exeter, a local jail rarely used to hold IRA prisoners. Hill was quickly moved on to Winchester and Wakefield while Sheridan endured nine months in the 'awful', ill-appointed Exeter where the Segregation Block resembled 'a subterranean dungeon'.[60] Sheehan was dispatched via Wormwood Scrubs to Parkhurst. McCluskey and McCartney were shifted to Winchester and very quickly into the punishment block for protesting the local conditions. Whereas McCluskey was shortly afterwards moved on to Wormwood Scrubs for an extended bout of solitary confinement, McCartney's refusal to co-operate with the staff and rejection of 'closed' visits resulted in his being detained in a 'strong box' cell in the Segregation Unit.[61]

Ronnie McCartney spent December 1978 and January 1979 in the 'strong box', during which time he was refused permission to attend religious services or use personal cash to buy Christmas cards for his family.[62] The adapted cell was soundproofed by reinforced doors and walls: a combination of solitary confinement and sensory deprivation which, prisoners claimed, facilitated physical attacks by staff. The Winchester variant was painted in brilliant white, which accentuated the impact of the overhead light being left on constantly, and resulted in the lasting impairment of McCartney's vision.[63] While the hardships endured by all IRA prisoners in England featured in republican organs, the perception that McCartney had been particularly maltreated resonated in political prints for several months. His progress was reported following transfer to Hull in February 1979.[64] His defiance in Hull, where he was held on 'E-List' in the Punishment Block, led to beatings and confinement in the 'strong-box'. The special cell consisted of a concrete bed behind a heavy double door which ensured 'no one could hear what was happening to you'.[65]

The highly visible and media-covered Gartree protest exposed the potential for violence within an overstressed penal environment. Overcrowding exerted strain across the network and ensured that prisoner pacification was a pressing matter in 1978 in the aftermath of expensive and embarrassing riots in the Dispersal System.[66] Brixton staff, as part of an ambitious POA strategy involving forty of Britain's 120 prisons, voted on 19 October to refuse admittance to an average of twenty-five remand prisoners per day from 5 November.[67] Such threats, in the context of prisoner restiveness, obliged Home Secretary Merlyn Rees to seek 'urgent' Cabinet approval for an inquiry into the grievances of Prison Service employees. This was granted on 2 November.[68] The POA were unequivocal in citing the Irish political dimension to the cusp of exaggeration, although many members would have realised that IRA personnel were due to give evidence in York Crown Court from 2 November when proceedings commenced against staff accused of offences committed during and after the Hull riot.[69] It was significant that warders did not overreact in terms of physical assaults when their ascendancy in Gartree was restored.[70]

In the advent of the Home Secretary's review, David Heywood, Assistant Secretary of the Society of Civil and Public Servants, pressed the case in a naked reference to the danger posed by IRA prisoners: 'Riots on the scale of the recent Gartree disturbances might break out at several prisons at the same time. Violent prisoners and IRA extremists would be delighted to exploit the situation'.[71] A joint letter to the Home Secretary from prison governors was similarly themed: 'If the present trend continues there will be a serious loss of control, which has to be quelled by armed intervention, with the probability of both staff and prisoners being killed'.[72] The allusion to an Attica - style massacre, if extreme and unprecedented in Britain, did not appear entirely unreasonable in the last years of the most violent decade of the century inside the country's prisons. PROP had predicted a major incident for years and was unsurprised by the near manifestation of armed intervention in Albany in May 1983.[73]

Questions of control lay at the heart of most serious controversies of the late 1970s and early 1980s. Inmates were conventionally punished for dissent and violation of regulations by temporary loss of privileges and remission of sentence. Punishments included imprisonment in detached or small spaces engineered to promote desocialization, discomfort, tedium and under stimulation. If mentally and often physically debilitating, the additional prospect of being 'sectioned' to 'hospitals' for long term and potentially even more severe maltreatment was omnipresent. PROP and other prisoner advocates alleged that 'kicking squads' and a psychotic element within the penal establishment abused and even staged 'suicides' of vulnerable and selected uncooperative prisoners. Psychotropic medicine, administered in either inappropriate dosages or forcibly by injection, was a widespread concern which went far beyond traditional jailhouse suspicions that the sedative Bromide was routinely added to liquids.[74] Dr. McCleery's admission, following relocation to southern Sudan, that 'problems of containment of psychopaths' led to the drugging of men showing 'no evidence of formal illness' on the Isle of Wight were publicised by the *Sunday Times* on 22 October 1978. Persistent allegations of untoward 'staff violence' towards prisoners and unsatisfactory inquests were not entertained by the insulated Home Office.[75]

Guardian correspondent David Beresford highlighted the retention of twenty-five Gartree rioters in a 'new unit' commissioned in 1975. 'Mystery' surrounded the function of the two - storey building which housed 'Twenty-five cells with a direct link to the prison hospital'.[76] Prisoners were convinced it had been conceived as a 'Control Unit' along the lines of that temporarily operated in Wakefield and that constructed but used in an alternate manner in Wormwood Scrubs. Official claims that the detached Gartree block was merely a high security 'segregation unit' did not mollify those familiar with the rebranded F Wing in Wakefield, where a regime of sensory deprivation operated, albeit without the strict schedule of modular progression which the formerly secret annexe had trialled.[77]

It was significant that the prisoners retained in what was described as simply 'temporary accommodation' in Gartree were inside another newly designated 'F Wing' which staffing problems had hitherto kept closed.[78] They were not, however, physically mistreated, and the contrast with Hull in 1976 was obvious. Labour MP John Prescott provided a direct connection given his role in negotiations, which resulted in the termination of the earlier protest in his Hull East constituency. His accurate prediction of unrest in Gartree, however, drew the ire of John Farr, Conservative MP for Harborough, who told his fellow Yorkshire man to keep 'his long nose' out of the affair.[79] By 1980 it was evident that the Prison Department, stymied in its sinister 'Control Unit' strategy, adapted the basic concept and infrastructure to regularize the *de facto* practise of prolonged solitary confinement. Harsh segregation was viewed as a vital tool in the arsenal of prisoner management and popular within the POA. The persistence of legal actions arising from the Wakefield prototype, however, sensitized its proponents to the importance of discretion, media - friendly terminology and institutional secrecy.[80] A case brought by Mickey Williams obliged the Home Office to release five hitherto secret documents on the Wakefield Control Unit despite claims by Home Secretary William Whitelaw that disclosure was 'injurious to the public interest'. Williams was ultimately unsuccessful as it was found that the *Prison Rules* he alleged to have been infringed were 'regulatory, not mandatory'.[81]

The Conservative orientated *Times* published an important feature by Home Affairs correspondent Peter Evans on 3 November 1978 which assessed the Home Secretary's announcement of the independent inquiry into Gartree. Evans noted that the penal system was in dire need of reform:

> For too long, prisons have been too low on the political agenda. Prisoners and prison officers have tended to feel that behind prison walls they are out of sight and out of mind. Part of the reason is the obsessive secrecy which has until recently surrounded the prison system. That has been broken by the increasingly articulate organisations representing prisoners' rights and more platforms on which to pursue them. Muffled by the Official Secrets Act, the prison staffs have lost a battle for public attention.[82]

Evans cited Martin Luther King's observation that 'riots are the voice of the unheard' in relation to the restive prison population, while warning of the danger of dismissing POA allegations regarding poor working conditions. The POA had threatened massive industrial action if their demands on back-pay and salary increases in lieu of their loss of lucrative overtime rates were not met. If, as Evans noted, penologists and psychiatrists increasingly dismissed the once inspirational mission of prisoner rehabilitation, the crude question of mere containment of supposed criminal contagion gained in importance. Evans averred that 'in overcrowded prisons, there is little chance of doing more than trying to make the system work'. Although avoiding discussion of the punishment and deterrent functions of incarceration, by the late 1970s, years of under-funding of the Prison Department ensured that loss of income for employees imposed additional hardships on persons deprived of liberty and quality of life. This diminution of experience was adjudged permissible, and the High Court endorsement of the Home Office definition of 'privilege' in March 1978 lessened the unwelcome prospect of the pace and extent of penal reform being driven by the domestic legal profession.[83]

Prisoners' advocates, including PROP, PAC and Sinn Féin, fully appreciated the utility of driving the agenda from within, even as international courts turned their attention to the Dispersal System. What the PAC had dramatically termed 'a wall of silence around Irish prisoners' was smashed by direct action in the form of hunger strikes, riots, roof occupations, passive 'sit-downs' and external pro-prisoner demonstrations.[84] IRA and Category A prisoners were central to this ominous evolution, as evidenced by the press and media attention devoted to such egregious incidents as the Albany and Hull 'riots' of 1976, and the persistent unrest in Gartree in 1978. As expressly intended, visible modes of prisoner protest projected from England's maximum-security institutions until 1980 could not be readily concealed. By November 1978 the men and women tasked with containing the once inviolate Prison Department domain, from which the glare of the popular media was hitherto excluded, had their own pressing concerns. The POA was motivated as never before to maximize its negotiating capital by stressing the widely appreciable dangers posed by the minor yet vibrant and menacing IRA cohort.[85]

Wormwood Scrubs, 7 October 1978

The arrest of Kenneth Gillespie of Oldcroft Road, London, on 7 October 1978 illustrated the multi-faceted nature of the IRA threat. Gillespie, a long term sentenced prisoner in Wormwood Scrubs, was on a week long pre-release parole ahead of planned emancipation in November when arrested in the vicinity of D Wing. On leaving the prison on 4 October, Gillespie was found to be in possession of addresses written on 'scraps of paper'.

These were clandestinely photocopied and replaced by staff who quickly ascertained that they related to the premises of licensed arms dealers. A surveillance operation was mounted on 7 October when, the Old Bailey heard, Gillespie drove a Ford Escort to the vicinity of D Wing and flashed his car lights. He was immediately arrested by police, who found a 130-foot rope inside the vehicle, which had been blackened with polish.[86] Angela Williams of Bollo Bridge Road, Acton, was questioned shortly afterwards following the discovery of a telegram she had sent to Gillespie in his lodgings. Williams, whose brother Nicholas Smith was another long term prisoner in D Wing, admitted handing over a 'heavy parcel' which had arrived in her Acton home from Dublin to a man she met in a local train station. The delivery had been arranged by phone and the man she encountered claimed to have been 'sent by her brother'. It was not proven that this was Gillespie. She gave him one of two Giro cheques which had arrived in the post from Dublin along with a registered letter containing £100. At trial in January 1980, prosecutor David Paget claimed that the sealed parcel delivered by Williams in Acton contained the modified rope, a detail of which she disclaimed all knowledge.[87]

Information on the incident emerged on 7 January 1980 when Gillespie was prosecuted. He pleaded guilty to conspiracy to aid the escape of four men from Wormwood Scrubs. The four were named in evidence as Nicholas Smith and IRA prisoners Paddy Mulryan, James 'Punter' Bennett and Stevie Nordone, who were all serving sentences of twenty years and over. Following Gillespie's conviction it was claimed that Wesley Dick had originated a plot which would have freed 'some of the most dangerous criminals in Britain', although the West Indian was not charged with any offence.[88] Dick, a politically motivated armed robber who had adopted the name Shujaa Moshesh in prison, had also been on good terms with Ray McLaughlin, who also encountered his co-defendants in the Category A circuits.[89] John McCluskey described him as 'the most politicized black prisoner that I've ever met in prison. He was constantly working to politicize other black prisoners and not only black. He worked with all the white prisoners he possibly could'.[90]

Dick was one of the three black radicals sentenced on 30 June 1976 for a misfired armed robbery attempt in London which precipitated the five day 'Spaghetti House' hostage - taking siege in Knightsbridge on 28 September 1975. Dick, Frank Davies and Anthony 'Bonsu' Monroe claimed membership of the socialist Black Liberation Army, an independent offshoot of the USA Black Panther movement, and insisted on political motivation when in custody. While the depth of this sensational identification was debated, the men consciously emulated the contemporary IRA by refusing to recognize the court and turning their backs on Justice Griffith-Jones in the Old Bailey. Advised by ex-Army major Sir Robert Mark and Commander

Ernest Bond, Griffith-Jones rejected the defendants' assertion of political and racial inspiration and imposed terms of seventeen to twenty-one years.[91] Dick had met the IRA 'Balcombe Street' group and 'some' of the Guildford Four when on remand in Brixton in 1975. On entering the Dispersal System, he had political discussions with Shane Paul O'Doherty and other assertive republicans. He acknowledged that there was 'a whole heap I learned when I was in prison, especially from people who were more conscious than me, mainly the Irish guys'.[92] According to the West Indian:

> In prison I was meeting people who were giving me the Irish liberation point of view. The first thing I noticed which impressed me was their commitment to the Irish struggle. They're not half way guys … Any kind of English hostility against black and Irish prisoners the screws will support because it's in their interest to keep prisoners divided as well as matching their own racism. We had a lot of political discussions, were involved in protests and strikes. They proved the level of their commitment. It was a learning process; I'm sure I learned more from them than they learned from me. They used to ask me questions about aspects of the black struggle.[93]

Such deep foundations underlay the spirit of cooperation divined in the attempted Wormwood Scrubs breakout of 7 October 1978. A search of Mulyran's cell on the night of the planned escape uncovered incriminating contraband. A manuscript map of D Wing, scale drawings of keys, pages extracted from a street directory showing the Wormwood Scrubs neighbourhood and a stolen driving license were found inside his record player.[94] The London court clearly accepted that Smith and the three IRA men had received the assistance of Gillespie in planning to escape. However, no 'proceedings' were initiated against the group in view of the 'length of the sentences they are serving'.[95] It emerged that a person acting on Mulyran's behalf had sent a telegram to Gillespie urging postponement of the bid, although this was evidently not received. Judge Michael Argyle sentenced him to four years' imprisonment on 11 January 1980 despite his unverified claim to have been subjected to 'veiled threats' from the republicans.[96] The trial occurred after a long interval and the time lag, coupled with the minimal attempt to bring charges, facilitated the Prison Department by downplaying the seriousness of an escape conspiracy of potentially major repercussions. Any successful collaboration between IRA Category A prisoners, politicized black prisoners and resourceful British organized criminals was a dire prospect *vis à vis* the efficacy of the Dispersal System and anti-republican propaganda. The Home Office must have noted that October 1978 was a month in which the IRA prisoners under their control were deeply implicated in rioting and viable escape plans. This was not the full extent of the republican challenge.

The Blanket Protest in England

The drama in Gartree prison temporarily overshadowed an historic development in Albany, Isle of Wight, where five IRA men commenced a blanket protest on 8 October 1978.[97] If the first major effort of its kind by the IRA in England since the 1940s, the methodology, mentality and stated objectives were exactly the same as its precursors. Refusal to wear prison uniform was the standard republican demonstration against criminal categorization. The death in Ireland of Tommy Mullins on 2 November 1978 served to remind the general public of the centrality of such modes of protest within the IRA. Mullins had undertaken a fifteen-day hunger strike and blanket protest when he was a republican prisoner in Wormwood Scrubs during the War of Independence, 1919–21. He went on to become a founder member of Fianna Fáil and retired as General Secretary of the party as recently as 1973.[98] In 1978 neither Fianna Fáil nor Fine Gael, the two largest political parties in Ireland, wished to be reminded of their shared armed republican heritage, despite separate annual political pilgrimages to Bodenstown, Kildare, the home of the grave of Wolfe Tone, 'father' of the ideology.[99]

In the course of a 'valedictory visit' by Irish Embassy First Secretary Richard 'Dick' O'Brien, David Blunt of the Republic of Ireland Department (RID) of the FCO was alerted to his concern 'with developments during the past few months in certain British prisons, especially HM Prison, Albany'. O'Brien demonstrated awareness that the 'unrest' on the Isle of Wight had been 'simmering for a while before being escalated by the July demonstrations'. In October 1978 the main fear expressed by the First Secretary was 'that we may be approaching an "H-Block" situation in this country'. A restricted digest of the meetings was passed to the Prison Department which rejected any justification of discrimination claims made by Irish prisoners in terms of either treatment or punishment.[100]

Albany had been at the centre of IRA complaints since April 1978 when visiting, and general penal conditions had deteriorated.[101] In a statement worthy of greater import than was granted, republicans claimed that matters in the complex were 'fast approaching those of the H-Blocks of Long Kesh'.[102] Irish Category A men received half-hour visits in tiny rooms attended by four prison officers and a policewoman if female visitors or children were present. Liam Baker took exception to a particularly obnoxious policewoman and lost all remission in consequence of his engagement in protests.[103] Britons, including Category A men, simultaneously enjoyed two-hour visits in a large hall with fifty tables and low-key staff supervision.[104] The contrast was by no means academic. Ray McLaughlin was fined for kissing his wife Mary goodbye in June 1978 and Eddie O'Neill was docked forty-nine days remission for claiming that a dog handler had called him an 'Irish bastard' in the exercise yard. Most of the IRA prisoners and one Loyalist were sent to the Punishment Block, after which the much-persecuted McLaughlin was shifted to Wakefield and O'Neill to Gartree.[105] 'Ghostings' were not isolated phenomena, and the universal withdrawal of facilities in Parkhurst due to industrial action by staff heightened tensions. The temporary closure of the prison's once heavily protected workshops exacerbated an already fraught situation. By early December over 200 men in three of the four wings felt obliged to boycott the extremely poor quality sustenance on offer.[106]

In the aftermath of the July cell - smashing protest, the remaining IRA men in Albany were deprived of chamber pots in their cells and did not receive replacement furniture.[107] Most declined to shave their beards from 18 July when informed that they would only be permitted to bathe only once per week.[108] They were denied permission to attend weekly Mass on Sundays to limit communication with other prisoners, but were granted access to religious services on other days.[109] This was ordinarily the responsibility of the Governor who under *Prison Standing Orders* was required to invoke Order 7A 3 (4) to disbar attendance. Circumstances determined that the option of rioting was impractical and a full-blown hunger strike was not warranted. Recourse to a protracted blanket-style protest on the core issue of repatriation was relatively appealing under the circumstances. Non-co-operation was the central concept. Strategic interests were addressed by IRA demands to be repatriated to their native country, while the initial cause of complaint against 'forms of discrimination' remained in focus.[110]

On 8 October 1978 Busty Cunningham, Tipp Guilfoyle, Tony Cunningham and Liam Baker demanded repatriation to Irish prisons where, despite the gruelling protest in the H-Blocks, their status as political prisoners would be much more defined. Family visits were generally less fraught in either of the two Irish jurisdictions than in England for prisoners who were not on protest. That fact that Baker had settled in Southampton and was married to a devoted Englishwoman was regarded as immaterial in view of the political context.[111] Ray McLaughlin had only just emerged from a unilateral blanket protest in Wakefield's F Wing and was incapable of resuming the tactic in support of Albany comrades, owing to what the PAC described as 'severe psychological disorientation'.[112] The Leeds branch of UTOM protested on his behalf outside the prison every Sunday. McLaughlin grew ill in Wakefield and had trouble with balance and speech when released to the wings.[113] In retrospect, the militant Irishman highlighted the typically 'bad communications' on the planning stages of the blanket protest, which may have altered the situation in Albany had he been in full health.[114]

It was pertinent that the trial of twelve prison officers who had savagely beaten McLaughlin and others in Hull was then underway.[115] Wakefield's IRA PRO contended that the Donegal man had been 'singled out by the prison staff for special treatment because of his participation in the Hull prison riot, and because he was one of the key witnesses'.[116] Tyrone's Gerry Cunningham, similarly, was also moved from London's tough Wandsworth prison to Wakefield ahead of the trial. He received 'plenty of verbal' in F Wing on arrival but was not physically assaulted.[117] The rare participation of IRA witnesses in a civil trial was cited as an explanation of the exceptional heavy security surrounding the sessions in York.[118] The stakes were high for all concerned. Mary McLaughlin, in a November 1978 interview recorded in Birmingham, claimed that the failure to convict staff for their actions following the Hull riot 'might lead to another'.[119]

Numerous Prison Officers were committed for trial at York Crown Court on 31 August 1978 to answer charges arising from one of the most important and destructive riots in modern British history.[120] Ray McLaughlin gave evidence on 25 January 1979, an ideologically challenging task for an Irish republican, who tended and were at times required under pain of Óglaigh na hÉireann sanction, to withhold personal recognition of the judicial competency of such forums.[121] Solidarity was expressed by other IRA men in Albany who, when 'on the blanket', withdrew their 'co-operation' from attending prison staff.[122] This oppositional stance placed an onus on their jailers to mediate the permanently unequal relationship *vis à vis* captors and captives, either within their own immediate terms, or those they deemed permissible by superiors. A robust equilibrium was thus established by the IRA in Albany whereby public and politically essential compromises in York were not only justified by the objective of achieving a higher objective, but were materially counterbalanced by harmful sacrifice within the intensely private Segregation 'Punishment' Block.

Whereas Shane Paul O'Doherty and a small number of IRA men had resorted to the blanket in England in previous years, the concerted co-operation of the Albany group marked a departure in scale and policy.[123] For pragmatic reasons, not least for clarity of key issues and the efficacy of republican propaganda, a blanket protest in Wormwood Scrubs was presented as an escalation of that underway in Albany. Mick Murray, who had just completed two weeks in solitary, joined Punter Bennett in refusing to wear prison clothes on 13 October.[124] He was held in solitary for twenty-four hours a day in a cell painted completely white.[125] The IRA in Wormwood Scrubs were irritated in the early part of the month when Paddy Mulryan was ghosted to Long Lartin and Eddie Byrne to Walton for alleged complicity in an escape attempt.[126] Newry man Byrne had been sent to Wormwood Scrubs in late 1978 from which he had come very close to liberating himself from two years earlier. He was placed in segregation and had his arm in a sling arising from an assault. Byrne was reputed to be 'refusing visits because of conditions there and threats against him and his wife by screws'.[127] An American Congressman who made overtures to the Home Office regarding Byrne's treatment was informed that the Irishman's 'behaviour since conviction has been poor ... [and involved] many offences against prison discipline'.[128]

The PAC offered direct support while campaigning politically at a strategic level. The 26 November 1978 commemoration of the Manchester Martyrs in London was identified as an opportunity to reiterate public backing for the interlinked demands of political status, amnesty and a British military withdrawal from Ireland.[129] An impressive turn out of 5,000 was achieved as most of the main leftist and union groups who had supported the July demonstration once again took to the streets. Chairman Peter Turton of the PAC called for a minute's silence 'for all the Irish political prisoners who have died in British jails'. Kevin Colfer of Sinn Féin (Britain) read a message from the Albany IRA men.[130] Ironically, the three 'martyrs' executed in Manchester in November 1867 had been convicted of taking part in the successful springing of two high-ranking Fenians from a prison van. The memorial in Moston Cemetery was the heart of republican events in Manchester in the 1970s and 1980s.[131] Marx, in fact, had organized a major public meeting in London seeking a stay in the execution of the doomed Fenians.[132] Among those who attended Moston every Easter were leftists who appreciated that an Irish Fenian living in Britain, John Connell, had written the words to the socialist anthem 'The Red Flag'.[133]

Baker, Guilfoyle and the two Cunninghams in Albany were kept in bare cells for twenty-three to twenty-four hours a day. Refusal to 'slop out' ensured that the staff regularly hosed them and their cells down in an ostensible and certainly robust attempt to improve sanitation. Infrequent escorts to the toilet obliged the men to dispose of human waste through the windows and, even if demeaning, the spreading of disinfectant in their cells was probably beneficial.[134] Normal bedding was withdrawn and replaced with hard boards, provided only at night, covering a concrete base. Deprived of blankets during the day, the men had to wrap themselves in prison towels. Protesting prisoners were generally entitled to attend the chapel, but this fleeting relief from a tedious, fetid and claustrophobic routine was prevented by the authorities who alleged they had been disruptive. The repudiation of this allegation by chaplain Fr. Parry proved insufficient to secure the restoration of access. Although offered alternate religious services in a specially designated cell, the four avoided setting a precedent that was tantamount to a major compromise of principle.[135] The Home Office, for its part, repeated in November 1978 that restrictions on attending Mass arose 'because their behaviour has threatened the good order of the establishment'.[136]

A Home Office briefing document prepared ahead of the 27 November 1978 visit of Taoiseach Lynch to London misrepresented England's 'blanket protest' situation as if it had arisen from a minor grievance by men with no political formation or aspirations:

Albany prison, on the Isle of Wight, has been particularly troubled in recent months by protests from Irish Republican prisoners. The point of contention has been the specially supervised visiting conditions applied in the interests of security to certain prisoners who present very high security risks. Not all Republican prisoners are subject to such visiting procedures, nor are all prisoners to whom the procedures apply Irish Republican prisoners. Certain Republican prisoners in Albany, however, have been protesting actively against the visiting arrangements since [25] April.

The protest started with a refusal by those concerned to work. Since then, they have also refused to go into the normal living accommodation in the prison, and, for certain periods, refused to collect their food, refused to use the normal sanitary facilities (a number of them have thrown the contents of their chamber pots at prison staff and over the floor of their cells) and, on occasions, refused to wear prison clothing. Where this behaviour has constituted offences against prison discipline, the offenders have been dealt with by the normal disciplinary procedures as any other prisoner behaving similarly would have been.[137]

Further discretionary pressure on the protesters was applied by means of restricting access to a newspaper to just one copy every two weeks. No personal property was allowed in the cells and mail deliveries were restricted to family members. Letters were removed by staff once they had been read and a single book a week was permitted on loan from the prison library.[138] The authorities appeared confident of breaking the resolve of the Albany men to persevere and elected not to separate them by transfers or short-term lie-downs, an arguably justifiable invocation of Rule 43.

Relocating militants was not invariably without repercussions. Punter Bennett, however, was sent from Wormwood Scrubs to Strangeways to separate him from the inflexible Mick Murray. This shift had the knock on effect of prompting the transfer of Eddie Butler from Strangeways to Winson Green. The Castleconnell, County Limerick man had been held in solitary confinement since the temporary closure of Leicester Special Unit in February 1978, and it appeared as if greater utilization of the local jails under Rule 43 was increasingly common.[139] In practical terms this ensured that Butler was held in isolation and subject to oppressive visiting conditions. Two 'closed' visits in the summer of 1978 and 1979 upset his family and matters only marginally improved from 8 May 1980 following the re-opening of Leicester SSU.[140] Murray was isolated in Wormwood Scrubs by virtue of being segregated when on his personal protest. He was by no means the only IRA man capable or willing to act. Jerry Mealy was also held in the London jail's solitary cells following transfer from Gartree in the aftermath of the October 1978 riot. In early December 1978 Mealy succeeded in entering a prison office with an iron bar and 'completely demolished everything possible within reach before voluntarily handing the iron bar back to his guards'. Sinn Féin reported that Mealy 'informed his guards that his action (demolition job) was his way of demonstrating his 'solidarity' with those picketing outside on behalf of all Irish POWs'.[141] The unwritten IRA policy of avoiding direct physical attacks on prison staff in England was then observed. Mealy had no qualms about utilizing force if necessary. He had violently resisted arrest when grappled by police in 1973 and managed to punch the then Conservative Home Secretary Robert Carr during a prison visit.[142]

The IRA men in Wakefield wished to express support for Martin Brady, who was also languishing in segregation arising from the Gartree riot. As intended, the bizarre environment inherited from the F Wing's days as England's most infamous 'Control Unit' disconcerted the Belfastman:

> You couldn't walk over that white line [in the yard]. If you walked over the line, you were sent in. 'Right, Brady, away you go'. That happened me many a time … You were walking in a circle, not thinking, you walked into someone else's exercise yard. They think you are trying to do something. 'Right, let's go here'. It was a strict regime there. They came down heavy … You weren't allowed cigarettes, you weren't allowed read magazines and you weren't allowed to get anything in. You were only allowed one letter a week … they took the bed off you at 8 a.m. until 7 p.m. at night. So you had nothing in your cell except a chair … When you got up you had your breakfast. Slopped out and did your exercises – press-ups etc. In the morning – the pipe was along the wall – in the winter it was freezing, in the summer it was boiling, but we got through that all right.[143]

The decision was taken that the republicans on the wings would engineer the means to join Brady in the block. On Christmas Day, 25 December 1978, Tony Clarke and Ray McLaughlin threatened to smash the windows of a staff office in C Wing before their unconventional wish was entertained. Similarly, Vince Donnelly, pulled the tie from a warder's uniform in D Wing to provide a minimal pretext for joining his comrades. The largely peaceful demonstration had an unexpected sequel in that the strange behaviour of the IRA prisoners sparked a security operation in the Wakefield vicinity.[144]

The experience of most Irish republicans in English jails continued to be anomalous. In late 1978 a petition was handed into the British Embassy in Dublin calling for the release of Fr. Pat Fell on the grounds that he had been eligible for parole in April 1977. Signatories included Rev. Michael Diden, President of St. Patrick's College, Maynooth, forty staff members and 500 students. Fr. Fell had been assistant priest at the All Souls' Church in Coventry and was sentenced to twelve years for his activities as a senior IRA member in the sector. His more junior co-defendant, Frank Stagg, had died on hunger strike in Wakefield in February 1976.[145] The FCO monitored the situation and offered to assist the British Embassy in Dublin 'on how to react to enquiries about the petition'.[146]

Fr. Fell was ultimately freed in July 1981, by which time his case at Strasbourg was progressing slowly towards the victory achieved three years later.[147] His profile had been relatively high in pro-republican sectors due to his clerical background and the incorrect acceptance by many that he was innocent. In New York, Michael Sheehan, columnist in the Clan na Gael paper *Irish World*, referenced his personal involvement in the campaign to emancipate IRA prisoners held in England in the mid-1940s. From September 1976, he interested himself in the fate of Fr. Fell and the privations endured by his English family. The story was subsequently front-page news.[148] Action had been required in London when Frank Maguire MP lobbied the Home Office on behalf of Bishop Thomas Joseph Drury of Corpus Christi, Texas who wished to visit Fr. Fell on 25 August 1978. Drury was en route to Rome and staying with Sr. Clarke whom, it was noted, was 'well known to P3 for her attempts to communicate with and visit IRA prisoners'. While Albany's Catholic Chaplain, Fr. Parry, raised no objection, his colleague, Fr. Masterson, an acquaintance of the bishop, advised 'he should not be permitted to visit Fell. He was apparently very pro-IRA, belonged to an American organization known as the [Ancient Order of] Hibernians, and had made some dangerous statements about the IRA in the American press'.[149] Rev. Cosmas Korb, OFM, a New York associate of Sr. Clarke, had launched a letter-writing campaign on behalf of the priest in December 1979.[150] Fr. Fell already had in excess of 300 contacts listed in his prison 'letter-sheets'.[151]

The visit of Taoiseach Lynch to Prime Minister Callaghan in London on 27 November 1978 inspired a round of consultations between the Republic of Ireland Department of the Foreign and Commonwealth Office and the Prison Department of the Home Office. Although occasioned by the necessity of face-to-face dialogue on the European Monetary System, it was appreciated that Lynch intended to 'bring up' the 'treatment of Irish prisoners in Great Britain'.[152] The British Embassy in Dublin had advised on 9 November that Ireland's Minister for Foreign Affairs had been challenged by Neil Blaney TD if he was 'aware that Irish political prisoners in British jails are still being held in solitary confinement under conditions which are an infringement of the Convention on Human Rights'. Swift of the DFA advised British diplomats that the question would be addressed in the Dáil on 15 November. This, coupled with ongoing queries emanating from the Irish Embassy in London, all but ensured Lynch was bound to request information in London.[153] A briefing document was compiled in part from correspondence sent by Lord Harris to Joan Maynard in July, supplemented by a Prison Department document of 21 November attributing much of the underlying problems to 'continuing claims made by their supporters outside prison that Irish Republicans convicted of criminal offences are "political" prisoners who should not be subject to the normal rules and regulations of prison life'.[154]

While the meeting of Lynch and Callaghan passed off without public discord, the Irish Embassy felt an obligation on 14 December 1978 to raise the treatment of Tyrone IRA prisoner Sean Campbell with the Republic of Ireland Department in Downing Street, London. David Blunt was informed that Campbell had cancelled a visit from his wife and three children in August 1978 when the Governor of Wandsworth refused to exercise his discretion to permit an extended time slot. Campbell regarded a counteroffer of an additional fifteen minutes for the reunion of a family separated for three years as unacceptable. The Embassy's Administrative Attaché related the Irishman's additional claim to have been denied permission to meet the Visiting Committee on 29 November 1978 where he intended to assert that 'letters he had sent to his mother and brother had not been received by them'.[155] Handwritten notes by Blunt acknowledged further serious allegations of impropriety, not least Campbell's accusation that a letter posted to the Irish Embassy on 7 March 1978 was among the correspondence 'destroyed by the Prison'.[156] While awaiting comment from the Prison Department on a possible diplomatic incident, Blunt responded to the Embassy query by posting a photocopy of the *Visiting Wandsworth Prison* leaflet to their nearby Grosvenor Place address.[157] The FCO and Irish Embassy omitted reference in their basic written exchanges to the highly germane fact that Campbell was party to a major ECHR case in Strasbourg and very much a 'special' Category A prisoner.[158]

By January 1979 the situation in Albany had gone from bad to worse. The republican magazine *IRIS* reported that the 'barbaric treatment' continued: 'Screws are still hosing out the cells, the POWs and their bedding with hot water, depriving them of their chamber-pots, and causing undue delays in permitting toilet usage'. The four faced mail restrictions, twenty-three hour lock up and remained barred from attending Mass in the main chapel'.[159] *IRIS* was edited by Fr. Parais O Duill, who had - first hand knowledge of the English prison system, arising from his efforts to save Frank Stagg's life in 1976.[160] He was also prominent in addressing injustice in Ireland. In March 1978 O Duill was denounced in the Special Criminal Court, Dublin, for his efforts to defend the four IRSP defendants framed by Irish authorities for the Sallins train robbery. His associate, Joe Stagg, brother of Frank, was also censured in the juryless court which had wrongly convicted the 'IRSP 4'.[161] O Duill's organizational ability and experience of prison issues made him the ideal chair of the influential National H-Blocks/ Armagh Committee, which acted as the key co-ordinating body for protests inspired by the blanket protests and 1980–81 hunger strikes.[162] His former IRA credentials lessened fears within the Republican Movement that persons interested primarily in opportunist 'anti-imperialist' politics lacking commitment to the

Armed Struggle would dilute the campaign. Advocacy of 'regard for human rights' by O Duill in March 1980 posed no threat to concurrent republican efforts.[163]

Prisoners and Armed Struggle

'The "Special Prisoners" in England' feature was carried by *Republican News* in January 1979 and concentrated on the harshness endured by Martin Brady in Wakefield. Two significant points were made by 'Oscair', which effectively signalled the leadership's policy towards the prisoners in England. Brady was cited as opining: 'Conditions will not improve much until a victory has been achieved over the H-Block issue at home in Ireland'. This addressed the uncomfortable but obvious fact that the Long Kesh campaign was being prioritized over a potential drive to highlight the injustices of the Dispersal System. It was important, however, to stress that the prisoners in England were not seeking pre-eminence and, in fact, were fully behind the grim struggles in Long Kesh and Armagh. 'Oscair' balanced the *de facto* downgrading of the England campaign with a declaration that 'The POWs in England must not be allowed to become the forgotten prisoners ... they are in need of support and solidarity'.[164] In Philadelphia, Pennsylvania, Mike Duffy of Irish Northern Aid compensated by organizing a 'Prisoners Writing Campaign' which annually channelled thousands of letters and cards to IRA members imprisoned in Ireland and England.[165] Quantities of *Irish People* and other Irish-American titles arrived into the English prisons where they were widely distributed, despite carrying detailed, uncensored 'war news' columns of a type eschewed by mainstream media.[166] From a British perspective, the *Irish People* newspaper was regarded as: 'Essentially Sinn Féin's *An Phoblacht* with any left wing comment laundered out so not to alarm more conservative Irish-Americans'.[167]

Statements from the PAC and RCG were increasingly uncompromising with respect to other groupings with whom they cooperated from time to time on the Irish question. The extremity of Long Kesh and 'similar conditions' in Albany increased their opposition to the perceived 'bourgeois' equivocation and moderation of the International Tribunal organization in particular.[168] The numerically small and avowedly 'independent' PAC was also concerned with ensuring it was not perceived as having a 'special relationship' with the more resourced RCG, despite close collaboration on several demonstrations and newspaper distribution arrangements prior to June 1979.[169] In restating the clear political agenda of the PAC, Kaye commented on 14 November 1978 that: 'The campaign of Irish prisoners for Prisoner of War Status in both England and Ireland is a crucial issue. Prisoners in this country have never had political status, yet they have never accepted criminalisation. The campaign of the prisoners in the H Block and the campaign of the women prisoners in Armagh have brought that central issue to a climax and to a crisis. There can be no standing on the sidelines, no impartiality'.[170]

The prospect of generating political pressure on the ground in England by uniting a spectrum of left wing organizations on the prisons theme ran into more serious difficulties in December 1978. Bomb attacks on commercial premises in Liverpool, Bristol, Coventry, Southampton and London on 17 and 18 December injured several civilians and fuelled a backlash against IRA tactics by groups which had hitherto offered conditional support. The blasts followed a lull in IRA actions and there had been no sustained series of major incidents since January/ February 1976.[171] Criticism from *Socialist Worker* and pro-People's Democracy *Socialist Challenge* was not unexpected, but the contention by the Worker's Revolutionary Party that the bombings were counterproductive struck a raw nerve. WRP organ *The Newsline* called on 19 December 1978 for 'IRA militants to immediately and unconditionally reject these terror tactics and those who advocate them'. This not only distanced the formerly staunch WRP from the IRA but encouraged activists to breach the constitution of Óglaigh na hÉireann.[172] Clann na hÉireann, representing the Official Republican Movement in Britain, sensed the discomfort of Sinn Féin in England and criticized the party's efforts, in what they described as 'frantically looking to the growing rag bag of Irish ultra-left organizations without finding the answers they seek'.[173] As with the CPGB, individual CNH members who did not migrate into the IRSP in the late 1970s were far more sympathetic towards those waging the 'armed struggle'.

The stance of the WRP contrasted with the unambiguous support offered by the PAC which, in a *Republican News* notice advertising the Bloody Sunday commemoration, declared its view that 'only an unremitting struggle against British Imperialism will bring Peace and Justice for the Irish people'.[174] The PAC message was printed directly above one placed by the IRA in Wakefield which expressed gratitude to those who participated in the commemoration and called for 'all organizations to unite on the issue of supporting the war for national liberation in Ireland'.[175] Inserts from the Irelande Libre group in Paris and the French Friends of Ireland could not cancel out the reverses sustained in relation to the English radicals. A subsequent assessment theorized that the PTA had minimized Irish engagement in political campaigns in England and 'left the field clear for the representatives of small groups who had no base in the Irish population'.[176] Certain 'far left' elements, it was claimed, retained an 'anti-Republican prejudice', which complicated the task of building support for the 'troops out now' position advocated by Sinn Féin.[177]

The National Joint Unit at New Scotland Yard, comprising detectives of the Metropolitan and detached provincial police Special Branches, coordinated 'enquiries and applications from police forces in Great Britain concerning people held under prevention of terrorism legislation'.[178]

Liaisons with the Heathrow Airport - based National Ports Office, Home Office, MI5 and individuals within Ireland's Special Branch provided scope for comprehensive surveillance, tracking and interdiction of known suspects. However, Irish communities in Britain believed that the danger of unjust convictions remained acute. This was illustrated on 26 January 1979 when thirteen Irish citizens were seized under the PTA in Braintree, Essex and remanded to Brixton. Those detained were members of the local 'Irish Society' whom the prompt combined efforts of lawyers Mike Fisher and Michael Mansfield ultimately kept out of prison. Fr. Brian Brady and Sr. Sarah Clarke responded with urgency to the situation while providing humanitarian assistance.[179]

Sr. Clarke mobilized many of her overseas contacts to intervene on behalf of those detained. A link provided by Fr. Faul in Paris alerted Rita Mullen of the Irish National Caucus in Washington DC. The INC was headed by Fr. Sean McManus, brother of Fermanagh ex-Republican MP Frank McManus. Such proactivity was not universally appreciated. Brixton's security vetted Catholic Chaplain, Fr. Evans, accused the nun of 'bringing the Catholic Church into disrepute'.[180] It transpired that the arrests had been sparked by the hunt for Gerry Tuite, a leading IRA activist from Cavan held responsible for several major incidents in 1978. He had stayed with one of those arrested in Braintree and was linked to a car hired in the area which was later found laden with explosives. Two small explosions had damaged police property in Braintree on 11 May 1977, but none of those detained faced charges in this respect.[181] Lack of physical evidence and confessions, as well as innocence of illegality, ensured that the Old Bailey jury rejected allegations that the thirteen were engaged in a conspiracy. Numerous persons charged in connection with IRA activities in England spent up to a year in maximum-security prisons prior to being tried and acquitted.[182]

Although less contentious in terms of media reportage in England, a wave of IRA attacks on prison officers in the North of Ireland was a major concern for imprisoned republicans and those by whom they were guarded. Ray McLaughlin was questioned about the IRA strategy in January 1979 in York Crown Court when giving evidence against Hull staff who had assaulted Irish and British prisoners. His argument that those working in the Six Counties were acceptable targets by virtue of being armed 'mercenaries who had chosen to take part in the attempted criminalization of Irish political prisoners' only marginally differentiated them from their colleagues in the Dispersal System.[183] Ultimately, the IRA decided that killing prison staff in England was an inappropriate use of resources and would probably lead to the deaths of imprisoned comrades. The organization was certainly capable of taking such severe action at will. On 3 February 1979 the Belfast Brigade shot Patrick Mackin, a Liverpool-Irish former head of the prison officers training school in Millisle, County Down.[184] There were then 350

IRA prisoners 'on the blanket' in Long Kesh enduring horrendous conditions of confinement, with many being routinely assaulted by staff.[185]

The IRA demonstrated that it had the personnel and ability in England to stage attacks of much greater complexity than close-quarter assassinations in early 1979. On the night of 17–18 January 1979, a bomb detonated at the Texas Oil terminal at Canvey Island, Essex, ruptured a tank containing 750,000 gallons of highly inflammable aviation fuel. Another bomb blasted a gasholder close to the Blackwall Tunnel, Greenwich, sending 300-foot flames into the sky. Secondary fires and explosions in the complex caused further damage; massive destruction was probably only averted at Canvey Island by the failure of the blasts to ignite the large quantity of aviation fuel which had flooded into a safety moat. Another bomb was found partly concealed on the M6 in Leicestershire, evidence of a considerable and diverse IRA offensive reach. A hoax warning, delivered with formal IRA credentials, threatened the Kennington Oval gasholder.[186] Paul Holmes was among the IRA prison population who had persistently advocated such tactics: 'They were an imperial power, and the only way that you could ever begin to rock them was to take the war to them'.[187]

The surge of attacks was featured on the front page of the launch copy of *An Phoblacht/ Republican News*, a weekly Sinn Féin newspaper which had just amalgamated the two main publications of the Provisionals.[188] Clann na hÉireann in Britain condemned the bombings and claimed: 'The strategic placing … show that they are quite prepared to wipe out hundreds, and even thousands of British workers at one fell swoop'.[189] This negative analysis, derived from often lethal factional hostility, was belied by the IRA's selection of high value, comparatively remote economic and communications targets, and their demonstrable ability to detonate substantial devices in virtually any location. Warnings had been phoned to the Press Association ahead of attacks, which cost in excess of one million pounds' worth of destruction. However, no casualties were inflicted. The Metropolitan Police, who defused one of the three London carbombs emplaced in December 1978, incurred additional costs by deploying 'hundreds of extra officers' in central London.[190]

Ray McLaughlin attended trial from Wakefield where the atmosphere remained particularly tense after months of direct and indirect clashes with staff. By January 1979 the immediate demands of the IRA group had narrowed to four points: normal visiting conditions, removal of four men from the E-List, access to educational programmes and use of the gym.[191] Agitation took many forms in the early months of the year, including the use of incendiaries. This also occurred in Parkhurst where the IRA were suspected without being directly credited of carrying out a series of destructive attacks. On 1 March a fire was started in the pantry, followed by another more serious blaze ten days later which 'swept through the library'.

Newport firemen responded and contained the conflagration within forty minutes, although its occurrence three hours after lock up suggested the use of timed incendiaries, an IRA hallmark.[192]

Physical fitness emerged as a major preoccupation of republican prisoners, primarily for the inherent aerobic and anaerobic benefits of maintaining health. Training was also used to foster discipline, self-regulated routine and bodily strength, qualities which imprisoned republicans wished to display to their captors. When McLaughlin returned from a month long 'lie down' in Armley in May 1979, his comrades pressed him to take a 'strenuous' one-hour run around the small prison yard with the ultra-fit Belfastman Tony 'Red Flash' Clarke. He recalled that the IRA wanted to establish that 'irrespective of whether they excluded us from the gymnasium or sent us on coolers, we intended to stay in top shape'.[193] Clarke was regarded as one of the best long - distance runners in the English prisons, while McLaughlin and Jimmy Ashe were also very athletic. Other Wakefield prisoners, not least Vince Donnelly and Paul Norney, were physically powerful and utilized their prowess when necessary.[194]

Brian Keenan

The IRA suffered a blow on 20 March 1979 when a car carrying GHQ member Brian Keenan was intercepted by the RUC near Banbridge, County Down, on the Dublin to Belfast road. Although reported in terms of a chance occurrence, it was actually a planned operation under the remit of 'Operation Hawk', a major RUC Special Branch drive against the upper tier of the IRA.[195] It was claimed that seventy members of the Special Branch and Special Patrol Group were involved, not counting British Intelligence resources.[196] Martin McGuinness was travelling south in the car behind Keenan and was detained for several days along with two companions. It has been claimed that Keenan had come into focus due to the heavy surveillance on McGuinness, and that the decision to spring the trap in Down arose from the availability of a warrant under the Explosives Substances Act, which had been secretly processed by the police in England.[197] Writers Liam Clarke and Kathryn Johnston noted the improbable theory that Keenan had been set up for arrest by associates and that his detention paved the way for Martin McGuinness and Gerry Adams to overcome internal opposition to the winding down of the Armed Struggle.[198]

Keenan had a markedly different interpretation of what occurred outside Banbridge and believed that he had survived an assassination attempt: 'They tried to write me off with a truck'. He averred that supporting police vehicles only deployed to pull his car over when an emergency defensive driving manoeuvre avoided a potentially deadly collision.[199] It was subsequently reported that Keenan's fingerprints had been found in a London safe house used by Brendan Dowd's ASU in 1974–5 and he was regarded as the director of the intense IRA offensive then underway in England. Following fruitless questioning in Castlereagh Interrogation Centre by the notorious Harry Taylor of the RUC Special Branch, Keenan was flown in a military helicopter to London on 23 March.[200] The flight to a Battersea landing pad was not without incident, and Keenan was amused when two RAF fighter jets buzzed the helicopter as it crossed the Irish Sea at low altitude.[201] Interrogation in Paddington Green, during which he remained silent, took an unusual turn when he was questioned about links to Russian Special Forces, Libya and the Algerian air force. This proved to be a line of argument advanced by the prosecution at trial to present him as a highly dangerous man connected to an 'axis of terror'. Brian Rose Smith and Michael Mansfield acted for his defense.[202] Bow Street Magistrates Court remanded him in custody on 26 March to answer charges of 'conspiracy to cause explosions' in England, and he was sent to Brixton to await trial in June 1980.[203] Keenan was posthumously described as being 'the principal organizer of the bombing campaign that rocked London in the mid-1970s'.[204]

Other factors connecting Keenan to the 1970s' England campaign were explicitly commented on following his death in May 2008. In 2010, retired RUC Detective Superintendent Alan Simpson elaborated on his previously more guarded published references to Keenan by naming him in relation to the December 1973 abduction of prominent West-German industrialist and consul Thomas Niedermayer from his Belfast residence. Niedermayer was seized by the IRA to increase pressure on the British Government to repatriate the 'Belfast Ten' group, several of whom were on hunger strike in the Dispersal System following sentencing for the March 1973 car-bomb attacks in London. In an unexpected and drastic turn of events, the unfortunate German perished from natural causes when in IRA captivity and was secretly buried.[205] Simpson's RUC and British Intelligence sources underpinned an additional claim that Keenan had in 1973 travelled to 'Libya, Lebanon, Syria and East Germany in a quest for arms. He spoke with Colonel Gaddafi'.[206] Similar points were made at his London trial seven years later, although nothing of substance was then established, and the well-travelled Keenan regarded the more fanciful assertions as 'crazy stuff'.[207] Former IRA Chief of Staff Eamon Doherty and Denis McInerney had carried out many of the international activities solely attributed to Brian Keenan.

Rise of the Conservative Party

The IRA had spent much of the 1970s waging a violent campaign against unstable Labour governments. Few within the leadership of the Labour Party dared to grapple with the Irish crisis and Tony Benn, one of the most outspoken figureheads, created some disquiet in early 1979 when he privately raised the prospect of a 'fundamental review' of British strategy in a letter to the Prime Minister. Callaghan's advisors suggested that a public debate of a 'Troops Out option' was highly dangerous in an election year and might invite an escalation of IRA attacks in England.[208] The discussion demonstrated the continuing concern in British government circles regarding local aspects of the conflict in Ireland. In this instance, the lexicon of debate was that formulated by British-based allies of Irish republicans.

James Callaghan's government fell on a vote of no confidence on 28 March 1979, heralding a General Election which Labour had little chance of winning. While the tide of support was inexorably running out for the Labour administration, the trigger for its dramatic fall was centred on the maltreatment of Irish prisoners. The appearance of the *Bennett Report* in March 1979 discomforted the generally amenable Gerry Fitt MP who cited its findings on the systematic brutalization of suspected republicans by the RUC as the reason for his abstaining during the crucial vote.[209] Frank Maguire also abstained on 28 March, as he had long threatened, in order to protest the manner in which IRA prisoners were being treated by the British authorities in England and Ireland.[210] The net result was that the Labour Government collapsed in 1979 on its handing of Irish political prisoners less than two years after an Irish Labour/ Fine Gael Coalition had been rejected by the Twenty-Six County electorate due to similar grounds.[211] Although only one of several factors in play, the formerly automatic pro-Labour votes of the Irish MPs for all intents and purposes equated to the balance of power.[212] Election events organised by the British Labour Party were disrupted across England by the RCG, for which they were lambasted by former TD Conor Cruise O'Brien in *The Observer*. In Croydon, Seamus O Mathuna received a cold reception from Merlyn Rees upon raising the subject of the H-Block crisis.[213]

The political landscape changed on 4 May 1979 with the resounding victory of the Conservative Party, which brought Margaret Thatcher to power as Prime Minister. The prospects of republicans making significant political headway with the most right wing British government in decades appeared remote. Thatcher's ascent had shortly followed a major personal setback when Irish socialist republicans blew up Airey Neave on 30 March 1979. Neave was not only her closest mentor during her ousting of previous party leader Edward Heath, but was intended to become Secretary for State for Northern Ireland. The sense of outrage within the establishment was sharpened by the fact that Neave had been killed by the INLA within the precincts of the House of Commons. Soviet - manufactured plastic explosives were detonated by a sophisticated mercury tilt switch which activated as Neave's car ascended the exit ramp of Westminster's underground carpark.[214] The INLA had originally targeted the incumbent Northern Secretary Roy Mason in his Yorkshire Labour constituency but switched their focus to his equally virulent Conservative counterpart during the election the which Tories appeared poised to win.[215] The organization had been in existence under various flags of convenience from 8 December 1974, but was only proscribed in Britain on 3 July 1979 under Section 1 (3) of the PTA (Temporary Provisions) Act 1976.[216] Neave was one of the most vocal Conservatives to publicly oppose British military withdrawal from Ireland and evidently believed that the IRA could be defeated.[217] Thatcher recalled his sudden loss in 1983, having survived an IRA attempt on her own life when in Downing Street: 'For some reason the death of a friend or family member by violence leaves an even deeper scar'.[218] In hindsight, moderate Tory John Wells told Thatcherite MP Alan Clark that 'the historic consequences of Airey's assassination could never be fully assessed' and had resulted in 'errors of judgment' in appointments to her first Cabinet in 1979.[219]

The killing shocked outgoing Prime Minister Jim Callaghan, who, on 2 April 1979 addressed his National Executive Council to warn that arising from 'the political assassinations that have taken place, particularly Airey Neave's, there is a risk to NEC members'. Yet Mason, openly despised by dangerous enemies in Ireland, had been spared by the INLA and no Labour Party politician was ever shot or bombed to death by the IRA. Callaghan's spiel digressed into the 'issue of Northern Ireland and terrorism', resulting in an extraordinary late office - declaration that opened blue water between the stated views of a man facing enforced retirement and the numerous courageous initiatives taken by his predecessor Harold Wilson: 'We should have as little difference as possible between ourselves and the Tories. I think there should be talks with both parties to discuss'. Tony Benn MP, a genial and perceptive diarist, was perturbed by this improbable conflation of incident and arguably pusillanimous bipartisanship on a matter of principle and practicality.[220]

Extensive use was made of the PTA to question, often harshly in respect to Paddington Green, IRSP members living in England. Deirdre O'Shea, a left wing political activist with IRSP connections, lost several teeth when assaulted in the London police base. In December 1984 she was deeply engaged in efforts to protect her veteran activist mother, Dr. Maire 'Betty' O'Shea, from prosecution in an INLA - linked operation in England.[221] Nick Mullen, student radical and a significant figure in IRA logistics in England in the late 1980s, was also detained for two days in Paddington Green in 1979 arising from the Neave assassination. Mullen was then involved with the IRSP, in which he encountered leading socialist republican personalities Naomi Brennan and Gerry Roche.[222] Personal connections heightened the sense of grievance for IRA prisoners in England. Billy Armstrong knew and respected the IRSP/ INLA leader Ronnie Bunting, who was killed by a pro-British death squad on 15 October 1980.[223] Bunting was one of a number of prominent IRSP and H-Block campaigners shot in 1979–1981, not least Noel Lyttle, Miriam Daly, John Turnly and Bernadette McAliskey. The involvement of British military personnel in collusion with embedded Loyalist auxiliaries was widely suspected, particularly when the integral involvement of UDA commander John McMichael was revealed.[224] Another leading UDA member and British agent, Robert McConnell, claimed SAS assistance in the assassination of Turnly.[225]

Suspicions of such illicit co-operation were raised by Billy Armstrong and others in England regarding the fatal shooting of National H-Block Committee member and QUB lecturer Miriam Daly on 26 June 1980.[226] Daly had cogently presented both academic and personal analyses of the Irish crisis in Newfoundland, Massachusetts and elsewhere to an extent that her advocacy induced concern from well wishers. If locating her home address did not present a major intelligence - gathering challenge for resourced opponents, the selection of a time when she could be accessed, interrogated and fatally shot without incurring reaction from locally positioned official combatants paid to spy on such prominent IRSP personalities indicated, at best, that uncommon luck had coincided with gross incompetence. The unusually professional *modus operandi* of Loyalists in such attacks struck imprisoned IRA men as demonstrative of direct British assistance. Co-operation between Loyalists and members of the British Army, UDR and RUC was evident in numerous other instances during the course of the Troubles.[227] When considering frequently random killings of Ulster Nationalists, Armstrong noted in March 1980: 'I think the B[ritish] A[rmy] and RUC have an agreement with the Loyalists to stay out of a certain area for a certain period of time'.[228] Self-confessed counter-insurgent, Albert 'Ginger' Baker, confirmed the reality of this scenario to several IRA prisoners whom he encountered in jail in England in the 1980s.[229]

The resurgent Conservative administration, acclaimed by Unionist MPs, was not diverted from its rigid Irish policy following the death of Neave. In July 1980 Thatcher described as 'disgraceful' a proposal of the Labour Party's NEC to investigate allegations of maltreatment in Six County prisons. Although criticized by ex-Prime Minister James Callaghan on the grounds that an enquiry could be misinterpreted as Labour acceptance of republican claims, Kevin McNamara, MP for Kingston upon Hull, Central, and John Maynard, MP for Sheffield, Brightside, urged support. The issue was raised in the context of an imminent Commons debate on a White Paper on devolving power in the North of Ireland. Within months the studied failure in London to address the crisis in Long Kesh, Armagh and Crumlin Road prisons had dire consequences for Anglo-Irish history.[230]

Confronting the reinvigorated IRA inside Britain's prisons and cities fell to William Whitelaw who, against expectations, was appointed by the Conservatives as Home Secretary on 15 May 1979.[231] Given his background as Secretary of State for Northern Ireland in the most violent years of the

Troubles, 1972–73, Whitelaw was well versed for a politician on the nature of the IRA threat in its totality. In July 1972 he had met much of the republican leadership in London alongside Martin McGuinness and Gerry Adams who, by 1979, were both influential in such circles.[232] Humphrey Atkins assumed the challenging post of heading the NIO at a time when the implications of the IRA's 'Long War' strategy for the 'Ulsterisation' policy were becoming apparent in both Britain and Ireland.[233] With over 350 republican prisoners on protest in Long Kesh in the spring of 1979, the priority of Sinn Féin's 'Smash H-Block' campaign in Ireland was clearly determined. In an inversion of standard perspective, the party held out the example of England as a warning of how the situation might unfold in the Six Counties: 'Remember the lingering deaths in English dungeons of Frank Stagg, Michael Gaughan, Noel Jenkinson and Sean O'Connell? Do not let the British kill any of the heroic "blanket men"'.[234]

Thatcher's administration attempted to establish common economic and political ground with the conservative Republican presidency of Ronald Reagan in the United States. Yet, ironically, the administration was eventually pressurised by the Irish American into addressing the situation in the Six Counties. The Irish question perennially troubled progressive forces across the Atlantic. Several key legal test cases taken in the USA during Thatcher's Downing Street years were impacted by the IRA campaign in England. In August 1978, Pete 'The Para' McMullen, an ex-British Army paratrooper from Derry who was wanted in England in connection with the IRA incendiary bombing of Claro Barracks, Ripon, Yorkshire on 26 March 1974, defeated efforts to extradite him to Britain from San Francisco, California. He had entered the country on a false passport in April 1978 following a stint in Portloaise for IRA membership. His lawyers asserted that there was a precedent for rejecting extradition on the grounds that his offence was political in character. The Californian court concurred, noting Britain's derogation from international conventions arising from the situation in Ireland.[235] Any such case in North America, however, distracted attention from the main 'secondary' zone of IRA related prison battles: England. By the early 1980s, a wide range of international jurisdictional concerns competed for the finite resources of the non-violent annexes of the Republican Movement worldwide.[236]

Among the details supplied to defence lawyers in the McMullen case was material collated by Paul O'Dwyer highlighting the 'brutal assault' on Fr. Pat Fell and hunger strike deaths of Michael Gaughan and Frank Stagg in English prisons in 1974–76.[237] When the definitive ruling on McMullen was given by the District Court of San Francisco on 9 May 1979, it was reported that the case was 'the first time that evidence has been admitted in an American Court concerning the jail conditions and the brutal treatment inflicted on the eighty-odd Irish prisoners in British jails'. O'Dwyer persuasively argued that extradition to Great Britain would be 'in contravention of the "cruel and inhuman" provisions of the United States Constitution'.[238] American focus on England competed with news from the much more violent Six Counties, yet was stimulated by such events as the annual National Graves Association Field Day at Gaelic Park in the Bronx, New York. Manager J.K. O'Donnell had hosted fundraisers for supporters of IRA prisoners in Ireland and England since the early 1950s in which the Irish Freedom Committee, Irish Republican Aid Committee, Irish Northern Aid and other bodies had generated substantial income. The 24 June 1979 gathering in the south Bronx was dedicated to fundraising for a memorial to the 'trinity of Mayo martyrs – Sean McNeela, Michael Gaughan and Frank Stagg, who died on hunger strike in Irish and English jails to secure political treatment and a measure of human dignity'.[239] Their deaths were annually observed, due in no small part to the common Mayo origins of leading New York lawyers Paul O'Dwyer and Frank Durkan, as well as their occasional client, IRA gunrunner George Harrison.[240] Tom Regan of the Clan na Gael descended Terence MacSwiney Club in Jenkintown, Philadelphia, was also a veteran of the War of Independence-era Mayo IRA.[241] In Cleveland, Ohio, another major Mayo emigrant destination, left wing INA leader Jack Kilroy hailed from a family which numbered 1940s IRA hunger striker Sean McNeela.[242]

Parkhurst, 22–24 March 1979

The Parkhurst protest began on the evening of 22 March 1979 when Sean Kinsella, Martin Coughlan, Gerry Small and Eddie Byrne got onto the roof of D Wing along with one non-political prisoner. Expert roof saboteur Roy Walsh, a tiler by trade, could not participate by virtue of being closely confined in the Punishment Block, although the attack by breaking through a skylight had been carefully planned. The men used a purpose-built ladder to get into position and caused extensive damage by stripping off tiles and hurling them to the ground.[243] Walsh had advised on an efficient methodology of loosening entire rows of tiles which had not been properly nailed in position and drilling holes in those that were well embedded to maximize the cost and effort of replacement.[244] Mick Sheehan had helped construct the ladder in the prison's engineering workshop and reported sick on the morning of the protest in order to be in position to provide those heading for the roof with blankets and food.[245] They acted to raise publicity on the conditions in H-Blocks, as well as the use of long-term solitary confinement against comrades in England.[246] Mainstream news reports covered a secondary purpose of highlighting ongoing frustration at the poor quality of meals supplied in Parkhurst, an issue which had led to periodic bouts of fasting by hundreds of men since December 1978. The IRA contingent in Parkhurst were aware that this aspect of the protest 'went down, very, very well with the other prisoners', some of whom they assisted with private and legal correspondence.[247] The republicans had also mounted seven-day fasts in support of repatriation and political status in February and November 1978.[248]

On 11 March 1979, the Republican Movement cited British Government statistics to claim 360 adherents were 'on the blanket' in Long Kesh while thirty-eight female members participated in Armagh Jail. Six prisoners in England were explicitly identified: Tony Cunningham, Liam Baker, Busty Cunningham and Tipp Guilfoyle in Albany, Mick Murray in Wormwood Scrubs and Punter Bennett in Strangeways, Manchester.[249] Tony Cunningham had lost close to 50 per cent of his bodyweight since being imprisoned for IRA activities in the Greater London area.[250] If the Parkhurst solidarity stunt was not as well noted as the 'token protest' of remand prisoners in Crumlin Road Prison, the incident, nonetheless, received press coverage.[251] In a gesture not calculated to assuage the concerns of the Home Office, Sr. Sarah Clarke, banned from entering the Dispersal System, was observed outside the complex 'waving up' at the IRA men.[252]

In keeping with past rooftop occupations, the Parkhurst IRA men unfurled banners referencing the major issues they wished to publicize. Two adjacent wings were immediately evacuated, giving lie to an unconvincing staff statement which claimed that the general body of the prisoners were unsympathetic.[253] In fact, approximately 100 prisoners refused meals in order to peaceably convey their support.[254] Walsh was adept at traversing and deconstructing slated rooftops. His advice and rudimentary training in sabotage techniques increased the efficacy of IRA roof invasions. The protesters ceased hurling slates to the ground at midnight but resumed their systematic destruction at 8.00 a.m. on 23 March. Power hoses were used in an ineffectual bid to dislodge or inhibit the men. When the group believed they had taken the action as far as practicable they surrendered on 24 March.[255] A stark official digest published in July 1980 purposefully concealed the agency of the IRA, if not the seriousness of the episode: 'One major demonstration at Parkhurst prison lasted three days and involved five prisoners who caused £50,000 worth of damage and rendered two wings of the prison unfit for habitation'.[256] The intact C Wing, hitherto used for Dr. Cooper's controversial experimental programme for prisoners with psychiatric issues, had to be pressed into service to house the maximum-security population. Improved sanitary facilities, not least showers, were acquired in consequence by those relocated from the antiquated and partially destroyed wings. Former occupants of C Wing selected for retention in Parkhurst were transferred into the Hospital Wing where no structured research could be undertaken. Ronnie McCartney, shifted from the Strong Box of Hull Prison, had threatened to resist incarceration in C Wing until its new role was explained.[257]

This level of impact, and its Irish political origination, probably explained why the punishments meted out to the five men in 1979 were unusual in character. Although legally entitled to impose terms of cellular or 'solitary' confinement, the Board of Visitors elected to instead nominate periods of 'loss of privileges' and 'non-associative labour'. This was tantamount to solitary confinement given that the 120 days spent in the Punishment Block did not technically constitute the traditional sanction. It was assumed by republicans that this represented a new degree of guile in the administration of punishment. Tellingly, the only non-political prisoner involved received just twenty-eight days, whereas the IRA men each lost 112 days' remission.[258] Boards retained much discretion and the Home Office claimed to have 'urged' rather than instructed compliance with revised regulations in 1977.[259] Sheehan's role was not exposed but he was quickly shifted to Wormwood Scrubs to spend seven and a half months in solitary.[260]

Reception staff at Parkhurst exacted a minor measure of revenge on Walsh on 3 April 1979 by seizing the vast majority of his record collection during his transfer into Wormwood Scrubs. He repaid their malign attention by initiating a further set of official correspondence with the Home Office which had to be processed by the Under Secretary of State. Using a 'Petition Form' that made no reference to the extraordinary context in which his move occurred, Walsh noted: 'I was transferred on Home Office instruction ... On passing through Reception at Parkhurst, the Reception Officer removed from my possession 34 LP (long-playing) records' on the technical grounds that only nine had been listed on his property sheet and they could, therefore, be confiscated.[261] The response of 11 May 1979 confirmed that the Secretary of State was 'not prepared' to return his albums.[262] Walsh learned on 29 May 1979 that while solicitors Woodford & Ackroyd of Southampton were unable to pursue his mooted case with the European Court, Alastair Logan of George E Baker & Co, Guildford, had consented to add his complaint to those already in preparation at his office.[263]

Hull convictions

The 1976 Hull riot created English legal history in York Crown Court on 15 January 1979 when Justice Boreham conceded that police background checks could be conducted to ensure that no juror had a criminal record. Sixty potential jurors had their names submitted to Central Criminal Records delaying the start to proceedings for over two hours.[264] Prosecutor Peter Taylor QC claimed that the thirteen defendants had assaulted prisoners in a 'deliberate exercise in retribution'.[265] Evidence on 17 January from one former Hull staff member then working in Wakefield claimed that the IRA had been 'in the forefront of the riot' and 'still had channels of communication from prison to the outside world ... IRA prisoners regarded themselves as prisoners of war'.[266] This apparent bid to highlight the extenuating circumstances in play revealed something of the perceived role of the state employees, eight of whom were found guilty on 4 April 1979 of 'conspiracy to assault' prisoners after the riot. All received token suspended sentences from Judge Boreham. Four co-defendants and Assistant Governor Douglas McCombe were acquitted in rulings which lessened the impression that the violence of prison staff at Hull had been co-ordinated from the top. Brian Cooke, a Principal Officer and chair of Hull branch of the POA, expressed disappointment at the outcome and predicted that the 'attitude' of his members towards prisoners 'would harden'.[267] Dick Pooley of PROP, by contrast, welcomed the unusual convictions which he believed to be historic in their implications.[268] The PAC were less enthusiastic and commented that a small number of those responsible for beating prisoners had received suspended sentences of 'derisory' proportions. If, as the PROP enquiry in London alleged, Irish and black prisoners had suffered disproportionate injury, the precedent of moderate punishment established in York did not auger well.[269] The *Observer* queried in relation to those convicted: 'Can the Prison Department claim to have any disciplinary standards at all if the men remain prison officers?'[270]

Gerry Cunningham, who had for tactical reasons set aside IRA reticence regarding court environs to give evidence at the trial, felt vindicated despite the partial nature of the legal victory. He had contacted his solicitor, Alastair Logan, and said 'Right, ok, take the case to court. These people were effectively criminals at large at the time they made their statements against me and I want my thirteen months [loss of] remission back'. Eventually, in the face of obstruction from the Board of Visitors, Cunningham was apprised that he was entitled to make periodic requests for the restoration of remission. Whereas the Tyrone man was willing to demand the lost time, he refused to seek it by the demeaning avenue of repeated BOV applications. This principled and politically informed stance ensured that Cunningham spent thirteen months longer in jail than was necessary.[271] He was ultimately and politely urged to exit Long Lartin in November 1988, a jail where he gained considerable influence among the prisoner population.[272]

The verdicts in York followed closely on the re-opening of Hull after a long period of renovation necessitated by the riot. Governor Parr was reinstated in what was interpreted by prisoners as a provocative move on the part of the Home Office. This view gained credence when the PAC ascertained, on the basis of reports from IRA prisoners transferred into Hull, that the stringent policies which had helped spark the riot were still extant. In the context of the minimal chastisement of men found guilty of assaulting inmates, republicans anticipated further grievances. Andy Mulryan, Ronnie McCartney and James 'Punter' Bennett were in Hull by May 1979, along with the innocent Dick McIlkenny of the Birmingham Six.[273] A minor fracas in C Wing over recreational facilities had already occurred without detriment to the administrators. McCartney followed a stay in the Punishment Block with a twenty-eight day 'lie down' in Armley and it was reported that the slightest infringement in Hull resulted in fourteen days' solitary confinement. With the doubling of staff on the wings from two to four, the risk of detection was raised in what remained a cloistered community.[274] When, in July 1979, Joan Maynard MP sought statistical information on breaches of *Prison Rules* at Hull in 1978, Whitelaw responded with an unconvincing claim that such data was 'not readily available'.[275] Minute details regarding Category A prisoners were, in fact, meticulously logged by dedicated staff members and available to members of the Home Office 'Category A Committee'.

Martin Brady, O/C of the IRA prisoners in Hull at the time of the riot, was returned to A Wing of the Yorkshire prison. His first impression was that the wing was being used as a 'punishment' area for 'anyone that was unruly' and that the prison as a whole was 'worse' than before.[276] Paul Hill was also transferred back to Hull and was in Brady's company when a very serious assault occurred in the TV room. An Australian prisoner reputed to have killed another inmate in Wakefield was badly burned when a man he had angered threw a pot of boiling water mixed with sugar over his body. The rudimentary facilities of the infirmary proved insufficient to treat the wounds inflicted and the Australian was quickly taken by ambulance to an outside hospital. Hill had noticed the attacker preparing the infusion in the kitchen but heeded Brady's warning to 'stay away from this'.[277]

Jackie Kaye addressed a Conference on European Political Prisoners hosted by Sinn Féin in Liberty Hall, Dublin, on 21–23 April 1979. Attention was drawn to the PTA, which had already resulted in the deportation of around 200 Irish people from Britain and 4,000 temporarily detained.[278] Pat McCarthy of the National Council for Civil Liberties in Britain appeared in a private capacity and explained how the PTA was being used to process exclusion orders against defence witnesses in political trials and increasingly targeted Britons who had protested Westminster's policy in Ireland. Des Warren, a communist trade unionist whose activism had resulted in prosecution for illegal picketing, addressed the theme. Warren was one of the 'Shrewsbury Three' jailed in 1973 and was widely regarded in consequence as a former political prisoner.[279] Fellow 'Shrewsbury Three' member, trade unionist turned actor Ricky Tomlinson, was less tolerant of mixing with IRA Volunteers in prison.[280]

Maintaining a physical presence in locations where IRA prisoners were held was an ongoing problem. Despite the best efforts of the small Tyneside Irish Solidarity Campaign, it required the input from Birmingham Sinn Féin's Pearse/ McDaid cumann to bring the numbers protesting outside Durham on 27 May up to a modest fifty. The Midlands delegation, aided by members of the city's UTOM group, traversed 430 miles to attend. Anne and Eileen Gillespie were in Durham, as was Hugh Doherty. Similar protests took place outside Wormwood Scrubs on 2 June, Wakefield on 24 June and Hull on

29 July 1979.[281] British-based supporters of the Gillespies realised that if spared the constant stress of being 'ghosted', the sisters were far from their parents in Gweedore, Donegal, and the only republicans in the all female H-Wing.[282] Unsympathetic authorities regarded them as having formed part of a Manchester 'sub group' of the major IRA network in Birmingham. It was noted that their brother, former resident of Manchester, was 'wanted in the UK' in relation to political offences but was living in the Twenty-Six Counties in 1978.[283] The FCO was, nonetheless, sensitive to public claims that the Irishwomen were either innocent or worthy objects of interest by Irish politicians. On 26 May 1978 HAJ Staples of the FCO reported that he had taken Donegal Fine Gael TD Paddy Harte 'mildly to task for having referred to the Gillespie case by name at last week's Ard Fheis'. According to Staples: 'He took this quietly and almost looked abash. He implied that he had let the name slip out unintentionally, and he had subsequently ensured that it did not appear in the written record'.[284]

The sisters improvised day-to-day strategies to preserve their personal security, composure, dignity and identity. To avoid seeking favour from a position of permanent disadvantage, both stopped smoking and never requested mail that they had reason to believe was arriving into Durham. Both took pains to dress and groom themselves as well as circumstances permitted. They guarded each other during alternate bathing sessions and countered the affront of strip-searching by nonchalantly discarding clothing before being ordered to disrobe. They only spoke Irish during exercise time on the yard and insisted on getting outside for the allotted time in virtually all weather conditions. Such stratagems irritated and confused staff, who at times encouraged disturbed prisoners to create trouble with the duo as a means of being shifted off a secure wing where the Irishwomen were required to remain. Friendly and fair-minded staff were either reprimanded or reassigned. Other factors were totally beyond the control of the Gillespies, not least disruptive cell shifts every month for eight years.[285]

NOTES

1. *Irish Times*, 7 October 1978.
2. Coggan and Walker, *Deaths in British prisons*, p. 209.
3. Martin Brady, 12 April 2008.
4. Ronnie McCartney, 12 April 2008.
5. *Times*, 29 July 1978. See 'Apologies to prison medical service doctors' in *British Medical Journal*, 9 August 1980, p. 463.
6. *Prison Service Journal* cited in *Times*, 20 November 1972. Many held in C Wing spent time in Broadmoor and Rampton. Wakefield, *Thousand days*, pp. 16–17. R Watson Lee, Chairman of the Board of Visitors, HMP Parkhurst, described C Wing as being 'pretty squalid' to Justice May who had visited four days previously. According to Lee: 'There are about 600 men in the prison system who should be in mental hospitals. This does not include the severely disordered psychopaths who are the lot of the Prison Service. We have about thirty prisoners who are mad and many others who are severely disturbed'. R Watson Lee to Justice May, 15 December 1978, NAE, HO 263/ 319.
7. Ronnie McCartney, 12 April 2008.

8. *Times*, 29 July 1978.
9. Bronson, *Bronson 2*, p. 275. Doug Wakefield was sent to the wing in September 1977 when there was an average of twenty inmates. He was convicted of killing a fellow prisoner in September 1978. Wakefield recalled: 'C Wing is ostensibly a psychiatric unit for prisoners who are in need of urgent and qualified help'. Wakefield, *Thousand days*, p. 17. See also Hill, *Stolen years*, p. 210.
10. Cited in *FRFI*, June 1984, p. 12.
11. See *World Medicine*, 9 September 1978 cited in *Republican News*, 13 November 1978.
12. *Irish Times*, 7 October 1978.
13. Hill, *Stolen years*, p. 199.
14. *Irish Times*, 7 October 1978.
15. Cited in *Sunday Times*, 22 October 1978. William Mullen examined allegations that Albany prison was being used for experimentation with drugs due to overcrowding. He cited Dr. McCleery's revelations and found that the high tolerance of prisoners resulted in the administration of doses that rendered the recipients almost catatonic. *Chicago Tribune*, 19 November 1978. The NIO subsequently admitted that Largactil was being used in the H-Blocks, allegedly with permission of the prisoners being dosed. *Irish Democrat*, March 1979. See also Cohen and Taylor, *Prison secrets*, pp. 71–2. For medical evidence of primary and secondary effects of Largactil see BMJ Group and Pharmaceutical Press, *British National Formulary*, March 2011 (London, 2011), p. 219.
16. *Guardian*, 23 October 1978.
17. *Report on the work of the Prison Department, 1983*, p. 58.
18. *Irish Times*, 7 October 1978. See *Chicago Tribune*, 6 October 1978. Prison historian Dick Callan noted that two prisoners were allowed liaise between A and D Wing in a bid to 'stabilise' the situation and that the three who visited Blake found him unharmed. Callan, *Gartree*, pp. 46–9. The Prison Department wrongly claimed in 1979 that the prisoners 'rejected an offer to send two of their number to see' Blake. *Report of the work of the Prison Department, 1978*, p. 23.
19. Martin Brady, 12 April 2008.
20. Ronnie McCartney, 12 April 2008.
21. 'John McCluskey part two: Gartree 1978' in *FRFI*, February 1985, p. 14.
22. Ronnie McCartney, 12 April 2008.
23. 'McCluskey part two: Gartree 1978' in *FRFI*, February 1985, p. 14.
24. *Times*, 7 October 1978.
25. Callan, *Gartree*, pp. 48, 54–5.
26. Eddie O'Neill, 19 July 2007.
27. Ronnie McCartney, 12 April 2008.
28. Hill, *Stolen years*, p. 201.
29. *Times*, 3 November 1978.
30. Ronnie McCartney, 12 April 2008.
31. *Times*, 7 October 1978.
32. See *Home Office Statement on the Background, Circumstances and Action Subsequently Taken relative to the Disturbance in D Wing at HM Prison Wormwood Scrubs on 31st August 1979; Together with the Report of an Inquiry by the Regional Director of South East Region of the Prison Department* (London, 1982), Appendix 8. A Circular Instruction issued on 29 May 1979 cited Prison Rule 44 and Standing Order 3E to advise on tactical aspects of MUFTI utilization. Ibid., p. 62. The units comprised a 'Section' of five men under the command of a Senior Officer. The use of more than one 'Section' entailed the formation of a 'Team' under the command of a Principal Officer. Ibid. The decision to disband MUFTI units was taken in November 1988. *Times*, 22 November 1988.
33. *IRIS*, 10 November 1979. See also *Guardian*, 2 November 1979.
34. *Report of the work of the Prison Department, 1978*, p. 24.
35. 'McCluskey part two: Gartree 1978' in *FRFI*, February 1985, p. 14.
36. 'McCluskey part two: Gartree 1978' in *FRFI*, February 1985, p. 14.
37. See *Irish Times*, 7 October 1978.
38. Hill, *Stolen years*, p. 201.
39. 'McCluskey part two: Gartree 1978' in *FRFI*, February 1985, p. 14.
40. McLaughlin, *Inside an English jail*, p. 47.
41. See Coggan and Walker, *Deaths in British prisons*, p. 204 and *Times*, 24 August 1978.
42. McLaughlin, *Inside an English jail*, p. 46.
43. *HC Deb 14 November 1978 vol 958 c136W*.
44. *Sunday Times*, 22 October 1978.
45. *HC Deb 22 November 1978 vol 958 c597W*.
46. *Guardian*, 24 May 1979.
47. *Times*, 2 November 1978.

48. Peter Evans, 'Why prison reform is long overdue' in *Times*, 3 November 1978. See also *Times*, 24 August 1978.
49. *Times*, 7 October 1978.
50. *Times*, 21 October 1978.
51. *Economist*, 7 October 1978.
52. *Guardian*, 15 November 1978.
53. *Irish political prisoners*, p. 94. Republicans believed that IRA men Brendan Dowd, Eddie Byrne and Paul Holmes had been drugged against their wishes on various occasions. Byrne claimed that he had been given Paraldehyde after the Albany 'riot' which rendered him unconscious for three days and left him disorientated for a further ten. See *The Irish Prisoner*, No. 6, September/ October 1979 and McLaughlin, *Inside an English jail*, p. 25. Byrne further claimed he was in 1977 'administered an unknown drug which resulted in experiencing hallucinations and feelings of suffocation. Since then I have refused to accept drugs which I fail to identify'. Eddie Byrne to the Editor, 25 July 1982, *Irish People*, 25 September 1982.
54. *Times*, 6 October 1978. Around 500 prisoners in Dartmoor, which then contained no IRA members, were locked down by staff on 6 October who feared a possible 'flashpoint' situation. *Times*, 7 October 1978.
55. *Report of the work of the Prison Department, 1978*, p. 23.
56. Martin Brady, 12 April 2008.
57. *Republican News*, 10 March 1979.
58. *AP/RN*, 29 July 1982.
59. *Republican News*, 25 November 1978. Brady found that his mail was subject to an extremely high level of censorship. Monthly 'closed' visits permitted to F Wing inmates were also conducted with an exceptionally intrusive staff presence. He felt obliged to refuse visits under the circumstances. Ibid., 21 January 1979. See also *IRIS*, 15 November 1978. Hill caught a glimpse of Brady taking exercise on his own and was buoyed to him walking 'with a cocky Belfast dander'. Hill, *Stolen years*, p. 203.
60. Hill, *Stolen years*, p. 202.
61. *Republican News*, 25 November 1978. McCluskey was held in a damp segregation cell prone to cockroach infestation for twenty-three hours a day. See Ibid., 24 March and 5 May 1979.
62. *IRIS*, 12 January 1979.
63. *Irish political prisoners*, pp. 73–4.
64. *Republican News*, 10 March 1979.
65. Ronnie McCartney, 12 April 2008.
66. In June 1978 Brixton contained 412 cells shared by two men and 315 cells shared by three. The total population was 1,032. *HC Deb 27 July 1978 vol 954 cc840–1W*. The Certified Normal Accommodation of Brixton was enumerated as 649 in October 1975, at which time it held 968 inmates. *HC Deb 14 October 1975 vol 897 cc668–73W*. In 1980 the average prisoner spent less than twenty-three days in Brixton ahead of trial, although certain prisoners, including all suspected IRA personnel, spent much longer. *Session 1980–8 ... 19 January 1981, HM Prison Brixton*, p. 77.
67. *Times*, 20 October 1978. See also *Times*, 22 August and 30 October 1978.
68. *Times*, 1 November 1978.
69. *Times*, 2 November 1978.
70. *Newsline*, 25 May 1983.
71. Cited in *Times*, 1 November 1978.
72. Cited in *Times*, 1 November 1978.
73. *Newsline*, 25 May 1983.
74. See Frank Norman to the Editor, *Times*, 25 October 1978 and PROP, *Prison Briefing*, No. 3, 1982.
75. PROP, *Prison Briefing*, No. 2, [London] 1982.
76. *Guardian*, 9 October 1978.
77. *Guardian*, 9 October 1978.
78. *Guardian*, 9 October 1978. PROP alleged Gartree staff had undertaken courses in the Wakefield Prison Officers Training School with a view to bringing their new unit on line. The Home Office dismissed this claim and Lord Harris criticized the airing of 'wild allegations' concerning the prison. Ibid. Harris visited the wrecked complex with John Farr MP. Construction of Gartree's £395,000 F Wing began in January 1976 during the tenure of Governor George Lakes and it operated as a Segregation Unit for seventeen years. Dick Callan, *Gartree, The story of a prison* (Leyhill, 2005), pp. 40–1, 48–9.
79. Quoted in *Guardian*, 9 October 1978. A disproportionate number of Prison Service staff hailed from Yorkshire and Scotland. It was a matter of official record that 'not many people born in London' worked in Wormwood Scrubs, Brixton or Wandsworth. See *Session 1980–8 ... 19 January 1981, HM Prison Brixton*, p. 81.

80. *Times*, 1 February 1980.
81. *Daily Telegraph*, 10 May 1980. See also *Guardian*, 25 November 1981.
82. *Times*, 3 November 1978.
83. *Times*, 3 November 1978. See also *Guardian*, 25 March 1978. Brixton, in 1980, had a notably high level of overtime due to the additional role of its staff in performing transport and security for court appearances. Around 80 per cent of persons rostered for free weekends were called in for duty until an industrial dispute led to more 'normal levels'. *Session 1980–8 … 19 January 1981, HM Prison Brixton*, p. 78.
84. Jackie Kaye to the Editor in *Irish Post*, 14 October 1975.
85. *Times*, 3 November 1978.
86. *Guardian*, 8 January 1980.
87. *Guardian*, 8 January 1980.
88. *Guardian*, 12 January 1980.
89. McLaughlin, *Inside an English jail*, p. 80.
90. 'John McCluskey speaks' in *FRFI*, March 1985, p. 14.
91. *Times*, 4 October 1975 and 1 July 1976 and *Camden New Journal*, 3 November 2011. Jenny Bourne, editor of *Race and Class*, knew Dick from his time working as a volunteer with the Institute of Race Relations, which published the journal. Nigerian Franklin 'Frank' Davies, who had a prior conviction for armed robbery, had attempted to join liberation movements in Zimbabwe (then Rhodesia) and Mozambique in the 1970s. In 1974 Dick attended the Sixth Pan African Congress in Tanzania. He died in a swimming accident in Africa shortly after being released from Wormwood Scrubs in August 1988. Medical student Anthony 'Bonsu' Monroe, also West Indian, ran a school for black children with educational difficulties. The attempt to rob the weekly takings of the Knightsbridge Italian restaurant went awry when a staff member fled to alert police and the trio initially refused to surrender. Angela Cobbinah, 'The Spaghetti House Siege of 1975' in *Camden New Journal*, 3 November 2011. See also Jenny Bourne, 'Spaghetti House siege: making the rhetoric real', *Race and Class*, October 2011 and Moysey, *Road to Balcombe Street*, pp. 102–4.
92. Interview with Shujaa Moshesh (aka Wesley Dick) in *FRFI*, January 1989, p. 8.
93. Moshesh in *FRFI*, January 1989, p. 8.
94. *Guardian*, 8 January 1980.
95. *Guardian*, 8 January 1980.
96. *Guardian*, 12 January 1980.
97. *Republican News*, 13 November 1978.
98. *Irish Times*, 3 November 1978.
99. Michael Keating TD addressed the Beal na Blath Michael Collins commemoration in Cork in August 1983 at which time he alluded to a new type of constitutional settlement in the presence of fellow ex-Fine Gael/ Labour Coalition leader Paddy Cooney. *Irish World*, 27 August 1983.
100. DG Blunt to BR Gange, 10 October 1978, NAE, FCO 87/ 763.
101. *Irish Voices*, p. 150.
102. *Republican News*, 30 September 1978.
103. *AP/RN*, 29 April 1982.
104. *Republican News*, 30 September 1978. IRA prisoners were allowed to receive a maximum of two adults and one child who were all subjected to being 'brushed down' on security grounds. The republicans, however, were intensively searched before and after all visits. The IRA did not contest press accounts that Baker had been jailed for 'conspiring to blow up the QE2 liner'. McLaughlin, *Inside an English jail*, p. 34. See also *The Irish Prisoner*, No. 5, June 1979, p. 3.
105. *PAC News*, June 1978. Fr. Pat Fell and the innocent Hugh Callaghan did not take part in the protest. The men in the block sent a message to the PAC/ Sinn Féin meeting in London on 5 May 1978. Ibid. O'Neill was subsequently placed in solitary confinement for kissing his mother goodbye. *Sunday Press*, 1 May 1983. See also Sr. Clarke, 'Ray McLaughlin', Clarke Papers (COFLA).
106. *Irish Times*, 2 December 1978.
107. Sr. Clarke, 'Albany Notes', Clarke Papers (COFLA).
108. *IRIS*, 15 November 1978.
109. *Irish News*, 1 November 1978.
110. *IRIS*, 15 November 1978.
111. *IRIS*, 15 November 1978. Tony Cunningham wrote to the *Daily Telegraph* to assert that he was not a member of the IRA and was seeking improved visiting rights rather than repatriation. *Daily Telegraph*, 26 June 1980. His weekly applications to attend Mass were rebuffed and he was in July 1978 kept in the Punishment Block after his term had expired. Sr. Clarke, 'Albany Notes', Clarke Papers (COFLA).
112. *Irish Times*, 19 October 1978 and *Republican News*, 25 November 1978. He claimed: 'The unit was designed to break you psychologically, to disorientate you. Everything's white in your [seven by twelve

foot] cell. The window faces north/ north-west, so that no sunlight ever penetrated. There's also a white wall twenty feet high around the unit, and from your window you can see just the white wall or the sky – you become an expert on the different moods of the skies. Every cell is like a little prison on its own. It's total isolation, you talk to nobody and the Screws are specially trained not to talk to you, or only in a very terse fashion. You couldn't hear conversations elsewhere, either'. Quoted in *AP/ RN*, 13 December 1984. He confided in his wife that 'if he was in there long enough that he thinks it could get to him. You have to be very, very strong minded … I think they are using this unit to find out what the prisoners are made of'. 'Interview with Mrs [Mary] MacLaughlin [sic]' in *Hands off Ireland!*, No. 5, January 1979, p. 13.

113. See *Irish political prisoners*, p. 73 and *Irish Post*, 16 September 1978.

114. McLaughlin, *Inside an English jail*, p. 46.

115. *Irish Times*, 30 October 1978. Tory MP Jill Knight was among those perturbed by such cases. When questioning David Taylor, Branch Chairman of the POA in Brixton in January 1981 Knight claimed: 'I am told it is very, very worrying to a prison officer that he can be now be at the receiving end of a prosecution at the instigation of a prisoner. This is something which was never intended to arise because the rules are such that no prisoner should be able to prosecute a prison officer'. *Session 1980–8 … 19 January 1981, HM Prison Brixton*, p. 82.

116. Wakefield IRA PRO to editor, *Irish News*, 13 November 1978.

117. Gerry Cunningham, 25 September 2007.

118. Thomas and Pooley, *Exploding prison*, p. 98.

119. Quoted in *Hands off Ireland!*, No. 5, January 1979, p. 14.

120. *Irish Times*, 1 September 1976.

121. *Irish Times*, 26 January 1979. Joe Duffy, Paul Hill and Gerry Cunningham also gave evidence. McLaughlin, *Inside an English jail*, p. 50. See also *Guardian*, 26 January 1979.

122. *Republican News*, 25 November 1978.

123. O'Doherty had maintained the protest in solitary from 10 September 1976 to 19 November 1977. O'Doherty, *Volunteer*, p. 203.

124. *Republican News*, 25 November 1978. Murray perceived his role, a resumption of earlier blanket protests, as 'against the repressive prison conditions all the Irish political prisoners are held under'. Ibid. See also *IRIS*, 21 July 1979.

125. *AP/RN*, 7 June 1980.

126. *Republican News*, 25 November 1978. Stephen Blake was sent to Wormwood Scrubs following a 'lie-down' in Bristol. John McCluskey also arrived due to his role in the October Gartree protest. Ibid.

127. *IRIS*, 12 January 1979. Governor William Driscoll described 'appalling conditions' in Walton in the aftermath of February 1979 violence in which five warders were injured. *Guardian*, 13 February 1979.

128. Cited in *Irish People*, 25 September 1982.

129. *Irish Times*, 19 October 1978.

130. *Republican News*, 9 December 1978. Turton represented the PAC at the communist inspired World Youth Festival in Havana, Cuba, in late July/ early August 1978. *Hands off Ireland!*, No. 5, September 1978, pp. 7–9. The PAC expelled both the IMG and SWP from the November 1978 organizing committee due to alleged factionalism. *FRFI*, September 1982, p. 11. See also PAC, Press Statement, 28 October 1978, Private Collection (O Mathuna).

131. Allen, Larkin and O'Brien were hanged outside the New Bailey, Manchester, on 23 November 1867 despite a sizeable campaign for commutation of their sentences. Their bodies were soon moved into the grounds of the then newly constructed Strangeways Prison. The Manchester Martyrs Memorial Committee, founded by local Fenian Seamus Barrett, erected the monument in the early 1900s. See Herbert, *Wearing of the green*, pp. 53–8.

132. Jackie Kaye, 'Case against the Tribunal' in *Hands off Ireland!*, No. 6, January 1979, p. 12.

133. See Quinlivan and Rose, *Fenians in England*, p. 166. Paul Hill taught the words to London armed robber Graham Little whom he first encountered in Wormwood Scrubs. He explained how the song had been sung during the Spanish Civil War in honour of a group of Republicans who fought to the death. This inspired Little to sing the song every morning at 6.00 a.m. Hill, *Stolen years*, p. 207. Ray McLaughlin heard Little's 'incessant chanting' during a lie-down in Bristol and feared 'it must be gibberish'. On raising it with him later and learning the true purpose of his recitation of what transpired to have been 'The Internationale', the two parted as 'the best of friends'. The Irishman was then reading Sean Cronin's biography of ex-IRA and Republican Congress leader Frank Ryan, a senior officer in the anti-fascist XVth International Brigade. Reamonn [Ray McLaughlin] to Eamonn [Eddie O'Neill], 1 November 1983, Private Collection (O'Neill). English prisoner Little endorsed the Bobby Sands portrait he painted and presented to the ISM with the slogan 'Solidarity'. *FRFI*, April 1984, p. 16.

134. *Republican News*, 25 November 1978.

135. *Republican News*, 13 November 1978. See also *IRIS*, 15 November 1978 and 21 July 1979.
136. 'Visit of the Taoiseach: 27 November 1978' enclosure with BR Grange to DG Blunt, 21 November 1978, NAE, FCO 87/ 763.
137. 'Irish Republican Prisoners', 21 November 1978, NAE, FCO 87/ 763.
138. *Republican News*, 30 September 1978.
139. *Republican News*, 10 February 1979 and *Irish political prisoners*, p. 71.
140. Sr. Clarke, Miscellaneous MSS, Clarke Papers (COFLA).
141. *IRIS*, 12 January 1979.
142. O'Donnell, *Special Category*, I, p. 113.
143. Martin Brady, 12 April 2008.
144. McLaughlin, *Inside an English jail*, p. 49.
145. *IRIS*, 6 December 1978.
146. DG Blunt to BR Grange, 23 November 1978, NAE, FCO 87/ 763. See also Grange to Blunt, 27 November 1978, Ibid.
147. *The Irish Prisoner*, No. 7 [1986].
148. *Irish World*, 4 and 11 September 1976. Frank Stagg's story also remained in the foreground in America where the IRA conviction of Patrick Stagg and Sinn Féin activities of George and Joe Stagg were reported in detail. See *Irish World*, 18 September 1976. Sheehan moved from Ireland to Australia in 1951 and was involved in the Anti-Partition League which De Valera had promoted worldwide. On resettling in the US he was greeted by George Harrison, Liam Cotter and other leading republican activists. *Irish World*, 6 September 1980 and 11 December 1982.
149. See 'Patrick Miles Fell: proposed visit by the Bishop of Texas' [n.d., 1978], NAE, FCO 87/ 763.
150. See Rev. Cosmas Korb to the Editor, *Irish World*, 4 December 1979. See also Clarke, *No faith*, p. 107 and *Irish Echo*, 18 August 1984.
151. 'Patrick Miles Fell' [n.d., 1978], NAE, FCO 87/ 763.
152. DG Blunt to BR Gange, 16 November 1978, NAE, FCO 87/ 763.
153. PJ Goulden to AL Free-Gore, 9 November 1978, NAE, FCO 87/ 763.
154. BR Gange to DG Blunt, 21 November 1978, NAE, FCO 87/ 763.
155. J Murphy to David Blunt, 14 December 1978, NAE, FCO 87/ 763.
156. D[avid] G B[lunt] MS notes, 14 December 1978, NAE, FCO 87/ 763.
157. David Blunt to John Neary (First Secretary), 21 December 1978, NAE, FCO 87/ 763. See also DG Blunt to M Paice (Home Office Prison Department), 18 December 1978, 14 December 1978, NAE, FCO 87/ 763. Blunt was also contacted regarding Stevie Blake to which he replied: 'Mr. Blake has certainly been moved from prison to prison a large number of times. Such moves are never made lightly and in Mr. Blake's case they have always been necessary in the interests of prison security or good order and discipline. The remedy seems to lie largely in Mr. Blake's own hands … in the event of a transfer, every effort will be made by the prison authorities to notify Mrs [Mary] Blake of her son's new location if a visiting order is outstanding'. Blunt to Neary, 4 December 1978, NAE, FCO 87/ 763. Mary Blake lived in Wolfe Tone Place, Letterkenny, Donegal. Dick [O'Brien] to Sherrard [Cowper-Coles], 9 May 1978, Ibid.
158. *Irish Times*, 10 May 1978.
159. *IRIS*, 12 January 1979. The paper averred: 'All the POWs retain their strength and determination in this struggle for their just demands and BASIC HUMAN RIGHTS'. The same issue carried a report of a meeting of major literary figures opposed to the situation in the H-Blocks. *IRIS*, 12 January 1979.
160. Fr. Piaras O'Duill, 12 July 2011.
161. See *Framed through the Special Criminal Court*, p. 34. Joe Stagg chaired the Irish Civil Rights Association until September 1978 when he resigned arising from his public comments concerning the allegedly excessive internal discipline of IRA prisoners in Portlaoise. *Irish Times*, 9 September 1978.
162. IRA prisoners in Long Kesh had reputedly made representations to the leadership of the Republican Movement to form such a body in the late 1970s. One claimed that the progression from 'no wash' to hunger strike had been deliberately delayed to permit time for the Committee to coalesce. See Maxwell Taylor and Ethel Quayle, *Terrorist lives* (London, 1994), p. 91.
163. See *An Phoblacht*, 8 March 1980 and Pat Walsh, *Irish Republicanism and Socialism, The politics of the Republican Movement, 1905 to 1994* (Belfast, 1994), pp. 172–8, 184.
164. *Republican News*, 20 January 1979.
165. Jim Panaro, 11 November 2009. See *AP/RN*, 8 January 2008. Duffy passed away in late 2007 at which time Ann O'Sullivan of the POW Department noted in his obituary that he had been assiduous in confirming prison addresses: 'Particularly important in relation to prisoners held in England. The process of "ghosting" … meant that we constantly had to trace the current whereabouts of these prisoners'. Ibid.
166. Martin Brady, 12 April 2008.

167. *Observer*, 28 March 1993.
168. See Kaye, 'Case against the Tribunal' in *Hands off Ireland!*, No. 6, January 1979, p. 10.
169. PAC Statement in *The Irish Prisoner*, No. 5, June 1979, p. 2.
170. Kaye, 'Case against the Tribunal' in *Hands off Ireland!*, No. 6, January 1979, pp. 11–12.
171. For a full listing of the attacks see *IRIS*, 12 and 21 January 1979. See also McGladdery, *Provisional IRA in England*, pp. 242–3 and Moloney, *Secret history*, p. 173. The incidents sparked a bizarre turn of events when an English policeman concocted a story of being fired upon by an IRA suspect in Farnham. The *Sun* headline on 18 December 1978 was 'Find Bald Eagle', a reference to Belfast republican Con McHugh who was then verifiably at home in Ireland. See *The British media and Ireland, Truth: The first casualty*, [London, 1979], p. 38.
172. *Newsline*, 19 December 1978. See also *Republican News*, 3 February 1979.
173. *The Irish Worker, Bulletin of Clann na hÉireann*, Vol. 1, No. 1, February/ March 1979.
174. *Republican News*, 21 January 1979.
175. *Republican News*, 21 January 1979. The PAC also campaigned on general issues concerning imprisoned republicans. It commissioned the short documentary 'Prisoners of War' which was sold from a Post Office box address in London. *Republican News*, 10 February 1979. See also *AP/RN*, 12 May 1979. The film was screened in Conway Hall on 6 April 1979. *The Irish Prisoner*, No. 5, June 1979, p. 5.
176. See Helen Stevens, 'Building an anti-war movement in Britain' in *AP/RN*, 18 August 1979.
177. Stevens, 'Anti-war movement' in *AP/RN*, 18 August 1979.
178. *Special Branch, Minutes of Evidence, Wednesday 23 January 1985, Association of Chief Police Officers* (London, 1985), p. 71. An official document noted: 'The Special Branch enquire into the implications of any offence connected with firearms and explosives unless it is immediately clear that there is no security interest. They also provide information about extremists and terrorist groups to the Security Service or in the case of Irish Republican extremists and terrorist groups to the Metropolitan Police Special Branch'. Ibid.
179. Clarke, *No faith*, pp. 59–64.
180. Clarke, *No faith*, p. 63.
181. *PAC News*, June 1977.
182. See Sr. Clarke, 'David McQuaid', Clarke Papers (COFLA). McQuaid, Anthony Walsh and Cyril MacLachlan were all acquitted of the charges for which Liam Baker and Punter Bennett were convicted in 1976. McQuaid was charged with conspiracy to contravene the Explosives Act on 24 November 1975 and cleared of wrong doing in Winchester on 26 November 1976. Ibid.
183. McLaughlin, *Inside an English jail*, p. 51. See *Guardian*, 26 January 1979.
184. *Lost Lives*, p. 775.
185. *IRIS*, 17 February 1979.
186. See *HC Deb 18 January 1979 vol 960 cc1998*.
187. Paul Holmes, April 2011.
188. December 1977 to April 1978 witnessed concerted efforts to suppress *Republican News* by the arrest of its writers and printers. In related moves, detention of Sinn Féin members working in the party's Belfast advice centres disrupted legal political activities by the organization. On 21 February 1979 charges ranging from IRA membership to conspiracy were dropped in relation to the twenty-one persons involved. See TOM, *The British media and Ireland, Truth: The first casualty* (London, [1979]), pp. 45–6 and Curtis, *Ireland and the propaganda war*, pp. 266–8.
189. *The Irish Worker, Bulletin of Clann na hÉireann*, Vol.1, No. 1, February/ March 1979.
190. *Report of the Commissioner of Police of the Metropolis for the year 1978* (London, 1979), p. 9.
191. McLaughlin, *Inside an English jail*, p. 50.
192. *Guardian*, 12 March 1979.
193. McLaughlin, *Inside an English jail*, p. 52. Vince Donnelly coined the nickname for the red headed Clarke when Jimmy Ashe obtained a pair of 'silver flash' running shoes. Ibid., p. 53.
194. McLaughlin, *Inside an English jail*, p. 53.
195. See Bell, *Secret Army*, p. 472. The arrests were by no means 'Irish luck'. Ibid.
196. *Sunday Times*, 29 June 1980.
197. Clarke and Johnston, *McGuinness*, p. 110. See also *Irish News*, 23 March 1979.
198. Clarke and Johnston, *McGuinness*, p. 111. Police agent Sean O'Callaghan reportedly 'co-operated' with Kathryn Johnston in producing his autobiography in 1998. Johnston and her husband Liam Clarke co-authored the McGuinness biography which advanced the controversial theory of Keenan's arrest. Clarke wrote for the *Sunday Times* which defended a libel action taken by Armagh republican Thomas 'Slab' Murphy with the aid of O'Callaghan and other witnesses. *Irish News*, 30 April 1998 and *Sunday Times*, 30 June 1995.
199. Brian Keenan, 26 May 2007.
200. Bell, *Secret Army*, p. 472. See also Nick Van Der Bijl, *Operation Banner, The British Army in Northern Ireland* (Barnsley, 2009), p. 112.

201. *Guardian*, 26 June 1980 and Clarke and Johnston, *McGuinness*, p. 111.
202. Brian Keenan, 26 May 2007.
203. *Irish News*, 26 March 1979.
204. *Irish Times*, 28 May 2008.
205. Alan Simpson, *Duplicity and deception, Policing the Twilight Zone of the Troubles* (Kerry, 2010), p. 65. Simpson claimed that Keenan was partly motivated by a 'personal grudge' arising from his acting as Shop Steward in the Grundig plant managed by Niedermayer. Ibid. In 1959–60 Keenan worked for English Elective (Guided Weapons Division) which manufactured the Thunderbird SAM in Luton. Brian Keenan to 'Peter Flynn' (Seamus O Mathuna), 10 December 1983, Private Collection (O Mathuna). See also Bernard Fitzsimons (ed) *Weapons and Warfare* (New York, 1978), Volume 23, pp. 2489–2490.
206. Simpson, *Duplicity and Deception*, p. 186.
207. Brian Keenan, 26 May 2007.
208. 'Behind closed doors, RTE One TV, 1 January 2010. Callaghan was conscious of his Irish heritage and often visited the Glandore, west Cork, holiday home of his son-in-law, Peter Jay. The appointment of Jay as Britain's ambassador to the US in 1977 was controversial. *Irish World*, 21 May 1977.
209. See contributions of Gerry Fitt MP to the biannual debate on the PTA. *HC Deb 21 March 1979 vol 964 cc1505–624* and Mason, *Paying the price*, p. 223. Judge Harry Bennett investigated allegations of police brutality in Castlereagh Interrogation Centre and Gough Barracks, Armagh. Dr. Robert Irwin, police surgeon with the RUC, claimed that 'roughly 150–160 prisoners have shown themselves to me with injuries which I would not be satisfied were self-inflicted'. Cited in Bell, *British Labour and Ireland*, p. 19. Information provided by republicans suggested H5 in Long Kesh contained 134 prisoners of 140 on the Blanket protest in March 1979. It was claimed that eighty-three republicans had been assaulted in late 1978. Faul and Murray, *H Block*, p. 65.
210. See Bell, *British Labour and Ireland*, pp. 1–2 and *AP/RN*, 14 May 2004. Fitt heavily criticized Roy Mason during the debate. In a patronizing and inaccurate account Mason claimed that Maguire was shamed into abstaining by Fitt's speech and was 'an amiable boozer whose contribution to Parliament was roughly nil. That he'd managed to get himself elected at all was a mystery'. Mason, *Paying the price*, p. 223. See also Ibid., p. 216. For Maguire's earlier interest in the Albany situation see *Irish Post*, 15 January 1977. Maguire visited Armagh Prison and Crumlin Road Prison on 2 July and 23 July 1979 respectively. Fr. Denis Faul and Fr. Raymond Murray, *The British Dimension, Brutality, Murder and Legal Duplicity in N. Ireland*, Booklet, November 1980, pp. 50–51.
211. See Geoffrey Bell, *Troublesome Business, The Labour Party and the Irish Question* (London, 1982), pp. 131–4.
212. For internal Labour Party and Conservative Party manifesto issues see Roy Hattersley, *Fifty Years On, A prejudiced history of Britain since the war* (London, 1997), pp. 269–75.
213. Seamus O Mathuna to Ruan O'Donnell, 14 April 2012, Private Collection (O'Donnell).
214. Holland and McDonald, *Deadly Divisions*, pp. 137–40, 236, *Observer*, 1 April 1979 and Potter, *Testimony to courage*, p. 213. Neave favoured a hard line in Ireland: 'There must be change in security tactics. The Army and the local security forces must be released from their present low profile and go on the offensive ... The time is ripe to smash the Provisional IRA'. Cited in Desmond Hamill, *Pig in the middle, The Army in Northern Ireland, 1969–1984*, (London, 1985), p. 198. See also *Lost Lives*, p. 779 and Mason, *Paying the price*, pp. 226–7.
215. Holland and McDonald, *Deadly Divisions*, p. 136.
216. *HC Deb 3 July 1979 vol 969 c509W*.
217. *Times*, 21 October 1978.
218. Margaret Thatcher, *The Downing Street years* (London, 1993), p. 415 cited in Bourke, *Ideas*, p. 414.
219. Alan Clark, *Diaries, Into Politics* (London, 2000), p. 303
220. Tony Benn, *The Benn Diaries* (London, 1995), pp. 467–8. Benn's political diaries recorded: 'We stood for a moment in Airey Neave's memory and Shirley Williams suggested sending a letter of condolence, which was agreed. Joan Lestor asked what was meant by an agreed response to terrorism. Did it mean capital punishment? Jim said no'. Ibid., p. 468.
221. Deirdre O'Shea, 2 October 2008.
222. Nick Mullen, 11 March 2012.
223. Armstrong to Wilson, 27 October 1980, Private Collection (Wilson). Armstrong had 'a few run ins with [Bunting] when he was a Stick [Official IRA member]'. Ibid. See also *Lost Lives*, pp. 840–41 and *Sunday Independent*, 12 August 2007.
224. See Holland and McDonald, *Deadly Divisions*, pp. 158–9, *Irish Echo*, 28 February 1981, *Guardian*, 31 October 1980 and 17 January 1981 and Gerry Fitt, *HC Deb 15 March 1982 vol 20 cc151–71*. For McMichael see Dillon, *Stone Cold*, p. 67. McMichael was second in command of the UDA when shot dead by the IRA on 22 December 1987. *Lost Lives*, p. 1103.

225. *Irish News*, 11 March 1982.
226. Armstrong to Wilson, 2 July 1980, Private Collection (Wilson). Armstrong admired Miriam Daly's political work and did not need to name her in a letter which addressed the strange circumstances of her assassination. See also *Lost Lives*, pp. 830–31. From the vantage of an English jail, it appeared to some IRA men in early March 1979 that the shooting of men within the psychopathic Loyalist 'Shankill Butcher' gang elicited condemnations of rank hypocrisy from Ian Paisley et al. Armstrong to Wilson, 6 March 1979, Private Collection (Wilson).
227. For forensic and judicial evidence of collusion see Anne Cadwallader, *Lethal Allies: British collusion in Ireland* (Dublin, 2013). See also Panorama, 'Britain's Secret Terror Force', BBC One, 21 November 2013.
228. Armstrong to Wilson, 3 March 1980, Private Collection (Wilson).
229. Noel Gibson, 22 August 2008.
230. Quoted in *Irish Echo*, 5 July 1980.
231. For date see Victory, *Justice and truth*, p. 16.
232. Anderson, *Cahill*, pp. 248–9.
233. See Moloney, *Secret history*, pp. 144–5.
234. 'Smash H-Block' leaflet reprinted in *Hands off Ireland!*, No. 7, April 1979, p. 11. In September 1979 the IRA PRO of H3, H4 and H5 also referenced the republicans who had died in 'their English dungeon' when on hunger strike. See *Hands off Ireland!*, No. 9, November 1979, p. 4. Jenkinson was convicted of bombing Aldershot Barracks in March 1972 and died in October 1976 from what comrades believed was medical neglect in Leicester Special Secure Block. *FRFI*, June 1982, p. 10.
235. Farrell, *Sheltering the fugitive?*, p. 82 and *Irish Times*, 22 October 1985.
236. *Irish World*, 12 March and 2 and 9 April 1983.
237. *Irish World*, 12 August 1978. Claro Barracks was the 38 Field Regiment Depot. McGladdery, *Provisional IRA in England*, p. 238.
238. *Irish World*, 2 June 1979.
239. *Irish World*, 9 June 1979.
240. See *Irish Echo*, 11 February 1984.
241. Information of Matt Regan, Philadelphia, 19 June 2014.
242. Information of Jack Kilroy, Cleveland, 3 July 2014.
243. *Irish political prisoners*, pp. 94–5 and *The Irish Prisoner*, No. 5, June 1979, p. 2. Walsh had been sanctioned with fifty-six days confinement on 2 February 1979 for attacking a prison officer on 24 January 1979. 'Walsh-BOV Adjudications' in A Aylett [For the Treasury Solicitor] to BM Birnberg & Co, 28 September 1990, Private Collection (Walsh).
244. Martin Coughlan, 24 August 2006.
245. Hayes (ed.) *In prison in England*, p. 23.
246. *Irish political prisoners*, pp. 94–5. Eddie Butler was one of the men whom republicans believed were being victimized. The Pearse/ McDaid and Jimmy Steele cumainn of Sinn Féin, plus the UTOM, picketed Winson Green on 3 March 1979. The retreat of nervous prison staff enabled the picketers to occupy the forecourt of the complex. See *Republican News*, 24 March 1979.
247. Sean Kinsella, 3 August 2007.
248. *Irish political prisoners*, p. 96.
249. Faul and Murray, *H Block*, p. 65.
250. *The Irish Prisoner*, No. 5, June 1979, p. 5.
251. Faul and Murray, *H Block*, p. 65.
252. Sean Kinsella, 3 August 2007.
253. *Irish Times*, 26 March 1979.
254. *Irish political prisoners*, p. 79 and *Republican News*, 31 March 1979.
255. *Irish political prisoners*, p. 96.
256. *Report of the work of the Prison Department, 1979*, p. 20.
257. Ronnie McCartney, 12 April 2008. An argument with a staff member in the Governor's office regarding the withholding of the Kathleen Largey Thompson album 'The Price of Freedom' resulted in McCartney's transfer to Wormwood Scrubs. Ibid. Her 'In Defence of the Nation' recording included the ballad 'Michael Gaughan' and 'Our lads in Crumlin Jail'. One Canadian production was distributed through Irish Northern Aid with 'all proceeds to Irish Republican POW dependents'.
258. *Irish political prisoners*, p. 96 and *AP/RN*, 20 January 1983.
259. *HC Deb 23 November 1978 vol 958 cc685–6W*. Home Office guidelines on adjudications contained 'provision' for accused prisoners to question prosecution witnesses and to invite supportive witnesses deemed acceptable to the Board of Visitors. Ibid.
260. Hayes (ed.) *In prison in England*, p. 23.
261. Roy Walsh to the Secretary of State, 6 April 1979, Private Collection (Walsh).

262. Secretary of State to the Governor, Wormwood Scrubs, 11 May 1979, Private Collection (Walsh).
263. Woodford & Ackroyd to R[oy] Walsh, 29 May 1979, Private Collection (Walsh).
264. *Guardian*, 16 January 1979.
265. *Daily Telegraph*, 16 January 1979.
266. *Guardian*, 18 January 1979.
267. *Irish Times*, 5 April 1979. The eight convicted were Anthony Bumstead, Malcolm Stevenson, George Clarke, Steven Hewson, Maurice Dudding, Andrew Wilson, Peter Watson and Kevin Burns. *IRIS*, 7 April 1979. The sentences, suspended for two years, ranged between two and nine months. *Irish Times*, 6 April 1979. The jury had failed to reach a verdict on 3 April. *Guardian*, 4 April 1979. Dudding had given evidence against Gerry Cunningham at a Leicester BOV proceedings arising from the riot. Alastair Logan, acting for the Irishman, endeavoured to refute untrue claims that he had looted 'other prisoners cells'. Gerry Cunningham to the Members of the Board of Visitors HMP Hull, 16 December 1987, Private Collection (Cunningham).
268. *Irish Times*, 5 April 1979. See also *Times*, 2 November 1978.
269. *AP/RN*, 26 May 1979.
270. *Observer*, 8 April 1979.
271. Gerry Cunningham, 25 September 2007.
272. Comment of Gerry Cunningham to author, Dublin, 24 November 2012.
273. *AP/RN*, 26 May 1979.
274. *AP/RN*, 26 May 1979. On 27 June Joseph Dean, MP for the Leeds constituency in which Armley was located, expressed concern that staff were working under 'tremendous pressures' and that 'other prisons ... could soon become flash points'. *HC Deb 27 June 1979 vol 969 cc438*.
275. *HC Deb 13 July 1979 vol 970 c312W*.
276. Martin Brady, 10 April 2008.
277. Martin Brady, 10 April 2008.
278. *IRIS*, 28 April 1979.
279. *IRIS*, 28 April 1979. The PAC film 'Prisoner of War' was shown in Pontypridd Polytechnic on 16 May 1979. Sinn Féin activist Gerry Mac Lochlainn, a resident of Wales, then addressed the students. *IRIS*, 16 June 1979. Although the IRA had a policy of eschewing attacks in Wales, police investigated a 'possible link' between the organization and 'Welsh extremists' in the wake of arson incidents in December. See *Times*, 15 December 1979. For Warren see *The Irish Prisoner*, No. 6, September/October 1979.
280. See Ricky Tomlinson, *Ricky* (London, 2004) and *Guardian*, 27 December 2014.
281. *AP/RN*, 9 June, 7 July and 18 August 1979.
282. *AP/RN*, 29 April 1982.
283. Memo, 31 October 1978, NAE, FCO 87/ 763.
284. HAJ Staples, 'Mr. P Harte TD and the Gillespie Sisters', Memo, 26 May 1978, NAE, FCO 87/ 763.
285. Ann and Eileen Gillespie, 7 June 2008.

CHAPTER 3

Resistance and Reaction

Eddie O'Neill was on the 'E list' in Gartree for much of 1978 following his attempted escape from Wormwood Scrubs. One of the additional restrictions imposed on his routine was that the light bulb in his cell burned night and day, ostensibly to facilitate spyhole observation of his behaviour. The net result was that O'Neill had great trouble resting, suffered chronic headaches and eventually developed the potentially fatal condition of 'sleep paralysis'. From late 1978 he was only sleeping for around half an hour a night, yet was still unsuccessful in persuading the Governor to relent on the lights policy. None of those on surveillance duty were sympathetic when witnessing his gradual and visible deterioration. Matters reached crisis point in May 1979 when the Tyrone man went deaf, lost the sight of an eye and became numb down the left side of his body. This was sufficient to warrant a transfer to Parkhurst Prison Hospital for two weeks of tests and treatment, which eventually led to his recovery.[1] It had emerged during his trial that O'Neill had visited the Isle of Wight when highly active in the IRA in England. This evidently prompted a perturbed Dr. Cooper, whom O'Neill encountered in the hospital in 1979, to say purposefully: 'I did not kill Michael Gaughan'.[2] Dr. Cooper's knowledge of republicanism evidently apprised him of the Fenian principle of holding enemies directly accountable for their actions. He survived IRA retaliation at a time when their imprisoned members assiduously pursued long-term plans that materialized, to the physical detriment of the Dispersal System.

Wakefield incendiaries, June 1979

A major security scare occurred in Wakefield on 26 June 1979 when IRA incendiaries set fire to a disused education block. An 'inch by inch' search of the locked - down facility led to the recovery of devices in 'all parts of the prison'.[3] At least two unexploded firebombs were found in workshops, which posed a direct threat to the prison industry sector and a challenge to the jail's Security Officers.[4] The estimated 'value of production' from the 'Prindus' trademark was £22.9 million in the financial year 1978–79, up from £20.5 million in 1977–78.[5] A statement from the Home Office claimed that armed police and dog handlers 'ringed' the prison in case the blazes were intended to divert attention from a breakout. Informed commentators knew, however, that the attacks were the work of the IRA, who had been agitating for years to highlight the maltreatment of their comrades in F Wing and elsewhere.[6] The attacks occurred just two days after a picket organized by Sinn Féin registered that access to educational programmes was one of the key demands of the republicans inside Wakefield.[7] Prisoners were theoretically entitled to 'education facilities' under Rule 29 (1), although the High Court affirmed the traditional discretion of governors extending to deny access.[8]

Merlyn Rees was obliged to discuss the incident in the House of Commons on 27 June and did so in terms that revealed something of the Establishment's modified view of imprisoned IRA members. The stress laid by Whitelaw on the allegedly minimal impact of the attacks was belied by the fact that he had been forced to answer questions on their nature in Westminster. The Home Secretary had previously commented on the importance of denying the IRA any form of publicity. Enoch Powell and other Conservatives had been anxious to address the propaganda dimension on the record of *Hansard,* despite the obvious danger of counter-productivity. However, it was clearly deemed politically beneficial to downplay the serious implications of what was undeniably a major breach of security. In a telling omission, no debate was recorded in June *vis à vis* the supposed causation of the unusual event, other than the bland circumstantial reportage that Wakefield contained 'many IRA prisoners' of whom 'well over half are lifers'.[9] In the North of Ireland, 377 men were either serving life sentences or being held at the Secretary of State's Pleasure by late 1980, out of a population standing at 2,506 on New Years Day.[10]

Whitelaw's low-key approach, even if pitched to calm nerves, implied that firebomb attacks on the fabric of the prisons of England and Wales should no longer be viewed as extraordinary in jails holding Irish republicans. The bedrock of the criminal justice apparatus in the United Kingdom was under IRA threat. Whitelaw recognized that the numerical proportion of republicans serving sentences of life imprisonment in a given prison was a significant factor. This was almost certainly informed by Home Office intelligence assessments derived from the massive data set generated by monitoring Category A prisoners. The organization's capacity for more ambitious coordinated action was raised by the less reserved Rees, who sought reassurance that 'there is not something going on in other prisons'. Fears were expressed for members of the public living in the vicinity of maximum-security institutions, an unsettling aside with overtones of the exaggerated concerns which inspired the *Mountbatten Report*.[11] Following realistic appraisal, it was decided in 1979 that the 'serious and costly damage' inflicted on Gartree's engineering workshops warranted their replacement with an innocuous shoemaking industry. This was suggested in part by the danger posed by the manufacture of 'illicit items' by men using prison machinery.[12]

The silent Home Office knew that the harassment of IRA men on 'E-list' was one of the main reasons behind the planting of the firebombs in Wakefield. It followed an incident when one of the four men in 'patches', Paul Norney, felt obliged to take a stand when deliberately locked into his cell without dinner after a work assignment. This affront impinged on fundamental principles and could not go unanswered by a man serving five life sentences imposed in May 1976. On failing to receive the desired redress from the staff through the normal channel of direct verbal appeal, the physical young Belfastman dismantled his metal frame bed and used the parts to smash and prise an opening through the cell door. After some exertion he climbed out onto the wing. Very few prisoners in Britain had exited their cells by this ingenious methodology and its viability raised serious questions. Norney, otherwise even-tempered and highly focused, received his food ration from startled prison staff, as well as a further six weeks of isolation in a soundproofed cell.[13]

The discovery of the incendiaries led to the immediate transfer of Vince Donnelly to Durham, Sean Hayes to Leeds and Ray McLaughlin to Manchester.[14] Yorkshire Special Branch, meanwhile, investigated the planting of the devices within their bailiwick. Those sent away from the prison on twenty-eight day 'lie-downs' were segregated upon return and required to attend interview sessions with the police. Tony Clarke and Ray McLaughlin, after time spent in Wakefield's F Wing, were jointly questioned in November when both refused to cooperate. In a similar vein, Donnelly's clear signals that he would not speak to local policemen were only accepted without equivocation when he threw a table at his putative interrogators. Arson charges were laid against Clarke, but quickly withdrawn as further fruitless enquiries continued and the unwelcome prospect of acquittal after more transparent criminal court proceedings loomed. Police interest, however, had a negative impact because the authorities used it as a pretext to prolong the solitary confinement of those under scrutiny.[15] This approximated to collective punishment in a very public IRA case that the police were incapable of resolving due to lack of evidence and the solidarity of the chief suspects. IRA prisoners in England believed that the planting of around twelve firebombs in Wakefield was a major success and that those responsible 'were gone and that was their victory.'[16] Eddie O'Neill was sent back to Wakefield in 1984, where he was kept apart from all other republicans in the prison.[17]

Ronnie McCartney had been on a twenty-eight day lie-down in Leeds in the summer of 1979, and on returning to Hull in July 1979, became embroiled in another visit related protest. On entering the room provided for political prisoners, the Belfast man noticed that a second table had been placed alongside the original one in order to increase the distance between his seat and that allocated to his wife. This redundant measure obliged the couple to raise their voices to converse, an additional loss of privacy which diminished the quality of the reunion. When he remonstrated with the Deputy Governor in the hope of receiving a compensatory normal visit, he was threatened that a screen would be erected.[18] He did not resort to extraordinary modes of resistance. The Albany blanket protest, meanwhile, dragged on into July when the IRA pinpointed Deputy Governor Mole as a particular problem.[19] It was alleged that he harboured 'racist tendencies' towards black and Irish prisoners and that attitudes had hardened within the prison administration following his transfer from Chelmsford. Whereas some latitude was then available in relation to Mass, this was generally not the case at times when Mole was on duty. Pat 'Tipp' Guilfoyle took action on this matter during a confrontation and threw the contents of his chamber pot over his adversary. 'Decorating' the Deputy Governor cost Guilfoyle three days in a strip cell with a canvas blanket, a punishment that required the invocation of Rule 45 by the governor.[20] Significantly, Sinn Féin alleged that the conditions in Albany were 'almost as grim as that of their comrades in the H-Blocks'.[21] The *Daily Telegraph* claimed that the men had acted 'on orders from their Dublin leadership', but this was not the case and denied in writing by Tony Cunningham.[22]

Warrenpoint and Mountbatten

The change of government in Westminster did not inhibit a march in London advocating British military disengagement from Ireland. Over 1,000 police escorted 10,000 persons down Oxford Street on 12 August 1979, including delegations from Young Liberals, as well as the Barnsley Trades Council, the Connolly Association and the Campaign for Democracy in Ulster (CDU). They were prohibited from entering Trafalgar Square, arising from the enforcement of a ban the Department of the Environment imposed in 1972, but heard speeches from Bernadette McAliskey, Michael Holden and ex-members of the British Army who had served in Ireland. If clearly a success for Sinn Féin and the UTOM leadership, the fact that it dwarfed those assembled outside the prisons indicated the relative importance of the issues to the pro-Irish lobby in Britain.[23] The IMG, SWP and 'British middle-class socialists' were criticised for taking part by the RCG, who lamented the missing anti-imperialist and explicit pro-IRA content of the event.[24] Elements within Sinn Féin hoped in August 1979 that 'war weariness' among the general British population would underpin a broad 'anti-war' movement.[25]

A protracted tour of the exterior of English prisons by the Pearse/ McDaid cumann of Birmingham Sinn Féin reached Wormwood Scrubs on 26 August 1979. They were joined by An Cumann Cabhrach and Sinn Féin delegations from Nottingham and London, as well as the UTOM. The prison held nine IRA members: Pat 'Paddy' Hackett, Anthony 'Ron' Lynch,

Liam McLarnon, Mick Murray, Stevie Nordone, Shane Paul O'Doherty, Roy Walsh, Gerry Young and Phil Sheridan. Murray had been on the blanket since October 1978 and was confined as a result in solitary.[26] Hackett was captured in 1976 after a premature explosion in which he lost his left leg and most of his right arm. This was a personal disaster for a 24-year-old man who regarded being 'badly injured and caught' as 'the worst possible' outcome of an IRA operation.[27] Tortured by two Special Branch officers when hospitalized in Fulhum, and further maltreated by warders and police when on remand in Brixton, he was an exceptionally determined prisoner who derived morale - affirming satisfaction from exercising dissent: 'We were political prisoners and we were there to cause as much disruption as we could'. An Irish - born police informer in London, who had attempted to entrap Angry Brigade anarchists in the early 1970s, fruitlessly manoeuvred to ingratiate himself with Hackett when both were being housed in B Wing.[28]

Hackett was held on a ground floor cell of D Wing owing to his serious unhealed injuries, which were evidently either neglected or de-prioritised by prison medical authorities. Partial immobility did not prevent him from smashing the windows of a staff office to answer their failure to return his cassette player in reasonable time. The machine required minor modification to ensure its recording function was inoperable but he took offence at the inexplicable delay. When called before Governor Norman Honey to account for his vandalism, Hackett followed IRA practise by refusing to state either his name or prison number. On turning to walk out in the midst of the session an irate Principal Officer roughly grabbed Hackett's damaged arm before he was escorted to the Punishment Block. News of this cruelty reached Young and Walsh on the wings, who deliberated before deciding to retaliate by striking the responsible warder with a ceramic chamber pot. This was achieved, and the man whom Walsh was told to intercept if he attempted to prevent Young's focused attack remained frozen with shock when it occurred. As the alarm sounded Young returned to his cell without further affray and received twenty-eight days in the Punishment Block for a premeditated, politically motivated assault.[29] Hackett frequently took direct action if provoked by men he regarded as antagonistic. Acts of resistance ranged from throwing boiling hot tea over a staff member who had discommoded him in the course of his duties to smashing the glass office windows where he had been repeatedly declined access to personal property related to his craftwork. He utilized a metal segment of his crudely manufactured false leg for the purpose. The validity of complaints underlying the destructive spree induced Governor Honey, whom he regarded as 'decent', to simply issue a recorded warning. The prudence of defusing an escalating situation involving a popular IRA prisoner contributed to its resolution.[30]

Two devastating IRA attacks on 27 August 1979 gained global coverage for the 'Long War'. The first killed Lord Mountbatten, a totemic figure within the Intelligence community and a first cousin of Britain's Queen Elizabeth II. He was blown up when sailing his yacht and drowned off Mullaghmore, County Sligo, in the northwest of Ireland.[31] Later that day a highly sophisticated double bomb - attack killed at least eighteen elite British soldiers at Warrenpoint, County Down. Admitted fatalities included sixteen members of the Parachute Regiment's 2nd Battalion based in Ballykinlar. Lieutenant-Colonel David Blair of the 1st Queen's Own Highlanders also died, one of the highest-ranking officers to have perished in the Troubles.[32] The impact of the bombings was considerable beyond the heavy loss of life in that it demonstrated a new level of IRA technical proficiency that endangered all military ground transport. The British Army increasingly relied upon helicopters to traverse republican areas of the Six Counties which minimized casualties at a price of ceding a large degree of control to their adversaries. Mountbatten's death, however, occluded that of the soldiers, and security arrangements for the funeral at Romsey Abbey on 5 September 1979 were extremely tight.[33] A wider reflection was further suggested by the decade - long and patently unsuccessful British deployment to Ireland under 'Operation Banner'. *Time Out* devoted its cover to the cost of Britain's engagement in the Troubles in its issue of 10–16 August 1979. The heading: 'Ten years of troops in Ireland, The failure of British peace keeping', struck a querulous note in a month of significant IRA escalation.[34] The routines adopted by Britain's front line NATO regiments and Special Forces in Ireland bore no relation to the function of actual 'peacekeepers' then operating under the aegis of the United Nations in Cyprus, Syria and Lebanon.

Taoiseach Jack Lynch travelled to London for an acrimonious meeting with Prime Minister Margaret Thatcher and to attend Mountbatten's funeral. When on vacation in Portugal the Corconian had castigated the killers as 'the real enemies of Ireland', a contentious pronouncement that did nothing to explain their extreme actions.[35] Given Callaghan's abject failure to respond to Lynch's historic White House - backed invitation of January 1978 for minimal commitment towards negotiations on the constitutional future of the Six Counties, the reaction of the right wing Conservatives to such hollow rhetoric was decidedly unpromising. Lynch addressed this short-term deficit of Anglo-Irish diplomatic cordiality by jettisoning years of Irish Government policy. The strategic consequences of a Taoiseach yielding ground, in public and private, were incalculable. Higher levels of security co-operation were agreed by Irish Civil Servants that increased the likelihood of republicans being extradited from the Twenty-Six Counties for trial in England and the Six Counties.[36] This did not immediately occur, and a subsequent Fianna Fáil Taoiseach, Charles Haughey, was less than enthusiastic on the matter. Contrary to the impression given by Irish and British official sources and the media, the Gardai and the RUC had closely interacted on a monthly basis since September 1974 at the latest, although the information flow was overwhelmingly directed at combating the IRA in the Thirty-Two Counties and Britain.[37]

Backlash in the prisons

Many republicans already within the Dispersal System were confronted with an angry backlash by prison staffs with high proportions of ex-military personnel. Hugh Doherty, serving what appeared to be open-ended solitary confinement without his radio in Durham, was given verbal updates of the Warrenpoint casualties by an English anarchist who shouted bulletins out his cell window. While being 'on a high' due to the military proficiency of the IRA, Doherty was mindful that he was on the eve of his first family visit in over fourteen months:

> Most of the screws were ex-soldiers and the tension was just [incredible], you could cut it with a knife ... I said I wanted to go for a bath there and the screw looked at me and said, 'are you mad?' They would have killed me. I wasn't giving them the opportunity. Then we got into the visitors room ... A big pile of screws, the usual. The screw says, 'you go on there'. My mother didn't come. It was a trap ... One of them in particular was giving me a hard time. One time I was there, he opened the [cell] door ... [which] was never opened on its own, there was always three screws ... He says to me, 'you were right' [about British Establishment disinterest in military deaths]. He had lost two of his comrades at Warrenpoint. ... but all the papers were about Mountbatten ... He says to me; 'Can I do anything? ... [although] I'll not help you escape'. He started to take me in books ... Any book I asked he would take in, so it was a lesson for him.[38]

British paratrooper Paul Burns, seriously wounded at Warrenpoint, noted that 'the tragedy of the massacre was rather overshadowed by the death of Earl Mountbatten' outside the airborne regiment. He was, nonetheless, among the injured survivors visited in Woolwich Military Hospital by the Prime Minister. The incidents in Counties Down and Sligo prompted an urgent reassessment of IRA capabilities.[39]

Eddie Butler was in Winson Green and, if housed on a wing, was locked down at least twenty-three hours a day. The 'atmosphere' was electrified by the news from Ireland, and Butler felt fortunate in retrospect to have avoided a beating. He learned, however, that Eddie O'Neill received a severe 'kicking' in the Punishment Block of the same prison. O'Neill, in fact, had been attacked prior to events in County Down.[40] The Tyroneman was 'roughed up a bit' entering Winson Green, 'but at 6.30 the next morning I was battered, kicked to pieces, broken ribs etc ... I woke up to find five or six of them beating me'. Such was the violence of the assault that one of his assailants suffered a broken arm. Rather than acknowledge staff initiation, O'Neill, who had been lying asleep when struck with batons, was preposterously charged with GBH. His injuries were such that he was kept 'out of circulation' for ten days and only allowed exercise at night while Alastair Logan tried to ascertain his whereabouts. It was five weeks before the immured O'Neill learned of Warrenpoint in the chapel from Butler.[41] Accounts of the IRA successes sparked an alert in the Parkhurst SSU when Johnny Joyce, a non-political prisoner of Irish extraction, warned republicans that staff intended to assault one of their number. O'Connell recalled:

> They were ready to kill you at that stage especially with Mountbatten … The screws were in your face a bit. It wouldn't have taken much to spark it off … Normally you'd be banged up for an hour or an hour and a half while the screws went off during the middle of the day. The rest of the day you'd be out of your cell. So we were going to be banged up [early] because the screws were going to have a service for Mountbatten. It was more or less a day of mourning. Someone asked why we were going to be banged up … If one of them came and attacked us they'd all come. We could have all been killed and they'd get away with it with the atmosphere at the time.[42]

Sean Kinsella was in F Wing, Wakefield, when news reached prisoners with radios, but not the IRA men being held under punishment conditions. Lacking direct verification, they disbelieved the details being relayed from distant cells. An exceptionally violent yet friendly prisoner shouted the accumulating death toll to Tony Clarke and Paul Norney: '6 Brits, 8, 10, 12, Jesus is he mad or what we thought?'[43] Newspapers were made available to republicans, and on being handed *The Guardian* to which he subscribed, Kinsella was astonished by the headlines. Isolation ensured there was minimal physical threat during exercise but the regime of collecting food singly in the presence of numerous staff was an obvious flashpoint: 'You could feel the atmosphere. They were standing at the top [of stairs] glaring at you. "This is it …we are going to be slaughtered here or killed"'. Kinsella was struck heavily on the back of the neck when climbing the stairs and then held by three or four staff and briefly beaten about the face and body before being thrown back into his cell. Comments from one of his assailants made it clear that several of his personal friends had just been killed in County Down. Concerns that this presaged a cell invasion and a 'real tanking' were unfounded.[44] Ann and Eileen Gillespie simultaneously experienced what they instinctively knew to be a 'dangerous time' in H Wing, Durham.[45] Such incidents occurred behind closed doors and rarely attracted publicity. Subsequent events in Wormwood Scrubs indicated that the Home Office, possibly cushioned by a right-of-centre Conservative Cabinet, wished to reinforce its grip on the flow of information from the Dispersal System. The London prison, a site of Sinn Féin demonstrations on 26 August, became the scene of a carefully planned confrontation five days later.

Wormwood Scrubs and Minimum Use of Force Tactical Intervention, 31 August 1979

Wormwood Scrubs was convulsed by disturbances at 9.55 p.m. on 31 August 1979 when the newly embodied and still mysterious Minimum Use of Force Tactical Intervention (MUFTI) squads attacked a sit-down protest by long-term prisoners of D Wing.[46] This marked a significant escalation in prisoner's rights issues as it appeared that the authorities were not only prepared to utilize maximum force in all occasions, but had secretly formed special units for the purpose. The Prison Department emphasised the role of training selected staff in the use of advanced techniques and riot equipment that were otherwise typical of the general personnel. The more neutral term 'team' was preferred to the militaristic 'squad', although the men grouped and attired to perform the duty very much resembled their counterparts in the paramilitary RUC and Metropolitan Police 'riot squads'.[47] Evidence produced by *The Guardian* established that the first use of the then unidentified MUFTI unit had taken place in Gartree on 6 October 1978, followed by an incident in Lewes Prison on 1 November 1978 when a sit-in protest was attacked. On 11 April 1979 a MUFTI squad was sent into Hull just over a week after prison officers were prosecuted for violent conduct against prisoners in 1976.[48] It emerged that the creation of the units by means of clandestine special training and disbursement of equipment had been prompted by the major Hull riot in 1976 in which IRA prisoners had been prominent.[49] Pro-republicans in England observed that the Wormwood Scrubs melee occurred within days of the death of Mountbatten and on the third anniversary of the Hull riot.[50] *The Guardian,* on 15 September 1979, noted: 'It is also alleged that some of the officers were intent on attacking IRA prisoners in revenge for the Mountbatten killings'. D Wing protesters may well have inadvertently played into the hands of authorities who were ready and willing to assert their new prowess.[51]

Tensions had been building in Wormwood Scrubs since February 1979 when staff refused to co-operate in escorting and supervising prisoners engaged in O Level, A Level and Open University studies. This followed the 6 February 1979 attack on a warder by a 'grossly disturbed' man subsequently committed to Broadmoor under Section 72 of the Mental Health Act (1959).[52] POA demands for increased manning levels were met by the drastic closure of the 'College' (Education Centre), where many of the more ambitious prisoners had pursued qualifications. A combination of financial retrenchment and staff indifference had already curtailed work and bathing opportunities. More seriously, time allotted for infrequent family visits was reduced to forty-five minutes. The quality of sessions was also problematic and republicans contended that they were being excessively strip-searched. On 8 August 1979 an IRA man reputedly informed Governor Honey 'that if "they" [i.e. republicans] were made to strip then staff would suffer'.[53] As matters stood it was claimed that 'the attitude and tolerance of staff at all levels had been adversely affected by the IRA roof - climbing incident in 1975'.[54] A pro-Irish politically motivated prison leader attributed the ultimate attack on protesters as the culmination of six months' aggravation:

> Sensing a threat to its authority because prisoners were generally co-operating with each other – unity amongst prisoners is the greatest threat to any regime's authority-slowly but surely tightened its grip on the wing. Petty rules which the staff used to turn a blind eye to were now enforced. An increasing number of prisoners found themselves charged with breaches of prison discipline for which they were given bigger fines, spent more days in the block or lost more remission than before. Basically, a repressive campaign was run by the staff to reinforce and increase their power.[55]

Keith Gibson, Regional Director of the Prison Department's southeast region, investigated the circumstances leading to the eruption, and on 22 April 1980 finalized a report that was not published for two years, when public interest had abated:

> There were four significant factors among the prisoners in D Wing; the London gangsters, who were referred to as 'Table 4' by virtue of the table they occupied on D1 landing; the IRA faction, which was perhaps the best organised and certainly the most politically motivated group within the Wing and able to exercise a degree of influence over the third faction, the black prisoners … The group of IRA prisoners and their supporters could be relied upon to participate in any challenge to the established authority, to attempt to maximise disruption and to exploit any conflict between staff and prisoners.[56]

Gibson deduced a fourth distinct clique on the wing whom he described as 'weak inmates', including sex offenders, who coalesced for self-protection. The acknowledgement that the 'IRA men … were the most organised' in Wormwood Scrubs at the time of the 'riot' and that the black prisoners had become 'increasingly politically conscious' were major and controversial statements.[57] There were twenty-six Category A men in D Wing in late August 1979 of whom at least six, including the innocent and ailing Giuseppe Conlon, were regarded as IRA members.[58] Gerry Young and other IRA prisoners realised that staff were attempting to spark trouble between republicans and gangsters by using their master keys after lock-up to switch personal goods between ground floor lockers. An accusation of theft was a major issue in prison culture. Alert to the ploy, Young recalled: 'In the mornings they asked if we had anything of theirs and we'd ask if they had anything of ours'.[59]

The accretion of grievances inspired co-ordinated action at 8.50 a.m. on 20 August 1979 when only thirty of approximately 280 D Wing prisoners reported for work. This followed the sudden reduction of Sunday visiting hours the previous day. A *de facto* prison leadership deputation comprising IRA man Gerry Young, London gangster 'Tony' and black prisoner leader Shujaa Moshesh attempted to present a list of nine complaints to Governor Honey in person, but were prevented from doing so by his subordinate, an Assistant Governor responsible for running D Wing.[60] Striking workers were informed that their arguments could be aired if they proceeded to the workshops which started at 10.30 a.m. As per agreement, Honey received the delegation that afternoon in order to discuss the situation. Most of the issues were relatively minor, including complaints concerning repairs to damaged cookers, high canteen prices and low private cash limits. Demands for the re-opening of the Education Centre, additional 'unspecified' privileges, extended evening association and liberalization of restraints on Category A prisoners, however, had the potential to pit the Governor against the POA and Prison Department hierarchy.[61]

Two points were particularly problematic: 'That IRA prisoners should be given the same facilities for Sunday visits as other prisoners in D Wing' and a demand that 'one senior officer and two officers be taken out of the Wing'.[62] Such overtures evinced a degree of common purpose amongst the long term prisoners who not only jointly advocated a uniquely Irish political prisoner demand, but sought to impose a veto on the rostering of individual staff members regarded as divisive. The Governor rejected this attempted interference in his administrative remit, along with the call for free association until 9.00 p.m., but agreed that 'one specially supervised Category "A" visit' would be permitted every Sunday. If by no means a major breakthrough, this reform ameliorated the conditions of the disadvantaged IRA grouping who were frequently denied Sunday visits on nominal security grounds. Crucially, feedback regarding the reasonable tone of the three hours of discussion encouraged a belief in D Wing that most of the nine demands would be met and that an ultimatum of two weeks had been communicated. Gibson asserted that Honey was unaware of any such 'time limit', but soon received intelligence of the resolve of prisoners to press for concessions he had no intention of delivering on 3 September 1979.[63]

A mood of latent threat evidently contributed to the rigid handling of several disciplinary incidents. An attack by a 'Table Four' gangster on a black prisoner in the Recess of D Wing on 23 August 1979 was attributed to a dispute over 'facilities' and, as such, had territorial implications. When a second gangster menaced the Wing Assistant Governor later that day, he followed his associate into the Segregation Unit before being transferred under Circular Instruction 10/ 1974 for a 'lie-down' in Canterbury. Several organized London criminals were then openly expressing their displeasure at the small minority of prisoners who had not participated in the 20 August work strike. The Governor consequently seized the opportunity to weaken their 'faction' by ghosting a further three on the evening of 24 August.[64] Three IRA men were due to be transferred on the evening of 31 August, but the plan was overtaken by events as the prisoners had determined that morning to mount a peaceful protest.[65] Prisoners had interpreted both actual and planned moves as contravening a strike resolution, understanding that none of those involved in the stoppages would be 'shanghaied'.[66]

If, as Gibson maintained, IRA and black prisoners attempted to fill the 'power vacuum' created by the temporary decimation of 'Table Four', no notable physical hostility manifested prior to 31 August 1979. Many influential and organized English criminals had been moved out and their IRA and black associates were conscious of their ongoing role in showing a united front to the authorities.[67] Gerry Young noted that 'other prisoners were coming to us and asking for back up'.[68] Stevie Nordone forcefully rejected claims that the IRA 'sought to obtain a degree of institutional power within the wing' or had been vying with others at the time in question.[69] The same spurious argument had been made in relation to Hull in 1976 when the authorities sought explanations of riot causation that exculpated the personnel and policies of the Prison Department. The Louth IRA man countered in April 1982: 'Our strength of organisation never has or never will be used to intimidate, pressurise or coerce any single or group of social prisoners … We show solidarity with all prisoners who struggle for better conditions in prison. We have a deep sense of solidarity with black prisoners because of the way they in particular are abused and maltreated by the large racist and fascist element within the Prison Officers Association'.[70] Moshesh, leader of the organized black prisoners in Wormwood Scrubs, dismissed Gibson's theory of a 'struggle for power' as 'a blatant lie'.[71]

The immediate trigger of the protest on 31 August 1979 was dissatisfaction with the continued disrepair of two electric cookers set aside for the use of the prisoners. This followed the confiscation that morning of improvised gym equipment from cells which staff may have feared could be used offensively.[72] An alternate explanation accepted by Irish republicans and black prisoners was that the senior staff incited rather than pre-empted a confrontation by provoking the most powerful prison groupings. To a suspicious mind, the seizure of property with combat utility lessened the ability of prisoners to defend themselves from an attack from staff which, if not carefully planned, was by no means spontaneous. The unprecedented scale of the MUFTI deployment that evening, and the unusual aggression displayed during and after the protest lent credence to sinister interpretations.

By 2.15 p.m. the Governor received confirmation from informers assisting the Security Principal Officer that prisoners in D Wing intended to mount a protest at 5.00 p.m. This corroborated intelligence that had been available since 1.30 p.m. and suggested the 'transfer of three IRA Category "A" prisoners' under CI 10/ 1974. Nearby Shepherds Bush Police Station was requested to mount 'low profile' surveillance on the 'external perimeter', freeing the maximum number of prison staff to attend to matters within its walls.[73] The Security Principal Officer informed Prison Department HQ, and at 3.30 p.m. the Governor contacted the Deputy Regional Director (Operations) to mobilize 'stand-by staff' from other Greater London - area prisons. This resulted in the assembly of MUFTI forces in Brixton (twenty-seven) and Wandsworth (nineteen), who were additionally reinforced by staff fully, partly or still untrained in the new counter-riot techniques from Pentonville (eleven), Coldingley (nine), Latchmere House (eighteen) and Ashford (twenty-five).[74] Ordinary Wormwood Scrubs personnel coming off their shift were retained in the complex from 4.30 a.m. By 5.16 a.m., A, B and C Wings were locked down after dinner, the majority of their staff were placed on 'stand-by for re-deployment' into D Wing. This generated a pool of another 248 reinforcements, including thirty-seven men rested ahead of night duty, exclusive of those already inside D Wing.[75]

Oblivious English prisoners, meanwhile, asked the IRA contingent to join a 'sit-down' after mealtime in order to disrupt lockup. This was readily agreed. Giuseppe 'Old Joe' Conlon was placed in his cell by fellow Irishmen while the actual IRA men in the prison congregated with those who protested from 5.00 p.m.[76] Most of the 280 men on the wing were involved; a heterogeneous group which contained 162 jailed for 'murder or some other act of homicide' and another thirty-five who had committed violent offences.[77] Twenty-one were regarded as 'mentally ill'.[78] Around 110 prisoners who had not already departed the communal areas of the wing simply ignored the PA announcement ordering them to 'clear the ones' and re-enter their cells for lock-up. Some reputedly responded with derisory jeers and many were observed congregating in a sector of the D1 landing. By 5.30 p.m. Governor Honey made an urgent request to the Deputy Regional Director (Operations) to assemble the London area MUFTI in the Administration Block of Wormwood Scrubs, which occurred at around 8.00 p.m.[79]

Matters had by then disimproved. At around 6.00 p.m. the Governor informed the Senior Assistant Governor that he would not receive a three-man prisoner delegation who wished to restate the demands delivered to him on 20 August. This created an impasse exacerbated by the extraordinary decision reached around 7.30 p.m. to unlock all prisoners who had not received their dinner or who had complied with earlier orders to go to their cells. This enabled scores of additional men to mingle with those already mounting the sit-down.[80] The gathering, however, was initially peaceful and the standard complement of prison officers and two Assistant Governors, Ritchie and Gregory-Smith, felt sufficiently confident of their personal safety to remain *in situ*. A number of staff members left the area around 7.00 p.m. for a scheduled rest period and no inkling of impending violence was in the air within the wing. Prisoners observed the arrival of twenty extra staff posted on the higher landings around 9.00 p.m. and it transpired that they had orders to keep the stairways open to provide access for the MUFTI.[81] Moshesh recalled the initially 'lighthearted' atmosphere which darkened 'when it was noticed that every five minutes or so two screws would come into the wing and take up a position around each landing office. Although our numbers had whittled away, there was still about 130 of us situated at one end of the wing but distributed on all four landings'. He and others understood from conversations with an Assistant Governor that a Home Office representative would make an appearance at 10.00 p.m.[82] Shane Paul O'Doherty was positioned on the fourth floor of the wing and noticed the sudden staff mobilization. He warned Gerry Conlon, whom he had previously endeavoured to assist in his campaign for exoneration, that 'there was an army of screws in riot gear packed into C Wing exercise yard'. The men had heard rumours of 'screws being bussed in' but expected renewed dialogue backed by threat ahead of all - out attack: 'Suddenly there was a terrifying noise, a hundred men all yelling together'.[83]

It was claimed that an Assistant Governor 'wrongly' informed prisoners at 10.00 p.m. that the Chief Officer was going to address the protesters. In fact, the men were not given a final warning over the PA to go to their cells, an incredible oversight explained by uncredited assertions that alarms had been sounded and the support teams feared for the safety of their colleagues inside the wing. Gibson ascertained that an Assistant Governor Class II was only informed by telephone 'just before 22.00 hours' that the Chief Officer and 'staff reinforcements' were *en route* to D Wing 'to order the demonstrators to disperse to their cells'.[84] Instead, at 10.03 p.m., at least three MUFTI teams drawn from six prisons and bolstered by 'untrained' local staff moved through the uproar of locked down C Wing and other access points into D Wing.[85] A MUFTI squad member recalled:

> We were lined up outside the Wing. The Chief went in. There was an awful lot of noise by then, outside. It is hard to put it across. We were standing outside, but the noise was outside with us. I suppose they were up at the windows. Again, I did not look. I just kept my head firmly screwed to the front and down in my collar. The Chief went in. There was a great big roar from somewhere – I am pretty sure it was from inside the Wing. The gates were thrown open and someone was shouting 'Get in. Get in'.[86]

The situation appeared concerted and brutal as helmeted MUFTI teams in heavy brown overalls and carrying shields and four - foot long 'riot staves' appeared in three gateways. They were the vanguard of less formidable contingents of 'ordinary' uniformed prison officers who rushed behind. They immediately batoned the surprised prisoners at random in what seemed a planned operation, despite official claims, backed by Gibson, that two MUFTI teams did not receive direct orders to 'enter the fray'. Gibson contended that 'sections and teams did not remain together as coherent units and individual officers left their sections and acted independently'.[87] Pat Hackett maintained that 'a lot of the prison officers had scarves around their faces so as they wouldn't be recognized ... and their [personnel] numbers gone'. He was rapidly ushered away from a table and into a ground floor cell where English associates with whom he took educational classes banged the door shut: 'The MUFTI squad were coming onto the wing ... when they arrived at the door, they were beating the hell out of the door with these big staves ... they were shouting "Get Mountbatten's killers!"'[88] Belfast republican Gerry Young recalled: '[It was] an entirely peaceful protest until they sent the MUFTI squad in. We were peaceful; we were just refusing to bunk up. They could have negotiated their way out of it very, very easily. They chose not to, they chose to send the MUFTI squad in ... helmets, visors, pads, a pretty fierce crew'.[89] Eyewitnesses claimed 'squads of warders came in, armed with batons, shields, helmets and padded jackets. The prisoners were unable to escape the onrush as the cell doors were locked ... some 'D' wing warders [on normal duty] ... unlocked cell doors to enable prisoners to escape [inside]'.[90] Moshesh watched as the MUFTI 'brutally assaulted every prisoner who had the extreme misfortune of being caught within their range. Within seconds the wing was in chaos, uproar and confusion'.[91] At least seven minutes of intense onslaught occurred in what the IRA and British prisoner advocates believed was an intentional demonstration of staff impunity.[92]

Conlon and others ran for the stairs leading to their cells: 'There was panic and pandemonium, the handrails on the narrow stairs were bending under the weight of men trying to get out of the way. The screws had a battle-cry, "Get the niggers! Get the Irish!"'[93] Before being dragged from a friend's cell by the hair, he saw Billy Power of the Birmingham Six being 'ambushed ... just picked up and kicked like a football along the threes, howling and screaming at the pain ... the ground floor was awash with blood'.[94] A Polish prisoner was one of a number of injured men 'slung' at random into Hackett's hitherto empty cell, which he had not been able to reach amidst the confusion. On returning he found there was 'blood everywhere, on the bed, on the floor, on the walls, the ceilings and everything'.[95] When checked by disciplined local staff later that evening, Hackett had to convince them that he had not been badly hurt. With some trepidation he acquiesced to their request to step out of his cell and was surprised on walking through two lines of prison officers that 'they never laid a hand on me'. Later he watched through his door spy hole as a Security Officer smashed his radio and sizeable quantities of eggs stored by prisoners in presses near the tables.[96]

Approximately sixty prisoners were hurt in the one-sided assault in contradiction of initial reports which variously claimed that none or just five had been injured.[97] Such was the cacophony echoing from the complex that nurses accommodated in nearby Hammersmith Hospital shouted over to the prison seeking news.[98] One of those present averred 'the riot squad went mad' and others described prisoners running a gauntlet of stave - wielding prison officers.[99] Many were isolated by virtue of being 'trapped' on the landings, particularly the higher levels of D3 and D4.[100] Persistent claims of the existence of a 'hard core ... not more than twenty-five men' who wished to engage in violence, and photographs of items regarded as weapons, did not accord with the casualty ratio and fact that there had been no physical confrontation prior to the entry of the MUFTI.[101] Roy Walsh had been among those who immediately ascended to D4 landing: 'After about two minutes I was forced to run a gauntlet of club - wielding prison officers ... at no time was I armed nor did I offer any resistance. I was struck several times on both shoulders and back, my right hand was bruised, my elbows were skinned and there was a cut on my left arm'. Forced into a cell with ten others, he was soon returned to his own where his injuries were noted.[102] Journalist David Beresford ascertained that a 'few warders' who were not involved in the attack opened cells for the beleaguered prisoners. Less sympathetic staff allegedly vented their anger by destroying taxpayer - funded recreation equipment and the limited private property stored by prisoners in temporary lockers on D1.[103] This aberrant escalation, unconnected with a mission to recover control, had also occurred in the aftermath of the Hull riot as the MUTTI members working in London must have known. Staff were permitted to exit the prison without being debriefed, an irregular circumstance that complicated police investigations.[104]

Republican sources succinctly referred to the August 1979 episode as a 'riot by warders'.[105] Sinn Féin acknowledged that all those held in D Wing Wormwood Scrubs were being neglected but argued that matters were 'even worse for the victimised political prisoners'.[106] At least four IRA men were physically injured, but only two with any reported degree of seriousness. Ron Lynch sustained a bloody scalp wound that required stitching.[107] It was not widely realised that Gerry Young also sustained a gash to the head that warranted stitches but went untreated. Two of his damaged fingers, a common result of instinctive protection of an endangered skull, were crudely strapped together with tape.[108] Roy Walsh was glimpsed with 'cuts on his head and blood on his clothes' when being removed from the prison along with Ron Lynch and 'Birmingham Six' prisoner Billy Power, who had received 'a few blows'.[109] Gerry Conlon, who had been dragged down stairs and kicked, saw blood seeping through a white sheet placed over one of the injured IRA men on a stretcher and feared he had been killed.[110] This was Stevie Nordone. Moshesh estimated that sixty-nine men needed stitches.[111]

A total of 143 prisoners were accused of committing 160 'riot' related offences, including 136 with the easily proven offence of disobeying a lawful order.[112] Thirty-three were quickly shifted to other prisons, spreading their insight into what had taken place among the prison population. Dispersion, paradoxically, stymied the task of systematic investigation by state officials.[113] It was subsequently considered unusual that the Board of Visitors did not commence its examination of what had occurred until 2 September.[114] Ron Lynch, who received head injuries when attacked on the floor, lost one month's remission. Other IRA men were 'ghosted' on lie-downs: Gerry Young was sent to Durham, Stevie Nordone to Strangeways, Roy Walsh to Wandsworth and Phil Sheridan to Winchester.[115] By 10 September, 122 prisoners were subjected to disciplinary charges and twenty-two punished by terms in 'segregation units'.[116] Local press accounts foregrounded the presence of 'murderers and terrorists' among those sanctioned in a manner which implied their guilt.[117] In the absence of accurate information, the assumption proved pervasive. An application for Emergency Civil Aid Certificate (aka 'legal aid') by Walsh was rejected on 19 October 1979 on the grounds that it was financially unjustifiable and that he had not only 'failed to establish any case in law', but was regarded as 'the author' of his 'own misfortune'.[118] When, on 20 November 1979, the Area Committee in Brighton 'appeared disposed to agree that the Local Committee had been wrong' in ascribing personal culpability to both Roy Walsh and Gerry Conlon, appeals against their separate negative legal aid grant decisions were dismissed.[119]

In an unsettling development at Wormwood Scrubs, all D Wing visits were cancelled until 13 September, and prisoners were denied access to chaplains, psychologists and probation officers. The authorities evidently sought to underline their ascendancy before reportage of what had occurred obliged restraint. The Public Relations Branch of the Home Office had been in contact with an Assistant Governor Class I around 10.20 p.m. on 31 August 1979, and although it was accepted that a factually incorrect estimate of injuries to prisoners was then related, Gibson found 'no record of the conversation' in official documentation.[120] Young was instinctively cautious in the days following the MUFTI attack when staff insisted that only two men at a time could use the shower block. He carried a Stanley blade for protection in case there was any attempted repetition of the brutalities of Hull in 1976 of which he had learned from eye-witnesses.[121] Relatives of 'Birmingham Six' prisoner Billy Power were among those refused entry to Wormwood Scrubs on 8 September during the lock-down period. The family of Pat Hackett were also turned away on 12 September 1979, the day before the quarantine expired.[122] Sr. Clarke visited Ron Lynch on 17 September 1979 along with his sister, Attracta Harkins, and others. Sr. Clarke spoke to the Cavan man and noted: 'He did not resist. He was just hit and put his hands up to protect his head. He was black and blue on his arms, thighs and legs'.[123] Lynch sustained two cuts to his head and told his visitors that 'the screws on the wing were as surprised as the prisoners' when the MUFTI attacked.[124] The drama in London distracted from an important step taken by Alastair Logan, who on 12 September 1979 served a writ on the Home Office in relation to the assaults inflicted on six IRA men in Albany in September 1976.[125]

Industrial disputes in 1979 promoted militancy within the POA. At an organizational level the Association disdained the specialized prison services which, according to the *Times*, rendered 'officers fearful that their job will be reduced to that of a turnkey'.[126] Fewer recruits were entering from the military along with a correspondingly higher input of persons with no prior experience of strictly disciplined hierarchy. It was assumed that prisoners, moreover, would infer from the show of force in London that they remained isolated and vulnerable, even if a string of ECHR decisions told in their favour. A reassessment of the situation by PROP in 1980 queried whether Governor Honey had lost control of elements of his staff. The theory seemed to explain English man Doug Wakefield's experience of intimidation and solitary confinement in late 1977, contrary to the express wishes of the Governor.[127] Kilroy-Silk MP averred that the prison was 'not controlled by the Prison Department but was run by prison officers for months after their clash with prisoners'.[128]

The Howard League for Penal Reform was dissatisfied by official commentary. Director Martin Wright called for an inquiry on 3 October 1979, as did PROP on 14 December 1979.[129] PROP had picketed the prison as early as 2 September 1979 to rebut the patently false Home Office statement that 'no injuries to prisoners or staff' had occurred.[130] On 10 September 1979 original claims of zero injuries were revised to admit that five prisoners had received 'very minor' abrasions. The ban on family visits was then described, equally disingenuously, as 'routine'.[131] The Prison Department did not obtain the Governor's report required under Standing Orders until 25 September, which, despite two supplementary documents and a meeting, 'no satisfactory account emerged'.[132] Eventually, it was conceded that fifty-four prisoners and eleven prison officers had been injured in the 'incident' at Wormwood Scrubs.[133] Alex Lyon, Labour MP for York and a former Home Office minister, later criticised the 'cloak of secrecy and fear' which had engulfed the truth of what had taken place in London's largest prison. He chaired the Labour Campaign for Criminal

Justice and endorsed prisoner claims of having been 'attacked' in the course of a 'peaceful demonstration' by 'a specially equipped squad of prison officers'.[134] Kenneth Daniel, General Secretary of the POA, admitted such a unit existed on 14 December 1979 and that its formation had been inspired by the Hull riot in 1976, when a perceived need for training in 'the handling of a disturbance which could ... develop into serious violence'.[135]

Lyon had a direct role in assessing the Prison Service arising from his membership of the House of Commons Home Office Affairs Committee, which, in November 1980, reviewed the tempestuous 'session' of 1979–80. He confronted Dennis Trevelyan, Director General of the Prison Department, with the results of his 'own investigations' into the Wormwood Scrubs 'riot', which controversially suggested that 'the cause of the difficulties was a limited number of very difficult prisoners, most of whom were Irish. The Prison Governor and the staff know it and you do not'.[136] The well-informed Lyon believed that the conflict in Ireland had yielded an IRA contingent whose presence in Wormwood Scrubs and elsewhere undermined the original concept and administrative model of the Dispersal System. He averred in the Commons on 10 November 1980:

> It is fairly certain, is it not, since the beginning of the difficulties in Northern Ireland and the more hardline prisoners you have got arising from the terrorist activities in the country [England], that the regimes in some prisons have noticeably hardened and created difficulties for prison staff? ... A number of very difficult prisoners who have thereby caused a change in the attitude of staff and prison governors in relation to things like the provision of free time, association or work, and where the difficulties have arisen they have arisen from a particular number of very difficult prisoners, some of whom are long-term violent types but a great many of whom seem to be people in prison because they have committed terrorist crimes.[137]

KJ Neale, Director of Regimes and Services, responded that Lyon's comments were 'true in operational terms' and that 'strain' had indeed been experienced. Neale insisted that the Prison Department maintained its commitment to enrich the educational and industrial 'opportunities' for long term prisoners. DER Faulkner, Director of Operational Policy, Prison Department, claimed to be 'not sure' if 'regimes have suffered as a result' but that his staff had 'tried to maintain the [original] regime'.[138] In 1980 Faulkner's colleague Neale visited the then pariah state of Turkey as part of a Council of Europe-backed initiative to provide 'technical assistance in regard to the development of penal environment and the problems of dealing with high-risk prisoners'.[139] This obviously extended to the IRA, the closest analogue of the violent separatist Kurdish PKK paramilitaries who ultimately emulated imprisoned Irish republicans by mounting protracted staged fasts to death. The PKK were specifically inspired by the 1981 hunger strike in Long Kesh, which was referenced during their major protests later in the decade.[140]

The high status and influence of Neale within the Prison Department was signalled by reports that he and Trevelyan had in July 1980 participated in a Directors of Penal Administration conference when the agenda for the successive 1981 session was set down. Neale was 'then given responsibility for reviewing the Standard Minimum Rules, preparing a provisional prospectus for the newly-formed European Committee on Co-operation in Prison Affairs, with Mr Shapland, Director of Prison Psychological Services, also preparing material for the 1981 session on developing specialisms in penal regimes'.[141] Trevelyan and Neale formed part of a Home Office delegation to Caracas, Venezuela, when the United Nations 6th Quinquennial Congress on the Treatment of Offenders and the Prevention of Crime was convened.[142] The experience, if not also perceived prowess of the Prison Department of England and Wales in confronting the challenges of politically motivated prisoners in their jurisdiction, was evidently valued far beyond the contested zone of Ireland and Britain.

The Howard League registered its concern at the dismissal of voluntary workers in Wormwood Scrubs who had criticized the response to a peaceful protest. Jonathan Pollitzer, a 'prison visitor' since 1976, was barred for taking part in a TV story on the 'riot'. Kay Douglas-Scott was suspended ahead of planned dismissal for speaking out.[143] One of those injured in the MUFTI assault was a man seen on a regular basis by Pollitzer who called for an independent enquiry and claimed that 'the Home Office has no public conscience whatever'.[144] Other prisons witnessed unusual behaviour by staff, and in December 1979 the outcry over a string of aberrant occurrences in Wormwood Scrubs coincided with situations in Wakefield, Styal and Broadmoor, where probation officers, visitors and welfare workers were denied entry. The exclusion of civilian and unpaid staff from several English jails was egregious and naturally viewed as a by-product of the controversy in London's main penal institution. A conclusive state - level inquiry was clearly required.[145]

William Whitelaw claimed in October 1979 that the Regional Director of the Prison Department's south-east region, Keith Gibson, had begun an investigation into an 'act of concerted indiscipline' and its aftermath. Scotland Yard initially declined to proceed until the Home Office had issued its own findings, but on 28 January 1980 received instruction from Whitelaw to conduct an inquiry.[146] This input was reaffirmed on 28 February 1980 in response to Gibson's assertion to the Home Office that he had been 'unable to make progress' owing to the emergence of *prima facie* evidence of 'criminal assaults'.[147] Labour MP Robert Kilroy-Silk, a member of the All-Party Penal Affairs Group, was then pressuring Whitelaw in the Commons.[148] The Home Secretary received the *Gibson Report* on 22 April 1980, which remained conveniently unpublished on the advice of the DPP, owing to concurrent police enquiries, until February 1982.[149] Police investigations raised issues in relation to ten unnamed prison officers whom, in December 1981, DPP Sir Thomas Hetherington, elected not to bring to court.[150] Gibson was ordered in the course of the month to 'write his report without completing his inquiries'.[151] The *subjudice* findings of the official inquiry by Detective Chief Superintendent Colin Wood were not released until 24 February 1982, a calming interval, when it was admitted that individual members of the local branch of the POA had adopted a 'punitive attitude towards prisoners'. It was then accepted that many 'incorrect statements' had been released which were 'not subsequently corrected'. The DPP was disinclined to revisit the question, which would have entailed politically and legally unwelcome assessment of the specifics of the affair and its underlying causation. Whitelaw's positive assurance that Prison Service Director General Dennis Trevelyan had taken action to reform areas of concern signalled that the Home Office wished to draw a line under the embarrassing episode.[152] All authoritative forums with oversight of the penal system, therefore, were united by early 1982 in their disengagement from a major episode with potential repercussions for the entire Dispersal System. Notwithstanding this studied detachment, the total absence of Wormwood Scrubs 'riot' incidents in the interim suggested that the challenge of imposing control on well-organized political and criminal prisoners was being approached in a subtler and more centrally directed fashion.[153]

NOTES

1. *Irish political prisoners*, p. 75.
2. Information of Eddie O'Neill, Clones, 3 August 2007.
3. *Irish Times*, 27 June 1979.
4. McLaughlin, *Inside an English jail*, p. 53.
5. *Report on the work of the Prison Department, 1978* (London, 1979), p. 40. According to the Home Office: 'The estimated loss on trading account in 1978–79 amounted to £4.9 million compared with a loss of £2.8 million in 1977–78', a differential explained in part by the deferment of the annual review of certain goods credited to the Prison Department. Ibid. The 'Prindus' brand was replaced with 'Prison Service Industries and Farms' in 1984. *HC Deb 31 October 1984 vol 65 cc983–4W*. PSIF also replaced the title Directorate of Industries and Farms. *Report on the work of the Prison Department, 1984/ 85* (London, 1985), p. 45.
6. *Irish Times*, 27 June 1979.
7. *AP/RN*, 7 July 1979.
8. Plotnikoff, *Prison Rules*, p. 65. Rule 29 (2) permitted the Home Secretary to issue 'direction' on prisoner access to education. Ibid.
9. *HC Deb 27 June 1979 vol 969 cc437*.
10. *Report on the Administration of the Prison Service, 1980*, p. 9.
11. *HC Deb 27 June 1979 vol 969 cc437*.
12. Callan, *Gartree*, p. 52.
13. McLaughlin, *Inside an English jail*, p. 53.
14. McLaughlin, *Inside an English jail*, p. 53.
15. McLaughlin, *Inside an English jail*, p. 54.
16. Eddie O'Neill, 23 July 2006.
17. Eddie O'Neill, 23 July 2006.

18. *IRIS*, 21 July 1979. Leeds contained a mere sixteen baths for 1,200 prisoners. *Times*, 26 March 1982.
19. *AP/RN*, 14 July 1979.
20. *IRIS*, 21 July 1979. For racism issue see *Times*, 6 September 1982. Chelmsford was badly damaged by fire on 20 March 1978, obliging the relocation of 246 prisoners. *Report of the work of the Prison Department, 1978*, p. 21. In 1983 Sir James Hennessy observed that Standing Orders, but not *Prison Rules*, described 'stripped rooms' as places 'available either to a medical officer or the governor for detaining an inmate who is violent, destroying property, etc ... normally ordinary cells from which the furniture is removed as the need arises. They usually contain a mattress on which the inmate may lie'. *Report of Her Majesty's Chief Inspector of Prisons, 1982*, p. 21. The Prison Reform Trust identified three main variants utilized under Rule 45: 'Three separately designated kinds of cell are used to confine prisoners deemed to be in need of physical restraint and isolation: the stripped cell (usually an ordinary cell equipped only with a mattress); the special cell (usually equipped with a double door, soundproofing and furniture which cannot cause injury); and the protected room (with a double door, soundproofing, padded walls, and no furniture)'. Plotnikoff, *Prison Rules*, p. 85.
21. *AP/RN*, 14 July 1979.
22. *Daily Telegraph*, 12 November 1979. See also Ibid., 26 June 1980.
23. *AP/RN*, 18 August 1979. For the ban see *Irish Times*, 4 August 1979. Lords Brockway, Kilbracken, and Milford supported the rally, as did the Association for Legal Justice and Connolly Association. Ibid.
24. *FRFI*, September 1982, p. 11.
25. Helen Stevens, 'Building an anti-war movement in Britain' in *AP/RN*, 18 August 1979.
26. *AP/RN*, 4 September 1979. For Hackett's ordeal in Brixton see Bridget Hackett and Family to the Editor, *Irish Press*, 1 February 1977.
27. Pat Hackett, 21 December 2007.
28. Pat Hackett, 21 December 2007. See also O'Donnell, *Special Category*, I, pp. 379–84.
29. Gerry Young, 8 March 2008.
30. Pat Hackett, 21 December 2007.
31. See *Lost Lives*, pp. 793–5. The remote controlled bomb also fatally wounded four civilians. Ibid.
32. Barzilay, *British army in Ulster*, IV, pp. 81–92. The Warrenpoint attack killed sixteen identified paratroopers. The C/O of the 1st Queen's Own Highlanders was also killed along with his radioman. In the aftermath of the explosion British troops shot wildly across the border killing a holidaying civilian who worked in Buckingham Palace. *Lost Lives*, pp. 797–8. See also Hamill, *The Army*, pp. 249–50. An RUC officer who attended a meeting with senior Gardai in Dublin Castle in 1980 was informed that Taoiseach Lynch regarded Warrenpoint as 'a political crime' and that inter-police cooperation had been prohibited. There was unease within the RUC that South Armagh men Brendan Burns, a senior IRA bomb-maker, and Joe Brennan, were charged with motoring offences 'despite traces of explosives being found on them'. *Irish News*, 14 March 2012.
33. Barzilay, *British army in Ulster*, IV, pp. 93–4.
34. *Time Out*, 10–16 August 1979.
35. Lynch cited in Keogh, *Lynch*, p. 419. Lynch's description of Mountbatten as a person with a 'remarkable record of service to mankind' would have found no favour in late 1940s India or Pakistan. A man who had been assigned twenty-four bodyguards at the expense of the Irish taxpayer in 1974 was clearly unwelcome in Sligo. Cited in Ibid., p. 419.
36. 'Behind closed doors', RTE One, 1 January 2010.
37. See Margaret Unwin, 'London and Dublin failed to focus on loyalist violence', *Irish Times*, 8 October 2013, p. 16. The formalization of upgraded links followed the Dublin/ Monaghan bombings in August 1974 in which British Intelligence had been implicated, and despite the fact that senior MI6 officer Michael Oatley and Minister for State Stan Orme had personally interacted with the UVF leadership before and after the worst anti-civilian attacks of the Troubles. Ibid.
38. Hugh Doherty, 23 June 2006.
39. Paul Burns, *A fighting spirit* (London, 2010), p. 66.
40. Eddie Butler, 21 December 2007. Butler spent ten months in Winson Green: 'You'd be locked up twenty-three hours a day. You got an hour's exercise, if it was fine, if it was raining you didn't. You got a shower once a week. Change of clothes once a week. Maybe library once a week for a few books. You had a radio'. Ibid. Three Winson Green staff were tried in March 1982 for the murder of prisoner Barry Prosser on 18 August 1980. *Times*, 6 and 17 March 1982 and *HC Deb 20 October 1981 vol 10 c92W*. In April 1982 Birmingham Six prisoner Billy Power, then in Wormwood Scrubs, claimed that the persons suspected of killing Prosser 'were the same warders involved in assaulting Irish POWs' in 1974. *AP/RN*, 29 April 1982. See also Richard Smith, 'Deaths in prison' in *British Medical Journal*, vol. 288, 21 January 1984, p. 209 and *FRFI*, February 1983, p. 9.
41. Eddie O'Neill, 19 July 2008.
42. Joe O'Connell, 7 June 2008.
43. Tony Clarke, 9 March 2008.

44. Sean Kinsella, 3 August 2008.
45. Ann and Eileen Gillespie, 7 June 2008.
46. *AP/RN*, 8 September 1979. In July 1980 the official account of the year 1979 acknowledged that the Wormwood Scrubs incident 'was the first occasion on which the deployment of such teams received publicity, although ... they have been used successfully to restore order at other establishments both before and after 31 August [1979] *Report of the work of the Prison Department, 1979*, p. 19.
47. *Disturbance in D Wing*, pp. 4, 9–10.
48. *IRIS*, 10 November 1979 and *Guardian*, 2 November 1979.
49. *Times*, 22 November 1988.
50. *Hands off Ireland!*, No. 9, November 1979, p. 7.
51. *Guardian*, 15 September 1979. Circular Instruction 12/79, issued in April 1979, came into force in the autumn, limiting a prisoner's private funds to £60 per annum. This was insufficient to cover minor luxuries and sundry purchases within the prison. Long-term prisoners had not been hitherto curtailed in the amount they could spend or nature of purchases, a boon some exploited to assist short-term prisoners. The new regulation was unpopular, as was another which prohibited personal underwear and footwear. Sr. Clarke, 'Wormwood Scrubs', Clarke Papers (COFLA). The Home Office claimed the reforms were intended to bring 'standardization' of personal possessions in Dispersal prisons, a view criticized by the Howard League. *Guardian*, 11 September 1979.
52. *Disturbance in D Wing*, p. 16.
53. *Disturbance in D Wing*, p. 17.
54. *Disturbance in D Wing*, p. 39.
55. Shujaa Moshesh, 'MUFTI riot at Wormwood Scrubs, A prisoner's account' in *FRFI*, June 1982, p. 11.
56. *Disturbance in D Wing*, p. 16. Gibson reported: 'There is no evidence that the demonstrations on 20 and 31 August [1979] were initiated or led by the IRA or any other single power group. However, it is clear that three dominant groups; the gangsters, the IRA and the black faction, had been instrumental in creating an atmosphere of unrest and instability in which prisoners were encouraged to challenge the authority of management and staff'. Ibid., p. 38. For claims of anti-black racism in C Wing in 1979 see *FRFI*, January/ February 1980.
57. *Guardian*, 25 February 1982.
58. *Disturbance in D Wing*, p. 4.
59. Gerry Young, 8 March 2008.
60. Moshesh, 'MUFTI riot' in *FRFI*, June 1982, p. 11.
61. *Disturbance in D Wing*, pp. 17–18.
62. *Disturbance in D Wing*, p. 18.
63. *Disturbance in D Wing*, p. 18.
64. *Disturbance in D Wing*, p. 19. Canterbury held a daily average of 373 prisoners but as many as 406 in the course of 1979. *Report on the work of the Prison Department, 1979*, p. 59.
65. *Disturbance in D Wing*, p. 20.
66. Moshesh, 'MUFTI riot' in *FRFI*, June 1982, p. 11.
67. *Guardian*, 25 February 1982.
68. Gerry Young, 8 March 2008.
69. Stephen Nordone to the Editor, *AP/RN*, 1 April 1982. Nordone claimed that 'about 70' D Wing prisoners took part in the protest. Ibid. See also Stephen Nordone to the Editor, *FRFI*, May 1982, p. 13.
70. Nordone to the Editor, *AP/RN*, 1 April 1982.
71. Moshesh, 'MUFTI riot' in *FRFI*, June 1982, p. 11.
72. *Disturbance in D Wing*, p. 20. The 'equipment' was typically wooden broom handles with plastic containers tied to each end holding either water or sand. Ibid.
73. *Disturbance in D Wing*, p. 20.
74. *Disturbance in D Wing*, pp. 21–22 and *Guardian*, 25 February 1982.
75. *Disturbance in D Wing*, p. 21.
76. Gerry Young, 8 March 2008. Giuseppe Conlon remained in his cell during the protest but was nonetheless deprived in its aftermath of the heating element he used to prepare his medical Complan diet. Clarke, *No faith*, p. 127.
77. *Times*, 25 February 1982.
78. *Guardian*, 25 February 1982.
79. *Disturbance in D Wing*, pp. 21–22.
80. *Disturbance in D Wing*, p. 23.
81. *Disturbance in D Wing*, p. 25.
82. Moshesh, 'MUFTI riot' in *FRFI*, June 1982, p. 11.
83. Conlon, *Proved Innocent*, p. 187.
84. *Disturbance in D Wing*, p. 25.

85. *Guardian*, 25 February 1982. For details of the specific tasking and actions of the various elements see *Disturbance in D Wing*, pp. 24–25.
86. *Disturbance in D Wing*, pp. 26–27.
87. Cited in *Guardian*, 25 February 1982.
88. Pat Hackett, 21 December 2007.
89. Gerry Young, 8 March 2008.
90. *AP/RN*, 18 September 1979.
91. Moshesh, 'MUFTI riot' in *FRFI*, June 1982, p. 11.
92. Wakefield, *Thousand days*, Appendix 3, p. 37 and Coggan and Walker, *Deaths in British prisons*, p. 193. In January 1979 the IRA PRO in Wormwood Scrubs understood that staff were irritated to have not received the 40 per cent pay increase granted to police in 1978. They were also deemed to harbour an anti-Irish and racist element. See PRO Irish Republican Prisoners of War to the Editor, January 1979 in *Hands off Ireland!*, No. 7, April 1979, p. 22.
93. Conlon, *Proved Innocent*, p. 187.
94. Conlon, *Proved Innocent*, p. 188.
95. Pat Hackett, 21 December 2007.
96. Pat Hackett, 21 December 2007.
97. *Irish Times*, 19 May 1980 and *Times*, 25 February 1982. Eleven prison officers were injured, evidently from been accidentally struck by the batons of their colleagues. *Times*, 25 June 1980. Gibson noted: 'It has being claimed that some prisoners who were not offering resistance were also struck with staves as the Mufti officers went past and that officers used more than minimum force necessary to return prisoners to cellular conditions'. *Disturbance in D Wing*, p. 27.
98. Conlon, *Proved Innocent*, p. 189.
99. Quoted in *Hands off Ireland!*, No. 9, November 1979, p. 7.
100. *Guardian*, 25 February 1982.
101. *Disturbance in D Wing*, p. 41.
102. Roy Walsh to the Secretary of State, 20 September 1979, Private Collection (Walsh).
103. *Guardian*, 15 September 1979. The ALJ in January 1975 secured affidavits which claimed that a Garda Superintendent had given orders for the systematic destruction of private property owned by IRA prisoners in Portlaoise. Riot - clad Gardai allegedly spent hours on the night of 30 December 1974 destroying radios, photographs, books, letters and other personal items. *Irish Times*, 28 and 31 January 1975.
104. *Times*, 25 February 1982.
105. *IRIS*, 10 November 1979.
106. *AP/RN*, 4 September 1979. Sinn Féin alleged that on 10 October 1979 four IRA prisoners sent from Portlaoise to the Curragh Military Hospital were roughed up and threatened by soldiers to such an extent that they requested to be returned to Laois prior to treatment. Ibid., 27 October 1979.
107. *AP/RN*, 27 October 1979.
108. Gerry Young, 8 March 2008.
109. Sr. Clarke, 'Wormwood Scrub notes', Clarke Papers (COFLA).
110. Information of Gerry Conlon, New York, 26 October 2013.
111. Moshesh, 'MUFTI riot' in *FRFI*, June 1982, p. 11.
112. *Disturbance in D Wing*, p. 33.
113. *HC Deb 15 November 1979 vol 973 cc713–4W*.
114. *HC Deb 30 November 1979 vol 974 c811W*.
115. *Hands off Ireland!*, No. 9, November 1979, p. 7. Sheridan was released and deported to Dublin in September 1980. Sr. Clarke, 'Phil Sheridan', Clarke Papers (COFLA). In an article carried by *AP/RN* Sheridan claimed that the disruption of ghosting within the Dispersal System had encouraged Irish prisoners to undertake self-directed education. He reported that 'informal lectures' and discussions were held by the IRA men to deepen their political knowledge. This had led to a growing 'socialist conviction' and 'awareness' among the cohort. Reprinted in Hayes (ed.) *In prison in England*, p. 25.
116. *Guardian*, 11 September 1979.
117. *[Acton] Gazette and Post*, 10 December 1981.
118. The Law Society to RP Walsh, 19 October 1979, Private Collection (Walsh). See also Alastair Logan to Roy Walsh, 2 November 1979, Ibid.
119. Simon Buckhaven to George E Baker & Co, 'Advice', 1 June 1981, p. ii, Private Collection (Walsh). The appeal in Brighton determined that 'the potential benefit … was insufficient to justify the proceedings having regard to the cost of proceedings and the effect of the statutory charge on what would be recovered or preserved in the proceedings'. AC Williamson (Area Secretary, The Law Society) to RP Walsh, 16 November 1981, Ibid.
120. *Disturbance in D Wing*, p. 28. See also *Observer*, 9 September 1979.
121. Gerry Young, 8 March 2008.

122. Sr. Clarke, 'Wormwood Scrubs', Clarke Papers (COFLA).
123. Sr. Clarke, 'Anthony [Ron] Lynch', Clarke Papers (COFLA).
124. Sr. Clarke, 'Wormwood Scrubs', Clarke Papers (COFLA).
125. Sr. Clarke, 'Albany', Clarke Papers (COFLA).
126. *Times*, 28 February 1982.
127. Wakefield, *Thousand days*, Appendix 3, p. 37. See 'My years in total solitude' in *Times*, 3 June 1982.
128. *Times*, 26 and 26 February 1982.
129. *Guardian*, 4 October and 14 December 1979.
130. Cited in Coggan and Walker, *Deaths in British prisons*, p. 193.
131. *Guardian*, 11 September 1979.
132. *Disturbance in D Wing*, p. 6. Governor Honey was assigned to Prison Department HQ in May 1980. He was preceded by his Governor Class III Deputy Governor 'for whom 31 August [1979] was the last day of duty at Wormwood Scrubs'. Ibid., p. 14.
133. *Times*, 19 December 1979.
134. *Times*, 15 December 1979.
135. *Times*, 15 December 1979.
136. *Administration of the Prison Service, Minutes of Evidence, Monday 10 November 1980*, p. 32.
137. *Administration of the Prison Service, Minutes of Evidence, Monday 10 November 1980*, p. 32.
138. *Administration of the Prison Service, Minutes of Evidence, Monday 10 November 1980*, p. 32. GW Fowler, Deputy Director General of the Prison Department expressed doubts whether a resolution of the Irish conflict would produce a resource or security dividend in the Dispersal System. Fowler, a former governor of Wormwood Scrubs, reaffirmed that the policy was to have 'a liberal regime within a secure perimeter'. Ibid.
139. *Report on the work of the Prison Department, 1980*, p. 62. A delegation of prison officers from West Germany was received that year by the Prison Department. Ibid.
140. See *Irish News*, 9 August 1997.
141. *Report on the work of the Prison Department, 1980*, p. 62.
142. *Report on the work of the Prison Department, 1980*, p. 61.
143. Coggan and Walker, *Deaths in British prisons*, p. 195. See also *Times*, 15 December 1979.
144. *Times*, 10 January 1980 and *HC Deb 13 December 1979 vol 975 cc1522–3*.
145. *Times*, 15 December 1979. Styal, located in Wilmslow, Cheshire, added twenty-three female places to its CNA in October 1979. *Report on the work of the Prison Department*, 1979, p. 57.
146. *HC Deb 30 October 1979 vol 972 c462W*.
147. *Times*, 29 February 1980. See also *Times*, 13 March 1980.
148. *Times*, 29 January 1980. See also *Irish Times*, 19 May 1980.
149. *Times*, 25 February 1982.
150. *HC Deb 1 May 1980 vol 983 cc628–9W* and Coggan and Walker, *Deaths in British prisons*, p. 196. Wood headed C1 Branch of Scotland Yard and investigated allegations of staff brutality with a team of six detectives. *[Acton] Gazette and Post*, 10 December 1981.
151. *Guardian*, 25 February 1982.
152. *Times*, 25 February 1982.
153. See *Times*, 6 March 1982 and *HC Deb 24 February 1981 vol 18 cc386–7W*.

CHAPTER 4

The May Committee on Prison Reform

Controversy surrounding the alleged drugging of prisoners on the Isle of Wight re-erupted on 29 October 1979 when the UK Southern Television's *Day to Day* TV programme claimed, contrary to evidence, that Dr Brian Cooper, Dr. Andrew Todd and Dr. Gordon Stewart had administered excessive chemical dosages to inmates of Albany and Parkhurst. This momentous charge was ultimately dismissed when the High Court vindicated all three medical practitioners. It was accepted that they had not prescribed Dalmane in the quantities unscientifically calculated by the concerned Peter Thompson.[1] Unconvinced relatives, friends and acquaintances of those regarded as having been inappropriately drugged were further aggrieved when the mental health of revered 1960s' London gangster Ronnie Kray necessitated his transfer to Broadmoor Hospital. 'Sectioning' was a distinctly ignominious denouement for a man renowned for having once wielded executive underworld power and who was celebrated by the popular press for enjoying the envied trappings of an elite criminal lifestyle. For many years after conviction in 1969, East London twins Ronnie and Reggie Kray, regardless of the media - hyped stigmatism attending their incarceration for serious offences and the contingent curtailment of their daily lives, were frequently consulted by contemporary and emergent metropolitan gangland figures. The influence of the twins permeated the culture from which they had been bodily excluded and in so doing reinforced and perpetuated their iconic status. An ex-prisoner claimed during a September 1983 TV-AM broadcast that Ronnie Kray's mental problems had spiralled towards the abyss of committal when he and his brother were 'suppressed by drugs' under the auspices of Dr. Cooper. This heartfelt accusation resulted in a further substantial libel damages award to Cooper when represented in the High Court on 27 March 1985. Justice Mann, a veteran of IRA trials, presided.[2]

The centrality of the highly erratic, intellectual and seemingly omnipotent Dr. Cooper to the Isle of Wight penal network, coupled with the dire reputation of Parkhurst's Hospital Wing, all but assured prison folklore notoriety. Other far-flung locations were simultaneously impugned by progressive voices for suspected psychiatric irregularities, indicating that the Englishman's sense of prerogatives of duty and personal idiosyncrasy were by no means unique. Few in his exalted position, however, had imbibed self-prescribed 'medicines' before fleeing naked, as watching prisoners contended, into the green belt abutting Parkhurst when under formal investigation for malpractice. Mike Fitzgerald and Joseph Sim, authors of the forthright *British Prisons*, related deeply disturbing accounts of inmates they portrayed in 1979 as having been harmed by inappropriate medical 'care' in the Dispersal System. This often-shocking publication invited dissenting commentary from liberal professionals, yet no dissenting bloc emerged even though vindication of their damning thesis proved elusive. Claims that three doctors had therapeutically mistreated George Ince, a bullion robber held in Gartree, were thrown out by the High Court on 31 July 1980.[3] Home Secretary Whitelaw had fronted strongly in the Commons on 3 December 1979 when refuting probing queries tabled by the tenacious Kilroy-Silk. With forensic exactitude, he insisted on the edited *Hansard* record that *'prisoners were not experimented upon'* (emphasis added) with Depixol and Modecote. An alternate narrative of the exchange asserted that the men had merely been involved in a 'study of the treatment given to a small group of prisoners in 1976'.[4] Brixton, according to the popular *Daily Mirror*, was another institution where 'litres' of the 'liquid cosh' were dispensed by compliant staff supervising Landing Three of F Wing and their solicitous charges. In an apparent attempt at balanced reportage, the lead journalist revealed that this was 'the section ... where most of the assaults on officers occur'.[5]

Parliamentary figures for 1979 enumerated the issue of 123,226 dosages of 'medicines' in Brixton, not counting 143,329 of psychotropic drugs, 30,020 hypnotic drugs, 33,141 chemicals affecting the central nervous system and 58,388 'other drugs and medicines'. The analytic value of these bald statistics was diminished by the fact that they revealed nothing of the strength or frequency of dosages to individuals. Yet, the implied prevalence of physical and mental illness in an average daily population of 916 appeared very high.[6] Dr. RC Ingrey-Senn, Acting Director of the Prison Medical Service, acknowledged that women jailed in Holloway Prison in London, who apparently collectively took imprisonment 'very badly', headed the national league table with an average of 274 dispensed dosages per person in 1981. A *World Medicine* editorial claimed: 'The practise of medicine in prisons is being perverted for purposes of political expediency with Home Office connivance'.[7] When architecturally reconfigured at massive expenditure in 1983–84, Holloway added new 'psychiatric facilities' and kindred specialised services that were more indicative of the true nature of female incarceration in England than its supposed gender - neutral facade in the past.[8]

Avenues of adverse publicity by opponents were limited, as expected, by Whitelaw who, in December 1979, vetoed a proposal for an independent consultative panel of physicians and psychiatrists to 'monitor the use of long-term sedation for difficult prisoners'.[9] This instrumental act of dissociation averred that no such occupational diligence was necessary. His prognosis gifted the whip hand of unilateral legal authority, within a notionally constitutional monarchy underpinned by mere statute law, to those who would not or could not investigate. Access to records of prison pharmacies, moreover, was withheld from applicants other than 'the responsible doctor', namely, staff in the pay of the Home Office who were reminded of their obligations to the Official Secrets Act (OSA). Within this rarefied environment, unqualified 'orderlies' issued 'stocks of medicine ... to prisoners who ask for them'. Whitelaw's caveat that this programme of devolved discretion was governed by the 'general' instruction of jail doctors and confined to non-prescription drugs did not accord with the experience of prisoner advocates.[10] Vetted Prison Visitors, as opposed to family members, were in 1979 prohibited from discussing 'prison conditions' with 'anyone outside the prison'.[11] Arcane and introverted Civil Service regulations and mores deterred OSA signatories from making disclosures during a period when serious grievances against state personnel were being alleged with greater frequency.

The May Committee Report, 31 October 1979

The resurfacing of a drugging controversy occurred at a sensitive time for the Home Office. On 31 October 1979 officials in their London Headquarters were preoccupied with the publication of the long awaited inquiry by Justice May into the operations of the Prison Service.[12] Advance information furnished to Home Secretary Whitelaw forewarned him of the backlash from the POA and other aggrieved stakeholders. Kenneth Daniel of the 22,000 strong union stressed dissatisfaction with salary rises that added just 6 per cent to third - stage scheduled pay increases.[13] Criticism of this order had been anticipated since February when it was held, conveniently, that the organization was less efficacious than those representing the police and fire brigade when striking 'a responsible balance between their duty and trade union bargaining'.[14] An IRA assessment of the imbroglio claimed 'since the POA lost their showdown with the Home Office, their ability to press their case ... has been greatly weakened'.[15] This was far from ideal in that it begged the question as to how militant prison officers in England and Wales would assert their industrial negotiating position. Stoppages and 'work to rule' might well diminish the all too finite quality of life available to imprisoned Irish Category A men and women. In the absence of immediate mortal threat to their jailed comrades in England, deployable IRA ASUs were unlikely to retaliate with the personalised lethality witnessed in Ireland. Deceptively enough, a watching brief seemingly yielded initiative to individual anti-republicans in England or those prepared to risk the forthright responses made in response to earlier attempted acts of intimidation. Whereas the maintenance of the status quo could never elevate the status of republicans detained in the UK, any modification of their situation, if dictated by state interests, necessitated painstaking evaluation in which all modes of resistance were deemed justified.

The Westminster Parliamentary Committee, announced on 17 November 1978, was chaired by Justice May who was instructed 'to inquire into the state of the prison services in the United Kingdom'. The committee spent the following ten months compiling depositions from a wide range of vested interests.[16] His small team were ostensibly receptive to unconventional proposals, including arguments for non-custodial sentences.[17] This option was rejected in October 1979 and Jerry Westall of Radical Alternatives to Prison (RAP) expressed disappointment with recommendations to double Prison Service capital expenditure in order to facilitate new jail construction. The antiquated Dartmoor complex, in theory capable of holding life - sentenced prisoners, was earmarked for decommissioning. Dartmoor had not confined Irish republicans since the 1940s when they had agitated for political status. Geoff Coggan of PROP and the NCCL were dejected as they hoped that the inquiry would address more fundamental issues than mere industrial relations.[18] By July 1980 the United Kingdom had 80 persons per 100,000 of its population behind bars, compared with 39.4 in France, 32 in Ireland (Twenty-Six Counties) and 13.4 in the Netherlands. Problems of overcrowding, therefore, were not simply a matter of insufficient cell capacity; they also clearly reflected a combination of national sentencing culture, parole administration and general penal policy.[19]

Justice May re-validated the Dispersal System in the wake of the most concerted prisoner unrest in decades. Dr Roy King, an informed critic of the evolution of British penal strategy post-*Mountbatten Report*, received national publicity on 25 May 1979 for his contention that the societal benefits predicted in good faith in 1968 had simply not materialized. Dr King, of the University College of North Wales, argued the adopted system was not cost effective and had very probably excited rather than inhibited prison violence. He recommended that Albany and Long Lartin should be renovated to accommodate 'high risk' prisoners while other jail facilities were modified to implement less severe daily regimes. This was a variant of declined Mountbatten proposals, albeit using two existing and relatively modern complexes in lieu of a single new super-maximum security 'fortress' located on the Isle of Wight.[20] The generally under-reported war in Ireland, or 'Operation Banner' as the Ministry of Defence privately designated what became its longest and most deadly deployment since 1969, naturally continued to exert stress on such deliberations. In February 1982 the Home Office was obliged to acknowledge that the potentially protracted presence of Irish republicans in English prisons was a further disincentive for a mooted 'Alcatraz' penitentiary: 'The regime in such a prison would be excessively custodial, that its inmates would despair, that there would be an explosive atmosphere inside and – especially now that there are so many IRA prisoners – that it would be particularly vulnerable to attack from outside'.[21] As in the 1970s, a relatively small number of republican men and women, denied official categorization as 'political prisoners' despite being accurately designated enemies of the British establishment, complicated basic UK policy on such fundamental issues as trial law, sentencing, parole and penology.

After an exceptionally detailed inquiry presented and received as bipartisan, the esteemed Justice May encouraged hugely increased spending on both new and existing prisons. His partly right-of-centre finding was counter-pointed by a jurisprudential orientated call to responsible court officials to minimize the number of custodial sentences handed down for minor offences and, specifically, against the invariably disadvantaged and mentally ill. This prospectus broadly accorded with the strategic plans of the Home Office, which in February 1979 oversaw a Prison Service budget of £275 million that included a proposal to build three new institutions. One additional jail was to be sited in Liverpool where Walton Prison remained a much-criticised 'local' facility.[22] In March 1980 Walton held 1,717 men in a fetid building with a CNA of 1,016; Winson Green in Birmingham, meanwhile, contained 1,075 despite a 596 CNA.[23] Such inherited commitments resulted in the construction of both Frankland and Full Sutton, near York, by the early 1980s, expensive initiatives that permitted the eventual downgrading of Hull and Wakefield from the Dispersal System.[24] Yet even Justice May, favoured in time by the Treasury, was not permitted full imprimatur or architectural blueprint. It was announced on 19 December 1979 that Parkhurst, far from being re-rated as either a Category B 'local' prison or dedicated criminal mental institution, would instead be 'modernised'.[25] Merlyn Rees, Shadow Home Secretary and the man who had appointed the judge in 1978, expressed qualified support for the conservatively toned report delivered to his desk.[26] Thus commissioned, empowered and followed, May was arguably the most significant British twentieth century penological czar since Mountbatten. In April 1990 the May Committee was retrospectively credited with having initiated a record billion pound sterling programme 'designed to bring conditions into line with the best found in other European countries'.[27]

The short-term efficacy of the *May Report* was cast into relief in September 1980 when Roger Attrill, Governor of Winson Green, Birmingham, opined that 50 per cent of the men in his charge should not be in jail. They included prisoners described as ranging from 'terrorists and vicious and violent professional criminals to minor fine defaulters and drunks'. Of the 4,093 prisoners in Winson Green between July 1979 and July 1980, 746 had never been previously incarcerated and 325 had one prior custodial sentence.[28] In a famous outburst in November 1981, Wormwood Scrubs Governor John McCarthy described his mission as 'manager of a large penal dustbin'. He claimed: 'I did not join the Prison Service to manage overcrowded cattle pens, nor did I join to run a prison where the interests of the individuals have to be sacrificed continually to the interests of the institution'. McCarthy queried why short-term prisoners were not being paroled and in so doing challenged the Home Secretary's commitment to reducing the prison population.[29] Conditions in Brixton remained appalling; three men shared thirteen by seven foot cells in which they were locked without toilet facilities for twelve hours every night and at other intervals of the day.[30]

The May Committee conceived a system of oversight whereby an amendment to the Prison Act of 1952, moved in the House of Lords by Lord Elton, created statutory provision for a HM Chief Inspector of Prisons. The new body was theoretically detached from the Home Office bureaucracy by virtue of reporting directly to the Home Secretary. On 1 August 1980 the ex-Chief Probation Officer of Inner London, William H Pearce, was nominated as the inaugural head of an Inspectorate that formally functioned from 1 January 1981.[31] His induction was eased by the decision of the National Executive Committee of the POA to suspend industrial action in January 1981, a boon which permitted the re-opening of most prison workshops.[32] This was counterbalanced by the extension of the remit of the Inspectorate to the Six Counties, although no meaningful interventions occurred in what the NIO described as a year of 'significant developments', which included the enervative 1980 Hunger Strike in Long Kesh.[33] Pearce remained in post until 4 January 1982 when the managers of the once sequestered system were attempting to adjust to the May reforms. Sir James Hennessy succeeded the deceased Pearce on 1 September 1982 following the 'advice of the Home Secretary' to 'the Crown'. He led, in theory, six full time and two part time inspectors, aided by a small secretariat.[34] Although May intended the Inspectorate to examine 'more general aspects of the work of the Prison Service', Hennessy was not initially in a position to fulfil this potentially important brief. Staff turnover in excess of 70 per cent in the course of one year impacted severely on administrative efficiencies due to lack of continuity and unfilled vacancies. The Inspectorate was, consequently, far from secure in its methodologies and competencies when beset by negative trends and sensational incidents that Justice May could not have reasonably foreseen.[35]

POW *Department*

The impetus to form the Prisoner of War Department of Sinn Féin came from the necessity of supporting the 'no wash protest' in the H-Blocks and Armagh, and was a logical outworking of the 1 March 1976 loss of political status. Republican ideology and discipline were exposed to pressure from state manipulation wherever prisoner cohesion was difficult to maintain. Armagh Gaol offered a stark example in 1979 when a combination of the new regulations, reduced frequency of women being convicted of 'scheduled' offences and release of those whose sentences had expired plunged the female republican population from seven to the lone Pauline Deery. She enjoyed the dubious distinction of retaining rights of a political prisoner. A Belfast comrade Liz McWilliams mused: 'Deery was in the whole wing on her own for about a year as she was the last one with political status. We used to see her sometimes and talk to her'.[36] The NIO demonstrated the new differentiation by preventing spatial segregation of Republicans, Loyalists and criminals, while withdrawing entitlements garnered in the early 1970s. As in Long Kesh, consensual and directed efforts to resist 'criminalization' were met with stern countermeasures. In March 1979 thirty-eight women in Armagh were subjected to twenty-one hour lock-up arising from their boycott of stipulated prison work. Additional punishments included loss of remission and the option of just one visit per month.[37] Following the May 1978 baton charge on prisoners of both sexes, poor conditions within the crumbling jail inspired further modes of dissent. On 7 February 1980 the taxing 'no wash' method of protest spread from Long Kesh to Armagh where male prisoners, in the wake of routine physical assaults and close confinement involving restrictive access to sanitation, resorted to the inherently harmful tactic of disposing of bodily waste by means of daubing cell walls and sluicing under heavy iron doors.[38] Sinn Féin expended increased, if limited, party resources on highlighting the odious situation. When remanded in custody to face charges of IRA membership in February 1978, Gerry Adams gained a strong personal sense of the negative trends inside North of Ireland prisons, as well as its potential political significance:

> Their campaign had been going on since 1976, and had escalated, and I was concerned by the lack of any sign of movement from the British. Our own agitation in support of the prisoners was clearly inadequate. Relatives' Action Committee had been formed from April 1976, but for all their Trojan work, they were not getting the political support from us that the issue demanded … the prisoners had been forced into a no-wash protest because their toilet facilities had been withdrawn … Conditions had rapidly become appalling.[39]

In the course of 1979, when Sinn Féin tactically opposed Bernadette McAliskey's independent efforts to campaign on the prison question, leading acolytes in Belfast had recognized the imperative of creating a committee that could collate and disseminate information on the prison struggle. Members were seconded from the party's Belfast based personnel, Ard Comhairle and staff of *AP/RN* who met weekly to address the crisis in the H-Blocks. The perceived utility of the strategy gained Ard Comhairle affirmation for a revamped POW Department with a Belfast committee concentrating on prisons in the Six Counties, and the Dublin equivalent focusing on the Twenty-Six Counties and England. This created a party

- controlled tier above the devolved RACs, with whom Jim Gibney had liaised, and the NHAC. Gerry Brannigan headed the Belfast office at 170 Falls Road, while Brendan Golden worked out of Sinn Féin premises at 44 Parnell Square, Dublin.[40] Sinn Féin operated a POW Information Office at 5 Blessington Street, Dublin, in November 1979, when the party adopted the platform of the 'five demands'.[41] The premisis in the capital became a hub of prisoner politics and was associated with an informal basement bar where fundraising and social events were hosted.[42]

An English based subcommittee was envisaged which, in the event, fore-grounded the painstaking work of Eddie Caughey's dedicated circle in Birmingham.[43] Caughey was the mainstay of An Cumann Cabhrach in England, and one of the few senior Sinn Féin officials in a position to venture back to Britain from James McDade's IRA funeral in Belfast on 23 November 1974. Fallout from the 'Birmingham Bombs', which that week caused numerous innocent deaths in the city centre, led to repeated attacks on his home and exposure to the full weight of the PTA.[44] Having endured seventy-two hours' detention in Castlereagh, he returned to England confident that the British authorities had no automatic right to serve him with an exclusion order in view of his residency in the country since 1947.[45] Pro-republicans continued to play their part across England and Long Lartin was picketed by the Pearse/McDade cumann of Sinn Féin, UTOM and RCG on 25 November 1979.[46] A meeting held on 22–23 September 1980, a year after the founding of the POW Department, noted that £20,000 had been invested in Belfast and Derry offices, lecture tours, events subvention and printed materials. 140 delegates, whose reports and later reflections were intended to improve the capacity of Sinn Féin to progress the prison struggle, attended the conference.[47]

Those most effected continued to act as circumstances dictated. In a percipient move, a new governor posted to Wakefield defused a potentially serious problem in November 1979 by allowing Ray McLaughlin and Tony Clarke to re-enter the main prison from F Wing. They had been held there following the June incendiary attacks and apart from month-long 'lie-downs' elsewhere. They had pondered their diminished options in the isolation unit and were preparing an attack on prison staff to force a change in conditions. In the tradition of Fenian and 1916 icon Tom Clarke, McLaughlin had written to his brother *'Is fearr an t-mreas no an t-uaigneas'*, a philosophical Irish phrase meaning 'strife is better than loneliness'. At best, assaulting warders or governors would have entailed heavy beatings, loss of remission and transfer to an external segregation unit. The chance of being retained in one of the grim 'strong boxes' was a distinct possibility. The incoming governor, from intuition, insight or chance, almost certainly pre-empted a violent incident by simply returning the two IRA men to the wings.[48] McLaughlin was then shifted to Durham on a 'lie down' in

December where he conversed with Eddie Butler and Frankie Fraser.[49] Matters remained highly strained in Wakefield. After a delay in releasing the news, it was admitted on 18 January 1980 that a serious incident had occurred the previous week in Wakefield, during which five prison officers were injured. *The Times* reported: 'IRA terrorists assaulted them with an iron bar and a hammer in protest against the transfer of other IRA prisoners'.[50]

Birmingham Six campaign in the USA

On 3 November 1979 the *Irish Post*, weekly paper of the expatriate communities in Britain, noted the intention of New York Congressman Hamilton Fish junior to petition the US State Department to press for the re-opening of the case of the 'Birmingham Six'. Fish had met in New York with Fr. Sean McManus and other leaders of the Irish National Caucus (INC), who drew upon research conducted by Fr. Ray Murray, Fr. Denis Faul and Sr. Sarah Clarke in Ireland and Britain to exonerate the wrongfully imprisoned men serving life sentences in England.[51] The INC cooperated closely with another 'Birmingham Six' advocate, Fr. Brian Brady, on institutional anti-Catholic sectarian discrimination in the Six Counties. Such foundations were vital to the establishment of the progressive 'MacBride Principles' which the Irish Government also initially opposed.[52] A secret communication regarding Irish diplomatic contact with the INC was approved by Taoiseach Jack Lynch and it was implied in 1985 that this amounted to a *de facto* endorsement of Ambassador Sean Donlon's less than cordial reception of Fr. McManus in Washington DC. Fr. McManus, for his part, had a tempestuous relationship with Donlon that flared in November 1979 in the course of a meeting in the US capital attended by Fr. Murray and his 'dear friend' Fish.[53] INA (aka 'NORAID') leaders alleged that Donlon had attempted to dissuade Fish from backing Fr. Murray's call to seek support in the Congress for the 'Birmingham Six'. Ireland's Foreign Minister Michael O'Kennedy, a member of Fianna Fáil, denied that this intervention stemmed from Government policy.[54]

The net effect of diplomatic briefings was that Irish officials in the US did not openly facilitate persons, politicians and organizations seeking to clear the 'Birmingham Six'. Irish-Americans divined the hand of Ambassador Donlon, who had played a key role in marshalling the powerful 'Four Horsemen' of Ted Kennedy, Tipp O'Neill, Hugh Carey and Daniel Patrick Moynihan in March 1977 in order to counteract US based supporters of the IRA and Sinn Féin.[55] The INC and INA were vociferous during the controversy surrounding the reappointment of Donlon to the US in 1980.[56] By coincidence, the Home Office shortly afterwards indicated that it was prepared to pay the six men damages for the injuries they had received following arrest. The gesture arose in the context of proceedings at the Court of Appeal where the West Midlands police had sought to overturn a High Court deliberation that the men were entitled to sue the force in whose custody they had been assaulted. A previous attempt to prosecute fourteen Winson Green staff members failed in 1977, a circumstance which tended to place the onus of responsibility on the police.[57]

'Operation OTIS', December 1979

On 12 December 1979 English police mounted a wave of raids on houses and flats used by Irish citizens. The search extended from London to Liverpool, Manchester, Birmingham and Southampton in what was presented as an effective employment of the PTA. Of the twenty-five arrested by the Anti-Terrorist Squad (C13), eleven were charged with offences under Section 11 regarding the withholding of information on 'acts of terrorism'. Eight of the ten were brought to trial and, although convicted, received suspended terms of imprisonment.[58] Early press accounts accepted Scotland Yard claims that an IRA pre-Christmas bombing campaign had been interrupted and the role of Commander Peter Duffy's Anti-Terrorist Squad was emphasised. NUJ member Paddy Prendiville, Assistant Editor of *Hibernia* magazine, was among those detained under the PTA in London during a holiday visit to his mother. He and the majority of those seized were released without charge.[59] Prendiville, a former TOM activist when living in England, had spent four days in custody in Leman Street Police Station following arrest at gunpoint in a Notting Hill flat by the Special Patrol Group. A hearing to assess the writ of *habeas corpus* sought by his solicitors was postponed for the critical four days and rendered moot in the interim by his release from custody.[60]

There were, however, active republicans arrested in the course of 'Operation Otis', a knowing term denoting an 'away team' derived from the police slang 'O[n] T[he] S[ide]' or extra-marital relations.[61] Information was obtained in the course of the enquiries pointing to a plan to rescue Brian Keenan from Brixton using a hijacked helicopter as he exercised in 'the cage'. This resembled in many respects the manner in which three high - ranking IRA men had been sprung from Mountjoy prison, Dublin, in October 1973.[62] Keenan supplied a detailed hand - drawn map of the prison and its environs which was recovered in a London room used by Belfast associate Bobby Campbell; Campbell had been under surveillance since visiting a house in Liverpool on 12 October 1979. At least thirty Special Branch and Anti-Terrorist Squad officers followed Campbell and close comrade Dickie Glenholmes. Eleven members of Campbell's extended family in England were arrested under the PTA, none of whom were prosecuted.[63] In the late 1970s Special Branch generally acted as the right arm of MI5 regarding 'intelligence and security within the United Kingdom' and were used for making arrests. F Branch, one of MI5's nominally civilian - recruited six departments, was formally tasked with 'countering "domestic subversion", whereas K Branch tackled 'counter espionage' in Britain.[64]

In leafy Holland Park, London, armed police from Scotland Yard's D11 branch netted Campbell and fellow republicans Gerry Tuite, Bobby Storey and Dickie Glenholmes, who were subsequently remanded in connection with the Brixton plot. It was claimed that the group practiced obtaining the helicopter needed for success and were on the eve of a 'dry run' to probe prison security measures on 13 December 1979.[65] Police reportedly intercepted a phone message in Belfast which indicated the planned movements of 'red light' Campbell.[66] The hyped-up armed D11 unit were 'less than subtle', according to those detained, when raiding the ASU staging post in Holland Park.[67] Police recovered two American Browning automatic pistols, ammunition and a street guide in which the location of Finsbury Park had been annotated. The four, assumed to be seasoned IRA Volunteers, were taken to Rochester Row Police Station for fruitless questioning. They were jointly charged on 19 December with conspiracy to cause explosions and possession of firearms. Having been deprived of their personal clothes, three of the men appeared in Lambeth Court wearing just blankets, an irregular circumstance criticized by defending lawyers Alastair Logan and Brian Rose-Smith.[68] Solicitor Mike Fisher, who had participated in the legal defence of the 'Balcombe Street' men believed to have been linked to Keenan, provided professional assistance despite open police hostility.[69]

Campbell had escaped from prison in Belfast in 1972 and spent eight months on the run from an eleven-year sentence for a politically motivated armed robbery before being recaptured. He was apparently closely watched on a number of trips between Ireland and the British capital in 1979.[70] On 11 May 1979 Storey was freed after a six day trial in Belfast when a judge in the juryless Diplock court found that he had 'no case to answer' in relation to an IRA attack on a British army patrol in Lenadoon in June 1977.[71] Glenholmes, although unconvicted in Ireland, had been interned in Long Kesh where, in August 1975, he shared Cage Three with Pat Magee and Rab Fryers, both of whom were subsequently jailed for IRA offences in England.[72] He had previously known Gerry Adams and both were present in Cage Four in October 1974 when much of the camp was razed.[73] In September 1977 Glenholmes was involuntarily flown to London for questioning in relation to the discovery of IRA war material in a container truck but was released without charge.[74] It was speculated that the munitions seizure 'may have prevented the start of a new Provisional IRA bombing campaign in Britain'.[75]

Gerry Tuite was described as 'one of the men on Scotland Yard's most wanted list' and had been sought under the *nom de guerre* 'Gerry Fossett' in February 1979.[76] Fossett was the patronymic and brand name of a famous circus that moved between Britain and Ireland. He was believed to have entered Britain in August 1977 and operated at a high level within the IRA.[77] Tuite hailed from Mountnugent, Cavan, and although descended from a large, staunchly republican family, was more active in the IRA in the 1970s than generally realised.[78] He was a major operative in the London area and a man whose skilful elusiveness merited the grudging 'master of disguise' tribute following arrest. Searches of several London flats used by Tuite turned up expertly concealed caches of firearms and bomb making equipment as late as May 1983. A haul at 144 Trafalgar Road, Greenwich, where police claimed he had resided between June 1978 and March 1979, provided the main evidence used to remand him to Brixton. He then lived with nurse Helen Griffiths who believed him to be German-Irishman 'David Coyne'. An Armalite rifle, sawn-off shotgun, nitro-glycerine traces and keys linked to vehicles used in London bombings in December 1978 were ultimately recovered, albeit not before August 1980.[79] Evidence of plans to subdivide a London ASU into two teams capable of simultaneous actions and documentation indicative of preparations in Liverpool were revealed in Dublin's Central Criminal Court on 7 July 1982.[80] The composition of the Greenwich haul indicated that it was the dump of an IRA engineering unit which utilized firearms for personal security. Police sources claimed that Tuite operated at various times with Belfast men Pat Magee and John McComb in the late 1970s when approximately 3.5 million pounds' worth of damage was caused by a sequence of sixteen IRA bombs in the London sector.[81]

Chrissie Keenan (nee Campbell) was arrested on 12 December 1979 in a friend's house in Bethnal Green when visiting London to see Brian Keenan in Brixton. Her London hosts, members of the RCG, were detained under the PTA but released without charge after their comrades demonstrated outside the police station and purposefully enjoined local MPs to intercede.[82] The Keenans had married in Luton, England in October 1960 before returning to Ireland in 1963. Chrissie Keenan was originally charged with withholding information and subsequently with the far more serious allegation of conspiracy to assist in a prison break.[83] There was, in fact, no evidence of any such enterprise. She later claimed: 'What they were trying to do was work on Brian and coerce him into giving them the answers they wanted. The detectives who were questioning us told Brian that, if he gave them the answers they wanted, then they would let his wife go home … it did not work'. Ironically, joint imprisonment in Brixton, albeit on different wings, ensured that the couple saw 'a lot more' of each other than usual when granted weekly visits in the jail.[84] Brian Keenan recalled: 'They put her in a cell above me in a man's prison which was the first time that that had ever happened and of course the purpose was that I would sign a statement of conspiracy to escape and she could go home … our first grandchild was born while she was in there and they kept her there above me until the trial'.[85]

London-Irish woman Jackie O'Malley was arrested on the same charges as Chrissie Keenan in Willsham Street, Notting Hill. This resulted from a visit from Bobby Campbell, when under close surveillance, who used her private phone to ring Belfast.[86] The capable O'Malley had worked as a Higher Executive Officer in the Ministry of Agriculture and had a long involvement in political activism, stemming from her background and North London upbringing where the Irish community was strongly established along the Northern Line tube environs extending from Camden, Finsbury Park and Finchley to Totteridge/ Whetstone. As a youth, O'Malley supported the civil rights - orientated Campaign for Democracy in Ulster and, from August 1971, the broad based Anti-Internment League. She moved into TOM in the mid-1970s, bringing organizational and administrative skills which future husband Michael Maguire of London Sinn Féin described as being 'badly needed in such ill resourced groups'. She was regarded as 'one of the principle organisers' of the sixty strong Labour Movement Delegation to Ireland in September 1976 and a key player in the International Tribunal on the British Presence in Ireland in 1978–79.[87] In July 1979 Ciaran MacAnali, Alastair Logan and Amalgamated Union of Engineering Workers leader Ernie Roberts participated in the Tribunal held in Conway Hall.[88] O'Malley was involved in bringing female relatives of the 'Blanketmen' from the North of Ireland to picket Westminster, Buckingham Palace and St. Paul's Cathedral.[89]

Press accounts of O'Malley being drawn into the Brixton plan 'on a romantic basis' were ill informed.[90] It was revealed upon her premature death in January 1999 that she had 'joined the republican movement in the late 1970s', a deep commitment suspected by the British authorities that detained her in connection with the Keenan venture.[91] MI5 and MI6 may not have discerned that O'Malley was centrally concerned in the transfer of confidential schematics of the 350-acre H-Block complex to Belfast republicans in whose possession they were eventually recovered.[92] The blueprints were of immense value to those seeking to plan escape from and attacks on the most secure prison complex in Western Europe. Fingerprints and taped phone conversations disclosed at trial established that Campbell, Glenholmes and Tuite had visited O'Malley's home during the mooted Brixton plot, as did her uninvolved friend Paddy Prendiville, whom she had known from TOM in England. British authorities ascertained that she had arranged the rental of the Holland Park flat for the use of an IRA ASU and had driven one of its members to Liverpool.[93] Marie Melia, sister of imprisoned IRA Volunteer John Melia and O'Malley's former flatmate, was detained as she arrived for work in London at 9.00 a.m. On 14 December 1979 Lord Justice Shaw and Mr. Justice Woolf of the Queen's Bench Divisional Court adjourned the case in relation to Prendiville, O'Malley and Melia who were granted leave to apply for writs of *habeas corpus*. Patrick O'Connor, representing Prendiville, claimed all three were being held incommunicado.[94] O'Malley and Whetstone bank worker Margaret

Parratt were further charged with conspiracy to cause explosions and the seriousness of the allegations, dropped in Lambeth Magistrates Court on 1 May 1980, was, in the short term, sufficient to rule out bail.[95] Parratt was Bobby Campbell's cousin. Her parents, Patrick and Anne Duffy, were separately arrested in Holloway Road but released without charge after a distressing period of detention.[96]

Brixton, January/February 1980

The common denominator between the seven defendants brought to trial in March 1981 was the charge of 'aiding the escape of a prisoner'.[97] Their experiences otherwise diverged. Provisional Category A prisoners O'Malley and Parratt were held with Chrissie Keenan in Brixton's maximum security D Wing: 'Up at the top of the prison on our own ... They had nowhere else to put us'.[98] The trio were the only women of 1,070 people crammed into the jail in February 1980 when the Certified Normal Accommodation was a mere 696. Glossing over this gender - centred and possibly politically inspired anomaly, the Prison Department simply commented in its annual review that Brixton had 'from time to time held Category A female prisoners'.[99] Women prison officers, nonetheless, had to be seconded from other institutions to guard the suspected republicans and, while the Governor proved open to arrangements which set the women apart from criminals on remand, the high rotation of the specially assigned warders required repeated renegotiation. The jailed republicans declined the nominal payment offered for cleaning their own cells on a point of political principle and were, contrary to expectations, allowed access to the association room monitored by cameras rather than staff. Any perceived concessions had to be weighed against fears of being suborned, coaxed or ultimately inured to ephemeral and ultimately compromising gestures. Strip-searching, if invariably degrading and attended with a sense of violation for the openly defiant, was generally restricted to occasions when the three were leaving the wing for visits or going to weekly committal proceedings in Lambeth. Regardless of arguably rational pre-emptive and psychologically inhibiting factors, this bodily intrusion served to aggrieve, motivate and consolidate an otherwise heterogeneous grouping. Following a distressing court day confrontation, O'Malley persuaded an unenthusiastic Assistant Governor that it was indefensible to insist that female prisoners be stripped naked on security grounds. If the authorities wished to avoid inciting the major outpourings of popular support stimulated by the maltreatment of sisters Dolours and Marian Price in Brixton in 1974–75, the unannounced decision to place staff inside the visiting room courted adverse reaction. In one such instance O'Malley registered her dissent by declining to see her mother and sister.[100]

None of the women had endured previous imprisonment and the psychological shock of robust detention in London was, at first, severe.

Chrissie Keenan, owing to her upbringing in the turmoil of the North of Ireland, understood certain essential dynamics. She was, nonetheless, deeply disconcerted by abrupt separation from her six children aged twelve to eighteen. Brixton was a frightening environment for most women: 'When we came out for visits for when we were going to court the men would start to shout abuse at us ... They had to clear the yard of all the men to allow us into the yard for one hour's exercise ... Every time we were brought our food, everyone else was locked up in their cells. The food was a disgrace ... we only saw each other when we got out to the Association Room'.[101] Englishman 'Hate them all Harry' Johnson, 'in for multiple murders' and consistently amenable to dialogue with IRA prisoners, convinced the more reprehensible 'ODCs' to desist from threatening the women.[102] Brian Keenan separately and ominously informed the Governor that 'his prison would go up' if the precious recreation time was unfairly disrupted for a second time.[103]

The judge accepted on 28 April 1980 that Chrissie Keenan could be bailed and permitted her to reside with her husband's relatives in England.[104] O'Malley and Parratt were granted similar terms on 1 May 1980.[105] Against expectations, O'Malley was the only one of the women to have bail rescinded on 1 June when the judge sent the defendants for trial. It was held that she represented a flight risk in her mother's home in Guildford, although the underlying explanation was probably knowledge of her deeper role in the affair. After an overnight stay in Holloway, she was driven over 200 miles at high speed to Risley Remand Centre in Cheshire. Risley was tightly regulated and O'Malley was allocated a cold cell where she spent at least twenty-three hours a day with constant light, limited reading material, few clothes and frequent verbal abuse from nearby male prisoners. She was not permitted to attend Mass and could mail just one letter a week. Legal meetings were extensively documented and she was interrupted when attempting to convey the severity of living conditions to her solicitor.[106] As the only Category A prisoner in the Centre, O'Malley surmised staff were 'all practising like mad for the next lot that go into Brixton'.[107] She petitioned the Home Secretary on 12 June 1980, claiming 'there is no doubt that I am being held under Rule 43 with an added "E" categorization'.[108] In extremis, O'Malley had embarked on a hunger strike on 11 June that produced no discernable reaction from her captors for five days. When visited by a patronising Medical Officer she was told: 'I know all about your organisation and the way your minds work. If you choose to starve yourself, no one here will lift a finger to help you'.[109] For someone conversant with the realities of hunger-striking, it was with great seriousness that O'Malley had resorted to such a drastic mode of protest. She did so with sufficient assiduousness as to permanently damage her health, which was already impaired by spinal osteo arthritis.[110] An extremely risky thirst strike escalation was pre-empted by a timely judicial decision to release her on bail of £60,000 on 19 June 1980.[111] In a letter to a friend in Dublin she explained: 'I'd given up all hope and resolved to cut out drinking as well ... Rather than go mad here I honestly felt it would be better to die'.[112]

The trial opened in the Old Bailey on 3 March 1981 after Justice Pain had replaced two jurors whose personal connections with the Troubles in Ireland were deemed too close for an impassive evaluation of evidence. David Jeffreys QC outlined the prosecution case against Brian Keenan, Chrissie Keenan, Bobby Storey, Bobby Campbell, Jackie O'Malley, Margaret Parratt and Dickie Glenholmes.[113] On 5 March Parratt and O'Malley seized the tactical option of altering their original pleas to 'guilty' in relation to the sole charge of conspiring to spring Brian Keenan from Brixton. This had remained the main allegation still standing against the pair who were, unusually for a case with IRA associations, released on bail ahead of sentencing.[114] Friends and relations speculated that the reduction in the seriousness of the original charges arose in consequence of Gerry Tuite's December 1980 escape from Brixton by the dramatically different mode of self-emancipation. This altered the political and public relations context of charges pertaining to the Keenan group who remained in close confinement.[115] Brian Keenan testified on 11 March 1981 that his wife 'was the last person he would have endangered' and ensured reportage of this comment by making an exaggerated claim that Brixton inmates could 'smuggle out anything they want to on a regular basis'.[116] Gerry Kelly recalled that while 'a legendary figure in the IRA', Keenan was 'not known for his diplomacy'. He had given his Belfast comrades a less than warm welcome when they arrived into Brixton on remand.[117]

Bobby Campbell and Dickie Glenholmes were on 16 March 1981 convicted of conspiracy to effect the escape of a prisoner and possession of a firearm. On the following day they received concurrent sentences of five and ten years on the two charges. Brian Keenan was convicted of the first offence; a verdict that indicated jury satisfaction that he was actively complicit. Bobby Storey, a six foot eight republican who had consistently denied guilt, was acquitted of all charges but sent for retrial by Justice Pain. He was eventually cleared and returned to Ireland where he was rearrested in Belfast on 20 August 1981. Storey was sentenced to eighteen years imprisonment for attempting to kill British soldiers in the North of Ireland.[118] This represented his seventh set of charges for republican activities in Ireland and Britain.[119] Chrissie Keenan was acquitted of wrongdoing in the Old Bailey, a benign result that not only restored her freedom but preserved the integrity of the family.[120] The three years handed down to her husband were added to the eighteen imposed in 1980. Although guilty, Brian Keenan was unfortunate in that previous sentencing in IRA cases in England generally entailed concurrent terms. In an unmistakable allusion to his perception of

Keenan's character, Justice Pain expressly dismissed the traditional norm as 'futile'.[121] Taking account of time served, O'Malley and Parratt received suspended sentences of eighteen months and one year respectively, as well as a fine of £1,000. This was a marked diminution on the worst-case prospect of conviction on all original charges. However, O'Malley's fast against the 'appalling conditions' endured in Risley badly strained her health.[122] Comrades observed that her confinement sapped her physical reserves and O'Malley was incapable of resuming her earlier dynamism. She married leading London based Sinn Féin member Michael Maguire in the Irish College, Rome, in 1995, but died prematurely in Kilburn on 10 January 1999.[123] Whereas Parratt had been deeply shocked by the intensity of police interrogations, one of those detained in Southampton was admitted to the local Acute Psychiatric Ward where he was visited by Sr. Sarah Clarke, Theresa Hynes and an NCCL member on 17 December 1979.[124]

Dickie Glenholmes was unperturbed by imprisonment in England and understood that pathfinding republicans of his acquaintance, not least Belfastman James 'Spotter' Murphy, had improved the situation from the nadir of the mid-1970s:

> By the time that I had arrived in jail [in England] Spotter [Murphy] had set the conditions and set the standards on how we were going to be treated. He knew it would be important that IRA Volunteers in London jails at that time should stick together because they would be picked on, they would be harassed and at any sign of trouble the famous ghosting would take place … We weren't to be messed with and it was through him, by the time I arrived, prisoners were respectful and actually came to understand why we were in prison. They realized we weren't there for self-gain, for self-glorification … The screws came to realize there's no use in antagonizing them republicans because on the two occasions that republicans decided to show what they were capable of, two English prisons lost their complete roofs.[125]

Giuseppe Conlon, January 1980

The ill health of Giuseppe Conlon, father of Gerry Conlon of the Guildford Four and one of the equally innocent Maguire Seven prisoners, had been an issue from the time of his detention. Conlon senior was excused a remand appearance at Guildford on 16 December 1974 when the prison governor provided a note to the court stating that he was suffering from 'pulmonary tuberculosis'.[126] He returned to Wormwood Scrubs on 26 January 1978 after a difficult and debilitating stay in Wakefield from April 1977. The scourge of TB was exacerbated by a security crackdown in the London prison in September 1979, during which long-term prisoners in D wing lost the right to prepare their own meals and his dietary health again declined. Gerry Conlon, once more in the same prison as his father, was prevented from purchasing supplements from the canteen for his use. On 28 November news that his second application for parole had been rejected proved demoralising for the elder Belfastman.[127] Pat Hackett interacted with Giuseppe Conlon in Wormwood Scrubs, where he played snooker, cards and 'Mastermind', and found him 'very grey ... as thin as a heron, very skinny and gaunt ... in very bad health'.[128]

Individual IRA men openly expressed their anger at the British policy of jailing innocents whilst the national and tabloid press bemoaned sentences imposed on self-confessed English drug smugglers overseas. Billy Armstrong sent a letter from Manchester prison condemning 'the framing of whole families during trials here in England' and the treatment of 'old Joe Conlon who was only off the plane from Ireland'.[129] The wrongful conviction of Conlon was regarded as a separate injustice to that faced by his occasionally wayward son.[130] IRA prisoners in Wormwood Scrubs had made a strong impression on Cardinal Basil Hume in late December 1978 when they insisted, in a face-to-face encounter, that both Conlons were entirely innocent.[131] Hume commenced an unstinting campaign to assist Giuseppe Conlon in March 1979 when he informed Merlyn Rees that he had 'little doubt in my own mind that he is innocent'.[132] Such sentiments may well have borne fruit if Conlon had not lapsed into terminal decline. Whatever pressure brought to bear via Irish diplomatic channels was done behind closed doors.[133] Sinn Féin regarded D Wing Wormwood Scrubs as one of the more oppressive prison environments in England and mounted a protest at its main gates on 24 December 1979, the last major demonstration of its kind during the decade.[134]

A short fast undertaken by Conlon to protest his innocence may have hastened his death, but the Irishman's chronic ill health had been obvious to all from his arrival in prison. On 31 December 1979 he was moved to an outside hospital for what was expected to be his imminent death.[135] British authorities had timed the demise of Sean O Conaill with morbid precision but erred in the case of Conlon. On 8 January 1980 it was claimed that the fifty-six year old Conlon had a 'bronchial' illness but was in 'no immediate danger' despite receiving the Last Rites.[136] By 11 January 1980 they seemingly grew impatient and he was taken from an oxygen tent to the far more rudimentary 'hospital' facilities of Wormwood Scrubs. The move, by a police - escorted public taxi rather than squads of heavily armed and manned vehicles, was improbably explained as a response to fears that the IRA might attempt a rescue. After one week in his cell Conlon was returned to Hammersmith Hospital where he lingered from 18 January until his death at 7.00 p.m. on 23 January 1980.[137] Prison doctor Horace Hudson gave evidence that Conlon's health had not been 'affected' by the transfer back from Hammersmith.[138] The 20 March inquest returned a verdict of death from 'natural causes' in preference to the alternate 'lack of care'.[139]

Official language on such matters was conventionally terse and impersonal. When questioned on the sequence of events in the Commons the Home Secretary simply stated: 'Mr. Conlon died in hospital on 23 January'.[140] Sr. Clarke, one of the last people to see him alive, perceived the Belfastman's terminal moments in more emotive terms: 'In his hospital room, gasping for breath, a dying man ... surrounded by men in uniform'.[141]

British Airways cited spurious 'security reasons' when refusing to fly Conlon's body to Belfast and the RAF at Brize Norton declined to assist when the casket arrived at their base.[142] It beggared belief that the corpse of an Irish prisoner jeopardized an RAF facility where nuclear weapons were stored and transited. The family eventually succeeded in paying Aer Lingus to convey the remains to Aldergrove, Belfast and were made aware that the Home Office would not extend financial aid. On being questioned on the prospect of compensatory payment, Whitelaw replied with the shortest response possible in the English language: 'No'.[143] For three days the coffin had 'gone missing' and had, in fact, arrived in Belfast on four occasions without being unloaded.[144] In the course of the third failed attempt to deliver the remains, a British army officer informed the frustrated undertaker that press awareness of their arrival made it impossible for his soldiers to cooperate. He reputedly remarked: 'We can't be seen handling the body of an IRA man'.[145] The bizarre conflation of alleged security, logistic and PR explanations suggested that Conlon's death in British custody was regarded in a similar manner to that of actual IRA men in 1974–76. A final punishment was levied on the bereaved and their supporters to counteract or possibly discourage the potential of paramilitary propaganda. If numbed to silence in January 1980, Gerry Conlon was subsequently traumatized when reflecting on the maltreatment of his father's body.[146] He was disconcerted to hear it had 'disappeared for almost a full week before mysteriously turning up at an SAS base in Herefordshire'.[147]

Cardinal Basil Hume noted in a pointed letter to Merlyn Rees that an avowed anti-republican priest, Fr. Vincent McKinley, conducted the funeral service in Milltown Cemetery on 29 January and that no IRA presence was recorded.[148] The contrast with the McDade, Gaughan, Stagg, Jenkinson and O'Conaill burials from English prisons was stark indeed. Informed sources deduced that this signalled that Conlon was either out of favour with the Republican Movement or had never been a member. RUC Special Branch appeared as indifferent in Belfast as they had when Conlon was arrested in England on explosives charges at which time they opted not to search his Cyprus Street home. Although the lack of an IRA dimension decreased media interest in the family interment, *Irish News* published a sombre photograph of the disconsolate mourners.[149] English prisoners who had befriended Conlon in Wormwood Scrubs sent a wreath.[150]

Joan Maynard continued to question the Home Office in February 1980 on its treatment of Conlon and in so doing added to the momentum of an *ad hoc* campaign to secure his posthumous exoneration.[151] Media, including the relatively progressive *Guardian*, persisted in describing the deceased with pejorative emphasis as a 'gaoled IRA terrorist'.[152] Parliamentarians John Biggs-Davidson, Christopher Price and Gerry Fitt shared Cardinal Hume's intuition that an innocent man had died in British custody. They were sufficiently agitated as to query the reliability of forensic practices in the Commons on 4 August 1980, a politically courageous stance given the fraught context and official endorsement of the flawed science.[153] On 24 March Sheffield MP Martin Flannery had made an unsuccessful attempt to query the extent to which the TLC procedure was being utilized and relied upon by the police but could not elicit a direct answer from the discomforted Home Secretary.[154] Flannery was one of several Labour MPs refused entry to Long Kesh.[155]

In February 1979 Republicans had petitioned Conlon's repatriation on humanitarian grounds, a line of argument they generally refused to assert in relation to adherents.[156] His death revived the animosity of imprisoned IRA members, one of whom exclaimed: 'The hypocrites who are supposed to be respectable men, are now coming out from under the slime and stone … who all of a sudden say they believed old Joe to have been innocent all along'.[157] Conlon's fate inspired additional public statements, all but ignored in the media, regarding others jailed for actions attributed to the IRA. On 27 February 1980 Brendan Dowd, Joe O'Connell, Eddie Butler and Harry Duggan reiterated their call for the release of the 'Guildford Four' by claiming, once again, responsibility for the bombings for which the group had been wrongfully convicted. The story was carried as the front page of *An Phoblacht/ Republican News* on 1 March 1980 and was timed to capitalize on the sense of unease caused by Conlon's demise.[158] The 'Balcombe Street' prisoners had encountered Giuseppe Conlon and the similarly wrongly imprisoned 'Maguire Seven' during joint remand periods in Brixton prison in 1976–77. O'Connell, constrained by strict IRA codes of internal security, attempted to reassure the psychologically distressed strangers 'who were not involved in anything' by bluntly stating 'we know the whole story'. The implication was potentially momentous. Years later O'Connell reflected: 'Not sure how much it impacted. Obviously they were able to go and tell their families and solicitor whatever; "There are IRA men in there who believe we are innocent". Probably gave them a boost to their situation that they were in. Course they went on in their trial to get sentenced'.[159] The incident had been covered in Irish-American prints, giving impetus to Fr. Piaras O Duill's prison-themed speech in January 1980 to the Annual Testimonial Dinner of Irish Northern Aid in New York.[160]

Pat Hackett, who was among the IRA prisoners present when the MUFTI attacked the originally peaceable Wormwood Scrubs 'sit-down' in August 1979, felt obliged to mount additional protests to draw attention to the maltreatment he endured. On 31 December 1979 Hackett decided that he had no choice but to commence a 'blanket protest' in D Wing in order to settle a long - running dispute over the compulsory wearing of prison garb.[161] He had forewarned staff as the self-imposed deadline of the New Year approached: 'I'm not wearing no more fucking uniforms' and on 1 January 1980 stripped off the prison - issue clothing and footwear.[162] Hackett was aware that his action did not constitute IRA policy in England and was disfavoured by the majority of republican prisoners who prioritized escape plans. Other short-term men, moreover, naturally wished to retain their remission entitlements which promised early release. The D Wing O/C, in order to maintain equilibrium, asserted no opinion on Hackett's initiative.[163]

This form of dissent was not a decision to be taken lightly by a man missing two limbs. Delays in providing appropriate prosthetics and the generally low quality of medical treatment available in prison ensured that the utility of those dispensed was absolutely minimal. Declining the uniform entailed punishment in the Segregation Unit in A Wing where he was relocated on the night of 2 January 1980. Four men escorted him out of D Wing after evening lock up and he found a line of many more awaiting his arrival in the Block.[164] Wrapped only in a sheet and barefoot, the partially disabled Hackett was obliged to negotiate broken glass shards, ice and snow during the cross compound move of 300 yards before being 'shoved into an extremely cold cell whose windows had been deliberately been left wide open'.[165] Within days, as milder weather returned, Hackett was shifted to the infamous 'oven' cell where the convergence of multiple hot water pipes raised the temperature to unbearable levels. His makeshift insulation of newspaper sheets was classed a breach of regulations in that it allegedly attracted cockroaches to a wing, which, as with all others in the prison, was permanently infested by insects and vermin.[166] If Hackett had managed to secure repatriation on health grounds to Portlaoise, uniforms and work assignments did not pertain.[167] Prison Chaplain Fr. Ennis visited him twice daily for a period vainly attempting to 'talk' Hackett 'out of the protest'. On being advised that the authorities would never relent Hackett countered: 'I'm not going to give in to them either'. This stance and a strong hint that he would go on hunger strike if his meals were tampered with were expressed in the full expectation that it would reach the ears of Governor Honey. Petty harassment continued and included a pointlessly destructive cell search in which books borrowed from the prison library were tossed in the air to fall on the ground.[168]

Ron Lynch was the first IRA prisoner released in England in the new decade. On exiting Wormwood Scrubs prison on 18 January 1980 he was deflected from pursuing the next chapter in his life by waiting police.[169] Sr. Sarah Clarke learned that he was 'held in [Rochester Row] Police Station two days – family not knowing where he was, asked to turn informer – he said that he never belonged to any organization and never would and would/ could not inform'. Once freed, deportation under the PTA loomed, and he returned of his own volition to Cavan in Ireland.[170] Arrested in April 1973 as one of the 'Coventry Seven', Lynch had been convicted of IRA activities alongside Frank Stagg, who died on hunger strike in Wakefield in February 1976. Co-defendants Fr. Pat Fell and Sean Campbell were badly hurt when attacked by staff members in Albany in September 1976.[171] If comparatively unscathed by the English prison experience prior to being batoned by warders in Wormwood Scrubs in August 1979, Lynch was by no means fortunate. The assault he endured resulted in additional loss of remission that pushed his emancipation from October 1979 to January 1980.[172]

The number and complexity of individual cases ensured that few specific examples were raised by advocates of repatriation. Given the wider context of Armed Struggle, republicans rarely campaigned on the issue in isolation. When on 27 January 1980 approximately 200 National Front and British Movement followers attempted to disrupt the gathering of 2,000 pro-Irish republicans in Birmingham, a cordon of 650 police secured the Bull Ring rally destination. Kevin Colfer of Sinn Féin insisted the 'Bloody Sunday' commemoration would endure and that the party and 'their socialist brothers' would march in support of the prisoners in the H-Blocks and Armagh. Addressing the English dimension fell to Pat Arrowsmith of TOM, who called for the granting of political status and repatriation of those held in England. The Birmingham crowd, which drew people from across the country, was only 1,000 less in number than that which marched at the same time from the Creggan to Free Derry Corner.[173] The IRA attempted to keep media reportage of the H Blocks focused on those jailed and from March to June 1980 suspended its lethal campaign against 'prison officials' in the Six Counties. The stated intention was to 'create a climate for a just settlement of the political prisoners' demands' and the termination of the policy was indicative of competing pressures and disappointed expectations.[174]

The PTA was employed on 30 March 1980 when Gerry Mac Lochlainn (aka 'McLaughlin'), a leading Sinn Féin organizer in Wales, was arrested and held in Brynmawr, Gwent. He was charged with conspiracy to cause explosions. Fifty-two people were detained as part of investigations into a wave of arson attacks on English owned properties in Wales.[175] Mac Lochlainn, however, was primarily suspected of Irish republican activities and moved in such open and legal circles when he was a student in Aberystwyth. Detained at Liverpool Airport under the PTA in 1975, he experienced periodic Special Branch attention and in 1979 organized anti-H-Block demonstrations in Wales. Mac Lochlainn formed Cyfeillion Iwerddon

(Friends of Ireland) to create an outlet for Welsh nationalists interested in the Irish question who did not wish to adhere to British leftist groups that were ambivalent regarding the constitutional status of Wales. Having founded a Sinn Féin cumman in South Wales, Mac Lochlainn challenged his arrest for selling *AP/RN* and attracted Welsh TV coverage for what was presented as a freedom of speech debate. His arrest in March 1980 coincided with a time of Sinn Féin expansion in Wales.[176] On 3 April Mac Lochlainn was moved from Pontypool to Luton police station in preparation to charge him with conspiracy to cause explosions the following week.[177]

Mac Lochlainn's associate, Jim Reilly, Sinn Féin Home Counties organizer, was arrested on 31 March 1980 in Highfield Road, Luton. He had previously defended himself from deportation on the basis that he had been domiciled in England for thirty-four years. The Luton seizure marked Reilly's fourth detention under the PTA, albeit the first on which serious offences were alleged. Both men had strong trade union affiliations, which the PAC cited as significant in that it foiled police efforts to have them dismissed from employment. Michael Holden, another leading Sinn Féin activist and Hemel Hempstead Branch Secretary of the Association of Cinematograph Television and allied Technicians (ACTT), had been held for a week in August 1978 on flying into Heathrow from Germany. The only evidence produced in Luton Magistrates Court on 6 April 1980 was a formal claim that Reilly and Mac Lochlainn had purchased radio parts, a charge which implied but did not establish complicity in bomb making.[178] A crowd of fifty supporters gathered outside the building, four of whom were arrested and charged under the Public Order Act for refusing a command to disperse.[179] Days of noisy protests continued as the 'Hands off Ireland!' organization and others rallied in solidarity.[180]

The men were remanded in custody to Leicester Prison where, contrary to general protocols for unsentenced inmates, both were held in solitary confinement and obliged to wear uniforms.[181] Reilly, asthmatic and stricken with chronic bronchitis, was refused his one-hour exercise slot for pausing in the yard owing to respiratory problems. Supporters alleged that police had removed property from their homes and 'wrecked' a fifteen seat minibus that Sinn Féin had purchased for the use of the Green Cross prisoner welfare organization in Belfast.[182] It was also claimed that police misled their families by claiming they were being held in Bedford while knowing that they were actually in Leicester. Sinn Féin had picketed Bedford Prison on 8 April, despite the arrest of several RCG/ 'Hands off Ireland!' allies in previous days.[183] The two republicans were bailed on 10 May 1980 on sureties of £10,000 each; this was a fortunate circumstance in that England and Wales did not apply the 110-day rule of maximum remand and IRA suspects frequently spent over a year in custody ahead of trial.[184] Mac Lochlainn divined that the authorities were perturbed by Reilly's ill-health and desirous to avoid another controversial death in custody.[185] The Home Office was under a degree of scrutiny owing to the rising trend in prison suicides: six in 1975, nine in 1976, seven in 1977 and 1978 and twelve in 1979. Tragically, twenty prisoners took their own lives between January and July 1980.[186] Temporary respite from imprisonment enabled Mac Lochlainn to organize a 'Bloody Sunday' commemoration in Cardiff on 25 January 1981.[187] Sir John Woodcock, Chief Constable of South Wales, was petitioned to ban a procession normally staged in London. An Anti-Nazi League contingent attacked 350 National Front members in the suburb of Llandaff despite the presence of 1,652 police. NF leader Martin Webster claimed his group wished to oppose 'supporters of the murdering IRA strutting through our streets'.[188] In December 1994 Woodcock investigated the sensational escape of five IRA men from Whitemoor SSU.[189]

Reilly's asthma and heart condition worsened during captivity. When remanded in custody staff allegedly withheld medicines leading to an emergency in which they were obliged to relent lest he succumb. His health did not recover following release and he became seriously ill in September 1980. After two weeks in hospital, Reilly died aged 54 on 26 September 1980.[190] As with Giuseppe Conlon, British Airways refused to repatriate the body from Heathrow to Aldergrove Airport, Belfast, citing what republicans regarded as insincere fears of Loyalist reaction in Antrim. The Irish semi-state carrier Aer Lingus, according to *AP/RN*, accepted the contract with the proviso that there be 'no republican tribute' upon arrival in Dublin Airport.[191] The memory of the Michael Gaughan demonstrations in June 1974 and the Frank Stagg fiasco in February 1976 evidently still reverberated in the Twenty-Six Counties. Reilly was buried in Milltown Cemetery on 3 October 1980 where the main oration was given by John Higgins, formerly of Luton Sinn Féin. Higgins had been released from Parkhurst on 9 March 1979 when his successful appeal against consecutive sentences reduced his term from ten to four years. Detained within the grounds of Parkhurst under the PTA, he was subject to an Exclusion Order and deported to Belfast after three days in Newport and Southampton police stations.[192] He opened a pub in Dundalk. Liam Hannaway and Jimmy Drumm represented the Republican Movement at Reilly's funeral. Fr. McKinley, who had refused to perform funeral services for IRA Volunteer Kevin 'Dee' Delaney, would not permit Reilly's coffin to be decorated with the Tricolour inside St. Peter's Chapel on the Lower Falls.[193]

Justice Purchas sentenced Gerry Mac Lochlainn to six years imprisonment on 16 April 1981 after the jury heard testimony from a 'secret witness … Colonel X' and were shown circumstantial evidence.[194] He was moved to A Wing, Wormwood Scrubs, separated from IRA members held on D Wing or, in the case of Paul Norney, the Segregation Block. One of the few Category A prisoners on the wing was Fowzie Nejad, a survivor of the bloody Iranian

Embassy siege. The Derryman was moved to Maidstone Prison in September 1981, a Category B establishment in Kent where he was the only long-term republican prisoner.[195] He corresponded with Billy Armstrong who, when in Wormwood Scrubs, wryly noted that Mac Lochlainn had been 'living in Wales when he was done on a diabolical charge of having a two way radio'.[196] The Court of Appeal reduced Mac Lochlainn's sentence to four years on 26 April 1982 on the basis that he had been charged under the wrong act and inappropriately associated with evidence pertaining solely to his deceased co-defendant.[197] Reilly's Sinn Féin membership card and other irrelevant political ephemera had been produced in court.[198] In Maidstone Mac Lochlainn commenced his punishment as a short term Irish political prisoner. His refusal to manufacture clothing for the MOD in February 1982 entailed loss of a week's remission and two days in solitary on more than one occasion.[199]

Easter commemorations inside the prisons were held whenever circumstances permitted. Writing from A Wing, Wakefield in April 1980, Billy Armstrong stated: 'My comrades and I always wear our Easter Lily on Easter Sunday and stand for a few minutes silence in commemoration for those who died in Ireland'.[200] This typically led to punishment, and Ray McLaughlin received three days in F Wing on this occasion.[201] Prisoners also marked the anniversary of the execution of Tom Williams, a man who rated alongside 1920s' martyr Kevin Barry for many Belfast republicans.[202] The event was very much in living memory and leading Sinn Féin fundraiser, Joe Cahill, had been reprieved from a death sentence arising from the same incident which sent 18-year-old Williams to the gallows in Crumlin Road. Williams had not fired the shot that killed RUC Constable Patrick Murphy in April 1942 and it was understood in some republican circles that Cahill was personally responsible.[203]

Although not part of the republican cadre in Durham, Anne Maguire may have been boosted by the broad 10 May 1978 'North of England Irish Prisoners Committee' demonstration in the town's Market Square. The Gillespie sisters were the only genuine republican women in the prison at a time where the wrongfully convicted Judith Ward, Carole Richardson and Anne Maguire were all present. Hugh Doherty was being held in solitary in the same prison.[204] Maguire had mounted a short fast in Durham on 18 February 1980 and was seeking vindication from the courts. She was, as such, unlikely to have accepted release on purely humanitarian grounds.[205] Ward, a former member of Britain's Women's Army Corps, had been wrongfully convicted of the M62 coach bombing in which twelve soldiers and dependents were killed. Initial concern by Sr. Sarah Clarke that the eccentric Ward was a 'Double Agent' were dispelled by her maltreatment by the judiciary and prison system.[206] Richardson, a young recreational drug user when interrogated for IRA incidents of which she had no knowledge, had been administered Pethidine to counteract hysteria and hyperventilation. At no time in prison did Richardson's demeanour or actions resemble that of a former member of the Republican Movement.[207]

Wormwood Scrubs, June 1980

The importance of addressing the MUFTI controversy in Wormwood Scrubs was illustrated by a rooftop occupation on 24 June 1980 when five D Wing prisoners climbed up from the laundry and tossed tiles onto the ground.[208] Ronnie McCartney, a veteran of the Gartree roof protest, was the only IRA participant in the overnight demonstration and received much publicity due to the ability of street level photographers to see the men and their banners.[209] He was one of fifty-four 'exchange' prisoners brought into D Wing after the August 1979 incident to replace men dispersed across the system.[210] McCartney found on arrival that 'the screws were really on top' and the environment was more oppressive than before. Governor Bob Duncan, with whom a form of rapport later developed, took 'real delight in sentencing' him 'to fourteen days, every fourteen days' for refusing to do prison work. He shared the Segregation Unit with habitual non-conformist Pat Hackett who remained 'on the blanket'.[211] English prison activist Micky Morris and IRA man John McCluskey informed McCartney that a roof occupation was planned and he consequently agreed to go to the workshops to enable participation. McCluskey, ironically, was then sent to the 'Punishment Block', leaving McCartney to represent the IRA in widespread ongoing protests organized by Britons.[212] They were not alone in seeking to highlight the true nature of the new regime and the National Association of Probation Officers had added their voice to calls to abolish MUFTI teams at their AGM in May 1980.[213] The core D Wing group acted in unison during exercise time to gain access to the laundry roof which they 'wrecked' and defended from staff attempting to challenge them physically. Having displayed signs reading 'MUFTI Mad Dogs' and 'D Wing-the Mean Machine', McCartney, John Wood, Billy Webb, Keith Kelly and Micky Morris descended at 3.30 p.m. on 25 June.[214] Predictably, McCartney received 'another beating' for his transgressions.[215]

In the last week of May 1980, during 'a rash' of suicides in the London prison, blanket protester Pat Hackett 'decorated' the Governor and other staff inspecting the Segregation Unit of A Wing, Wormwood Scrubs.[216] Staff unlocked his door at 8.00 a.m. and one shouted 'Hackett, put down that pot'. Two warders appeared with fire buckets filled with water and successfully goaded him with racist insults and aggressive feints to grab and then toss the hitherto untouched chamber pot towards his abusers. Prisoners could never hope to triumph in such circumstances and the all but inevitable response was a relay of several buckets thrown over his body, including one with disinfectant and another with hot water. With his floor flooded to a depth of two inches, the drenched Hackett reasoned that he could be left as he was for some time without alleviation. He did not apprehend physical assault as he was aware that the Board of Visitors was in session in A Wing and that 'civilians' would never be permitted to witness such a scene. After a period of making 'a racket', Assistant Governor Morrison arrived around 3.00 p.m. and provided him with dry bedding. The denouement proved to be a charge of assaulting staff, a near comical allegation against a man possessing just two fully functional limbs. He was docked 120 days' remission and given twenty-eight days 'cellular confinement'.[217]

Observing the unwritten understanding pertaining to resistance in solitary confinement, the Tipperary man had taken pains when throwing a container of urine towards the approaching Governor and colleagues to avoid drenching the mattresses confiscated from fellow prisoners which had been stacked in the corridor by staff.[218] On serving his notional additional punishment on 15 July, Hackett was driven under heavy escort to Wakefield in Yorkshire.[219] He recalled the minutes in which his three years in London terminated: 'Suddenly there was a door banging against the cell and they came charging in on top of me, pinned me to the table and put handcuffs on me ... some of them talking amongst themselves outside my cell saying "he'll last six months and that's all"'. This development separated him from Dubliner Mick Murray who was also on a 'blanket' protest in the Segregation Block. Murray had previously interacted with Hackett when both were on D Wing but contact in solitary confinement was fleeting and verbal in nature.[220]

Hackett, an intelligent and resourceful republican, keenly understood the importance of penetrating the barrier of censorship maintained around the Dispersal System by the Home Office. He managed on several occasions to smuggle detailed accounts of his dire personal experiences to the Republican Movement, which attempted to champion his case with publicity, propaganda and a dedicated campaign. Arrival into Wakefield in a coarse blanket on 15 July 1980 prompted a formulaic ritual in which the prison staff of a notorious institution attempted to convince the Irishman to wear the regulation uniform. His refusal could have come as no surprise and arrangements were in place to house him in the segregation unit in F Wing. Hackett, probably the single-most physically disadvantaged IRA man in England, was consequently confined in the most hated block in Britain.[221] In a statement carried by *An Phoblacht* he claimed:

> It is completely separated from the rest of the jail and is self-sufficient with even its own private exercise yard ... Unlike other normal prison wings, only one side of F wing contains cells and all those cell windows face out into the exercise yard, while the side which would be facing the main prison contains nothing but a blank wall. The exercise yard runs the full length of the wing – about 20 feet wide and

surrounded by a high wall. The wall opposite our cells was painted white with weird designs in darker colours at intervals along its length and at night powerful lights were shone onto it so that it was never really dark in our cells ... I experienced constant and very irritating noise, it was only turned off during sleeping hours ... The cells were about 6ft by 10 and the furniture consisted of a chair, a press which also acted as a table and the metal bed frame which was bolted to the floor ... I was kept in complete isolation. If I happened to see another prisoner, we were not allowed to speak ... There was no heating in the cells and for the first couple of months I had only a small hand towel to keep myself warm during the day.[222]

Hackett was permitted the use of his blanket during the day from October and on 18 November was transferred to the hospital unit following an altercation with staff.[223] Over three years into solitary confinement, Hackett reputedly had no communication except with 'the prison warders at whose hands he receives frequent harsh treatment'.[224] Amnesty International queries were answered by Home Office assurances that the situation was 'within prison rules' and derived from his refusal to conform.[225] There was no sense of compassion in play and a prison doctor in Wakefield reputedly advised him to 'go on hunger strike as he would make a lovely corpse'.[226] Among those held in F Wing were Alex Casson and Bob 'The Cannibal' Maudsley, both of whom had killed other prisoners. Noel Gibson was the sole IRA man with whom any contact was possible. He noticed that Jimmy Ashe had carved his name into a wooden bed frame. A stint in Wakefield's prison hospital, where he was evidently relocated to prevent an Irish embassy official seeing the harsh conditions of F Wing, was enlivened by emergency evacuation arising from a fire started by the occupant of the adjacent cell. During a brief period of fire control, Hackett met IRA prisoner Michael MacLochlainn.[227]

After two years in Wakefield, Hackett was moved via Windsor to more suitable yet dangerous confinement in Parkhurst's Hospital Wing.[228] He was told on arrival in July 1982 that if he abandoned the 'blanket' protest he could go onto the wings. This was rejected. Conditions, however, were generally better than the austere north of England, not least regular access to outdoor exercise. Among the IRA prisoners he encountered arising from their sporting and minor injuries were Harry Duggan, Paul Holmes, John McCluskey, John McComb, Eddie Byrne, Stevie Nordone, Billy Armstrong and Gerry McDonnell. The national prison medical role of the centre ensured that Hackett also met famous English prisoners such as Reggie Kray and 'Yorkshire Ripper' Peter Sutcliffe. Hackett regarded Sutcliffe as a 'lunatic' and was displeased when he gave his young niece a Yorkie chocolate bar in the visiting room. Princess Anne, a member of the British Royal Family, also visited in an informal capacity, leading to opportunist calls from the republicans such as 'what about the Birmingham Six?'

Hackett recalled 'she was well able to give back lip herself'.[229] In March 1984 Dr. Cooper's diagnosis of paranoid schizophrenia was instrumental in moving Sutcliffe from Parkhurst to Broadmoor Hospital. Home Secretary Leon Brittan authorized the transfer under the Mental Health Act upon advice received from Cooper and Broadmoor's medical director, Dr. John Hamilton.[230]

Marian Price was released from Armagh Jail on 30 June 1980 after seven years of a life sentence imposed in Winchester, England. Price was in very poor health owing to the onset of anorexia nervosa and as such a deserving recipient of therapy available in the Twenty-Six Counties.[231] Prison Chaplain Fr. Ray Murray warned she was 'in danger of death' and it was reported that Price additionally suffered from TB, a debilitating legacy of the Brixton hunger strike. Her release occurred under the terms of a pardon extended in the form of a conceptual 'Royal Prerogative of Mercy', rather than a more conventional emancipation 'on license'.[232] British sources insisted, however, that she had been 'freed on license' and, unconvincingly, that her serious medical state had 'no connection with her hunger strike'.[233] Unionist politicians protested but most must have privately appreciated that the overt humanitarian context served to alleviate pressure on British authorities when under scrutiny from Strasbourg.[234] Republicans ascertained that the day of the announcement was less than twenty-four hours prior to the scheduled release from Armagh of the first female 'no wash' protester, Rose McAllister, an event which would otherwise have garnered more press attention.[235]

Dolours Price was described in Fr. Murray's annual chaplaincy review as being in 'appalling condition', yet NIO clemency was not extended.[236] She was one of just three women republicans in Armagh Prison entitled to 'special category status' in C Wing from whence Governor Scott was endeavouring to remove them in order to join the protesters in A Wing or conformists in B Wing.[237] The Price family in Andersonstown, Belfast, informed well-wishers that they were endeavouring to 'keep everything quiet' to facilitate the rehabilitation of the underweight Marian and hoped for emancipation of her sister.[238] News of the release of Dolours Price from a Belfast hospital on 22 April 1981, to which she had been transferred when unwell from Armagh, 'pleased' her co-accused, Billy Armstrong. Health grounds had been cited for the decision, a medically related humanitarian dimension utterly absent from the experience of IRA prisoners in England.[239] A British press synopsis of the NIO statement noted that the early release of Price was '"on license ... In accordance with well-established policy" and was by royal prerogative'.[240] In the early 1980s, the Prices represented the sole example of advantage being gained by life - sentenced IRA prisoners repatriated from England. The first of their sentenced 'Belfast Ten' co-defendants to be released in Britain, Liam McLarnon, was taken from Long Lartin and deported to Ireland in August 1984, having served twelve of a fifteen-year sentence.[241] Fame and notoriety in the 1970s followed the sisters in the decades ahead when both were referred to in the print media using the prefix 'Old Bailey bomber'.[242] After years of ill-health, Dolours Price died suddenly in Dublin aged 61 in January 2013.[243]

Punished for the Albany Riot, Eddie O'Neill had struggled to regain his health in solitary confinement in Winson Green following his sojourn in Parkhurst Prison Hospital. His refusal to either deliver or collect his bedding in the Punishment Block, an assertion of political status, ensured that he was lying on a basement floor with no furniture, radio, books or possessions other than a pencil and notebook. Months living in such conditions approximated to prolonged sensory deprivation and he experienced hallucinations which, having discounted the probability of being secretly drugged, made him question his sanity. Frustration at the lack of escape opportunities played a major part in O'Neill's case until the phase of irrationality gradually passed. On being moved to a normal wing in Parkhurst, he spent much of 1980 rebuilding his physical strength by running and weight lifting.[244]

Hugh Doherty, who had spent more time in Durham than any other male IRA Volunteer, was moved back to Winson Green in June 1980, arising from what appeared to be either a planned assault by staff or a dangerous overreaction. As he was being returned to his cell following a search, one of the escorting prison officers unexpectedly struck Doherty heavily from behind. He recalled: 'Of course the row got up in the cell and they tried to smother me. I remember I was in the mattress. I was fighting but you can only fight so many, you can only go so much. I remember just starting to black out'. On reflection, Doherty surmised that the search and escort team had panicked when he resisted the initial attack. He doubted that his assailants consciously intended to kill him but attributed his survival to the timely intervention of a professional Principal Officer from Liverpool. An extended 'lie-down' in Winson Green immediately followed, where he conversed with Eddie O'Neill from afar and ascertained that John McCluskey was elsewhere in the prison.[245] The Birmingham jail retained its reputation for brutality, but even Doherty was surprised when staff members 'went around' on 24 December 1979 and 'smashed all the cells for Christmas Day'.[246] Eddie Butler had been 'swapped' for Doherty in Durham, having been held in solitary confinement in Winson Green and Strangeways until February 1980 due to the closure of Leicester SSU. He met 'Mad' Frankie Fraser in Durham, who was on good terms with several IRA prisoners and exercised sufficient influence to be moved to a cell beside Butler. It was some time before the roster of Category A prisoners in the block to one of three small caged enclosures set aside for exercise enabled direct conversation. The two men raised the ire of staff responsible for mail distribution by receiving colossal numbers of seasonal cards.[247]

Wilkinson and Wakefield

Britain's prison population reached its highest level in March 1980 when 44,800 were incarcerated, and progressive commentators such as Robert Kilroy-Silk predicted increased agitation.[248] The May 1980 inquest into the death in custody of George Wilkinson highlighted issues encountered on a regular basis by IRA prisoners in England. Part of the fall-out of Wilkinson's demise on 5 December 1979 in Walton jail, Liverpool, was the revelation that Governor Driscoll had offered him a 'reversion' programme of graduated re-integration in Durham prison, based on the three month blocks developed for the Control Units.[249] Driscoll outlined the plan in May 1979, four years after the ostensible abandonment of the earlier version. As matters transpired, the oppressive working of Rule 43 hastened Wilkinson's death in Walton.[250] A 24 November 1981 decision of the Court of Appeal ensured that a case taken in May 1980 by Mickey Williams did not go to the House of Lords where additional information on the Control Unit in Wakefield would have been aired.[251] The much publicised May 1980 inquest heard that Wilkinson had been kept for eighteen months in a special white – painted cell with wire doors. A wall had been constructed outside his window to block natural light and the limited prison yard 'view'.[252] It was noted that Wilkinson, an armed robber, was regarded as an aggressive prisoner who had mounted a hunger strike and on two occasions seized hostages. He evidently crossed a threshold by taking a Principal Officer captive in Parkhurst in 1976. Amongst other privations, he was given pointless electric shock treatment and segregated for eighteen months. Unsurprisingly, the combination of 'ghosting', isolation and unjustified medication resulted in his detachment from the general prisoner population.[253] Terry Munyard reported that Wilkinson was shifted 'as far away from his family … as possible' and moved on ten occasions in his last four years in the system. For much of the time he was held in isolation and 'heavily sedated with a cocktail of psychotropic drugs – at one stage he was on 900mg of Largactil a day'.[254]

Wilkinson's story was associated by the *Times* in November 1981 with that of Doug Wakefield, a convicted killer held in Hull's 'Cage' under the punishment block.[255] Segregation was described in 1980 as 'damp ground floor or basement cells, double barred, double doored, cockroach ridden and inadequately lit'.[256] The pair came to symbolize the undercurrent of brutality within the Dispersal System, a role which numerous IRA prisoners were eminently qualified to fulfil, although rejected as suitable exemplars by the British press and most penal advocates. Sentenced to life in May 1974, Wakefield had a reputation for violence against staff and was singled out for harsh treatment.[257] In August 1975 he closed himself into his Long Lartin cell with a Principal Officer hostage and he was wrongly assumed to have played a role in the following year's Hull riot.[258] Rule 43 was invoked to facilitate the infliction of informal punishment. Ghosting on twenty occasions in six years, denial of writing privileges and general harassment inspired Wakefield to smuggle his story out of jail on sheets of toilet paper. He briefly surfaced in April 1977 when housed for six months on D Wing of Wormwood Scrubs and feared in 1980 that he would ultimately be killed by either deliberate neglect or direct assault presented as 'suicide'.[259] Segregated after September 1978, the month in which he stabbed and strangled another Parkhurst prisoner to death, he claimed that 'prison guards have told me that they could after the Hull riot now hang me and get away with it'.[260] Few knew his whereabouts at any given time and those that did were in a poor position to communicate details to others. His predicament when in Long Lartin stirred John McCluskey to pass messages through his visitors in order to stage a protest on Wakefield's behalf. McCluskey was returned to Wormwood Scrubs in consequence.[261]

PROP opened an office in Caledonian Road, London and in July 1980 published Wakefield's provocative *A thousand days in solitary* with the aid of Warwick University faculty. The author had an IQ of 150 and was a member of Mensa.[262] The pamphlet posed uncomfortable questions for the Home Office about several deaths in custody and staff violence towards British prisoners. The preface contributed by a PROP writer noted similarities with the experience of IRA men: 'Most prison deaths are the culmination of long drawn out torture and medical neglect – Noel Jenkinson and Sean O'Connaill [sic] amongst the many Irishmen who have suffered, and continue to suffer, such conditions'.[263] While no IRA prisoners were either forcibly drugged with regularity or subjected to electrotherapy, the semi-secret routine of 'ghosting', isolation, visitor disruption and staff hostility were typical.

Overcrowding, pay grievances and problems posed by the 'decaying fabric' of England's Victorian prisons led to discord during the autumn between the Home Office and the Prison Officers Association, who threatened to strike.[264] The need for essential renovations in Brixton and Wormwood Scrubs led to specialized parts of the prison operations being transferred to other sites. Governor John McCarthy's 'penal dustbin' comments in November 1981 courted controversy but did not result in an expected reprimand from Home Secretary William Whitelaw.[265] Staff in the sprawling London prison had a poor reputation in republican circles and it was noted that Palestinian political prisoner Fahad Mihyi had been badly injured in an unprovoked assault within sight of disinterested prison officers.[266] Stories alleging abuse of prisoners in a system widely recognized as being overpopulated and afflicted by staff disputes prompted occasional commentary from the British Establishment. On 10 October 1980 Lords Brockway and Avebury pressed Lord Belstead in the House of Lords in relation to 'the chaos there now in the prisons'.[267] Arising from reporting limitations, Belstead was incapable of providing precise numbers of those segregated under Rule 43 but furnished estimates of 1,054, 1,187 and 1,322 as the average so designated for the sample months of August 1977, 1978 and 1979. While this did not necessarily indicate a higher utilization of Rule 43 given rising overall prison occupancy, it confirmed that that more men were indeed being held in locations where, if rated Category A, no privileges could be extended. Avebury was unequivocal in his view that 'segregation is a form of punishment which is inflicted on a prisoner without any charges being preferred against him, without his being given an opportunity of a hearing before a tribunal of any kind'.[268]

Albany and Leicester

The situation in Albany, where Liam Baker and Tony Cunningham had been 'on the blanket' since October 1978, was featured in *AP/RN* on 7 June 1980. Pat 'Tipp' Guilfoyle smuggled a letter to the newspaper in May describing the struggle between the IRA prisoners and Governor Mole. Deprived of exercise and held in solitary, Baker and Cunningham were said to be 'pale and weak' and in no position to exert pressure on the inflexible authorities.[269] IRA comrades, however, started a sustained campaign of arson and triggered alarm bells that summoned police into the jail to investigate. The TV room was torched and the second major fire set since May adding credibility to numerous hoax alarms which the prison staff attributed to the republicans without evidence. Tension levels were high in the prison and Guilfoyle reasoned that the two D Wing men who threw chamber pots over the Governor were not beaten in solitary owing to fear that maltreatment would incite a riot. A sit down protest in the exercise yard by forty men passed off peaceably. Various ploys were used to coax the IRA prisoners into acceptable modes of behaviour. Lord Longford was allowed visit 'Tipp' Guilfoyle and Busty Cunningham when they were in solitary, a move which the Tipperary man believed had been intended to weaken their resolve. In a separate initiative Guilfoyle was promised temporary relocation to a mainland England prison in order to receive accumulated visits in June if he complied with staff instructions.[270]

The IRA in Albany faced considerable challenges in airing their claims. In the first instance, the culture of secrecy which shrouded Home Office direction of the Prison Department made it difficult for any prisoner to attract media attention. The newly instated right wing Conservative Government was ideologically disinclined to facilitate open or wide ranging discussions of prison controversies in the House of Commons. The logistics of the Irish conflict also obliged Sinn Féin and its allies to concentrate on the strategic issues in play in the Six Counties. When, on 14 June 1980, the 'Voices for withdrawal' conference convened in Conway Hall, London, delegates and 300 attendees were shown a filmed interview with ex-Blanketmen Joe Maguire and Fra McCann. Prominent speakers, not least Peter Hain, Clive Soley MP, Phil Flynn, Jack Bennett, Geoff Bell and Mick Martin (Chair of the Hammersmith and Kensington Trades Council), addressed the major question of the British military presence in Ireland rather than the local, underreported and comparatively marginal theme of Irish political prisoners in Wandsworth and Wormwood Scrubs.[271]

Brendan Dowd was moved to the reopened Special Unit in Leicester in late May 1980 following sixty-two days' solitary confinement in Winchester prison. A letter smuggled to a comrade from Winchester was carried by the PAC journal *The Irish Prisoner* in which Dowd commented on the political landscape. The Kerryman was 'glad' to hear of the publicity being generated by the H-Block/ Armagh protest. An assertion that Liam Cosgrave and Jack Lynch 'covered up the truth' about the Dublin and Monaghan bombings of May 1974 was contentious, although his claim that they would 'face justice' would have been interpreted by the security services of Britain and Ireland as a threat.[272] Dowd was highly conscious of the propaganda value of such letters and intended to damage British state interests.[273] Eddy Butler and Brian Keenan soon joined him in the small ground floor SSU.[274]

Brian Keenan, the 38-year-old IRA GHQ member who had liaised with Dowd's London ASU in the mid-1970s, was sentenced to eighteen years imprisonment by Justice Kenneth Jones on 25 June 1980. Attorney General Sir Michael Havers QC headed the prosecution in the Old Bailey but after making what *Time Out* reported as a 'somewhat puzzling opening' delegated the task to two subordinates.[275] The only physical evidence produced in court was a partly completed *Daily Mail* crossword fragment recovered in an IRA safe house in Scarisbrick Drive, Liverpool. Handwriting expert David Maurice Ellen declared the entries to be the work of the Irish man, whose fingerprints were apparently matched with a partial set recovered many years earlier from a damaged vending machine in Luton. Acquitted on two of the four charges, Keenan's conviction rested on a ten to two jury majority from 'a vetted panel'.[276] This divide probably accounted for the comparatively light sentence of eighteen years for incidents the prosecution had attributed to the multiple life - sentenced 'Balcombe Street' men. The four were the most recent Irish republicans to appear in the famous court.[277] In a two hour 'speech from the dock', Keenan admitted staying with Hugh Doherty in a London flat in November 1975, but disingenuous claims of innocent purposes were disbelieved.[278]

The paucity of hard evidence encouraged speculation ahead of the trial that a 'mystery informer' would appear in court. Writing in *Hibernia* magazine, David Brazil surmised that the person 'may turn out to be another Irish prisoner already convicted in Britain, trying to do a belated deal for favourable consideration by the parole board'. This did not occur in 1980 or at any time during the Long War in England, and such stories were regarded as part of a psychological strategy to disconcert the IRA.[279] *Guardian* security correspondent Nick Davies reported that the prosecution 'overplayed its hand' in terms of its most sensational unproven allegations against the defendant and had difficulty winning the jury on more substantive points.[280] Much was made of the dramatic production in evidence of 'three bank notes, one Libyan and two Irish, all roughly torn in half'. It was assumed the bills were examples of a code system linked to Colonel Gaddafi's North African regime and linked to an alleged shipment of weaponry planned for August 1979.[281] The Arabic note was actually Lebanese, which Keenan had hoped might provide grounds for an appeal when misidentified by the Prosecution. The well-travelled trial judge recognized the currency and immediately settled the matter.[282] Alleged connections between Irish republicans and international militants, occasionally well grounded, were highly newsworthy in Britain.[283]

Time Out queried whether the jury had been influenced by a trial 'conducted with such a high level of security' and quoted defending QC Michael Mansfield on the possibility that such factors could 'intrude'.[284] One juror was sufficiently nervous as to object to the demeanour of Keenan's wife and mother who were then instructed by the judge to sit out of her line of sight in the public gallery. Mansfield's request that the jury be discharged on the basis that they were susceptible to regarding the defendant as 'a dangerous man' was not entertained.[285] Left wing supporters asserted: 'British imperialism was determined to jail Brian Keenan and it did so with the minimum of legal formality'.[286] Although restricted to a minor role in the trial, the initial presence of the Attorney General indicated its perceived importance to the Establishment. Havers had entered the Commons as Conservative MP for Wimbledon in 1970 and was a close ally of Margaret Thatcher. He was credited with having 'led for the Crown' in the trials of the Birmingham Six and Guildford Four and despite justified concerns that all ten were innocent, was appointed Lord Chancellor by Thatcher in 1987.[287]

Proceedings in the Old Bailey touched on a number of strands of IRA activity in Britain in the 1970s. Keenan managed to avoid conviction on two charges of conspiracy to cause explosions in Liverpool with Tony Clarke, who had been sentenced to fourteen years imprisonment in September 1977 for possession of war material.[288] Another man was detained in Liverpool at the time of Clarke's arrest but deported to answer unconnected political charges in Belfast. Former republican internee Gerry 'Blute' McDonnell was convicted in June 1986 of planning major IRA attacks in England.[289] The *Evening News* commented that Keenan 'was behind the eighteen bombings and shootings which terrorised London and the Home Counties for months and only ended in the Balcombe Street siege' in December 1975. Such reportage ensured that the Belfast man entered the Dispersal System with a reputation.[290] He was described variously as an 'IRA mastermind' and the 'IRA's Mr. Evil', destined for imprisonment in a 'specially built security wing at Gartree jail'.[291] The *Guardian* named Keenan as the IRA's Director of Operations and 'architect of carnage'.[292] Details emerged of his alleged plans to mount a bombing campaign against the British Army on the Rhine in West Germany in early 1974 and his role in receiving thirteen tons of weaponry in batches from Libya in 1975.[293] He was accused by British Intelligence sources cited by *The Observer* in 1986 of arranging explosives training for 'Brighton Bomber' Pat Magee in the Middle East. Truth was not separated from fiction in both the courts and the media while the Republican Movement declined to comment.[294] If perplexed by certain exaggerations entertained in court, Keenan believed the judge had acted fairly and conceded that the recovery and utilization of the crossword fragment was 'quite a good piece of collated information'.[295]

The IRA in the SSUs

Brian Keenan had already served eight months in jail for IRA membership imposed by the Special Criminal Court in Dublin on 8 November 1974; he adapted quickly to the new environment in England.[296] His first long-term place of detention, Leicester Special Unit, was dissimilar from anything in use in Ireland. Ghosted temporarily to Durham in December 1980, Keenan encountered permanent lighting, closed visits and being shifted between cells that were freezing cold or overheated.[297] Projecting a degree of stoicism was psychologically advantageous under such circumstances. He quipped in late 1982 that he was 'regarded by most of my fellow POWs as a short timer. My sentence is only twenty-one years'.[298] Isolation in Leicester minimized face-to-face contact with fellow republicans and rendered Keenan indisposed to make public general comments on the IRA in the Dispersal System.[299] Among the men Keenan encountered during a decade inside the 'Submarine' were Donald Neilson, Harry 'Big H' MacKenney and bullion raider Mickey 'The General' McAvoy.[300] London-Irish man McAvoy was charged on 8 December 1983 with masterminding the theft of £26 million in gold bullion from the Heathrow headquarters of Brink's-Mat on 26 November 1983.[301]

One former IRA associate, Hugh Doherty, was moved amidst considerable security from Winson Green to Parkhurst SSU on 4 July 1980, where he re-encountered Harry Duggan and Joe O'Connell. A number of English prisoners he had known in Leicester SSU, including Freddie Sewell and Johnny Joyce, were also present, as was Cyril Burke and armed robber Dave Martin, whose penchant for wearing elaborate disguises boosted his press profile. Doherty noted that the 'English were always falling out', but this did not prevent co-operation on planning escapes and matters of mutual interest.[302] Harry Roberts was present for a time and regarded by republicans as a 'very interesting character' who 'helped us a lot'.[303] London gangsters were especially open minded: 'If you weren't attacking them outside … 99 per cent of them, more or less would say, "The British Army shouldn't be in Ireland but we don't agree with bombs going off or with blowing up innocents". They didn't mind how many police you killed or judges ... or if you were attacking screws ... But there would be a hostile reaction say if something [perceived as indiscriminate] happened'.[304] Living for years in proximity to up to eight others convicted of serious offences had benefits and demerits. IRA men in the oppressive 'units', whether Parkhurst, Leicester or the later Whitemoor facility, were present in numbers out of all proportion to the general Category A population. Left to schedule their own hours, Parkhurst SSU offered a workshop, classroom, kitchenette and a small, enclosed exercise yard. The men ignored instructions to avoid conversation with prisoners housed on the wings who often approached the compound. Lifers could not be effectively sanctioned for such trivial misdemeanours.[305] Leicester SSU was described by the Home Office as having 'physical conditions [that] are not very satisfactory for long-term inmates. There is little natural light in the central recreation area and the ceiling is low, giving a somewhat cramped feeling to the unit, which over a long period could become claustrophobic'.[306]

In his Home Office Research and Planning Unit Report completed in 1988, Roy Walmsley noted that men assigned to SSUs by the Director General of the Prison Service were generally 'major spies', 'major "terrorists" (eg offenders sentenced to long terms of imprisonment for causing explosions)', 'notorious offenders who have killed in the commission of crime' and other intelligent Category A prisoners with the capacity to initiate or benefit from escape attempts. In October 1987 the fourteen men inside the two operational units comprised under 4 per cent of the 369 Category A prisoners in England and Wales. In the decade since October 1977 a mere sixteen men had been selected by Prison Service Headquarters for SSU confinement, eight of whom were IRA 'bombers' and just four 'well-resourced robbers'. According to Walmsley: 'It is considered that all of these men could well have been the subject of a rescue attempt if they had been located in a dispersal prison'.[307] Nine men, most of those transferred out of the SSUs and into the Dispersal Prison, spent between five and ten years in the facilities. IRA prisoners, Walmsley ascertained, 'tend to spend longer than the average', a factor which skewed statistics on the average stay of all SSU men given the disproportionate number of republicans.[308]

Joe O'Connell compared Parkhurst SSU to a 'small ... two storey building, like a big solid house for all the world ... Quite a big exercise yard and a green house and a garden. There was more activity [but] ... you were contained. They weren't in your face all the time like in the ordinary prisons'.[309] Prisoners were allocated cells on the upper storey after 1976 and had access to various rooms for exercise, hobbies and education. The visiting room shared with 'high risk prisoners' in the main prison provided fleeting opportunities for contact that did not pertain to Leicester.[310]

Staff generally avoided confrontation in the manner which occurred with frequency in 'local' prisons and many, by virtue of having undergone well paid secondment to Magilligan and Long Kesh in the Six Counties in 1972–80, were personally acquainted with IRA members.[311] The IRA in English prisons referred to such men as 'the bounty hunters' and 'mercenaries' without particular animus.[312] Escape was often discussed, particularly with one English prisoner with Irish heritage, but the issue of external resources was critical in view of the island location: 'A helicopter was talked about. The other [plan] was a blasting, as the Unit was very close to the perimeter wall. That would have involved major help from the outside. It just wasn't possible. Plans going nowhere because the back up you needed wasn't there and the Isle of Wight was more difficult as well. Getting on to it and the whole area would have been hostile territory'.[313]

Wormwood Scrubs, 9 August 1980

A smuggled letter written by John McCluskey detailed a series of dramatic incidents in Wormwood Scrubs in August 1980. The constant flashpoint of visiting rights and the continued insistence on 'closed' visits for republicans prompted the Monaghan man and Paul Norney to climb onto the roof of the prison on 9 August, where they remained for twenty-three hours. Other stated concerns of the weekend protest encompassed recent 'warder brutality' in C Wing and 'solidarity with the IRA and the H-Block blanket men'.[314] Reaching the roof was no mean feat as the overnight occupation on 24–25 June 1980 had resulted in £20,000 damage and the increased vigilance of staff.[315] The Dispersal System could not readily cope with the steady toll of structural damage within an overcrowded and limited maximum-security network. By accident and design, a number of circumstances aligned to make the IRA protest not only viable but unusually effective on 9 August 1980. In the course of the day, fifteen prisoners and nine staff were injured in fighting which broke out when around seventy inmates refused to comply with instructions to leave the exercise yard. None required hospitalization but the incident was exactly what the MUFTI, used with great cost to the reputation of the Home Office in August 1979, had been designed to confront.[316] A PROP spokesman concurred with the views expressed by Kilroy-Silk MP that conditions had deteriorated in the facility since the previous year.[317]

Sinn Féin marched on 9 August from Shepherds Bush to Wormwood Scrubs to mark the return to the neighbourhood prison of John McCluskey, a former leading member of Hammersmith's Terence MacSwiney cumann. The precise timing was suggested by the anniversary of the introduction of internment in the Six Counties in August 1971. In west London, up to 150 demonstrators met Helen O'Brien, McCluskey's sister, on approaching the prison at Ducane Road. She rushed to notify the press by phone of the impending roof occupation.[318] Within forty minutes McCluskey and Norney climbed onto the roof of the laundry building and displayed a 'Victory to the IRA' banner to the acclaim of friends in the yard.[319] Rough handling of prisoners on exercise and back on the landings disposed six men to barricade themselves into their D Wing cells. Three announced that they were on hunger strike and one reportedly slashed his wrists. McCluskey and Norney, meanwhile, spent twenty-four hours on the low roof before coming down to inevitable punishment.[320] The Bank Holiday weekend was further enlivened the following day when relations of McCluskey and London based Irish supporters returned to the prison. Organizer Jim McDonald recalled: 'The [Special] Branch knew by the Sunday [10 August] that we wouldn't go away. That there was going to be a vigil there all the time'.[321] The demeanour of police outside the prison was more intimidating than the preceding day. Protesters included London Sinn Féin's Jan Taylor, a former member of the British Army and an English IRA Volunteer, fined for selling republican propaganda in Hammersmith on 9 May 1984. Although Taylor had sold *AP/RN* and other political titles in the venue for eight years, Section 2 (1) (b) of the PTA was invoked in Horseferry Road Magistrates Court. He was jailed for planting bombs in London in the early 1990s.[322] McCluskey claimed in hindsight that the point of the exercise was to 'show them that Republicanism hadn't died'.[323]

On climbing down from the roof McCluskey and Norney were immediately placed in the Segregation Unit along with two Englishmen where, on 15 August 1980, four republicans 'smashed up' their cells to extend the action.[324] The response of the vigilant staff was swift and violent. At 7.20 p.m. McCluskey was summoned into the corridor where he spotted around twenty prison officers, including men wearing the white shirts of Principal Officer and Senior Officer grades. Several carried staves and McCluskey immediately grasped he was going to be assaulted. He recalled: 'They all seemed to jump on me. They were kicking me and hitting me with their fists ... I was dragged down to the Special Cell at the end of the segregation unit, which was about fifteen yards away from where my cell was. They were kicking and punching me all the way down. In the Special Cell they ripped the clothes off me with such force that the clothes were torn. They were beating me all the time'.[325] A cursory examination by a doctor soon followed when McCluskey was naked and disorientated. He was given two vomit stained blankets for overnight cover but no bedding. The Board of Visitors came to the cell on 16 August and appeared 'unconcerned' at his extensive bruising which made it difficult for McCluskey to either sit or stand. Two days later he was charged with damaging his cell and, ludicrously, assaulting the prison officers who had subjected him to the prolonged attack. Only one of those he was accused of attacking was identified in the documentation.[326] Paul Norney was also 'beaten up' by staff and 'had to spend sometime in the Prison hospital'. The BOV approved his punishment of 112 days solitary confinement.[327] This was a comparatively fortunate outcome. McCluskey contended that part of the photographic evidence presented to a magistrate had been fabricated as the images of his wrecked cell showed an electrical wire running from the shattered conduit lying close to the wire reinforcement running down the steel door. His threat to contest any attempt to frame him for attempted murder by means of electrocution in an outside court, backed by his sending an intercepted letter to Hammersmith police, may have influenced the internal decision to drop the potentially very serious charge.[328]

The story of the latest bout of unrest in Wormwood Scrubs resurfaced on 21 August 1980 when PROP announced that educational and external staff had been 'placed on stand-down' in the prison to facilitate a search for weapons and ammunition. This produced an 'imitation firearm' which, other than promising a momentary advantage of intimidation, had little purpose if not used in an escape attempt. The Deputy General Secretary of the POA, Peter Rushworth, grasped the opportunity to dismiss PROP allegations of staff brutality and tensions in the advent of the anniversary of the MUFTI riot as 'the usual hysterical nonsense'.[329]

The IRA, Sinn Féin and PAC

The IRA was a far more coherent and organized body in the English prisons in 1980 than it had been in the early 1970s. Years of individual and collective action had created an environment in which republican prisoners were rarely subjected to physical attacks from warders and British criminals. While there were many exceptions to the mutual live and let live approach, systematic assaults had become uncommon where they had once been almost routine. Joint protests between Irish and British prisoners commensurately increased in frequency, ambition and scale, particularly when the contribution of the IRA to long-term campaigns to improve penal conditions was recognized by the leading elements of the English prisoner hierarchy. Ephemeral bouts of friction arose in rare instances when IRA activities in Britain aggrieved segments of the prison staff and criminal population. Life - sentenced prisoner Norman Parker observed: 'On my travels from one top-security jail to another, no matter how the regimes might differ, there was always one constant. At recreation time and exercise time out on the prison yard or sports field, the IRA prisoners would always congregate together. The most senior IRA man in the jail would automatically be the commanding officer, for these were men who considered themselves to be prisoners of war, not convicts. He would 'hold court' with the other IRA men. Although they did mix quite widely with other prisoners at other times, these meetings were solely for IRA members'.[330] Parker was essentially correct, although the leadership situation was necessarily much less rigorous than in the jails of Ireland's two jurisdictions.

The gradual winding down of the PAC in England in the early 1980s deprived Irish republican prisoners of the backing of a small but dynamic political ally. The core of mainly English volunteers who had devoted time and resources in organizing meetings and demonstrations, as well as publishing occasional newssheets and magazines, relinquished their demanding duties. Their major publication, *Irish Voices from English jails, writings of Irish political prisoners in English prisons* appeared in December 1979 in the form of an inexpensive paperback with a photograph of IRA protesters on the roof of Gartree in July 1978.[331] The introduction paid tribute to the men and women who 'from behind prison bars ... have carried on the struggle for the liberation of their native land'.[332] The broader based TOM continued to represent a British progressive perspective on the Irish conflict and its consequences for those inside the Dispersal System. Sinn Féin (Britain) responded to the changed circumstances by expanding the role of An Cuman Cabhrach personnel. Eddie Caughey, the Birmingham based veteran republican, issued *P.O.W., Bulletin of the Irish Political Prisoners in Britain* under the auspices of the POW Department (Sinn Féin), Britain.[333] The November 1980 edition of the *POW Bulletin* summarized the operations of the Dispersal System and noted that IRA prisoners in Hull, who had refused visitors in May, had been moved on the basis of a rumour that a mass escape had been planned in October. In a break with general PAC practise, the *Bulletin* separately listed prisoners who had been wrongly convicted due to 'an incidental connection with the war in Ireland'.[334] If frequently alluded to by republicans, the prospect of successfully campaigning on their behalf in English courts was so remote in the context of other immediate priorities as to militate against critical engagement.

The POW Department, headquartered in 5 Blessington Street, Dublin, had in April 1980 issued *Irish political prisoners in England, Special Category 'A', An account of prison life in England based on the experiences of Irish Republican John Higgins imprisoned between 1976 and 1979.*[335] Sean Mac Stiofain, former Chief of Staff and ex-IRA prisoner in England, claimed 'this pamphlet must be read by every Republican, it should be discussed by every Sinn Féin cumann'.[336] Caughey was also well qualified to promote the title in Britain, having spent a year on remand in Brixton facing charges in the case which resulted in his co-defendant Higgins being sentenced to ten years imprisonment.[337] The account drew heavily on PAC publications and established the claim of the party to primacy in the sensitive prisoner arena. The booklet served to remind that Sinn Féin was the authoritative voice on the subject at a time when the overall role of the POW Department was boosted by the Republican Movement, owing to the mounting severity of the prison struggle in Ireland. Offices were maintained in the Falls Road, Belfast and Cable Street, Derry, in addition to the satellite services provided by Caughey in Birmingham.[338]

The PAC joined forces with Sinn Féin in late September 1980 to commemorate the tenth anniversary of the major Coalisland to Dungannon Civil Rights march in Tyrone. Jackie Kaye represented the prisoners in England in an event dominated by the H-Block/ Armagh protest and heavily supported by the East Tyrone RAC, IRSP and numerous allied groups. Kaye, who had consistently connected the struggle for political status to the resolution of the overall conflict, claimed: 'We can stand together and fight together like today and bring them all home'. Frank Maguire, more familiar than any other MP with the English situation, confined his contribution to the prisoners of Long Kesh whom he had recently visited in wretched circumstances of the 'no-wash' protest.[339] Maguire was not permitted to enter Portlaoise by the Irish authorities, a 'tough line' in the view of the FCO, which reinforced the NIO and Home Office policy of denying Oireachtas TDs and Senators access to prisons in the Six Counties and England.[340] Even if deemed desirable, it would have been impossible for Sinn Féin in Britain or the PAC to elevate the situation facing the prisoners in England over the much wider and immediately threatening scenario in the Six Counties. This mirrored the situation in the Twenty-Six Counties, where the regime at Portlaoise, less severe in 1980 than during the tenure of the Coalition Government ousted in 1977, could not be automatically compared with Long Kesh. Sinn Féin, moreover, was complicit in concentrating on the Irish dimension. In late February 1980 a 'comm' smuggled out of the H-Blocks and addressed to the 'PEOPLE OF ENGLAND' outlined the nature of the 'dirty protest [sic]' without reference to IRA prisoners in Britain.[341] Similarly, issues of the London *H-Block/ Armagh Committee Bulletin* covered the Long Kesh situation in great detail, along with accounts of other developments in the North of Ireland, with no mention of the IRA in local English prisons. Such men were, however, deeply affected by the worsening crisis.[342]

NOTES

1. *Times*, 1 August 1980.
2. *Times*, 28 March 1985.
3. *Times*, 1 August 1980. Dr. Charles Smith, Dr. Donald MacKay, Principal and Assistant Medical Officers, as well as Consultant Psychiatrist Norman Low, were Gartree staff defended in the High Court. Ibid. See also *Irish Times*, 7 October 1978. The Ince case had been raised in the Commons in March 1977 when the Home Secretary noted Civil Service regulations complicated the ability of Gartree staff to rebut 'misleading' allegations on their conduct. HC Deb 3 March 1977 vol 927 cc262–3W. The fortunes of Ince were followed by the PAC. See *PAC News*, August/ September 1977.
4. HC Deb 3 December 1979 vol 975 c14W. The exchange in the Commons concerned an article by Dr McCleery in the *Prison Medical Journal*, No. 18 (June, 1978). Ibid.
5. *Daily Mirror*, 31 October 1979.
6. *Report on the work of the Prison Department, 1980*, p. 111. Brixton contained an average of 916 prisoners in a jail with a Certified Normal Accommodation of 682 in 1980. Ibid., p. 80.
7. *World Medicine*, 30 October 1982, p. 28.
8. *Report on the work of the Prison Department, 1983*, p. 86.
9. HC Deb 20 December 1979 vol 976 c291W.
10. HC Deb 21 December 1979 vol 976 c436W.

11. *HC Deb 21 May 1980 vol 985 cc217–8W*.
12. *Report of the work of the Prison Department, 1979* (London, 1980), p. 1.
13. *Guardian*, 1 November 1979.
14. *Observer*, 8 April 1979.
15. Eddie O'Neill to [Lord Avesbury], 'Albany Document', 18 July [1983], Typescript, Private Collection (O'Neill), p. 2.
16. *Report on the work of the Prison Department, 1978*, p. 79. Members of the committee included Sir Myles Humphreys JP, Chairman of the Northern Ireland Police Authority and ex-Unionist Lord Mayor of Belfast; Michael Bett, Director of Personnel at the BBC and Sir John Nightingale, ex-Chief Constable of Essex and Chairman of the Police Council. *Report on the work of the Prison Department, 1979*, p. 77. King was one of three external academics appointed in September 1983 to the Prison Department's Control Review Committee. *Report on the work of the Prison Department, 1984/ 85*, p. 42.
17. *Daily Telegraph*, 21 February 1979. In March 1979 the Howard League urged greater reliance on non-custodial sentences and better training of prison staff. *Guardian*, 16 March 1979. Delegates of the Board of Visitors in Winson Green described the Home Office as a 'faceless organisation' which seemed to have 'no conception of everyday problems of prison life'. *Guardian*, 21 March 1979.
18. *Guardian*, 1 November 1979.
19. *New Statesman*, 19 September 1980.
20. *Guardian*, 25 May 1979. See also Roy D King and Kenneth E Elliott, *Albany: Birth of a prison-end of an era* (London, 1997).
21. *Guardian*, 19 February 1982.
22. *Daily Telegraph*, 21 February 1979.
23. *Report on the work of the Prison Department, 1980*, p. 3.
24. *Guardian*, 19 February 1982. The opening of Frankland, near Durham, was expected to alleviate the 'deplorable' conditions in Leeds. *Times*, 26 March 1982. It was the first purpose - built new generation Dispersal Prison and had been due for use in 1980. Soldiers of the Green Howard Regiment worked in the jail that year when parts of the complex received prisoners displaced by POA industrial action. Construction of Full Sutton, then planned for Category B prisoners, was due to commence in April 1982. *Report of the work of the Prison Department, 1978*, p. 16 and *Report on the work of the Prison Department, 1980*, pp. 56–7. See also *Economist*, 7 February 1981. It was alleged that alcohol, tobacco and drugs were 'easily available' in Frankland. *HC Deb19 January 1981 vol 997 c18W*. In December 1978 approval was granted for a twelve cell 'special' unit in Full Sutton where eight cells would be used at time to permit maintenance. Walmsley, *Special Security Units*, p. 24.
25. *Daily Telegraph*, 20 December 1979.
26. *Guardian*, 1 November 1979.
27. *Times*, 9 April 1990.
28. *New Statesman*, 19 September 1980.
29. John McCarthy to the Editor, *Times*, 19 November 1981.
30. See '208 prisoners' to the editor, *Guardian*, 11 December 1981.
31. *Report on the work of the Prison Department, 1980* (London, 1981), pp. 2, 72.
32. *Report on the work of the Prison Department, 1980*, p. 40.
33. NIO, *Report on the Administration of the Prison Service, 1980* (London, 1981), p. 7. The annual report of the Prison Service of Northern Ireland printed on 13 November 1981 included a memorial notice to GF Cox and WG Burns: 'prison officers' who had 'died following terrorist attack in 1980'. Ibid., [p. 5]. For details of the IRA killing of Cox and Loyalist killing of Burns see Chris Ryder, *Inside the Maze, The untold story of the Northern Ireland Prison Service* (London, 2000), pp. 191–2, 226–7. Prison Service members carried out 'industrial action ... in support of their colleagues in Great Britain' in October 1980, moves which obliged the temporary staffing of a jail facility in Foyle, County Derry, by the RUC and British Army after 1 November 1980. *Report on the Administration of the Prison Service, 1980*, p. 8. Further connections between the two prison jurisdictions stemmed from the practice of sending newly appointed Assistant Governors in the Six Counties for 'a period on attachment at the Great Britain Prison Service College at Wakefield'. Ibid., p. 11. Five members of Boards of Visitors and Visiting Committees, additionally, received training in the English institution. Ibid., p. 31. On 15–25 June 1981 the Chief Inspector and a small team examined the circumstances of the Crumlin Road jailbreak, finding a 'failure of the security system' and 'human error', as well as insufficiently 'rigorous' searching of 'professional visitors'. *Report of Her Majesty's Chief Inspector of Prisons for England and Wales, 1981* (London, 1982), p. 9.
34. *Report of Her Majesty's Chief Inspector of Prisons, 1982*, p. 1.
35. *Report of Her Majesty's Chief Inspector of Prisons, 1982*, p. 3.
36. Liz McWilliams in Brady et al (eds.) *Stories of Republican Women*, p. 252.

37. Sinn Féin POW Department, *This baby is being body-searched in Armagh ... her mother and other POWs are being strip-searched,* pamphlet ([1984]), p. 6.
38. Sinn Féin, *Body-searched in Armagh,* p. 6.
39. Adams, *Before the Dawn,* p. 279.
40. 'Sinn Féin P.O.W. Department, Report', n.d. [1980?], Private Collection (O Longain). For Gerry Brannigan and Gerry Adams see De Baroid, *Ballymurphy,* p. 222. Adams had stressed the importance of prison issue in discussions with Ruairi O'Bradaigh during the 1978 Ard Fheis: 'We formed a small committee to take care of the prison protests and we regrouped the POW department ... by October 1979, we had our act together'. Adams, *Before the Dawn,* pp. 280–81.
41. *IRIS,* 10 November 1979.
42. Eoin Dougan, 17 July 2013.
43. *IRIS,* 10 November 1979.
44. Eddie Caughey, 16 September 2008.
45. *Irish News,* 6 December 1974.
46. *AP/RN,* 22 December 1979.
47. 'Sinn Féin P.O.W. Department, Report', n.d. [1980?], Private Collection (O'Loingain).
48. McLaughlin, *Inside an English jail,* p. 54.
49. McLaughlin, *Inside an English jail,* p. 56.
50. *Times,* 18 January 1980.
51. *Irish Post,* 3 November 1979.
52. *Irish Times,* 27 October 1986.
53. McManus, *My American Struggle,* p. 143.
54. See *Irish People,* 9 November 1985.
55. See Keogh, *Lynch,* pp. 413–4. For INA clashes with the Irish Ambassador see Jack McCarthy and Martin Galvin to Sean Donlon, 12 March 1980 in *Irish World,* 22 March 1980. See also Fr. Sean McManus, *My American struggle for justice in Northern Ireland* (Cork, 2011). Kennedy, O'Neill, Moynihan and Carey exerted considerable influence in the Democratic Party and were closely briefed by Donlon and DFA. If deemed hostile towards the IRA, O'Neill had advocated the Congressional embargo on the supply of weapons to the RUC and Carey supported economic sanctions on Britain if it failed to show 'some willingness to initiate moves towards peace'. *Financial Times,* 4 May 1979 and *Spartacist,* No. 14, August-September 1979.
56. See *Irish Echo,* 12 July 1980.
57. *Irish Post,* 1 December 1979.
58. *HC Deb 18 March 1981 vol 1 cc336–74.* For a list of twenty-seven persons detained, including four aged twelve to sixteen and the visiting boyfriend of Bernadette Duffy (Margaret Parratt's sister), see *RPFPC, Relatives and Friends of Prisoners Committee,* Typescript newsletter, December 1979.
59. *Irish News,* 13 December 1979. See also *Irish World,* 22 December 1979.
60. *Irish Democrat,* January 1980. Prendiville was astounded when detectives falsely claimed they could 'connect' him to the INLA assassination of Airey Neave and IRA bombings in London. Ibid. Prendiville recalled the raid led by Detective Inspector Beck: 'Two thunderous bangs on the door (it had been broken down) were followed by the thump of running feet in the hallway, and three pistol toting men (one in uniform) burst through the living room door followed by several others ... I spent the first 24 hours in a filthy cell, completely naked for the first few hours as all my clothes had been taken off me'. He was interrogated on six occasions for more than two hours in the course of just forty-eight hours in Leman Street Police Station. *Hibernia,* 20/ 27 December 1979, p. 8.
61. *Daily Telegraph,* 15 December 1979.
62. O'Donnell, *Special Category,* I, p. 137.
63. *Guardian,* 4 March 1981.
64. *Times,* 20 September 1983.
65. See Clarkson, *Moody,* p. 138.
66. *Magill,* August 1982, p. 14.
67. Gerry Kelly, *The Escape, The inside story of the 1983 escape from Long Kesh prison* ([Belfast], 2013), p. 12.
68. *Irish News,* 11 January 1980 and *Times,* 5 March 1981.
69. *Guardian,* 28 January 2015.
70. *Times,* 18 March 1981.
71. *AP/RN,* 19 May 1979. Storey was interned between April 1973 and April 1975. He was remanded in custody for alleged IRA activities between March and October 1976 and again for a brief period in March 1977. Rearrested and beaten in August 1977, Storey was held until charges collapsed in December 1977. On 11 April 1978 he was held in connection with the Lenadoon incident. Ibid.
72. Fr. Raymond Murray, *The shame of Merlyn Rees, 4th year of internment in Ireland, Long Kesh, 1974–1975,* pamphlet, (Cavan, 1975), p. 52. Glenholmes' cousin, Francis Fitzsimmons from the Short

Strand, was one of three IRA Volunteers killed in a premature explosion on 16 October 1976. *Lagan enclave*, p. 86.

73. Adams, *Before the dawn*, p. 238.

74. Michael Maguire, 'Jacqueline O'Malley (1949–1999): A London-Irish Republican Militant', MS Draft (23 January 2014), Private Collection (O'Donnell). John Lawlor, a west Dublin haulage contractor living in Ballymore Eustace, Kildare, was shot dead by IRA in a city quayside pub on 7 September 1977. He had recently met a Belfast man near Luton to receive a container of arms and explosives from Dublin but the load was not that expected. Lawlor was questioned by Gardai in Naas on 27 August when explosives, two Armalite rifles and five revolvers, were found in a haulage depot in Manor Street, Dublin. War material was also recovered in Kildare. Lawlor was released after three days in custody. After his shooting further raids occurred in Rathcoole, County Dublin, Carrick-on-Shannon in Leitrim and in Sligo. Two men and a woman were questioned in Paddington Green on 23 September 1977 under the PTA, including a 44-year-old Short Strand man arrested in Belfast on 20 September and moved from Castlereagh to England. The IRA divulged that Lawlor had been 'instrumentally involved in the seizure and had gratuitously given important information to the authorities'. *Irish Times*, 9 September 1977. See also *Irish Times*, 8 and 10 September 1977 and 26 May 1981.

75. *Irish Times*, 9 September 1977.

76. *Times*, 15 December 1979.

77. *Guardian*, 14 July 1982.

78. Mick Tuite, father of Gerry and an IRA member, married Jane Dermody, sister of wanted republican Paddy Dermody, on 30 September 1942. Their wedding in Mountnugent, Cavan, was raided by the Special Branch who fatally shot Dermody and injured guests. Detective MJ Walsh was mortally wounded in the incident and leading Belfast IRA man, Harry White, was seriously injured. MacEoin, *White*, pp. 112–17. Dermody was a close associate of Dick Goss, a former IRA 'S Plan' prisoner in England, who was executed in Portlaoise on 9 August 1942. *Last Post*, p. 156. On 2 May 1983 a flat in North Road, Highgate, London, was found to contain a small IRA explosives dump. Tuite had rented the property in 1979 and the 15lbs of gelignite discovered under floorboards four years later was 'weeping' when recovered. *Guardian*, 19 December 1983.

79. *Irish Times*, 14 July 1982. Items recovered in Greenwich were linked to the car bomb that detonated outside the Oasis Club on 18 December 1978 and another defused in Windmill Street. Police claimed a mini-cassette tape found in the flat listed potential targets, including William Whitelaw, Lord Carrington, Enoch Powell and Airey Neave. Ibid. It was stated in 1983 that the voice in the tape was that of Belfastman John McComb. *Times*, 27 June 1986. McComb, from the Short Strand, had been held in Cage 12, Long Kesh, in the 1970s. He wrote a letter published in *Republican News* on 23 August 1976 which stated: 'The present generation will not fail, the flame of freedom has been lit, the Provisionals will see to it that it will never be extinguished'. The cassette tape storing IRA intelligence referred to ten industrial sites on the Mersey River including three oil depots. Other targets under surveillance included rail installations carrying nuclear waste, troops trains and military bases. Many high - profile individuals had been closely observed. *Irish Times*, 7 July 1982.

80. *Irish Times*, 8 July 1982.

81. *Times*, 11 June 1986. See also *Times*, 3 June 1993, *Daily Telegraph*, 11 May 1983 and Clarkson, *Moody*, p. 168.

82. O Mathuna to O'Donnell, 14 April 2012, Private Collection (O'Donnell).

83. *Keenan*, p. 4 and *Guardian*, 26 June 1980.

84. Chrissie Keenan in Brady et al (eds.) *Stories of Republican Women*, p. 345.

85. Brian Keenan, 26 May 2007.

86. Maguire, 'Jacqueline O'Malley', Private Collection (O'Donnell). Maguire was detained under the PTA in London on 4 December 1984 and questioned about Sinn Féin and aspects of his writings for Irish media on the SAS. The IBRG highlighted his case. *FRFI*, January 1985, p. 13.

87. *AP/RN*, 25 January 1999.

88. *AP/RN*, 14 July 1979 and *Irish World*, 14 July 1979. Chrissie Keenan was remanded in custody for six months and subjected to a strict regime of twice - daily signing in a police station. Clarke, *No faith*, p. 94. Ernie Roberts, MP for Hackney North and Stoke Newington, countered the Tory view of the H-Blocks. He stated in the foreword to an 'Information on Ireland' pamphlet that 'The solution to the Irish problem is political. It is a United Ireland'. *H-Blocks, The truth, a reply of H.M. Government* (London, [1980]), n.p.

89. Jenny Payne, 2 July 2008.

90. *Times*, 18 March 1981.

91. *AP/RN*, 25 January 1999. For the Labour Movement Delegation see *Troops Out*, No. 2, Winter 1976, pp. 2–3. The visitors met leading activists including Seamus Costello of the IRSP/ INLA, Phil Flynn of Sinn Féin, Michael Farrell of People's Democracy, Fr. Des Wilson and Bernadette McAliskey. Ibid. In Belfast

O'Malley met Bobby Storey, representing the Falls Road Taxi Drivers Association, and community worker Dickie Glenholmes. Maguire, 'Jacqueline O'Malley', Private Collection (O'Donnell).

92. Maguire, 'Jacqueline O'Malley', Private Collection (O'Donnell).
93. Maguire, 'Jacqueline O'Malley', Private Collection (O'Donnell).
94. *Daily Telegraph*, 15 December 1979.
95. *Irish News*, 11 January 1980.
96. *RPFPC, Relatives and Friends of Prisoners Committee*, Typescript newsletter, December 1979. Anne Duffy was Bobby Campbell's aunt. His uninvolved brother-in-law, Bernard Cassidy, was one of three people arrested in Liverpool. Two brothers of Dickie Glenholmes, Joe and Samuel, were arrested in Birmingham but released without charge on 15 December 1979. His brother-in-law Liam Martin was arrested in Southampton and subject to a deportation order. Ibid. Holloway Governor Joy Kinsley was subsequently appointed to the top position in Brixton. *Times*, 23 May 1983 and 7 December 1984.
97. *Times*, 4 January 1980.
98. Chrissie Keenan in Brady et al (eds.) *Stories of Republican Women*, p. 346.
99. *House of Commons Home Affairs Committee, Session 1980–81, Administration of the Prison Service, Minutes of Evidence, Monday 19 January 1981, HM Prison Brixton* (London, 1981), p. 76. In October 1981 F Wing was closed for refurbishment resulting in a temporary reduction of inmates to 581 in November 1980. Ibid.
100. Maguire, 'Jacqueline O'Malley', Private Collection (O'Donnell).
101. Chrissie Keenan in Brady et al (eds.) *Stories of Republican Women*, p. 346.
102. Chrissie Keenan in Brady et al (eds.) *Stories of Republican Women*, p. 346. The colloquial term 'ODC', meaning 'Ordinary Decent Criminal', was widely understood in the 1980s and used by Viscount Brookeborough in the House of Lords. *HL Deb 15 March 1984 vol 449 c945*.
103. Maguire, 'Jacqueline O'Malley', Private Collection (O'Donnell).
104. Chrissie Keenan in Brady et al (eds.) *Stories of Republican Women*, p. 346. She was permitted to return to Belfast but required to arrange two sureties of £5,000 and report to a police station in London. Sr. Clarke, 'C[hrissie] Keenan', Clarke Papers (COFLA). The charge of conspiracy to cause explosions was dropped in the case of Parratt on 24 April 1980. Sr. Clarke, 'Margaret Parratt', Clarke Papers (COFLA).
105. Maguire, 'Jacqueline O'Malley', Private Collection (O'Donnell).
106. Maguire, 'O'Malley', Private Collection (O'Donnell).
107. Jackie [O'Malley] to Anon, 12 June 1980, Private Collection (Maguire).
108. Petition of Jackie O'Malley, 12 June 1980, Private Collection (Maguire).
109. Maguire, 'O'Malley', Private Collection (O'Donnell).
110. *AP/RN*, 25 January 1999.
111. Maguire, 'Jacqueline O'Malley', Private Collection (O'Donnell). Two sureties of £10,000 were posted to secure bail. Sr. Clarke, 'Jackie O'Malley', Clarke Papers (COFLA).
112. Jackie [O'Malley] to Anon, 12 June 1980, Private Collection (Maguire).
113. *Guardian*, 4 March 1981.
114. *Times*, 6 March 1981. O'Malley retained friends in the Labour Party, including Laois native Oliver 'Hammy' Donoughue, who had been involved in legal pro-Irish campaigning since the 1960s. Information of Oliver Donoughue, Dublin, 30 August 2008.
115. *AP/RN*, 25 January 1999.
116. *Times*, 12 March 1981.
117. Kelly, *The Escape*, pp. 12–13.
118. *Times*, 18 March 1981 and Coogan, *IRA*, p. 533. Bobby Storey and Larry Marley were two of the main planners of the mass H-Block escape of 25 September 1983 when nineteen of thirty-eight IRA men made a clean break. Bell, *Secret Army*, pp. 543–4. The appointment of Storey as an Orderly in H7 was described as a 'serious' error by British investigators. *Report of an Inquiry ... HM Prison, Maze*, p. 65. After committal hearings in England Storey was sent to Bristol where he went on a short fast before being returned to Brixton ahead of the trial. Sr. Clarke, 'Robert Storey', Clarke Papers (COFLA).
119. Kelly, *The Escape*, p. 12.
120. *Daily Telegraph*, 17 March 1981 and *Times*, 18 March 1981.
121. *Times*, 18 March 1981.
122. *AP/RN*, 25 January 1999.
123. *AP/RN*, 25 January 1999, Mass Card of Jacqueline O'Malley-Maguire and Michael Maguire to Ruan O'Donnell, 9 March 2012, Private Collection (O'Donnell).
124. Sr. Clarke, 'Margaret Parratt', Clarke Papers (COFLA). See also Sr. Sarah Clarke, Statement, 19 December 1979, Clarke Papers (COFLA).
125. Dickie Glenholmes, *Remember our Volunteers Committee 2008*, DVD. Murphy was 55 when charged in relation to offences associated with the Dowd/ O'Connell ASU. *Times*, 7 May 1976. By chance

Murphy knew John Smyth, father of Sean Smyth and Anne Maguire of the 'Maguire Seven', from life in west Belfast. In London Murphy socialised with Hugh Maguire, brother-in-law of Anne Maguire (nee Smyth) but never alluded to his IRA activities. Sean Smyth, 2 June 2009.

126. *Irish News*, 17 December 1974.

127. *HC Deb 11 February 1980 vol 978 c413W*, Coggan and Walker, *Deaths in British prisons*, p. 113 and Clarke, *No faith*, p. 95.

128. Pat Hackett, 21 December 2007.

129. Armstrong to Wilson, 25 July 1978, Private Collection (Wilson).

130. Armstrong to Wilson, 6 March 1979, Private Collection (Wilson).

131. Victory, *Justice and truth*, p. 14. Cardinal Hume had been lobbied over the winter by Sr. Sarah Clarke and the RPPC to examine the Irish political prisoner issue. Her approach was handled in December 1978 by Fr. Richard Atherton, the Head of the Catholic Chaplains in the prison service and, as such, an employee of the Home Office. Fr. Atherton had an acrimonious meeting with Sr. Clarke who regarded his negative attitude as typical of Catholic chaplains working in English jails. Clarke, *No faith*, pp. 111–12, 126–7.

132. Cardinal Hume to Merlyn Rees, 26 March 1979 in Victory, *Justice and truth*, p. 15. Monsignor George Leonard, Personal Assistant to the Cardinal for Non-Diocesan Affairs, investigated the Maguire Seven case. Ibid.

133. Clarke, *No faith*, p. 93.

134. *AP/RN*, 21 January 1980. Around eighty protesters were addressed by Kevin Colfer of Sinn Féin, Michael Holden of An Cumann Cabhrach, Alan Woods of TOM and speakers from the Woman and Ireland Group, RCG and RCT. The SWP also participated. Ibid. Republicans claimed that Deputy Governor Scott had admitted he was acting under 'Home Office instructions' in denying visits to IRA prisoners in D Wing on Sundays. Hayes (ed.) *In prison in England*, p. 32.

135. *Irish World*, 19 January 1980.

136. *Guardian*, 8 January 1980.

137. *Irish political prisoners*, pp. 56–8. At various times Conlon had been held in Winchester, Brixton and Wakefield. See also Coggan and Walker, *Deaths in British prisons*, pp. 99–100. Sr. Clarke understood that his inability to properly prepare the Complan mixture taken in lieu of prison rations presaged an 'enforced hunger strike'. On seeing the condition of his father just prior to the hospital relocation Gerry Conlon smashed up the dispensary. Clarke, *No faith*, pp. 127–8. See also Sr. Clarke, 'Giuseppe Conlon', Clarke Papers (COFLA) and Conlon, *Proved Innocent*, pp. 191–3. When taken from Wormwood Scrubs for medical treatment in Grendon Underwood, IRA member Gerry Young was heavily escorted. The convoy of vans, police cars and unmarked vehicles laid on for security was involved in serious motorway crash on the return leg: 'I thought the cops came out of holes in the ground'. Gerry Young, 8 March 2008.

138. *Guardian*, 21 March 1980.

139. See Coggan and Walker, *Deaths in British prisons*, pp. 114.

140. *HC Deb 31 January 1980 vol 977 c707W*.

141. *Guardian*, 14 February 1995.

142. *Irish Times*, 26 January 1980. Home Secretary William Whitelaw claimed that Conlon might have been freed if he had survived hospitalization. *Irish Times*, 28 January 1980. In December 1978 his colleague Merlyn Rees affirmed that it was 'long standing practice to consider recommending the exercise of Royal Prerogative of Mercy in the case of a terminally ill prisoner'. This was not extended to Conlon, who personally opposed humanitarian intervention on the grounds that he was innocent. *HC Deb 8 December 1978 vol 959 cc126–7W*. See also Coggan and Walker, *Deaths in British prisons*, p. 101.

143. *HC Deb 7 February 1980 vol 978 c287W*.

144. Clarke, *No faith*, p. 130.

145. Quoted in *Guardian*, 12 October 2010.

146. *Guardian*, 12 October 2010.

147. Gerry Conlon quoted in *Irish News*, 18 September 1997. See also Conlon, *Proved Innocent*, p. 195.

148. Hume to Rees, 24 January 1980 in *Victory, Justice and truth*, p. 17. Fr. McKinley had the previous week refused to admit the coffin of IRA Volunteer Kevin 'Dee' Delaney into the same church. During his service for Conlon he expressed the hope that 'justice will be done' in relation to other wrongfully convicted members of the family. *AP/RN*, 2 February 1980. See also *Tirghra*, p. 226. A commemoration for Delaney in Armagh Goal resulted in the wrecking of cells by staff. Brady et al (eds.) *Stories of Republican Women*, p. 230. For Fr. McKinley and the ICPO see *The Irish Commission for Prisoners Overseas, 2nd Annual Report, 1986/ 87* (Dublin, 1988), p. 16.

149. See Brendan Murphy and Seamus Kelters, *Eyewitness, Four decades of Northern life* (Dublin, 2003), p. 49. Photojournalist Brendan Murphy, who had known Conlon as a customer in the bar he once owned, noted 'few media were present'. Ibid. See also 'One more body, The murder of Giuseppe Conlon' in *FRFI*, March/ April 1980, p. 11.

150. *AP/RN*, 2 February 1980.

151. *HC Deb 11 February 1980 vol 978 c413W.*

152. *Guardian*, 21 March 1980.

153. Victory, *Justice and truth*, p. 22. Tory MP Sir John Biggs-Davison stated his belief that Conlon was 'innocent' in the Commons in March 1981. See *HC Deb 18 March 1981 vol 1 cc336–74*. A group styling itself 'Saor Uladh', a name used in the 1950s and 1960s by a Tyrone/ Monaghan/ Donegal centered IRA splinter, had sent him a letter-bomb in 1972, although responsibility was never determined. On 22 June 1981 a low-powered incendiary was posted to his House of Commons address in a brown 'jiffy bag', one of seven devices delivered to British persons connected to the Long War that year. Conservative ally Jill Knight MP received a posted 'bomb' during the sequence claimed by the 'ERA', an acronym presumed to denote 'English Republican Army', yet attributed to 'a single crank' by the Scotland Yard unit which failed to determine responsibility. *Guardian*, 23 June 1981. Biggs-Davison supported 'Operation Banner' and claimed: 'If we lose in Belfast, we may have to fight in Brixton or Birmingham … what is happening in Northern Ireland is a rehearsal for urban guerilla war more widely in Europe, particularly in Britain'. Cited in Revolutionary Communist Group, *The road to communism in Britain, Manifesto of the Revolutionary Communist Group* (London, 1984), p. 70.

154. *HC Deb 24 March 1980 vol 981 c388W.*

155. Faul and Murray, *H Block*, p. 114.

156. *Republican News*, 10 February 1979.

157. Armstrong to Wilson, 3 March 1980, Private Collection (Wilson).

158. Hayes (ed.) *In prison in England*, p. 15.

159. Joe O'Connell, 7 June 2008.

160. See 'Address of Fr. Piaras O'Duill' in *Irish World*, 26 January 1980. Irish National Caucus in Washington DC issued a condemnation of Conlon's treatment before and after death on 28 January 1980. Fr. Sean McManus accused the British Government of acting 'in a such a callous, inhuman and even murderous manner' and called for a boycott of British Airways. See *Irish World*, 9 February 1980. For reaction of the American IRA INC (Pittsburgh) and Ancient Order of Hibernians see *Irish World*, 19 April 1980.

161. *AP/RN*, 19 August 1982.

162. Pat Hackett, 21 December 2007.

163. Pat Hackett, 21 December 2007.

164. Pat Hackett, 21 December 2007.

165. Statement from Patrick Hackett, n.d. [1981] in Hayes (ed.) *In prison in England*, p. 28. One of the accompanying prison officers refused to close the window which Hackett discovered, by means of climbing on top of the metal frame bed, to have a warped frame preventing it from being latched. He blocked the gap with newspapers to reduce the cold air intake. Ibid.

166. Hackett, n.d. [1981] in Hayes (ed.) *In prison in England*, p. 28.

167. Murray, *State Violence*, p. 101.

168. Pat Hackett, 21 December 2007.

169. *The Irish Prisoner*, No. 9, June/ July 1980, p. 2.

170. Sr. Clarke, 'Coventry Seven', Clarke Papers (COFLA). See also Sr. Clarke, 'Anthony [Ron] Lynch, Clarke Papers Ibid. Pat O'Neill, one of the wrongfully convicted 'Maguire Seven', was released from Parkhurst on 8 April 1980, four days later than expected. Owing to the confusion, O'Neill was not met at the airport in Dublin. Sr. Clarke, 'Pat O'Neill', Clarke Papers (COFLA). Tommy Cooper, released from a three-year sentence, was arrested outside Aylesbury prison and served a deportation order on 9 May 1978. Sr. Clarke, 'Tommy Cooper', Clarke Papers (COFLA). See also *The Irish Prisoner*, No. 9, June/ July 1980, p. 2.

171. *FRFI*, May 1982, p. 13.

172. Sr. Clarke, 'Coventry Seven', Clarke Papers (COFLA) and Miscellaneous MSS, Ibid.

173. *Guardian*, 28 January 1980. See Herbert, *Wearing of the Green*, p. 171.

174. *AP/RN*, 14 June 1980.

175. *The Irish Prisoner*, No. 9, June/ July 1980, p. 4. Mac Lochlainn had been arrested in Cardiff on 15 September 1979 at a meeting attended by Sinn Féin, RCG, UTOM and SWP supporters under Section 5 of the Public Order Act. RCG leader Terry O'Halloran, using his 'Marlowe' alias, chaired the event. Police contended that the distribution of the *Hands off Ireland!* newsletter and a Sinn Féin pamphlet on the H-Block crisis was illegal. The charges were subsequently changed to the lesser allegation of causing an obstruction. Ibid., p. 6. See *Hands off Ireland!*, No. 10, April 1980, p. 20. O'Halloran claimed that the persons arrested during the Luton picket were associates when 'the police attacked, kicked and pushed the demonstrators down the ramp'. *Guardian*, 9 April 1980. See also Chris Fraser, 'Police attack on Welsh Republicans' in *FRFI*, July 1982, p. 13.

176. Mac Lochlainn to O'Donnell, 27 April 2011, Private Collection (O'Donnell).

177. *Guardian*, 8 and 9 April 1980.

178. Michael Holden, 23 June 2008 and *The Irish Prisoner*, No. 9, June/ July 1980, p. 7. Holden was questioned on a series of Red Army Faction bombings on NATO bases in the Rhineland despite having

visited Lubeck and flying from Hamburg. See Michael Holden, 'PTA, A weapon to harass the Irish people', *Hands off Ireland!*, No. 7, April 1979, pp. 7–9. See also RCG, *The Attack on Jim Reilly and Hands off Ireland!*, Pamphlet, 1978. Innocuous personal, as well as political themed materials, were seized from his home and one of his work lockers at Kodak Ltd broken into. Holden, 23 June 2008.

179. *Irish Press*, 8 April 1980.
180. *Guardian*, 8 April 1980, *Evening Post*, 5 April 1980 and 'Hands off Ireland! Defence Campaign', Leaflet, [April 1980], Private Collection (O Mathuna).
181. Rule 20 (1) stated: 'An unconvicted prisoner may wear clothing of his own if … tidy and clean'. Plotnikoff, *Prison Rules*, p. 52.
182. *The Irish Prisoner*, No. 9, June/ July 1980, p. 7.
183. *Guardian*, 9 April 1980.
184. Gerry Mac Lochlainn, 2008, 'Event timeline', Coiste Archives. For 110 rule see Ruth Allan, National Association of Probation Officers to the editor, *Guardian*, 16 December 1981.
185. Gerry Mac Lochlainn to Ruan O'Donnell, 27 April 2011, Private Collection (O'Donnell).
186. *Times*, 30 June 1980.
187. Mac Lochlainn to O'Donnell, 27 April 2011, Private Collection (O'Donnell).
188. *Guardian*, 26 January 1981.
189. *Guardian*, 19 December 1994.
190. Michael Holden, 23 June 2008 and *AP/RN*, 4 October 1980.
191. *AP/RN*, 11 October 1980.
192. *Irish political prisoners in England*, p. 97. Higgins, who had lived in Luton since 1959, was close to reaching the twenty-year residency requirement that would have made exclusion legally impossible. He appealed the decision and it was claimed that Merlyn Rees took the trouble to formally reject the application on his last day in the office of Home Secretary. On 11 March 1979 Higgins was served with an Exclusion Order, obliging him and his English born children to depart for Ireland. They left behind their family home and a promising electronics business. Ibid. William Higgins, sixty-two year old father of John, was detained under the PTA on 9–10 April 1980. Sr. Clarke, 'John Higgins', Clarke Papers (COFLA) and *The Irish Prisoner*, No. 5, June 1979, p. 2.
193. *AP/RN*, 11 October 1980 and *Tirghra*, p. 226.
194. *FRFI*, May/ June 1981, p. 14.
195. Mac Lochlainn, 'Timeline', Coiste Archives, Dublin.
196. Armstrong to Wilson, 10 September 1982, Private Collection (Wilson).
197. *FRFI*, May 1982, p.12.
198. *FRFI*, May/ June 1981, p. 14.
199. *FRFI*, March 1982, p. 12.
200. Armstrong to Wilson, 21 April 1980, Private Collection (Wilson).
201. *The Irish Prisoner*, No. 9, June/ July 1980, p. 2.
202. Armstrong to Wilson, 10 September 1982, Private Collection (Wilson). For execution of Williams see *Irish News*, 2 September 1942. Irish communities in Britain contributed to the reprieve campaign.
203. See Jim McVeigh, *Executed, Tom Williams and the IRA* (Belfast, 1999), Chapter Four.
204. *AP/RN*, 24 May 1980. For Ward's trial see *Times*, 9 October 1974.
205. *AP/RN*, 1 March 1980.
206. Sr. Clarke, 'Judith Ward', Clarke Papers (COFLA). Ward undertook a short hunger strike in February 1983. Ibid.
207. *FRFI*, August 1986, p. 12.
208. *Times*, 25 June 1980.
209. *Irish Times*, 26 June 1980 and *AP/RN*, 28 June 1980.
210. *The Irish Prisoner*, No. 9, June/ July 1980, p. 3. IRA prisoner Jerry Mealy was one of nine men who signed a letter on the Wormwood Scrubs dispute sent to the paper. Ibid. McCartney was sent on a 'lie-down' to Wandsworth but returned to Wormwood Scrubs in August 1980. Sr. Clarke, 'Ronnie McCartney', Clarke Papers (COFLA).
211. Ronnie McCartney, 12 April 2008.
212. Ronnie McCartney, 12 April 2008.
213. *Times*, 25 June 1980.
214. *FRFI*, July/ August 1980.
215. Ronnie McCartney, 12 April 2008.
216. Pat Hackett, 21 December 2007.
217. Hackett, n.d. [1981] in Hayes (ed.) *In prison in England*, p. 28. Hackett had been using his ninety pence allowance to buy Mars bars and biscuits for McCartney, deprived of all privileges, which he concealed for collection behind a shower unit. After some weeks staff discovered this arrangement and simply confiscated the supply. Hackett responded by adulterating a packet of Bourbon biscuits and laughing at outraged staff who fell victim to the prank as they threw buckets of water over him in his cell. McCartney, 12 April 2008.

218. Pat Hackett, 21 December 2007.
219. *AP/RN*, 27 May 2010. See also Ibid., 28 June 1980.
220. Pat Hackett, 21 December 2007.
221. Hackett, n.d. [1981] in Hayes (ed.) *In prison in England*, p. 28.
222. Hackett, n.d. [1981] in Hayes (ed.) *In prison in England*, pp. 28–9.
223. Hackett, n.d. [1981] in Hayes (ed.) *In prison in England*, p. 29.
224. Bridget Hackett to the Editor, *Irish Times*, 18 January 1982.
225. Hayes (ed.) *In prison in England*, p. 26.
226. Mrs Bridie Hackett quoted in *AP/RN*, 19 August 1982.
227. Pat Hackett, 21 December 2007.
228. *AP/RN*, 27 May 2010.
229. Pat Hackett, 21 December 2007.
230. *Times*, 28 March 1984.
231. *The Irish Prisoner*, No. 9, June/ July 1980, p. 1 and *FRFI*, July/ August 1980, p. 15.
232. Murray, *Hard time*, p. 75. For details of the pardon and controversy arising from the May 2011 re-imprisonment of Marian Price see Pat Finucane Centre to the Secretariat of the Committee on the Prevention of Torture, Council of Europe, 22 March 2012, www.patfinucanecentre.org. Northern Secretary of State Owen Paterson authorized the detention of Price in Maghaberry prison in relation to a Derry 1916 commemoration attended by members of the Real IRA. Anphoblacht.com., 18 May 2011. In 1982 the Home Affairs Committee noted: 'The Home Secretary is constitutionally responsible for recommending the exercise of the Royal Prerogative of Mercy to grant either a free pardon, the effect of which is that a person is relieved, as far as possible, of all penalties and other consequences of his conviction, or the remission of all or part of the penalty imposed by the court'. *House of Commons, Sixth Report of the Home Affairs Committee, Session 1981–82, Miscarriages of Justice ... 20 October 1982*, p. iv. See also Ibid., p. 1.
233. *Guardian*, 1 May 1980.
234. Tim Pat Coogan, *On the blanket, The inside story of the IRA prisoners' "Dirty" protest* (Dublin, 1980), pp. 136, 216. Renowned Dublin artist Robert Ballagh designed the cover image of the first edition. Danny Morrison retrospectively commended the publication as 'an important contribution to raising public awareness about the protest'. Morrison (ed.), *Hunger Strike*, p. 10.
235. *AP/RN*, 3 May 1980.
236. Murray, *Hard time*, p. 75.
237. *AP/RN*, 24 May 1980.
238. Albert Price to George Harrison, n.d. [c. June 1980], Harrison Papers, New York University. Price sent his regards to 'all my friends' in New York. Ibid.
239. Armstrong to Wilson, 1 May 1981, Private Collection (Wilson). This contrasted with the precipitous release in Ireland of the Intelligence community - linked Littlejohn brothers. Armstrong to Wilson, 29 September 1981, Private Collection (Wilson). See *Guardian*, 21 April 1981.
240. *Guardian*, 23 April 1981.
241. *Irish Post*, 18 August 1984. McLarnon, aged 17 when arrested in March 1973, spent four years in solitary confinement. Although convicted as part of the 'Belfast Ten', Roisin McNearney was not sentenced in view of her assistance to the prosecution. Ibid. His deportation was viewed as 'a case of the HO carrying on in the usual bloody minded fashion'. Joe O'Connell to 'Peter' (Seamus O Mathuna), 19 August 1984, Private Collection (O Mathuna).
242. See *Irish News*, 20 November 2013.
243. *Irish News*, 25 January 2013.
244. Eddie O'Neill, 19 July 2007. O'Neill's symptoms approximated to those defined as 'Confinement Psychosis ... a psychotic reaction characterized frequently by hallucinations and delusions, produced by prolonged physical isolation and inactivity in completely segregated areas'. GD Scott and Paul Gendreau, 'Psychiatric implications of sensory deprivation in a maximum security prison' in *Canadian Psychiatric Association Journal*, Vol. 14, No. 4, pp. 338.
245. Hugh Doherty, 23 June 2006.
246. Hugh Doherty, 23 June 2006. Doherty was released from solitary in Winson Green in August 1980. Sr. Clarke, 'Hugh Doherty', Clarke Papers (COFLA).
247. Eddie Butler, 21 December 2007.
248. *Irish Times*, 26 June 1980
249. *New Statesman*, 30 May 1980 and Wakefield, *Thousand days*, p. 1.
250. See Wakefield, *Thousand days*, Appendix 2, p. 36. Hugh Doherty had conversed with Wilkinson when both were in Durham: 'They say he died on hunger strike ... I remember talking to people who heard the noises the night he died [in Liverpool]. I'd say they [i.e. guards] went in and beat him to death. You know, he was a giant of a man'. Hugh Doherty, 23 June 2006.
251. *Guardian*, 25 November 1981. Ex-Labour Minister Michael Meacher, MP for Oldham West, wrote to Prime Minister Thatcher in response to NCCL information on Control Units. Meacher alleged

their development was a 'spectacular' example of the 'Whitehall ploy' whereby policies given outline ministerial approval were implemented without referral for final authorization. *Guardian*, 14 April 1980.

252. *Times*, 20 November 1981.
253. Wakefield, *Thousand days*, p. 33.
254. *New Statesman*, 30 May 1980. Terry Munyard detailed the plight of Wilkinson whom, an inquest found, had been held 'for 18 months in two cage-barred white painted cells, one of which had a wall specially built outside the window to cut him off from the outside world'. Ibid.
255. *Times*, 19 and 20 November 1981.
256. Wakefield, *Thousand days*, p. 3.
257. See Charles Bronson 2, *More porridge than Goldilocks* (London, 2009), pp. 53–4.
258. Wakefield, *Thousand days*, p. 10.
259. Wakefield, *Thousand days*, p. 2.
260. Wakefield, *Thousand days*, p. 34. See also *Times*, 3 June 1982.
261. John McCluskey, 2 August 2007.
262. *Sunday People*, 23 May 1983.
263. Wakefield, *Thousand days*, p. 1.
264. *Times*, 25 September 1980.
265. *Times*, 20 November 1981. Jill Jones, Chair of the Board of Visitors at Wormwood Scrubs, backed McCarthy's observations. See also *Times*, 6 March 1982 and Coggan and Walker, *Deaths in British prisons*, p. 202.
266. Hayes (ed.) *In prison in England*, p. 32. Prisoners were taken following a surge in Middle East related violence in London in 1978. Incidents included the assassination in July of ex-Iraqi Prime Minister General Al Naif, a grenade attack on the car of the Iraqi ambassador, assassination of PLO official Said Hammami and a machine gun assault on an El Al coach in Mayfair. *Report of the Commissioner of Police of the Metropolis for the year 1978*, pp. 9, 13, 29 and 49. The detention of two Sinn Féin members in Orly Airport, Paris, on arrival from Beirut in 1981 led to British speculation that they had spent 'several months' with the PLO in Lebanon. Irish police sources described Denis Donaldson and Liam Kelly as 'minor members of the Provisional movement'. *Guardian*, 29 August 1981. In December 2005 Donaldson was revealed to be a long term 'turned' British agent as well as Sinn Féin's Head of Administration. *AP/RN*, 16 December 2005 and *Irish Times*, 12 March 2015.
267. Lord Brockway in *HL Debates, 10 October 1980*, p. 713.
268. Lord Avebury, *HL Debates, 10 October 1980*, p. 714.
269. *AP/RN*, 7 June 1980. Guilfoyle noted that two recent editions of the republican paper had been withheld encouraging him to speculate that there may have been information on Albany in the issues. Ibid. Baker was reputedly suffering from a neck complaint. *The Irish Prisoner*, No. 9, June/ July 1980, p. 2. Flynn had attended a public meeting in the House of Commons on 24 January 1978, less than a month after being detained in Liverpool under the PTA. *Socialist Challenge*, 19 January 1978.
270. *AP/RN*, 7 June 1980.
271. *AP/RN*, 21 June 1980. Ruth Addison, ex-chair of the National League of Young Liberals also spoke. Ibid. Soley, former probation officer and Labour MP for Hammersmith North, a constituency with a large migrant Irish population, had a long term interest in conditions in Wormwood Scrubs and other prisons. See *Times*, 20 November 1981 and *HC Deb 20 July 1984, vol. 64, cc 633*. For his investigation of Armagh Prison in the 1980s see Murray, *State Violence*, p. 108. Flynn, active in republicanism since the 1950s, was regarded by Brian Keenan as a 'very capable man'. Brian Keenan to 'Peter Flynn' (Seamus O Mathuna), 25 July 1984, Private Collection (O Mathuna).
272. Brendan Dowd to Anon., [c. April 1980] in *The Irish Prisoner*, No. 9, June/ July 1980, p. 2.
273. Brendan Dowd to the Editor, n.d. [1989] in *The Irish Prisoner*, No. 16 [1989], p. 17.
274. Sr. Clarke, 'Leicester', Clarke Papers (COFLA).
275. *Time Out*, 7 July 1980.
276. *Guardian*, 26 June 1980. Keenan had lived in Corby and Luton between 1960 and 1963. Ibid.
277. Hayes (ed) *In prison in England*, p. 9, De Baroid, *Ballymurphy*, p. 234 and *Irish Echo*, 12 July 1980.
278. *Guardian*, 26 June 1980.
279. *Hibernia*, 5 June 1980.
280. *Guardian*, 25 June 1980.
281. Clarke and Johnston, *McGuinness*, p. 111.
282. Brian Keenan, 26 May 2007.
283. See 'Arab link feared in Neave bomb', *Observer*, 1 April 1979. Official IRA and Worker's Party republicans developed communications with North Korea. Leading figure Sean Garland, General Secretary of the Worker's Party, met President Kim Il Sung in North Korea in 1984. *Dublin Evening News*, 13 June 1989.
284. *Time Out*, 7 July 1980.

285. *Guardian*, 26 June 1980.
286. *FRFI*, July/ August 1980.
287. 'Lord Havers', *Times*, 3 April 1992.
288. *Sunday Times*, 22 May 1983. Clarke was described as 'a junior member of the key IRA cell organized by Brendan Dowd and Joseph O'Connor [sic]'. Ibid. Keenan's photograph had been found on a forged driving license recovered in the 'Liverpool bomb factory at 91 Scarisbrick Drive'. *Guardian*, 26 June 1980.
289. *Guardian*, 12 June 1986.
290. *Evening News*, 25 June 1980. See also *Guardian*, 26 June 1985.
291. *Daily Mirror*, 26 June 1980.
292. *Guardian*, 26 June 1980.
293. *Sunday Times*, 29 June 1980. The source quoted by the 'Insight Team' in relation to the alleged West Germany conspiracy, Peter 'The Para' McMullen, was a former British Army paratrooper who had been wanted in England for IRA attacks in the early 1970s. Ibid. For McMullen's alleged links to Keenan see McKee and Franey, *Time bomb*, p. 5.
294. *Observer*, 15 June 1986.
295. Brian Keenan, 26 May 2007.
296. *Guardian*, 25 June 1980.
297. Sr. Clarke, 'Brian Keenan', Clarke Papers (COFLA).
298. Quoted in *AP/RN*, 20 January 1983.
299. Brian Keenan to 'Peter Flynn' (Seamus O Mathuna), 10 December 1983, Private Collection (O Mathuna). Keenan noted: 'I only hear a few things when POWs or other prisoners pass this way on lie-downs and then only in snatches of conversation. All other information is gleaned from press & personal letters. I do know, however, that our people are moved about a lot on lay downs & that there are some very racist screws in some of the dispersals'. Ibid.
300. Brian Keenan, 26 May 2007.
301. *Times*, 12 July 1984. See Wensley Clarkson, *The curse of Brink's-Mat, 25 years of murder and mayhem* (London, 2012).
302. Hugh Doherty, 23 June 2006. David Martin, a 'gunman' serving twenty-five years, was found hanged in Parkhurst SSU on 13 March 1984. He had quarrelled with child-killer Donald 'The Black Panther' Neilson and was in 'suicidal mood'. *Times*, 22 May 1984 and *FRFI*, April 1984. Neilson was a veteran of Britain's colonial wars of the 1950s and 1960s. Renwick, *Hidden wounds*, pp. 40–41. Dr. Cooper, who gave evidence at Martin's inquest, was later that month involved in the decision to relocate 'Yorkshire Ripper' Peter Sutcliffe from Parkhurst to Broadmoor Hospital owing to 'paranoid schizophrenic' state of mind. *Times*, 28 March 1984. Martin had escaped from Marlborough Street Magistrates Court on 24 December 1982 having been charged with the attempted murder of a police officer. Armed detectives shot a man in Kensington whom they believed to be Martin. *Daily Telegraph*, 15 January 1983 and *FRFI*, February 1983, p. 1.
303. Joe O'Connell, 8 June 2008. Londoner Norman Parker claimed in relation to the IRA in Parkhurst: 'They kept very much to themselves and never gave anyone cause to fall out with them. They were polite and eminently trustworthy. Their crimes apart, they were principled men. I never heard of any of them pulling strokes. In a world where we were surrounded by potential enemies, we had nothing to fear from the IRA. Some of our crowd didn't like them. Understandably, they strongly disapproved of the IRA's habit of planting bombs in places where civilians could get hurt'. Parker, *Complete Parkhurst Tales*, pp. 300–301. Roberts was released in November 2014. BBC One TV News, 12 November 2014.
304. Joe O'Connell, 8 June 2008.
305. Hugh Doherty, 23 June 2006.
306. Walmsley, *Special Security Units*, p. 33.
307. Walmsley, *Special Security Units*, p. 28.
308. Walmsley, *Special Security Units*, p. 29.
309. Joe O'Connell, 7 June 2008
310. Walmsley, *Special Security Units*, p. 34.
311. Hugh Doherty, 23 June 2006.
312. Eddie O'Neill, 23 June 2006. For use of the same term in the H-Blocks in December 1979 see Sam Millar, *On the brinks*, (Galway, 2003), p. 92.
313. Joe O'Connell, 8 June 2008.
314. John McCluskey to Anon, [c. August 1980] in *AP/RN*, 18 October 1980.
315. *Report on the work of the Prison Department, 1980*, p. 35.
316. *Times*, 12 August 1980.
317. *Times*, 12 August 1980.
318. Jim McDonald, 2 July 2008.

319. *Guardian*, 11 August 1980.

320. *Guardian*, 11 August 1980. See also Ibid., 12 August 1980.

321. Jim McDonald, 2 July 2008. McDonald was a leading member of Sinn Féin in London from the 1970s to early 2000s. Born in Galway and raised in Clare, Cork and Dublin, he emigrated to England in 1961. Sinn Féin, *2014 Le Cheile*, programme, pp. 56–7.

322. *FRFI*, June 1984, p. 16 and *Independent*, 15 January 2006. See also Terence MacSwiney Cumann, West London to Comrades, 18 April 1984 and Jan Taylor to Comrades, 16 May 1984, Private Collection (O Mathuna). A member of Kilburn Sinn Féin and the Trade Union Committee on the PTA, Taylor had been arrested in November 1976 when protesting the 'so called' Peace People's march in London. Several demonstrators were assaulted by police. He was charged in Bow Street court on 1 February 1977 with breaching the peace, resisting arrest and possession of an offensive weapon for which he was fined £30 and bound to keep the peace for three years. *PAC Bulletin*, March/ April 1977.

323. John McCluskey, 3 August 2007.

324. McCluskey to Anon, [c. August 1980] in *AP/RN*, 18 October 1980. Other IRA prisoners in Wormwood Scrubs in the summer of 1980 included Pat Hackett, Liam McLarnon, Ronnie McCartney, Jerry Mealy, Mick Murray, Shane Paul O'Doherty and the innocent Gerry Conlon and Billy Power. *The Irish Prisoner*, No. 9, June/ July 1980. Mealy, transferred to the London prison after the Gartree rooftop protest of July 1978, was moved to Wandsworth owing to 'tension in [Wormwood] Scrubs'. Sr. Clarke, 'Jerry Mealy', Clarke Papers (COFLA).

325. McCluskey to Anon, [c. August 1980] in *AP/RN*, 18 October 1980. See also *FRFI*, November/ December 1980, p. 13.

326. McCluskey to Anon, [c. August 1980] in *AP/RN*, 18 October 1980.

327. Sr. Clarke, 'Paul Norney', Clarke Papers (COFLA).

328. John McCluskey, 3 August 2007.

329. *Times*, 21 August 1980.

330. Parker, *Dangerous people*, p. 118.

331. *Irish voices from English jails, writings of Irish political prisoners in English prisons* (London, 1979). The book was expanded from a special issue of *Irish Prisoner* Magazine. Ibid., p. 11.

332. *Irish voices*, p. 11.

333. See *P.O.W., Bulletin of the Irish Political Prisoners in Britain*, Special Edition, November 1980. Caughey's former Birmingham Sinn Féin associate Eddie Fullerton became founding chairman of the Inishown RAC, Donegal, on 12 October 1980. *AP/RN*, 18 October 1980. One of twenty children, Fullerton had migrated from Slediren, Buncrana, to Birmingham in teenage years where he married in 1958. He sold *An Phoblacht* in the city until 1975 when the fall out of the Birmingham bombs prompted a return to Donegal. Elected in 1979 to Buncrana Urban District Council and Donegal County Council, Fullerton was one of only ten Sinn Féin councilors in the jurisdiction. He was a member of the Donegal Comhairle Ceantair of which Brendan Magill, former head of Sinn Féin in England, was Secretary. *AP/RN*, 15 August 1981. Fullerton was assassinated in Buncrana in 1991 in an attack attributed to Loyalists. *AP/RN*, 15 January 2009 and 'Fullerton', TV documentary, TG4, 5 January 2010.

334. *P.O.W. Bulletin*, November 1980. See also Sr. Clarke, 'Hull', Clarke Papers (COFLA). Governor Lewis claimed in October 1980 that two low flying sightings of a helicopter near Hull were part of a plot to spring IRA prisoners. Republicans transferred into the prison after the pre-emptive segregation of the republicans were also isolated. *FRFI*, January/ February 1981, p. 11.

335. [John Higgins et al], *Irish political prisoners in England, Special Category 'A', An account of prison life in England based on the experiences of Irish Republican John Higgins imprisoned between 1976 and 1979* (Dublin, 1980).

336. *AP/RN*, 24 May 1980.

337. See *PAC News*, June 1977.

338. *Irish Political Prisoners in Britain*, p. 6.

339. *AP/RN*, 30 September 1980. Other major speakers included Miriam Daly of the IRSP, Bernadette McAliskey, Tony Gildernew of Tyrone RAC and Sinn Féin's Mary Nelis. Ibid.

340. AE Huckle to RA Neilson , 6 March 1978, NAE, FCO 87/ 762.

341. 'DEMAND POLITICAL STATUS-SMASH H-BLOCK', Private Collection (Renwick). See also TOM press release, 'Fleet Street blanket protest', 27 February 1980. Ibid. For unrest by political prisoners in Limerick Jail and Portlaoise see *Guardian*, 2 September 1982. Moral support offered by left wing TD Tony Gregory then posed a threat to the minority Government of Charles Haughey. Ibid.

342. See [London] *H-Block Armagh Bulletin*, No. 3, 19 June [1980]. See Philip Boxberger, 'Tony Gregory, TD, Talks to the Bru', *The Bru, The Larkin Unemployed Centre's Monthly News*, Vol. 1, No. 2 [1989], pp. 6–7.

CHAPTER 5

The IRA in England and the 1980–1981 Hunger Strikes

The 1980 H-Block Hunger Strike

Informed sources appreciated that the Republican Movement was edging towards a major stand on political status in late 1980. On 23 September 1980 ex-'Blanketman' Fra McCann, who had entered the US irregularly as a result of his conviction for IRA offences, told the rapt Boston State House that 'a hunger strike at one of the most notorious prisons is imminent and could lead to deaths'.[1] For those conversant with matters left unstated in Boston, psychological distress and an ominous sense of dread accumulated in tandem. English humanitarian Pat Arrowsmith, who had fasted in support of the hunger-striking Price sisters in June 1974, addressed a London audience on 3 October sponsored by the moderate 'Charter 80' grouping. An eclectic panel that included English born Anglican Bishop Colin O'Brien Winter of SWAPO, Eamonn McCann of the SWP and Paddy Bond of the Connolly Association, supported the rally. Speakers included Kevin McConnell of National Smash H-Block Campaign and Labour MPs Tony Benn, Eric Heffer and Jock Stallard.[2] A vicarious 'broad front' had undeniably assembled in England. When the window of positive political intervention by the British Executive was reduced to a mere two days, Cardinal O Fiaich risked straining the patience of his private republican contacts by asking them to postpone the protest while he conferred with Secretary of State Humphrey Atkins.[3] This proved impossible, not least in that the prerogative of agency and discretion had passed to those within the H-Blocks. The latitude already granted to the Primate by the leadership was not insignificant in that the IRA had already called a cessation in its deadly campaign against prison staff in order to 'facilitate mediation'. Any further delay threatened to retard if not derail forward momentum. The danger of projecting a sense of weakness to the NIO ahead of substantive negotiations was a major factor. Strategist Danny Morrison reflected: 'The British government refused to budge and thus began the 1980 hunger strike'.[4]

On 27 October 1980 IRA men Brendan Hughes, Tommy McKearney, Ray McCartney, Sean McKenna, Leo Green and Tom McFeeley, as well as the INLA's John Nixon, commenced a concerted campaign to achieve political status by a fast to the death.[5] The initial seven were selected to represent primary republican sectors in the Six Counties, but their number deliberately replicated that of the signatories of the 1916 Proclamation in defiance of the punishment for 'treason' against the British Crown.[6] The specific requirements sought by political prisoners in 1980 included entitlement to wear their own clothes, additional freedom of association and recreation time in lieu of convict work duties. Communication with family and friends, a constant concern, was addressed by reasonable demands to post one letter and receive one visit per week. Regarding their actions as both unavoidable and justified, the men required restoration of forfeited remission on par with persons who had not been docked arising from protests. Enumerated in the form of the 'five demands', this assertive charter encompassed the traditional self-definition of republican political prisoners.[7] Participation by the INLA reflected the larger organization's conception of 'the broad front' in which 'republican and socialist political prisoners' had equal status, as well as IRA acceptance of their personal commitment.[8] The evolution of a 'Smash H-Block' campaign into a more structured National H-Block/ Armagh Committee guided by republican veteran Fr. Piaras O Duill, enabled disparate civil and human rights groupings to interact.[9]

Government moves to pre-empt the action in Long Kesh by what was described as a 'compromise' of allowing prisoners wear 'civilian style clothes' rather than uniforms was announced on 23 October 1980.[10] The NIO, according to its own administration, had decided to introduce 'prison-issue civilian clothing to replace the old denim uniform' prior to the commencement of the fast. They reported: 'Clothing is supplied on a personal basis in a variety of colours and styles'.[11] If centrally procured, the stockpile remained on the shelf at the moment of truth. Interpreted by the IRA as an inadequate token response to their more ambitious and meaningful demands, the fast commenced as planned on 27 October.[12] Among those who addressed a mass rally in Dublin the previous day was the charismatic orator Joe Stagg. His presence outside the GPO on O'Connell Street, headquarters of the Irish Volunteers, Irish Citizen Army, Cumman na mBan and Hibernian Rifles during the 1916 Rising, and his fraternal relationship to the deceased militant Frank Stagg, was highly symbolic.[13] As the protest stretched into weeks and then months, supporters anticipated fatalities and tragic emotional funerals. Republican perceptions of the hunger strike in Ireland were crucial as it informed the logic of the decision to option a drastic contingency. Derry's IRSP newsletter queried whether participants would 'join the ranks of M[a]cSwiney, Gaughan and Stagg', who had attained iconic status in the republican communities as high - profile prison casualties. While eclipsing the death of Tyrone's Sean McCaughey in Portlaoise in May 1946, the focus on men who had succumbed in England indicated that the 1970s Dispersal System provided the most cogent role models for their comrades in Derry in 1980.[14] Reportage of the ordeals of Gaughan and Stagg had created much greater ferment in the Twenty-Six counties than that of Mac Stiofain in 1972 or, indeed, the dozens who had fasted to extremity in the Curragh and Portloaise in the mid-1970s.[15]

Billy Armstrong was sent from Wakefield to Durham on a twenty-eight day lie-down in September 1980 and shifted to Wormwood Scrubs on 8 October. This necessitated the usual notification of correspondents regarding the change of address, a lag in receiving personal possessions and the re-organization of planned visits.[16] The move had been long sought but, ironically, coincided with two fresh points of concern. The first was word that a hunger strike had begun in the H-Blocks. Mention of Brendan 'Darkie' Hughes on a London radio news bulletin struck a chord with those acquainted with the former Belfast Brigade Operations Officer. Claims that 150 men had joined the protest ensured that many IRA prisoners in England had personal ties to Long Kesh which exceeded common bonds of incarceration for republicanism.[17] Monaghan's Sean Kinsella had escaped from Portlaoise in August 1974 with Derry man Tom McFeeley.[18] In Albany Roy Walsh and Ronnie McCartney, stirred by equally profound links, formed a compact 'to do something here' and decided to maximise hoped - for publicity by waiting until the strike had matured.[19] Both men were under close observation: Walsh had 'decorated' a prison officer in Hull on 31 October 1979 following punishment for possession of 'contraband' on 11 September 1979.[20]

The hunger strike proved a stringent test of the capacity of British support groups and ostensible political allies. A new strand of activism emerged centred on the 'five demands', and it was argued that the *de facto* concessions granted to the IRA in Portlaoise in 1977 provided a basis for a similar accommodation in Ulster.[21] Birmingham TOM braved a suspiciously lightly policed National Front counter-demonstration, during which journalists were pelted by neo-fascists, to steer a torchlight procession into the city centre on 27 October 1980.[22] A TOM delegation received a briefing in Sinn Féin's Dublin headquarters from Tom Hartley, Director of the POW Department, on 3 November. Richard Behal, Director of Sinn Féin's Foreign Affairs Bureau, also spoke to a gathering which attracted supporters from Britain, France, Germany and the Netherlands.[23] The party's Ard Fheis in the Mansion House, Dublin, was predictably dominated by prison issues. English socialist republican Dr. Rose Dugdale, who had fasted in Limerick Prison in 1975 in support of the 'Belfast Ten', attended shortly following her release in October 1980.[24] Dugdale had made at least one attempt to escape from Limerick, a feat last managed by the ingenious Behal in 1966. Arising from their background, the pair delivered highly credible commentaries on pertinent prison issues.[25]

Undeterred by the menacing Birmingham episode, approximately 5,000 marched from the Embankment to Camden via Downing Street on

15 November 1980 where ex-members of the British military delivered a document advocating the removal of UK armed forces from Ireland. The London event occurred under the auspices of the 'Committee for Withdrawal' and marked the 60th anniversary of the partition of Ireland. The Committee was a sub-grouping of the Young Liberals, which had formed in 1979 to back the 'troops out' argument of TOM and others. Events in Long Kesh altered the tenor of one of the most successful British rallies on the Irish question in some years.[26] Sinn Féin's account of the main London demonstration concentrated on the radicals who rallied under the banner 'Don't let the Irish prisoners die!'. The party optimistically viewed the comparatively large turnout as indicative of improved British consciousness of the injustices underpinning the Irish conflict. Diminished by the PTA, Sinn Féin had been present in London in the form of proxies and fellow travellers. Lily Fitzsimmons of the Belfast RAC addressed the crowd, as did Nora Connolly O'Brien, daughter of the revered Hiberno-Scottish 1916 martyr James Connolly. Fitzsimmons and Connolly O'Brien intimated a strong message of Republican Movement approval and ideological continuity on the gathering. Turf Lodge activist Fitzsimmons was a comparatively familiar name in Britain's leftist circles owing to the coverage of the RAC by the RCG in their *Hands off Ireland!* campaign.[27] TOM had forty-four branches across Britain, including eight in the London metropolitan area. Co-operation between IRA and INLA supporters in the US proved less straightforward owing to disputes concerning pro rata disbursement of funds raised by touring relatives and associates.[28]

Left wing Britons, not least Paul Foot, and pro-Irish Liberals such as Frank Filgate also spoke in London. Foot criticized the editorial policy of the *Daily Mirror,* for which he occasionally worked as a correspondent. Labour MP Ernie Roberts chaired proceedings at Camden Town with the backing of fellow parliamentarian Clive Soley. Roberts was unequivocal in supporting the demands of the hunger strikers in the H-Blocks, a valuable endorsement given the more general official purpose of the demonstration. Long-term Irish advocates participated, including pacifist Pat Arrowsmith. The CPGB, often reluctant to confer approval on Sinn Féin, was represented in the person of Chris Myant, Assistant Editor of the Moscow backed *Morning Star.*[29] The paper had described the assassination of vehement anti-communist Airey Neave as an act of 'barbarism'.[30] Gordon McLennan, General Secretary of the CPGB, had nonetheless signed the 'Charter 80' petition backing the 'five demands' in February 1980.[31] Many republicans were unimpressed. IRSP supporter and future IRA member in England Nick Mullen discounted the *Morning Star* for being 'revisionist ... on the Irish question'.[32]

British Conservatives were re-sensitized to the prospect of Irish republicans gaining ground and Jill Knight MP remained consistently hostile towards any perceived concession to the IRA. On 10 November 1980 she questioned Prison Department Director General DJ Trevelyan on allowances for family visits to republicans in her capacity as a member of the Home Affairs Committee of the House of Commons. As part of a general discussion on Prison Department finances at a time when an increase of custodial sentences threatened to derail the unfulfilled reforms promised by the May Committee, Knight cited the case of a woman who brought her children from Birmingham to Parkhurst every two weeks to visit 'an IRA prisoner'. Her sources implied that the family travelled by rail, stayed in hotels and that 'substantial sums' were involved.[33] Avoiding discussion of an arguably unpopular case study, Trevelyan responded by making a 'more general point' in which he noted the dual factors of limitations on family visits arising from 'security classifications' and the practise of Home Office support for just one per month under any circumstances. The Director, more than most administrators, was aware of the additional privations imposed on Irish Category A prisoners and their families.[34]

The successful London rally was followed by a stunt in Westminster Cathedral on Sunday 17 November 1980 when four blanket wearing protesters attended Cardinal Basil Hume's services to register their opposition to his call for the IRA and INLA prisoners to abandon the fast. As had occurred in the 'Belfast Ten' hungerstrike of 1974–5, the Catholic Hierarchy in England was both vocal and proactive in declaring its firm opposition to Irish republicans at home or abroad. The impact of the crisis on Sinn Féin in England was also measurable and on 22 November Birmingham republicans staged a two-hour picket at Winson Green prison in a bid to convey their anger over the H-Block situation.[35] A march in Dublin on 28 November 1980 attracted over 12,000 people and was followed within the week by another that summoned 30,000 to the gates of the British Embassy in the affluent south city suburb of Ballsbridge.[36] Mairead Farrell, Mary Doyle and Mairead Nugent joined the IRA strike in Armagh prison on 8 December 1980 and, in so doing, mounted the first major female republican protest of its kind since that of Dolours and Marian Price in Brixton in 1974. The fraught context in which the Armagh escalation occurred ensured that the once vivid London precedent was virtually ignored.[37]

Roy Walsh and Ronnie McCartney selected 18 December 1980 for a freezing roof top protest in Albany but were interdicted by staff who discovered their prepared kit during cell raids. Walsh was dispatched for punishment in Bristol while McCartney was sent to Winchester.[38] If all had gone as planned, Albany would have been in the news the following day when a further heavily marshalled picket on Thatcher's Flood Street home in Chelsea passed off without untoward incident. Protesters were urged to consider the plight of Maurice (aka Michael) Ward, a non-political Dubliner on a solidarity hunger strike in Brixton.[39] Ward had been detained in Southend in April due to passport irregularities when travelling from Germany to Ireland. He was remanded in custody in Brixton where he was attacked by criminals. Incriminating press reports named him as a person of interest to the RUC in Belfast regarding political offences, although no such charges were laid. On 30 October Ward followed an individual impulse to begin fasting in support of the 'five demands'. He was visited in Brixton by Fr. Cagney and a Dublin based solicitor.[40]

All such activity rallied available republican support in England towards the critical situation in Ireland and, as such, diminished agitation on what was perceived as the less urgent task of aiding the prisoners within the Dispersal System. Ward was in earnest and piqued the interest of radical solicitor Brian Rose Smith, the Revolutionary Communist Tendency (RCT), National H-Block/ Armagh Committee and the Irish Embassy in 17 Grosvenor Place, London. Diplomats relayed the substance of the British Government position to Ward and on 11 December senior Irish official Gerard Corr evidently convinced him to desist. The Irish man had by then lost four stone, almost a third of his body mass, and had accentuated the danger of dying by a short thirst strike. Ward, however, recommenced the protest on 13 December. Ann Gillon of the RCT contacted Sr. Sarah Clarke on 18 December to report that he was 'mentally coherent & determined to carry to the death if possible'. The prospect of Ward perishing in Brixton was negated on 18 December when a statement carried by *Republican News* in Belfast announced the cessation of the fifty-three day hunger strike.[41] Over thirty IRA and INLA prisoners in Long Kesh and three female IRA prisoners in Armagh Jail began taking food the following day.[42]

Newry man Sean McKenna, one of the first batch of seven hunger-strikers, had been administered the Last Rites on 18 December when comatose in Musgrave Park Hospital. This occurred an hour before the thirty-four page NIO document, which had been on the table for several days, was unilaterally accepted by Brendan Hughes.[43] The Republican Movement then claimed that Northern Secretary Atkins, in the light of a Commons debate on 4 December, had provided the basis of a deal which was centred, in the first instance, on acceptance that political prisoners could wear their own clothes. Cardinal O Fiaich and others hinted that further concessions were in prospect, including the restoration of lost remission to protest participants. This boon had been previously conferred on those who had proved incapable of staying the course but, as with other aspects of the intense discussions surrounding the matter, had not been formally agreed in London.[44] Danny Morrison understood that the British Government 'promised to introduce progressively a liberal prison regime' but that this undertaking was 'reneged' upon as soon as the protest ceased.[45] In Winchester's concrete 'Strong-Box', Ronnie McCartney was 'pleased but not pleased'; lives had been preserved but nothing of political substance secured.[46]

Within days of the cessation it was clear that the IRA had been outmanoeuvred by the NIO and powerful British stakeholders for whom the definition of 'civilian style' clothing differed markedly from reasonable expectations. Brightly coloured oversized trousers and shirts reminiscent of circus costumes were offered instead of normal attire, an unsophisticated technique employed in Manchester Prison in 1976 to test Sean Kinsella's resolve following sentencing.[47] The ruse implied NIO contempt for the prisoners and was read by many of those in the line of fire as a calculated provocation. In Long Kesh Sam Millar and other 'blanketmen' who had bridled with frustration when ordered to maintain restraint in the H-Blocks during the crisis were appalled: 'All the years of torture and torment ... for an inimical "agreement" that wasn't even worth the paper it was printed on'.[48] Recently advanced IRA O/C, Bobby Sands, grappled with the harsh realization that this brinkmanship ensured the continuation of the blanket protest and greatly enhanced the stark prospect of an even more concerted hunger strike. Sands knew he was destined to be the first fatality if the 'Five Demands' were not conceded in London.[49]

Parkhurst escape attempt, 18 December 1980

A potentially major escape from Parkhurst was prevented when Sean McKenna was dying in Long Kesh. With two wings out of commission due to comprehensive IRA roof deconstruction, the remaining republican prisoners confined within the complex considered inflicting structural damage on the intact A, B and C Wings. This ambitious sabotage programme was under preliminary consideration when, against the backdrop of the Long Kesh and Armagh protests, London gangsters offered to include republicans in a daring break out. The plan hinged on a corrupt prison officer who regularly exchanged prohibited goods which he delivered into the prison for cash. Once the man consented to have his 'security key' moulded, a variety of escape options became viable. Plasticine supplied for creative art was used to make a crisp key impression which was smuggled to outside contacts. The perfect copy obtained enabled the bearer to open cells as well as internal doors within the wings. Exiting the building became the main concern as the formidable challenge of the Isle of Wight sea barrier had already been addressed. A seagoing craft lay secreted in a convenient coastal location on a trailer. Eddie O'Neill was offered the choice of making his own way from the English mainland or accompanying the Londoners to Spain in the light aircraft they intended to acquire from a Hampshire airfield. Lacking an extradition treaty with the UK, Spain was a legally safe and often lucrative haven for organized British criminals in the 1970s and 1980s.[50]

The men ascertained that a Security Officer holding the vital 'pass key' opened an outer gate in the early morning to allow staff into the building where they could ascend the floors and have breakfast in the kitchen area of the still locked-down facility. The plan required a sympathetic canteen worker, who was allowed to move through the otherwise carefully controlled internal gates, to go to O'Neill's cell around 5.00 a.m. and receive the copied 'security key' needed to unlock the Irish man's door from the outside. This would be handed back. Once at liberty on the unsupervised landing O'Neill planned to release those selected for the bid. They intended to lock the kitchen staff in the vacated cells, and having thus replaced them, encourage the coerced Security Officer to escort them via gates he alone could unlock. The escapers could walk out of Parkhurst with additional hours of winter darkness to cover their progress by boat to the south coast of England. Whereas the plan allowed some minor leeway on the Isle of Wight, crossing the sea channel required favourable tides and weather. The hiatus waiting for the right moment, however, spelled disaster as it became clear in hindsight that staff had, at the very least, learned of O'Neill's inclusion. Without warning his cell door was 'smashed in' and he was 'dragged away to the block'.[51] It transpired that the remorseful staff accomplice had confessed his complicity. A variant of the ambitious plan was utilized in January 1995 when three British prisoners exited Parkhurst without raising the alarm. They were only thwarted by failure to find a local aircraft with sufficient fuel to reach the mainland.[52]

Staff lost no time 'ghosting' O'Neill and other republicans out of Parkhurst on 18 December 1980. During the ferry crossing to Southampton he recalled his indignation: 'The screws [were] talking about the hunger strike being over and that they had given up and that they'd got nothing'. Of more immediate concern was that the escape and sabotage contingency had both been prevented. After a short 'lie-down' in a Wandsworth punishment cell emptied of furniture by day and any source of stimulation at all other times, O'Neill was returned to the re-opened Hull Prison in Yorkshire. Stevie Blake, Tony Madigan, Martin Coughlan and Noel Gibson were among the IRA contingent present by early 1981. Held on his own on a wing prior to the arrival of Stevie Nordone, O'Neill, unusually, was not required to attend compulsory work assignments. While no explanation was proffered it seemed likely that the authorities did not with to tempt fate by admitting an IRA engineer suspected of expensive acts of sabotage and with a track record in escape attempts to a modern machine workshop. The success of Parkhurst staff undoubtedly saved the Home Office major embarrassment, particularly in the light of contemporaneous events in London.[53]

Escape of Gerry Tuite, 16 December 1980

The escape from Brixton of Gerry Tuite in the early hours of 16 December 1980 delivered a blow to the prestige of the Prison Department. His arrest in December 1979 had been hailed as a coup for Scotland Yard, who had identified the Cavan man as one of the most important republicans in Britain.[54] Remanded to Brixton with Dickie Glenholmes, Bobby Storey and

Bobby Campbell, the men faced common charges relating to a plan to spring Brian Keenan from the same prison.[55] The more serious offences alleged against Tuite concerned a wave of bomb attacks in the London area in 1978 that he was assumed to have organized.[56] Early reports of the escape claimed that he had joined forces with two English men who broke through the walls separating their adjoining cells before tunnelling into the outer wall of Tuite's cell. IRA involvement attracted international coverage and Tuite was the only man named in the account carried by the *Chicago Tribune*.[57] Clan na Gael organ *Irish World* noted from America that the 'pre-Christmas publicity campaign to alert the public' of the danger posed by Tuite was 'unprecedented'.[58] The Prison Department acknowledged the incident as one of its 'significant events' of the year.[59]

Tuite was originally remanded to A Wing in December 1979 with others accused of planning to fly Keenan out of Brixton's more secure D Wing using a commandeered helicopter. He co-operated with friendly English men in order to obtain escape paraphernalia needed to break through the wall of his top tier cell. On scrapping away the plaster layer to access the brickwork, Tuite exposed a new type of rendering over steel mesh. He sent word of this discovery to a construction industry contact in Ireland who advised him that the material was impervious to cutting with available tools, but could be removed by drilling holes in the metal and then prising back the strips with a screwdriver until it snapped. Surveillance or human agency warned staff that a serious escape attempt was nearing implementation, and lacking the equipment required to proceed, Tuite pre-empted inevitable discovery by requesting a cell shift on the basis that his neighbour was noisy. This was granted and it was some weeks before the exploratory damage came to light. The Irish man was immediately suspected and promptly moved to the ground floor of D Wing that had been specially adapted to contain Category A prisoners in the wake of the *Mountbatten Report*.[60] In 1969 a team of 'specialist' soldiers had failed to find appreciable weakness prior to its commissioning.[61] Tuite, by contrast, was utterly determined to break out and prior to leaving A Wing, organized the smuggling of a .45 calibre revolver into the prison using contacts available to an Englsih man facing a life sentence. The high-powered weapon was detected in Reception and events overtook the arrival of its replacement which he intended to brandish in a rush to the gate. He nonetheless managed the singular feat of convincing a Security Officer to carry an art box containing three hacksaw blades into D wing. The SO evidently believed that the request for assistance heralded a tentative step towards conformity and neglected to X-ray the cardboard container.[62]

The Irish man entered a part of the prison housing numerous well-known occupants, including the sole survivor of the Iranian Embassy hostage siege.[63] The annexe generally held fifteen Category A men who were guarded by a Senior Officer and seven staff, one of whom was tasked with keeping vigil overnight when the area was locked down.[64] Principal Officer J Denyer was responsible for running D Wing.[65] Governor Michael Selby viewed the sector as being similar to other special units where the balance of security and humane treatment ideally permitted 'greater association and greater freedom within a very tight boundary'.[66] Tuite's involuntary wing shift led to an enforced reunion with Brian Keenan who occupied a cell on a higher landing adjacent to seasoned English bank raiders, 'Big Jim' Moody and Stan Thompson. Jimmy Moody, whose mother was Irish, was a prolific and physically imposing armed robber with a capacity for extreme violence. A former associate of South London's feared Richardson gang, he later joined the 'Thursday Mob', which netted over two million pounds. He was additionally regarded as a top underworld assassin.[67] Essex man Thompson was one of the most successful prison escapers in Britain, having exited Dartmoor, Chelmsford and Brixton between 1966 and 1971.[68] 'Alleged contract killer' Henry 'Big H' MacKenney (aka 'McKenney') occupied the end cell of their row and proved amenable to the plans of the conspiring group.[69] Keenan, Thompson and Moody intended to escape by breaching two adjacent cell walls in order to enable the occupants of all three to exit the building by a single opening in the exterior wall.[70] Tuite was briefed by Keenan on developments to date and steps were taken to arrange his inclusion. They discussed the option of blowing the outer cellblock wall using South African C4 plastic explosives stockpiled in London.[71]

It was imperative that Tuite was moved to the strip of cells on the upper floor where Moody and Thompson were located and, specifically, into the one occupied by MacKenney. The English man was attending trial daily at the Old Bailey. This required careful negotiation with a much-feared and highly intelligent individual who effected the exchange in June 1980 by informing staff that he was not gelling with the others on the landing. Tuite had befriended MacKenney for whom he obtained specialized aviation reference books and offered advice on his legal affairs. The Irish man promised assistance in dissuading a key witness from appearing in court in return for facilitation.[72] Crime writer Wensley Clarkson theorized that MacKenney would have been killed if he had refused to cooperate.[73] Such a move would have been counterproductive, even though the general reputation of the IRA dissuaded casual potential informers from compromising many months of painstaking work. A republican account claimed: 'One point in Gerry's favour was that the rest of the remand prisoners were in terror of Gerry following the hysterical reports in the British gutter press'.[74] Republicans, however, possessed various means to assist other prisoners and Tipp Guilfoyle asserted in court on 6 November 1980 that 'supergrass' John Childs had spoken to him of his desire to frame MacKenney.[75] An unexpected incident occurred in D Wing, meanwhile, when Tuite spotted a newly transferred prisoner returning from a visit with an illicit lighter which he used in front of others. This uncharacteristic and therefore suspicious display aroused Moody's keen self-preservation instincts and he immediately administered a severe beating to a presumed stooge who was never seen again.[76]

Placating MacKenney had an unexpected benefit as Tuite, feigning indifference, had insisted that he would only willingly exchange cells if those allocated to the English man were redecorated. This was agreed. A can of white emulsion paint was skilfully purloined, providing the precise shade needed to hide evidence of illicit drilling and prising. Moody's external contacts supplied a sufficient stock of screwdrivers, masonry drill bits, hacksaw blades and superglue to meet other requirements. His brother Richard was in June 1981 convicted of smuggling such supplies.[77] Tuite obtained a valuable makeshift tool once provided with a table suitable for laying out large - format jigsaw puzzles. A tubular bar was cut from its frame which, when mounted on the end of a broom handle, created a highly effective brace for the drill bit. The segment was reattached when not in use.[78] A routine emerged during which one man worked on the wall separating Tuite's cell from Thompson's while the others made themselves visible to staff and kept watch. Searches were neither as frequent nor as thorough as might have been expected and the team progressed at a rate that would have been impossible in the Dispersal System. Wooden lockers were screwed into position against compromised brickwork in order to conceal openings and contraband. When paint became available it was used along with cardboard and tape to disguise damage caused to the seventeen inch thick walls.[79] Keenan was inconveniently embroiled in a dispute with Brixton staff and was suddenly moved to Wandsworth. He was convicted of IRA offences in England in June 1980 and transferred into the Dispersal System.[80] Tuite, meanwhile, toiled steadily on a second wall breach that permitted, once complete, access to an exterior roof area. The final major step entailed Moody cutting into Thompson's cell.[81]

Moody and Thompson quietly opened their shared wall on the night of 14 December, intending to exit via Tuite's onto the roof of the extension outside. The Londoner found that he could not manipulate his muscular upper torso through the hole separating Thompson's cell from Tuite's. The IRA man, however, had wisely delayed smashing the perilously thin plaster layer standing between the interior of the prison and the roof until both accomplices had entered his cell. This precaution enabled Moody and Thompson to mask the breaches and wait for the next night when the extra work of widening the inter-cell access could be carried out. Thompson appeared in St. Albans Crown Court later that day and subsequently discovered that he had been acquitted. Against all odds, the security of the plan held up and all three broke out of Brixton at around 3.15 a.m. on 16 December.[82] Exiting the prison necessitated avoiding CCTV detection, scaling a twelve-foot mesh fence and the seventeen-foot outer wall. Careful observance of apparent blind spots and timing of dog patrols, as well as sheer good fortune, was required to traverse the outer wall undetected. The men advantageously utilized scaffolding planks and rope left in the vicinity of the boundary wall by work crews.[83] A blanket was used to cover and cross the wire fence, although the serendipitous availability of wooden boards obviated the need to use their purpose - made grappling apparatus. Trusted associates were tasked with engineering subtle distractions inside the prison at a critical moment and the trio were not missed for seven hours. The only major problem encountered was the non-appearance of the car intended to speed them away from the locality, a probable result of the last minute change in date. The fact that Brixton was an inner city jail, however, ensured transport options and the men succeeded in hiring a 'mini-cab' taxi within minutes.[84] The driver told police that he was searching for a pre-booked fare and that his passengers were dropped beside a vehicle positioned in Herne Hill in which they left the city having paid £5 for a £1.50 journey.[85] The taxi man was not questioned for five days after notifying the authorities of his innocent role but was then grilled for seventeen hours until they cleared him of complicity.[86]

After lying low in a cottage in Kent, Thompson decided to surrender in the light of his acquittal in St. Albans Court *in absentia*. He presented himself in a Brixton police station with a solicitor on 19 December.[87] Tuite and Moody, meanwhile, passed between a succession of IRA and underworld safe houses before chancing passage across the Irish Sea to Ireland.[88] Commander Peter Duffy, of Scotland Yard's Anti-Terrorist Squad, posed with Tuite's wanted poster claiming that he was a 'dedicated and dangerous' man who might resume IRA activities in England.[89] He was described in dramatic terms as possessing a limp and 'burns down the left side of his body'.[90] Although many IRA engineers received wounds from premature explosions, Tuite's scars stemmed from a serious car crash in June 1976 which required him to use crutches for over a year. By the time it was realised that he had left England, the propriety of hyping his profile as a prime 'public enemy' was under review.[91]

Tuite absconded while a sizable protest organized by the RCG and TOM mustered on Jebb Avenue outside Brixton. London-Irish woman Annette Maloney, who had lived in North Armagh with her husband in 1976–78, was part of a crowd which assembled with banners. They observed scenes of commotion around the prison that led them to expect multiple arrests. Solicitors' phone numbers were hastily distributed and some in attendance assumed the sirens and police traffic were laid on 'to frighten us from further pickets'. A friend arrived at the scene and on the basis of early news reports explained that Tuite had 'done a runner'.[92] Strabane Sinn Féin activist Michael Cunningham was travelling by Tube with three of his young children and a niece, preparing to visit his imprisoned brothers, Gerry and Busty, when manhandled by passengers arguing over who had spotted him first. One of the children had noted the close resemblance between their father and Tuite's ubiquitous wanted poster and uttered 'look, here's Daddy'. Although quickly resolved by a uniformed policeman, Cunningham was for once reassured that he was being shadowed by the more discrete and armed Special Branch.[93] Sr. Sarah Clarke was travelling to Brixton with a parcel for Tuite when she heard the extraordinary news. A letter posted to her convent by the then missing Irish man arrived on 16 December 1980.[94]

Within weeks of Tuite's disappearance the *Guardian* deemed it desirable to assert that there was 'no evidence that he attempted to link with the London [IRA] active service unit allegedly responsible for a gasworks explosion, a car-bombing, and the attempted assassination of Mr. Christopher Tugendhat, the EEC Commissioner in Brussels'.[95] A gas depot in the London suburb of Bromley-by-Bow was bombed on 30 December 1980. The catalogue of high - impact international activity occurred in the midst of the detonation of two 10b high-grade gelignite bombs that 'wrecked' the Territorial Army Centre in Hammersmith and injuring five persons on 2 December. The Ministry of Defence had warned of IRA actions 'if the [H-Block hunger] strikers win no concessions, or because of revenge if any of them should die'.[96] *The Observer* dismissed any putative role by Tuite as 'extremely unlikely', speculating that England based ASUs using supplies smuggled via France were operating in the London sector.[97] This sober assessment followed misguided *Sun* predictions of a 'Christmas Bloodbath if one of the hunger strikers dies'.[98] No such indiscriminate cause and effect ever informed IRA strategy. William Whitelaw, when questioned in the Commons by Jill Knight, instructed Gordon Fowler, Deputy Director General of the Prison Service, to convene an enquiry in the midst of shrill press reaction to the breakout.[99] The outline report was released with the assent of Attorney General Sir Michael Havers QC on 2 February 1981 and led to the reassignment of Governor Michael Selby and Assistant-Governors RJ Perry and JH Dixon.[100] Lord Longford, who had visited Selby during his joint investigations into jail overcrowding with Lord Hutchinson in 1980, regarded him as 'one of the most enlightened governors ... [who] committed the unpardonable sin of having allowed a prisoner under his aegis to escape'.[101] Anthony Pearson, formerly Governor of Gartree, succeeded Selby in Brixton in January 1981.[102]

The assessment of the most serious escape scandal in England since that of George Blake in 1966 identified the probable demerits of holding maximum - security remand prisoners in a single location for over a year ahead of trial. This implied that familiarity with staff, routines and environment favoured potential escapers and, if entirely logical, deflected attention from politically sensitive discussion of 'human error' and 'antiquated' infrastructure. Less informed criticism was aired by rightwing MPs. In response to Whitelaw's cautious presentation in the Commons, Alan Clark, Conservative Member for Plymouth, Sutton, queried if Tuite had been remanded in Brixton 'as opposed to a more distant high security location for the convenience of relatives who wished to visit' and whether 'particular privileges in this field are being allowed to IRA prisoners?' Knowing the privations endured by republican and many non-political Category A prisoners, Whitelaw credibly denied the extension of 'special privileges' to the Irish contingent.[103] The Home Secretary did not then divulge that the Prison Department had in 1979 raised concerns as to Brixton's suitability for accommodating the assigned numbers of Provisional Category A prisoners.[104] The published version of the report, however, highlighted perceived failures in administrative routines within D Wing, leading to the creation 'in practice of a no-go' area for the staff.[105] Serial escaper Stan Thompson described this contention as 'entirely untrue', leading to a familiar divergence in basic information between prisoner witnesses and their Home Office employed captors. Thompson's 'whitewash' argument was also at odds with the opinion of David Evans, Assistant General Secretary of the POA, who surmised that other prisons had ceded undue local control to their inmates.[106] Trevelyan, Director General of the Prison Department, concurred in respect of his attribution of blame to 'human error at all levels' in a complex where 'physical security' did 'not equate to that at the dispersal prisons where sentenced Category A prisoners are held'.[107] This was axiomatic given the primary function of Brixton as a short term prison for men remanded in custody.

Staff vigilance was particularly acute in early 1981, with negative consequences for the IRA and all other Category A men. Administrative problems caused by poor communications with the England prisoners wrong-footed Sinn Féin in late January 1981 when *An Phoblacht* carried a call for British action on transfers to Irish prisons while publishing an incomplete list of the men and women under discussion.[108] By February 1981 protocols for incarcerating Irish republicans had been further tightened and more stringently observed. As matters stood, Category A men were escorted on a wing by two warders and, if moving between buildings, an additional guard dog and handler. In the event of a court appearance in the Old Bailey, they were accompanied by seventy-five Metropolitan Police, as well as at least one Principal Officer and two other senior staff drawn from the Prison Service.[109] Two prison officers and a Deputy-Governor were detailed to attend 'closed' visits, and the familiar disruption of 'ghosting' and solitary confinement on 'lie-downs' continued.[110] In Parkhurst SSU Joe O'Connell hailed Tuite's feat as 'a huge coup' and regretted that he too had not prevailed when in Brixton.[111]

Tipp Guilfoyle was placed in solitary under Rule 43 in Wormwood Scrubs when items regarded as useful for an escapee were found in a nearby cell. The Governor candidly explained that he would be dismissed if another

Irish prisoner managed to break out.[112] Such additional duties strained the Prison Service which, in early 1981, resulted in Brixton staff mounting a 'work to rule' protest and declining to admit new inmates.[113] 'Discretionary' visits in Wormwood Scrubs were curtailed and Guilfoyle received a letter from the habitually frank Governor McCarthy which stated: 'My reason [for refusing additional visitors] is that I think you and [Paul] Norney both still have your beliefs and that these inevitably make you against the prison system'.[114] This accurate assessment did not extend to pro-British agents imprisoned in England. Billy Armstrong claimed in February 1981 that 'most of the so called Loyalists in this country have all got the red band [i.e. orderly] jobs, which means they get taken off the CAT A book. There are one or two who are still on the book, but even then they are given ordinary visits whilst we are on "specials"'.[115]

A national manhunt for Tuite was launched in the Greater London area where Scotland Yard distributed 16,500 posters with his picture and the unnerving caption: 'Terrorist Alert. This Man Must Be Caught'.[116] Police checked traffic streams and raided homes of identified republican supporters. Sr. Clarke was visited in the La Sainte Union convent where she had accommodated many Irish visitors, unknown to her disapproving superiors, but not to her occasional correspondent Gerry Tuite. She was due to enter hospital for TB treatment.[117] Commander Duffy warned on 16 January 1981 that the IRA in the London area possessed 'a substantial supply of explosives' and were poised to follow up their recent attack on Uxbridge RAF base.[118] This coincided with news that Tuite's associate and 'suspected IRA bomber' Pat Magee was free to depart the Netherlands after three months detention.[119] British authorities had unsuccessfully sought the Belfast man's extradition to England to face fourteen charges of 'plotting and conspiring' and possession of arms and explosives in 1978 and 1979. These included blasts for which Tuite and John McComb were convicted although the actual operational permutation of those concerned was not ascertained in court proceedings.[120]

Born in Belfast, Pat Magee moved with his parents to England aged 4 and spent his youth in Norwich, East Anglia. He could speak with a convincing English accent. Magee returned to Belfast in 1969 and lived in the embattled Unity Flats housing project where he was detained several times on suspicion of IRA involvement.[121] It was claimed he was a leading IRA engineer in North Belfast prior to being interned in Long Kesh between June 1973 and November 1975.[122] Magee was reputedly 'the subject of constant army attention' upon release and in April 1977 underwent interrogation in Castlereagh Holding Centre when microswitches were uncovered in the home of his girlfriend. After being assaulted for three hours, an RUC man held a revolver to his head and threatened to supply his photograph and details to a UVF death squad. The Black Taxi hired to send him home was rammed *en route* by an armoured military Land Rovers, injuring three occupants.[123] The recovery of Magee's fingerprint in Greenwich in 1979 indicated to Scotland Yard that the Belfast man had interacted with Tuite's circle. He was then, however, detached from the IRA and residing in Holland, where he lived legally under a valid passport issued in May 1979.[124] In 1980 Dutch judges dismissed an extradition warrant on the grounds that they did not recognize the vague 'conspiracy' type charges accepted in British courts.[125] Tuite was named in the Commons in March 1981, when a fugitive, as the person suspected of carrying out bomb attacks known as 'Operation Oxo'.[126] McComb had received a ten year sentence for politically motivated armed robbery in 1972 and was tried in relation to the London attacks in the Old Bailey in May 1983.[127] Media sources later alleged that Magee availed of Brian Keenan's contacts with Middle Eastern radicals to obtain advanced training.[128]

The London escape and spate of IRA attacks stimulated international media attention on the England campaign and related matters. On 14 February 1981 the pro-republican *Irish World* covered the paroling in England of IRA prisoner Sean Canavan on its front page, a story which normally would have been relegated to a much less prominent slot in the American weekly.[129] Andrew Bennett, Labour MP for Stockport North, elicited information from the Home Secretary that Canavan had been paroled in November 1980, having served just four of a ten year sentence for conspiracy to cause explosions in England.[130] This was highly unusual for any Category A prisoner as it was widely understood that Circular Instruction 116/68 deprived them of the right to standard parole.[131] IRA prisoners were very rarely downgraded to Category B, let alone Category C, which would have shortened the structured pathway to parole as envisaged by the *Mountbatten Report*. The fact that Canavan had been permitted to reside in Britain was contrary to the general practise of deporting ex-IRA prisoners to one of the two jurisdictions in Ireland.[132] If Canavan's experience represented a rubric for achieving early parole, a republican defendant in England was expected to publicly renounce their ideological allegiance, admit to having committed relatively minor offences under duress, co-operate with the prosecution at trial and avoid prison militancy when convicted. He was atypical. Only Roisin McNearney, whose documented assistance to the Crown during the trial of the 'Belfast Ten' in Winchester Crown Court in November 1973, was known to have received greater leniency. Sr. Clarke noted: '[The Irish] Embassy rang before his release for information on him. Canavan was fighting his deportation on grounds of danger to his life'.[133] Whereas the attention focused in the Commons by Andrew Bennett MP was indicative of parliamentary curiosity regarding extraordinarily liberal treatment, the publicity generated in vigilant Irish-American circles implied concern of a different order, as the Department of Foreign Affairs was cogniscent. On

5 August 1981 Peter Short, a Belfast republican convicted of IRA arms possession offences in Southampton, was given a week long parole from Blundestone Prison in Norfolk. He was released in December 1981.[134] Short had received a ten year sentence in 1974 and would not have been automatically rated Category A in the first instance.[135]

The escape of Tuite came at a propitious moment for republicans in that it generated positive propaganda just as the dispiriting October-December 1980 hunger strike drew to a close on a less than satisfactory basis. Tuite was prevailed upon to make a dramatic public intervention on 4 October 1981, as matters had further deteriorated in the H-Blocks, when interviewed at a remote location by Eamonn Mallie of Downtown Radio, County Down. The Cavan man related his remarkable story with uninhibited candour. The *Sunday Times* carried excerpts of the scoop which prompted an *Irish Times* assertion that the Gardai were 'helping British to find IRA escaper'.[136] This mutually beneficial disclosure did nothing to alleviate his notoriety but Tuite managed to remain on the run until arrested by the Special Branch in Drogheda on 4 March 1982.[137] The London trials of September and December 1980 were contemporaneously cited as a successful utilization of the PTA and linked to the surge of IRA attacks which had taken place in December 1978. Bobby Campbell and Dickie Glenholmes received ten-year sentences in March 1981 when Bobby Storey was acquitted.[138] On 25 September 1983 Storey was credited, along with Gerry Kelly, Larry Marley and Bik MacFarlane, with masterminding the spectacular mass escape of thirty-eight IRA men from the H-Blocks, the most secure prison complex in Western Europe. Kelly had come tantalizingly close to this feat on several occasions, including the December 1974 attempt in London when he reached the top of the outer wall of Wormwood Scrubs.[139]

Notwithstanding the Keenan trial losses, previously imprisoned IRA members demonstrated continued capacity for targeted aggression on 28 December 1980 when two suspicious devices discovered in Albany over the Christmas period were examined by police forensic teams. One was identified as an incendiary while the other, a tin can containing electrical components, appeared to be a partially assembled blast bomb. The finds received national coverage when the *Times* reported that Albany housed 'several IRA terrorists'.[140] The subsequent recovery of an Irish Tricolour flag fashioned from a bed sheet and, separately, a homemade rope ladder, encouraged speculation that an 'escape bid' had been pre-empted in which a firebomb would be used as a diversion. The more plausible explanation of sabotage alongside a roof top protest was not entertained.[141] Kilkenny IRA man Kevin Dunphy, who had twice planted car bombs in Heathrow airport and was convicted of possession of illegal war material found in Kilburn on 20 August 1974, could not be directly implicated in the finds. The seizure of a quantity of match-heads in his Albany cell in December 1980 nonetheless inspired a failed attempt to charge him with making incendiaries. Having been allocated from Wormwood Scrubs to Parkhurst, Dunphy returned to the London prison in the summer of 1981.[142] He had previously been badly beaten in his cell in Parkhurst when staff unlocked his door to admit waiting criminal assailants. Paul Holmes and Andy Mulryan were attacked the same day in the yard, although assisted in their vigorous self-defence by London prisoners of Irish ancestry.[143]

March 1981

Advocates of prisoners' rights in England and the IRA in particular were boosted by the March 1981 decision of the European Commission of Human Rights in Strasbourg to investigate allegations made by Fr. Pat Fell. The priest was then in Parkhurst and approaching the end of the fourteen year sentence he had received in November 1973 for IRA activities in the Midlands.[144] He had previously been in the news in December 1980 when treated for non-infectious TB that he had contracted in Parkhurst.[145] By then the English born priest had been denied parole on six occasions. Fell's contention that he had been denied access to adequate medical care and legal advice following the Albany 'riot' of September 1976 was deemed to warrant attention in Strasbourg. This breakthrough ensured that the pioneering advancement of an application by Sean Campbell was no fluke and that the questions raised by Irish republicans in the Dispersal System would not be easily discounted.[146] In November 1982 the European forum upheld the complaints lodged by Campbell and Fr. Fell, a ruling anticipated and pre-empted by important Prison Department reforms required by the High Court in London.[147]

Chronic overcrowding in British prisons was controversial in March 1981, and while the Government was insufficiently solvent to spend the £720 million recommended by the May Committee to redress the need to additional infrastructure, Conservatives were instinctively indisposed to alleviate the situation by non-custodial sentencing and selective releases.[148] Repatriation of political prisoners would have provided a minor degree of amelioration had it not been ruled out in effect if not also in policy. The *Irish Post* on 14 February 1981 covered the story of the transfer of two British army sergeants who had been sent to England following conviction for a notorious double killing in Ireland. This was counter-pointed by Sr. Sarah Clarke's Relatives and Friends of Prisoners Committee (RFPC) claim that William Whitelaw had reneged on the alleged Home Office promise to repatriate the remainder of the 'Belfast Ten'.[149] Once 'retired' from the convent from which she had actually been expelled, Sr. Clarke moved into housing in Kentish Town and invested much energy under the banner of the RFPC in providing 'a 24-hour service' to the families of Irish political prisoners in England. The group offered a degree of protection from the misapplication of the PTA and liaised as necessary with the NCCL and the Irish Embassy.[150]

In January 1981 soldiers Stanley Hathaway and John Byrne confessed in a Belfast court to causing the deaths of Michael Naan and Andrew Murray near Newtownbutler, Fermanagh, on 23 October 1972. At the time of the killings the pair were sergeants in the 1st Argyll and Sutherland Highlanders, and while on duty fatally knifed the two victims in what became known as the 'pitchfork murders'.[151] It was publicly speculated that other members of their unit, 13 Platoon, D Company, played a role in concealing the bodies of the Irish men. The soldiers were veterans of the brutal Aden counterinsurgency in 1967 and received life sentences for murder with the opportunity to serve them in Britain.[152] They were rapidly transferred from Crumlin Road.[153] By the end of the year, fifty-four British soldiers and five Loyalists had been flown home, whereas approximately sixty republican prisoners who wished to be repatriated remained inside the Dispersal System. Gerry Kelly, Hugh Feeney, Dolours Price and Marian Price were the only republicans moved to Long Kesh and Armagh Prison as part of a pact negotiated to terminate the 1973–74 hunger strike in Brixton, Gartree, Wormwood Scrubs and Parkhurst.[154] The recently convicted soldiers followed numerous British Prison Officers who had been seconded to the Six Counties until late 1980 and were sent back to England and Scotland in the midst of a decrease in the numbers of maximum-security prisoners.[155]

Henry 'Big H' MacKenney, amongst the most feared prisoners in England, remained on good terms with the IRA in the early 1980s. A situation arose when a New Zealand cocaine addict was cited by *The News of the World*, which had dispatched a female journalist to interview him behind bars, as intending to inform on the IRA men in Parkhurst. This was dismissed by the republicans as absurd as the man possessed neither the knowledge nor the inclination to do so. The story, nonetheless, unnerved the New Zealander who, if irrational and mentally vulnerable, was by no means paranoid. An English gangland assassin had indeed offered to act as a proxy for the IRA. This highly experienced individual accosted Hugh Doherty by a stairway and suggested: 'Youse grab him and I'll kill him'. The gesture was declined but the sudden demise of the putative informer within a short period created a stir: 'He was dead. It looked in the papers that we must have done it. It was nothing to do with us, he was on cocaine … it was either that or a massive heart attack'.[156]

Long Kesh Hunger Strike, March to October 1981

The abrupt termination of the first hunger strike in late December 1980 and the widely held view that the IRA and Sinn Féin had been cheated by the NIO set the stage for a further contest in March 1981. In a major step, the 'no wash' campaign was abandoned to ameliorate day to day living conditions in the prisons, although the concurrent 'blanket' and 'no work' protests continued.[157] Contrary to assumptions, the republican leadership was firmly opposed to a fast to the death and Gerry Adams bluntly informed the newly instated H-Block O/C: 'We are tactically, strategically, physically and morally opposed to a hunger strike'.[158] Undeterred by analysis from Adams that the British would not compromise, the prisoners were determined to act. Bobby Sands had assumed a central position from fellow Belfast man Brendan 'Bik' MacFarlane and implemented a modification of the strategy that had been in evidence in late 1980. Carefully vetted volunteers, selected in part to reflect the geographic remit of Northern Command, were committed to join the protest in regular, staged intervals rather than *en masse*. This signalled that a protracted struggle was anticipated in which deaths could be expected in the event of failure to convince the NIO to relent on the 'five demands'. As before, the INLA contingent was fully engaged and Antrim INLA Volunteer Patsy O'Hara was scheduled to follow the South Derry IRA leader Francis Hughes. The fast commenced as announced on 1 March 1981 when Sands refused food on the fifth anniversary of the removal of special category status in the Six Counties.[159]

This step had been anticipated by the Republican Movement and garnered significant international attention and independent acts of solidarity.[160] Women IRA prisoners in Armagh Gaol, however, lacked the numbers and state of health to sustain the physiological and psychological rigours of a further protest.[161] The Armagh predicament was necessarily and publicly addressed in view of the 1980 precedent. The prospect of the fatal strategy migrating to England, however, remained a closely guarded secret. Approximately seven IRA prisoners in Albany and Long Lartin volunteered to join the Hunger Strike and communicated with the leadership on the matter with the assistance of a suitable family visitor. A list of names was submitted as per the selection process in the North of Ireland. Tony Clarke, in separate exchanges with ill-fated Long Kesh protester Joe McDonnell, recalled: 'Word came straight back that in no uncertain terms, "nobody goes on it". You were told you were taking away from this [H-Block protest]. You could see the wisdom'.[162] This was a non-negotiable instruction as General Order No. 4 of the Constitution of Óglaigh na hÉireann dictated: '(a) Volunteers are forbidden to undertake hunger strikes without the express sanction of General Headquarters. Maximum penalty for breach: Dismissal'.[163] The minimal room for manoeuvre in Ireland did not apply to England.

Bobby Sands, the most famous hunger striker of the twentieth century, felt a deep affinity with the two Mayo IRA men who had died in England in June 1974 and February 1976. All three had campaigned for political status using the same drastic and ultimately lethal methods. Soon after release from his first sentence in Long Kesh in April 1976, Sands had joined the Twinbrook

Sinn Féin cumann in Belfast, which had recently organized a march in support of Stagg.[164] The party had been weak in the neighbourhood due to the relative strength of the Official IRA after a feud in 1975.[165] On returning to the new H-Blocks without the protection of political status, he became involved in the 'blanket' protests which presaged the major hunger strikes of 1980 and 1981. He characterized his situation in terms of waging a war against 'the monster's army' and in an article smuggled out for publication in *Republican News* on 7 October 1978, alluded to his position in the continuity of prison struggle. Sands wrote: 'I remember, and I shall never forget, how this monster took the lives of Tom Ashe, Terence MacSwiney, Michael Gaughan, Frank Stagg and Hugh Coney … tomorrow I'll fight the monster and his devils again!'[166] Hugh Coney, East Tyrone Brigade IRA, was shot dead during an escape attempt from Long Kesh on 6 November 1974.[167] Sands possessed a keenly historical mind and both embodied and extolled the militant republican ideology of succession, continuity and lasting contribution through martyrdom.[168] While non-traditional use of the warm and familiar 'Tom' for Ashe connoted a sense of personal interest with a long - deceased icon, the fate of Sands and the contemporaneous IRA men who died in England frequently intersected. When on the blanket in July 1979, Frank Maguire MP came to Sands and Brendan Hughes and told them stories of visiting the ailing Stagg in Wakefield in 1976.[169] It is unclear to what extent this vivified an already perceived sense of connection in the mind of Sands, but there are indications that the Belfast man was deeply moved. On 3 March 1981, two days into the resumed Hunger Strike, *Irish Times* journalist Brendan O Cathaoir gained access to Sands and listened as he told him in Irish of the inspiration provided by MacSwiney, Gaughan and Stagg.[170]

Sands was acutely aware of the symbolic potency of his own death and privately expressed a wish to be buried in the Republican Plot in Leigue, County Mayo. According to Irish-American biographer Denis O'Hearn: 'Sands had thought a lot about where he would be buried and at one point he asked his lawyer to draw up a legal document backing up his request to be buried in County Mayo, next to Michael Gaughan and Frank Stagg … Sands insisted that he was being neither "naïve" nor "morbidly flamboyant", but that he had serious personal reasons for the request'.[171] One practical reason concerned a female member of the Sands family who moved to Dundalk in the late 1970s, arising from an alleged incident involving incendiaries north of the Border. Sands indicated that this was a factor as to why he 'wanted [to be] buried down there' in Mayo. He continued: 'I think I'm going to die and again I'm not playing at bravado or egotism'.[172] Ultimately, it was the death of Frank Maguire on 5 March 1981, and the decision of his bother Noel Maguire to forgo the opportunity of an assured parliamentary succession, that brought Sands to international attention. News of Maguire's death was reputedly well received in the Prison Officer's Social Club in the H-Blocks by men who could not divine its consequences. Visiting RUC officer Kevin Sheehy was shocked to see how the prison staff 'cheered and shouted sectarian abuse at the screen'.[173]

On 9 April 1981 Sands received 30,492 votes to secure the Westminster seat of Fermanagh/South Tyrone, which independent republicans Frank Maguire and Frank McManus had previously held. Habitual SDLP supporters in the constituency had contributed approximately 10,000 votes. The victory was later described by Sinn Féin Vice President Daithi O'Conaill, a strategic - minded republican, as a demonstration that the electorate 'stand with the political prisoners'.[174] Yet Gerry Adams, Jim Gibney, Danny Morrison and other Sinn Féin leaders had taken what they regarded as a major gambit in nominating a prisoner candidate, knowing that rejection at the polls would devastate republican morale. A senior IRA leader in Belfast greeted news of the triumph with the comment: 'That's worth twenty bombs in England'.[175] Many believed the newfound status of Sands as an MP would transform negotiations with the NIO, but no discernable increment of merit emerged.[176] In England persons irritated by the allegedly pusillanimous bi-partisan policy adopted by the Labour Party occupied their South London HQ and displayed a banner urging 'Victory to Bobby Sands MP'.[177] Morrison was among those who perceived 'armed struggle' as a strategy involving 'the ballot box and the Armalite' without using that precise wording. In an English cell, unconvinced lifer Billy Armstrong quipped: 'Something that wasn't in the *Little Red Book* [by Mao Tse Tung]. An Armalite bullet travels faster than the ballot'.[178] The widely circulated pamphlet *The writings of Bobby Sands* was published in April 1981 by the Sinn Féin POW Department in 5 Blessington Street, Dublin, in a bid to raise public consciousness if not also solidarity. The compilation of short articles smuggled by Sands to *Republican News* and later *AP/RN* included his reflections on the hunger strike deaths of Gaughan and Stagg. Readers were invited by the publishers to obtain copies of *Irish political prisoners in England: Special Category 'A'*.[179]

Several strands of negotiation and consultation continued behind the scenes, including a message from Pope John Paul II, urging Sands to desist. It was delivered by the Pope's Irish born envoy, Fr. John Magee, who subsequently briefed Secretary of State Humphrey Atkins.[180] This high - level input from the Holy See was intrinsically significant, even if other factors were in play. Ireland's highly eccentric Papal Nuncio from 1969, Archbishop Gaetano Alibrandi, had a reputation as a 'noted Provisional IRA sympathiser' with a consistent track record in siding with fasting republicans. The Sicilian had pressurized the Irish Government during hunger strikes in 1972, when Sean Mac Stiofain was languishing in the Mater Hospital, Dublin, and in 1977 when Martin Ferris and other IRA prisoners protested in Portlaoise. Alibrandi had been personal secretary to Cardinal Giovanni

Battista Montini who, in 1963, became Pope Paul VI. Senior DFA official Sean Donlon, subsequently Irish Ambassador to the USA, recalled the nuncio's 'very testy relationship with three taoisigh – Jack Lynch, Liam Cosgrave and Garret FitzGerald'.[181] Dermot Nally, Secretary to the Irish Government, informed his British equivalent, Cabinet Secretary Sir Robert Armstrong, that Taoiseach Haughey wished to assist 'in any way he could'. This rare overture from the leader of 'green' Fianna Fáil was pregnant with the risk of leak-driven malign interpretation. It was clarified by Dublin that the offer stemmed from 'purely ... humanitarian' inspiration. Crucially, Armstrong inferred from the communication that 'the Irish government did not want us to meet the [IRA] demands for political status'. The British were encouraged to consider either inviting or drawing the European Commission of Human Rights into the controversy, but this did not occur.[182] No ECHR investigation could have affirmed the probity of holding prisoners in the regime of squalor, routine assault and deprivation maintained at Long Kesh. In 1983 tentative diplomatic interaction between Armstrong and Nally, endorsed by both Thatcher and FitzGerald, outlined the draft parameters of joint Anglo-Irish policy which culminated in the Anglo-Irish Agreement of November 1985.[183] Republicans viewed the AIA as a desperate bid by the two governments to minimize the rising constitutionalist profile of Sinn Féin, very much an outworking of the 1981 crisis.[184]

Persons backing the 'five demands' protested outside Durham prison on 18 April 1981 'in solidarity with the H-Block hunger strikers and the Irish political prisoners held there'. London based pro-republicans staged a simultaneous 'hunger strike picket' at Wormwood Scrubs where they had marched from a rally in nearby Shepherd's Bush. A separate event planned for Brixton was cancelled due to police intervention and resulted in an alternate gathering on the steps of Westminster Abbey. The sixty people who mounted a twenty-four hour fast on Good Friday remained *in situ* outside Westminster. Another contingent fasted in Finsbury Park in the midst of the annual Easter fair in a district of the capital home to many of London's 400,000 plus Irish born residents.[185] Similar vigils, fasts, 'black flag' parades and political gatherings took place in Manchester, Leeds, Nottingham, Glasgow and other British urban centres over the summer months.[186] Glasgow was a long-term centre of Irish republican strength and a city where the Irish Tricolour flew regularly in the grounds of Celtic Football Club.[187]

IRA prisoners in Wormwood Scrubs made their major protest on Sunday, 26 April 1981 as Bobby Sands neared death in the H-Blocks. Martin Coughlan, Paul Norney and Billy Armstrong staged an overnight rooftop protest. Armstrong recalled: 'We felt it our duty to do something before they let him die rather than after'.[188] *The Times* conceded that the three 'category A prisoners [were] normally held in strictest security' and it was evident that major embarrassment had been caused.[189] The group knew they were being scrutinised and Norney, wearing distinctive yellow E-List 'patches', very closely indeed. This was turned to advantage when, by arrangement, Norney walked ahead of the others during yard exercise time. Armstrong and Coughlan lagged behind and then casually presented themselves at a monitored gap in the fenced area which provided access from the yard to a nearby toilet block. The two IRA men loitered outside the facility until they were not being directly observed and received a boost onto the low roof of the building from companion Sean Smyth of the innocent Maguire Seven. Having pulled back the barbed wire defence and gone prone, Armstrong noticed that staff were still totally unaware of what had occurred. Norney was silently signalled from the low vantage, and on making a further lap of the yard with hundreds of others, calmly walked over to join his concealed comrades. Smyth again assisted the ascent before moving away.[190]

Supporters arrived outside the jail with Tricolours and, despite being buffered by a strong police presence, added to the drama of the occasion. Wormwood Scrubs was particularly suited to actions of this kind as much of the upper portions of the jail complex were visible from local roads. This ensured that the British press obtained photographs of the event which were carried in the Monday tabloids, as well as normal radio and television coverage.[191] The presence of civilian witnesses may have restrained the authorities, whom, the IRA were later informed, attempted to recruit prisoners to confront the protesters. This would have been interpreted as a severe provocation. Coughlan issued a challenge to irate prison officers: 'If anyone puts his head up above the parapet he'll get the head off'.[192] Armstrong understood that a senior prison officer had previously thrown a man off a roof protest, breaking his legs. He recalled: 'He was welcome to come onto the roof. We had nothing to lose after all ... we were throwing bricks, scaffolding, everything down on them ... We wrecked the roof and flooded a brand new laundry'.[193] Heavy rain deluged the four IRA men in Wormwood Scrubs between 10.00 p.m. on Sunday and 9.30 a.m. on Monday when they descended to face inevitable punishment.[194] The protesters were 'weighed off' on 1 May, earning fifty-six days in the segregation block and the loss of ninety days remission.[195] John McCluskey was sent to Canterbury on a twenty-eight day 'lie-down', but the others remained inside the London prison. The IRA men in D Wing were still confined when it was reported that Sands had died on 5 May.[196]

Meanwhile, a large attendance had rallied in Kilburn on 26 April at an event organized by the London H-Block Armagh Committee. They defied the just implemented twenty-eight day ban on processions in the city resulting in a melee on the High Road when police used their transport vehicles and commandeered buses to confront oncoming marchers. Hundreds chanted 'Bobby Sands MP' when attempting to break the police cordon. Around forty were arrested during the scuffles on the Kilburn High Road and the related impromptu sit - down protest outside Brondesbury railway station.[197] A full-blown riot was eminently possible under the circumstances and the public was reminded of the continued IRA presence in the capital on the same day when Barry Porter, Conservative MP of Bebington and Ellesmere Port, received an explosive package in the post.[198]

Gerry Cunningham and other IRA prisoners made it onto the roof of Long Lartin on 4 May 1981 in a similarly well-planned move. He had previously smuggled a letter out of the prison where Martin Brady and Paul Holmes were present, as well as brothers Paddy and Andy Mulryan. The five republicans expected an intensification of political violence in both Irish jurisdictions arising from the dismal events in Long Kesh. While Haughey and Thatcher were predictably disparaged, the most serious invective was reserved for the SDLP leadership, 'Hume, Fitt and Co', who were harshly described as 'vultures' for their alleged wish to 'rob the dead of their glory and wear it as a crown upon their own heads'.[199] Having not received instructions to the contrary, the five proceeded to mount a protest during which some fasted. With careful preparations, the men held out until 10 May. RCG leader David Yaffe noted 'other prisoners united to prevent any attack on the POWs'.[200] Cunningham was on good terms with Italian, Palestinian, Turkish, Swiss and Iranian prisoners. His main English acquaintance was a Hells Angel leader who 'had a lot of sympathy for the republican cause'.[201] Non-political Irish prisoners were quickly neutralized by staff who moved them into segregation, but the pre-arranged assistance of foreign and British prisoners negated this strategy. Cunningham recalled:

> We were being well fed and well looked after by lowering a rope down to the windows underneath and they were putting food in … We broke into a loft and so we had plenty of shelter …. We'd got everything we needed and we were prepared for the long haul. But we got a communication, from the outside, they said that we were to come off the hunger strike and come down off the roof. That we were taking attention away from the hunger strike… We were contemplating coming down anyway because … there's always dissent … We all expected to be shanghaied out of the prison and again back to Wandsworth or whatever but they decided to keep us. And we all stayed in the [punishment] block.[202]

Disaster was narrowly averted when a prison officer grabbed and tugged heavily on a food line passing from an English supporter to an IRA man on the roof. The republican was pulled off balance and almost fell to probable instant death. Paul Holmes recalled: 'We later spoke to the Governor about this, he came up to see us. He had a window on some adjoining landing. And we told him that we would actually destroy the prison completely, the roof we were on. And he promptly gave us his word that the screws could never attempt to do that again. And nor did they'.[203] For differing reasons, the Republican Movement leadership in Ireland and Prison Department in London were united in avoiding the consequences of IRA deaths in England in May 1981. Long Lartin republicans were then on reasonable interpersonal terms with many staff members, yet were ultimately surprised at the relative mildness of the manner in which they were treated on climbing down.[204]

News of the death of Sands was badly received in Parkhurst on 5 May 1981, where Irish prisoners on the wings refused to attend work and those in the Special Security Unit staged a three day fast. Hugh Doherty recalled: 'The hardest time to be in jail was during the Hunger Strikes … you didn't know what to do. You were told on the outside that you weren't to get involved in hunger strikes … [and] all during that period, you could feel the tensions on the wings. The screws didn't know what was going to happen'.[205] Protesters on the wings were sanctioned by the standard means of 'ghosting': Ray McLaughlin was moved to Winchester and Paul Hill to Canterbury.[206] McLaughlin was afflicted with painful memories and recalled how the death of Stagg in February 1976 cast 'a dark shadow'. He had then played a role in encouraging Jerry Mealy to desist from his near fatal fast in Long Lartin.[207] Tony Madigan in Albany was similarly afflicted by the 'personal' loss of Stagg.[208] Gerry Young's sense of grievance was accentuated by the fact that he had interacted with Stagg in IRA circles in the English Midlands prior to their separate arrests. Young was one of those who had been on hunger strike for ten days in Gartree along with Gerry Cunningham and Paddy Mulryan in 1976.[209]

Many ordinary British prisoners instinctively identified with Sands as a principled non-conformist. Paul Hill noted: 'They support Bobby Sands. They support the miners during the [1984] strike, anyone who fights back'.[210] In the Segregation Block of Hull Noel Gibson listened to the uproar which greeted a visit by William Whitelaw: 'A significant number were shouting "Remember Bobby Sands!" It was incredible. I think this was credit to the Irish prisoners who had passed through the prison. The existing ones that were there. The prisoners felt this, they were screaming at him … That was a tremendous thing to happen. We created an affinity'.[211] International political prisoners were also affected. In South Africa's Robben Island prison, life - sentenced African National Congress leader Nelson Mandela annotated his calendar: 'IRA martyr Bobby Sands dies'.[212] Around 100,000 people attended the funeral procession and interment during what Fr. Des Wilson described as 'one of the most significant events we have seen in West Belfast since the beginning of the "troubles"'.[213] Photographs and images of the IRA firing party in Milltown Cemetery were transmitted around the world.

By 13 May 1981, when Armstrong was again in a position to write letters in Wormwood Scrubs, Derryman Francis Hughes had died and both

Ray McCreesh of the IRA's South Armagh Brigade and Patsy O'Hara of the INLA were nearing death. He conceded: 'Thatcher seems to be still dogmatic on her stand of no political status'.[214] The 'place' of Hughes was taken by IRA prisoner Brendan McLaughlin, the sixth man to commence fasting.[215] Faced with a seemingly intractable impasse and a conviction that 'we have enough martyrs', Armstrong believed that the Prime Minister should be 'shown the *road* … and that goes for all her lackeys'. Anger at the British Establishment extended to the Irish Government which was also blamed for virtual collusion. If prison censors missed the unsubtle death threat raised *vis à vis* Thatcher, they must have registered Armstrong's hope that '[Garret] Fitz[Gerald] and quite a few more [would] get it'.[216] A letter approved by republican prisoners in Wormwood Scrubs reproved the Prime Minister as culpable while relating the slogan 'British Troops Out of Ireland!' to the wider left wing objective of 'Thatcher Out!'[217] The RCG were incensed, as was John Hume of the SDLP, to learn that Labour's shadow Northern Secretary, Don Concannon, visited Sands on the eve of his death to confirm that his party concurred with Conservative opposition to granting political status. Concannon had served in the Labour administration which abolished 'special category' in March 1976.[218] His intervention in Long Kesh was castigated by Britain's 'Spartacist' tendency as a 'contemptible' act, a harsh denunciation by a hardline body which regarded Labour as marching 'in lockstep with the Tory murderers' while Tony Benn and Leo Abse adopted an allegedly sentimental 'troops out call'.[219]

Militant sentiments were fuelled by powerlessness and isolation. There were also myriad personal factors. Billy Armstrong had been a Belfast Brigade comrade and friend of Joe McDonnell who died on 8 July 1981.[220] Public anger at his demise fuelled a major riot in Dublin on 11 July during which Gardai, backed by the Irish Army in reserve, prevented a 10,000 strong crowd engulfing the British Embassy in Ballsbridge.[221] Other IRA men in England had long term associations arising from chance and upbringing. Tony Clarke had been a close childhood friend of McDonnell's with whom he was arrested by the RUC for fighting when teenagers.[222] Liam McLarnon, Armstrong's co-accused in 1974, had known Sands.[223] Liam Baker, deeply committed to the Albany 'Blanket Protest', met McDonnell 'long before he was in the IRA', arising from his sojourns working in the south of England. Baker's brother Paul served seventeen years in Long Kesh and, in sharing the hardship of republicans held in the H-Blocks, was kept in mind from afar. Liam Baker had directly assisted ex-Long Kesh O/C Brendan Hughes on transatlantic IRA business out of Southampton.[224] Ronnie McCartney was not only 'a very good friend' of McDonnell but knew Danny Morrison 'very well'. The collective impetus was not simply derived from personal grief, past intimacy and camaraderie, but from their keen desire to make a meaningful political contribution. McCartney lodged a will with Alastair

Logan ahead of his intended hunger strike participation in Albany alongside Brian McLoughlin and others.[225] Sean Smyth, who tended to avoid direct participation in jail protests, 'got involved' in the Albany agitation during the hunger strike and went from supplying his IRA associates with tobacco to joining them in the Segregation Block.[226]

The IRA in England could not have known that on 9 August 1981 Bik MacFarlane had written to Gerry Adams warning that the 'IRSP [i..e. INLA] have no further replacements' due to lack of numbers to join the deadly protest in the H-Blocks.[227] Following the death of Derry man Mickey Devine on 20 August 1981, no additional INLA members participated and the real situation began to become clear to the public.[228] The men in Albany had correctly inferred from printed reports in the *Irish Times* and other sources that the socialist republicans were on the verge of withdrawing altogether. This altered context repositioned the overture from Albany and serious preparations were undertaken while awaiting word from Belfast and Dublin. To prevent a family member intervening, as had just occurred in Long Kesh, McCartney nominated a close personal friend upon whom he could 'rely' as power of attorney. Such contingencies were nullified when a firm instruction came from Belfast that no action should be taken as the Movement 'couldn't manage a hunger strike in two places'.[229]

While the IRA prisoners in England heeded the instruction, matters took a different course in Australia where new branches of the H-Block/ Armagh Committee had been formed to reinforce the existing Irish National Association. 29-year-old Eamonn 'Ned' O'Connor appeared outside the British Consulate in Sydney on 9 August 1981 to announce what transpired to be a thirty-nine day hunger strike in support of the 'five demands'. He desisted when a message from the Republican Movement in Ireland urged him to relent, although some press accounts highlighted the more acceptable explanation that the decision followed pressure from Cardinal Freeman.[230] His debilitating solo run had obliged the NIO to provide briefing documents to British diplomats due to attend the 30 September to 2 October 1981 Commonwealth Heads of Government meeting in Melbourne. NIO official RA Harrington redrafted the final version when O'Connor's resumption of eating defused a potentially serious protest. The death of Bobby Sands had entailed short fasts and work stoppages in Melbourne, Adelaide, Sydney and beyond.[231]

Reliable information on the conduct of the hunger strike was impossible to obtain in Wormwood Scrubs due to restrictions on television and newspapers. IRA prisoners believed on the basis of strange lapses and discontinuities in their correspondence that their incoming and outgoing mail was being diverted, even if passed by censors.[232] Policy on newspaper distribution varied from prison to prison. Whereas Wakefield permitted *An Phoblacht* in 1978, Manchester did not. Wakefield, however, changed its rules in April 1980 when only titles sent directly from approved newsagents were admitted.[233] Prisoners in Parkhurst in December 1982 were allowed *An Phoblacht/ Republican News*, Irish-American papers and the republican *IRIS* newssheet, anonymously edited by Fr. Piaras O Duill. Radio coverage, however, compensated for the occasional shortfall in print journalism for those in a position to receive broadcasts on the wings and SSUs.[234]

The levels of public sympathy accruing to Irish republicans in 1981 gravely concerned conservative elements in Westminster and Whitehall. Tory rightwinger, Ian Gow, Parliamentary Private Secretary to Margaret Thatcher from 1979 to 1983 and MP for Eastbourne, encouraged Humphrey Atkins in June 1981 to consider the intravenous feeding of the hunger strikers. If pursued, the suggestion would have revived the acrimonious debate on state intervention which had been dormant since June 1974 in the aftermath of Michael Gaughan's sudden death in Parkhurst. There were, however, powerful advocates of such a policy change. Foreign Secretary Lord Peter Carrington, a man with strong connections to British Intelligence, reasoned that 'force feeding' was justified to counteract the negative publicity tarnishing Britain's reputation internationally.[235] Carrington had, in 1971, officially, if discretely, defended the use of 'deep interrogation' methods to Merlyn Rees during the torture of the predominately civilian 'hooded men' in Ballykelly Barracks. He had been targeted by the IRA in England in 1978–79 and in 1981 received backing for his hard line stance from Lord Privy Seal, Sir Ian Gilmour, albeit against the consensus within the NIO, where the practicalities of forcible feeding by means of a drip had been assessed.[236] Another rigid Conservative, Alan Clark, subsequently gave one of what he regarded as his 'best speeches' on Sands in the Commons.[237] Clark was an intimate of Gow and lamented his assassination by the IRA in Sussex in July 1990. The NIO, meanwhile, secretly sought means to force the 'capitulation' of at least one hungerstriker without force-feeding. On 1 June 1981 RA Harrington recommended identifying 'the best candidate ... and then go to some lengths to organise pressure on him ... before his condition becomes critical'.[238] The impact of Sean McKenna's situation at the termination of the 1980 hunger strike may have offered a rough prototype. The leadership of the Republican Movement had every reason to suspect their British Establishment enemies of ruthless and insincere posturing during negotiations. Long term recriminations were all but assured under the circumstances.[239]

Sr. Sarah Clarke 'looked after' Kieran Doherty's mother on her trip to London on 26 July 1981 and met his father when visiting Long Kesh. The nun was fully in favour of the protest objectives: 'I was in sympathy with the hunger strikers' demands – as far as I was concerned they were political prisoners and many would never have been in gaol if it hadn't been for the grave absence of human rights in their society'.[240] This social and political connection infused Doherty's death on 2 August 1981 with added personal poignancy. He died after seventy-three days of starvation during which time he was elected Sinn Féin TD for Cavan/Monaghan. The by-election this initiated in conjunction with the June 1981 General Election victory in Louth of IRA prisoner Paddy Agnew, threatened to destabilize the Fine Gael/Labour Coalition Government who returned to the Dáil on 11 June 1981.[241] Sr. Clarke's republicanism and compelling sense of justice was affirmed by a trip to Belfast, Derry and Donegal in August 1981, where she became acquainted with many of the families who travelled to England to see imprisoned relatives.[242]

The sense of urgency engendered by the crisis created ephemeral bursts of activity around English prisons and on 23 August 1981 Sinn Féin held simultaneous pickets at Wakefield, Durham, Leicester, Parkhurst and Albany.[243] Further rallies organized by Sinn Féin in Luton, Blackpool and London attempted to draw attention to the overall prisoner issue. Owen Carron was the guest of honour at the Luton event in the People's Park on 26 September 1981[244] The RCG were also energetic picketers and harsh critics of what they internally regarded as the Labour Party's 'murderous legacy in the Six Counties'.[245] Behind the scenes, Labour leader Michael Foot urged the Prime Minister to consider a 'softening of her position' whilst projecting a bi-partisan image in the Commons.[246] Thatcher had openly rejected US Senator Edward Kennedy's call for 'flexibility' with a blunt statement that her Government would not be 'yielding to coercion'.[247]

The advancement of Garret FitzGerald to the office of Taoiseach on 30 June 1981 restored to the front rank of national politics a man who had served as Minister for Foreign Affairs in the previous Fine Gael/Labour Coalition. FitzGerald, however, held the key position in 1981, and as an innate liberal was invulnerable to the extremist tendencies of Paddy Cooney, Paddy Donegan and Conor Cruise O'Brien, who collectively imbued the mid-1970s' precursor with a pronounced right wing character. The temporary ousting of Charles Haughey, whose constitutional republicanism won the grudging respect of adversary Margaret Thatcher, opened the door to improved Anglo-Irish dialogue, if not co-operation. The Irish conflict remained in central focus owing to the ongoing Long Kesh crisis and an early sign of a new disposition to seek consensus on such matters was signalled when Ireland's Attorney General Peter Sutherland stated his support for the extradition of wanted republicans to Britain.[248] A test of this unpopular facilitation loomed in October 1981 when the first extradition warrant of a political nature since 1970 came before the Supreme Court in Dublin. Deliberations on a High Court appeal with no proven IRA dimension, as had been mooted, terminated in a manner which indicated that the traditional definition of a 'political offence' would be indefinitely maintained.[249]

Plans in Hull

IRA prisoners in Hull made a concerted effort to contribute to the general conflict by escaping and carrying out acts of sabotage during the hunger strike. Eddy O'Neill regarded the period as 'the most surreal in my lifetime … You were absolutely totally helpless to do anything. Standing on the sidelines and watching it was like watching the inevitable. Hoping that it didn't turn out that way'.[250] Inaction was not an option. Tuite's triumph in Brixton confirmed the immense propaganda potential of a breakout and O'Neill had identified a possible weakness on the wing to which he was confined in the converted double cell space that functioned as the Welfare Officer's room. One of the doors inside the office was sealed, creating a physical and visual barrier between the main area and what had been a cell with a standard barred window. If he and Stevie Nordone managed to access the space during association, it would be relatively easy to conduct preparatory work to simplify cutting or jacking the bars 'if the opportunity arose'. Careful investigation revealed that the lock mechanism was the exact match of that used in the kitchen and a common key opened both. Covered by an associate, O'Neill unscrewed and removed the entire kitchen lock assembly during Association, stripped it down in his cell and made the measurements required to manufacture a functional key. The lock was refitted before it was missed and a new key, ingeniously fashioned in two sections and joined by a screw, was readied for use. Unfortunately, an observant British prisoner had grasped what had occurred and requested a loan of the key in order to break into the Welfare Office and view his private file. The IRA men refused and 'sat on it for a while' to see if the irate and disappointed man approached the authorities.[251]

Meanwhile, plans progressed to detonate a substantial blast incendiary in the main workshop where a wood mill had been established to manufacture furniture. Quantities of flammable materials were collected and concentrated in a particular area of the plant. Over many trips, portions of a large firebomb followed and were assembled as a device was timed to explode at midnight. This would minimize the chance of unwanted collateral damage. Success promised the destruction of the expensive plant and adjacent smaller workshops. When it failed to detonate at the appointed hour, days were allowed pass to see if it had been discovered before IRA members carefully retrieved it for detailed examination. On three occasions the risk - laden and physically dangerous process was repeated as nothing could be found to indicate that either the watch timer or detonation arrangement were in any way defective. IRA men with engineering skills concurred that it should have worked. Suspicions that a normally 'friendly' non-political prisoner had 'disarmed the device in some manner' went unproven and what may have been the largest bomb planted in an English prison remained inert. The lack of repercussions indicated that outright betrayal was not a factor and the combination of increased 'lie-downs' and denial of work assignments appeared simply prudent measures by staff as the hunger strike drew fitfully towards a close.[252]

Kevin Colfer and Eddie Caughey of Sinn Féin, much involved with the prisoner issue in England, had joined forces with political allies in the hunger strike rally held in Luton on 19 September 1981.[253] By then the outworking of the H-Block crisis had permeated Britain's Labour Party, which in the course of its conference that month, edged closer to a position of advocating military withdrawal and Irish reunification. Owen Carron, who had succeeded Sands as MP for Fermanagh/ South Tyrone on 20 August 1981, was well received at a series of public events after arrival at Heathrow on 17 September 1981.[254] Carron had attended Manchester University and was comfortable in an English political and media milieu. He had been expected to make 'maximum use' of his parliamentary entitlements when elected.[255] Such was the progress among the moderate left by February 1982 that Tony Benn was in a position to claim that the Labour Party 'came out with the objective of a united and independent Ireland'.[256] Membership of TOM boomed as a sense of purpose and opportunity was grasped by the reinvigorated and allied Sinn Féin.[257]

A rare statement attributed to 'Irish POWs in England' was disseminated on 26 September 1981 which reaffirmed their collective endorsement of the leadership of the Republican Movement in the midst of a difficult year. The 'full support' of the men and women concerned was conveyed to a segment of the British public through the pages of *Fight Racism!/ Fight Imperialism!* and other channels. No text had been or could be universally agreed upon given the logistics entailed but the import of the message was non-controversial and did not spur individual derogations once published. Essentially, the IRA prisoners nominated Sinn Féin, the National H-Block/ Armagh Committee and the IRSP as bodies entitled to represent their viewpoints on prison affairs, alongside 'people who are genuine'. They rejected calls from the CPGB and SWP in England and the Worker's Party in Ireland to terminate the military campaign:

> Continue with the war until such times as the British Government declares its intention to withdraw from Ireland, militarily, politically and economically ... We now ask you our comrades to keep intact the committees that have been formed to further the demand of Repatriation for the Republican prisoners in this country ... we intend [to] challenge the British Government by any means necessary to win the right to serve our sentences in Ireland.[258]

Ideological opponents in the Official Republican Movement were variously hostile, ambivalent or sympathetic towards the position. Dessie O'Hagan held the view that an insufficient number of IRA and INLA men had perished. Vituperation of this order did not sit well with former IRA Quartermaster General and Army Council member Mick Ryan, who in 1981 managed North American fundraising from San Francisco.[259]

The strike gripped Ireland and focused the attention of the international community on the conflict to an unprecedented degree. The simple fact that over 100,000 persons marched in Belfast on the day of Sands' funeral shattered the credibility of a concerted propaganda campaign to portray the Republican Movement as isolated and on the verge of defeat. Black flags had been flown in parts of London's East End.[260] Far from being the IRA's 'last card', as Thatcher famously remarked, the hunger strike secured a new threshold of support. She insisted in a letter to Ernie Roberts MP that 'the Government will not negotiate terms for ending the hunger strike either with the prisoners or their representatives'.[261] In fact, various lines of dialogue were then functioning with her express endorsement. The deaths of Mickey Devine and Kevin Lynch of the INLA and Thomas McElwee, Joe McDonnell and Martin Hurson of the IRA had occurred by 3 October 1981 when Bik MacFarlane ordered a halt to the most significant prison protest in Irish history.[262] 23-year-old Pat Sheehan, who had survived fifty-five days without food, was moved to a military hospital.[263] Far from being coerced into silence by the IRA, parents of a number of comatose hunger strikers had exercised their prerogative of intervention from 20 August with a view to saving the lives of their adult children. As the position of the NIO strengthened, the mounting losses and immense psychological strain of maintaining the endeavour disposed the republican leadership to call a halt.[264] In hindsight, the PRO of the Wormwood Scrubs IRA prisoners divined a degree of consistency in the British strategy:

> Even after 10 deaths we find it absurd that there are still some people who think these deaths are for 'petty' trivial prison reforms, when in fact what is happening in the Blocks goes to the very core of the whole Irish struggle. For some years the 'war machine' has been engaged in a brutal policy within the prisons (and towards the POWs held in English prisons) in the foolish thinking that if they break the prisoners mentally then those on the streets engaged in armed struggle will fear the prisons, to such an extent that the struggle will die on the streets. They have been only too happy to know the Irish people have been getting the facts of the brutality and inhumane treatment from inside the prisons. This insane logic is now in action on the streets itself, with men, women and children being battered with plastic bullets. The message is stark, do not question our rule ... Thatcher will not break the people's will in Ireland, nor will it ever be broken. If anything all she has done is unite the masses ... The 'machine' does not have cells cold or brutal enough to break the will that will not be broken.[265]

Officially, the hunger strike failed in that the five demands had not been conceded prior to the cessation. The true picture was more complicated and Northern Secretary James Prior announced meaningful concessions on clothing as early as 6 October 1981. A combination of NIO reforms and a new strategic direction by IRA prisoners yielded significant dividends. All terms sought by the hunger strikers were effectively granted in the months following the cessation of the protest. Consequently, the IRA further diminished its violent campaign against prison staff and adopted what appeared to be a more pragmatic relationship with the H-Block hierarchy. Segregation was achieved by the unwillingness of nervous Loyalists to occupy the same wings as IRA men coming off years of 'no wash' and 'blanket' protest. Remission of sentence was restored to a controversially favourable 50 per cent and visiting conditions were liberalised. The less rigorous regime of late 1981 and 1982 facilitated the historic IRA mass breakout of 25 September 1983.

Streets were by then dedicated in honour of Sands in many cities, not least Paris, Nantes and Saint-Etienne in France, and Florence in Italy.[266] In Nantes, the 'Committee for Bobby Sands' claimed responsibility on 2 November 1981 for a bomb attack on the Royal Navy survey ship *Hecate*.[267] French navy divers responded to reports of an explosion near the moored vessel and found a 6lb bomb on a raft positioned under its hull. Left wing Cork republicans had in April 1971 destroyed a launch belonging to the 2,898-ton parent ship.[268] Ambassador Sir Jock Taylor was uninjured when the British Consulate in Hamburg, Germany, was bombed in mid-November 1981. Italian Red Brigades blasted the British Chamber of Commerce in Milan to avenge Sands, while other pro-IRA elements bombed a British car dealership in Zurich, incinerated a British owned club in Oporto and threatened the British Embassy in Athens.[269] Irish political strategist Dr. Martin Mansergh noted: 'Francois Mitterand, just before he became President of France in 1981, went on a protest demonstration about the hunger strike'.[270] An effort to recover lost ground in the United States went badly awry in New York in June 1981 when a massive and noisy crowd directed by Martin Galvin of Irish Northern Aid disrupted the visit of British royals Prince Charles and Lady Diana to the Lincoln Centre in Manhattan. The IRA and Sinn Féin attracted solidarity from an unusually wide spectrum of international political opinion encompassing the far left and liberal tendencies to the militant right. Fresh avenues of political development beckoned.[271]

Repercussions; ODCs and remission

Re-orientating the heterogeneous sympathetic groupings in Britain towards the interests of republicans imprisoned in England was a major step given the deep-seated factionalism, fatigue and diminished resources in play.

Other factors complicated the situation. When news of the hard - won IRA successes filtered back to the Dispersal System in England, the inmates of several prisons attempted to secure identical entitlements by citing the British Government's contention that paramilitary prisoners in the North of Ireland were merely 'criminals'. PROP on 21 October 1981 disclosed the existence of substantial petitions from Long Lartin, Albany and Parkhurst.[272] From May 1981 non-political Wormwood Scrubs prisoners were publicly querying why '"conforming" prisoners in England are entitled to one-third remission, even though they are better behaved in most cases have been convicted of less serious offences' than the IRA in the Six Counties.[273] It was estimated that 160 imprisoned republicans in the H-Blocks and Armagh would be 'freed immediately' when 50 per cent remission was restored in the North of Ireland.[274] Grievances of envious English prisoners were cited as the major inspiration behind co-ordinated strike action on 18 January 1982 when 270 of 289 men in Albany refused to attend work assignments. In Parkhurst 141 of 245 prisoners protested at the same time, as did sixteen in Long Lartin and six in Hull.[275] On 24 February 1982 it was reported that five prisoners on C Wing of Wormwood Scrubs had 'barricaded themselves' into a cell and refused meals for four days to protest their restricted access to lawyers.[276]

The drawn out sequence of deaths in the H-Blocks led to a temporary loss of purpose among the IRA men in Long Lartin, which bordered on demoralization once the protest ceased. This arose from their sense of 'close affinity with the hunger strikers', many of whom were personal acquaintances as well as comrades. A generally strong 'unit' was vigorously resurrected in 1982 following a therapeutic 'sabbatical'. Having devoted nine months to managing a prison soccer side, which triumphed in the local league, Gerry Cunningham renewed his political activism and was joined by his brother Busty Cunningham following his gruelling 'blanket protest' in Albany. Relocation had enabled him to move beyond a principled but potentially futile protest centred on a tactic phased out by the IRA in Long Kesh and Armagh. This, in turn, encouraged the relieved authorities to permit the reunion of the brothers without the appearance of bending to republican coercion. The presence of his sibling relieved Gerry Cunningham of part of his anxiety regarding their parents who for years had divided their visits from west Tyrone to shuttling between the Isle of Wight, Long Lartin and London where another close relative resided. Also significant was the arrival onto the wings of a veteran Belfast republican Jimmy 'Spotter' Murphy, who encouraged the re-coalescence of the militant core. By then the fruits of the Long Kesh hunger strike provided an additional inspiration: 'They got some recognition of their speciality, of their political genus ... They got something out of it but it was a terrible price to pay ... we resurrected the unit and we carried on working'.[277]

Repatriation

In September 1981, Eamonn O'Doherty, brother of Derry IRA prisoner Shane Paul O'Doherty, made a proposal that irritated republicans in Wormwood Scrubs. It was claimed that the strategy involved using IRA men in English prisons 'as a block to get his brother home'. Part of the problem, as viewed by Billy Armstrong, was that Shane Paul O'Doherty 'along with [Lord] Longford, [Bishop] Daly and a few other goody goodies tried to blacken our cause'.[278] It was pertinent that the Derry republican had apologized to the 'innocent' victims of his actions in 1976, a notably early gesture of its kind, but badly strained relations with the IRA by undermining its justification for waging the conflict in 1978. He subsequently attempted to work through Fr. Gerry Ennis of the Prison Chaplaincy Service, approved by the Home Office, to send written apologies to persons who had been targeted in the letter bomb campaign of which he was the prime mover. This represented a further increment of alienation from the republican community. One disgruntled recipient of an apology divulged the low-key overture to *The News of the World*, a tabloid which reported the story with near comic opprobrium.[279] After release, IRA lifer Roy Walsh told British journalist Peter Taylor: 'The only regret I've got is getting caught, and I would say that every republican prisoner regrets getting caught. For actually doing what I did, no, I've no regrets'.[280] More generally, the recently conceded liberalization of prisoners' mail privileges enabled O'Doherty to be considerably more prolific in disseminating his arguments on repatriation. An *Irish Press* article described his endeavours as 'a new campaign ... by the relatives and friends of the prisoners'. This well intentioned coverage inappropriately aggregated his industrious endeavours, however general in scope, to those separately initiated by the Republican Movement.[281] His energetic and extensive work was referred to without rancour by prisoner advocate Owen Carron as 'an individual campaign to highlight his case'.[282] The tactic was not without intrinsic merit. Noel Jenkinson had rendered himself a nuisance to the Home Office in the early 1970s by sending numerous, cogent letters of protest which required filing and formal processing. The Derry man and other republicans pursued this laborious course with alacrity when restrictions on letter frequency were definitively rescinded.[283]

Attention was drawn to O'Doherty's situation on 15 April 1981, against a backdrop of ferment in the H-Blocks, when it was reported that he was petitioning the European Commission for Human Rights arising from alleged breaches of Articles Seven and Fourteen of the Convention, which safeguarded family life and freedom from discrimination. He had already been obliged to suspend work towards an Open University degree in Social Science owing to the lack of educational facilities.[284] SDLP leader and MEP John Hume had written to the Northern Secretary in relation to the O'Doherty case on 18 and 26 May 1981 when the Six Counties were convulsed in the aftermath of the death of fellow MP Bobby Sands. Hume had formed a benign connection with the O'Dohertys in Derry and attempted to secure a commitment from the British Government to repatriate their life - sentenced relative from Gartree. No definitive response was forthcoming until 30 November 1981 when Lord Gowrie of the NIO furnished an appraisal in which he revealed that a 'detailed review of our whole policy on transfers' had taken place.[285] Gowrie was on familiar ground and had been deeply engaged over the autumn in the H-Block hunger strike, duties which extended to direct contact with families of prisoners nearing death.[286] Hume was obliged to transmit the negative decision to Eamonn O'Doherty, but the substance of the reasoning was significant as it affected all IRA prisoners in England.[287] Shane Paul O'Doherty was not unmindful of IRA associates with whom he was confined in Gartree in January 1982 when he publicized the fact that five were 'undergoing long periods of punishment in solitary confinement' under Rule 43.[288]

Gowrie confirmed in his report to Hume that 'it has been the practise of successive Northern Ireland administrations not to accept prisoners who had been sentenced in Great Britain for terrorist-type offences'. This was an admission or claim that the Home Office did not necessarily have the final say on whether such men and women would be repatriated. In outlining the selfish concerns of the NIO, Gowrie argued that 'prisoners with paramilitary associations' had a 'disruptive influence on the smooth running of any prison' and posed 'a constant threat to security'. Such factors, he claimed, rendered the NIO disinclined to accept those sentenced in Britain.[289] Gowrie politely dismissed submissions highlighting O'Doherty's 'change of heart' on the grounds that this retrospective political reorientation did not comprise 'compassionate circumstances' of sufficient exceptionality as to warrant special treatment. Family interests evidently carried very little weight in such deliberations, even though the wellbeing of relatives and dependents originally underpinned the logic of repatriation legislation.[290] In 99 per cent of cases, IRA prisoners were not granted temporary escorted parole to attend the funerals of parents or weddings of immediate relatives.[291]

The position advanced by the NIO in November 1981 asserted that it would veto transfers of paramilitaries from English prisons for reasons of security that superseded normal humanitarian concerns. This was a convenient defence as events in the H-Blocks since 1 March 1976 and the 10 June 1981 mass escape of IRA men from Crumlin Road Prison represented incontrovertible examples of a crisis in Six County facilities. By expressing its own agency and longstanding policy on repatriation, the NIO alleviated pressure which had been brought to bear on the Home Office by progressive MPs, church leaders and international human rights bodies in England. Gowrie's final comment to Hume, however, contained a familiar message by identifying the 'violence in both Northern Ireland and Great Britain' as an impediment to progress. The primacy of political considerations from a British perspective over any judicial, humanitarian and penological interest remained a constant feature of the Irish conflict. The IRA clearly remained strategic prisoners in the early 1980s if convicted in England.[292]

Ex-internee Paul 'Dingus' Magee was one of eight IRA men who escaped from Crumlin Road Jail on 10 June 1981. He received a life sentence *in absentia* two days later for killing SAS Captain Herbert Westmacott in Belfast; as did Angelo Fusco, Robert Campbell and Joe Doherty. Westmacott was shot dead on 22 May 1980, leading a unit of eight plain-clothed SAS men in an assault on an Antrim Road house they believed had been occupied by republicans.[293] They attacked the wrong doorway and came under defensive IRA rifle and machine gun fire from an adjacent building. The 'M60 gang' possessed the standard US Army medium machine gun and were described by Justice Hutton as 'ruthless and highly dangerous'.[294] Their escape, which entailed hijacking vehicles and a fighting retreat from pursuing RUC and British Army units, represented a propaganda coup for the IRA. Dingus Magee appeared shortly afterwards in public at the annual Wolfe Tone commemoration in Bodenstown, Kildare, and a photograph of the moment was republished from *AP/RN* in *Fight Racism! Fight Imperialism!* in August 1981.[295] Jailed in Portlaoise, Magee disappeared upon release to avoid extradition until arrested in June 1993 in England following the fatal shooting of a policeman.[296] Doherty was detained in New York on 18 June 1983 where his prolonged detention in the Manhattan Correctional Centre on a minor pretext spawned the most vigorous individual pro-prisoner campaign of the Troubles in the USA.[297] IRA prisoners in North America, Ireland and the UK were frequently the public face of the Republican Movement and their fortunes were chartered by hostile and friendly media to a degree that served to enhance their political importance.

NOTES

1. *Irish World*, 4 October 1980. See also Ibid., 29 November 1980 and 18 October 1980.
2. *Irish Echo*, 4 October 1984. For 1974 see *Times*, 10 June 1974. Arrowsmith had addressed a pro-H-Block rally on 1 January 1980 in her capacity as a member of Amnesty International and a 'well known pacifist'. Messages were received from Paul O'Dwyer and Vanessa Redgrave. *IRIS*, 12 January 1980. For Bond's CPGB 'Irish Committee' background see Matt Treacy, *The Communist Party of Ireland, 1921–2011, Volume 1: 1921–1969* (Dublin, 2012), p. 225. The RCG were critical of the IMG, SWP, TOM and Charter 80 and 'opportunist compromisers' for failing to give 'full and unconditional support to the POWs'. RCG, 'Our line on the Hunger Strike and the support campaign in Britain', 27 October 1980, Private Collection (O Mathuna).
3. *Irish World*, 25 October 1980.
4. Morrison (ed.), *Hunger Strike*, p. 17.
5. McFeeley's family sent a message of support to the 5 May 1978 London meeting on the prisoners in England organized by the PAC. He had recently undertaken a short hunger and thirst strike in Long Kesh. See *PAC News*, June 1978 and *AP/RN*, 1 November 1980. For McKearney's extensive republican connections see *AP/RN*, 6 December 1980. His sister Margaret was the subject of a deeply hostile tabloid campaign in England in 1975 when described as 'the most dangerous woman in Britain'. Ibid. See also McKee and Franey, *Time bomb*, p. 399.

6. *Irish World*, 1 November 1980.
7. *Report on the Administration of the Prison Service, 1980*, p. 16.
8. See IRSP, *Republican Socialist Programme for Ireland*, pamphlet, p. 5. The IRSP claimed: 'Determined INLA prisoners not only forced the issue of opposition to the Merlyn Rees policy of criminalization in the prisons, but led that opposition by example'. Ibid., p. 3. For Sinn Féin views of a 'broad front' in the UK see *AP/RN*, 18 August 1979.
9. See *Magill*, August 1981.
10. *Globe and Mail*, 24 October 1980.
11. *Report on the Administration of the Prison Service, 1980*, p. 8.
12. *Globe and Mail*, 28 October 1980.
13. *Irish World*, 1 November 1980.
14. *IRSP Hunger Strike Bulletin*, No. 1 [1980].
15. For international coverage of the June 1972 protests in Crumlin Road Prison and the Curragh see *Irish World*, 3 June 1972.
16. Armstrong to Wilson, 22 September 1980, Private Collection (Wilson). The detention of two Belfast women upon arrival in England was also troubling for those anticipating family visits in a country where so many innocent persons had been framed. Maureen O'Hara was quickly released but her traveling companion was questioned without a solicitor. Ibid.
17. Armstrong to Wilson, 22 September 1980, Private Collection (Wilson).
18. *AP/RN*, 1 November 1980.
19. Ronnie McCartney, 12 April 2008.
20. 'Walsh-BOV Adjudications' in A Aylett [For the Treasury Solicitor] to BM Birnberg & Co, 28 September 1990, Private Collection (Walsh).
21. The 'Charter 80' and 'Information on Ireland' groups co-operated to issue a leaflet entitled *H Block & Armagh, The case for urgent action*. The publication was designed to address British based supporters of the five demands. See also Tim Pat Coogan to the Editor, *Guardian*, 31 October 1980.
22. Mary Pearson, 'Marching in England' in Morrison (ed.) *Hunger Strike*, pp. 86–88.
23. Agenda, 'Ireland: International Solidarity Conference: Nov. 3–4 1980', Private Collection (Renwick).
24. *Irish World*, 5 November 1980.
25. *Irish Times*, 13 October 1980.
26. *AP/RN*, 22 November 1980. Charter 80 organized a forty-eight hour fast outside Downing Street on the weekend of 14–15 November to highlight the demands of the Long Kesh protesters. English allies included Pat Arrowsmith, Lord Gifford and Ricky Hall, a former British soldier who had served three tours in Ireland. *Irish World*, 15 November 1980.
27. See Lily Fitzsimmons to the Editor, *Hands off Ireland!*, No. 5, September 1978, p. 23 and 'Statements and reports from Belfast RAC' in *Hands off Ireland!*, No. 6, January 1979, pp. 4–5.
28. *Irish Echo*, 9 August 1980. Fitzsimmons, a leading member of the RAC, retrospectively noted the singularity of events in English prisons *vis à vis* what was in the offing in Ireland with the loss of political status: 'I can still recall our anger and dismay in 1974 and 1976 when, first Michael Gaughan and then Frank Stagg died on hunger strike in jails in England. We thought then, because of the massive protests all over Ireland and the bad public image of the British government abroad, that it could never happen again. How wrong we were'. Quoted in *Left Republican Review*, August 2001, p. 4. See also 'H-Block, A mother's account' in *Prison Struggle, Paper of the Relatives Action Committee*, March [1980], p. 6.
29. *AP/RN*, 22 November 1980.
30. *Morning Star*, 31 March 1979. See Reed, *Key to the British Revolution*, pp. 330–31.
31. Troops Out Movement Press Release, 27 February 1980 and 'Charter 80 Human Rights for Irish Political Prisoners', Private Collection (Renwick). See also *Irish Post*, 23 February 1980
32. Nick Mullen, 11 March 2012.
33. *House of Commons Home Affairs Committee, Session 1979–80, Administration of the Prison Service, Minutes of Evidence, Monday 10 November 1980*, p. 28.
34. *Administration of the Prison Service, Minutes of Evidence, Monday 10 November 1980*, p. 29.
35. *AP/RN*, 22 November 1980.
36. *Irish World*, 29 November and 13 December 1980.
37. *Irish World*, 6 December 1980. See Mary Doyle, 'The feelings are still raw' in Morrison (ed.) *Hunger Strike*, pp. 23–30 and Sile Darragh, *'John Lennon's Dead', Stories of Protest, Hunger Strikes & Resistance* (Belfast, 2011). The Armagh hunger strike ended on 19 December 1980 when confirmation was received that Brendan Hughes had ordered a cessation in Long Kesh. See Sinn Féin, *A Woman's Voice*, No. 1, May 1988.
38. Ronnie McCartney, 12 April 2008.
39. *Irish World*, 20 December 1980.
40. Sr. Clarke, 'Maurice Ward', Clarke Papers (COFLA).
41. *Report on the Administration of the Prison Service, 1980*, p. 8. See also *Irish World*, 27 December 1980.

42. *Report on the Administration of the Prison Service, 1980*, p. 16.
43. See O'Malley, *Biting at the grave*, pp. 28–33.
44. *Irish World*, 27 December 1980.
45. Morrison (ed.), *Hunger Strike*, p. 17.
46. Ronnie McCartney, 12 April 2008.
47. Sean Kinsella, 3 August 2007.
48. Millar, *On the brinks*, p. 104.
49. See Moloney, *Voices from the Grave*, pp. 238–43, RK Walker, *The Hunger Strikers* (Belfast, 2006), pp. 155–6, Morrison (ed.) *Hunger Strike*, p. 17 and *Irish World*, 3 January 1981.
50. Eddie O'Neill, 19 July 2007.
51. Eddie O'Neill, 19 July 2007.
52. *Independent*, 10 January 1995.
53. Eddie O'Neill, 1 February 2008.
54. *Times*, 15 December 1979.
55. *Guardian*, 4 March 1981.
56. *Irish Times*, 17 December 1980.
57. See *Chicago Tribune*, 17 December 1980.
58. *Irish World*, 3 January 1981.
59. *Report on the work of the Prison Department, 1980*, p. 7. Whereas only one additional prisoner escaped from Brixton, a Category B establishment, a total of twelve escaped in England in 1980. No Category A prisoners broke out of a Dispersal Prison or Special Wing that year. Ibid., p. 36.
60. Tuite, 11 September 2009. See also *Times*, 18 December 1980.
61. *Times*, 18 December 1980.
62. Gerry Tuite, 11 September 2009. Other IRA prisoners learned of Keenan's input: 'Brian didn't take part but he was part of the planning'. Joe O'Connell, 8 June 2008.
63. *Guardian*, 3 February 1981.
64. *Times*, 3 February 1981. D Wing had a Certified Normal Accommodation of 303 men. *Disturbance in D Wing*, p. 14.
65. *Times*, 31 July 1981.
66. *Session 1980–8 … 19 January 1981, HM Prison Brixton*, p. 89.
67. *Guardian*, 8 July 1991 and *Evening Standard*, 2 June 1993. It was claimed that 'Moody was number one enforcer for the Richardsons, did freelance 'work' for the Krays and became probably the most feared gangster ever to emerge from the London underworld'. Wensley Clarkson, *Gangs of Britain* (London, 2008), p. 98. He was tried with the Richardson gang in 1967 and although acquitted of serious charges was found guilty of manslaughter the following year. *Guardian*, 3 June 1993. See also *Times*, 10 April 1981. The Richardsons also had Irish family connections. See Eddie Richardson, *The last word, My life as a gangland boss* (London, 2005), pp. 12–13. Moody was shot dead in June 1993 in the Royal Hotel, Hackney, at which time he was believed to have participated in the bloody Brindle/ Daly/ Arif underworld feud. Another participant, Dubliner Michael Boyle, had been in the IRA in the late 1960s and 1970s. Boyle was captured after wounding Tony Brindle. See *Guardian*, 25 March 1997.
68. Clarkson, *Moody*, p. 139 and *Irish Times*, 17 December 1980.
69. Clarkson, *Moody*, p. 139.
70. Brian Keenan, 26 May 2007.
71. Gerry Tuite, 11 September 2009. See also *Sunday Times*, 4 October 1981.
72. Gerry Tuite, 11 September 2009. See also Clarkson, *Moody*, p. 139. Prison celebrity Charles Bronson wrote: 'Big H McKinney [sic] killed five … but did he? Some say he was a London hit-man, all 6ft 7in of him … John Childs, the supergrass, went Q[ueen's] E[vidence] on Big H, putting him away for life'. Bronson, *Bronson 2*, p. 230. Press sources claimed that MacKenney's 'friends outside' understood he did not wish to join the escape attempt in December 1980 and secured a cell change on the basis that the one he had been allocated was too cold. *Guardian*, 3 February 1981. When in Parkhurst SSU MacKenney was described as having been 'convicted of gangland contract killings'. *Times*, 22 May 1984
73. See Clarkson, Moody, p. 140.
74. *The Irish Prisoner*, No. 15 [1988], p. 14.
75. *Guardian*, 7 November 1980.
76. Gerry Tuite, 11 September 2009.
77. See *Times*, 29 December 1980 and *Guardian*, 17 February 1981. Richard Moody and Stan Thompson were charged in connection with the escape in Camberwell Magistrates Court on 27 December 1980. The men received eighteen months and a twelve-month suspended sentence respectively on 30 June 1981. *Times*, 29 December 1980 and 1 July 1981.

78. Gerry Tuite, 11 September 2009. Tuite claimed that the first drill was powered by a pencil sharpener with a handle extended by a coat hanger. In two weeks nine holes in an approximate area of one and a half inches was drilled. Advice from Moody improved the efficacy of the device by combining metal tubing, a masonry bit and a broom handle. *Irish Times*, 5 October 1981.

79. See Clarkson, *Moody*, pp. 141–2.

80. *Irish Times*, 17 December 1980.

81. *Irish Times*, 5 October 1981.

82. Clarkson, *Moody*, pp. 144–5. See also *Guardian*, 1 July 1981.

83. *Guardian*, 8 July 1991. See also *Guardian*, 3 February 1981.

84. Clarkson, *Moody*, pp. 146–8. The men had left dummies stuffed with newspapers to indicate that they remained in bed. *Guardian*, 3 June 1993. A grappling hook rig was not used owing to the fortuitous availability of planking. *Guardian*, 1 July 1981. This account claimed that Moody 'planned the escape'. Ibid.

85. *Guardian*, 3 February 1981.

86. *FRFI*, January/ February 1981.

87. *Guardian*, 20 December 1980.

88. Clarkson, *Gangs of Britain*, pp. 101–2. He was sometimes referred to as 'Mick the Irishman' and was shot dead in Homerton on 1 June 1993 when still on the run. He was suspected of having killed David Brindle in August 1991, a member of a leading London criminal organization. Ibid., p. 104 and *Evening Standard*, 2 June 1993.

89. *Guardian*, 19 December 1980.

90. *Guardian*, 18 December 1980.

91. *Guardian*, 14 July 1982.

92. Annette Maloney, 23 June 2008. Maloney's Kerry - born mother Nora formerly hosted leading Sinn Féin activist Sean Grealy in London. Two of Grealy's Dublin based siblings had been involved in the February 1959 springing of Kildare IRA man Seamus Murphy from Wakefield Prison. Ibid and Aine Grealy, 13 November 2005.

93. Michael Cunningham, 2 August 2007.

94. See endorsed envelope of Gerry Tuite to Sr. Sarah [Clarke], Clarke Papers (COFLA).

95. *Guardian*, 28 January 1981.

96. *Guardian*, 11 December 1980. See also McGladdery, *Provisional IRA in England*, p. 243.

97. *Observer*, 11 January 1981.

98. *Sun*, 16 December 1980.

99. *Irish Times*, 17 December 1980 and *HC Deb 18 December 1980 vol 996 c256W*.

100. See *Daily Mail*, 3 February 1981 and *The Economist*, 7 February 1981. See also Callan, *Gartree*, p. 54. Selby had been questioned by Jill Knight MP the previous month during a Home Affairs Committee investigation into Prison Service administration. He answered her query regarding alleged extra 'privileges' enjoyed by Category A men in Brixton as follows: 'You can have total security by having all closed visits, but I think this is inhumane and the country rightly takes this risk. It was decided when special wings were set up that the regimes should be those of separation and segregation'. *Session 1980–8 … 19 January 1981, HM Prison Brixton*, p. 88.

101. *HL Deb 21 March 1984 vol 449 c1337*.

102. *Times*, 3 February 1981.

103. *Times*, 3 February 1981. The remand period of twelve to eighteen months of the three men involved in the escape was described as 'an outrage in a civilized society'. *Guardian*, 18 December 1980.

104. *Times*, 23 February 1981.

105. *Report of an Inquiry by the Deputy Director-General of the Prison Service into the escape of three prisoners from HM Prison Brixton on December 16, 1980* (London, 1981) quoted in *Times*, 31 July 1981.

106. *Times*, 31 July 1981.

107. *Report on the work of the Prison Department, 1980*, p. 11.

108. Armstrong to Wilson, 2 February 1981, Private Collection (Wilson).

109. *Session 1980–8 … 19 January 1981, HM Prison Brixton*, p. 93 Governor Selby of Brixton argued that 'if there was a secure court nearer to Brixton it would save police time and improve security from the point of view of attacks from other terrorists and gangs'. Ibid.

110. See Hayes (ed.) *In prison in England*, p. 4.

111. Joe O'Connell, 7 June 2008.

112. Hayes (ed.) *In prison in England*, p. 29 and Sr. Clarke, 'Pat 'Tipp' Guilfoyle, Clarke Papers (COFLA). Guilfoyle received a press apology when an agency report of an Appeal Court session incorrectly associated him with 'pub bombings' in Manchester and Birmingham. It was admitted that there had been 'no Manchester pub bombings' and that he was in Winson Green prison when the 'Birmingham incident' occurred. *Guardian*, 6 January 1981.

113. *The Economist*, 7 February 1981.
114. Cited in *AP/RN*, 29 April 1982.
115. Armstrong to Wilson, 2 February 1981, Private Collection (Wilson). The poor 'quality & quantity' of food in Wormwood Scrubs in early 1981 disposed Billy Armstrong to decline meals and eat the more palatable alternative of bread and jam. Armstrong to Wilson, 2 February 1981, Private Collection (Wilson).
116. *Guardian*, 27 July 2005.
117. *Guardian*, 14 February 1995.
118. Quoted in *Irish World*, 17 January 1981.
119. *Irish World*, 17 January 1981.
120. *Irish World*, 17 January 1981. See also *Guardian*, 10 January 1981.
121. *Observer*, 15 June 1986 and Bishop and Mallie, *Provisional IRA*, p. 337.
122. *Times*, 11 June 1986. In Long Kesh, Cage Two, in 1974. Patrick Magee, *Gangsters or Guerillas? Representations of Irish Republicans in 'Troubles Fiction'* (Belfast, 2001), p. 1.
123. *Guardian*, 12 June 1986.
124. *Guardian*, 12 June 1986.
125. *Times*, 11 June 1986.
126. *HC Deb 18 March 1981 vol 1 cc336–74*. See also *Times*, 27 June 1986.
127. *Daily Telegraph*, 13 May 1983.
128. *Observer*, 15 June 1986.
129. *Irish World*, 14 February 1981. Canavan, a factory machinist in Harlesden Gardens, London, was arrested on 28 April 1976 and remanded to Brixton. He received a ten-year sentence from Justice Melford Stevenson on 8 November 1976 for conspiring to cause explosions between January and December 1973. See Sr. Clarke, Card Index, Clarke Papers (COFLA) and *PAC News*, June 1977. He was 'the first IRA man to be paroled from a British jail' since March 1973, an issue raised in the Commons. See *HC Deb 5 February 1981 vol 998 c164W*. Canavan pleaded guilty on 8 November 1976 and was understood by Sr. Clarke, who shared his Galway origins, 'to have made incendiary bombs which did not work'. His appeal for a reduction in sentence failed on 8 November 1977 and his initial application for parole was rejected two years later. Sr. Clarke, 'Sean Canavan', Clarke Papers (COFLA). See also O'Doherty, *Volunteer*, p. 201. Trial reports claimed: 'It was said that he had been ordered to join the IRA and did so out of fear. He was taken to training camps in the Irish Republic where he was shown how to use various automatic weapons, including machine guns, and how to make landmines, time bombs and firebombs. His instructor was an Englishman from Birmingham'. *Sunday Telegraph*, 8 February 1981.
130. *Sunday Telegraph*, 8 February 1981.
131. *AP/RN*, 29 April 1982.
132. *Sunday Telegraph*, 8 February 1981.
133. Sr. Clarke, 'Sean Canavan', Clarke Papers (COFLA).
134. Sr. Clarke, 'Peter Short', Clarke Papers (COFLA).
135. O'Donnell, *Special Category*, I, p. 249.
136. *Irish Times*, 5 October 1981. See also *Sunday Times*, 4 October 1981.
137. *Irish News*, 5 March 1982 and *Irish Times*, 14 July 1982.
138. *Trials by ordeal*, p. 108. Glenholmes, when in Long Lartin, was advised by the Catholic Chaplain to 'have nothing to do' with Sr. Sarah Clarke. Clarke, *No faith*, p. 112.
139. McKeown, *Out of time*, Chapter ten.
140. *Times*, 29 December 1980.
141. *Guardian*, 29 December 1980.
142. Sr. Clarke, 'Kevin Dunphy', Clarke Papers (COFLA).
143. Paul Holmes, April 2011.
144. *Irish Times*, 21 March 1981.
145. *Irish Times*, 3 December 1980. See also Fr. Raymond Murray and Fr. Denis Faul, *Parole for Fr. Patrick Fell*, pamphlet (Armagh, 1980) and Clarke, *No faith*, pp. 85–6.
146. *Irish Times*, 21 March 1981. In February 1981 Reg Freeson MP sought figures from the Home Secretary on the number of Albany prisoners charged with offences in the course of the previous twelve months. *HC Deb 9 February 1981 vol 998 c249W*.
147. *Times*, 13 November 1982.
148. *HC Deb 5 March 1981 vol 1000 cc400–1*.
149. Clarke, *No faith*, p. 113 and *Irish Post*, 14 February 1981. In December 1981 the preface to Prison Standing Order No. 5 was amended to uphold the right of a prisoner for social contact with persons outside. This was deemed a preemptive reform spurred by an anticipated negative ruling from the ECHR. *Irish News*, 21 January 1983.
150. *Irish Post*, 17 March 1984.

151. Louis Leonard Sinn Féin Cumann, *The 'Pitchfork' murders, Uncovering the cover-up* (Fermanagh, 2012). At the time Hathaway and Byrne were transferred to England it was noted that a group of British Army paratroopers previously jailed for theft had decided to serve their sentences in B Wing of Crumlin Road Prison. *Irish Times*, 10 January 1981. Five Black Watch Regiment soldiers involved in killing and concealing the death of seventeen year old Leo Norney in September 1975 were sent to Scotland to serve their sentences. *Republican News*, 26 February 1977.

152. Dillon, *Dirty War*, p. 157. See *AP/RN*, 24 January 1981 and *Lost Lives*, pp. 286–7.

153. *Irish News*, 22 November 1982.

154. *Guardian*, 15 April 1981. See also *Irish Echo*, 7 March 1981.

155. *Report on the Administration of the Prison Service, 1980*, p. 8.

156. Hugh Doherty, 23 June 2006.

157. See *Irish Post*, 7 March 1981. See also *Guardian*, 3 March 1981, Millar, *On the brinks*, pp. 105–6 and Thomas Hennessey, *Hunger Strike: Margaret Thatcher's battle with the IRA 1980–1981* (Dublin, 2014).

158. Adams, *Before the dawn*, p. 290.

159. *Irish News*, 30 December 2011.

160. See *Irish Echo*, 14 March 1981.

161. See Brady et al (eds.) *Stories of Republican Women*, p. 232 and Darragh, *Stories of Protest*, pp. 116–18.

162. Tony Clarke, 9 March 2008.

163. Cited in O'Brien, *Long War*, p. 294.

164. O'Hearn, *Sands*, p. 98

165. Feilim O hAdmhaill, 6 August 2008. Feilim O hAdhmaill, an Irish speaking youth who had visited Sands in Long Kesh in 1976 and later worked alongside him in Twinbrook's Sinn Féin Cumann. Destined for imprisonment in England in the 1990s, O hAdhmaill's father participated in the 'S-Plan' bombing campaign in 1939. Feilim O hAdhmaill, 6 August 2008.

166. *Republican News*, 7 October 1978. The article was reprinted in Bobby Sands, *The writings of Bobby Sands, 1954–1981* (Dublin, 1981), p. 32.

167. *Lost Lives*, p. 488 and *AP/RN*, 14 October 1999.

168. Dick Barrett, one of four senior IRA and IRB leaders executed by the Free State forces on 8 December 1922 during Ireland's Civil War, viewed himself in similar terms. Hours before being shot in Mountjoy Prison he wrote: 'I am prepared to die and glad that I die in the same cause as Tone, Emmet, Pearse and Charlie Hurley'. Dick [Barrett] to his family, [8 December 1922] in Martin (Bob) O'Dwyer, *Seventy-Seven of Mine said Ireland* (Cork, 2006), p. 90. Barrett's litany spanned republican leaders who had been executed in 1798, 1803, 1916 and 1921. See *Last Post*, p. 118.

169. O'Hearn, *Sands*, p. 236.

170. O'Hearn, *Sands*, p. 338. David Beresford of the *Guardian* was also present but omitted an account of the visit from his *Ten men dead* publication. See also *Irish Times*, 5 March 1981. Sands noted in his secret diary that he 'couldn't quite get my flow of thoughts' during the meeting with O Cathaoir and Beresford. Bobby Sands, *Skylark sing your lonely song, An anthology of the writings of Bobby Sands* (Dublin and Cork, 1982), p. 155. The entry for 6 March 1981 reiterated the point: 'Thomas Clarke is in my thoughts, and MacSwiney, Stagg, Gaughan, Thomas Ashe, McCaughey'. Ibid., p. 159. Clarke, identified in an anonymous H-Block 'comm' as 'THE GREATEST FENIAN OF ALL' was revered by the 'blanketmen'. 'Demand Political Status-Smash H-Block', Private Collection (Renwick). Sands was emerging as a figure of note and a short story attributed only to a 'young writer [who] has been on the blanket for over two years' appeared in *IRIS*, 14 July 1979. See also Sands, *Skylark*, pp. 103–5.

171. O'Hearn, *Sands*, p. 375.

172. Cited in Beresford, *Ten men dead*, p. 40.

173. Kevin Sheehy, *More questions than answers, Reflections on a life in the RUC* (Dublin, 2008), p. 67.

174. *AP/RN*, 9 September 1981. O Conaill spoke during the annual Mayo hunger striker tribute to McNeela, Gaughan and Stagg. Ibid.

175. Jim Gibney quoted in Feeney, *Sinn Féin*, 291.

176. De Bariod, *Ballymurphy*, p. 238.

177. *Time Out*, 8–14 May 1981.

178. Armstrong to Wilson, 6 July 1982, Private Collection (Wilson).

179. POW Department, *The writings of Bobby Sands was published in April 1981*, Pamphlet (Dublin, 1981), p. 36. See also [Bobby Sands], 'The Lark and the freedom fighter' in *AP/RN*, 3 February 1979.

180. *Irish Times*, 31 December 2011. Atkins evidently declined an offer conveyed by Sands through Fr. Magee to 'suspend' his hunger strike for five days as part of negotiations with the NIO. *Irish News*, 29 November 2013. See also Thomas Hennessey, *Hunger Strike: Margaret Thatcher's Battle with the IRA* (Dublin, 2013).

181. *Irish Times*, 22–23 September 2012.

182. Sir Robert Armstrong, Minute, April 1981, Margaret Thatcher Foundation cited in *Irish Times*, 27 April 2013. Armstrong was privy in the course of the hunger strike to information passed between Northern Secretary Humphrey Atkins and Derryman Brendan Duddy who acted as an intermediary for the IRA leadership. Ibid.
183. BBC News, Northern Ireland, 3 January 2014.
184. [Danny Morrison], *The Hillsborough Agreement, The text of the Bobby Sands Commemorative lecture given by Danny Morrison in Twinbrook, Belfast on Sunday 4ᵗʰ May 1986*, Pamphlet (Dublin and Belfast, 1986), pp. 6–10.
185. *AP/RN*, 25 April 1981.
186. *AP/RN*, 18 July 1981.
187. *Hands off Ireland!*, No. 10, April 1980, p. 19.
188. Armstrong to Wilson, 13 May 1981, Private Collection (Wilson). Coughlan had spent much of 1980 in Albany, from whence he was sent on a 'lie down' to Winchester in March. *The Irish Prisoner*, No. 9, June/ July 1980, p. 2. See also *AP/RN*, 17 October 1985.
189. *Times*, 28 April 1981.
190. Martin Coughlan, 24 August 2006.
191. Armstrong to Wilson, 2 February 1981, Private Collection (Wilson). See also *AP/RN*, 18 July 1981.
192. Martin Coughlan, 24 August 2006.
193. Billy Armstrong, 'Fighting all the way' in *AP/RN*, 22 February 2001.
194. Armstrong to Wilson, 1 May 1981, Private Collection (Wilson).
195. Armstrong to Wilson, 1 May 1981, Private Collection (Wilson). See also *AP/RN*, 17 December 1981.
196. *Times*, 6 May 1981 and Hayes (ed.) *In prison in England*, p. 27.
197. *Times*, 27 April 1981.
198. *Times*, 27 April 1981.
199. Gerry Cunningham, n.d. [May 1981] in Hayes (ed.) *In prison in England*, p. 29. In October 1980 Holmes had been refused compassionate parole from Wormwood Scrubs to visit his terminally ill mother, Eileen Holmes, in hospital in Belfast. The request, unusually, was backed by a petition from hospital staff to Home Secretary William Whitelaw. *AP/RN*, 11 October 1980.
200. *FRFI*, April 1982.
201. Gerry Cunningham, 25 September 2007.
202. Gerry Cunningham, 25 September 2007.
203. Holmes, April 2011.
204. Holmes, April 2011. They believed 'the screws had a modicum of respect for us' arising from their comparative self-discipline, rejection of hard drugs and political formation. Holmes, who had been severely beaten following a Gartree altercation, knew some in Long Lartin who avidly read *An Phoblacht/ Republican News*. Ibid.
205. Hugh Doherty, 23 June 2006.
206. Hayes (ed.) *In prison in England*, p. 27.
207. McLaughlin, *Inside an English Jail*, p. 9. Few IRA men were acquainted with the full story of the Mayo man's death and details emerged from many sources over time. Billy Armstrong befriended an English radical prisoner, John Masterson, who was evidently 'a very good friend of Frank Stagg whilst up in the hospital in Wakefield'. Armstrong to Wilson, 19 May 1983, Private Collection (Wilson).
208. Tony Madigan, 7 March 2008.
209. Gerry Young, 8 March 2008.
210. Hill, *Stolen years*, p. 200.
211. Noel Gibson, 24 August 2006.
212. See Mark Moloney, 'Nelson Mandela, A hero among heroes' in *An Phoblacht*, January 2014, p. 6.
213. Fr. Des Wilson, 'Changed Utterly' in *Fortnight*, No. 183 (October/ November 1981), pp. 5–6.
214. Armstrong to Wilson, 13 May 1981, Private Collection (Wilson).
215. *Chicago Tribune*, 15 May 1981. McLaughlin withdrew from the hunger strike after fourteen days when a perforated ulcer threatened additional severe medical complications. He was replaced by Martin Hurson. Within two days the Sinn Féin decision to run prisoner candidates was announced in the Twenty-Six Counties. Kieran Doherty, Joe McDonnell and Martin Hurson were nominated by the National H-Block Committee for the constituencies of Cavan-Monaghan, Sligo-Leitrim and Longford-Westmeath. INLA prisoner Kevin Lynch was nominated for a Waterford seat. *Chicago Tribune*, 30 May 1981. Caoimhghin O Caolain was Director of Elections in the 'H-Block campaign of 1981' and in June 1997 took the Cavan/ Monaghan Dáil seat held by Kieran Doherty at the time of his death in Long Kesh. 'Profile' in *Cairde Sinn Féin*, November 1997, p. 2. Hurson had worked for two years in England prior to joining the IRA in his native Tyrone and being jailed in 1976. Francis Hurson told an RCG interviewer in London on 19 September 1981 that his brother, who died after forty-six days fasting on 13 July 1981, firmly believed 'the British government shouldn't be in Ireland'. Francis Hurson quoted in *FRFI*, October/ November 1981, p. 2. See also *Tirghra*, p. 240. Dundalk supporter Mrs Una Toal, a prolific correspondent of IRA prisoners in England, attended Lynch's funeral with

Irish-American sympathizers. Una Toal to Noel Gibson, Kevin Dunphy and Con McFadden, 10 March 1983, Private Collection (Dunphy).

216. Armstrong to Wilson, 13 May 1981, Private Collection (Wilson).

217. 'Republican POW Wormwood Scrubs' in *FRFI*, July/ August 1981, p. 15.

218. O'Hearn, *Sands*, p. 368 and RCG, *Manifesto*, p. 71. See also Robert Clough, *Labour, A Party fit for Imperialism* (London, 1992), p. 120.

219. *Spartacist*, No. 33, June 1981, p. 1.

220. Armstrong to Wilson, 28 July 1981, Private Collection (Wilson).

221. *Irish Times*, 12 July 1981.

222. Tony Clarke, 9 March 2008.

223. *AP/RN*, 29 April 1982.

224. Liam Baker, 3 March 2008.

225. Ronnie McCartney, 12 April 2008.

226. Sean Smyth, 2 June 2009.

227. Bik [MacFarlane] to 'Brownie' [Gerry Adams], 9 August 1981 in Beresford, *Ten men dead*, p. 298.

228. Aidan Hegarty, *Kevin Lynch and the Irish Hunger Strike* (Belfast, 2006), p. 141 and Holland and McDonald, *Deadly Divisions*, pp. 183–4.

229. Ronnie McCartney, 12 April 2008.

230. *AP/RN*, 7 June 2001. See also Facebook.Com/AustralianIrishRepublicanHistoryProject.

231. RA Harrington, Briefing, 21 September 1981, PRONI/NIO/12/253.

232. Armstrong to Wilson, 13 May 1981, Private Collection (Wilson). *An Phoblacht* was temporarily banned after the April 1981 protest and the *Andersonstown News* only available intermittently. Armstrong to Wilson, 28 July 1981, Private Collection (Wilson). Similar claims by prisoners of D Wing, Wormwood Scrubs, were vindicated in October 1982 when Lord Elton admitted 'some incoming mail had not been issued, and some outgoing mail had not been posted'. *HL Deb 25 October 1982 vol 435 cc385*.

233. Armstrong to Wilson, 21 April 1980, Private Collection (Wilson).

234. Armstrong to Wilson, 16 December 1982, Private Collection (Wilson).

235. See *An Phoblacht*, January 2012, p. 15.

236. *Irish Times*, 31 December 2012, p. 7 and *Times*, 27 June 1986. IRA surveillance of Carrington noted his home address, daily movements, transport and personal security. *Irish Times*, 7 July 1982.

237. Clark noted on 5 April 1982: 'Three of my best speeches-on [KGB agent Anthony] Blunt, on Bobby Sands and on the NATO commitment'. Alan Clark, *Diaries, Into Politics* (London, 2000), p. 314.

238. Cited in *Irish Times*, 31 December 2012, p. 7.

239. See Richard O'Rawe, *Blanketmen, An untold story of the H-Block hunger strike* (Dublin, 2005).

240. Clarke, *No faith*, pp. 95–6.

241. *Times*, 11 September 1981.

242. Clarke, *No faith*, p. 96.

243. *AP/RN*, 1 August 1981.

244. *AP/RN*, 19 September 1981.

245. O Mathuna to O'Donnell, 14 April 2012, Private Collection (O'Donnell). See also 'RCG statement to London H-Block/ Armagh Committee strategy meeting', 2 August 1981, Private Collection (O Mathuna).

246. Hattersley, *Fifty years on*, p. 292.

247. *Chicago Tribune*, 15 May 1981.

248. Farrell, *Sheltering the fugitive?*, p. 95.

249. Farrell, *Sheltering the fugitive?*, p. 96. Maurice Hanlon was accused by British police of handling explosives in London in 1971. The Longford man claimed the material was the property of the IRA and in so doing warranted classification as a political offence. Justice Doyle heard the extradition request in the High Court in 1974 but delayed issuing a decision until October 1980. The Supreme Court in October 1981 assessed other details casting doubt on the subversive aspect while avoiding comment on the validity of Hanlon's reasoning. Ibid., p. 95.

250. Eddie O'Neill, 1 February 2008.

251. Eddie O'Neill, 1 February 2008.

252. Eddie O'Neill, 1 February 2008.

253. *AP/RN*, 3 October 1981. See also *Irish Democrat*, May 1981.

254. *AP/RN*, 26 September 1981.

255. *Observer*, 23 August 1981. See also *Irish Democrat*, October 1981 and *Guardian*, 20 January 1986.

256. *Irish Post*, 27 February 1982. Benn spoke in relation to a meeting of the Labour Committee on Ireland and the Committee for Withdrawal from Northern Ireland, which was backed by fellow MPs Joan Maynard, Clive Soley, Eric Ross, Stuart Holland, Les Huckfield, Denis Canavan, Bob Parry, Ernie Roberts, Sid Bidwell, Stan Thorne and MEP Richard Balfe. Ibid.

257. *Irish Times*, 12 October 1981.

258. 'Extracts from a statement by Irish POWs in England (26 September 1981) in *FRFI*, November/ December 1981, p. 13.
259. Mick Ryan, 23 July 2007.
260. *Irish Democrat*, June 1981.
261. Quoted in *Observer*, 23 August 1981. See *Guardian*, 29 April 1989. Jill Knight MP misinformed the Rotary Club of Chicago that 'the IRA is a very hard taskmaster .... If you didn't go on a hunger strike when you were told to, you wouldn't last very long, and neither would your family'. Knight claimed that the concept of human rights has 'gone dreadfully wrong' and was manipulated by 'terrorist groups' and 'professional agitators'. *Chicago Tribune*, 7 October 1981.
262. Walker, *Hunger Strikes*, p. 188.
263. *Chicago Tribune*, 5 October 1981. See *Guardian*, 17 January 1998.
264. The twenty-two IRA members spanning Thomas Ashe to Mickey Devine who died on hunger strike were commemorated by a Yann Goulet decorated granite slab in Glasnevin Cemetery, Dublin, on 20 May 1983. Fr. O Duill, who had participated in the funerals of Gaughan and Stagg, blessed the new National Graves Association memorial in front of a crowd of 500. *Irish Times*, 21 May 1984.
265. 'PRO Republican POWs Wormwood Scrubs' in *FRFI*, September 1981.
266. See *Saoirse Nua*, Spring 2012 and Morrison, *Rebel columns*, pp. 149–51. IRA women in Armagh Gaol campaigned for the improved terms yielded in Long Kesh by the NIO by means of workshop sabotage and disruption. See Brady et al (eds.) *Stories of Republican women*, p. 232. In August 1984 Loyalists in Magilligan mounted a fast to achieve segregation from IRA prisoners. The Loyalist Prisoners' Association claimed the IRA was 'virtually in control' of the Derry prison. *Irish Times*, 31 August 1984. See also *Irish Times*, 11 September and 4 October 1984.
267. *Guardian*, 3 November 1981.
268. O'Donnell, *Special Category*, I, p. 45.
269. *Chicago Tribune*, 25 November 1981 and *FRFI*, May/ June 1981, p. 2.
270. Mansergh, *Legacy of History*, p. 405.
271. Martin Galvin, 14 April 2014. A planned US visit by Princess Margaret was cancelled. *Spartacist*, No. 34, July 1981, p. 8.
272. Hayes (ed.) *In prison in England*, p. 8. See also *FRFI*, February 1982, p. 13.
273. Cited in *Times*, 19 January 1982.
274. *Chicago Tribune*, 5 October 1981.
275. *Times*, 19 January 1982.
276. *Daily Telegraph*, 24 February 1982.
277. Gerry Cunningham, 25 September 2007.
278. Armstrong to Wilson, 29 September 1981, Private Collection (Wilson). Armstrong had refused to co-operate with Eamonn O'Doherty when he came to visit him in Wakefield. Ibid. See O'Doherty, *Volunteer*, p. 101. He had attended St. Columb's College, Derry, with Vince Donnelly. Eamonn O'Doherty to the Editor, *Irish News*, 12 January 1984. Republicans distrusted Fr. Ennis in Wormwood Scrubs for his refusal to endorse the claims of the Birmingham Six to innocence. John McComb, 5 August 2008.
279. O'Doherty, *Volunteer*, pp. 215–6.
280. Roy Walsh quoted in Taylor, *Provos*, p. 155.
281. *Irish Press*, 29 January 1982. In March 1978 Gerry Young was informed that he was not permitted to correspond with Una Caughey, the fiancée of IRA prisoner Ray McCartney, arising from 'security reasons'. J Page (Home Office) to George E Baker & Co, Private Collection (Caughey).
282. *AP/RN*, 29 April 1982.
283. See O'Donnell, *Special Category*, I, pp. 426–7.
284. *Guardian*, 15 April 1981.
285. Lord Gowrie to John Hume, 30 November 1981 in Hayes (ed.) *In prison in England*, p. 16. O'Doherty was reclassified as Category B and moved to Blundeston Prison, Suffolk, in March 1983. *Derry Journal*, 19 March 1983. Anne Maguire was reportedly changed to Category B in July 1983. *Irish News*, 7 July 1983. In September 1985 the Home Office announced that O'Doherty would be repatriated from Wormwood Scrubs to an Irish prison. *Times*, 5 September 1985.
286. *Guardian*, 5 October 1981 and *Irish Times*, 30 December 2011.
287. John [Hume] to Eamonn [O'Doherty], c. December 1981 in Hayes (ed.) *In prison in England*, p. 17.
288. Shane O'Doherty to the Editor, *Catholic Herald*, 17 January 1982. He regarded Gartree in the early 1980s as 'a prison in which physical force and/ or reputation went a long way and there were a lot of fights'. Shane Paul O'Doherty to the Editor, *Irish Times*, 5 December 1989.
289. Gowrie to Hume, 30 November 1981 in Hayes (ed.) *In prison in England*, p. 16.
290. Gowrie to Hume, 30 November 1981 in Hayes (ed.) *In prison in England*, p. 16.
291. See S[herard] L Cowper-Coles [RID, FCO] to R[ichard] A O'Brien [First Secretary, Irish Embassy], 3 May 1978, NAE, FCO 87/ 972.

292. Lord Gowrie to John Hume, 30 November 1981 in Hayes (ed.) *In prison in England*, p. 16. Gowrie referenced the Crumlin Road breakout on 10 June 1981 as the 'recent escape from Belfast Prison'. Ibid. See De Baroid, *Ballymurphy*, p. 244.

293. *Lost Lives*, p. 827.

294. *Guardian*, 13 June 1981. For an account of the escape of Joe Doherty, Dingus Magee, Gerry Sloan, Tony Sloan, Michael McKee, Robert Campbell, Pete Ryan and Angelo Fusco from Crumlin Road Jail see Joe Doherty, *Standing proud, writings from prison and the story of his struggle for freedom* (New York, [c. 1991]) pp. 103–6, Magee, *Tyrone's Struggle*, pp. 253–4 and *Guardian*, 11 June 1981. Ryan was shot dead by pro-British agents in Coagh, Tyrone on 3 June 1991. Oliver Kelly, a former internee in Long Kesh and solicitor for several IRA defendants, was detained under the PTA for three days arising from the Crumlin Road breakout. His brother John Kelly had been one of the founders of the Provisional IRA. *Guardian*, 12 June 1981 and *Tirghra*, p. 332.

295. *FRFI*, July/ August 1981, p. 16.

296. *IRIS*, August 1989, p. 47, *AP/RN*, 11 October 1990 and De Bariod, *Ballymurphy*, p. 244.

297. See Holland, *American Connection*, p. 170.

CHAPTER 6

Prisoners, Politics and Repatriation

Parkhurst attacks, 1981

Facets of prison life germane to the overall Dispersal Prison subculture invariably impacted on Irish republicans in England. Racial tensions in Parkhurst occasionally imperilled IRA members who resolutely opposed the white supremacist dimension of British prison gangs. Acts of interracial solidarity, both moral and physical, were appreciated by the often beleaguered minority traditions. Black activist Shujaa Moshesh recalled an incident in which

> an English prisoner attacked an Irish prisoner. There was only one or two other Irish prisoners in the prison, so they were outnumbered. The Irish guy and the English prisoner were moved to the Scrubs. It's generally known that these Irish guys do not mess about; they are serious guys. It would have come down to a full-scale war if … some kind of peacemaker hadn't intervened … We black guys heard about it and we were prepared to go on to the side of the Irish guys.[1]

Belfast man Francis (aka Felim and 'Feely') McGee was stabbed to death in C Wing in Parkhurst on 10 July 1981 by the insane Johnny Patton.[2] The non-political victim, due for release in the near future, had been on good terms with IRA and English prisoners. A horrified Paddy Joe Hill watched as McGee was 'murdered at breakfast in front of me'.[3] The IRA ascertained that a group of racists had paid the violent Patton to kill Gerry Young arising from his vociferous objection to their attempt to marginalize black prisoners. When, in the course of the previous night, Young was found to be unexpectedly in the company of fellow republican John McCluskey, Patton demurred. Fearing loss of face, a major liability in professional criminal society, he decided to kill the unsuspecting McGee when he was momentarily isolated the following morning.[4] McCluskey witnessed the attack: 'It was savage – knifed him through … [the back. Patton] pointed up to the landing, pointed up to one of our prisoners [Young] and said, "you are next"'.[5] Patton previously killed an inmate in Wakefield in 1977 and received a second life sentence in Winchester for fatally stabbing McGee.[6] Held in extreme conditions of confinement in Wakefield's F Wing, Patton was found hanged in his cell as a presumed suicide.[7]

Manipulating unstable prisoners to assault republicans by cash and drug supply inducements rarely paid dividends. Billy Cockill, who had been involved in attacking 'Birmingham Six' prisoner Gerry Hunter, was stabbed to death.[8] Mentally ill prisoners were also deliberately utilized. Liam Baker, who when in Gartree threatened a man inculpated in the November 1974 Brixton attack on Eddie O'Neill, was set up for assault by staff in Albany after being unlocked from the Segregation Block to attend Mass. Watchful prisoners summoned the alarm when they heard the commotion which followed Baker being struck on the head from behind in the Recess. Fearing major acts of retribution from the IRA, a senior staff officer politely requested that the aggrieved Belfast man attend an unscheduled dental appointment the following morning. When escorted to the office for notional, unnecessary treatment, Baker was shown the official file of his deranged attacker whom, he gleaned, Broadmoor and Rampton had declined to accommodate. The intent of the unorthodox disclosure was to dissuade republicans from automatically mounting a violent retaliation: 'They knew rightly we were going to come back'. Divergent opinions among Albany staff in this instance both occasioned and defused a dangerous situation.[9]

John McCluskey was injured in Parkhurst on 10 September 1981 in what appeared to be a sequel to the botched attempt on the life of Gerry Young. He was slashed in the back by an Irish psychopath known as 'The Pig' Boyle, a native of Donegal, as he queued for breakfast. Boyle had surprised and stabbed prisoners in the past. McCluskey, however, sensed the approach of his assailant: 'He came down the landing and he came tearing towards me'. Prior warning from an Irish man that Boyle had procured an edged weapon in the workshop amplified McCluskey's normal intuition and vigilance during the morning ritual: 'When I heard he had a knife for me, I expected what was going to happen – I was half ready. It is very difficult when you are watching but because I was half ready for him it probably saved my life … The knife actually touched me'.[10] Blade wounds to his back proved to be superficial due to his lightning responses of evasion and counterattack. The incident nonetheless precipitated McCluskey being severely scalded by his instinctive attempt to use a pot of boiling water to drive his armed attacker away. Both men were badly hurt. McCluskey was hospitalized and withheld information of his medical situation from his family until his livid injuries had begun to heal. Staff were by no means sympathetic as the Monaghan man had a long history of prison activism and had been moved to Parkhurst in July 1981 for an alleged assault on a prison officer in Wormwood Scrubs. A combination of reputation, cohesion, alliances, pre-emptive action and promised retaliation minimized orchestrated attacks on the IRA in England in the 1980s.[11]

Irish in Britain Representation Group

The Irish in Britain Representation Group (IBRG) was founded in October 1981 in Nottingham, arising from correspondence carried by the *Irish Democrat* and *Irish Post*. Desmond Greaves, John Martin and others argued that the culturally orientated Federation of Irish Societies (FOIS) had failed to adequately represent its grass roots constituents in the UK. Founding members Gearoid MacGearailt and Pat Reynolds attracted support from the Connolly Association in developing a small but dynamic and politicized body capable of direct advocacy of persons harmed by the PTA, miscarriages of justice, strip-searching and anti-Irish discrimination.[12] The leftist IBRG promoted a 'troops out now' policy which had hitherto divided TOM and declared that the British Government should 'withdraw-immediately and unconditionally-from Ireland (militarily, politically and economically)'.[13] The FOIS, stung by the open criticism and the underlying merit of certain assertions, in 1982 declared that the PTA had 'stifled healthy political comment by the Irish community in Britain'.[14]

Impetus from the hunger strikes spurred the revival of the Manchester Martyrs commemoration in the English city, where the IBRG had an active cadre. Although barred from Moston Cemetery by the Catholic Bishop of Salford, as had occurred in November 1974, the march proceeded to the Fenian Arch near Belle Vue.[15] A similar boost to the Sinn Féin - organized Bloody Sunday commemorations in late January 1982 brought 1,500 pro-republican marchers to the Rag Market in Birmingham when police cited a threat from the National Front to prevent its occurrence in Coventry.[16] The National Front was in precipitous decline from its peak strength in the late 1970s, although it remained organized in many English cities and had numerous adherents within the Prison Service.[17]

The involvement of numerous English-born and long-term Irish migrants in Britain in the IRA frustrated Home Office efforts to draw upon the deportation clauses of the PTA. One of the more prominent prisoners, Jerry Mealy, had survived the protracted hunger strike which had killed Frank Stagg in Wakefield in February 1976.[18] Remission lost for his involvement in the Gartree rooftop protest of July 1978 was restored by court order and Mealy was consequently eligible for release to his Luton home in October 1981. On 29 October 1981 Mealy was taken to Evesham Police Station where he was held overnight before being moved to Redditch. He understood that an Exclusion Order was being sought that would have deported him to Ireland without his Luton family. This did not occur when it was established that his length of residency in England immunized him from the PTA clause. He was instead allowed to return to Luton on 4 November 1981 where he resettled with his English wife and engaged in Irish cultural life.[19]

Another nonconformist, Roy Walsh, remained in almost constant trouble with his various jailers from 1980–81. He had spent much of 1980 in Hull, apart from a month in solitary in Armley, which commenced just before a visit from his wife, two children and sister who had spent £400 travelling to England from Divis Flats, Belfast.[20] The governor of Hull travelled to Manchester on 17 October 1980 to attend a BOV hearing on alleged 'contraband' being discovered; the subsequent discovery of a Parker Pen in his Albany cell on 4 December 1981 resulted in a further twenty-eight day 'lie-down' in Bristol.[21] Supporters believed the real reason for his punishment was because a segment of rope had been found in his possession on the Isle of Wight.[22]

Paddy Hill hunger strike, October 1981

The prospect of achieving justice for the Birmingham Six diminished in 1980–81. In January 1980 Lord Denning, Master of the Rolls, announced that a civil action, which the Birmingham Six wished to press against the West Midlands and Lancashire police, could not proceed. Denning famously commented:

> If the six men win, it will mean that the police were guilty of perjury, that they were guilty of violence and threats, that the confessions were involuntary and were improperly admitted in evidence and that the convictions were erroneous. That would mean the Home Secretary would either have to recommend they be pardoned, or he would have to remit the case to the Court of Appeal. This is such an appalling vista that every sensible person in the land would say 'It cannot be right these actions should go any further'. They should be struck out.[23]

While this was a body blow to Paddy Hill in Long Lartin, the October 1981 decision of the House of Lords to uphold Denning's judgement appeared to be 'the end of the road' in terms of legal routes to justice.[24] It also terminated access to state funding towards legal costs. Brendan Mac Lua, Clare born editor of the *Irish Post* and a Sinn Féin member in his youth, persisted in asserting their innocence.[25] When Denning retired in 1982, Lord Bridge of Harwich was in the running to succeed him as Master of the Rolls until outpaced by Sir John Donaldson. As Justice Bridge in 1975, he had sentenced the innocent Birmingham Six to life terms, a duty he was reputed to have been 'unhappy but not guilty about' following their ultimate vindication. Bridge had entered the legal profession without the platform of university education and gained his first distinction in 1950 'in the chambers of the future Lord Widgery', architect of the 1972 'Bloody Sunday' whitewash which Lord Saville repudiated in 2010.[26] By accident or design, the collective actions of the intimate circle of Widgery, Bridge and Denning between 1972 and 1981 safeguarded Britain from potential international censure. In retrospect, it appeared probable that extraordinary measures were resorted to within the upper echelons of the judiciary of England and Wales to minimize the legal blowback from 'Operation Banner' in Ireland.

Hill was in Albany, following a surprisingly positive short stay in Winson Green, when he decided to take action on 31 October 1981. He had formed a mistaken impression that the rest of the Birmingham Six had agreed to commence a hunger strike if the House of Lords upheld Denning's ruling. Ronnie McCartney advised against using a classic IRA mode of protest which had recently led to ten deaths in the H-Blocks.[27] The pair had met earlier in the year when on punishment 'lie-downs' in Bristol.[28] McCartney told his visiting fiancée Una Caughey that '[IRA] prisoners did their utmost to prevent him [i.e. Hill] going on the H[unger] Strike'.[29] Although the *Irish Post* covered the story on 14 November 1981, its seriousness was not widely apparent. The *Irish Times* reported on 25 November 1981 that Hill was on his thirty-second day without sustenance and had been moved to the hospital wing in Parkhurst six days previously.[30] He was described in a neutral - toned article as 'England's Hunger Striker'.[31] The fast spanned forty-one days and ended when Dr. Cooper convinced Hill he was in fact the only man on what appeared to be a doomed endeavour. This, in the context of supportive communications from Sr. Clarke and the comradely discouragement of IRA prisoners, tipped the balance.[32] If extreme, the gambit attracted international reportage to the irregular case of the 'Birmingham tavern bomber [sic]'.[33] Republican accounts of Hill's protest reasserted that persons jailed for the Guildford, Birmingham and M62 'coach bombing' were entirely innocent.[34]

Hill was moved to Gartree in February 1982 where, believing he had nothing to lose, became more aggressive in defending his interests. Amongst other episodes this entailed Hill using a hammer to smash numerous sewing machines in response to being fined £3 for a minor infraction.[35] Shane Paul O'Doherty, who was then regarded as having moved beyond IRA membership, befriended the desperate Hill in Gartree. O'Doherty encouraged the Belfast man to recommence a letter writing campaign and advised on basic techniques geared to maximize the chances of such communications being taken seriously. Of equal if not greater importance was the introduction O'Doherty provided to the talented solicitor Gareth Pierce, who visited Hill in late 1982.[36] Within two years Hill personally contacted around 120 members of the Commons and Lords, as well as numerous other interested parties. The prodigious legal work of Pierce, and the fundraising assistance provided by Sr. Clarke's Relatives and Friends of the Prisoners Committee, assumed central importance to the campaign for exoneration.[37]

October/ November 1981

On 16 October 1981, pro-republican supporters of Labour Greater London Council (GLC) leader Ken Livingstone protested outside his offices to endorse his 'right to speak out on Ireland'. Although technically unconnected with the much criticised GLC, a *cause célèbre* of British Conservatives, Sinn Féin members living in the capital reassembled the following day outside Brixton prison in the hope of heartening IRA prisoners on remand. They did so once again on 18 October on the perimeter of Wormwood Scrubs in order to emphasise the unresolved question of repatriation of political detainees. In Cambridge University on 19 October, Tomas Mac Anna, Director of the prestigious Irish National Theatre in Abbey Street, Dublin, spoke against a motion which upheld the validity of Westminster's trenchant opposition to 'demands of the hunger strikers'.[38] The British right, as well as sections of the Labour group on the GLC, criticized Livingstone's endorsement of official negotiations with the IRA and INLA. Mac Anna cherished lifelong patriotic sentiments and had participated in Irish Civil Rights Association events in his native country in 1972.[39] Contemporaneous mainstream reportage did not extend to the all - but - invisible Pat Hackett who was alleged to have received 'constant petty harassment' during the month of October when denied permission to see the dentist without donning the detested prison uniform. The Irish man's exercise time was limited by an apparent 'shortage of staff'.[40]

A spate of IRA operations in London forced circumspect discussions of the organization in the Commons on 27 October.[41] Two aspects of the attacks were played down in that the type of devices utilized in England for the first time included a radio-detonated bomb and another fitted with a sensitive anti-handling mechanism. A coach returning soldiers from guard duty in the Tower of London to Chelsea Barracks was bombed at Ebury Bridge on 10 October, killing passing civilians John Breslin and Norah Field. Additional non-military casualties and in excess of twenty members of the First Battalion, Irish Guards and Second Battalion, Scots Guards were wounded.[42] An under-car bomb gravely wounded the Commanding Officer of the Royal Marines, Lieutenant-General Sir Stuart Pringle, the following week.[43] Republican tactics shifted on 26 October when a booby-trapped bomb exploded as Kenneth Howarth of the Metropolitan Police attempted to defuse it at a commercial premise in Oxford Street. Howarth, who had served with distinction in Ireland with the RAOC, received a posthumous George Medal. Numerous other attacks and elaborate hoaxes stretched the police and intelligence forces in the London region to the greatest extent in years.[44] Whitelaw's claim that month that there were sixty-nine IRA prisoners in the Dispersal System was clearly intended to reassure MPs of the success of British counter-measures, although the continuance of the stepped-up campaign against military and political targets into November demonstrated its limitations.[45]

On 13 November 1981 a sizable IRA bomb wrecked the Woodhayes Road property used by Sir Michael Havers in Wimbledon, southwest London. Having reviewed the damage Havers claimed that he would have been killed if not absent in Spain at the time of detonation. Inferences would have been drawn that commercial, political, military and police targets had been attacked in London within a four week span using markedly different bomb schematics. The apparent attempt on the life of prime target Havers fell on the eve of the assassination in Belfast of hardline Ulster Unionist MP Rev. Robert Bradford.[46] Between 14 and 19 November an RUC man was injured in Newry and another died of wounds sustained in Tyrone. Two UDR members were shot dead in Derry and Strabane. During the same period an Orangeman was killed when bravely trying to protect the intended IRA target Rev. Bradford, and two unfortunate Nationalists were shot at random by the UVF in Belfast and Lurgan.[47] The England campaign coincided with a sustained effort by the IRA in the Six Counties to pressurize its perceived enemies. In the Greater London area police teams' trawling of over 251,000 lock-up garages and premises yielded two corpses and quantities of criminally amassed loot, yet nothing connected to the IRA.[48]

Qualified Reform

Indications that the British Government was on the verge of taking important decisions on the rights of prisoners were present from 2 August 1981 when the Home Office announced change was imminent.[49] However, Liberal Peer Lord Avebury maintained public monitoring of England's prisons on 20 October 1981 by highlighting his frustration that a photocopy of *Home Office Instructions, Prisons Standing Orders* obtained in the House of Lords Library had been removed from a sealed package he had posted to a Parkhurst prisoner. On pressing the matter, Avebury was informed that the public had no entitlement to view the directives that supplemented *Prison Rules*. The Home Office explained: 'It contains management instructions as well as prisoners' rights. It is really provided for the use of the governor and his staff'.[50] Avebury consequently issued a complaint to the European Commission for Human Rights claiming that Article 8 (2) of the European Convention had been violated. This unexpected and unusual stance from a member of the upper chamber added a further strand of inquiry to what remained a highly secretive prison operation.

IRA prisoner Pat 'Tipp' Guilfoyle was also in the news in October 1981, arising from his ongoing clashes with the Home Office. Guilfoyle learned that month, when in Wormwood Scrubs, that his father had passed away in Manchester. This followed the fatal injury of his mother in a house fire in the northern English city in November 1977. Permission was granted on that tragic occasion for a brief visit to Widdington Hospital, a very rare circumstance for an IRA prisoner in England. He was not allowed attend the funeral service.[51] In what marked a second untypical concession, Guilfoyle was granted a few hours parole from Wormwood Scrubs four years later to witness his father's interment. He spent the entire time handcuffed to policemen while snipers and guards armed with shotguns ringed the cemetery.[52] Governor John McCarthy had exercised positive discretion in favour of the Irish man, even if the quotient of compassionate consideration was fixed at a bare minimum. His IRA comrades had doubted this would be granted.[53] It may not have been immaterial that the case lodged on behalf of the Tipperary man in Strasbourg was then inching towards a hearing which some commentators predicted would end in 'a defeat for the United Kingdom'.[54] This pertained to a serious assault in Winson Green in November 1974, but other grievances raised formally by Guilfoyle threatened to draw ever-increasing attention to the Prison Department from European courts.

The relatively conciliatory attitude towards Guilfoyle contrasted with the harshness experienced in Wormwood Scrubs by Sean Smyth. He had been moved to London from Albany on applying for a visit from his family.[55] The innocent Belfast man, jailed along with the Maguire family grouping, suffered the tragedy of the death of his son on 11 June 1981. Smyth had not realised his son was gravely ill in hospital until visited by his wife in Wormwood Scrubs, but he was refused permission to travel to Belfast. He was further denied compassionate parole to attend the funeral.[56] Similarly, Brian McLaughlin was in Wakefield in August 1981 when he learned that his mother had died in Ireland. His sister was apprised by the Home Office that parole to attend the funeral might be granted 'if my mother was buried near Wakefield'.[57] Security, if actually deemed a major impediment to temporary releases connected to the deaths of close family, would have been addressed by transfer to the purpose built H-Blocks in Long Kesh, County Antrim. It was standard NIO practice to enable IRA prisoners in Long Kesh and Armagh to attend family funerals. No escape attempts or opportunist attacks on prison staff occurred in an environment containing numerous IRA members and active supporters. Republicans appreciated the importance of respecting such special arrangements and rarely exploited bail conditions when on remand.[58]

A major advance in the rights of prisoners occurred on 1 December 1981 when Standing Order 5 of the rules of the Prison Department liberalized regulations governing correspondence. In a response to a planned question, Whitelaw announced that inmates in England and Wales could now 'correspond with anyone, subject to certain specified objections'. The main restriction was reasonable in that it enabled a Governor to intercept letters concerning 'activities which present a real and serious threat to the security or good order of any prison'.[59] However, prisoners were permitted to 'mention' alleged maltreatment and jail conditions without waiting for the judgement of internal procedures. They were, however, obliged to initiate their complaints within such channels. This reform gave legal and practical effect to the *Golder* judgement reached in February 1975 in the European Court of Human Rights, a matter subsequently pressed in Strasbourg by the solicitors of IRA prisoners held in England.[60] Republicans in Gartree surmised the amendment to the preface of Section 5 of the Prison Standing Order No. 5 was impelled 'under pressure of an imminent ECHR judgement'.[61]

As recently as December 1980 the Court of Appeal under the presidency of Lord Denning had ruled that prison authorities were permitted to read and, if deemed necessary, 'stop letters passing between a prisoner and a solicitor'. The judgement had arisen in relation to Guilfoyle's assertion that as a petitioner to the Human Rights Commission in Strasbourg, his correspondence should pass uncensored out of Albany.[62] From December 1981 prisoners could correspond freely with their solicitors and virtually all others as they saw fit. Whitelaw made no reference to the Strasbourg dimension during his speech and did not reference his previous parliamentary exchange on the matter with the dogged Kilroy-Silk in March 1980.[63] On 25 March 1983 the ECHR ruled unanimously that the UK had not only breached Article 8 in their routine censorship and delaying of prisoners' mail, but had violated Article 13 by denying such writers 'an effective remedy before a national authority'. Namely, the automatic steering of prisoners' complaints to the Board of Visitors was inadequate given restrictions on the panel to impose binding decisions.[64] An even worse record was possible in view of the Prison Department's disinterest in adhering to the European Standard Minimum Rules (ESMR) for prison administration as urged by the Prison and Borstal Governors in December 1981. ESMR required the provision of single cell occupancy and 'adequate' in-cell sanitary facilities, conditions that could not be met in England and Wales due to the dual factors of custodial sentencing culture and available infrastructure.[65]

Repatriation, however, was another matter. Overtures to the Home Office by Minister for Foreign Affairs James Dooge were reported on 10 January 1982 as resulting in a restatement of the British Government's opposition to further transfers of Irish republicans. Approximately eighty-seven persons were concerned, of whom seventy-seven would have potentially qualified for parole if serving their sentences in Irish prisons where more generous remission was standard. Neil Blaney, Independent Fianna Fáil TD for Donegal, had pressed Dooge to seek a resolution and, in the light of the negative response from London, outlined his allegations that Category A republicans were being maltreated.[66] Sr. Clarke had sight of an important statement on the matter sent by Whitelaw to Kilroy-Silk and the Home Secretary was in the news in April 1982 arising from a major statement.[67] *Guardian* journalist David Beresford publicised the story on 2 April 1982 which claimed that 'the government is pursuing an admitted policy of discrimination against some Irish prisoners in Britain by refusing to allow them to serve their sentences in Northern Ireland'.[68] The South African had a strong track record on writing about IRA prisoners and was the only British based correspondent permitted to meet with Bobby Sands in the H-Block the previous year. His account of the 1981 hunger strike, *Ten Men Dead*, was well regarded by republicans who had facilitated his research to the extent of disclosing smuggled 'comms'. Whitelaw's letter spelled out the new reasoning for an established practice of discrimination:

> Where a prisoner has been convicted of a terrorist offence the balance is heavily weighted against transfer .... The movement of people from Ireland to commit terrorist offences is a matter which understandably excites strong feelings and deep concern and the return on a routine basis of those convicted of such offences to Northern Ireland to serve their sentences would justifiably provoke public anxiety ... The return of a terrorist to a prison system where he might be regarded as a hero by a substantial proportion of his fellow inmates might well diminish, and be seen to do so, the deterrent value of the punishment imposed for the offences.[69]

The prospect of an IRA prisoner gaining overt political status by repatriation had been addressed by Merlyn Rees and Roy Mason in 1975–6, but their 'criminalisation'/ 'Ulsterisation' solution had begun to unravel in late 1981 and early 1982 as important concessions were won by the IRA in the H-Blocks. The IRA, moreover, had demonstrably not been defeated. The much vaunted cellular H-Block complex at Long Kesh nullified earlier Home Office claims that overcrowding and security issues in the Six Counties had influenced its position on repatriation. The 'deterrence' factor cited by Whitelaw, however, was a constant and credible position, albeit one that fell within the remit of the judiciary at time of sentencing, rather than the Home Office when in custody of the prisoner. Whitelaw acknowledged that the circumstances of detention in England were part of the state's overall response to the republican threat. The logic of the Home Secretary's 1982 argument was that the IRA prisoners in England were indeed differentiated from criminals and that British national and political interests required the Home Office to disregard its own regulations and guidelines pertaining to the general prison population.[70]

Alastair Logan's analysis of Whitelaw's newly expressed position was significant in view of his centrality to litigation involving Irish republicans in England:

> The Government's attitude was that all applications for transfer to Northern Ireland were not blocked as a matter of policy but would be considered and granted in cases of exceptional hardship or upon exceptional compassionate grounds. Experience showed ... [this] did not apply, for instance, to the terminal illness of a child, wife or other close relative, the death of a close relative, or the fact that relatives were too elderly or infirm to visit from Ireland because of the strains upon them of travelling. Accordingly, questions were asked in the House of Commons

by various MPs designed to establish upon what criteria the Government would exercise its discretion to transfer ... it became clear as a result of a reply given by the Home Secretary in [April] 1982 that it was a policy decision not to permit the transfer to Northern Ireland of anyone convicted of 'terrorist offences'. The articulated reasoning being that if those who felt that they could come across to this country and commit such offences knew that they would not be transferred back to Northern Ireland if arrested and convicted and sentenced to imprisonment they might be less likely to undertake such ventures.[71]

The general state of British prisons was very much in focus in April 1982 when parliamentarians debated the best means to reduce the burgeoning number of sentenced and unsentenced persons in custody. Whitelaw had signalled in May 1981 that around 7,000 could be discharged if short-term prisoners were granted entitlement to parole and other reforms, including the imposition of lesser sentences, were implemented to limit new intakes. This proposal did not survive the rightist posturing of the ensuing Conservative Party Conference. Lord Longford was frank in April 1982 when he told the House of Lords 'it is now generally admitted that the overcrowding of our prisons and the resulting squalor is a disgrace to our civilisation'.[72] Of the 46,000 men held in England and Wales in early 1982, 4,900 were housed three to a cell and 11,000 two to a cell of dimensions the austere Victorian architects deemed suitable for one. Lord Elystan-Morgan claimed that the 'maximum tolerable figure' for incarceration in England and Wales was 'only' 37,000.[73]

Lord Gardiner, the former Lord Chancellor whom the IRA had tried to kill in Belfast in June 1981, was the first to broach the subject of the Irish dimension during the Lords debate.[74] He observed that republican prisoners in Northern Ireland were theoretically eligible for 50 per cent remission of sentence in a jurisdiction where standard parole procedures had been declared unworkable. Generous parole was being considered in Britain as a means to alleviate prison population pressure but this was not countenanced in relation to the IRA prisoners. Gardiner correctly noted in the debate that the *de facto* recognition of political circumstances in the North of Ireland was resented within the long-term criminal prison population in England. He claimed that a prisoner spokesman in a recent barricading protest had queried: 'Why should we be treated worse than you treat IRA prisoners in Northern Ireland?'[75] The *Times* had carried a similar message in May 1981 and PROP in November 1981 had presented a petition from Parkhurst men which specifically requested the 'five demands' drafted by the IRA in Ireland. On 18 January 1982 well co-ordinated work stoppages by prisoners in Albany, Parkhurst, Long Lartin and Hull reiterated the call for 'parity' with the IRA in Long Kesh and Armagh. The most compelling Home Office explanation was that the two penal systems were 'not compatible', although this was undermined by the practice of transferring selected inmates.[76] PROP insisted that prisoners were aggrieved that 'regulations and '"privileges" applying to one category of prisoner in one part of the United Kingdom should not differ from those applied elsewhere ... The Government ties itself in knots over Northern Ireland'.[77]

The Republican Movement in March 1981 authorized filmed interviews with Richard MacCauley and Joe Austin of Sinn Féin in which the optimistic prospect of IRA prisoners in England deriving benefit from a victorious hunger strike campaign in Ireland had been raised. MacCauley expressed scepticism that any such boon would accrue given past crises in the English prisons and ongoing Home Office resistance to the much simpler utilization of repatriation.[78] Yet the legacy of articulating the rights of political prisoners *vis à vis* Long Kesh, Armagh and Crumlin Road proved far more enduring among the ODC population in England than could have been expected. This was necessarily a secondary issue for Sinn Féin in Ireland, as well as its subsidiary in Britain, but one that its strategic allies on the left could and did avidly endorse. Austin, when probed in 1981 on his reputedly negative attitude towards certain British fellow travellers, clarified that 'solidarity' was highly valued among those who did not 'masquerade as the revolutionary left'.[79] He diplomatically did not identify the groupings regarded as exploitative and insincere.

The debate came a matter of weeks after Whitelaw had issued a public and significant statement on the differentiation accorded IRA prisoners by the Home Office.[80] The retention of IRA prisoners in England, if not specifically intended to deter further attacks by their comrades, was nonetheless informed by public sensitivities towards perceived concessions to those convicted. Gardiner's comments in the Lords reaffirmed that a policy had been adopted to address the vested interests of the British state. Such essentially political concerns were entirely logical from London's perspective, if at variance with oft-repeated assertions that no 'special' categories of political prisoners existed in a regime that was ostensibly governed by universal *Prison Rules*. At the very time that IRA prisoners in the H-Blocks were gradually receiving the 'five demands' for which ten republicans had died between 5 May to 20 August 1981, the Home Office and its allies in Britain were disposed to publicly acknowledge an aversion to repatriate those held within the Dispersal System. For all intents and purposes, the belated success of the 1981 hunger strike campaign in Ireland elicited a more transparent discussion of related matters in Britain in 1982.

Comparisons on judicial and penal affairs within the various jurisdictions linked to Westminster were inevitable in 1982 and the longevity of the conflict in Ireland ensured transference of important issues in both directions across the Irish Sea. Viscount Ingleby grasped the nettle of repatriation during the Lords debate. Although first raised in relation to the estimated

350–500 prisoners eligible for exchange, the topic had not been mooted in the Irish context. However, Ingleby asked the Minister if he would

> take a fresh look at the request by IRA prisoners who are in prisons in this country to be transferred to prisons in Northern Ireland so that their families can visit them without long and expensive journeys? Family visits to those who are in prison must be an essential lifeline. I feel that this is something which should not be made difficult without very careful study. It is not only the prisoners themselves but their families who are being penalised. I understand that for this reason British soldiers convicted of offences in Northern Ireland serve their sentences in this country.[81]

Lord Longford supported the remarks in a rare endorsement of the republican viewpoint in the Upper House.[82] Retention of the IRA prisoners, ironically, aggravated the crisis of the Dispersal System. In its report for 1982 the newly appointed Chief Inspector of Prisons, Sir James Hennessy, captioned a section 'Dangerous Prisoners', which primarily concerned the approximately 1,750 people serving life-sentences. This represented a ten-fold increase in real terms since the 1960s. Given that the Irish republican dimension was numerically very small, their disproportionate profile in the first paragraph was significant:

> We visited a number of prisons this year which were holding extremely dangerous prisoners. They came from all kinds of backgrounds. Among the most dangerous (although they are scattered throughout the dispersal prisons) were those convicted of terrorist activity, including the eighty or so convicted in connection with events in Northern Ireland. It is this group that would perhaps pose the greatest risk to society if they were to escape.[83]

Prison Welfare

Sr. Clarke's main welfare role in the early 1980s, within and beyond the RFPC, was to attempt to locate Irish people who 'had disappeared' during visits to England as a result of being seized under the PTA. Most resurfaced after a day or two of being held incommunicado in or near ports of entry. Clara Reilly, a former member of the Association for Legal Justice, aided Fr. Brian Brady and Fr. Denis Faul in tracking such persons once they had been reported missing by relatives in the North of Ireland. Very little media coverage was devoted to allegations of maltreatment of uncharged Irish travellers by British state employees. The same Belfast based group liaised with Sr. Clarke to assist relatives of prisoners held in England during long-planned visits. A small network of mainly Irish migrant families provided accommodation when possible. English liberals also donated transportation services. The visiting families otherwise had to brave the vagaries of seeking bed and breakfast rooms near the predominately rurally located prisons, services which were often illegally denied.[84]

Wrongful imprisonment was a very real concern and an issue raised with increasing frequency in the 1980s. On 1 January 1982 the cover story of the *New Statesman* boldly claimed that Carole Richardson of the Guildford Four was 'spending her eighth New Year in prison – for a crime she didn't commit'.[85] Chris Mullin's article proclaimed the four to be 'innocent'. He noted, amongst many other apposite details, that 'normally IRA prisoners refuse to recognise a British court' whereas Brendan Dowd and Joe O'Connell had taken pains to go on record in order to admit responsibility for the Guildford and Woolwich explosions.[86] Mullin also surveyed the cases of the Maguire family for whom the PTA had functioned in a pernicious manner.[87] The task of overturning years of sensational and untrue reports of the interlinked cases remained considerable. The *Daily Mirror* had described the 'Guildford Four' as 'convicted IRA killers' in October 1977. This was emphasised in an article which revealed that the High Court was deemed an unsafe venue for their appeal leading to the use of the Old Bailey amidst 'the tightest security screen ever imposed on an English court'.[88]

Sr. Sarah Clarke and Theresa Hynes of the RFPC co-authored a letter on the prisoner issue which was widely publicized in the *Irish Times* on 1 March 1982.[89] Section IV of Pope John Paul II's *Familiaris Consortio* encyclical of November 1981 was interpreted by Sr. Clarke as an endorsement of the type of pastoral work on prisoners undertaken by the RFPC. This provided welcome moral support in the midst of interminable wrangling and dispiriting hostility she had encountered when attempting to liaise with prison chaplains.[90] Identified recipients of the private version and its covering note included Cardinal Tomas O Fiaich, Bishop Dermot O'Mahoney and Archbishop Dermot Ryan of Dublin, as well as politicians Brian Lenihan TD and Neil Blaney, MEP. The twin track overture to church and state was no coincidence.[91] O Fiaich remained one of the most overtly political cardinals in modern Irish history and in late 1980 had made clear that the jurisdiction of the Papal Nuncio in Dublin should not be superseded in respect to any part of Ireland by the representative of the Holy See in London.[92] The cardinal was the only member of the Catholic Church upper hierarchy to meet privately with republican leaders in the early 1980s.[93] If arising in part from the stimulus provided by Papal commentary on prisoner's dependents, the central argument of the powerful letter was distinctly temporal. Sr. Clarke and Hynes contrasted the generally impressive concern demonstrated by British authorities for nationals imprisoned overseas with the comparative apathy and disdain of their Irish counterparts. They claimed: 'Irish women … are dragging their children across Ireland and the Irish Sea to the remotest corners of England, at regular intervals, staying a few days in a bed and breakfast to get a half hour or an hour's daily visit under extremely harsh conditions … The long journeys and constant switching of prisons and the varying harshness of visiting conditions are part of the policy of punishing the prisoner further by punishing his innocent family and relatives'.[94] The inevitable severe stress on marriages and family relationships was fore-grounded without exaggeration.

Increased publicity, coupled with the direct support of Cardinal O Fiaich and Fr. Denis Faul, spurred Sr. Clarke to seek to establish a more formal Catholic Church role in assisting the families of prisoners in both England and Ireland. Rev. PJ Byrne, Secretary of the Irish Episcopal Commission for Emigrants, facilitated the inclusion of the Irish Chaplaincy Scheme in London, which was directed by Galwegian Fr. Bobby Gilmore. On 19 April 1982 Rev. Byrne and Fr. Gilmore met Sr. Clarke in Dublin to pledge support. Sr. Clarke was concerned that some republican families would query the change of heart on the part of the Chaplaincy which had formerly been noted for its alleged 'hostility to Irish prisoners'.[95] She briefed Gerry Corr of the Irish Embassy on developments and was optimistic that a 'voluntary ministry' would be formed in Ireland to mirror the work of her circle in England. Sr. Clarke understood the necessity of establishing family support groups on both sides of the Irish Sea and she, more than any other individual, possessed first - hand experience of the issues involved.[96] Fr. Gilmore had served as a Columban missionary in the Phillipines prior to 1979 and readily supported campaigns in aid of persons wrongly convicted in England as well as against the PTA.[97]

Special Category Dáil candidate

While the Republican Movement considered standing Dolours Price, when imprisoned in Brixton and on hunger strike, as an abstentionist candidate in West Belfast in 1974, the less complicated decision was taken to run her republican father, Albert Price, in her stead. He diverted votes from Gerry Fitt and helped establish what became a strong Sinn Féin electorate.[98] In February 1982, however, Joe O'Connell was nominated for the Clare constituency in the Dáil elections despite his presence in Parkhurst. Sinn Féin claimed the Clare man, a native of Kilkee, had 'led the most successful IRA unit ever to operate in Britain' which had carried out 'more than fifty attacks' until key members were arrested in December 1975.[99] He secured a modest vote share on 18 February 1982. Fellow Clare man and London ASU member Harry Duggan regarded the electoral gambit as a political mistake as his comrade had spent too long away from the country to attract significant votes.[100] Sinn Féin, however, had partly viewed the promotion of the H-Block issue as a means to re-engage and expand its potential support base in the Twenty-Six Counties. North Tipperary Sinn Féin organizer Pat O'Donnell recalled the 'titular' participation of individuals who had 'prominent social or political reasons from the past'.[101]

If republicans were manoeuvring to maximise their non-violent propaganda options in February 1982, so too were the penal authorities of the British Establishment. The final decision to dispense with legal proceedings against MUFTI squad personnel who had suppressed the 31 August 1979 Wormwood Scrubs 'sit-down' protest was publicised on 25 February 1982.[102] With uncanny timing, the generally perceptive and progressive *Guardian* published a substantial feature article on 19 February 1982 which praised the penal regime managed by Wakefield Governor Ian Dunbar.[103] This was fortuitous for the Prison Department in that a notoriously harsh facility in England was singled out as being 'the most relaxed and trouble free regime of any' Dispersal System jail. Journalist Melanie Phillips cited the demeanour of the small IRA contingent in order to illustrate the comparatively serene ambiance:

> Mr Ian Dunbar, governor of Wakefield top security prison, lounged against the railings on one side of the prison landings. It was association time, when prisoners leave their cells and mingle with each other. Around him milled some of the most violent and dangerous prisoners in Britain. An IRA bomber complained about his visiting arrangements. These really should be improved, said the young man mildly, considering he had 27 years of his sentence still to run.[104]

No mention was made of the IRA incendiary attacks in Wakefield in June 1979 or the prior ordeal of Frank Stagg and many others in the infamous 'F-Wing'.[105] While Wakefield in February 1982 did indeed contain sixty to seventy Category A prisoners, in contrast to the twenty to thirty in most Dispersal Prisons, the concentration of life - sentenced sex offenders in its long-term population was not addressed. Indeed, Wakefield's 'Rule 43 wing' was the 'national resource for prisoners segregated under Rule 43 at own request'.[106] This was significant in that such detested individuals were by no means as volatile, assertive or cohesive as either the IRA or organized criminals in maximum-security facilities. In reality, the creation of an 'atmosphere' described by one prison officer as 'magnificent' in Wakefield was due in large measure to the outlook of its comparatively moderate governor, unique offender profile and Prison Department strategy.[107]

Owen Carron prison tour, 22–24 February 1982

Owen Carron, elected MP for Fermanagh-South Tyrone on 20 August 1981 in succession to the deceased Bobby Sands, fore-grounded the prisoner issue during his three-day visit to England in February 1982. He had recent personal experience of detention and on 22 January 1982 appeared in court in Buffalo, New York, charged with attempting to illegally enter the US from Canada. Leading Sinn Féin member Danny Morrison was separately detained on the same charges at Niagara Falls. Western and Upstate New York were centres of considerable pro-Irish support, not least in Buffalo, Rochester, Oswego and Albany. The pair were due to address an Irish Northern Aid fundraiser in New York City on 24 January despite the fact that Carron was barred by the State Department from entering the country.[108] Both men were nonetheless bailed. Non-attendance of the invited prominent guests did not prevent the INA from raising $50,000 in the Astoria-Manor Hotel, Queens, New York, news of which was reported in England in the advent of Carron's trail - blazing trip to England.[109]

Returned with a 2,230-vote majority as an 'Anti-H-Block Proxy Political Prisoner', Carron was effectively an abstentionist Sinn Féin MP.[110] Access to the prisons was by no means automatic for any MP who did not take their seat, but the Home Office did not press such technicalities in early 1982. From 22 February 1982 Carron was unimpeded when interviewing IRA prisoners in Leicester, Albany, Parkhurst, Hull and Wakefield.[111] He was greeted on arrival in Birmingham by Eddie Caughey who had devised an itinerary in which he could not fully participate by virtue of being denied security clearance. Although acquitted of the arms offences for which he was arrested with John Higgins in May 1976, Caughey was a past associate of numerous IRA members and remained a leading Sinn Féin activist.[112] He was shocked to learn from information forwarded by Ronnie McCartney and Liam Baker that the then unbalanced Gerry Conlon of the Guildford Four had made 'terrible [unfounded] accusations' about him under severe stress of wrongful imprisonment.[113]

In Leicester Special Security Block Carron met IRA lifer Brendan Dowd who related a blackly comic story of his failed efforts to obtain KRM Short's *The Dynamite War, Irish-American Bombers in Victorian Britain*. Dowd recalled that the Governor stated: "'I can't allow people to take refresher courses in my prison" to which he replied: "What makes you think I've forgotten what's in my head?"'[114] Dowd revelled in his subversion of authority within the Dispersal System and on occasion anonymously distributed bomb schematics through prison libraries. This was contrary to IRA practices but, according to Ronnie McCartney, rationalized as a strategy to 'terrorise them in such a way that they'll have to move us somewhere together'.[115]

Carron was struck by the incongruity of being politely served tea in the presence of two avid staff note-takers when sealed into the compact SSU by 'six electronic doors'. Brian Keenan pointedly did not complain about the claustrophobic conditions in which he lived since June 1980 but encouraged Carron to promote repatriation. He also sent messages to his family in Ireland. Eddie Butler and three other republicans were held in the unit, a high proportion of an expensive small facility. The published report of the visit by Seamus Boyle stressed the prisoners' endorsement of Sinn Féin's greater participation in 'social and economic issues' which they monitored by reading *AP/RN*.[116] On 23 February 1982 Carron and Caughey moved through Southampton to Albany on the Isle of Wight where Tony Clarke, Roy Walsh, James 'Punter' Bennett, Stevie Blake, Jimmy Ashe, Noel Gibson and Ray McLaughlin were IRA Category A prisoners. The innocent Hugh Callaghan of the 'Birmingham Six' was also in the prison. Gibson and Walsh were life sentenced with the remainder of the IRA men due for release and deportation within a few years despite loss of remission. Clarke impressed upon Carron that the situation was replicated in many English jails, lending a degree of urgency to resolving the fraught question of repatriation. Ashe suggested the formation of a dedicated committee, a requirement which had been addressed in part by the revamping of the POW Department.[117]

Much of the general experience of the IRA in English prisons was encapsulated in Albany. Walsh, who had been brutally force-fed in November 1973, suffered from stomach complaints but was initially denied access to the X-ray machines available in nearby Parkhurst. The fate of republican prisoner Sean O'Conaill was recalled, a man deemed to have succumbed to misdiagnosed cancer owing to 'lack of medical attention'. Blake had recently arrived from Hull where he received no visits from his Donegal relatives for over three years: 'Every time he has one arranged he is moved to some other location'. Gibson had not received a visitor for four years and was generally unwilling to expose his family to the trauma and inconvenience entailed. McCartney, shouldering the responsibility of being O/C of the group, had been moved twenty-five times in the first seven years of a life sentence. His warning that 'the men are prepared to take a stand on repatriation' was intended for a wider audience than his distinguished visitor and readers of the republican print media.[118] McCartney noticed that Carron seemed somewhat 'over awed' by the environment and bemused by having to check his legally held handgun into security at Reception.[119]

The Albany 'blanket protest', however, had recently and suddenly ended, resulting in the relocation of four men associated with England's longest joint enterprise of its kind. Liam Baker recalled: 'My bed was lying beside the door. The woman from the Visiting Committee she said: "I think it's time to end it". Next thing, 'bingo': Busty [Cunningham] got shipped out. Tony Cunningham ... Raymond McLaughlin. They were all shipped out. I was the last one. I was sent to Gartree ... When I got to Gartree I met the Governor, which is unusual. He said, "are you going to keep this up? ... This isn't the same as Albany". Says me, "well I don't know that, I won't be wearing any clothes, I'm only wearing them because ye brought me here"'. Sean Kinsella, IRA O/C in Gartree, was given time to discuss the situation with Baker in private and the new arrangement of token cooperation was cemented when the two Category A republicans were permitted to occupy adjacent cells. In retrospect it appeared that the Albany authorities did not wish to perpetuate a protest so firmly associated with political activists into a fourth year and either orchestrated or reacted to timely advice from the Visiting Committee.[120] The resolute Busty Cunningham regarded the incident as an acceptable de-escalation: 'We never won, we never gave in … it was a stalemate'. Other IRA prisoners discerned a moral victory.[121]

In Parkhurst Carron entered the SSU to converse with Joe O'Connell, Harry Duggan and Hugh Doherty who shared the intentionally cramped environs with a Libyan and an Iranian. Duggan confronted staff on their unusually oppressive demeanour on the day and it was claimed that their studied 'work to rule' approach prevented Carron from meeting O'Connell face to face. In the main wings, the slow rate of facilitation ensured that he had only time to see Fr. Pat Fell and Gerry Young. As in Albany, the subtext of prisoner opinion as relayed in *AP/RN* was that contesting elections in the Twenty-Six Counties was not an unwelcome strategy, even if the scale of the challenge and selection of candidates required reflection.[122] In Hull on 24 February 1982 Carron met John McCluskey, Eddie O'Neill, Stevie Nordone, Tony Madigan and Dickie Glenholmes. They expressed concern for Mick Murray who remained in the Punishment Block, maintaining a unilateral four and a half year long 'blanket' protest'.[123] Madigan had known Murray from Birmingham's republican scene but could not convince him to return to the wings, despite inviting punishment in order to make direct contact.[124] This sacrifice was a regular occurrence and the men took turns keeping Murray company. McCluskey ascertained from a shouted conversation that the Dubliner believed he was being drugged, a serious allegation which few Category A prisoners would have discounted. Murray was refused permission to see Carron as it would have entailed donning prison uniform. While the alternative of granting the MP access to the Punishment Block was not acceded, special permission to write to him on 11 August 1982 assuaged Murray. Hull also contained Paddy Maguire senior and Paddy Armstrong, whose innocence was restated by Carron.[125]

The Fermanagh man moved on to Wakefield where Brian McLaughlin of Muldonagh, County Derry, Mick Reilly and Gerry Small were held. All three had been convicted in relation to IRA activities in the English Midlands. Reilly, whose father hailed from Ardoyne, was serving a ten year sentence for possession of incendiaries in Birmingham.[126] In the prison hospital Carron met Paddy Hackett who had been on the 'blanket' since 1 January 1980. He wished to be repatriated to the H-Blocks and advocated a more leftward stance by Sinn Féin.[127] He was instead moved to the Hospital Wing, Parkhurst, on 4 July 1982, just ahead of a planned visit by an Irish Embassy official.[128] The IRA PRO in Hull published a letter of thanks to Carron in the RCG paper *Fight Racism! Fight Imperialism!* which also urged readers to assist his efforts to achieve repatriation.[129] Although underplayed in the Irish national media, Carron's hectic tour represented a rare first - hand inspection of English prison conditions by an elected Irish parliamentarian. Carron, furthermore, as a member of Sinn Féin's Ard Chomairle, was automatically part of the leadership of the Republican Movement. He had met around thirty of the fifty-four sentenced republican prisoners jailed in England and confidently asserted that all requested transfer to prisons in the North of Ireland.[130]

In Gartree Shane Paul O'Doherty was frustrated by the lack of demonstrated diplomatic attention to the repatriation question and other aspects of prisoners' rights. A scheduled visit with the First Secretary of the Irish Embassy in London went ahead in Gartree on 3 March 1982, despite the efforts of staff to 'goad' the Derry man into refusing by insisting on direct observance and additional searches of his clothes and documentation. This consultation yielded no tangible improvements. According to O'Doherty, 'the interest and representations of Dáil Deputies and Irish Euro MPs have never materialized'.[131] He repeated his criticism the following year when his mother was neglected by prison staff on arriving in Evesham to visit him in Long Lartin. In a negative allusion to the abandonment of the beleaguered Six County Nationalists by the Irish Government in August 1969, he correctly predicted that official Irish channels would 'stand idly by', despite Britain signing the European Convention on the Transfer of Sentenced Persons.[132] Ireland was indeed the last European Union member state to ratify the Convention in July 1995.[133]

Gerry Tuite and the Criminal Law Jurisdiction Act

The Special Detective Unit in Ireland scored a coup on 4 March 1982 when Gerry Tuite, the Cavan IRA member who had escaped from Brixton in December 1980, was arrested by Detective Sergeant John Biggins in Dyer Street, Drogheda.[134] His seizure precipitated a series of historic developments when the juryless Special Criminal Court in Dublin invoked previously unused legislation to remand Tuite to Portlaoise on charges arising from offences he was accused of committing in England.[135] This had been envisaged in 1974 during the negotiations which produced the ephemeral Sunningdale Executive.[136] Following an initial court appearance on 6 March, Tuite made legal history on 13 July 1982 when he became the first Irish citizen sentenced in the Twenty-Six Counties for a scheduled offence committed in an overseas jurisdiction.[137] Mainstream American magazine *Newsweek* described the verdict as 'a landmark in Anglo-Irish judicial cooperation' which they imagined 'infuriated the IRA'.[138] The legislative framework for this departure was indeed Section Four of the Criminal Law Jurisdiction Act (1976), which enabled courts of the Republic of Ireland to utilize the Explosive Substances Act of 1883 to convict Tuite of possession of such materials in London between June 1978 and March 1979. Sinn Féin decried the move as 'further collaboration' with Britain on the part of 'the Free State government'.[139] Appalled by the 'increased collaboration' between Dublin and London, Harry Duggan reflected that the prosecution of Tuite was 'one lasting result of Sunningdale'.[140]

Justice Hamilton was undeterred by the fact that English police had failed to recover key items of evidence against Tuite until 26 August 1980 as the finds were regarded as pertaining to the date range presented in the indictment. Sean MacBride SC and Patrick MacEntee SC argued in vain that the defendant should have a jury trial, as would have been the case in England, and that the Special Criminal Court lacked jurisdiction to proceed with two sets of charges, committals and books of evidence.[141] After eleven days of proceedings guided by prosecution counsel Kevin O'Higgins SC, Tuite received ten years imprisonment. A separate charge of conspiracy to cause explosions in England was deferred until 6 October 1982. 'Conspiracy' charges of this nature, however, were not covered by the 1976 legislation and Tuite faced no real prospect of additional consecutive convictions.[142] He could not be tried for escaping from Brixton on the grounds that only jailbreaks which had occurred on the island of Ireland were prosecutable. In handing down the initial conviction, however, Hamilton was obliged to reassert the legitimacy of the juryless Special Criminal Court which, from 1972, had operated at the behest of Government under the aegis of the Offences Against the State Act (1939).[143] The revalidation of the controversial forum was further bolstered by the rejection of Tuite's appeal.[144] British authorities, nonetheless, were impressed at what Northern Secretary James Prior termed the 'remarkable event' in Dublin which occurred in the midst of an Anglo-Irish discord arising from the Irish Government's criticism of London's handling of the Falkland Islands/ Las Malvinas crisis.[145] David Maurice Ellen, Principal Scientific Officer in the 'handwriting and documents' section of the London Metropolitan Police, had given important forensic evidence against Tuite in Green Street, Dublin. Ellen had previously been instrumental in the conviction of Brian Keenan.[146] In all, seventy British based witnesses had appeared in an Irish court where they were not required to convince a jury of any assertion inimical to the defendant.[147]

Utilization of the CJA after a pregnant pause of six years indicated that the Irish authorities were prepared to co-operate more closely than before with Britain's counter-insurgency agenda. Charles Haughey had criticized the draft legislation when it came before the Dáil and was reputed to have 'orchestrated a secret attempt to shelve the act's operation' after Tuite's conviction.[148] Kieran McMorrow, wanted for questioning by British police in connection with fifty-nine bombing incidents in England, was not extradited following arrest on the Cavan/Fermanagh border on 23 March 1977. This would have been a test case for the CJA had the incidents occurred after the legislation was adopted.[149] Fianna Fáil were in power on 22 July 1982 when the IRA killed eleven soldiers in central London. Fine Gael, who won the November 1982 General Election were much less reticent. Garret FitzGerald then specifically referenced the Tuite precedent as an example of 'the vital importance of the extraterritorial legislation' in combating the IRA.[150] Charles Haughey also condemned the London fatalities but remained reluctant to promote what remained a disfavoured option. Only thirteen persons were tried under the CJA in Dublin prior to 1989 despite frequent and public British references to the presence of wanted IRA men in the Twenty-Six Counties.[151]

The CJA proceedings in the Special Criminal Court were deemed to be preferable to tackling the legal and political minefield of extradition. Ireland's Extradition Act (1965), affirmed by the Supreme Court in Dublin, remained a bulwark against the deportation of republican prisoners to UK jurisdictions until 17 March 1984 when INLA leader Dominic McGlinchey was delivered into the hands of the RUC on the border within eighteen hours of arrest in Clare.[152] Sending IRA suspects out of the country to England, however, was rejected as late as December 1988 when, despite the irritation of Thatcher's Conservative Government, their Irish counterparts refused to extradite alleged IRA quartermaster and gunrunner Fr. Paddy Ryan.[153] The Tuite case had proven that evidence amassed by Scotland Yard could achieve prosecution in Ireland, although the British Prime Minister dismissed a suggestion from Irish Attorney-General John Murray that this legal process could apply to Fr. Ryan.[154] Murray justified his refusal to extradite Fr. Ryan on the grounds that the priest could not be assured a fair trial in England and would face 'conspiracy' laws that did not apply in Ireland.[155] This stance obliged British Attorney-General Sir Patrick Mayhew to reconsider the CJA offer.[156]

The momentous potential of the Tuite conviction was not realised in that numerous republicans who had been named by Scotland Yard and other British agencies as having come under suspicion for IRA operations in England were not brought before the courts in Dublin. Whereas the politics of extradition prevented the appearance of IRA suspects in London, the effectively ignored CJA alternative equally failed to accumulate sentenced prisoners in the Twenty-Six Counties. Notwithstanding the special consideration of the Brehon Law Society and other legal structures who provided free and reduced cost services, fighting extradition was expensive and drained much of what had been generated in North America and Australia.[157] The prospect of additional IRA members entering the Dispersal System at the behest of Irish and American courts also commanded propaganda and news coverage which might otherwise had remained dedicated to those already *in situ.*

Fr. Pat Fell

The story of Fr. Pat Fell was revived as newsworthy in April 1982 ahead of his anticipated release on 10 July. The English man had been sentenced to twelve years imprisonment in 1973 for his role in running the IRA in Coventry and his emancipation was delayed by loss of 579 days remission arsing from his participation in the Albany sit-down protest in 1976. Fr. Fell's allegations of improper conduct on the part of the prison authorities were under investigation in Strasbourg in 1982. His British nationality, however, posed an immediate problem for the London government in that it made it impossible to issue an Exclusion Order under the PTA. In the event, the decade - long residency in Donegal of his English father, Harry Fell, disposed the Wolverhampton born priest to migrate to Ireland where he recommenced clerical duties.[158] England based Irish language writer Donal Mac Amhlaigh had in March 1982 written from Northampton proposing that Fr. Fell be given a 'presentation on his release' to acknowledge his 'mental and physical suffering'. Although carried by the *Irish Post* in London, the 'Irish in Britain' addressed by Mac Amhlaigh were far too legally exposed to endorse his suggestion.[159]

Success in the preliminary stages of his Strasbourg cases entailed Fr. Fell's appearance at the court on 20 September 1983 when he and Sean Campbell gave evidence concerning alleged breaches of Articles 6 and 8 of the European Convention on Human Rights. Campbell, following a prison shift from Long Lartin to Bristol, was released and deported on 31 March 1982. In token adherence to *Mountbatten Report* principles, the Tyrone man had been reclassified as Category B on 19 March 1982.[160] A different Home Office section still refused to disclose his prison medical records to George E Baker & Co solicitors.[161] Mary Campbell and her three children abruptly ceased highly stressful three monthly interval visits to various parts of England.[162] Already literally scarred from staff assaults, Sean Campbell suffered a debilitating stroke in Ireland six months later which friends and family attributed to the physical abuse received in Albany in September 1976.[163] He was one of the main speakers at an anti-internment commemoration rally in Coalisland on 8 August 1982 when he 'thanked the crowd on behalf of his comrades still incarcerated in Britain's hell-holes ... and asked them to continue as it served as an inspiration'.[164]

Fermanagh-South Tyrone MP Owen Carron's second visit to the IRA prisoners in England began on 6 April 1982 and continued from where he had left off on 24 February. Once again hosted by Eddie Caughey, Carron was driven 200 miles from Birmingham to Durham where thirty-three women in H-Wing lived in close proximity to 900 male prisoners. The innocent and distraught Anne Maguire was permitted to meet him in a small room used for visiting lawyers. She maintained that Irish prisoners were being denied equal access to 'cumulative' visits with immediate family and that she was only permitted to see her wrongly imprisoned husband Paddy Maguire, then in Wakefield, every three to four months. Carron then met Judith Ward, who complained of a lack of intellectual stimuli within a 'very strict' regime.

This issue was later campaigned for with much success in Durham by IRA prisoners Martina Anderson and Ella O'Dwyer. Ward had been framed for the M62 'coach bombing' in 1974. In April 1982, however, the only IRA women in Durham remained Eileen and Anne Gillespie, who arrived in the prison in February 1975 after ten months in Risley Remand Centre. Carron noted the very close bond between the sisters and their conspicuous use of Irish for cultural affirmation and privacy.[165] They anticipated being released and deported to Ireland in August 1983.[166]

Carron moved south to Gartree on 7 April 1982 where, he mused, the exterior was reminiscent of the perimeter of Long Kesh. Governor Booth met the MP on arrival before the planned consultations took place 'in a small supervised visiting room off the normal large visiting room'. Although not 'closed', meetings with IRA prisoners occurred, as usual, under circumstances that did not apply to the vast majority of Category A men.[167] He met Tipp Guilfoyle, Sean Hayes, Eddie Byrne, Liam Baker, Sean Kinsella and Shane Paul O'Doherty. The presence elsewhere in the prison of Paddy Joe Hill of the 'Birmingham Six' was apparently 'concealed' from Carron by the authorities. Hayes had not received a visitor for five years owing to his refusal to subject his Dublin family to the Special Branch vetting required by the Home Office. He urged an escalation of the conflict in Ireland and England. Baker's situation had marginally improved in Gartree as he had spent four years in solitary, mostly 'on the blanket', in Albany.[168] IRA O/C Kinsella made a suggestion which, following dissemination in *AP/RN*, assumed the function of political kite-flying: 'He thought there was ambiguity on the political involvement of the Republican Movement and that the leadership would have to make a decision on the policy of abstentionism'.[169] This significant comment provided a glimpse of the type of unrestricted discussion taking place among the imprisoned IRA cohort in England, a direct parallel to the H-Blocks and Portlaoise but in a much less stratified environment. The 'individual campaign' of O'Doherty was equally untypical and, if not fully endorsed by the IRA leadership, was not in any way opposed. Carron noted that the Derry man had succeeded in getting his claim for repatriation considered in Strasbourg and undertook to provide him with the addresses of specific politicians.[170]

Carron travelled sixty miles from Gartree to Long Lartin where he hoped to meet Gerry Cunningham, Busty Cunningham, Liam McLarnon, James 'Spotter' Murphy, Paul Holmes, Andy Mulryan, Paddy Mulryan, Peter Toal, Tony Cunningham, Martin Brady, Con McFadden and wrongly convicted prisoners Johnny Walker, Gerry Hunter and Gerry Conlon. The size of the republican grouping and visiting arrangements ensured that not all were seen. The plight of the three innocent men was raised by Holmes, an issue which, in the light of Lord Denning's ruling, remained one of sensitivity. Carron personally ascertained that Hunter was hopeful that a re-examination of forensic evidence would lead to exoneration and in April 1982 understood that Patrick Mayhew, Minister for State at the Home Office and future Secretary of State for the North of Ireland, was engaged. Gerry Conlon claimed that his wish to see the Irish MP had been impeded, an allegation which lent credence to the belated realisation that Paddy Joe Hill's presence in Long Lartin had been deliberately obscured.[171] Repatriation, however, was the main point of consensus. Gerry Cunningham outlined his letter - writing campaign on the subject and stressed that it was being sought 'for political not humanitarian reasons'.[172] This perspective was reinforced on 7 April 1982 when Carron arrived into D Wing of Wormwood Scrubs in London. Billy Armstrong and Paul Norney, both described as 'determined', echoed what Cunningham had told Carron.[173] Armstrong, shortly afterwards moved to Parkhurst, impressed on Carron that he was 'not to be considered under compassionate grounds' and that the IRA men demanded their right 'to go home as POWs'.[174] The MP was accompanied to the wing and during the visits by Assistant Governor Deane, who must have observed the sense of unanimity and purpose among the Irish contingent who additionally numbered Kevin Dunphy and the innocent Billy Power, Paul Hill, Sean Smyth and Dick McIlkenny.[175]

Smyth remained highly aggrieved by the refusal of parole in June 1981 to attend his son's funeral in Belfast, a circumstance unlikely to have occurred in Long Kesh. Denied access to Mass and restricted in terms of exercise time, Smyth was permitted just one inter-jail visit in six years to Durham to see his sister, Anne Maguire.[176] He was not, however, 'ghosted' as was common for actual IRA members. Conditions in Wormwood Scrubs were deteriorating and reductions in exercise time, attributed to staffing shortages, convinced prisoners that it was turning into 'a punishment nick'.[177] Coughlan raised the fact that Norney had been beaten up by staff in every prison he had been held in and made the deliberately ambiguous comment that 'sooner or later someone will get killed if something isn't done'.[178] The final leg of the inspection tour brought Carron and Caughey to Maidstone, which, as a Category B institution, had a less rigorous regime. Sole republican prisoner Gerry Mac Lochlainn overcame initial resistance to participate in full - time education.[179] His wish to pursue a degree in philosophy was supported by many Kent University students but fuelled the wrath of the *Sun* tabloid. The Press Council censured the hazardous allegation that the Derry man was 'one of the most important Provisional IRA organisers in Britain' the following year.[180] Mac Lochlainn had not been charged with IRA membership although the substance of the claim regarding political prominence was warranted in relation to Sinn Féin in England and Wales, which remained a legal entity.

The tour reconfirmed that the Irish prisoners wanted to be located closer to their families, some of whom were married to women who had visited them under much less taxing circumstances when interned in Long Kesh. Armstrong's case was raised in *AP/RN* later that year when the added costs of travel to Parkhurst and the 'awkward geographical position' of the Isle of Wight inhibited relatives from visiting.[181] Comfort was taken from compensatory news from the English prisons: Mary Walsh was reassured that Roy Walsh was 'in with some other Belfast ones' in Albany. Martin Coughlan's mother understood her son was 'always in trouble, but he's popular' in Hull.[182]

Those who intermittently assembled outside Durham were oblivious to an unreported 'battle of wills' between staff and the Gillespie sisters on H-Wing during the summer. Nationalist fervour sparked by the uneven British campaign in the Falklands in May/ June 1982 evidently inspired staff to withhold food from the two republican women. Rather than request dinner, the duo went for seventeen days without being fed, claiming that they were 'not hungry' when they knew all food had been previously distributed. Successes of the Argentinean Air Force and Navy against the Royal Navy in the South Atlantic enabled the sisters to get their 'digs in' when watching censored TV coverage. They recalled at such times the 'terrible things' said by staff and prisoners in relation to the 1981 hunger strikers. Major IRA operations were also tension filled occasions: '[You] put on your shields and face them, you knew the minute you heard the news that there was going to be a backlash ... You had to stick it out and make the best of it'.[183] The dire standard of medical care threatening the health of all women in H-Wing took a sinister turn when it transpired that a female doctor was plotting to contaminate the water supply consumed by the sisters. This was pre-empted by IRA prisoners held elsewhere in the complex who arranged for outside contacts to convey a strong warning to her LSD - producing boyfriend.[184] Overt acts of solidarity, however, were more common. TOM gained publicity on 10–11 July 1982 when they picketed Durham, Wakefield, Hull, Wormwood Scrubs, Leicester, Brixton, Maidstone, Albany and Parkhurst as part of a campaign to press the Government to relent on repatriation. An estimated seventy-four republican prisoners were being denied permission to serve their sentences in Ireland.[185] Delegations of TOM marched the following month in Belfast during the annual Anti-Internment rally in early August.[186]

Official British statistics claimed that English prisons housed 'about 80 prisoners ... for terrorist type offences connected with the troubles' in July 1982.[187] Although specifics were deliberately withheld, it was claimed in February 1981 that 111 people had been 'arrested and charged with terrorist activities' since March 1973. It was then claimed that there was 'no breakdown by Scotland Yard or the Home Office of how many were Irish terrorists or how many were imprisoned'.[188] The contrast with the treatment of Irish men and others convicted of criminal offences was extreme. In June/July 1982 Birmingham-Irish man Martin Foran spent forty-seven days on the roof of Nottingham Prison to protest what he insisted was a wrongful conviction for armed robbery. On 11 July he watched as six men, one of whom had been convicted of murder, scaled the low security prison and escaped over the wall from unlocked huts in the compound.[189] In correspondence with the Irish Embassy and the FCO in 1977, Valerie Foran alleged that 'her husband is being unfairly treated because he is Irish and that certain prison officers had stated that Mr. Foran was a member of the IRA'.[190] Proven membership of the IRA, even for those not convicted of political offences, was deemed to have bearing on a man's eligibility for parole, particularly if there was 'evidence on his prison record to connect him with that organization'.[191]

Three actual former Midlands IRA activists, Tony Madigan, Brian McLaughlin and Eddie Byrne, attempted to reintegrate into society in the summer of 1982. Madigan, who in May 1975 received a ten-year sentence for conspiracy to cause explosions, was released from Hull on 8 June 1982. He had just completed an Open University degree, which had been facilitated by the Governor in Albany where he had spent most of 1978 to 1981. Madigan spent four days in the Punishment Block of Hull prior to release where he parted ways with Mick Murray. Sr. Clarke learned that on exiting prison Madigan was 'given the statutory £23 in silver rather than [pound] coins'.[192] Born into a Galway family in Birmingham, Madigan could not be excluded under the PTA. This enabled him to visit Sr. Clarke on London on 3 July 1982 and pursue postgraduate studies at North London Polytechnic. He was heavily if discretely involved in the campaign to prevent National Front organizer Pat Harrington from gaining influence in a predominately left-leaning institution.[193] Brian McLaughlin was released from Wakefield on 7 July 1982 having served seven of the ten years imposed in 1974 for bombing offences. He had spent time in all seven 'Dispersal' prisons and six 'local' prisons, including Winson Green, Liverpool and Bristol on Rule 43 imposed twenty-eight day 'lie-downs' in solitary. Special Branch detectives informed him on 5 July that he was being deported to the Six Counties and faced a £1,000 fine and five years imprisonment if he returned to Britain. Armed plainclothes police met him at the gates of Wakefield and drove him to Leeds Airport for a Belfast bound flight.[194]

Another former member of the Midlands IRA, Eddie Byrne, addressed a lengthy letter to republican supporters on 25 July 1982 refuting Home Office claims that his 'ghosting' on seventeen occasions since February 1975 had only occurred when 'absolutely necessary'. He argued that if security emergencies pertained, the near impregnable Segregation Blocks of the same prisons would have sufficed, as was routine in the H-Blocks of Long Kesh. Byrne recalled: 'On the occasion of each of these seventeen transfers I would awake one morning during pre-dawn hours to find several staff surrounding my bed. My thoughts in those first moments of opening my eyes were many and often totally irrational; horror, fear, disbelief, sometimes even that gut feeling of terror ... worst of all your naked vulnerability'.[195] Byrne confided that his 'psychological state' provided 'ample poof that a policy of disorientation has and continues to be pursued' against his best interest. He had declined unfamiliar medication since 1977 when given an unknown drug which caused intense mental and physical discomfort. In July 1982 he remained adamant that the authorities aimed to 'force political prisoners to accept psychiatric drugs'. This was denied by the Home Office. His parting comment, however, revealed deep-seated anxiety: 'If I am forcibly committed to a mental institution, I want you to know that the British motivation is political'.[196] Byrne's admission of psychological trauma put a personal name, if not a human face, on consistent IRA claims of maltreatment.[197]

Hyde Park bombing, 22 July 1982

The 22 July 1982 car bomb planted by the IRA on South Carriage Drive, Hyde Park, fatally injured four mounted members of The Blues and Royals on their way to Horse Guards Parade Ground. A second attack later that day in Regents Park mortally wounded seven members of the band of the 1 Royal Green Jackets, a unit which had lost four men in Camlough, Armagh, in May 1981.[198] Crossmaglen republican Danny McNamee was wrongly convicted of taking part in the radio-controlled London bombings in October 1987, but the verdict was quashed on appeal in December 1998. In the interim McNamee briefly escaped with IRA prisoners from Whitemoor Special Unit in September 1994.[199] The July 1982 attacks received heavy international reportage and re-established the lethality of the IRA's England activities. *The Washington Post* and *Newsweek* both noted the alleged significance of Tuite's conviction and the presence of Northern Secretary James Prior in the American capital on a dual mission to deter support for the IRA and to encourage investment.[200] The fact that all the fatalities were military personnel belonging to regiments with extensive experience in the Six Counties was distinctly underreported.[201] British authorities ascertained similarities with techniques of the South Armagh IRA and the Special Branch mounted 'Operation Find' to locate those responsible.[202]

The Hyde Park bombing was described as an 'IRA Massacre' in the *Daily Mirror* headline of 21 July 1982. London-Irish man Patrick Maguire junior, the youngest of the innocent 'Maguire Seven', was perturbed by the double bombings which occurred within earshot of his flat. He braced himself for an aggressive visit from the Bomb Squad which, to his surprise, did not materialize. A chance visit from a police burglary unit, however, led to the discovery of a number of bullets he had purchased at a local market in contravention of the Firearms Prohibition License.[203] Speculation regarding the timing of the attacks extended to a theory that they were in 'reprisal' for the conviction in Dublin of Gerry Tuite and intended to undermine the visit of Northern Secretary James Prior to the US.[204] The CPGB, WRP and SWP all described the bombings as counter-productive and ill-conceived, much to the irritation of the RCG, who endorsed the IRA tactics.[205]

The renewed deadliness of the IRA campaign did nothing to lessen the challenges endured by its adherents in the Dispersal System. Noel Gibson's mother travelled from Laois to Wormwood Scrubs, London, to see him in August 1982 when in rapid decline from terminal cancer. They had not met for four years due to Gibson's refusal to accept 'closed' visits. Opportunities were further lessened by his frequent incarceration in punishment blocks for his constant defiance of staff authority. Moved to London from Parkhust in June 1982, he mounted a twelve-hour rooftop protest to highlight what he regarded as unacceptable visiting conditions. This resulted in sixty days solitary confinement. In late July his wife and daughter visited for the first time in four years, an experienced which encouraged him to see his mother.[206] He recalled: 'There was no distinction made between a prisoner and relatives. They were seen as one group and treated with great hostility ... You were worried about their safety. There was also never guarantee that you would be there when they arrived. I was ghosted to other prisons several times when I had visits organised'.[207] With Sr. Sarah Clarke's assistance Mrs Lily Gibson arrived at Wormwood Scrubs only to be refused entry. Her son had not been apprised of her state of health and rejected the restrictive arrangements for their mooted reunion. The Irish Embassy was contacted at Sr. Clarke's behest and short visits of twenty-five minutes duration were arranged for the two successive days even though the contested glass partition remained. This situation increased Gibson's militancy and he was greatly aggrieved when his mother passed away in Laois on 23 October 1982.[208] Sr. Clarke learned he 'punched a Governor in face and got 61 days in solitary ... He was angry at the way they treated his mother when she visited before she died'.[209]

Republicans were aware that Mick Murray, one of the long term 'blanket' protesters held in a succession of punishment blocks, had not seen his wife or six children in five years.[210] Damian O'Rourke wrote an emotionally charged feature on Pat Hackett in the 19 August 1982 edition of *AP/RN*, which served to remind people that some IRA prisoners remained 'on the blanket' despite the improvement of conditions in the H-Blocks. In October 1980 Minister of Foreign Affairs Brian Lenihan, a man of constitutional republican sympathies, had inadvertently agreed to look into Hackett's predicament in the H-Blocks at a time when he was languishing in Wormwood Scrubs. Neil Blaney and Frank Maguire had earlier encouraged Hackett's family, sister Bridget and mother Bridie, to persevere in a private campaign. Bridget Hackett was visited in Shannon, County Clare, by Sinn Féin's Sile Darragh in advance of the *AP/RN* piece.

Former Armagh Goal IRA prisoner Darragh advised: 'If Sinn Féin are seen to head such a campaign [for repatriation] the results would be negative ... let the campaign be seen to be organised by the relatives, Sinn Féin could work away in the background'.[211]

The Irish embassy in London were eventually persuaded of the merits of sending an official into Wakefield but by the time this was arranged Pat Hackett was moved to better conditions of confinement in Parkhurst. In late July 1982 Mrs Bridie Hackett travelled to the Isle of Wight from Nenagh, Tipperary, to see her son and found he was permitted three hours exercise a day in the prison garden, albeit from the grim Hospital Wing:[212]

> He gets no medical treatment there. They stuff him with tablets and he told me he is afraid they are trying to turn him into a dope [addict]. He is being detained with severely mentally-ill patients ... He told me that the doctor in Wakefield had once advised him to go on hunger strike as he would make a lovely corpse ... He is determined not to give up his blanket protest until his demands are met. He wants only to be treated like a human being. He will not wear a prison uniform because he is no criminal. He wants repatriation to his own country for himself and all other republicans POWs.[213]

If governed by a less structured regime than generally enjoyed by Category A prisoners in the Dispersal System, Parkhurst's Hospital Wing was a notoriously unpredictable and violent environment. In the months preceding the visit of his mother and sister Michelle in late July, Pat Hackett heard 'terrible screaming and shouting' from a prisoner enduring physical assault. On banging his chair against the cell wall to raise the alarm, Hackett was removed by staff to spend the night in a cell with a 'filthy mattress'. He learned two days later that the person he had endeavoured to assist was deceased. Hackett was held close to the hated 'Yorkshire Ripper' Peter Sutcliffe, whose offences against women resulted in a series of attacks by other prisoners, including James 'JC' Costello. Danger was omnipresent and IRA lifer Paul Holmes, who had been slashed by a deranged Turkish prisoner, was one of the few permitted to visit Hackett in the Hospital Wing.[214] Generally, Hackett found the staff 'helpful and courteous' in comparison with those he had encountered in Wakefield and Wormwood Scrubs.[215]

Bridget Hackett, meanwhile, had been invited by Seamus Brady to a meeting in Iveagh House, Dublin, with an official of the Department of Anglo-Irish Affairs. Brady, former editor of the pro-republican *Voice of the North* newsletter and a close friend of Neil Blaney, was firmly in the 'green' Fianna Fáil camp.[216] They met on 28 July despite the unexplained non-appearance at the Heuston Station rendezvous of another invitee, Eamonn O'Doherty, whom Brady wrongly feared had been arrested. In Iveagh House Mr King of the DFA confirmed his familiarity with the Hackett case and revealed he had received correspondence on the matter from Clive Soley MP. King informed Bridget Hackett that negotiations on repatriating her brother were complicated by 'Mrs Thatcher's victory in the Falklands – she hasn't come back down to earth yet'. Although treated 'with some respect' by the Home Office, he claimed that the Irish Embassy found 'at present talks with them were very difficult'.[217] This was an understatement. The Falklands/Las Malvinas conflict strained Anglo-Irish relations due to the strong and overt line taken by Taoiseach Haughey for a negotiated settlement, a viewpoint which obliged Britain to use its veto to uphold foreign policy objectives on the United Nations Security Council. Britain's ambassador in Dublin, Sir Leonard Figg, reported to London in July 1982 that 'As with the [1981] hunger strike, the Falklands issue touched raw nerves in Ireland and reminded us yet again of the virulence in some quarters of anti-British feeling'.[218] World War Two RAF veteran Figg, appointed in 1980 by senior Intelligence figure Lord Carrington, lost faith in Haughey as a possible ally for improved Dublin/London diplomatic connections.[219]

On 5 August 1982, four days ahead of a planned visit to Parkhurst by a London embassy official, Bridget Hackett reported a significant aspect of the Dublin briefing to Sr. Clarke. She claimed King had stated: 'Agreement had been reached among all the members of the European Parliament, including Britain, that prisoners be sent back to their own respective countries to serve their prison sentences there. However, in her agreement to this, Britain has added the stipulation that this would not apply to political prisoners'. Brady added that the advancement of the legislation, assiduously promoted by Blaney, was anticipated in October/November 1982 and that the 'battle would continue for the return of the Irish [political] prisoners and would probably take another year or two'. In private, Brady informed Hackett that King had limited scope for manoeuvre, as 'the politicians don't want to know'.[220] A proposal to engage Charles Haughey and Minister for Social Welfare Dr. Michael Woods in a bid to extend subvention of travel to families with prisoners in England did not bear fruit.[221]

The gradual trend towards political hegemony in the European Economic Community brought increased co-operation between Irish and British MEPs on matters of mutual interest. As predicted, Neil Blaney MEP achieved a personal victory in September 1982 when he succeeded in massing the necessary twenty-one signatures required to table an emergency debate in the European Parliament on the issue of prisoner repatriation. The family dimension was stressed in a motion which claimed 'with regret that numbers of Irish Republican prisoners are serving long sentences in jails in Britain and are not permitted to opt for transfer to prisons near their homes'.[222] Backing was received from numerous British Labour MEPs, including ex-Cabinet Minister Barbara Castle, Alf Lomas, Richard Balfe and Roland Boyes.[223] The Department of Justice in Dublin, meanwhile, made

Blaney aware in the midst of his initiative that the government was moving towards tackling the same question by means of the draft Convention of the Council of Europe under discussion in late October. Ireland and Britain, as Council members, were part of a process that would permit convicted persons to serve their sentences in their own country if tried abroad. It was envisaged that member states would sign the Convention and potentially resolve a controversy that had periodically unbalanced Anglo-Irish relations since 1969.[224]

Brent East Labour MP Reg Freeson reaffirmed his agreement in a letter to William Whitelaw which sought the extension of the nominally 'standard practice' of repatriation to fifty-four Irish prisoners.[225] The Irish Government, however, proved remarkably reluctant to implement the Convention and ultimately lagged years behind Britain. The disjunction between two countries sharing an open yet partly militarized border complicated the process of transferring prisoners into the Twenty-Six Counties.[226] Councillor Liam Bradley questioned Northern Secretary James Prior on the issue in the course of the MP's surprise visit to Derry on 10 November 1982. When challenged to explain the marked imbalance in transfers of British military personnel convicted in Ireland and republicans jailed in England, Prior differentiated the two elements on the basis that the soldiers had been 'sent' whereas the IRA had gone abroad voluntarily. This ingenious excuse had a rational basis but did not accord with the official version of decision making on the matter coming from the Home Office and NIO.[227] The British Government was less likely to face public political questioning from Dublin following the 25 November 1982 General Election in Ireland, which returned Garret Fitzgerald's Fine Gael party to power in coalition with Labour's Dick Spring.[228]

In Albany IRA prisoners had joined with Britons around 1 September 1982 in the dumping of food, plates and utensils to protest the poor quality of fare. Republican sources alleged that whereas the non-politicals were essentially unpunished, the IRA men received twenty-eight day 'lie-downs'. Tony Clarke and Ronnie McCartney were sent to punishment cells in Durham for a particularly stringent routine of twenty-three hour lockdown. McCartney, who had functioned as O/C in Albany, was moved on to Hull when the period expired. This comprised his twenty-fifth prison move since conviction in May 1976. In defiant mood he proclaimed: 'I am a Republican 24 hours a day and even if I come out in a box they will never break me'.[229] By early December 1982 the IRA contingent in Albany was restored to consist of Punter Bennett, Stevie Blake, Tony Clarke, Joe Duffy, Ronnie McCartney, Ray McLaughlin and Roy Walsh.[230]

The importance of disseminating news of the Dispersal System in the US was not lost on Eddie Byrne in Parkhurst who corresponded with American supporters arising from a letter - writing campaign encouraged by the INA organ *Irish People*. 'NORAID' collected funds on behalf of republican dependents and was involved in a wide range of solidarity work in America.[231] Another England based IRA prisoner, Brendan Dowd, wrote from Leicester on 4 December 1982: 'I received letters and cards from many wonderful people in the USA especially from around N[ew] Y[ork]. I apologize to all of them because it is not possible for me to write to each of them. I hope they will understand … pass my greetings and apology to our friends in the USA'.[232] Paul Norney, writing from Albany, drew on his harsh personal experiences in England when responding to a correspondent linked to the main INA forum. He attributed the massive sentence imposed on him and the denial of compassionate parole to attend the funerals of his parents as symptomatic of 'Britain's hatred of those who rebel against them for what is rightfully theirs'.[233] The December 1981 easing of letter writing restrictions greatly augmented the distinctive contributions of IRA personnel.[234] A further impetus to letter writing occurred in December 1983 when the strong Ancient Order of Hibernians organization in Bergen County, New Jersey, commenced a humanitarian project 'directed to the Irish prisoners in British and Irish jails'.[235] The extensive and national AOH, whose affiliated Hibernian Rifles had taken part in the 1916 Rising in Dublin, possessed significant influence in the running of several major St. Patrick Day parades where IRA prisoners were honoured in the 1980s.

Republicans in various jails corresponded with each other to exchange news of local conditions, mutual acquaintances and political viewpoints.[236] It was also permissible for Category A men to send letters to those denied Special Branch or Home Office clearance to visit in person. West London Sinn Féin activist Jim McDonald, when rejected by the Home Office as an authorized visitor to Gerry Cunningham in Long Lartin, was expressly informed by the Governor in November 1983 that he could 'write letters to him at the above address'. A mutual friend, Jim Treanor, who also knew Cunningham prior to his arrest for IRA activities, was permitted into the prison.[237] Cunningham, Con McFadden and John McCluskey all kept in close postal contact on Sinn Féin affairs with McDonald, whom all three had known when at liberty in London. McFadden was obliged to apologize for not sending a Christmas card in 1983 when Wakefield staff limited him to a total of twenty needed for family purposes. McFadden suspected that many of the letters he posted had 'gone astray'.[238]

Published Christmas greetings in republican prints were dedicated to numerous IRA prisoners in December 1982 in three classic formats: short messages from immediate family, notices to groups of men being held together and notices to those who hailed from the same locality. John McCluskey in Hull was recognized by the Republican Movement in Fermanagh along with Seamus McElwain and Jim Lynagh, held in Long Kesh and Portlaoise respectively. McElwain and Lynagh rejoined the IRA when free to do so and were separately killed by British Special Forces in April/May 1987.[239] Waterford Sinn Féin similarly listed Kevin Dunphy in Wormwood Scrubs and life - sentenced Eamon Nolan in Portloaise. Both had connections with the city and county. The Sheils family of Moross, Donegal, who were deeply involved in prisoner support activity, remembered Hugh Doherty and Con McFadden, arising from shared links with Ireland's northernmost county. Chrissie Keenan, acquitted of political offences in London in 1981, expressed regret that she could not spend time with husband Brian Keenan in Leicester SSU. The Terence MacSwiney Cumman of Sinn Féin, West London, greeted former associates Busty and Gerry Cunningham, Eddie O'Neill and Con McFadden, who had been jailed with the 'Uxbridge Eight' in March 1975. In the detailed listings of *AP/RN*, Volunteers imprisoned in England were fully integrated into the world of republican prison losses and accorded annual recognition in consequence.[240]

IRA numbers in the Dispersal System in early December 1982 amounted to two women in Durham and forty-six men in ten locations. Other than the anomalous and reduced four year sentence imposed on Maidstone prisoner Gerry Mac Lochlainn, terms included sixteen of 'life', a factor guaranteed to keep the England situation in the endgame of conflict resolution. Due to a combination of multiple and consecutive sentences, as well as important acquittals, Brian Keenan in the Leicester SSU possessed a twenty-one year sentence. Ten other IRA men were serving twenty years, one had sixteen years, two had fifteen years, seven had fourteen years and five received terms of twelve years. Kevin Dunphy in Wormwood Scrubs received a unique twelve year, six months sentence, while four men were serving ten-year terms. The spatial distribution pattern managed by the Prison Department ensured that ten were in Long Lartin, nine in Parkhurst (including the SSU) and eight in Albany. Six men were in Hull and just four in Gartree, a temporarily low complement. Three men were in the Leicester 'submarine' SSU and a further three in D Wing, Wormwood Scrubs. One man in Maidstone and two women in Durham's H-Wing were unusually isolated, as was Gerry Small, the solitary IRA prisoner in Wakefield.[241]

The difficult situation regarding prison visits was raised in a feature article in the Christmas issue of *AP/RN*. Patsy Armstrong of Moyard, Belfast, told a journalist: 'I've more or less got used to him not being here, even at Christmas time ... It was much harder when the [five] children were very young. I was trying to get over before now but it would be far too expensive'.[242] Billy Armstrong was then in Parkhurst, close to Albany where Roy Walsh, another of the 'Belfast Ten', was being held. Mary Walsh and her three children were equally disadvantaged in terms of travel to the distant Isle of Wight. Stevie Nordone had visited her son Paul Nordone in Hull on 14 December 1982 for the first time since 5 December 1979. The trip from Dundalk to the north of England was expensive for families with average or low incomes. It was also highly inconvenient. Mrs Nordone quipped: 'If he was in Long Kesh ... sure, you'd cycle up'. He and many others were adamant to minimize the sense of pressure within families to brave costly travel, hostile reception, strip-searching and oppressive visiting conditions.[243]

Mary McLaughlin, whose husband Ray was held in fourteen jails in twelve years from 1974, experienced moderately better visiting conditions after 1978 when glass partitions were emplaced with less frequency: 'I was actually shaking when I got my first visit where I was able to sit beside him. For four years I hadn't touched this person and now I could hold his hand and embrace him. Although there was always two screws sitting just yards away. It was hard to have everyday conversations ... They would interrupt your conversation if they didn't like what you were talking about'. She knew staff were capable of extreme acts, having seen her husband in the aftermath of severe beatings in Winson Green where he had spent eighteen months on remand. Ray McLaughlin had insisted that she refuse visits if threatened with strip-searching. At other times, she arrived to find he had been moved that morning:

> It was not unusual to get up early in the morning to leave for your visit. You would have yourself all built up for it. Of course you were also looking forward to the visit but on arrival to the gaol you would have been told Raymond was moved. I would have felt so let down and there was nothing you could do about it. You had travelled for miles for nothing. I would have gone home emotionally drained. You had to just pick yourself up and get organized to go visit whatever gaol Raymond was in the following week.[244]

NOTES

1. Moshesh, *FRFI*, January 1989, p. 8.
2. *Irish Post*, 17 October 1981. Charlie Bronson was in Parkhurst when McGee was killed: 'McGhee copped it in the back with a 7in chib in the dinner queue. As he lay dead on the floor, cons just stepped over him as if he was a bag of spuds. Nobody sees anything in Parkhurst'. Bronson, *Good prison guide*, p. 105.
3. Paddy Joe Hill, University of Limerick, 18 March 2014.
4. Vincent Donnelly, 27 July 2006 and Eddie O'Neill, 19 July 2007.
5. John McCluskey, 3 August 2007.
6. *Guardian*, 17 February 1982.
7. Bronson, *Good prison guide*, p. 105.
8. Information of Paddy Joe Hill, University of Limerick, 18 March 2014.
9. Liam Baker, 3 March 2008.
10. John McCluskey, 3 August 2007.
11. Sr. Clarke, 'John McCluskey', Clarke Papers (COFLA).
12. Herbert, *Wearing of the green*, p. 177. See 'The Irish in Britain must organize', *Irish Democrat*, September 1981, p. 1.
13. IBRG 'Northern Ireland' Policy Statement, Issued from IBRG 'Northern Ireland' Policy Conference held on Saturday 20th September 1986 in Birmingham, England (1986). The IBRG, headed in 1983 by John Martin (President) and Jim King (Chairman), backed an immediate British military withdrawal from Ireland.

14. Cited in Sean Sorohan, *Irish London during the Troubles* (Dublin, 2012), p. 81.
15. *AP/RN*, 3 December 1981.
16. *AP/RN*, 4 February 1982.
17. Brian Baldwin, a senior prison officer in Manchester, was National Education Officer and Northern Organizer of the British National Party (BNP). He had previously been a member of the National Front (NF) and other far-right organizations. Baldwin claimed that over seventy of the 300 officers at Strangeways were NF members. Other prisons with significant cadres included Walton, Wakefield and Risley Remand Centre. The wearing of NF tiepins and badges was not deemed to contravene uniform codes as was commonly noted by Irish prisoners. Some affected a militaristic image by wearing their caps pulled tightly onto their heads. *Republican News*, 13 August 1977 and *Guardian*, 15 November 1976.
18. *Daily Telegraph*, 30 January 1976.
19. Sr. Clarke, 'Jerry Mealy', Clarke Papers (COFLA).
20. 'Roy Walsh', Clarke Papers (COFLA).
21. 'Walsh-BOV Adjudications' in A Aylett [For the Treasury Solicitor] to BM Birnberg & Co, 28 September 1990, Private Collection (Walsh).
22. 'Roy Walsh', Clarke Papers (COFLA).
23. Cited in Hill, *Forever lost*, p. 179.
24. Hill, *Forever lost*, p. 185. The Lords decision was confirmed by Lord Diplock after whom the juryless courts in Belfast were named. *The case of the Birmingham 6*, TOM poster, 1986.
25. Clarke, *No faith*, p. 83.
26. 'Lord Bridge of Harwich', *Times*, 26 November 2007.
27. Hill, *Forever lost*, pp. 186–7. McCartney advised: 'Paddy, if you go on hunger strike mate, you can't come off it, because what you are doing then is you are giving them a parameter of what they can work with, what they can negotiate with the brinkmanship etc'. Ronnie McCartney, 12 April 2008. When in Bristol with Ronnie McCartney in 1981, Paddy Hill observed: 'He was then beginning to question the IRA's use of violence, and within a few years was to break from the organization altogether'. Hill, *Forever lost*, p. 182.
28. Hill, *Forever lost*, p. 182.
29. Sr. Clarke, 'Patrick Hill', Clarke Papers (COFLA).
30. *Irish Times*, 25 November 1981. See also *Times*, 25 November 1981.
31. *City Limits*, 20–26 November 1981.
32. Hill, *Forever lost*, pp. 186–9 and Clarke, 9 March 2008.
33. *Chicago Tribune*, 25 November 1981. See also *Irish People*, 5 December 1981.
34. *AP/RN*, 19 November 1981.
35. Hill, *Forever lost*, p. 190. There were six IRA prisoners in Gartree in January 1982, five of whom were in solitary under the GOAD rule. *Newsline*, 16 January 1982.
36. Hill, *Forever lost*, p. 194. O'Doherty had already attempted to assist Dick McIlkenny and Billy Power, whom he encountered in Wormwood Scrubs. O'Doherty, *Volunteer*, p. 217.
37. See Patrick Joseph Hill to the Editor, *Irish People*, 11 August 1984.
38. *AP/RN*, 22 October 1981.
39. *Irish Press*, 15 December 1972.
40. *AP/RN*, 19 November 1981.
41. *HC Deb 27 October 1981 vol 10 cc721–4.*
42. *AP/RN*, 17 October 1981, *Observer*, 11 October 1981 and *Times*, 8 March 1985.
43. *Irish People*, 24 October 1981. The attack on Pringle was noted in Ballymurphy where Royal Marine Commandos had shot up a house they raided seeking to detain an IRA firing party which had honoured hunger striker Joe McDonnell on 10 July 1981. Local republican Paddy Adams was one of those wounded and arrested. De Baroid, *Ballymurphy*, pp. 245–6. For Howarth see Peter Birchall, *The longest walk, The word of bomb disposal* (London, 1997), p. 19. UXB expert Peter Gurney, who had seen Howarth's lifeless body, defused an IRA bomb planted in Debenhams on Oxford Street on 26 October 1981. *Times*, 8 March 1985. Fourteen IRSP members were detained in Paddington Green and Rochester Row police stations under the PTA on 4 November 1981 but released without charge. *FRFI*, November/ December 1981, p. 1. When convicted of the Chelsea Barracks bombing in the Old Bailey on 7 March 1985, it was claimed that Thomas Quigley and Paul Kavanagh had used a 300-foot command wire to detonate the bomb. *Times*, 8 March 1985.
44. See McGladdery, *Provisional IRA in England*, pp. 117–8 and *AP/RN*, 22 and 29 October 1981.
45. *HC Deb 27 October 1981 vol 10 cc721–4.*
46. *AP/RN*, 19 November 1981.
47. *Lost Lives*, pp. 886–8.
48. *Irish People*, 5 December 1981.
49. *Times*, 3 August and 2 December 1981.

50. *Guardian*, 21 October 1981. Avebury corresponded with Gerry Cunningham in Long Lartin and Fr. Fell in Parkhurst *AP/RN*, 29 April 1982 and *Irish People*, 17 April 1982. The Peer also assisted the violent prisoner and convicted killer Doug Wakefield. *Times*, 3 June 1982. See also Editorial, *New Law Journal*, Vol. 133, No. 6120, 9 September 1983, pp. 793–94.

51. See O'Donnell, *Special Category*, I, p. 488.

52. *AP/RN*, 29 April 1982. See also *AP/RN*, 17 October 1985.

53. Armstrong to Wilson, 21 October 1981, Private Collection (Wilson).

54. *Guardian*, 15 December 1980.

55. Sean Smyth, 2 June 2009.

56. *AP/RN*, 29 April 1982. See also *Irish Post*, 26 February 1983. On 25 April 1980 Albany staff removed Smyth's glasses and watch during a pre-visit search and withheld his property until it was over. A farcical but legally serious charge of cultivating drugs in his cell in December 1980 was dropped when the plant transpired to be shamrock. He was moved to Wormwood Scrubs in January 1981. Sr. Clarke, 'Sean Smyth', Clarke Papers (COFLA).

57. *AP/RN*, 29 July 1982. See also Sr. Clarke, 'Brian [Donal] McLaughlin', Clarke Papers (COFLA).

58. In February 1973 Susan Loughran was released from Armagh Gaol for four hours to attend the funeral of her brother John. This occurred despite NIO objections and a civil action being taken by female republican prisoners arising from their maltreatment in the aftermath of a riot. Brady et al (eds.) *Stories of Republican Women*, p. 88. John Loughran was one of four men, including IRA Volunteer Tony Campbell, shot dead by British Army snipers in the New Lodge district. *Lost Lives*, p. 326 and Relatives for Justice, *New Lodge Killings, 40th year anniversary*, pamphlet (Belfast, 2013). Janet Murphy, from the 'Bone' area of Belfast, was similarly granted six hours to attend the funeral of her brother. She too was accompanied by Chaplain Fr. Ray Murray. Brady et al (eds.) *Stories of Republican Women*, p. 233. An early republican prisoner in England, Joe Farrington, was in March 1973 denied one day parole from Stafford to visit fatally ill father in Birmingham. He died in Dublin in December 1973 and parole was again refused despite an established release date of August 1974. *The Irish Prisoner* [1975], p. 5.

59. *HC Deb 1 December 1981 vol 14 cc100–1W*.

60. *Irish Times*, 16 December 1976.

61. *Irish News*, 21 January 1983.

62. *Guardian*, 15 December 1980. Guilfoyle's lawyers had appealed in response to a High Court dismissal of his complaint regarding interference with correspondence pertaining to his ECHR action. *Irish Post*, 20 December 1980. Denning disapproved of prisoners taking cases against staff. In a 1972 case involving the Home Office he stated: 'If the courts were to entertain actions by disgruntled prisoners, the governor's life would be made intolerable. The discipline of the prison would be undermined'. Cited in Tim Owen, 'Prison Law: 1' in *Legal Action*, January 1987, p. 10.

63. *HC Deb 3 March 1980 vol 980 c63W*. Kilroy-Silk raised the issue owing to the concurrent discussions on prisoners' correspondence taking place in the European Commission. Ibid. The House of Lords determined in March 1982 that Albany's Governor was in contempt of court when he blocked a letter from a prisoner to his solicitor. *Times*, 5 March 1982.

64. *Times*, 26 March 1983. Reuben Silver had complained in connection with correspondence impeded between 1972 and 1976. He died in 1979. Ibid.

65. See *Times*, 21 April 1983.

66. *Evening Press*, 10 January 1982.

67. Cited in Clarke, *No faith*, p. 40. See also *Double sentence*, [p. 16].

68. *Guardian*, 2 April 1982.

69. Quoted in *Guardian*, 2 April 1982.

70. *Guardian*, 2 April 1982.

71. Alastair Logan to Roy Walsh, 18 January 1984, Private Collection (Walsh).

72. *HL Deb 28 April 1982 vol 429 c867*.

73. *HL Deb 28 April 1982 vol 429 cc867–901*

74. *Irish Times*, 15 June 1981. An IRA statement of 14 June 1981 read: 'We meant to kill Gardiner, the political architect of the criminalization policy, and the H-blocks. The device fell off the car and failed to explode'. A three-pound booby trap bomb was found on a pavement where a vehicle being used by the former Lord Chancellor had been parked during a visit to Queen's University Belfast on 13 June 1981. Ibid. Lord Gardiner had been a long - serving President of the Howard League. See McGladdery, *Provisional IRA in England*, pp. 243–4. Chief Justice Lord McDermott was wounded by the IRA after an appearance at Ulster Polytechnic in 1977 and Chief Justice Lord Lowry survived an ambush outside QUB in March 1982. In earlier incidents the IRA shot dead Judge Rory Conaghan and Resident Magistrate Martin McBurney in September 1974. Resident Magistrate William Staunton was mortally wounded in October 1972. The INLA placed a boobytrap under the car of Judge Roy Watt in November 1982 and in January 1983 the IRA killed Judge William Doyle. *Irish Times*, 6 January

1984 and *Lost Lives*, pp. 319, 934. For the attempt on the life of Judge Tom Travers see *Irish World*, 14 April 1984.

75. *HL Deb 28 April 1982 vol 429 cc867–901.*

76. *Times*, 19 January 1982.

77. PROP, *Prison Briefing*, No. 1, 1982.

78. Richard MacCauley in '"We live in our areas, our people know us", Interviews with Provisional Sinn Féin', Booklet (London, 1981).

79. Joe Austin in 'Interviews with Provisional Sinn Féin'. Austin elaborated: 'We are not critical of the revolutionary left in England. We are critical of those who masquerade as the revolutionary left ... we rely considerably on solidarity from all over the world, and of course solidarity from England ... We would see the revolutionary left as basically being ambassadors for the English working class. The Brits have very successfully portrayed the struggle in Ireland as being a struggle between the Irish working class and the English working class. Well that simply isn't true; it's a capitalistic ploy, an imperialist ploy. The struggle in Ireland is between the Irish people and the ruling sections of the English. Ibid.

80. *Guardian*, 2 April 1982. See also *Irish Times*, 3 April 1982.

81. *HL Deb 28 April 1982 vol 429 cc867–901.* Ingleby had evidently visited at least one IRA prisoner in a 'remote' location. Ibid.

82. Lord Elton, Undersecretary at the Home Office, was questioned as to whether the refusal to repatriate IRA prisoners was in contravention of Rule 37. Lords Hilton, Hunt, Underhill, Brockway and Kilbracken took part in the discussion. *Irish Post*, 26 February 1983. Brockway, Gifford, Longford and Kilbracken had also jointly appealed to then Northern Secretary Humphrey Atkins on behalf of Pauline McLaughlin when she fell ill in Armagh Prison. *Guardian*, 8 November 1980. She was only five stone when released 'on medical grounds' in January 1981. *Guardian*, 11 January 1981.

83. *Report of Her Majesty's Chief Inspector of Prisons, 1982*, p. 15.

84. Clarke, *No faith*, pp. 82–3. Fr. Faul was in disfavour with the Republican Movement due to his perceived interference in negotiations with the NIO during the 1981 hunger strike and subsequent condemnations of political violence. See *AP/RN*, 19 November 1981. The ALJ had in January 1975 protested the detention in Dublin under the OSA of ex-Clann na hÉireann organizer Gerry Doherty following his deportation from Scotland. Doherty had been a high profile Official Republican Movement prisoner in England. *Irish Times*, 9 January 1975.

85. *New Statesman*, 1 January 1982.

86. *New Statesman*, 1 January 1982, p. 7.

87. See also *Irish Democrat*, January 1982.

88. *Daily Mirror*, 10 October 1977.

89. *Irish Times*, 1 March 1982.

90. Clarke, *No faith*, pp. 112–4. See also Eamon Andrews to the Editor, *Catholic Herald*, 9 July 1982.

91. Clarke, *No faith*, p. 114.

92. *Irish World*, 25 October 1980. The issue arose in the context of a proposal to raise the diplomatic status of UK relations with the Holy See. Ibid.

93. Adams, *Hope and History*, p. 29.

94. See Clarke, *No faith*, pp. 114–5.

95. Clarke, *No faith*, p. 116.

96. Clarke, *No faith*, p. 117.

97. Sorohan, *Irish London*, pp. 149–50.

98. O'Donnell, *Special Category*, I, pp. 159–60.

99. *AP/RN*, 11 February 1982. O'Connell had been arrested in Monaghan in 1972 and Wexford in 1973 resulting in sentences for IRA activities in the Curragh and Mountjoy.

100. *AP/RN*, 11 March 1982. Sinn Féin may have been anxious to rival the IRSP which, in June 1981, stood H-Block INLA prisoner Tom McAllister in the constituency. McAllister polled an impressive 2,120 first preference votes. Ibid., 11 February 1982. For the wounding and arrest of McAllister in 1978 see Holland and McDonald, *Deadly Divisions*, p. 127.

101. Interview with Pat O'Donnell, Tipperary, 3 March 2009.

102. *Times*, 25 February 1982.

103. *Guardian*, 19 February 1982.

104. *Guardian*, 19 February 1982.

105. *Irish Times*, 27 June 1979.

106. *Report on the work of the Prison Department, 1984/ 85*, Appendix No. 3, p. 102.

107. *Guardian*, 19 February 1982. Wakefield, in addition to being the main training centre for prison officers, contained the 'Rule 43 wing-national resource for prisoners segregated under Rule 43 at own request'. *Report on the work of the Prison Department, 1978*, p. 67.

108. *Guardian*, 23 January 1982.

109. *Observer*, 24 January 1982.
110. Flackes and Elliott (eds.) *Political Directory*, p. 388.
111. *AP/RN*, 11 March 1982.
112. See O'Donnell, *Special Category*, I, p. 385–6.
113. Eddie Caughey, 16 September 2008.
114. *AP/RN*, 11 March 1982. The book concerned Fenian bombing attacks in England in the 1880s. See KRM Short, *The Dynamite War, Irish-American Bombers in Victorian England* (New Jersey, 1979). Dowd criticized Sinn Féin for printing an Irish language account of Kerry Easter commemorations in 1982 and for retaining 'religious services' as part of the ceremonies. He also disapproved of giving 'a platform to our enemies, such as ... a former IRA Volunteer who on finding himself in prison, now rejects the use of force and claims to be a pacifist'. Brendan Dowd to the Editor, *AP/RN*, 20 May 1982. Seamus Boyle's account of Carron's tour was reprinted in full by Irish Northern Aid in the US. See *Irish People*, 27 March 1982.
115. Ronnie McCartney, 12 April 2008.
116. *AP/RN*, 11 March 1982. See also Sr. Clarke, 'Leicester', Clarke Papers (COFLA)
117. *AP/RN*, 11 March 1982. A fifteen-stanza poem by Ray McLaughlin, 'Paradoxical View', was printed as a full page in the subsequent issue of the paper. *AP/RN*, 18 March 1982. It was discovered in March 1982 that the Hull censor destroyed letters sent to republicans that 'he did not like'. A letter sent by Tony Madigan's mother reached him with an added Red Hand of Ulster symbol drawn beside her home address. In Ireland this would have constituted a death threat. Sr. Clarke, 'Hull', Clarke Papers (COFLA).
118. *AP/RN*, 11 March 1982. Blake's sister had arrived in Bristol in the summer of 1980 for an arranged visit to find he had been moved. His mother complained to the Irish Embassy and in January 1982 Niall Blaney, a fellow Donegal native, made additional representations. In Albany in January 1982 Blake's mother found he had been ghosted to Hull. Sr. Clarke, 'Stephen Blake', Clarke Papers (COFLA).
119. Ronnie McCartney, 12 April 2008.
120. Liam Baker, 3 March 2008.
121. Busty Cunningham, 2 August 2007.
122. *AP/RN*, 11 March 1982 and 3 December 1981.
123. *Irish News*, 1 March 1982.
124. Tony Madigan, 7 March 2008.
125. *AP/RN*, 19 August 1982 and Eddie O'Neill, 1 February 2008. Roy Walsh recalled: 'You'd go down the block for various minor charges and you say, "Mick, what about you? Are you coming back?" "No", he wouldn't budge'. Roy Walsh, 9 March 2008.
126. McLaughlin, *Inside an English jail*, p. 26 and *PAC Bulletin*, March/ April 1977.
127. *AP/RN*, 11 March 1982.
128. *AP/RN*, 19 August 1982. Armstrong had a knee operation in Parkhurst prison hospital in January 1983 and detested the place so much that he returned to the wing at the earliest opportunity. Armstrong to Wilson, 5 February 1983. Hackett believed Wakefield staff attempted to 'set' him up by allowing a lone prison officer into his cell while others waited outside view: 'They thought I was going to swing at yer man. They could have probably fucked me down the stairs, into the basement cells'. Pat Hackett, 21 December 2007.
129. PRO Republican Prisoners Hull Prison to the Editor in *FRFI*, April 1982, p. 15.
130. *Guardian*, 2 April 1982.
131. *Derry Journal*, 26 March 1982.
132. *Irish Post*, 17 September 1983. O'Doherty's 68-year-old mother was not collected by prison transport in Evesham on 10 August as had been arranged and thereby missed a rare visit with her son who had waited in ignorance of what had gone wrong. Ibid. See also *Irish Times*, 13 February 1984.
133. *Irish Times*, 22 July 1995.
134. *Irish Times*, 6 March, 8 March and 14 July 1982.
135. *New York Times*, 7 March 1982 and *The Irish Prisoner*, No. 15 [1988], p. 14.
136. *Guardian*, 15 December 1988.
137. *Guardian*, 14 July 1982.
138. *Newsweek*, 2 August 1982. In 1980 an attempted CLJ prosecution of Jim Lynagh, Aidan McGuirk and Lawrence McNally for shooting UDR man Henry Livingston in Armagh failed in the Special Criminal Court. The first convictions under the CLJ were secured in December 1981 when two men who had escaped from Crumlin Road Prison, Bobby Campbell and Michael Ryan, were convicted. See Michael Farrell, *Sheltering the fugitives? The extradition of Irish political offenders* (Cork, 1985), pp. 77–9. See also *Irish Times*, 11 May 1987.
139. *AP/RN*, 11 March 1982.
140. Harry Duggan to 'Peter' [Seamus O Mathuna], 10 August 1986, Private Collection (O Mathuna).

141. *Irish Times*, 30 June 1982. See also *AP/RN*, 15 July 1982 and *Observer*, 7 March 1982.

142. *Times*, 4 January 1989.

143. *Irish Times*, 14 July 1982.

144. *Independent*, 8 July 1991.

145. *Irish Times*, 17 July 1982.

146. *Irish Times*, 8 July 1982.

147. *Irish Post*, 24 July 1982.

148. *Guardian*, 15 December 1988. See also *AP/RN*, 1 July 1982 and Joyce and Murtagh, *The Boss*, pp. 208–9.

149. *Irish World*, 26 March 1977. McMorrow defected from the First Battalion, Irish Guards, in late 1969. Ibid. March 1982, when Tuite was recaptured, also witnessed the arrest in Dublin of Derry republican John McKeever. The Derryman, a self-described former member of both the Official and Provisional IRA, had previously informed the British media that he had been engaged in 'the military campaign in England between 1975 and 1979'. Quoted in *Guardian*, 25 May 1982. He received a three year jail sentence for arms possession and membership of an illegal organization in the Special Criminal Court on 24 May 1982. No attempt was made to extradite him to England in relation to any offences for which he was uncharged. Ibid. McMorrow, when in Limerick Prison, was one of 220 men granted Christmas parole from Twenty-Six County jails in December 1984. *Irish Times*, 22 December 1984.

150. *Irish Times*, 21 July 1982.

151. *Guardian*, 15 December 1988.

152. *Guardian*, 6 August 1984.

153. *Guardian*, 15 December 1988.

154. *Guardian*, 15 December 1988. Thatcher queried whether the personal security of British witnesses, under no compulsion to testify, could be guaranteed if they agreed to appear in Dublin's Special Criminal Court. Ibid.

155. *Times*, 4 January 1989.

156. *Times*, 4 January 1989.

157. See *Irish World*, 5 February 1983. At the INA (Irish Northern Aid) Annual Testimonial in Queens, New York, in February 1983, Sinn Féin Ard Comhairle member Martha McClelland averred: 'If we lose these trials, we would lose much more that just four men in jail. We would lose a very important battle in America'. *Irish World*, 5 February 1983.

158. *Irish Times*, 13 April 1982. Fr. Fell was relocated to Canterbury prison from Parkhurst ahead of release, a move which he regarded as 'the final vindictive straw', as it prevented him completing Open University studies. In a letter to the Relatives and Friends of Prisoners Committee, Fr. Fell described the Category B prison Canterbury as 'a veritable zoo'. Quoted in *Irish People*, 17 April 1982. Fr. Fell was dramatically compared to Jeremiah O'Donovan Rossa and Tom Clarke. Peadar McAleer to the Editor, *Irish Post*, 27 February 1982. See also *Irish People*, 24 July 1982 and Sr. Clarke, 'Fr. P[at] Fell', Clarke Papers (COFLA).

159. See Donal Mac Amhlaigh to the Editor, *Irish Post*, 20 March 1982.

160. Governor of Bristol Prison to Mary Campbell, 19 March 1982, Private Collection (Campbell).

161. Alastair Logan to Sean Campbell, 24 August 1982, Private Collection (Campbell).

162. Mary and Terry Campbell, 2008.

163. *Irish Post*, 3 September 1983 and *AP/RN*, 29 April 1982.

164. *AP/RN*, 12 August 1982. Campbell's comments were echoed by Peggy O'Neill. Eddie O'Neill, then in Hull, was referred to by Owen Carron. Ibid. Campbell, elected to Cookstown District Council for Sinn Féin in 1997, died in Tyrone on 13 December 2002. Magee, *Tyrone's Struggle*, p. 548 and *AP/RN*, 30 January 2003. Tyrone National Graves erected a memorial to him in Brocagh Cemetery.

165. *AP/RN*, 29 April 1982.

166. *Irish Post*, 3 September 1983.

167. *AP/RN*, 29 April 1982.

168. *AP/RN*, 29 April 1982. Hayes had refused to take visits 'behind Perspex' in Wakefield where he spent three months in solitary protesting the prison policy. Members of the family living in Raheny, Dublin, had been cleared to visit but could not proceed due to his militancy. Sr. Clarke, 'John [Sean] Hayes', Clarke Papers (COFLA).

169. *AP/RN*, 29 April 1982. Abstentionism was a major issue yet reaffirmed at the November 1984 Ard Fheis in Dublin. *Irish People*, 10 November 1984.

170. *AP/RN*, 29 April 1982.

171. *AP/RN*, 29 April 1982.

172. *AP/RN*, 29 April 1982. Toal was due for release in September and Murphy in October 1982. Gerry Hunter, described in press accounts as a 'pub bomber [sic]', failed to re-open his case by means of civil proceedings against police he correctly claimed had extracted a false confession. On 19 November 1981 the House of Lords upheld the decision issued by Lord Diplock on behalf of the Court of Appeal

that 'once a matter has been determined by a court of competent jurisdiction, it cannot normally be challenged, except by the ordinary processes of appeal'. *Guardian*, 20 November 1981. Andy Mulryan won the Long Lartin marathon in 1983, covering twenty-six miles in three hours, nineteen minutes. Patrick Mulryan to [Anon], *Irish People*, 9 July 1983.

173. *AP/RN*, 29 April 1982. Sr. Clarke had been granted permission to visit Norney in early March 1982 only to have the order rescinded without explanation. Sr. Clarke, 'Paul Norney', Clarke Papers (COFLA).

174. Armstrong to Wilson, 16 November 1982, Private Collection (Wilson). The Howard League had promoted the Belfast man as a 'special' case owing to his large family in May 1978. Wright to Brockway, 16 May 1978, Clarke Papers (COFLA).

175. *AP/RN*, 29 April 1982.

176. *AP/RN*, 29 April 1982. Fr. Gerry Ennis was Catholic Chaplain of the prison, assisted by Sister Agnes. A feature on Wormwood Scrubs claimed 'there is daily RC communion in D Wing'. The *Illustrated London News*, June 1982.

177. Armstrong to Wilson, 7 April 1982, Private Collection (Wilson).

178. *AP/RN*, 29 April 1982.

179. *AP/RN*, 29 April 1982. J Court, Training Principal Officer in Brixton in 1980–81, supported 'remedial education and teaching people to read and write and so on' as well as men completing low level studies in progress. He did not, however, accept that prisoners should conduct Open University courses: 'I wonder how many of these people would have taken advantage of this education on the outside as much as they do inside. I think we may finish up with educated crooks ... In my view it is a waste of money'. *Session 1980–81 ... 19 January 1981, HM Prison Brixton*, p. 98. See also Sr. Clarke, 'Gerry McLaughlin', Clarke Papers (COFLA).

180. *Guardian*, 26 August 1983.

181. *AP/RN*, 21 December 1982. Patsy Armstrong explained: 'I was trying to get over [to Parkhurst] before now but it would be far too expensive so close to Christmas. I'll be over to see him, I expect, around February'. Ibid.

182. *AP/RN*, 21 December 1982. Mrs Coughlan lived in Killarney Street, Dublin. Her previous visit to Hull irritated the staff who 'didn't like it' when she sang the 1920s rebel balled 'The Lonely Woods of Upton' in the visiting room. Ibid. Roy Walsh was admitted to Parkhurst Prison Hospital on 2 March 1982 for examination in connection with abdominal pains by a Consultant Surgeon six days later. Following additional X-rays on 9 December, further treatment was prescribed. SJ McCarthy to George E Baker & Co, 20 April 1982 and 10 February 1983, Private Collection (Walsh). A set of X-rays taken in Wandsworth on 13 October 1983 in relation to a suspected trapped nerve in his neck was mislaid. George E Baker & Co, 1 December 1983, Private Collection (Walsh).

183. Ann and Eileen Gillespie, 7 June 2008.

184. Ann and Eileen Gillespie, 7 June 2008.

185. *Irish Post*, 3 July 1982. TOM by 1983 subordinated pickets to other forms of 'prisoners work' due to organizational problems. TOM Minutes, 1 February 1983, Private Collection (Renwick).

186. *AP/RN*, 12 August 1982.

187. *HC Deb 26 July 1982 vol 28 c349W*.

188. *Sunday Telegraph*, 8 February 1981.

189. *Times*, 13 July 1982 and Sr. Clarke, 'Martin Foran', Clarke Papers (COFLA).

190. AJ Canning to SL Cowper-Coles, 24 February 1978, NAE, FCO 87/ 762.

191. Janet Thompson to SL Cowper-Coles. 25 January 1978, NAE, FCO 87/ 762. Thompson wrote in relation to Albany prisoner Stephen Harris, jailed for assault on 12 May 1977, having been 'questioned by police officers about his possible involvement with the IRA, but no evidence was found to substantiate charges'. Ibid. Foran's case was advocated by IRA prisoners who believed him to be innocent. See Noel Gibson to 'Peter Flynn', 7 July 1987, Private Collection (O Mathuna).

192. Sr. Clarke, 'Tony Madigan', Clarke Papers (COFLA).

193. Tony Madigan, 7 March 2008.

194. *AP/RN*, 29 July 1982.

195. Byrne to the Editor, 25 July 1982, *Irish People*, 25 September 1982.

196. Byrne to the Editor, 25 July 1982, *Irish People*, 25 September 1982. See also Eddie [Byrne] to Frank [J. Byrne], 22 August 1982 in *Irish People*, 9 October 1982. Byrne had corresponded with MPs Jock Stallard and Michael O'Halloran in 1980, arising from what he regarded as unreasonable use of Rule 43. Sr. Clarke, 'Eddie Byrne', Clarke Papers (OFSA). O'Halloran hailed from Doonbeg, Clare. *Irish Echo*, 14 March 1981.

197. See O'Neill 'Albany Document', p. 1.

198. *Lost Lives*, pp. 908–9 and Van De Bijl, *Operation Banner*, p. 148. The Royal Dublin Society sent the largest single donation, £300,000, to assist the families of those killed and injured. White-Spunner, *Horse Guards*, pp. 570, 577. A squadron of the unit commanded by Major Andrew Parker Bowles

had been the first to enter Free Derry in 1972. Four troopers were killed in Belfast during a tour of duty in 1976 and at least three more died at the hands of the IRA prior to the attack in London. The Blues and Royals generally operated with either Saladin or Ferret armoured cars but were also used as infantry in Ireland. See Van De Bijl, *Operation Banner*, p. 147. Seven horses also perished in London. 'Sefton', a badly injured animal which survived, became a household name and in the eyes of some, 'a symbol of the struggle against the IRA'. *The Irish Emigrant*, 8 October 2012. See also White-Spunner, *Horse Guards*, pp. 576–7 and *Irish Independent*, 6 September 2013.

199. *Lost Lives*, p. 909.

200. *Washington Post*, 21 July 1982 and *Newsweek*, 2 August 1982. A Boston paper covered the story with a headline 'IRA's bombs bring world attention back to Northern Ireland'. The article claimed 'technically, it was a considerable coup in the enemy's heartland'. *Christian Science Monitor*, 23 July 1982. See also *Guardian*, 22 July 1982.

201. For approving commentary on the attacks see *Irish People*, 31 July 1982.

202. Toby Harnden, *'Bandit County', The IRA & South Armagh* (London, 1999), pp. 238–9. For named suspects, including a Belfast man jailed in Dublin on 21 January 1983, see Fleming and Miller, *Special Branch*, p. 156.

203. Maguire, *My father's watch*, pp. 330–31. His father, Paddy Maguire, spent nearly ten years in prison and emerged in early 1984 intending to sue the British Government. *Irish Echo*, 5 May 1984.

204. *Christian Science Monitor*, 23 July 1982. See also *Washington Post*, 21 July 1982.

205. See *FRFI*, September 1982, p. 2, *Morning Star*, 21 July 1982, *Newsline*, 21 July 1982 and *Socialist Worker*, 24 July 1982. In January 1979 the CPGB condemned the IRA bombing of Canvey Island gasholders in London as 'politically primitive' yet in June 1980 hailed the MK (ANC) attack on three SASOL oil refineries near Johannesburg, South Africa, as 'their most spectacular blow'. *Morning Star*, 19 January 1979 and 3 June 1980. Leading post-apartheid South African politician Kadar Asmal acknowledged that the IRA had materially assisted MK in the famed SASOL bombings. *Irish Times*, 29 August 2011.

206. *Irish Post*, 7 August 1982. Prior to the London move, Gibson spent fifty-six days in Parkhurst Segregation Block owing to the discovery of a hacksaw blade in his cell. Rosalie Gross to the Editor, *Irish People*, 17 July 1982. Gross was related to Ray McCartney and corresponded with many IRA prisoners in England. Ibid. A forty - strong group protested outside Long Lartin on 15 August 1982. *Irish People*, 4 September 1982. See also *AP/RN*, 4 November 1982.

207. Noel Gibson, 24 August 2006.

208. Clarke, *No faith*, p. 95 and *Irish Post*, 6 November 1982.

209. Sr. Clarke, 'Noel Gibson', Clarke Papers (COFLA).

210. [Hackett] to [Clarke], 5 August 1982, Clarke Papers (COFLA).

211. [Hackett] to [Clarke], 5 August 1982, Clarke Papers (COFLA).

212. *AP/RN*, 19 August 1982. O'Rourke's article was reprinted in INA paper *Irish People* which subsequently encouraged a letter-writing campaign by Irish-American supporters to the IRA prisoners in England. *Irish People*, 28 August 1982. Eddie Byrne and Brendan Dowd were among those whose correspondence was subsequently published in America. *Irish People*, 18 December 1982.

213. Bridie Hackett quoted in *AP/RN*, 19 August 1982. Bridget Hackett claimed: 'My brother is now in his third year of solitary confinement – total isolation – his only communication being with the prison warders at whose hands he receives frequent harsh treatment … Amnesty International have recently described his prison conditions as "cruel, inhuman and degrading"'. Bridget Hackett to the Editor, *Irish Times*, 18 January 1982.

214. [Hackett] to [Clarke], 5 August 1982, Clarke Papers (COFLA). Holmes had an operation for a perforated eardrum when in Wormwood Scrubs in September 1980. Sr. Clarke, 'Paul Holmes', Clarke Papers, COFLA. For Costello see *FRFI*, June 1984, p. 12.

215. [Hackett] to [Clarke], 5 August 1982, Clarke Papers (COFLA).

216. See Coogan, *The IRA*, p. 280. The *Irish Press* and, more incongruously, England's *Daily Express* had employed Brady as a journalist. Ibid. See also *Irish Press*, 1 May 1987.

217. Bridget [Hackett] to Sr. Sarah [Clarke], 5 August 1982, Clarke Papers (COFLA).

218. Cited in *Irish Times*, 31 December 2012. See Joyce and Murtagh, *The Boss*, pp. 162–8.

219. Charles Lysaght, 'Leonard Figg' in *Sunday Independent*, 14 September 2014.

220. Bridget [Hackett] to Sr. Sarah [Clarke], 5 August 1982, Clarke Papers (COFLA).

221. Bridget [Hackett] to Sr. Sarah [Clarke], 5 August 1982, Clarke Papers (COFLA). See also *HC Deb 18 March 1980 vol 981 cc123–4W*.

222. *Derry Journal*, 1 October 1982.

223. *Irish News*, 19 October 1982. See also *Irish News*, 16 January 1983.

224. *Derry Journal*, 1 October 1982.

225. *North West London Press*, 29 October 1982. The figure of fifty-four prisoners tallied with the TOM estimate and excluded persons regarded as innocent. See Cath Haywood, TOM (Birmingham) to the Editor, *Irish People*, 2 October 1982.

226. *Sunday Tribune*, 27 May 1984.
227. *Irish News*, 22 November 1982. See also Eamonn O'Doherty to editor, *Derry Journal*, 23 November 1982.
228. *FRFI*, January 1983, p. 1.
229. *Irish People*, 23 October 1982.
230. *Irish People*, 11 December 1982. Duffy (aka Mooney) had been due for release on 6 August 1982 but with the loss of 810 days remission for rioting, for which he was additionally punished with 308 days in solitary confinement, his sentence was effectively elongated. By February 1983 he had lost 1,028 days of remission, giving a revised release date of 22 May 1985. In 1979 Duffy declined to accept £1,500 paid into a court fund by the Home Office in respect to injuries he had received. Maryellen Cantlin to the Editor, *Irish People*, 5 February 1983.
231. The Mission Statement of Irish Northern Aid stated under the heading 'Objectives': 'Irish Northern Aid is an American-based non profit organization formed to alleviate the suffering of the dependents of Irish political prisoners through An Cumann Cabhrach in Dublin and affiliates such as Green Cross in Belfast'. *Irish People*, 24 December 1983.
232. Brendan Dowd to Geri Mulvey-Nostrand, 4 December 1982 in *Irish People*, 18 December 1982.
233. Paul Norney quoted in Maryellen Cantlin to the Editor, *Irish People*, 22 January 1983. Cantlin sent over seventy cards to IRA prisoners in Ireland and England. Ibid.
234. See *HC Deb 3 March 1980 vol 980 c63W*.
235. *Irish People*, 17 December 1983. Non-IRA prisoners, such as Patrick 'Paddy' Maguire in Wakefield, were also assigned or received pen pals. See Rose Ahearn to the Editor, *Irish People*, 4 February 1984.
236. Jennifer McCann to Kevin Dunphy, 26 November 1983, Private Collection (Dunphy). McCann was being held in C2 Wing, Armagh Prison. Ibid.
237. Governor (Long Lartin) to Jim McDonald, 2 November 1983, Private Collection (McDonald).
238. Con McFadden, 18 December 1984, Private Collection (McDonald).
239. See *Tirgrhra*, pp. 278, 291 and *Irish Times*, 11 May 1987. Lynagh, a Sinn Féin member of Monaghan Urban District Council, was tried for IRA membership in the Special Criminal Court, Dublin, on 28 November 1981. His co-defendant was John Joe McGirl, Chair of Leitrim County Council. *FRFI*, January 1982. McElwain polled well for Sinn Féin in the Cavan/Monaghan Dáil constituency in February 1982 when a remand prisoner in Crumlin Road Jail. *FRFI*, March 1982.
240. *AP/RN*, 21 December 1982.
241. *Irish People*, 11 December 1982. For Small see also Ibid., 5 February 1983. Maidstone was a Category B prison where Mac Lochlainn claimed: 'I have made friends among the criminals here, but I don't have very much in common, being a political prisoner'. Gerry [Mac Lochlainn] to Patrick [Anon], in *Irish People*, 4 June 1983. His sentence for conspiracy to cause explosions had been reduced to four years on appeal. See Sr. Clarke, 'Gerry McLaughlin', Clarke Papers (COFLA).
242. *AP/RN*, 21 December 1982. The financial costs accruing to the Armstrongs had been noted by the Howard League when urging the repatriation of Billy Armstrong and his co-accused. Director Martin Wright was aware that her necessarily infrequent visits to Parkhurst cost £120, of which only £20 was covered by the DHSS. See Martin Wright to Fenner Brockway, 16 May 1978, Clarke Papers (COFLA).
243. *AP/RN*, 21 December 1982.
244. Mary McLaughlin, 'A long and painful road', http:/www.cunamh.org. (20 January 2013). In November 1974 Mary McLaughlin had observed the dire conditions of the 'Birmingham Six' in Winson Green: 'They would have had black eyes; blood stained shirts, and bruises and cuts all over their bodies'. Ibid. On 5 July 1978 she arrived in Wakefield from Birmingham to find that her husband had been moved two days previously to Durham. A 'closed' visit was arranged in Durham. Sr. Clarke, 'Ray McLaughlin', Clarke Papers (COFLA). Close family members of Billy Armstrong, Stevie Blake, Martin Coughlan, Pat Hackett and Paddy Armstrong were similarly disobliged in this period. See Sr. Clarke, 'Michael McLaughlin', Clarke Papers (COFLA).

CHAPTER 7

The Broad Front and Mutiny in Albany, 1983

The IRA in Hull had planned to enliven the New Year period by mounting an escape in which they had invested months of development. Harassment of Stevie Nordone's visitors from Ireland over the holiday period, however, endangered the entire bid. Having been thwarted in plans to bomb the prison's main furniture workshop the previous year, republicans on the second floor re-orientated their energies towards breaking out. Eddie O'Neill arranged the smuggling of special blades, maps and a type of radio suitable for concealing contraband. By the autumn of 1982 he had drawn upon basic knowledge of plumbing and his dexterity with tools to decommission his cell's cast - iron radiator without attracting notice. Select incisions into the pipes eventually enabled him to rotate the heavy radiator to the point at which it lay flat on the floor and could be gradually drained of its putrid water. As the unit flanked the exterior wall, O'Neill's ability to manipulate its position provided access to brickwork which was generally concealed. The slow work of cutting into the masonry commenced, covered, in part, by Nordone's newfound interest in leather craft and hobbies that generated tapping sounds. An average of two hours' labour and a half hour of camouflage work could be achieved on most nights. Damage was covered by large paper sheets starched in sunlight to render them dry and seemingly inflexible once attached to wall. Bread, putty and paint disguised the cuts that compromised the radiator, which was quietly repositioned every night.[1]

As winter approached, O'Neill was inconveniently cell swopped with a puzzled Iranian whom the IRA requested not to make an issue of the fact that the radiator did not function. Another republican prisoner was moved into the cell before O'Neill was returned. He pulled his table in front of the work area and covered it with a sheet and tossed clothes just in case a staff member entered after lockup. Just such an infrequent visit materialized while O'Neill was prising the brickwork, but the momentary warning of approach by a conciliatory staff member offering tea proved harmless owing to the precautions and pretence of engaging in physical exercise. When the opening was ready, efforts were made to acquire a hook to dislodge nearby bricks, as well as rope and general escape equipment. The plan entailed using the cover of a foggy night, to which northerly Hull was prone in wintertime, to close with and scale the outer fence without being spotted by the three cameras trained on the sector.[2]

Nordone was shocked to discover on 2 January 1983 that the first of five consecutive visits from his mother, sister and Austrian fiancée had been cancelled. Having returned to the second floor, he and O'Neill glimpsed the disconsolate trio in the distance beyond the front gate. They demanded an explanation from the Principal Officer who disclaimed any knowledge of the reasoning of his security colleagues and declined to ascertain this when requested. A second attempt to remonstrate ended badly when Nordone lost his patience and threw a heavy table into an office wall. Staff dashed into the area and began striking the two republicans. O'Neill had nothing personal against those with whom he grappled and was surprised when one began to aggressively drive his boot onto his lower leg in an effort to break the limb. A Manchester prisoner alerted the wing and, as alarm bells sounded, the landing became 'swamped with guys'. The removal of the Irish men from the melee did not resolve the issue as British prisoners threatened to 'wreck' the prison if an explanation justifying the root cause of the incident was not forthcoming. Repercussions were also promised if the IRA men were beaten in the Punishment Block. When, after unusual delay, Nordone and O'Neill were lodged in the punishment cells near 'blanketman' Mick Murray, no further violence materialized.[3]

A short 'lie down' in Durham ensued but the indisposition to accuse the Irish men of assaulting staff, as opposed to simply 'fighting', revealed 'they wanted to play it down a bit because it was embarrassing'. The men were, however, under heightened observation and advancing the escape was all but impossible in the short term. An overhead if innocent discussion about the mechanical efficiency of a watch O'Neill had repaired proved the final straw, as it was misconstrued as an indication that he had manufactured an incendiary or explosive device.[4] This misfortune ensured that O'Neill was unlocked and sent to the Segregation Block with Nordone and Glenholmes. Yet no incendiaries had been laid down by the IRA, prompting alternate explanations of the sequence of events. Sr. Sarah Clarke ascertained that the willingness of Glenholmes to speak to a BBC 'Newsnight' crew doing a documentary on the Dispersal System was deemed to infringe the malleable accusation of threatening 'Good Order and Discipline'. He was moved to Walton on 30 January 1983 under Rule 43 where he was held in a strongbox and wore only a towel due to his politically informed refusal to don a modified 'E List' prison uniform bearing yellow 'patches' and stripes.[5] Glenholmes was sent on to Long Lartin in preference to Hull.[6] Eddie O'Neill and John McCluskey, it was reported, were similarly treated in Hull in order to prevent them being filmed or interviewed by the state - funded media. They were moved on Rule 43 'lie downs' to Armley and

Durham.[7] O'Neill, in fact, was repeatedly shunted to and from Durham for four months of solitary confinement before being transferred to Albany. He returned to the Isle of Wight with a concealed 'escape kit' of small hacksaw blades and blanks for keys.[8] The Hull - centred documentary was broadcast on 8 March 1983 without input from Kevin Dunphy, Con McFadden or Noel Gibson.[9] Several prisoners were angered and surprised when the Hull programme featured a contribution from Loyalist Albert Baker.[10]

In a New Year greeting to American supporters, Albany IRA prisoners stated the following for publication in Irish Northern Aid's *Irish People*:

> As this phase of the struggle for independence enters its fourteenth year with the Republican Movement as steadfast and determined in its revolutionary course, we Republican Prisoners wish to take this opportunity to thank all those Irish Americans who have made this course possible. However small the contribution – physical, moral or financial – each can by happy in the knowledge that their contribution helped drive a nail into the coffin of British Imperialism in Ireland … we would warn again against complacency and apathy due to recent military and political successes made by the Republican Movement; indeed, we ask for a redoubling of effort, to consolidate and build on past successes.[11]

In keeping with past communications intended for the surface North American support base, the IRA men concentrated on strategic questions, rather than the minutiae of their specific concerns. Questions surrounding repatriation and visiting conditions were subsumed into larger issues of generic concern to all imprisoned republicans, and published extracts from the correspondence of individual prisoners in England generally cited particular injustices to illustrate the travails of the overall political prisoner element in the Dispersal System. As before, major articles on the prisoners in England were reprinted from *AP/RN* and, as such, had the imprimatur of the Republican Movement.[12] The surge in trans-Atlantic correspondence surprised and gratified numerous IRA recipients in England. Liam Baker wrote from Gartree to *Irish People* to acknowledge the 'thousands' of letters and cards flowing into the prisons from international supporters, Americans in particular. Baker accurately claimed that the unprecedented scale of the inflow was permissible owing to Home Office reforms pressed by the ECHR and that the new phenomenon ensured that 'morale among the Republican prisoners was strengthened'.[13] Hugh Doherty, Joe O'Connell and Harry Duggan sent a similar joint message from Parkhurst SSU to the same paper via one of their correspondents.[14] Kevin Dunphy expressed gratitude for being 'flooded with messages of solidarity' in Wormwood Scrubs where Paul Holmes also received copious mail.[15]

Parkhurst, early 1983

Steve Bundred and twenty-six GLC Labour councillors issued invitations to Gerry Adams and Danny Morrison to speak in London following their success in the 20 October 1982 Assembly elections in the Six Counties.[16] They were two of the five Sinn Féin candidates returned when the party contended the Assembly elections for the first time, garnering 10 per cent of the first - preference votes cast.[17] This would have provided an early test on the ability of the Sinn Féin leadership to engage politically inside Britain, even if the party maintained its prohibition on direct participation in the House of Commons. Adams, along with Martin McGuinness and Danny Morrison, were issued with Exclusion Orders by Home Secretary William Whitelaw on 8 December 1982. Section 4 (1) of the PTA was invoked to prevent them meeting Labour Party MPs in London six days later. It was unclear in February 1983, however, whether this situation could be maintained in relation to a Westminster MP.[18] The IRA in Parkhurst were among the republicans who wished to put this to a the test by requesting that Adams visit his jailed constituents on the Isle of Wight.[19] The steady rise in electoral support for Sinn Féin concentrated minds on the prospect of the party winning Westminster seats in the June 1983 General Election.

In February 1983 the IRA group in Parkhurst consisted of Billy Armstrong and Eddie Byrne on C Wing, Bobby Campbell on B Wing and Paddy Hackett in the Hospital Wing, where he remained 'on the blanket'.[20] Campbell reported to friends in Belfast: 'I try to make things as easy as possible for him ... but there's little anyone can do. I've had a few visits with him, he's in good spirits, considering his condition'. He had little success having letters published in *An Phoblacht* and was one of a number concerned with their ongoing isolation. He confided to a correspondent: 'We POWs don't know what is happening re the Movement' and where it stood on the unresolved repatriation demand.[21] The question of an elected Sinn Féin delegation touring Parkhurst was temporarily settled in March 1983 when it was confirmed that the necessary Home Office authorization would not be forthcoming.[22]

This sense of detachment was exacerbated by the perceived heterogeneity of England based support groups. Campbell was unsure as to which enjoyed the endorsement of the republican leadership and at a loss to devise a programme that would enable them to speak with 'a united voice'. The logistic challenges of direct, private contact were considerable, and men like Campbell were unfamiliar with many of the personalities who strove in various ways to improve the conditions of IRA prisoners.[23] There could be no unanimity in a body as diffuse as the IRA in English jails and a story concerning 'wee Ronnie [McCartney]' left most of his comrades 'in the dark' *vis à vis* the real situation.[24] Campbell, being sent on a twenty-eight day lie-down to Winchester in March 1983 and then to Hull, illustrated the nature of such problems. Those who remained in Parkhurst anticipated an intake of other men from Hull, but in the event it was Armstrong who received the '10/74' to Winchester in May.[25] This was a direct result of smashing colour television sets.[26] Unknown to the authorities, Campbell had seriously assaulted a Greek psychopath who had stabbed a number of prisoners in unprovoked attacks and rashly conspired to attack the Belfast man in Parkhurst.[27] Campbell claimed that he and Paul Hill had been sent from Parkhurst to Winchester under Rule 43 in order to deprive them of access to a BBC TV production. He explained:

> The authorities here see me as a threat politically, especially after my letter appeared in *AP/RN* calling for anti-imperialist groups in Britain to unite. When word leaked out in Parkhurst that a television crew was coming, a lot of the prisoners asked me and other political prisoners what was the best way to get across to concerned people outside what was going in these prisons. The authorities know that the Irish political prisoners are respected among the prison population and this was another reason for the move.[28]

Such pre-emptive actions were as effective as the Irish Government's use of Section 31 of the Broadcasting Act, which severely limited legal republican perspectives from the national media. The State denied Sinn Féin the standard prerogatives of constitutional parties while the commercial sector undermined its reach by refusing to distribute and stock its publications. Censorship extended into other organs of the Republic of Ireland. None of those badly beaten by staff in Portlaoise in February 1983 during a dispute over loss of entitlements had open access to journalists who, with rare exceptions, were barred from entering prisons.[29]

By the time Armstrong returned to Parkhurst, relatives of the England prisoners had published a letter in *An Phoblacht* urging political action on repatriation. They too averred that the Movement appeared apathetic, although the fact that the party's organ carried the criticism indicated that the leadership accepted the validity of the low level campaign.[30] In June 1983 McCartney arrived in Parkhurst and strongly refuted the substance of the 'rumour' which had circulated in Belfast the previous month regarding his allegiance. His presence clarified the situation for his comrades but resulted in the shifting of Roy Walsh to Gartree.[31] Campbell, meanwhile, had been involved in a run-in with a former professional boxer in Hull who made derogatory comments about the IRA in the presence of Liam Baker. A group of friendly Liverpool men, including a man serving life and a biker, insisted on taking positions along with Baker at the base of a stairwell leading to the offending party while Campbell remonstrated with the man in his cell. Baker was surprised to see that one of those assisting the republicans had come armed with a bayonet - style blade.[32]

Ken Littlejohn and the IRA in Gartree, 25 January 1983

Stories emerging from the Dispersal System had a familiar ring to those who followed such events. In January 1983 a Gartree IRA man wrote to the *Irish News* to detail the experiences of his elderly mother who encountered typical problems when attempting to visit him in January 1983. The cancellation of Irish ferry services due to bad weather on 5 January forced his brother to drop out of the planned visit on financial grounds. His widowed pensioner mother flew to Manchester, the most convenient airport to rural Market Harborough, to whence she travelled by train and taxi on 7 January. Late arrival ensured a truncated visit of just forty-five minutes, her first in six months. A planned visit for the following day was declined on the grounds that there were no additional places available for 'Special Supervised Category A' men. A two-hour visit on 9 January completed the particularly expensive 'blocked' visit series.[33] The Chief Inspector of Prisons had warned in March 1982 of the 'considerable resentment' of long-term prisoners in relation to the withdrawal of services. The 'original concept of a liberal regime' had been compromised and serious unrest predicted in a prison where two of the four wings, C and D, remained out of action in early 1982, arising from the 1978 riot.[34] Other more immediate sources of conflict occurred from time to time, leading the IRA prisoners to consider the possibility that they were being encouraged to take actions which would result in much closer control than routinely warranted by Category A status. The situation continued to deteriorate in 1984 at which time the IRA suspected that the POA was attempting to engineer a response that would facilitate a crackdown.[35]

Ken Littlejohn (aka Austen/Austin) was arrested on the M6 in Staffordshire on 15 March 1982 on suspicion of being one of three armed men who expropriated £15,000 from a man in North Wingfield, Derbyshire. He was convicted of armed robbery in Nottingham Crown Court on 16 July 1982 and sentenced to six years imprisonment by Justice Drake.[36] The development revived republican anger at his *agent provocateur* activities in Ireland with brother Keith in the early 1970s. The £67,000 netted from the Allied Irish Bank on 12 October 1972 was the largest total in the history of the state. The fact that it entailed an early 'tiger kidnapping' of the unfortunate bank manager's family was also significant in that it represented a new threshold in paramilitary 'finance' operations.[37] Ken Littlejohn had received a twenty-year sentence in Dublin on 3 August 1973 while his brother Keith was given fifteen.[38] Although conspicuously heavy sentences for the non-fatal offences with which they were convicted, republicans correctly predicted that they would not be served due to their links with British Intelligence.[39] Keith Littlejohn was isolated from republican prisoners in Mountjoy but was on one occasion accosted and beaten.[40] Their former patron, Lady Pamela Onslow (nee Dillon), received a two-pound bomb in the post at her

Kensington home from the IRA in 1982.[41]

The brothers escaped from the Basement of B Block of Mountjoy Prison on 11 March 1974 but Keith injured himself during the breakout and was recaptured when recognized by an off duty prison officer on the street. Otherwise, the escape was remarkable for exposing the sudden lack of security on C and D Wings, not least in the operation of wall patrols.[42] Ken Littlejohn seemingly hid for a number of days in the Howth area of County Dublin before crossing the border and making his way via Amsterdam to England.[43] Bizarrely, he was harboured in Alum Rock, Birmingham, by National Front member Thomas Watt, who gave evidence against members of the wrongfully convicted 'Birmingham Six' in June 1975. Littlejohn was found in Watt's home on 11 December 1974 and was quickly returned to Mountjoy Prison.[44] The men were released on compassionate grounds on 18 September 1981 when Anglo-Irish relations were strained by the Conservative Government's management of the H-Block crisis. Fine Gael Minister for Justice Jim Mitchell ordered their emancipation.[45]

When in Gartree in January 1983, Littlejohn made approaches to Birmingham Six inmate Paddy Hill seeking incriminating information on the IRA; a bold initiative given his acquaintanceship with one of the witnesses who had appeared for the prosecution in 1975. The English man was regarded by republicans as an MI6 asset, if not a former agent, and his overture courted danger. Indeed, one Gartree IRA prisoner had published a letter in the *Irish News* in January 1983 which denounced the Littlejohns as 'British spies', a clear threat to their wellbeing.[46] According to Hill: 'Not long afterwards he was attacked by IRA men in the jail who gave him a savage beating'.[47] This took place on 25 January 1983 and led to a case in Leicester Crown Court on 25 June 1984 in which Hill and other Gartree prisoners agreed to testify for the defence. The English man received twenty stitches to his head and was sent to Leicester to recuperate. Gartree Acting Governor John Clark claimed four IRA prisoners were responsible.[48]

The IRA defendants participated to an unusual degree in court, despite enduring protracted terms of solitary confinement and 'ghosting' in the interim. Hayes was put on Rule 43 on at least forty occasions by 1983 when it was known colloquially in the prison system as 'the Paddy Rule'.[49] Hayes and Kinsella were held in Winson Green in the summer of 1983, where their solicitor Alastair Logan was one of very few visitors permitted to enter.[50] Supporters viewed prison shifts as a tactic to damage their 'excellent morale' ahead of the trial.[51] This sinister yet unverifiable claim represented the most positive interpretation. Sr. Clarke privately queried if the added frequency of transfers in the advent of the trial was 'to make legal visits difficult', an allegation likely to peak the interest of the ECHR.[52] Prison shifts under CI 10/1974 were by no means as common as the general public believed. Between January 1981 and May 1982 Lord Avebury discovered that a total of 112 men were moved in England and Wales. In thirteen of the seventeen-months, the numbers ranged between just three and seven, although ten to sixteen prisoners were shifted in four individual months. In theory governors of 'local' prisons were 'required to confirm ... that there are no exceptional problems that would make it impossible for the prisoner to be accommodated'.[53]

In the case of Category A IRA prisoners, this entailed being held in segregation, although the liberal use of Rule 43 ensured that even this notional consideration could be set aside at will. Officially, a mere 2 per cent of prisoners in England and Wales were held under the provisions of Rule 43 in England and Wales in the early 1980s, including those who had been segregated for their own welfare.[54] The Chief Inspector of Prisons had recommended in 1984 that Rule 43 be used as 'a short term measure' and it was evident that IRA prisoners fell within what he regarded as the 'rare cases' meriting more prolonged segregation. In assessing the overall question of segregation it was averred: 'If Rule 43 inmates could not be returned to their normal location or could not be released from custody in a matter of months, we recommended that they should be transferred to units specially designed to cater for those longer term inmates who were particularly difficult to handle or who required protection'.[55]

It transpired that Littlejohn had made a serious error by approaching fellow A Wing prisoner Wesley Dick, aka Shujaa Moshesh, in an apparent bid to enlist his support in an anti-republican conspiracy. Dick served his sentence as a political prisoner and was fined for a period of two months for refusing to work in the sewing workshop in Gartree. His IRA friends in B Wing, Liam Baker, Jimmy Ashe, Sean Kinsella and Tipp Guilfoyle, with whom he constantly interacted as a comrade, ensured that he was kept well supplied with personal goods.[56] Dick told the court in Leicester that Littlejohn had informed him on the night before the assault that he had brought together a group of fifteen prisoners who planned to attack the republicans.[57] This was denied at trial by Littlejohn, who also disputed having said 'I would hang every goddam one of them if I could'. He did, however, repeat his allegations that he had been recruited by British Intelligence to infiltrate the Official IRA in 1971 and plotted to have Provisional IRA Chief of Staff Sean Mac Stiofain assassinated.[58] Liam Baker carefully checked on the allegations against Littlejohn with non-political associates before the final decision was made to pre-empt the Englishman's efforts to 'get a team up'.[59]

In keeping with the unwritten prisoners' code on public informing, Littlejohn declined to identify his assailants in open court, claiming to have been surprised when attacked from behind.[60] In actuality, Liam Baker, Sean Kinsella, Sean Hayes and Tipp Guilfoyle deliberately carried out the January 1983 assault in full view of everyone present in the exercise yard. It was

IRA policy in England to openly attack hostile ringleaders, generally in a one-on-one basis.[61] A number of Londoners moved of their own accord to screen the republicans from nearby staff.[62] Kinsella 'grabbed him around the throat' and recalled: 'We gave him a good flaking ... We did it in front of all the other prisoners; we did it to show that if anyone was going to attack IRA prisoners there'd be a comeback. We weren't going to take things lying down'.[63] Guilfoyle, who was not laden with a life sentence, claimed in court that he had taken no direct part. In a carefully planned attack the IRA men used table legs, a bottle and a 'sharpened brush handle' to inflict minor injuries when a fatal assault was eminently achievable.[64] The men simply decided that it was unnecessary to kill Littlejohn. On being verbally chastised after the incident by a prison officer, Kinsella reputedly retorted: 'It's your fault, he should not have been here with us'.[65] Another staff member, whom Baker had encountered in Albany, seemed amused that the IRA men had managed to obtain table legs.[66]

Kinsella refused to plead to the charges in Leicester yet freely admitted that he had organized the attack and specified it was on the grounds that Littlejohn was attempting to incite other prisoners to assault republicans.[67] When Guilfoyle was asked why he had not informed staff of the grievance he replied 'Prison officers have given me more kickings, and more scars on my head than Littlejohn will ever get from the IRA'.[68] On 28 June 1984 Kinsella, Baker and Hayes received four years each from Justice Skinner for injuring Littlejohn. Guilfoyle was acquitted when the jury failed to reach a majority verdict on his role.[69] In the time intervening the attack and resultant trial, Guilfoyle was moved between Winson Green, Gartree, Walton, Parkhurst and Leicester. A November 1984 trial in Leicester was postponed for 'security reasons' related to the imminent visit of Queen Elizabeth II to the city.[70] He was afterwards returned to Parkhurst and sent on to Wandsworth. His retrial for the Littlejohn incident took place on 26 February 1985 and he was once again found not guilty on 1 March, a circumstance that entailed his release within the year.[71] Kinsella was moved from Wormwood Scrubs to Frankland in March 1985 and returned to the new dispersal prison on 15 May 1985 after a month 'lie-down' in Armley.[72]

New tactics pursued by the IRA in the H-Blocks following the 1981 hunger strike greatly improved day to day conditions of confinement. The 'no wash' (aka 'dirty protest') had ended and the core elements of the 'Five Demands' were in place by early 1983. Confinement in Portlaoise was less advantaged but by no means the confrontational environment it had been in the mid-to-late 1970s. Accordingly, the attention of Sinn Féin began to revert to the IRA in the Dispersal System where no progress had been achieved on political status, repatriation and visiting conditions. A significant article in *AP/RN* in January 1983 claimed:

Perhaps it is not surprising, especially given the daily pace of events in the North and, in particular, the long drawn-out prison struggle in the H-Blocks and Armagh – that the Irish POWs in England have been relegated to the back of the collective republican consciousness, being remembered only on specific occasions such as Christmas or whenever one of them is released ... at some stage, and in some fashion, the plight of these POWs will have to be faced up to collectively by republicans, even if only to ensure that their situation – separate in the majority of cases from their families in England, and serving savagely long sentences, is not neglected.[73]

The paper, however, was mildly criticised in some quarters for devoting insufficient coverage to the theme. A specific objection was lodged *vis à vis* the lack of wordage devoted to the 26 January 1983 debate in the House of Lords where it was resolved to deny republicans automatic right of repatriation.[74] Humanitarian Lord Hylton posed a query on the Order Paper of the Lords asking the Government 'whether the spirit and intention of Prison Rule 31 is not contravened by the prolonged refusal to transfer certain prisoners from British to Northern Ireland prisons'.[75] This was answered by Lord Elton, Undersecretary of State at the Home Office, and former holder of the equivalent position with the NIO. In view of his status and prior experience, Elton's responses to Hylton and several other Liberal lords amounted to a significant statement at a time when the IRA and INLA had secured advances in the aftermath of the 1981 hunger strike.[76] In justifying the question put to the Government, Hylton specified the strain placed on marriages and family cohesion, whereas Lord Hunt adverted to additional factors, such as arduous, time consuming and expensive travel to the Isle of Wight from 'distant places like Derry and Fermanagh'. Lord Brockway urged special consideration of men with ill relatives incapable of availing of cumulated visits in England before Kilbracken raised the contrasting situation pertaining to military offenders in the North of Ireland. Soldiers were deemed to warrant repatriation to England on the grounds that they were not convicted of 'terrorist offences' and had gone to Ireland 'in pursuit of their duties under orders'.[77]

Elton acknowledged that while general prison practices and regulations pertained to the overall matter, which were addressed by the Home Secretary on the basis of individual merits, the substance of what had been asked related to 'prisoners convicted of terrorist offences committed in this country [England]'. This entailed consideration of 'the management of the prison population in Northern Ireland', where tensions had been raised by disruptive Republican and Loyalist efforts to achieve segregation, alongside the administration of the Dispersal System in England. The core of the argument against automatic invocation of Rule 31 was that there were 'particular obstacles to a transfer to Northern Ireland if a prisoner has committed an offence on behalf of a paramilitary organisation and there is no clear evidence that he has severed his link with that organisation'.[78]

This expressly separated the IRA from persons convicted of criminal offences from the equation. The Home Office definition of severance was indicated by the claim that Shane Paul O'Doherty, who had been advocated on such grounds by Viscount Inglesby, did not qualify. Elton stated that O'Doherty 'continues to refuse to comply with prison rules' and that this was interpreted as meaning there was 'no convincing evidence to suggest' his departure from the IRA.[79] If nothing else, the debate proved that the IRA was still very much regarded as a discrete and dangerous element within the Dispersal System. Those aspiring to repatriation, moreover, were given to understand that conformity in England was a pre-requisite to consideration by the Home Secretary of transfer. In a subsequent private but official correspondence with Islington South and Finsbury MP Chris Smith, Elton dismissed a circumstance of great relevance by stating 'there is no power to transfer prisoners to serve their sentences in the Republic of Ireland'.[80]

Sinn Féin responded, albeit indirectly, when Owen Carron MP spoke out against the 'ghosting' of Dickie Glenholmes, Eddie O'Neill and John McCluskey from Hull to 'lie downs' in Liverpool and Durham. Carron claimed that such 'unexplained movements' were 'a common form of harassment used almost exclusively against Irish political prisoners in England'. There was no real equivalent in Ireland and the policy represented a point of demarcation in the overall prisoner issue. As always, the wider picture demanded attention and Carron simultaneously raised recent incidents of prisoner maltreatment in Armagh Jail and Portloaise.[81] Republican supporters in England attempted to maintain pressure by picketing Hull on 22 January, a gesture which Ronnie McCartney appreciated whilst arguing for Sinn Féin (Britain) to prioritize the primary question of 'the development of the struggle in Ireland'.[82]

McCartney's intervention from Hull adverted to an occasionally bitter debate surrounding statements from Sinn Féin (Britain) which reasserted the party's sole right to speak 'officially' on behalf of the IRA prisoners in England. Left – leaning IRA men such as Bobby Campbell, then in Parkhurst, interpreted such declarations as a slight upon other 'anti-imperialist pro-Irish liberation groups' in Britain and urged 'tolerance'. Repatriation was identified as the single-most pressing issue, and this too created tensions. Campbell claimed: 'No POW wants and expects any deviation from the war effort, be it the military or political side of the struggle, because of the conditions we are suffering, but it must be said that Sinn Féin, both in Ireland and Britain, could do better where the interests of the POWs are concerned'.[83] He implied that the absence of clear leadership direction on the relative importance of a repatriation campaign had created 'divisive arguments' among the prisoners who would accept 'whichever course is adopted'. The prisoners, he argued, required much more information on party policies and positions.[84] This call was echoed by an *ad hoc* grouping of relatives of Belfast IRA prisoners held in England in mid-May.[85] By early June the same group insisted that the men were 'political hostages' who were entitled to repatriation as 'a right' as opposed to 'a concession'.[86] A further group of three women were inspired to echo an initiative which Sinn Féin accepted by virtue of facilitating its expression.[87]

If concerned by the pace of policy formation and general communications on political affairs from Sinn Féin Headquarters in Dublin, Campbell and, therefore, the Parkhurst coterie, were conscious of their immediate roles. He noted:

> The vast majority of us here try to express our actions as republican POWs at all times. We play our small parts as best we can by facing the repressive administrations here at every opportunity we see. Some concentrate on the spreading of information on how the prison system uses drugs on those seen as politically aware prisoners and a large number keep foreign solidarity groups and individuals informed as to the Brits' torturous and murderous actions. When necessary we operate against the enemy in violent terms of action – we can't all be level-headed and calculating all the time. On occasions we have protested (rarely newsworthy from the Brits' point of view) in support of actions at home in Ireland. I believe the POWs carry our flag proudly.[88]

Owen Carron commenced his second round of English prison tours on 28 February 1983, just four days after Campbell's assessment from Parkhurst. Carron went to Gartree and found modest improvements since his previous visit: 'A screw sat in the doorway and supervised the visit. The screws used to sit at the table but over the years the lads kicked up so many rackets that now they sit at the door'.[89] This minor yet meaningful reform was maintained notwithstanding the IRA prisoners' attack on Kenneth Littlejohn. In Hull on 29 February 1983 Carron met with Stevie Nordone, who once again drew attention to the solitary protest of Mick Murray, and Martin Coughlan, who was dissatisfied with Sinn Féin's handling of the repatriation question. Paul Holmes and Ronnie McCartney were also in Hull, as was Con McFadden, recently arrived from Wormwood Scrubs where he had fasted for twelve days in the Segregation Unit with no publicity to register his dissent.[90] February 1983 also witnessed a co-ordinated prisoners' work strike in Parkhurst and Albany during which inmates had demanded the new parole privileges which had been conceded to the IRA in the North of Ireland arising from the 1981 hunger-strike.[91]

The planned visit to Leicester SSU on 1 March 1983 was cancelled when it was learned that Brian Keenan and Brendan Dowd were receiving visitors. Carron instead travelled to Styal Prison in Wilmslow, Cheshire where Ann and Eileen Gillespie had been located in 1982 ahead of their release in August 1983. The sisters were in the news the following month when denied compassionate parole to attend the Donegal funeral of their father.[92]

From 11 March 1983 Sr. Clarke held the view that her original concept of volunteer clergy running a twenty-four hour service to assist prisoners' families was unviable. It appeared to her that the Chaplaincy in London had not accepted her perspective on the allegedly poor level of service being provided by the Home Office - cleared chaplains in English prisons and that they were consequently unwilling to manage the type of grouping she had advocated. Ultimately, much of the envisaged voluntary work was undertaken from 1985 by a different body, the Irish Commission for Prisoners Overseas (ICPO) and Sr. Clarke surmised that if unsuccessful in bringing her ideal project into being, she had, nonetheless, achieved a general improvement in the situation through focused lobbying.[93] The effort was described by *The Catholic Herald* of 9 July 1982 as 'that most unpopular cause of all ... Irish convicted prisoners in British jails'.[94] Support was then received from Eamon Andrews, the Irish born celebrity presenter of *This is your Life,* one of the top - rated television programmes in Britain.[95] The ICPO was a subsection of the Irish Episcopal Commission for Emigrants and worked under Fr. PJ Byrne and Nuala Kelly out of offices in Lower Abbey Street, Dublin.[96]

Cardinal Tomas O Fiaich, Archbishop of Armagh, made an important statement on the prison situation in England on 7 April 1983 in the course of an address to the congress of the Irish Episcopal Commission on Emigration. The Cardinal stated his conviction that there were Irish prisoners in England serving sentences for offences they had not committed. He specifically raised the cases of the Birmingham Six, Guildford Four and Maguire Seven. Much of the immediacy and confidence of his assertion derived from fact-finding visits to Styal and Long Lartin prisons on the weekend of 2–3 April.[97] O Fiaich also recommended that long-term Irish prisoners be granted transfers to the North of Ireland and in so doing gave his backing to a major bone of contention of IRA support groups. He also implicitly criticized the Home Office in calling for the immediate notification of families whose imprisoned relatives were being moved between English prisons.[98] One, Sean Smyth of the Maguire Seven, had been highlighted in February when his wife Theresa was informed on the eve of the fourth of six long-planned visits to Wormwood Scrubs that he had been shifted to Wakefield.[99] Smyth was moved five times in nine years on what he described as the 'roundabout' used for Irish Category A prisoners.[100]

Conservative MP Michael Mates challenged the validity of O Fiaich's intervention during an interview on RTÉ radio on 8 April. Mates claimed there was 'general acceptance' that the Birmingham Six were 'guilty men, who actually caused murder and mayhem in Birmingham on that infamous day in 1975 [recte 1974] when it all happened'. If undoubtedly accurate *vis à vis* the media created ill-informed perspective of the wider British public on the convictions, Mates was erroneous on the basic facts of the events under discussion. His expressed view that those who committed offences in what he termed 'mainland Britain' should serve their sentences in England, however, was entirely legitimate as a personal opinion even if not reflected in the formal regulations of the Home Office which permitted repatriation.[101] Mates had served in Ireland in the capacity of a senior Intelligence Officer attached to the British Army and he spoke with the authority of the British Establishment in 1983. His criticism of O Fiaich, and the invective of sectarian elements of Irish Unionism, however, backfired spectacularly if intended to quash suspicion of significant wrong doing in British courts. The moderate Nationalist *Derry Journal* decried unequivocally the 'intemperate outbursts' on what it regarded as valid and informed criticism.[102]

In a February 1983 letter to the Relatives and Friends of Prisoners Committee, Paddy Joe Hill of the Birmingham Six claimed 'we have been condemned to die in prison for a crime we did not commit and if we are to die in these hell holes, then I for one, would rather die fighting on hunger strike'. A commencement date of 1 June 1983 was declared, although this did not eventuate. Hill had fasted for forty-one days in 1981 and the prospect of him emulating the tragic Frank Stagg, who mounted four sustained hunger strikes prior to dying in Wakefield in February 1976, was exceptionally serious. He and others evidently took heart from the groundswell of support rising in Ireland, Britain and the USA.[103]

The Cardinal's comments greatly encouraged those who had campaigned on behalf of republican and wrongfully convicted prisoners in England. Deaglan O hAodha, a student activist in Trinity College, Dublin, joined with others to seek the support of Tony Gregory TD in raising two questions on O Fiaich's allegations in the Dáil.[104] One of Gregory's first public political acts was to march in support of IRA prisoners arrested in England in 1969. He was also a former member of the Official Republican Movement and IRSP. Charles Haughey had already expressed concern in relation to the Home Office decision to deny short-term parole to Ann and Eileen Gillespie from Styal Prison on the occasion of the death of their father, Owen 'Owney Mor' Gillespie, in Bunbeg, Donegal on 15 April 1983. The sisters were due for release within four months and William Whitelaw's claim in April 1983 that parole was declined owing to the jurisdictional complications of providing a British escort was deemed unduly petty. Fianna Fáil TD Pat 'The Cope' Gallagher, later to wed Ann Gillespie, was highly critical: 'We in Fianna Fáil will make it known to the British in the strongest possible terms that if they are interested in strengthening relationships between Ireland and England, this was an excellent opportunity for them to show good faith. This they did not do and for this we condemn them'.[105] Transfer to Styal had entailed a security reclassification for the sisters who described the facility as 'a group of houses ... a semi-open prison'.[106]

The rejection of representations from the Department of Foreign Affairs, via the London embassy, gave substance to a broad range of critical voices.[107] Unusually, Fine Gael was represented in the form of Paddy Harte TD, an energetic Border anti-republican who had been elected in the Gillespie family constituency. Harte had visited the sisters in Durham in the late 1970s when his parliamentary status, coupled with FCO recognition that his was 'a personal friend of the family', induced the Home Office to make an exception to its policy of denying TDs access to prisoners detained in the Six Counties and England.[108] His 1983 intervention and that of Derry's SDLP MEP John Hume, although consistent, led to accusations of political opportunism from republicans.[109] The Gillespie funeral was attended by prominent republicans including the recently emancipated Fr. Pat Fell, Daithi O Conaill, Joe Cahill and Sinn Féin Vice President Gerry Adams. The presence of Neil Blaney, MEP and independent TD, was inoffensive to these men in view of his strong track record on the National Question. Other public figures, not least Bishop Edward Daly of Derry, were engaged on behalf of the Gillespie family, adding to an increasingly rare panoply of state, secular, clerical and republican sentiment.[110] The sisters were released on 29 August 1983 and were greeted in Dublin airport by a large crowd of well-wishers.[111] Ruairi O'Bradaigh met the sisters in Bundoran and described them as 'the longest serving women Republican prisoners in history'.[112] Press photographers captured scenes which could only have dismayed opponents of the IRA:

> Hundreds of people, including relatives, friends and supporters, clapped and cheered as the sisters were carried shoulder-high from the arrivals gate. And there [were] bonfires blazing, bands, car cavalcades and crossroads meetings in Donegal that evening as enthusiastic friends and neighbours welcomed them home.[113]

At Easter 1983 Cardinal O Fiaich had formed a highly favourable opinion of Shane Paul O'Doherty in the course of a prison visit: 'We had a very sincere heart to heart conversation and like all the other priests who have met him, I was very impressed by his honesty and openness and prayerfulness'. This added impetus to his public comments on Irish prisoners in England, which generated a flurry of media attention. He reflected in January 1984: 'Suddenly ... and for a few weeks I was very hopeful as many papers carried articles and TV and radio became interested'. The attention, however, was not sustained and resulted in no short term dividends. O Fiaich attributed this to press reaction to the mass breakout from Long Kesh, a major embarrassment to the British authorities, and renewed IRA activity in England, which limited the prospects of accruing public empathy.[114]

Several Belfast women with close male relatives in jail in England accused the SDLP of engaging in Westminster electioneering at a time when the party was allegedly at 'a low ebb' due to the growth in support for Sinn Féin since 1981.[115] A specific line of attack emerged when Dickie Glenholmes, whose wife Lily was one of those engaged in advocating the rights of IRA prisoners in England, referenced what he regarded as the hypocritical or hostile decision of the SDLP to contest the Fermanagh-South Tyrone constituency held by Sinn Féin's Owen Carron and previously by republicans Bobby Sands and Frank Maguire.[116] Both Carron and Maguire had been demonstrably more committed to agitation on the prisons issue than SDLP MPs, although Paddy Devlin and John Hume had assisted at various times. Perceived injustices were neither academic nor remote. In April 1983 Glenholmes had been denied compassionate parole to attend his mother's funeral in Belfast from Long Lartin. This followed the March rejection of an application from Gerry Young to travel to his father's funeral services in the same city from the Leicestershire prison.[117] Glenholmes was one of a number of IRA prisoners in England with experience of incarceration in the North of Ireland. When in Long Kesh in the 1970s Glenholmes was photographed alongside Gerry Adams as they posed with prominent republicans Ivor Bell and Kevin Hannaway.[118] In the event of the death of immediate family, all would have qualified for compassionate parole in the North of Ireland.

With increased political and press interest in Ireland, accounts of the hardships suffered by the relatives of prisoners proliferated in the regional and mainstream media. Fergus Hall interviewed Josephine O'Neill, mother of Parkhurst prisoner Eddie O'Neill, in late April 1983. Hall found Mrs O'Neill visibly 'tense' in her home near Coalisland, Tyrone, following the 'trauma of looking at her son locked up so far away'.[119] She knew he was being regularly moved between prisons without explanation and generally experienced disruption of his mail and other supposed entitlements. Such were typical IRA Category A experiences. Immediate, personal grievances were also in play and O'Neill had served over a month in solitary confinement for embracing his mother, contrary to prison policy.[120] His London based sister, Ursula Hayes, appreciated first hand the myriad stresses of visiting different parts of the Dispersal System. Regarding the Isle of Wight: 'If you missed one connection, that was it. One ferry would have been too early and the next ferry would have been too late. So it was a rush'.[121] Informal networks of associates and supporters attempted to redress the particular hardships faced by elderly parents and women with small children. In 1983 Hayes was contacted by Sr. Clarke, with whom a bond of friendship had formed, to provide overnight accommodation to Geraldine Bailey when the Belfast woman's fiancée Tommy Quigley was on remand in Brixton.[122] Fourteen persons remanded as 'Provisional Category A' on 'terrorist type offences' went untried for periods of nine to twelve months between 1980 and 1982.[123]

The Irish Government received unwanted inspection of its judicial affairs on 7 April 1983 when it was reported that Nicky Kelly intended to protest the 'uncompromising attitude' of Fine Gael Minister for Justice Michael Noonan by going on hunger strike in Portlaoise. Kelly had gone on the run after the forty-first day of his trial at the Special Criminal Court, which terminated in the wrongful conviction of his two co-accused, Brian McNally and Osgur Breathnach, whose sentences were quashed in 1980 when the Court of Criminal Appeal accepted their 'confessions' had been obtained by severe physical and mental abuse. On returning from exile to Ireland in expectation of exoneration, Kelly was not only detained but frustrated in seeking the same consideration bestowed on McNally and Breathnach on technical grounds. The Supreme Court erred in upholding his original conviction and the twelve-year sentence imposed in absentia. The fact that all three IRSP men had been framed by their captors for the 1976 Sallins train robbery carried out by the Provisional IRA aroused the interest of Amnesty International. Kelly's innocence was conceded by the Irish state on 28 April 1992 when he was granted an exceptionally rare Presidential Pardon.[124] The IRA had publicly admitted the heist as early in May 1980, although the Irish judiciary ignored the implications of an unusual statement of responsibility in the absence of charges against its membership.[125] After thirty-eight days of refusing food, Kelly abandoned his hunger strike on 7 June 1983, during which time supporters in England including the IRSP, TOM and RCG picketed Ireland House, the Irish Embassy and the Irish Tourist Office.[126]

A very broad section of Irish society had been convinced of Kelly's innocence, including Cardinal O Fiaich and Fr. Ray Murray who had been critical of the prison policies of the NIO and Home Office. In London, TOM, RCG and the Young Liberals were united in their advocacy of justice for Kelly and support for a withdrawal of British Military forces from the North of Ireland.[127] The Sallins prisoners, like the 'Birmingham Six', had been wrongly suspected of politically motivated offences carried out by the IRA. The Law Society of University College Cork appointed Kelly Honorary Vice-President of the society in 1983.[128]

A new Broad Front?

On 19 April 1983 IRA prisoners in Albany endorsed a complicated process of realignment taking place within Britain's numerous pro-republican groupings. The impetus derived from the 20 November 1982 conference in Caxton House, organised by the North London Irish Solidarity Committee.[129] The stated aim, as outlined by David Yaffe (aka Reed) of the Revolutionary Communist Group, was the formation of a national Irish

Solidarity Movement by means of achieving a 'real unity – based on the common interests of the Irish people and the British working class in the defeat of British imperialism'.[130] Tariq Ali had called for such an initiative in July 1970 but the task of marshalling disparate Trotskyite militants in concert with the Republican Movement proved elusive.[131] Alastair Logan, Helen O'Brien and Michael Holden provided information and analysis on the prisoner dimension in Caxton House and ensured an Irish republican input from the outset.[132]

The London event was followed on 12 March 1983 by a 'national demonstration' which provided encouraging signs that a coalition formed on the basis of shared anti-imperialism could be created. A crowd of 600 activists marched through North London and converged in Euston Road before attending a rally chaired by leading RCG member Terry O'Halloran (aka 'Terry Marlowe' and 'John Fitzgerald') in Whittington Park. Joint support for Irish self-determination, abolition of the PTA and campaigns of the 'Irish POWs' bound the RCG-backed Irish Solidarity Committees of Scotland and England to Essex University Students Union, Bristol TOM, Luton Sinn Féin, Bangladesh Workers Association and Organisation of Iranian Peoples Fedaii Guerillas. Messages from Irish, Scottish and Welsh political prisoners were read to reportedly 'enthusiastic applause'.[133]

The ISM was projected as an umbrella organization linking Irish Solidarity Committees across the country which, crucially, were to comprise an interface between the notoriously fractured far left in Britain. It was envisaged that input from disparate campaigns, such as humanitarian groups opposed to the use of plastic bullets, were be incorporated even if their sponsors did not fully endorse the RCG view of the ISM as a vehicle for 'the anti-imperialist position on Ireland'.[134] The core ISM demands were encapsulated in the phrase 'Victory to the Irish People! Troops Out Now! The Right of Repatriation for all Irish POWs!'[135] The well-qualified London-Irish man Terry O'Halloran, who hailed from Pimlico, was one of the 'principal architects'. O'Halloran worked as a journalist, rising to chair of the London Freelance Branch of the NUJ and belonged to the organization's Ethics Council.[136] Nineteen IRA prisoners and the wrongly convicted Paul Hill sponsored the initiative. John McCluskey from Hull stated:

> We appeal to all those political groups and individuals who claim to support the right of self-determination for the Irish people to come together and help form an Irish Solidarity Movement. By showing full support with the Irish struggle you will also be helping the British working class, we are fighting the same enemy as you, i.e. 'the British ruling class'.[137]

Attended by the RCG, Revolutionary Communist League, East London TOM and two Sinn Féin cumainn (Wolfe Tone and Connolly/Keegan), the event was ignored by the CPGB, International Socialists and Connolly Association. The detachment of the Stalinist CPGB was predictable given its consistent failure to engage with the Irish conflict as a body and that of the Connolly Association, explained by its preference for independent campaigning. However, the estrangement of the core of the TOM and International Socialists was problematic given their past centrality to pro-Irish agitation. The 20 November 1982 gathering succeeded in initiating a network of Irish Solidarity Committees which, if by no means well subscribed by the full range of possible constituents, was sufficient to launch the ISM on 2 October 1983.[138] It was in this context of concrete advances and clear reverses that an analysis of the situation was sent to the Liverpool ISC in April 1983 in the name of the IRA prisoners in Albany.[139]

It was clearly significant that the militant RCG, publishers of *Hands off Ireland!* had continued its open dialogue with the Republican Movement in the early 1980s in the pages of its *Fight Racism! Right Imperialism!* monthly newspaper. Noel Gibson regarded the openly sympathetic title, produced to high professional standards, as 'the best newspaper published in this country'.[140] With the gradual winding down of the once dynamic PAC, the activist core of RCG maintained a distinct presence in radical pro-Irish politics in Britain alongside the much larger TOM, Connolly Association and Sinn Féin (Britain). The Albany document noted that the RCG had offered unequivocal 'militant support to the Irish war for national liberation' and that over 100 of its members had been arrested for producing and distributing published propaganda. This track record was interpreted as putting the political 'credentials' of the RCG 'beyond question', and the organization believed the publicity work of Marlowe *et al* had contributed to the Home Office retreat from staging 'mutiny' hearings.[141] Accordingly, Helen O'Brien, sister of IRA prisoner John McCluskey, Michael Holden of Luton Sinn Féin and Liz Hill, mother of the innocent Paul Hill, were among those who addressed a preliminary demonstration on 1 October 1983 on the weekend of the ISM formation. Vince Donnelly encouraged the step: 'Ireland's victory is your victory, the cause of Irish workers is your cause – let's win this victory together'.[142]

More qualified support was given by Irish republicans to the Revolutionary Communist Party and its Irish Freedom Movement (IFM) front on the grounds that it appeared to be 'a party controlled grouping'. Although not cited, the contention that the RCP was vulnerable to accusations of selfish interests was reminiscent of past unease with 'entryist' tactics favoured by the IMG and similar Trotskyist bodies.[143] The republican perspective in April 1984 called for the amalgamation of the RCG backed ISM and RCP controlled IFM to create an 'impeccably democratic' campaign for 'three demands'.[144] By then the ISM had promoted communications with IRA prisoners in England by a means of correspondence and had drawn up practical guidelines in order to minimize Prison Department scope for censorship and sanctions.[145] From February 1983 a *Newsletter* produced for 'internal circulation' within the ISM was sent to IRA members in English prisons, resulting in closer ties than before.[146]

The 'demands' formulated in Albany articulated the thinking of numerous IRA prisoners in England *vis à vis* their position in the ongoing Long War: '1. complete British withdrawal from Ireland, 2. self-determination for the Irish people, 3. repatriation for all POWs to Ireland'. The specific interests of the prisoners in England were addressed in two further 'stipulations': '1. no political demands whatever will be asked of the Irish Republican Army i.e. a tactical ceasefire etc. *The war goes on regardless.* 2. no pseudo-humanitarian calls for a ceasefire in England as a quid pro quo for our repatriation, the continuation of the liberation war takes precedence over our repatriation'.[147] The conditions and terms delineated represented a bold effort to stimulate action from the confines of the Dispersal System. Origination with IRA prisoners in England, however, all but guaranteed disharmony with Sinn Féin Headquarters in Ireland where the challenge of addressing the conflict as a totality was Herculean in extent.

Confusingly, individual cumainns of Sinn Féin (Britain) were aligned with both the ISM and IFM in 1984, and the IRA men imprisoned in England deemed it necessary to petition the leadership in Dublin to bestow 'full-hearted support' for a potentially major merger.[148] John McCluskey recalled: 'We were trying to create a line of solidarity between Irish political prisoners in Britain and groups on the outside. We were trying to voice our views, even to our own organisations, on how things should be done'.[149] Other IRA prisoners, not least close friends and republican socialists Ray McLaughlin and Eddie O'Neill, were determined that no single body could assume the mantle of 'claiming … the Republican imprimatur' in Britain. As joint authors of the 'Albany letter', the pair had a deep interest in ensuring that its content was not subject to 'distortion' and contested one TOM-sourced perspective which indicated that 'POWs are no more than receivers and transmitters of Brit left politics'.[150] TOM produced a detailed response to its critics noting that the organization had 'through consistent work over the last ten years, … help[ed] create the basis which now exists, for a broad withdrawal movement, which is called for by the Republican Movement in Ireland'.[151]

Brian Keenan had offered constructive criticism of the formative stages of the ISM strategy from the confines of Leicester SSU with special reference to its capacity to address the 'bitter enmity … between groups professing to be in the revolutionary left'. Holding that the 'struggle in Ireland' could not be won 'without the help of sincere revolutionaries in this country, acting in total harmony with each other', he asserted that 'until the struggle in Ireland is successfully brought to a revolutionary phase there is no hope at all of a successful start' in Britain.[152] Drawing on his background as a trade union

Shop Steward in Belfast, Keenan did not believe that forging a joint far left position on the prison struggle in England would suffice:

> If the SLISC envisage solidarity then much work must be done in that respect. It is not enough to hope that the POWS etc can be a sufficient catalyst for that solidarity. The catalyst must be ideological and at the same time pragmatic. In the final analysis the revolutionary must have the ability and respect to motivate vast numbers of people. The constant bickering at the moment seems to me a microcosm of that inability to motivate ... I fully understand the problems you will have and I am fraternally with you. I do not, however, believe that it is necessary, nor indeed revolutionary correct, that I as a POW should be asked to publicly endorse a committee or organisation outside the one to which I am totally committed. Revolutionary comrades will always come together naturally at the right time and place. The catalyst must come from within.[153]

Competition for Sinn Féin's attention in England and perceived lack of direction from Dublin derived, at least in part, from the manifestation of a damaging rupture within TOM/ UTOM in the late 1970s. TOM was the original and most significant pro-Sinn Féin organization in Britain and one with strong ties to the party from its foundation in west London in 1973. The Albany group were harshly critical of TOM's allegedly 'reformist' leadership which, it was argued, underestimated the perniciousness of British imperialism in Ireland, to the point that it was diverted into 'humanitarian solutions'. It was not entertained that the failure of Sinn Féin (Britain) to gain influence in the UK trade union movement during periodic IRA offensives in England and CPGB resistance had been addressed by TOM in a manner that invited questions of its militancy. Certain TOM branches identified as 'progressive' were urged to combine with the ISC and build a coalition attracting 'every shade of political opinion from progressive social democrats leftwards to Revolutionary Marxism'.[154]

IRA prisoners in England took pains to ensure that the positions adopted by loose groups in various prisons was not perceived as oppositional to Sinn Féin in Ireland or Britain. From the Kent Wing of Maidstone Prison, Gerry Mac Lochlainn endorsed the programme in a purely 'personal capacity' in order to sidestep potential questions of organizational preference.[155] Vince Donnelly in Albany observed in his private communication with the RCG: 'We pledge our support as individuals and not as any stated faction. We all regret that unconditional support is not at the moment forthcoming from Sinn Féin'. This was attributed to the views of a 'few' promoting an exclusively 'nationalist solution' whom, he believed, 'will have to eventually bow to the majority'.[156] As before, the 'unconditional support' consistently offered by the RCG for the Republican Movement appealed to Bobby Campbell in Parkhurst.[157]

Eddie O'Neill recalled that the 'broad front' advocacy of the Albany prisoners was 'anathema ... to the Movement' whereas both *Andersonstown News* and *Irish News* were intrigued. The attempted inclusion of the far left in Britain certainly questioned Sinn Féin policy. In the light of the major internal party reforms of 1986–87, its authors reflected that while their recommendations made from the wings and SSUs in England had not been adopted in full, the 'philosophy was expounded' in a way that 'allowed us to open up our minds'.[158] Long Kesh, Portlaoise and Armagh also contributed important political commentaries, albeit in a generally more discrete and manageable fashion informed by numbers, structures, tradition and modes of communication. In June 2001 Martin Mansergh, a leading Irish Government advisor in the 1980s and 1990s, noted: 'The prisons had also enabled some at least on all sides time to study and discuss both their basic political philosophy and their tactics. It has to be acknowledged that some of the most creative thinking and impulses in the peace process came out of the prisons'.[159]

When the RCG pressed forward with the ISM march and conference in October 1983, the tactics of repression developed in Ireland for application in Britain were very much in evidence, as the far left had long predicted. The Tory Government stood its ground against the anti-nuclear campaigners in Greenham Common in 1985, initiated secret contingencies to destroy the mining unions in 1984–85 and utilized the PTA and other legal measures to inhibit protest marches in 1984.[160] The spectre of plastic bullets, CS gas and *agent provocateurs* being transferred from the North of Ireland to British soil was suddenly very credible as progressive forces in the UK had long feared and predicted. Solidarity was also extended across the Irish Sea to a degree that inspired close examination by British authorities. A sequesters' investigation into the National Union of Mineworkers funds lodged in Irish banks allegedly resulted in the discovery of £3 million owned by the IRA.[161] Miners participated in ISM/TOM delegations to Belfast in August 1984 and the Manchester Martyrs' rally in November 1984.[162] In Wakefield Vince Donnelly mused that the 'wholehearted response' of the Irish at home and in Britain would be an 'eyeopener for the sizeable number of ex-army personnel from mining communities'.[163]

Glasgow Sinn Féin launched the monthly *Republican Bulletin* in November 1983 which, from the outset, carried news of the IRA prisoners held in England. This was logical given the base of the grouping in Scotland's sizable republican community and the heavy commitment of local bands to Irish political events across Britain.[164] The timing of the launch coincided with plans to initiate a 'Prisoners of War Campaign' in London to secure 'five demands'. While details remained tentative in late 1983, the objectives were understood in November to encompass the release of Pat Hackett 'on medical grounds', the release of 'prisoners framed by the British police', the repeal of the PTA, 'repatriation on demand for all POWs' and 'an end to solitary confinement and control units'.[165] This was subsequently approved by the AGM of Sinn Féin in Britain and launched in London in February 1984 on the anniversary of the death of Frank Stagg. Alastair Logan supported the campaign.[166]

The *Republican Bulletin* was also a platform for An Cumann Cabhrach/ Prisoners Aid (Britain), which was organized in Glasgow by Tony O'Mara. All monies raised in Scotland by the grouping were expended on the forty plus IRA prisoners then in England and a target of £1,000 in donations was set in November for the Christmas 1983 'special payment'. More generally, An Cumann Cabhrach financed the purchase of reading and educational materials for the prisoners and attempted to defray the costs of prison visits throughout the year. This was expressly to 'help the POWs keep in contact with the outside world'.[167] The Troops Out Movement, with twenty-one branches in England, seven in London, three in Scotland and two in Wales in 1984 offered significant support to the 'five demands' initiative across Britain.[168]

John McComb

The Irish conflict and the capacity of the IRA to operate in England ensured further trials and arrivals into the Dispersal System. John McComb was seized in the Short Strand, Belfast, on Sunday 24 January 1982. His detention, linked to a city based informer, was described as 'a significant arrest' and led to brief speculation that he was the fugitive Gerry Tuite.[169] McComb received a ten-year sentence on 6 December 1972 for IRA armed robberies which financed prisoners' dependents funds. Elder brother Hugh 'Huggy' McComb had been previously jailed as a leading republican activist in the Short Strand/Markets district and their mother, Cecilia, had at least one of her four sons behind bars between October 1971 and July 2000.[170] John McComb 'reported back' to the IRA once released in August 1977 and operated in England with Gerry Tuite the following year when 'on the run'. They returned to Ireland in 1979 where McComb took up residence in Dundalk on the Louth/Armagh border. Risking discovery, he returned to Belfast during the 1981 hunger strikes, partly to be near his young family at a time of great instability. English voices overheard in Castlereagh Interrogation Centre alerted him to the imminence of being dispatched on an RAF flight to Northholt airfield in London. Confirmation of his actual identity resulted in his transfer to Paddington Green on 25 January 1982, where Scotland Yard attempted questioning in relation to numerous economic bombings in the late 1970s. Lambeth Magistrates Court remanded McComb in custody to Brixton on charges of conspiracy to cause explosions.[171] He reappeared in Marylebone Court on 28 January 1982 in the presence of heavily armed police. Proceedings were exceptionally perfunctory and reportedly took just 'one minute'.[172] Haste may have played a part in the revelation during committal proceedings on 13–14 September 1982 that seventy-two detonators recovered in Trafalgar Road had been transferred to Woolwich Arsenal, contrary to earlier claims that they had been destroyed.[173]

Attacks attributed to the IRA ASU of which McComb had been a member were among the most costly and disruptive carried out by the organization in England. This may have had bearing on his unusually confrontational induction to imprisonment in London. McComb received vindictive treatment in the Reception Area of Brixton where his clothes were ripped from his body in full view of a cynical churchman. A Scottish staff member who recognized him from secondment to County Antrim struck him heavily on the back of the head and quipped 'you're not in Long Kesh now, McComb'. The seemingly cultivated sense of menace deepened when his asthma inhaler was confiscated: 'I remember the screw throwing it into the waste paper basket: "We don't care if you fucking die tonight you bastard!" And I just looked up, lying on the floor naked, and there's a Church of England chaplain sitting laughing'. Held for a time in a ground floor 'Punishment Block', McComb was momentarily disconcerted by the thought that it was a 'normal' cell from which daylight was barely visible through rows of steel grilles. He was later allocated the one from which Tuite had escaped in 1980: 'They showed me the big cement mark on the wall. They said, "have a look at that, you're not going where he went, you're going nowhere"'.[174]

His twenty-seven months on remand were utterly different to his years in Long Kesh prior to the abolition of political status. Isolation was an unwelcome new experience which he countered by attending Mass on Sundays and ecumenical religious meetings on Wednesday evenings. This enabled social interaction with Billy Power and Dick McIlkenny of the 'Birmingham Six' who, unlike McComb, were indeed devout Christians. He was appalled by the attitude of the Catholic Chaplain, who openly agreed that the pair were innocent without feeling any onus to advance their campaign for exoneration. An exercised McComb called the priest a 'hypocrite' when he refused to support his letter format petition, intended for circulation among all the religious denominations, on that grounds that it might jeopardize the ecumenical sessions.[175] McComb was unimpressed by the chaplain's claim to have 'turned Shane [Paul O'Doherty] around … brought that man to Redemption'. This was not only untrue given the Derry man's personal inspiration but also indicative of a mindset disposed to undermine republican cohesion in England. The Chaplain had been attached to Wormwood Scrubs during the August 1979 'riot' and refused to corroborate multiple prisoner complaints of maltreatment as it contravened Home Office practices and came under the auspices of the Official Secrets Act.[176] Gerry Cunningham and Ray McLaughlin had previously failed to interest the cleric in cases regarding the maltreatment of prisoners in the London jail.[177]

John McComb was tried in the Old Bailey on 9 May 1983 for offences associated with the London based cluster associated with Tuite between November 1978 and January 1979. Fingerprints recovered from a copy of *Who's Who* and maps of English cities in the Trafalgar Round, Greenwich safe house used by the ASU were linked to the Belfast man by prosecuting QC David Jeffreys.[178] An audio tape recording was described in court as a 'hit list' owing to its mention of prominent Establishment figures such as Lord Carrington, Enoch Powell, Michael Heseltine and William Whitelaw, as well as Sir Hugh Fraser, who had been previously targeted by Brendan Dowd's ASU in October 1975. The inclusion of Airey Neave indicated that the presumed IRA intelligence dated from the period prior to March 1979 when the MP was assassinated in the House of Commons by the INLA.[179] Evidence heard in court served to remind the British public of the acute threat posed by the IRA in their native land. The drama of the occasion soared when the Anti-Terrorist Squad claimed to have found ten pounds of nitro-glycerine and other explosive materials in a flat on North Road, Highgate, just one week prior to the trial. The quantity recovered was sufficient for numerous IRA attacks. McComb was convicted on 26 May 1983 by a jury split 11–1 and sentenced to seventeen years imprisonment.[180] Andrew Collins, Junior Treasury Counsel, was subjected to vitriolic comments attributed to opposing counsel and leaked to the *Daily Telegraph* for pursuing his professional duty to defend the Irish man. Collins was subsequently vindicated.[181]

In sending a polemical address carried by the *Irish People* on 14 May 1983, Ronnie McCartney furthered the process of the England IRA prisoners aligning themselves openly with the objectives of the overall Republican Movement. McCartney's historically informed communication praised the ongoing efforts of the North American INA and their supporters for 'assisting us in many ways' and urged them to 'keep the faith'. He invited a negative comparison of the records of 'the likes of [Charles] Haughey, [John] Hume and [Garret] Fitzgerald with that of Michael Flannery, Gerry Adams, Owen Carron or any other Republican representatives'. In belligerent tones informed by Terence MacSwiney's IRB ideology he continued: 'Republicans are willing to make all the necessary sacrifices to ensure that our sovereignty is recognized and upheld ... while the Free State politicians are willing to sacrifice nothing'.[182] In signing off with the *Tiocfaidh ár Lá* slogan popularised by Bobby Sands in 1981, McCartney alluded to the fact that the conflict was ongoing and that Irish-America should take its lead from men like Flannery rather than the unmentioned anti-IRA 'Four Horsemen' and the Irish Embassy in Washington DC. If McCartney's message from a Hull cell was addressed to sympathisers, it was, nonetheless, perceptive and rational.[183] In private McCartney was unsuccessfully seeking assistance in obtaining a bolt cutters and outside assistance to convey escaping prisoners to safety from one of the most inaccessible prisons in Britain.[184]

The economics of visiting prisoners in England did not improve in the early 1980s and most families with relatives in the Dispersal System struggled to manage 'blocked' visits of two or three days duration a few times a year. Sinn Féin argued in 1983 that the British Government should be obliged to finance thirteen family visits per year. The problem of 'closed' visits also remained. In Long Lartin, TOM claimed, a Category A prisoner could be accompanied on the journey from cell to visiting area by two dog handlers and 'at least five prison officers'.[185] This typically entailed moving slowly through seven door systems to reach a set of particularly small rooms where two to three staff would listen and observe all proceedings. One room used by IRA prisoners measured approximately eight by nine feet, whereas non-political prisoners housed on the same wings were permitted to see friends and family in a much larger space where the furniture and security arrangements gave 'an air of normality'. Protesting such discrimination in any meaningful way incurred formal and casual penalties. Prisoners sacrificed a great deal, according to TOM, 'because the screws will smash everything up'. Making a stand in the visiting area was more dangerous in that the summoning of a 'MUFTI squad' by staff promised chaotic and violent confrontation.[186]

The Albany Riot, 19–25 May 1983

The IRA played both overt and subtle parts in fomenting the historic Albany Riot of May 1983, the most destructive prison disturbance of the decade. This stemmed from a number of factors, not least the rotation of an especially experienced cadre of IRA prison activists into the prison. Moreover, Ray McLaughlin, Tony Clarke, Roy Walsh, Punter Bennett and Stevie Blake had been present at least intermittently for over a year in which advantageous knowledge and contacts accumulated.[187] Walsh had completed yet another stint in Winchester in the interim.[188] Paul Norney was moved in followed by Vince Donnelly from Parkhurst and Eddie O'Neill from Hull. After years of solitary confinement and Victorian prisons, the modernity and open spaces of Albany were a 'sort of freedom' for Norney.[189] This strengthened a grouping which had lost Jimmy Ashe, who was released on 18 January 1983, and reunited several co-conspirators. Norney and O'Neill had mounted an ambitious escape attempt from Wormwood Scrubs on 7 October 1977.[190] The presumably unintended net effect of concentrating republican militants was their unusually potent capacity to act with decision whenever opportunity occurred. The men could scarcely comprehend that the Home Office had permitted this to materialise and surmised that the vexatious tempo of 'ghosting' had by chance produced a perfect storm scenario.[191]

Donnelly immediately grasped the situation: 'It was one of the greatest mistakes that the Home Office made ... they had nine of the most rebellious IRA prisoners ... together at the one time ... I suppose it was a permutation of moving and swopping'.[192] O'Neill was also surprised to find so many of 'the most militant' IRA prisoners in a comparatively liberal prison. Such men viewed imprisonment as 'another stage of the war' in which 'every day was combat day when you could do something', yet Albany, above all others, had occupied a position close to the optimum IRA objective since 1978 when members discussed an ambitious plan of destruction in response to the beatings of comrades two years earlier.[193] Matters began to coalesce in 1983 when Donnelly met McLaughlin on the yard and listened as he urged an additional rationale for major action: 'We are all in [jail] four, five or six years now, or whatever. They are getting cocky with us ... It's time we done something'.[194] In 1981 Donnelly had stabbed the Governor of Hull in the neck with a poisoned and sharpened nine inch nail in response to a one-sided bout of pressure and was eager to play his part in Albany.[195]

Paul Hill of the Guildford Four was present in Albany. While the victim of wrongful imprisonment in 1974, his formative republican politics and strong record of prison activism resurfaced for the third time in Albany. He had just returned from 'lie-downs' in Canterbury when the IRA capacity peaked.[196] Sean Smyth of the 'Maguire Seven' shared a wing with Clarke and Bennett. Innocent of IRA activities in England, Smyth had a background in the Official Republican Movement in the Lower Falls area of West Belfast and frequently participated in prison actions.[197] He was released unvindicated in August 1983 and took pains to publicize the difficulties faced by the Irish based relatives of republican prisoners in England.[198] On 19 October 1989 his conviction was declared to be 'unsafe'. Smyth recalled: 'I was the only prisoner who left Wormwood Scrubs at 7.00 a.m. in the morning. They came to my cell around 5.00 or 6.00. They made me a suit. I wanted a shirt and tie and the money I'd saved up. They sent me out of prison with two black bags'.[199]

Perennial friction regarding prison food assumed unusual proportions in Albany in the early months of 1983. Hill described the glutinous slop as 'unrecognisable ... stewed pulp' and so low in quality as to suggest that the authorities were striving to discomfort the prisoners.[200] He was one of the organisers of a short 'food strike' which resulted in yet another 'lie-down' in Winchester.[201] McLaughlin was apprised of an incident in late January when a 'Cockney' prisoner in C Wing inadvertently sparked a near riot of 100 men. A simple complaint about the 'atrocious' food resulted in an aggressive overreaction by a staff member to which the Londoner responded by tossing his food over the man who had pushed him bodily. Ten men were then 'skull dragged to the block' for solitary confinement.[202] An attempt to cultivate an informer among the generally cohesive Londoners in early February resulted in the stabbing of the man who rebuffed the prison officer's approach. Staff allegedly circulated a dangerous lie that the uncooperative man was a 'pervert', resulting in his being knifed shortly afterwards in the course of a relatively minor disagreement.[203] Prisoners' views of staff were further eroded in April 1983 when the wives of three men expecting visits were singled out for strip-searching. Visits to IRA prisoners were already fraught with tension.[204]

Cliques within the staff appeared to have private agendas. McLaughlin, acquainted with a number of black prisoners and the politically motivated 'Spaghetti House Siege' trio in particular, noted the strangely moderate response to a further stabbing in March when a white prisoner injured a black associate.[205] Although the matter was non-racist in character, the inexplicable leniency extended towards the white aggressor evinced a tolerance, if not approval, of what the Irishman described as 'the fascist element of National Front prisoners'.[206] The IRA noted the occurrence of 'several serious knife attacks' and the manner in which they were handled.[207] McLaughlin, when rejecting press claims of a purely 'IRA initiated action', believed that at least two of the interracial stabbings 'were instigated by the prison staff'.[208] Officially, the Chief Inspector of Prisons found 'no evidence of direct discrimination' in the course of 1983 when 25 per cent of the inmate population was classified as belonging to 'ethnic minorities'.[209] In June 1982 black prison leader Shujaa Moshesh (formerly Wesley Dick) assessed the IRA contribution:

> The authorities … particularly victimise Irish POWs who had been subject to many vicious assaults, excessive durations of isolation and much psychological intimidation in the attempt to crush their resistance. The strong determination of the Irish POWs to resist the innately oppressive policies of the prison system has been a powerful source of inspiration to many others, including myself.[210]

By the spring of 1983 it was evident that 'all the ingredients for a major confrontation' were present in Albany.[211] Donnelly recalled: 'We realized at that stage that we could get a lot of English fellas, particularly North of England fellas to do something'.[212] Albany, according to O'Neill, was 'always a tinderbox ready to go. We were going to help it on its way. Back in [March 19]78 we had plans, as a consequence of what happened to Sean Campbell in [September] 1976 … to destroy that prison. We just couldn't get it [activated] in 1978 when we were there'.[213] The main cause of postponement was that too many of the intended participants were sent to the Punishment Block for 'petty reasons'.[214] Yet the IRA motivation remained strong and memories of 1976 permeated the entire system. On arriving into Brixton John McComb was accosted by friendly British prisoners who had been in Albany and were tasked with cleaning up the spur: 'They told me not only about mopping the blood off the floor and the walls, they had to mop the blood off the ceiling ... That changed everything and that led on the Albany thing [in 1983]. People think that they just went up and wrecked the roof but ... the whole rationale was this is pay back time'.[215]

A basic strategy was devised to undermine the prison administration by motivating ordinary British prisoners to rally in support of the better conditions they deserved. The IRA recognized that English class politics, reliant on conservative traditions of social deference and acceptance of authoritarianism, was inhibiting prisoners from self-assertion. To this end the IRA men in Albany consciously set about subverting the prison population by greatly increasing the supply of 'hootch' – illicit alcohol. Donnelly, Martin Brady, Jerry Mealy and Roy Walsh had prized reputations as 'master brewers' and, following a plan of action, the men imparted once private recipes and methodology to avid English acolytes. In a humorous move with serious overtones, Donnelly utilized his calligraphy flair to present signed certificates of 'graduation' to students. He was amazed when some displayed them proudly on their cell walls, a fact which did not go unnoticed by staff.[216] The initiative probably inspired the canard made during the riot that the IRA had corrupted impressionable young drug addicts by manipulating the exploitative prison market. As prison staff well appreciated, republicans regarded the production of 'hootch' within their own circles as a kind of 'release valve' which others tended to fill with illegal narcotics with more unpredictable results.[217] The outcome was a surge in alcohol production and consumption in Albany, which, inevitably, manifested in additional clashes with prison staff arising from misbehaviour, cell searches and disciplinary proceedings.

Two separate strands of IRA ambition were played out in Albany. One centred on the workshops, which they intended to totally destroy in a broad effort involving agitated British prisoners. McLaughlin and Donnelly had much experience of machine sabotage and concentrated on this project which, if successful, would serve to avenge the brutal attack on Albany's IRA cohort in 1976. A second conspiracy entailed a long held plan of mounting a roof top protest. Albany, as a modern prison, did not have the fragile antiquated tiles previously smashed in massive quantities by republican protesters in Wormwood Scrubs in 1978 and Parkhurst in 1979. Prison roofs, however, provided vantages for the display of banners while the act of breaking onto the forbidden area was by no means an insignificant achievement for Category A men. Norney and O'Neill had discussed this option with a view to pressing their ongoing demands for repatriation.[218] Ultimately, workshop protests in May 1983 facilitated a general melee in which the occupation and scaling of B Wing became viable. The result was a prison riot on par with Parkhurst in 1968 and Hull in 1976, during which millions of pounds of damage was inflicted on a major Dispersal System asset. The status of the prison and unprecedented real time television coverage added to the impact of the interlinked incidents. In retrospect, the Albany episode was a turning point in the Prison Department's attitude towards life - sentenced IRA prisoners in England. A senior POA member later queried why nine republicans were assigned to wings where there were already five political prisoners from other organizations. The Home Office learned from its mistakes in this instance and did not replicate the apparently happenstance convergence.[219]

The mid-term sequence of events culminating in the Albany Riot of May 1983 began in February when the vast majority of men joined a wider 'strike' to demand 'equality of treatment with prisoners in Northern Ireland'.[220] In early 1982, 210 of the approximately 279 prisoners in Albany had signed a petition seeking the 50 per cent remission available in the North of Ireland to IRA and INLA prisoners in the aftermath of the 1981 Hunger Strike. Many went on the wider Dispersal System strike from 18 to 20 January 1982.[221] This glaring 'sense of injustice' observed by Geoff Coggan of PROP in 1983 was, he believed, 'a specific incitement to protest and riot', which compounded problems across the Dispersal System arising from overcrowding, poor sanitation and inadequate educational facilities.[222] Such factors, aggravated by a sinister medical regime run by Dr. Cooper, induced Britons John Bowden and Jimmy McCaig to hold Assistant Governor Gerry Schofield hostage in his office on 4–5 January 1983.[223] Albany witnessed two-day work stoppages on 28 February and 1 March owing to the denial of 50 per cent parole and the decision making process which pertained. By early May the Albany protesters were part of a series of simultaneous strikes involving over 650 men in Parkhurst, Wakefield, Gartree, Hull and Long Lartin.[224]

Albany, ironically, was the most modern and, after Long Lartin, harmonious jail in the network. Long term prisoners had single occupancy *en suite* cells, generous association time, recreation rooms, access to playing pitches and relatively disciplined staff.[225] It also contained a high proportion of Category A prisoners acutely attuned to work management issues and parole entitlements. While both immediate and on-going grievances were certainly additional causative factors in Albany, it could not be denied that the influence of the H-Block crisis had disrupted the Dispersal System as never before. Serious unrest in Albany dated from 12 May 1983, although this went unreported in contemporary press accounts which, owing to state - imposed censorship, lacked information emanating from the Category A hard - core protagonists. Liberal media outlets noted that details of 'peaceful, and therefore largely unreported protests' had gradually seeped into the public domain 'rather like news from nowhere'.[226] O'Neill, former O/C of the IRA's 'Uxbridge Eight', privately compiled a detailed analysis dated 18 July 1983 regarding 'the world within the walls' in the advent and course of the riot. This was furnished to interested parties on the outside and specifically to Lord Avebury and journalist Nick Davies. The document was privately imparted in order to counter Home Office claims that no terms had been agreed to end the protest. The Tyrone man was then awaiting sentence on charges of 'mutiny' which could have added many years to his sentence and subtly understated the IRA contribution to the overall situation. He noted:

> That finely honed oppressive machinery – Albany penal administration is the connection between all the acts of protest. There was no plan or strategic plotting behind what occurred at Albany, regardless of what has been said. Each act was a spontaneous and natural reaction to an arbitrary/ vindictive/ punitive penal policy with respect to all aspects of prison life. Prisoners have endured without any possible remedy thro[ugh] the normal channels, a prison policy that is both physically and psychologically destructive to their well being. That an explosion of pent up frustration should occur in any of the dispersal prisons in hardly surprising … Albany like all dispersal prisons is/ was an explosive situation … because a body of human beings were being systematically crushed (by a Machiavellian regime for its own ends) towards exploding point.[227]

O'Neill theorised that the staff overused Rule 43 and imposed petty sanctions to 'lean on' prisoners with a view to inciting reaction that would justify severe countermeasures in which the ascendancy of the POA would be demonstrated. Events in Hull and Wormwood Scrubs in 1979–81, he believed, had exposed the weakness of higher 'prison management' during a period when the grass roots POA had lost ground in service - related wrangling with the Home Office. *Prison Rules* provided sufficient powers for even junior staff to traduce prisoners, who, lacking effective communications and legal standing, were placed in 'a hopeless and invidious situation'.[228] If this could be achieved in Albany, in many respects designed to function as the most humane Dispersal System prison, staff stood to counter the trend in which legal judgements affirming human rights and the influx of civilian professionals had steadily eroded POA authority in the late 1970s and early 1980s. The POA had, since 1980, instructed its members 'not to cooperate in any internal investigations which may be held following allegations by prisoners against staff' under CI 14/1980.[229]

Jimmy Murphy, a non-political D Wing prisoner who rejected press assertion of IRA instigation of the riot, arrived from an eight-week stay in Parkhurst in April. He claimed overall responsibility for the May riot, in which he played an active part, lay with

> the racist inhuman prison system with their policy of division on the basis of race, their incitement of prisoners to inform on each other under promises of transfers to goals like Maidstone and promises of parole etc, intimidation of prisoners by

indiscriminate use of the 10/74 lie down rule … and hatred especially towards anyone who is politically educated and aware. Never have I felt so much hatred as there is at Albany.[230]

Although dismissive of exaggerated claims of IRA conspiracy in Albany, Murphy's agenda during the riot conjoined the H-Block inspired quest for 50% remission and overall 'parity in conditions with Northern Ireland', with localised demands regarding food quality, staff brutality, overuse of Rule 43 and legal representation at Home Leave Board Meetings.[231] Scottish prisoner Robert McGhee, who arrived into Albany from Winchester on 8 May 1983, similarly, 'put the blame on the Prison Authorities … which are occurring in most of the prisons'. He had 'never entered a prison with so much tension as Albany, you could feel it going through the gates of reception'.[232]

The refusal of prisoners to work in the mailbag-sewing area on 12 May 1983 was one in an intermittent series of protests against what many regarded as an unworthy task reminiscent of Victorian era convictism. The men knew that much of the product was quietly discarded and that the real purpose had more to do with establishing conformity rather than generating saleable output. Albany's new sewing facility was referred to as 'the punishment shop' and it was abnormal for long-term prisoners to be assigned to carry out the 'degrading and demeaning task'.[233] News that the facility was being commissioned, Hill recalled, 'was considered an insult and an attempt to provoke the prisoners'.[234] The Chief Inspector of Prisons reported in October 1984: 'One of the major causes of the discontent which had led to the disturbance was the employment of prisoners on the sewing of mailbags – an occupation many consider to be unsuitable for long term prisoners'.[235] Republicans tended to accept engineering and woodworking assignments, with the exception of Ministry of Defence contracts, as it practised useful skills while providing access to tools and materials.

The motivation of staff issuing direct orders for ten men to report for work in the sewing shop in May 1983, therefore, raised serious questions. McLaughlin's Category A 'Red Book' contained a consistent record of non-compliance in other prisons yet he, alone of the IRA group, was required to muster. Hill, officially regarded as an IRA member by the Prison Department, was ordered to the mailbag production area and entailed the penalties for his refusal.[236] Donnelly, meanwhile, was dispatched to a different workshop despite his notoriety as one of the most effective saboteurs in England. In a move which must have confounded staff, McLaughlin accepted the summons to the sewing shop. In retrospect it was revealed that he and Donnelly were working to their own subversive agendas and were correctly identified by informers as 'ringleaders' of what transpired.[237] An impromptu meeting was held in the sewing shop in which all concerned agreed to immediate strike action. This stand was repeated the following day despite direct instructions from a Principal Officer.[238] As had occurred during earlier series of stoppages, prisoners branded as troublemakers were singled out for solitary confinement under Rule 43 or 'ghosted' out of the prison under Circular Instruction 10/74. The pool of men downing tools, therefore, continually changed, although the mode of dissent and motivation to reject the stigmatism of reduced social and penal hierarchy remained constant. McLaughlin was transferred to Bristol on the weekend of 14–15 May, whereas Donnelly went to Norwich.[239] The facility in Norwich was normally used as a remand centre for men and youth offenders, a circumstance used to justify the detention of IRA prisoners in solitary confinement referred to as merely 'segregation'.[240] Roy Walsh remained, although he was held in solitary confinement for throwing the contents of a food trolley at a group of otherwise disinterested prison officers.[241]

Instead of backing off, the Albany prisoners organized a major work strike for Monday, 16 May 1983, which only ten or so men ignored. The prison was 'shut down' arising from the boycott, probably to forestall acts of vandalism in the expensive workshops which seemed likely given the very high degree of dissent among its putative labour force. The 'lock out' was repeated on 17 May as numerous men were docked their paltry wages of sixty pence to one pound. This clampdown was evidently intelligence - directed and had the desired effect of preserving the facilities, although the corollary of retaining hundreds of restive men on their wings jeopardized the entire prison.[242] Several B Wing prisoners who complained that they were being denied free association time on the afternoon of 17 May were reprimanded. None were contrite and the evening was enlivened by the burning of a cell belonging to one of the 'blacklegs' who were later rewarded with relocation in non maximum-security prisons. Additional use of CI 10/1974 ensued without nullifying the groundswell of malcontent.[243] This calculated affront to the authority of newly instated Governor Peter Meech occurred in the context of frustrated prisoner requests to meet a representative of the Board of Visitors, a channel formally prescribed by the Prison Department for airing grievances.[244] By 18 May it was understood that around 100 men had been disciplined by loss of pay and remission. Hill and numerous others were fined the equivalent of a week's wages: 'The whole prison was on charges'.[245] The imposition of regulatory punishments indicated that the new Governor, promoted from the non-dispersal HMP Durham, was as unsympathetic to prisoner opinion as his predecessor. Detachment was his prerogative. His firmness, however, proved counter-productive as it had the presumably unintended effect of worsening an unstable situation.[246]

The dispute extended into Wednesday 18 May, when a second member of the small group who had reported for work as normal had his cell burned in C Wing. By chance, a man mounting a five-day hunger strike in A Wing to highlight his failure to receive a special 'medical diet' elected to commence a drastic thirst strike. He reputedly cut a 'pitiful' figure on the landings when ordered out of his cell under pain of punishment. Hitherto compliant inhabitants of A Wing determined following discussions with other parts of the prison to join a rare and highly symbolic 'general strike' on 19 May. This move toward concerted, consolidated action would have perturbed the Home Office and no information on what was in prospect was conveyed to the media. On A Wing O'Neill understood that the administration had wisely relented when the lone protester was provided with appropriate food around 11.05 a.m.[247]

A degree of momentum had, nonetheless, been achieved, and four prisoners at the centre of the mailbag strike climbed onto the roof of the sewing workshop during an exercise period on the early evening of Thursday 19 May.[248] Irish Traveller Jimmy Mohan, Robert McGhee, Jimmy Murphy and another man took up their position around 6.45 p.m. McGhee and Mohan were on good terms with the Irish republicans and were actively assisted by IRA members riled by the dispatch that day of Donnelly on a twenty-eight day 'lie-down' to Norwich. In a serious and unreported escalation, the men began smashing the workshop roof and those of four nearby buildings.[249] Hill had provided 'truncheons' which were fashioned by a friend in the wood mill from table legs. The protesters were expected to act quickly when masked and then melt back into a throng of friends, screening their re-entry into a crowd during exercise period. The IRA, when staging illegal and armed Firing Parties at republican funerals in Ireland, used this generally effective technique. The plan was discarded when the men did not relinquish the chance to inflict serious damage while their associates, including Hill, 'massed together to block the screws'.[250] Prisoners insisted on remaining in the yards for the allotted exercise period before returning to the wings and informing the Chief Prison Officer that violence would not be used by the four protesters against staff. This undertaking was intended to convey a threat of repercussions if the men of the roof were attacked by staff during the hours of darkness.[251] No effort was made to confront the men who 'worked like navvies all night'.[252] Tension levels remained extremely high, particularly when prisoners glimpsed MUFTI personnel congregating inside the prison between 8.00 and 9.00 p.m. on 19 May: 'That night most prisoners remained awake. Most blocked their doors and remained dressed, for it was felt that some action was going to happen. The prison was "alive" throughout the night'.[253]

When unlocked for morning association at 9.30 a.m. on 20 May the prisoners immediately noticed augmented staff levels on the landings with all the attendant friction this invited. They were not permitted to go to the workshops even if so disposed. By 10.30 a disagreement with staff flared in B Wing, leading to possibly purposeful and officious intervention by 'management'. Resentment against those who had broken the strike was demonstrated by fouling the handles of their cell doors. Angry scenes developed when prisoners refused direct orders from staff to clean up the mess caused by unidentified persons. An alarm bell was also smeared with noxious human waste. Hill, who assisted the collection of supplies for those wrecking the roofs, learned that his associates were tearing the sleeves off their jerseys to use as masks, 'a sure sign that they were preparing to riot'.[254] This duly occurred when a man placed on a charge for refusing to clean the tarnished alarm bell grabbed a brush handle and began smashing glass in a stairwell. Clarke assessed him as 'a sound fellow. He would have done a few things for you if you needed anything done'.[255] Solidarity of this nature copper - fastened IRA aid to British prisoners on the wing. The riot began when a source from A Wing reported that MUFTI squads were 'forming up' to enter the building.[256]

A Wing prisoners, including O'Neill, had been permitted into the yards to take exercise as normal, where they immediately noticed the 'heavy presence of screws' and extra dog handlers at 11.15 outside B Wing.[257] He carried a pillowcase full of supplies under his shirt which he had intended tossing up to the men still occupying the workshop roofs:

> At that moment from behind me came an explosion of sound, B Wing literally blew apart. I watched for about 30 sec[ond]s and decided to deliver the food I had. I did this and on turning to walk back to opposite B Wing I spotted visored figures, MUFTI, peering from behind [the] gym. On spotting me they ducked back... [I] then decided to go down to B Wing door and see inside and warn the prisoners.[258]

The presence of numerous vigilant and well prepared prison officers made it impossible for most of the men on the yard to regain access to A Wing. A sufficient quotient of Albany's 279 prisoners were, nonetheless, *in situ* in B Wing, which they quickly seized. An estimated sixty to 100 men then gained control of C Wing. Information provided to the press claimed they 'began smashing fittings, furniture and windows' in B Wing before extending the destruction into C Wing.[259] The eruption was not, however, as carefully planned as it appeared and the precautions taken by the authorities probably prevented A Wing from experiencing similar events. The fact that the bulk of its inhabitants were in the yard when the riot commenced was a prime consideration.

After a hurried conversation with O'Neill, who remained on the yard, Norney joined Clarke in leading militants, who had been virtually trapped inside B Wing, in a dash up to the top floor of the building. Norney recalled: 'We barricaded the wing up, set fire to it, smashed the place up, clambered onto the roof'.[260] They jacked heavy steel gates off their hinges and mountings and overcame all internal security obstacles. Bennett, convicted of gunrunning, advised others on techniques used in Long Kesh for removing the hated doors. There was little interference from staff, most of whom, as generally occurred in such situations, had either rushed to the ground floor or exited the building to avoid being injured, marooned or taken hostage. Sex offenders also ran into the open to avoid unrestrained jail justice. Several had their possessions smashed in vacant cells by men determined to inflict a modicum of retribution.[261] Hill was to the fore in the B Wing rampage: 'In the bath house we ripped out the baths to drop on the screws on the lower landings, forcing them to scatter. They regrouped and shouted up threats, calling us out by name. They said that when they got me they were going to break my legs. We ignored them. The destruction continued'.[262]

The men hurried to fill the stairwell with high tech electronic doors they had levered off frames and other debris before the MUFTI regained the upper hand. A dismounted steel door was used as a battering ram to smash through a section of the outer wall and a breach large enough for a man to climb through was opened. This provided access to the roof and the means to assist others milling around the yards.[263] A bed board was used to secure a rope lowered from an aperture to the yard where O'Neill waited. Although less fit than normal due to a debilitating lie-down in Durham, O'Neill climbed and pulled himself up the exterior of B Wing and onto the roof. The Tyrone man reached the third floor of the building unaided before being passed a plank he needed to cross from one ledge to another. He boosted Stevie Blake to safety and was then pulled up. MUFTI squads were evidently distracted at ground level as they prepared to move in and confront the rioters. O'Neill's precarious ascent was closely followed by English man Michael 'Mickey' Browne, who was regarded as simply 'going for a riot'. With a line firmly secured, Norney and Clarke crossed onto the roof from the breach they had helped create, as did five other prisoners.[264]

The ten included non-political English, Irish and Scottish prisoners along with Fahad Mihyi, a well-disposed Jerusalem born member of the Popular Front for the Liberation of Palestine-General Command. The PFLP, led by George Haddash, were best known in Europe for the 1970s, actions of their proxy, 'Carlos the Jackal'. William Baldock, Charlie McGhee and Peter Knight were serving sentences of seven years or less and were courted heavy punishment for men nearing parole.[265] Armed robber McGhee had featured in earlier Albany protests and was on good terms with many republicans. Norney claimed: 'If I was in trouble with anyone, Charlie would be there at my side. He wouldn't leave you alone if he thought I was going to get into hassle with anyone. He'd be with me'.[266] McGhee had been involved in an incident in Parkhurst in 1976 when he had chased prison officers out of the wing with a knife. His friend and prison celebrity Charlie Bronson recalled that 'Winney loved a fight'.[267] Michael Jamieson, however, was serving five life sentences for a particularly vicious murder spree and was described in the press as a 'baby-faced butcher'.[268] Norney regarded Jamieson as 'a nasty piece of work' but accepted his right to participate, even if the media fixation with his offences tended to tarnish the grouping.[269] Michael Browne and another prisoner remained with the IRA men.[270] Clarke was curious to find a total stranger on the roof. He asked the young Englishman:

> 'What you come up for?' It was funny like. He says, 'I only came in yesterday'. 'How long are you doing?' 'Three years' he said. I said, 'Get yourself down them stairs. You are going to lose all your remission. Go on'. 'Oh, no chance' he said. And he started banging away. An English guy – a smashing lad. And he ended up staying with us to the death.[271]

The men made use of the respite to gather batons, food, ropes, radios, batteries, sheets, blankets and paint for the days ahead.[272] Hydration was not a concern as they had direct access to two massive 2,000-gallon water tanks from which they removed brick ballast. Considerable water damage had already occurred in B Wing owing to the destruction of the bathing area. Releasing almost 4,000 gallons of water into the heart of the building was a potentially devastating option. Burning the roof was also a distinct possibility, arising from the surprise discovery when holes were smashed into its surface that it was constructed with wood and strawboard sealed with tar. It was, therefore, highly combustible and Clarke revelled in the chance to unsettle watching staff: 'Waving matches ... at the screws. Letting them know – if you come up here – that is going off'.[273] The men reasoned that they could survive a conflagration by retreating to the concrete platform supporting the huge water tanks. In the event of being stormed by military Special Forces, Norney advised McGhee, with whom he had shared many tight corners, on a drastic contingency: 'They are going to shoot you anyway; just fucking grab one and jump off the roof with him'.[274] O'Neill fully concurred.[275] Buoyed by the realisation they were acting from a position of strength, the prisoners attempted to explain their actions. One of the first banners unfurled read: 'Prison reform, Parity with Irish prisoners' in reference to the protests of February 1983 in support of parole entitlements won by the IRA and INLA in Long Kesh.[276] The four men who had ascended the lower workshop roofs during the early evening of 19 May came down at 4.30 p.m. on 20 May having engineered as much destruction as possible in what became a radically changed prison environment. Robert McGee and Jimmy Murphy were defiant and wrote to *FRFI* from the Winchester Segregation Block seeking a 'full enquiry' into the Albany disturbances.[277] They were dispatched to other prisons while the protests continued.

Staff reinforcements from Parkhurst and Camp Hill prison on the Isle of Wight rushed to contain the uncontested perimeter while reinforcements from the Hampshire police arrived in numbers. With the outer defences secured and police patrols mounted to guard against opportunist breakouts, the major task of regaining control of the complex was addressed. Many of those held in Albany had connections to organized crime and the IRA and this significant outside network factor encouraged the imposition of a five-mile air exclusion zone to counter the threat of helicopters or light aircraft attempting to carry escapers off the island.[278] The decision to deploy the MUFTI squad for its most high - profile action since the disastrous Wormwood Scrubs 'riot' in August 1979 was not without political risk and was subsequently commended by the POA as having saved the jail from being 'wrecked beyond repair'.[279] The initial counterattack in Albany focused on C Wing shortly after 12.00 p.m., where MUFTI teams, assisted by ordinary warders, ran into vigorous resistance. Advancing officers were met with 'a barrage of missiles including doors, sinks, glass and blocks of wood from the damaged furniture'.[280] Seven prisoners were reportedly injured in C Wing while the makeshift weapons wielded by their associates were evidently ineffective given that just one prison officer suffered concussion and a broken jaw despite wearing a specialised helmet and padded protective clothing. Around forty-seven prisoners were locked into C Wing cells as the focus shifted to sealing off the already 'badly damaged' B Wing. This was achieved after around three hours of bitter fighting. A further fifty-one prisoners were immediately shipped to the English mainland.[281]

The MUFTI penetrated the B Wing stairwell barrier and pursued those not immediately overrun towards the upper landings. Hill found himself separated from the 'main body' and was trapped by ten 'screws in full riot kit … They crashed down on me using their riot shields, and dragged me and another prison to a secure cell'. He was later taken handcuffed to the Reception Area, strip-searched and driven off to Parkhurst. Other than verbal abuse and 'rabbit punches' he was not mistreated after capture, a circumstance he attributed to the 'lessons of Hull'.[282] Counterattacking MUFTI teams cleared the landings of B Wing and from the roof O'Neill 'personally witnessed them assaulting prisoners'. This occurrence, the IRA men believed, led to subsequent damage limitation by the authorities fearing yet another scandal.[283] Early estimates put the cost of repair at £1 million, including £250,000 to rebuild the workshops and an art room.[284] From the vantage of July 1984 the Director General of the Prison Service praised the 'last resort' operation as an example of the 'correct use of MUFTI tactics'.[285] The Prison Department's annual report for 1983 devoted twenty-four lines to an incident regarded as 'serious' and expensive without reference to the IRA.[286]

The suppression of the most serous prison riot in England since Hull in 1976 revealed the centrality of the minority IRA element once the centre of action shifted from the wings to the rooftops. Ten prisoners remained on the roof of B Wing by 21 May. They included O'Neill, Clarke, Norney and Blake who displayed a banner identifying themselves as 'IRA political prisoners'.[287]

Elsewhere in the jail Punter Bennett and Roy Walsh were not in a position to join their comrades on the roof. *Sunday Times* coverage emphasised the gravity of offences for which the Irish men had been convicted and noted: 'Prison authorities regard IRA men as among their most politically aware, and therefore potentially dangerous inmates. To minimise their influence they are regularly moved at short notice around the country's seven top-security jails'.[288] The POA was unequivocal in condemning the IRA's 'sick brand of anarchy' as the root cause of the riot, although the self-serving theories of Albany staff regarding the organization's methods and intentions were ill founded if not deliberately cynical.[289]

A perceptive feature by *Guardian* journalist David Beresford explained the rooftop protest as 'a public manifestation of a long running' question of 'the treatment of Irish prisoners in England'. As Beresford noted, Home Secretary William Whitelaw had asserted that the retention of IRA prisoners in England was partly conceived as an 'additional deterrent' to those considering participation in the organization's military campaign in the country. Failure to repatriate, however, created security problems owing to the nightmare scenario of a successful IRA escape. The contingent resort to excessive 'ghosting', and oppressive visiting conditions certainly deepened the pre-emptive strategy while motivating dissenting republicans to discomfort, embarrass and antagonize their captors.[290] Repatriation separated the IRA from the general concerns of the Category A population but the 'more politicised' republicans were, nonetheless, 'in the vanguard of prison reform', as evidenced by the thirty plus complaints lodged with the ECHR. Beresford mused that the Home Office, if not other Government bodies, would view the eventual resolution of the repatriation impasse 'with some relief'.[291]

The specific agenda of the protesters had crystallized on the roof and fell into two segments in recognition of IRA and general prisoner issues. The 'major grievances of the Irish Political Prisoners' were summarized as the demand for repatriation and tolerable visits. Repatriation, as was known by all informed parties, would in the case of the Six Counties entail the acquisition of a form of political status that if not as well defined as had been the case prior to March 1976, was nonetheless superior to the situation prevailing until 1981–82. The point on visits decried 'the policy of alienating ... [IRA] prisoners, from society in general and their family and friends in particular by the use of special visiting arrangements'.[292] The second schedule of demands, numbered one to thirteen in the document given to the Home Office on 25 May 1983, was partly informed by events in the North of Ireland, but also raised concerns solely germane to the Dispersal System. One criticised 'lack of parity in conditions' with prisoners in the North of Ireland, a matter with relevance for clothing, visitors, association time, compassionate parole and exercise. Failure to operate 50 per cent remission was also correlated with the Six Counties' norm for political prisoners. Several grievances concerned the lack of transparent communications and decision-making processes within the prisons in England, particularly in relation to the administration of seemingly 'arbitrary' punishment. Health, work pay and diet were all raised, as was the objectionable 'apartheid quality of "Cat[egory] A" and "Special Cat[egory] A".'[293]

The prisoners on the roof decided to allow 'safe conduct' on 21 May 1983 to prison officers moving in and out of the prison, passing over the chance to drop masonry and debris from a commanding height. The gesture was intended to permit the conveyance of food supplies to the remaining prisoners as staff had requested. They persuasively argued that they did not wish to remove permanent fencing at the rear of the prison in order to reach a secondary entrance. This was agreed in the spirit of keeping the roof occupation peaceful and the men initially failed to notice that security staff had exploited their chance to bring cumbersome jacking equipment and heavy planking into the complex. Accordingly, the men watched as the materials needed to attempt forced entry to the rooftops by the locked steel access doors were unloaded into the building. This sleight of hand was viewed as a threat to their lives in view of the acute angle of the roof slope and resulted in an immediate and forthright change of policy.[294] As the truck departed the prisoners dropped a concrete block which was carefully timed and aimed to land behind the driver: 'There was no attempt to kill anyone. It was just a lesson, "You'll never come back this way again". It was dropped on the back end of the cab – not the front and it went straight through'.[295]

On the night of 21–22 May the protesters were informed that military personnel were inside the prison. This was not unexpected and did not alter the situation except in the increased probability of fatal violent confrontation. The IRA men had noted that Margaret Thatcher's Conservative Government, despite heavy Royal Navy losses, was seeking re-election and that the imperialistic euphoria fuelled by the Falkland Island (Las Malvinas) conflict had probably raised public tolerance for muscular state intervention. PROP believed that it was 'remarkable' that an Attica style prison massacre had not already occurred in England.[296] The IRA desired no such loss of life, but by virtue of being personally inured to the true face of British counterinsurgency, prepared for the worst. Prisoners arrayed rows of bricks taken from the water tank structures to use for defence if attacked by the MUFTI or other forces at any time. They attempted to sleep during the day to maximize vigilance at night when training, equipment and the prospect of surprise otherwise advantaged their opponents. No serious negotiations were opened as the prisoners had no desire to relinquish their position and the Home Office was evidently unprepared to enter formal discussions. A tentative overture from a Principal Officer on the morning of 21 May failed to impress when a simple request for a pen and paper to record their grievances was rebuffed. A counteroffer to hear an oral version was rejected.[297] The men could be seen by journalists in low light 'walking about on the roof, carrying makeshift batons'.[298]

The reticence of the prisoners was informed by their cumulative experience of dishonoured negotiations. This resolve, coupled with possession of ample food and water in full view of TV cameras, necessitated sophisticated Home Office countermeasures. When, on the morning of Sunday 22 May, a Deputy Governor approached soliciting their 'surrender', the men 'politely told [him] not to bother talking'.[299] Later in the day three men who felt they had gone as far as they wished agreed arrangements to withdraw. Baldock, McGhee and Knight descended by a hydraulic lifting platform to commence punishment.[300] The Deputy Governor returned that evening to reopen the communication begun by his Principal Officer but the continued opposition to receiving a hard copy document from the prisoners negated all chance of progress. The administration was evidently anxious to repudiate any justified rationale for the protest or to enter forms of dialogue in which the action could be perceived as having extorted concessions. His repeated offer to accept 'surrender' without terms was calmly 'blanked'. In the course of the night the men observed 'unknown persons in MUFTI dress' closely inspecting the roof from ground level.[301]

A final attempt to induce capitulation and purely verbal transmission of unverifiable terms was made on 23 May when a Principal Officer and a Catholic clergyman approached the prisoners. After various consultations, basic writing materials were provided and the prisoners agreed to furnish their demands at 2.30 p.m. when the mechanics of a climb down would be discussed. The draft document, however, was retained at the appointed hour, owing to the additional proviso that its transference would only follow a 'guarantee' of personal safety for the signatories. The men also required phone contact with trusted MPs Owen Carron and Joan Maynard, as well as investigative journalist Nick Davies. A further reversion to an unseen command element followed, resulting in the counteroffer to allow the prisoners write letters to the three MPs after coming down. This was unsatisfactory as it was held that the Prison Department would not necessarily either disclose the nature of terms being sought or reveal their decisions in response.[302]

The standoff immediately became more fraught. A banner claiming that the authorities had essentially rejected an interim settlement was countered by what quickly matured into a concerted programme of disinformation. The media were informed that the IRA prisoners, regarded as pariahs by many ordinary Britons, had not only declined negotiations but had thrown bricks at staff. This, according to O'Neill, 'was a lie', although the protesters were certainly prepared to face an imminent assault:

> Meanwhile works, screws and others are preparing equipment: staging, [high power] hoses etc, all the necessary equipment to be prepared for an attack upon us. By this time it was evident that plans were afoot. The Home Office was regularly pointing out that it was an IRA protest and that we had weapons stored to attack prison officers. It was quite clear from the false statements issued to the press on Monday [that] public opinion was being manipulated.[303]

The return of the clergyman and Principal Officer was regarded as a mere 'diversion' intended to distract their attention from the sinister build up in the yards and lower floors of B Wing. At this point there was nothing to be lost from relaying outline terms to the delegation who, critically, received permission to record O'Neill's dictation in writing. A reply was promised by 7.30 a.m. on 24 May but this was interpreted as mere subterfuge to conceal a full-scale assault on the roof between 5.00 and 6.00 that morning.[304] As far as the prisoners were concerned, the main outstanding threat was posed by the military, quite possibly the SAS or other Special Forces, whom they believed were poised to strike. Activity was visible in Parkhurst and a helicopter hovered near the men containing a tactically equipped squad in black hoods:

> That evening we could see the military usher away the television crews – they were on a hill. They were looking into the prison and could see everything. They ushered them all away and things changed dramatically … We suspected they were going to do something in a big way … One of the screws came to us and said, 'Listen lads this is big. We need to sort this out. It's out of our hands. You know what I mean? Can you not see a way to resolve it?' We weren't interested at that stage. I remember talking to Paul Norney and saying it could be the case that they'll shoot us. It was a big, big issue. It was all over the news. So we prepared ourselves as best we could. We lined up with bricks piled high. If they did come up there is no doubt we were going to throw them over the side. We looked at that aspect and had decided that that was the way it was going to go. We had decided we weren't going to back off from that threat.[305]

In the manuscript account smuggled to Avesbury and Davies O'Neill claimed:

> They had planned an assault on the roof, it failed [or] was postponed because we had taken steps to render their equipment useless at the point of attack, and were, as they realised, aware of what they were up to since all seven prisoners were posted on various parts of the roof throughout the night. They didn't finally postpone their attempt until just before 7.00 a.m. [on 24 May] and at 7.15 the P[rincipal] O[fficer] returned and said there was no answer but he would be back at 1.30 [p.m.] … He returned at 12.15 p.m. and told us that we should listen to the 1.00 news and that W[illiam] Whitelaw would be making a statement and that would be our answer.[306]

Sinn Féin MP Owen Carron, whom the protesters had been denied direct contact with, issued a public offer on 24 May to mediate with Home Secretary Whitelaw. This was declined, radio reports of which spurred the IRA men to daub a banner 'Willie Whitelaw electioneers with prisoners' lives'.[307] Whitelaw stated in response to the Sinn Féin overture that there was 'no question of mediating with convicted terrorists' in Albany whom he intended to face down by severing their supplies of food and water. Carron warned that the situation on the Isle of Wight was 'long running' and should be properly addressed 'before someone lost their life'.[308] Mortality was discussed on the roof once the men became convinced that the groundwork had been laid in both propaganda and practical terms to storm their makeshift positions. A strong media presence from around 1.00 p.m., however, may have stemmed any impulse to attempt an exceptionally dangerous operation and by 3.30 p.m. movements observed from the roof suggested a winding down of preparations. Valves were shut off and power hoses taken away.[309] Watching press, meanwhile, witnessed the systematic demolition of the brickwork surrounding the two massive 2,000-gallon water tanks on a roof described in the *Times* as 'heavily damaged'.[310]

By 24 May the top floors of all occupied prison wings were cleared to prevent the transmission of additional supplies to the roof. Prisoners had been hitherto observed receiving food from a bucket attached to ropes or wire.[311] Clarke was amazed that it had taken the authorities so long to address the situation.[312] Some confusion surrounded the identity of those responsible for the stream of rations. It transpired that two of the most diligent helpers were political prisoners from El Salvador, regarded by the British authorities who arrested them in Heathrow as members of Cuban Intelligence.[313] Antonio Sanchez and Luis Garcia Fernandez were jailed for seven years in June 1982 and claimed membership of the El Salvadorean FMLN.[314] Another political prisoner, Libyan Nageeb Gasmi, was also credited by the IRA with being 'especially helpful'.[315] On arrival into Albany Gasmi had sought out the IRA and when introduced to Tony Madigan had 'stood to attention and saluted', much to the Irish man's surprise.[316] The Home Office was picketed that day by the ISM/RCG, as well as the IFM, RCL and South London TOM, who brandished a banner bearing the legend 'Support Albany Prisoners Demands'. This and a second picket two days later attracted minimal reportage, although police saw fit to push the demonstrators across the road and prohibit their use of megaphones.[317]

By chance, the annual conference of the Prison Officers' Association met in Scarborough on 24 May at the height of the Albany crisis. This provided a timely platform for prison staff to air their opinions which, due to the newsworthiness of the ongoing rooftop occupation, gained wide reportage. Albany POA member Roy Richards was quoted as posing the rhetorical question 'whether the terrorists, the bombers and the maimers of modern society should be given a free and easy type of prison to use at their playthings?' He contended that the IRA corrupted 'impressionable drug-reliant prisoners' and that the riot was the result of a 'broad based policy of total disruption' by Irish republicans.[318] POA Chairman Colin Steel concurred with Richards and was critical of the Prison Department's policy of accommodating criminals along with 'very sophisticated politically orientated prisoners'.[319] Generally, the POA disapproved of relatively moderate prison regimes and preferred the concentration of Category A prisoners in 'a specially built jail where they could be controlled more easily'.[320] The 'fortress' envisaged by the *Mountbatten Report* in 1966 had been repeatedly rejected by the Prison Department owing to the great cost and security risk entailed. The organization also sought the recruitment of an additional 2,500 prison officers and disputed Home Office claims that the Dispersal System was 'considerably below capacity'.[321] The concentration of all IRA prisoners in England would have involved less than 100 men and women in late 1983 when the Irish Government held approximately 120 IRA and forty INLA prisoners in Portlaoise.[322]

Comments by Richards, carried by the *Daily Telegraph* and *Times*, sensationally alleged IRA manipulation of the illegal drug supply to gain control over malleable criminals. He claimed that 'drug reliant prisoners ... will do anything to pay off their debts which they owe for a drug habit fed to them by the IRA'.[323] This 'dirty slander' was rejected by the pro-IRA RCG as a POA gambit to 'divert attention from the real issue: the prisoners' struggle for their basic democratic rights'.[324] The Home Office, which periodically denied the baleful effect of chemical dependency in the prisons, knew that an infinitesimal fraction of IRA prisoners utilized soft drugs in England. While some of this exceptionally small minority may well have traded with others, no republicans were either formally accused or punished for engaging in marijuana supply within the prisons, even though such charges carried a high propaganda premium. It was patently absurd to attribute millions of pounds' damage in Albany to this exotic source and the Prison Department notably did not endorse such unsound theories. The official view of St. Anne's Gate, carried in the same print media reports as the bizarre comments of Richards, was that ordinary prisoners obtained personal supplies smuggled by visitors and by feigning illness to acquire dispensed medicines.[325]

PROP highlighted the gross improbability of illicit drugs being distributed on a major scale by the single-most surveilled and frequently searched element within the prison population. Coggan, if concerned to ensure that the IRA's engagement at Albany did not overshadow the wider issues of incarceration in England, observed that the major prisoner grievance regarding drugs, as before, was their fear of being forcibly or irresponsibly dosed by the authorities.[326] Hill, in fact, had been personally threatened with the 'liquid cosh' and, implicitly, by transfer to the feared Hospital Wing when shifted to Parkhurst from the ruins of B Wing.[327] The IRA view was that the publication of misleading comments on the origins of the protest comprised 'disinformation' to distract attention from the violence used to quell the occupation of B and C Wings and obscure the mismanagement of the facility.[328] They appreciated that Albany was neither purely a 'Republican conspiracy' nor mere anarchic explosion. The IRA suspected that the timing of the dissemination of novel anti-republican propaganda, however outlandish in nature, could have been intended to lessen criticism, if not justify a lethal assault on the roof of B Wing.[329] This concurred with the sympathetic RCG analysis and was linked to the 'thinly veiled threat' of the Home Office on 24 May that it did not 'at this stage ... want to do anything which could cause unnecessary injury or death'.[330]

In a by then familiar cycle, the Principal Officer and clergyman returned to the scene at around 5.15 p.m. on 24 May and after two hours of being virtually ignored succeeded in passing on the message that the prisoners terms were being treated in the Home Office 'with the utmost priority'.[331] O'Neill took the opportunity to relay a personal message to Governor Meech, whom he had previously encountered face to face only weeks before when both were in Durham. Meech was apprised that the IRA 'were aware of their plans' to prepare public opinion for a potentially deadly attack on the protesters and that the net effect of the 'strategy of lies and misinformation' was to imbue the action with 'an aim and quality it did not possess'.[332] The protesters not only intended to vigorously contest the roof if attacked but had unlimited water and sufficient food on hand to comfortably survive for at least two weeks. The Tyrone man increased the only non-violent pressure he could bring to bear at the time by insisting that no further dialogue would take place if their reasonable demands were dismissed.[333] In discussion with his comrades Norney reasoned: 'They were going to kill us if we had stayed any longer. They would have killed one or two of us ... I said, "let's go down; we have gone as far as we have gone". So we all agreed'. The crucial point was that the protest has achieved considerable coverage as all remaining participants had decided to risk death if violently confronted.[334]

A reply was received at 10.30 p.m. in the form of a letter read by the interlocutors. The men were assured that the Home Secretary guaranteed their personal safety and that Owen Carron would be contacted by phone when they alighted. Carron was also to be informed that Governor Meech had received a document from the protesters and that this would be shared with Nick Davies of the *Guardian*. A final commitment was made to apprise their families of the location of where they were shifted.[335] Within an hour the terms were agreed with minor additions stipulating the provision of a medical examination, shower, fresh clothing, hot meal and personal property suitable for use in the 'local' prisons to which they were heading.[336] This was agreed by 11.45 p.m. and discussions then turned to the all-important minutiae of managing of the descent without the stigma of capitulation. O'Neill knew from experience that the authorities with whom he had interacted in good faith would probably renege on the substance of the negotiations, yet he drew strength from the knowledge that at least forty persons had witnessed the hard - won deal. The IRA complement was defiant as there had been 'no unconditional surrender, so the moral victory was ours'.[337]

The men unfurled a newly produced blanket banner at 9.30 a.m. on 25 May to encourage public identification with their aims and to bind the authorities to at least part of the negotiated agreement. It read: 'Protest ends at Noon – Statement to press from Governor will follow'.[338] A second new banner was displayed at 11.30 asserting 'Long-term prisoners' grievances to be issued to the press'.[339] The pressurized authors probably did not realise that the Home Office was already engaged in nimble defensive posturing. A London based spokesman insincerely claimed 'we were surprised to see the banner go up', in reference to the painted sheet announcing the cessation of the protest. This falsely implied that the cessation was a unilateral decision by the prisoners for which no terms had been agreed.[340] Several men holding the roof had in fact raised the classic revolutionary clenched fist salute when declaring their intent to descend. Such gestures were captured on film by vigilant media situated less than 500 metres away. As 12.00 p.m. approached, four men walked to the edge of the precipitous roof and began to climb down, leaving three comrades *in situ* listening to a radio. It was speculated that the last of the group were Irish men waiting for the BBC time signal in order to honour their statement of intent to the letter. In actuality, the IRA men possessed functional watches and were fully aware of the correct time. At 12.17 p.m. the republicans descended from the heights to cheers from British prisoners retained in a complex depleted of half its normal residents.[341]

Staff, accompanied by representatives of the Board of Visitors, as they requested, received the prisoners. They were not assaulted, as generally occurred in such situations, and waited to see if the authorities would honour the terms agreed.[342] One of the first signs that the Home Office had no intention of implementing the desired reforms came when the men were deprived of civilian clothes, watches and their only hardcopy of the terms document. O'Neill appreciated that the concurrent suppression of the Home Office version, which was not forwarded to either Davies or Carron contrary to the deal, reduced claims of the very existence of a negotiated settlement to a matter of vying elements of vastly differing capacity. On 26 May O'Neill urgently addressed the task of recreating the original from memory and succeeded in setting down a 'fair copy' that was '97 per cent correct'.[343] The Irish dimension was highlighted on the same day when an inquiry team arrived to conduct a major investigation. *The Irish Times* noted: 'The team will be looking at the grouping in [the] British jail of IRA prisoners, who were blamed for organizing the six-day protest'.[344] Albany was damaged to the point that it had to be 'taken out of use for repairs and redevelopment'.[345]

'Mutiny' and isolation

PROP, which had tended to play down the centrality of the IRA to the Albany protest, warned in its aftermath of what appeared to be a new Home Office policy regarding Irish republicans. *Newsline* reported that the Prison Department was not only stepping up its 'transfers of Irish prisoners from prison to prison – always without warning' but was utilizing 'local' jails to the extent that they were 'scattered outside as well as inside the dispersal system'. Unfamiliar prisons, such as Shrewsbury, Canterbury, Winchester, Lincoln and Bristol, alongside larger Category B complexes in Manchester, Liverpool and London, were increasingly selected. It was claimed that this stemmed in part from the reorganization of P3 Division of the Prison Department at Eccleston Square, London.[346]

As the weeks unfolded, a distinct new pattern of prisoner isolation emerged leading pro-republican sources to allege that Belfast families with relatives held in England were 'anxiously awaiting news of their loved one as the first reports filter through of a ruthless backlash being unleashed on them by jail authorities incensed at the dramatic Albany Jail protest'.[347] Journalist Nick Davies reported: 'Irish prisoners are now believed to be scattered not only through the seven top security "dispersal" prisons but also in local prisons ... which make no claim to have facilities for Category A inmates ... The suggestion now is that 10/74 is being used to move Irish prisoners simply because they are Irish and without tackling the niceties of whether there is any evidence of trouble making'. A Prison Department source denied any such policy existed and commented: '"I'm not saying it's wrong"'.[348]

In April 1984, however, 'Amendment No. 2' of CI 10/1974 was circulated to governors which effectively encouraged much greater use of isolation on a reactive as well as pre-emptive basis. They were informed that provision for increased use of 'secure cells' for 'troublesome prisoners' had been made and that 'steps have been taken to provide more cells' in local prisons. Paragraph Two read: 'Cells will be available on a Regional basis such that there are on average at least five cells available for each dispersal prison'. Fifty cells in Local Prisons were set aside for Dispersal Prison utilization with Gartree being allocated the highest total of seven for its complement.[349] Governors were reminded of their authority to dispatch persons 'because of an imminently explosive situation caused by his actual or impending disruptive behaviour'. Paragraph five set down a form of negative equalization of treatment: 'No greater privileges than any other "subversive" prisoner at the local prison' would be provided and 'they will bring with them none of the additional possessions normally allowed to long term prisoners'.[350]

The ISM obtained a copy of the restricted document and in May 1984 noted: 'An alarming trend is taking place towards a harsher, strictly secure and punitive prison policy'.[351] Moreover, the July 1984 publication of *Managing the Long-Term Prison System* by the Home Office Control Review Committee, established by the Home Secretary in September 1983, confirmed a new pre-emptive vigour to combat 'subversive' prisoners. Among the recommendations was that the routine application of CI 10/ 1974 be extended to Category B prisons outside the Dispersal System. This encouraged the protracted isolation of those deemed troublesome in such jails and normalized the use of solitary confinement for those transferred in on 'lie downs'.[352] Initiated during the tenure of Director General W Brister, his successor from March 1985, CJ Train commented that the report had been 'widely welcomed within the Service'.[353] The CRC paper recommended that 'a number of small units should be established to hold long term prisoners who present serious control problems'.[354]

Other precautions were taken to assist prisoner control and the RCG, a body with excellent lines of communications to the Dispersal System, alleged 'the regime at Albany has been extremely repressive ever since the major protest … The prisoners are kept in small groups "never more than 25 in one place" even in the exercise yard and they are guarded by large numbers of prison officers'. Confidential documents leaked to the *Observer*, meanwhile, established in the case of at least one Albany prisoner that private legal correspondence had been illegally intercepted and copied. It was alleged that the Parliamentary Ombudsman had been misled on seeking to investigate such claims and that the person at the centre of the controversy had been kept in 'prolonged solitary confinement' by instructions which 'by-passed' the Board of Visitors.[355]

Roy Walsh had been in segregation when the Albany Riot commenced and was subsequently sent to Parkhurst prison hospital owing to a stomach problem; here he was treated as if he had been a ringleader of the violence. By October 1983 he had been moved for twenty-eight day 'lie downs' in Canterbury, Winson Green, Wandsworth and twice to Gartree. He was sent to Gartree's Punishment Block for fifty-seven days when a particularly obnoxious prison officer, one of the seven crowding a small room containing his wife and two children, succeeded in goading him into a physical reaction on 7 July 1983.[356] Mary Walsh claimed the room was 'no bigger than a bathroom'.[357] Her husband had reputedly given the offending staff member five minutes to 'go out or get carried out' and ultimately broke the jaw of a man who claimed to be acting under the governor's instructions.[358] Sr. Clarke learned that the 'family visit [was] very bad, one hour under v[ery] bad conditions. Roy got angry and hit out at an officer'.[359] Ronnie McCartney viewed the episode in its overall dynamic: 'They tried it on and then you had to confront them and the only way to change things was to confront them'. In this instance the Gartree authorities soon relented and permitted the use of a much better appointed boardroom but Walsh was singled out for special treatment.[360]

Walsh incurred an additional penalty on 7 July 1983 for smashing 'the contents' of Segregation Unit 5 where he was sent for 'striking' the prison officer in the Visits Room. Twenty-one days 'cellular confinement' and forty-two days 'stoppage of earnings' were imposed.[361] The Irish man admitted he had 'punched' a man twice warned to back off 'in the face' but claimed to have only initiated the secondary destructive protest 'after being told that the rest of my visits had been cancelled'.[362] Eight prison officers were assigned to watch Walsh at close quarters as he showered. Held under unwarranted 'E List' conditions in Winson Green, deprived of clothes in a cell with a constantly shining red light, he was refused reading materials and access to the chapel. This elevated level of harassment was protested by the Relatives and Friends of Prisoners Committee in London.[363] An attempt by a solicitor to see Walsh in Hull on 8 November 1983 was refused, at which time he had been deprived of his watch, money and personal property.[364] Ray McLaughlin, described by the *New Statesman* as a 'well known Irish prisoner', but without his political affiliation, was sent from Bristol to F Wing, Wakefield, on 25 July 1983.[365] Militants Stevie Blake, Shane Paul O'Doherty and Shujaa Mosesh were present in the wing in early 1984.[366]

Home Offices responses to the Albany riot exceeded even the emergency measures instituted in the aftermath of Hull in 1976. An estimated fifty-one IRA prisoners were 'ghosted' to new prisons or 'lie-downs' in June/ July 1983, all of whom were inducted with periods of solitary confinement.[367] In what appeared an intentionally vindictive practice, at least six men were moved on the eve of scheduled visits, adding family distress to general disruption. One was allegedly beaten by prison officers.[368] The specifics of the backlash were monitored by the Relatives and Friends of Prisoners Committee which gleaned a pessimistic trend of mounting extremity. Previously, lengthy terms of solitary and loss of remission were the norm for long term prisoners who had been directly engaged in protests. However, in June 1983 it was speculated that the Home Office aimed to reduce correspondence entitlements for all Irish Category A prisoners to one letter per month from a relative and abolish 'accumulated' visits frequently availed of by visitors from Ireland.[369] Other forms of pressure had been introduced without public fanfare. It was not until April 1984 that Terry Davis, Labour MP for Hodge Hill, discovered that the Home Office had issued a Circular Instruction in 1980 limiting visitors to any remanded Category A prisoner to immediate family, solicitors and MPs. This was the ongoing *de facto* situation for IRA prisoners and the Prison Department alteration, as admitted by Lord Elton, harmonized arrangements in a negative manner for the whole top security class.[370]

Twenty-one of the thirty-two men charged arising from the Albany disturbances were brought before BOVs between 22 June and 31 August 1983. Four were found 'not guilty' and twelve were not adjudicated owing to the suspension of the proceedings by the Prisons Department.[371] All four IRA activists who had taken to the roof, however, faced comparatively rare charges of 'mutiny', as did Bennett and Hill who had simply rioted inside B Wing.[372] Bennett had been badly beaten and was transferred to the Hospital Wing of Wormwood Scrubs where he still remained over a month later.[373] Whereas protesters could generally expect to be sanctioned by loss of remission, fines and segregation by standard BOV 'adjudication', the Home Office elected to additionally charge twenty-eight men with 'mutiny' under Rule 47 (1) of the *Prison Rules*.[374] The *Irish News* accurately described this as an 'extremely serious charge' which permitted 'unlimited loss of remission'.[375] While the exact definition of the term was not specified, Rule 47 (1) declared 'A prisoner shall be guilty of an offence against discipline if he mutinies or incites another prisoner to mutiny'.[376] In the context of what Category A prisoners regarded as the excessive use of Rule 43, men could spend unprecedented periods in solitary confinement. On 14 July 1983 Stevie Blake was docked 670 days remission, which effectively added six years to his sentence in addition to fifty-six days solitary confinement. This distinguished him as the most punished Albany rioter. Tony Clarke lost 500 days remission as well as receiving fifty-six days in solitary, during which time he was assaulted in Strangeways.[377] Bennett was docked 456 days of remission and given fifty-six days in solitary on 19 July 1983.[378]

Clarke followed Hill into Strangeways in Manchester while both Norney and Miyi were taken to Durham.[379] The cell occupied by Norney, too small to take a prison - issue bed frame, was reputedly 'seep[ing] with damp' and akin to 'living in a tomb'.[380] On 11 June 1983 Clarke was reportedly in solitary confinement and deprived of fresh clothes since the roof protest. His family lived in Lenadoon where the local paper, *The Andersonstown News*, described him with evident communal pride as the person who had 'led' the famous protest.[381] The car park of the 'Busy Bee' shopping complex in Andersonstown, close to the much-raided Prisoners' Dependents Club (aka 'PD') and the GAA Casement Park grounds, was a major staging area for West Belfast protests during the Troubles. O'Neill was dispatched to Brixton where, on 23 June 1983, he was charged with 'mutiny' arising from the Albany action in accordance with Rule 47 (1) of the *Prison Rules* (1964).[382] He corresponded frequently with Stevie Blake and Ray McLaughlin in Wakefield, who collectively fed information into a communications network that included the *Fight Racism! Fight Imperialism!* group and other progressive allies outside Sinn Féin.[383]

Paul Hill had sent letters to his family in Belfast explaining the turn of events and while staff denied interference it transpired that all replies had been returned to sender on the untrue basis that the Irish man was 'not known at this address'.[384] He derived a measure of satisfaction by apprising a particularly unfriendly prison officer living in Stockport that he would 'sooner live here than in your home'. This had the effect of encouraging more acceptable interaction and may have contributed to Hill's success in achieving temporary transfer to Wormwood Scrubs for long - delayed accumulated family visits.[385] Clarke and Hill subsequently fended off a weak 'shiv' attack in the yard by a young and deranged prisoner whom they magnanimously assisted by refusing to depose evidence of the incident. Hill had correctly interpreted the muffled sound of glass being broken the previous night as a harbinger of danger. His putative assailant, nonetheless, managed to fashion the shard into a potentially lethal weapon and smuggle it into a closely supervised yard without detection.[386]

The Strangeways men were among the former Albany rioters concentrated in Wormwood Scrubs to appear before the Board of Visitors for 'adjudication'. Hill recalled: 'The Governor and the members of the Board of Visitors sat, guarded by screws, around a table in an office off the block. One by one, men were taken from their cells to make their brief appearance before the kangaroo court. I sat in my cell and waited my turn'. A prisoner in a nearby cell, however, threw a bucket of week - old urine onto the floor the moment he was unlocked. Faced with such a visceral repudiation of authority and decorum, the shocked BOV promptly 'fled' the wing.[387]

'Mutiny' and the Boards of Visitors

The 'mutiny' factor demanded a focused prisoner response and one English man, Jimmy Tarrant, took a case of great ramifications for Category A prisoners. Divergent progressive elements readily grasped that devolving such serious powers to an untrained Prison Board of Visitors appointed by the Home Secretary, which functioned in camera in a forum where prisoners were denied legal representation and the power to either call or question witnesses, was an affront to civil rights. This viewpoint was supported by Edwin Lever, Vice-Chairman of the Association of Members of Boards of Visitors, who averred: 'These are matters which should be dealt with by an open court' and that persons faced with the prospect of spending an extra year behind bars merited professional legal defence.[388] Prisoners found guilty of 'mutiny' under the 1974 amended Rule 51 were regarded as having committed an 'especially grave offence' and could be punished with 'unlimited forfeiture of remission'.[389] In a parallel move, Jimmy Anderson, wary of being 'set up' as the 'ringleader' of unrest in Wormwood Scrubs, petitioned the High Court for his right to obtain legal advice and representation at the semi-secret BOV proceedings.[390]

Tarrant *et al* were aware that the ECHR had criticised the general nature of the Boards of Visitors but identified a credible specific complaint on the question of entitlement to legal aid. An application for the grant by Tarrant to the High Court induced Justice Popplewell to order a review of BOV proceedings on 12 August 1983.[391] This brought the schedule of BOV actions to an abrupt halt, largely as it was held that the ECHR would ultimately condemn the Home Office. It was not immaterial that the Strasbourg court was due to ratify its decision in favour of Sean Campbell in September 1983, in which his loss of 500 days remission arising from the 1976 Albany disturbance was interpreted as contrary to natural justice.[392] While all sentences imposed by the prisons BOV remained extant pending the decision of the High Court, segregation was maintained wherever it had been imposed. Charlie McGhee and Chris Scales, two of those acquitted of mutiny, were returned to solitary confinement.[393] The Popplewell ruling nonetheless checked the Home Office in its bid to punish the protesters and publicity in the *Guardian* and *New Statesman* deepened the discomfort of the Prison Service by confirming that Eddie O'Neill had indeed transmitted negotiated terms to the authorities.[394]

Other prisoners observed High Court developments with keen self-interest, not least men facing charges for another underreported incident on 16 June 1983 when twenty-five inmates of D Wing, Wormwood Scrubs, occupied its top landing at 4.30 p.m.[395] Category A man Jimmy Anderson explained: 'Rumours had been coming in that the men in the Albany Demo had been badly mistreated by the guards. In an attempt to draw attention to this a group of D Wing prisoners including me decided to stage our own protest ... [no] IRA men or ex Albany prisoners took part ... for tactical reasons.[396] This act of identification went further than normal in that the seven chosen protesters stated their support for 'parity with Irish Prisoners' in the North of Ireland and 'Repatriation of all Irish Prisoners of War on demand'.[397]

Five Prison Officers were locked into an office and barriers placed on the landing prior to the ascent, a humiliating reversal which may have informed the violent tenor of subsequent events. The men on the roof were attacked by up to eighty London region MUFTI members who appeared from three stairwells and spent approximately ten minutes beating the protesters. Anderson was twice knocked unconscious and sustained injuries to his shoulder and left eye. The Governor directed that his handcuffs be removed in the Segregation Block strip cell where he had just been kicked and punched.[398] The seven were given terms of forty-two to 168 days solitary confinement.[399] In retrospect the Prison Service claimed to have been relieved that 'courage shown by staff ... managed to contain what would otherwise have developed into a far more serious confrontation'.[400] From the vantage of July 1984 the Director General of the Prison Service praised the 'last resort' operation as an example of the 'correct use of MUFTI tactics'. Principal Officer Ronald Dixon was personally awarded a Certificate of Commendation by the Home Secretary for leading the counterattack.[401]

Another Wormwood Scrubs prisoner, Tommy Tangney, was punished for climbing onto the Laundry roof at 2.00 p.m. on 24 June to draw attention to the dangerous situation facing his friends in Segregation. In keeping with the new Home Office resolve, Tangney was heavily attacked around 5.00 p.m. by at least fifteen staff in full view of prisoners watching from C and D Wings. After three days in the Prison Hospital he joined his comrades in the Segregation Block.[402] Tangney received 112 days in solitary. In the light of such developments, the High Court was obliged to consider applications from three members of the aggrieved Wormwood Scrubs grouping alongside a further Albany - related case taken on behalf of prisoners sentenced for mutiny in the prison prior to the 12 August moratorium.[403] Anderson's lawyers, having won a judicial review of his case in July, successfully resisted Prison Service plans to have the charges against him dealt with by a 21 September Board of Visitors hearing.[404]

Complaints aired by Wormwood Scrubs prisoners Tommy Tangney, Jimmy Anderson and Chris Clark were considered by Lord Justice Kerr and Mr. Justice Webster on 8 November 1983 alongside those of Albany prisoners Jimmy Tarrant and Roy Leyland.[405] The main finding of the Queen's Bench Divisional Court concerned the charge of 'mutiny' and its adjudication under *Prison Rules* regulations by Boards of Visitors. It was reported: 'In most, if not all mutiny charges, questions were bound to arise as to whether collective action was intended to be collective. Where such questions arose, as in the present cases, no board of visitors, properly directing itself, could reasonably decide not to allow a prisoner legal representation'.[406] As the various boards had not exercised their discretionary authority on the question of permitting legal representation, including the option of self-advocacy by a prisoner addressed in Rule 49 (2), the court quashed the verdicts reached in the five cases which had been referred.[407] Although the judgement did not restrict the provision of legal assistance to persons facing 'exceptionally grave' charges, it was understood that only such cases would be affected. With 115 BOVs hearing 3,500 disciplinary hearings per year, the potential administrative costs were immense.[408]

Punishing men under the useful tool of segregation under Rule 43 was an obvious alternative to pressing complicated 'mutiny' charges, although the relatively large numbers involved in riot type situations posed logistic challenges for a system in which the *Prior Report* claimed sanctioned 'only a very small proportion of the prison population' in this manner. In late October 1983 a mere 114 men were technically confined under Rule 43 of England's 31,700 male prisoners, of whom approximately 50 per cent were isolated for less than two weeks. Just eight men in late October 1983 had been 'segregated for more than six months', although this low total was misleading in terms of the actual incidence of isolation. Prison establishments retained the option of sanctioning those deemed to have contravened discipline by imposing periods of cellular confinement. This, however, was limited to fifty-six days and required BOV adjudication with all the new legal oversight and court directions being applied.[409]

The Prison Department acknowledged that the judgement in *R v Board of Visitors HM Prison Albany ex parte Tarrant and others* required a 'major change in the arrangements for adjudications'.[410] Justice Webster had openly expressed his approval of 'charges of mutiny' being heard in the criminal courts. Home Secretary Leon Brittan was obliged to respect the Divisional Court ruling and the newly defined strictures of 'Webster criteria' which were transmitted to governors and BOV chairpersons.[411] On 29 November Brittan informed the Commons that he had 'decided to set aside all the disciplinary awards made by the board in respect of offences committed during the disturbance' at Albany. Twenty-eight prisoners would not be tried for 'mutiny'. This major setback was tempered by his announcement of an invitation to the Chief Constable of Hampshire to 'investigate any criminal offences' which had occurred on 19–25 May 1983.[412] Brittan also instructed the Prison Department to respond to the new entitlement of legal representation for adjudicated prisoners by having the Governor 'represented by a lawyer'.[413]

Corresponding IRA prisoners in Liverpool, Wakefield and Brixton, who were informed by legal documents provided by Alistair Logan, closely followed news of the Tarrant precedent. George E Baker & Co distributed a briefing document headed 'Judicial Review, Re: Albany Board of Visitors Adjudication' which summarized in eleven paragraphs recent legal developments and advised on how and when clients should petition the Home Secretary if appropriate.[414] Blake had followed the advice of Logan when summoned before the BOV in Manchester: 'It will certainly do more good on our behalf, and make people more aware of what is taking place in their prisons in the good name of the choice words "British Justice"'.[415] Justice Webster, who gave the leading judgement in the Divisional Court, also responded in a manner favourable to remand prisoners in 1984 when he accepted that the Home Secretary was required to consider a prisoner's right to receive legal and family visits when deciding on appropriate locations for transfer. Citation of 'operational and security' grounds, however, remained sufficient to justify immediate non-notified movement of any Category A prisoner to a different premises.[416] In practice, it was clear by February 1984 that the courts were unprepared to process a potentially massive number of BOV related judicial reviews unless proceedings had been initiated within three months of the sitting. Whereas courts retained discretion to conduct reviews on a longer term basis, Alastair Logan advised Roy Walsh that this would almost certainly not extend to a re-examination of the the harsh BOV rulings arising from the Wormwood Scrubs 'riot' in 1979.

Paul Norney was placed in solitary confinement in Durham where he had served 162 days by 4 November 1983. His isolation, therefore, continued after he had completed the fifty-six day punishment imposed by the BOV.[418] Under Rule 48 (2), prisoners facing adjudication on disciplinary charges could be segregated, although the prolonged solitary confinement of Norney following the hearing was untypical.[419] The authorities evidently viewed the standard BOV punishment as a mere prelude to continued segregation, which could be defended under Home Office regulations by citing the application of Rule 43 to 'Good Order and Discipline'. Gerry Adams bluntly described this treatment on 23 November as 'continuous torture', a loaded term chosen to elicit attention from Amnesty International and the ECHR.[420] The perspective of Strasbourg was not immaterial and the Divisional Court ruling in *Tarrant* had the effect of pre-empting a negative ECHR judgement in June 1984 on the basis of complaints made by two IRA prisoners attacked by Albany staff in September 1976.[421] Yet for month after month Norney was permitted to exercise for up to one hour a day in a particularly small 'yard'. He claimed in a letter to the *Guardian*: 'If I stand in the centre of the cell and stretch out my arms, I can easily rest the palms of my hands on the two side walls. Five short paces take me from the back wall to the cell door. I have no bed in the cell, I have a mattress which must be removed or upended against the wall during the day to enable me to move about'.[422] Lord Elton, with Home Office ministerial responsibility for prisons, admitted that such conditions were 'very restricted' but rejected accusations that Norney was being persecuted for his involvement in the Albany riot. Republicans suspected that his harsh confinement was a form of revenge exacted by the Home Office in response to the embarrassing reverse in the High Court.[423] The tide of legal review was decidedly flowing against the British Government, which had accumulated eight separate findings of violating the European Convention on Human Rights by the Strasbourg authority in March 1983.[424]

The Queen's Bench Divisional Court delivered a further blow to the *modus operandi* of the Prison Department on 21 December 1983 when Lord Justice Robert Goff and Mr. Justice Mann ruled that Jimmy Anderson, one of the Wormwood Scrubs 'mutiny' prisoners, had been wronged on 13 July when the Assistant Governor prevented him from consulting his legal advisor. Anderson had wished to examine the prospects of taking legal action against staff whom he claimed had assaulted him during the disturbances of 16 June but was not allowed confer with Ms Akester, an articled clerk of BM Birnberg & Co. The justices concurred that 'unimpeded' access to a solicitor was 'an inseparable part of the right of access to the courts' and that prison regulations on pursuing allegations of staff malfeasance through all internal mechanisms, following the *Raymond v Honey (1983)* judgement, amounted to 'impediment'.[425] The Prison Department interpreted the Honey ruling as requiring its governors to provide prisoners with 'facilities for private prosecutions in much the same way as for civil litigation'. In response to *R v S of S for the Home Department ex parte Anderson* the Prison Service instructed that legal consultations must be permitted even if a prisoner had not 'raised the matter through the prescribed internal channels'.[426] Anderson had been represented by Edward Fitzgerald who later engaged in numerous cases involving Irish republican prisoners.[427]

Billy Armstrong was moved from Albany to Parkhurst and held in isolation and 'in patches'. Armstrong's efforts to resist this extended to a hunger strike which succeeded in that he was moved on to Winchester and held in isolation.[428] He was subsequently returned to Parkhurst.[429]

The dramatic events at Albany and Wormwood Scrubs reopened public discussion of the rationale of the Dispersal System as the outworkings of the May Committee remained in abeyance. *The Times* reflected on the high cost of the Albany riot with the fact that two of the three 'sieges' in D Wing, Wormwood Scrubs, entailed life - sentenced prisoners taking hostages.[430] The then pending legal clarification on the punishment for 'mutiny', if not specifically addressed in the feature 'Tougher prisons for prison toughs', represented a further setback for the concept of humane control of inmates within a secure perimeter. Jonathan Uzzell, 'No. 3 [Governor] at Wormwood Scrubs', rebuked Leo Abse who had admitted deliberately undermining the *Mountbatten Report* with the red herring of plans to employ armed guards in his provocatively explicit autobiography, *Private Member*. As a Labour MP and member of the Advisory Council on the Penal System, Abse pursued his personal libertarian agenda by countering 'the military absurdities of Mountbatten' *vis à vis* the 'fortress' concentration model. This contributed to the adoption of 'dispersal' policy variant which, despite modification in practise by the Prison Department, had not prevented major riots at Gartree in 1978 and Albany in 1983. *The Times* claimed: 'It is now widely accepted that the dispersal system does not work' and noted that fear of another revolt in Gartree had led to staff locking down 'top security' prisoners fourteen hours per day.[431]

Although impolitic for conservatives to foreground the disproportionate role of the IRA in fomenting disruption, a 'source' in the Prison Department implied their potency when addressing Home Office approved countermeasures: 'Top ranking IRA men are being held in special security wings at two prisons with no more than 20 to each'.[432] This indicated that the SSUs were still regarded as providing additional protection against Irish republicans who were theoretically entitled under the 'dispersal' mode of incarceration to relative freedom inside a high secure perimeter. A Prison Department spokesman claimed that republicans held on the wings were not subjected to heightened prison shifts but that 'you hear more about Irish prisoners being moved because their relatives contact the Irish newspapers'.[433]

Gerry Adams and the prison visit ban, July 1983

The Westminster General Election on 9 June 1983 returned Margaret Thatcher's Conservative Party to Government with a reduced majority and produced an extraordinary result when Sinn Féin Vice President Gerry Adams was elected MP for West Belfast. Unseating former SDLP leader Gerry Fitt, as well as surpassing the vote of the party's main Belfast contender Dr. Joe Hendron, enabled Adams to start the process of consolidating a natural Sinn Féin constituency where the IRA received considerable communal support.[434] Fitt was elevated to the House of Lords on 21 July and moved his primary domicile to London. On 2 July 1983 Adams wrote to Home Secretary Leon Brittan querying the veracity of media reports that he had been banned from British prisons.[435] The logic of 'excluding' an elected member of the Assembly and Imperial Parliament from entering 'Britain' undermined cherished Unionist perceptions of the Six Counties as an integral part of the United Kingdom. An irritated Fitt had previously described those excluded as 'victors in the controversy'.[436]

It was held following review in Belfast and London that the obvious 'parliamentary privilege' argument would not be invoked by Sinn Féin in relation to members who had not taken their seats. This followed private consultation by Brittan with Northern Secretary Jim Prior and further advice from NIO officials who supported the contention that persons offering opinion in 'support of violence' could and should be differentiated from members of 'constitutional parties'.[437] On 21 July 1983, as Home Office deliberations continued, Adams addressed the topical issue of the 'conditions' imposed on the sixty IRA prisoners in England and their families in Ireland. He acknowledged overtures from prisoner's relatives and revealed he had sent messages to both the Home Office and the Governor's Office in Gartree.[438] Adams revealed that he had written to the IRA cohort in England and referred to the numerous 'framed up' Irish and English civilians.[439]

The subject was to the fore in London on 27 July 1983 when, accompanied by Joe Austin, Adams addressed his first public meeting as an MP out of Ireland in Finsbury Town Hall. He announced that he intended to use his nominal right as a member of Westminster to visit IRA prisoners in England and that Sinn Féin planned to form a 'repatriation committee' to work towards this end. Chris Smith, Labour MP for Islington South, qualified his approval for much of what Adams had said yet raised the ire of a section of the 350 people in attendance by repudiating the legitimacy of political violence.[440] Adams clearly intended to pursue the hands-on approach developed by Owen Carron between August 1981 and June 1983, who was no longer in a position to demand entry into British prisons having lost his Fermanagh-South Tyrone seat to ex-UDR Major Ken Maginnis. As a 'H-Block' candidate, Carron was not technically a 'Sinn Féin' MP and consequently side - stepped the attention drawn by Adams.[441]

The *Guardian* predicted that the presence of Adams inside the Dispersal System would 'embarrass the [British] Government' and were soon proven correct.[442] An ingenious pretext to prevent this materializing was signalled by Brittan on 28 July 1983 when the Home Secretary announced that the MP for West Belfast would be deprived of his traditional prerogative to visit prisons in England and Wales on the grounds that he was 'a member of an organisation which openly espouses the use of violence for political ends'. It was inferred that this allegation alluded to Sinn Féin, prompting accusations of 'gross hypocrisy' from Carron who when holding the same position had visited the majority of IRA prisoners in England.[443] The refinement received front-page reportage in the Clan na Gael organ in the USA, in addition to rare international coverage of the repatriation question in the *New York Times*.[444] The British press conceded that the outright ban was 'unprecedented' in England, a further negative historic step arising directly from the Irish conflict.[445]

Brittan's powers extended to nullifying Standing Orders enabling Westminster MPs to enter prisons and Adams, it was revealed, had been barred without notification prior to his Finsbury appearance. The Home Office explained that the access granted to Carron resulted from his election in the mode of an independent anti-H-Block candidate, rather than as a representative of Sinn Féin. The NIO issued a statement of concurrence providing a uniform basis for the closure of all prisons in the Six Counties and England to Sinn Féin MPs, if not also other elected members.[446] This manoeuvre struck deeply at Sinn Féin's prospect of keeping IRA prisoners in the limelight, a setback seconded by the subsequent Home Office decision to serve Adams with an Exclusion Order from the United Kingdom under the PTA. In this respect the Home Office evidently concurred with the republican contention that no part of Ireland lay within the United Kingdom.

Irish Post editor Brendan Mac Lua used his popular 'Frank Dolan' column of 27 August 1983 to aver that up to forty innocent persons may have been jailed in England. He queried, in anticipation of the November 1983 meeting between Thatcher and FitzGerald, whether Britain's endorsement of the Council of Europe's convention for the transfer of prisoners 'be extended to Irish political prisoners in Britain?' In a perceptive comment Mac Lua equally questioned the commitment of the Irish Government to sign the accord given that Foreign Minister Peter Barry 'appeared unaware' of the convention when interviewed in London.[447]

The August 1983 annual Anti-Internment rally in Andersonstown, Belfast was attended by international prison solidarity groups, including 200 TOM and over eighty US visitors. Irish Northern Aid Chairman Martin Galvin accused the Irish Government of abandoning the Northern Nationalists at a time when, he further alleged, the British Government was pressuring the American authorities who wished to render assistance. In front of a 2,000 strong crowd which included observers from Birmingham Trades Council, he claimed Irish-Americans had 'rallied perhaps as never before' to resist a US version of "criminalization".[448] The tone of the event was belligerent and Sinn Féin leader Danny Morrison addressed British withdrawal with the powerful phrase: 'There is the boat and the box. We want them to take the boat'.[449]

Mary Pearson of Birmingham TOM on 7 August 1983 was an invited speaker at the annual rally in West Belfast where she announced the 'particular emphasis on Irish prisoners in English jails' that year. TOM supported such persons by assisting their families on visits across the Irish Sea.[450] A reflective TOM analysis published in 1983, when the organization was ten years old, surveyed the prison situation in the context of a decade of political violence. Even as the impact of the 1981 H-Block hunger strike reverberated, British based republicans singled out 'the 'forgotten' prisoners' in England for special mention. According to TOM: 'The prisoners who had suffered the most, those in English jails, have largely sought not to impose their plight on the Republican Movement. They're not likely to see Ireland again until the struggle is over'. With military victory and amnesty well in the offing, TOM advocated the Sinn Féin Ard Comhairle policy of campaigning in the future for repatriation as was generally extended to sentenced British military personnel and Loyalists. The familiar litany of hardships was detailed in *Close to home, Lessons from Ireland*. These included the then self-evident dangers of isolation, bad health care, 'ghosting' and uniquely bad visiting conditions.[451]

The PTA, a major source of disruption to those pursuing legal pro-republican activities, was refined in March 1983. Earl Jellicoe's review of the November 1974 PTA addressed the operation of coercive legislation which the liberally inclined Home Secretary Roy Jenkins had described as 'draconian', even as he steered its progression through Westminster without a division. In March 1983 a new bill proposed a series of changes to the 1974 and amended 1976 legislation, including the removal of the phrase 'Temporary Provisions' from the formal title to facilitate a proposal that the Act become renewable at five-year intervals.[452] Other adjustments were ostensibly positive, not least the attempt to make Exclusion Orders subject to three year review instead of being indefinite. Persons who had lived in Britain for over three years, rather than the original twenty years, cold not be excluded. 'Withholding' information, moreover, remained an offence, albeit insufficient to warrant arrest.[453] Liberal William Pitt, MP for Croydon North-West, noted that the PTA had not prevented 1982 being the 'worst year since 1975 for terrorist outrages' and reluctantly supported the legislation.[454] Few expected the colourful Earl Jellicoe, godson of King George V and World War Two commander of the Special Boat Squadron in the Mediterranean theatre, to make comprehensive amendments to Britain's most useful coercive instrument.[455]

One of the main arguments cited against concentrating IRA and other Category A prisoners in a 'fortress' prison was the danger of a mass breakout. This remained a theoretical concept in the Six Counties until 25 September 1983 when thirty-eight republicans exited the H-Blocks of Long Kesh in an incident described by the *Independent* as 'the most spectacular IRA breakout'.[456] Belfast Crown Court claimed it was a 'well planned and concerted military type operation' and Northern Secretary Jim Prior resisted calls for his resignation.[457] The spirits of the IRA in England were raised by the event and several of those centrally involved were acquainted. Gerry Kelly, one of the leaders of the attempt, was the former inmate of Brixton and Wormwood Scrubs who had been on hunger-striker in 1974–75 prior to repatriation. Another key figure, Bobby Storey, stood trial in the Old Bailey in 1981 on charges of attempting to spring Brian Keenan from Brixton.[458] In the 1990s Storey was named in the House of Commons under Parliamentary Privilege as the IRA Director of Intelligence.[459] Ex-H-Block IRA O/C Brendan 'Bik' MacFarlane also made good his escape through South Armagh and was named in December 1984 in connection with a major republican kidnapping centred on Leitrim, which sparked a national police and military operation.[460] Prominent republican escaper Gerry 'Blute' McDonnell had been deported from England in June 1977 following detention in Liverpool. He was arrested in Glasgow in June 1985 with part of an ASU credited with an attempt to assassinate Margaret Thatcher in Brighton.[461] The brazen and monetarily rewarding IRA seizure of businessman Don Tidey in Dublin on 24 November 1983 prompted the embarrassed Irish Government to secretly explore the possibility of reintroducing internment without trial if their British counterparts acted in tandem. While the extraordinary proposal gained no traction, preliminary discussions identified the Curragh Military Camp in Kildare and Armagh Prison as suitable sites to hold large numbers of untried prisoners.[462]

Sir James Hennessy, Chief Inspector of Prisons, was appointed to investigate the H-Block escape on 26 September 1983, a significant input given multiple calls for a Home Office shift in penal policy towards a re-concentration of Category A prisoners.[463] The inquiry lasted until 12 January 1984, and consumed, as Hennessy noted, 'all our meagre resources' due to its scope and urgency.[464] Massing IRA prisoners in England, however, posed particular difficulties in the early 1980s as it would have indisputably confirmed their 'special category' as holders of political status in all but name. In the aftermath of Gerry Tuite's escape from Brixton, *The Economist* rationally argued: 'If a large number of IRA prisoners were kept together, they would be able to make political protests as they do in H-blocks of the Maze prison in Belfast'.[465] Logistical issues also pertained in view of the fact that the men who fled H7 overcame all internal obstacles and a secondary garrison of 150 British soldiers who comprised the Prison Guard Force.[466]

Hennessy noted a number of 'lessons' from the H-Block disaster which he related to the 'custody and control of dangerous prisoners' in the Dispersal System. He observed that the main gain complex at Long Kesh was exposed as being physically deficient as a security barrier, a weakness replicated in England where certain Victorian prisons possessed 'defects ... hidden behind impressive facades'. Many were 'listed' historic buildings where reconstruction and modernization options were limited. Building additional perimeter gateways in such institutions was regarded as expensive but unavoidable if the risk factor was to be reduced. The Chief Inspector believed search procedures of prisoners, visitors and buildings were insufficiently frequent to screen effectively for contraband. He implied that if the IRA could acquire firearms inside the formidable H-Blocks they might well do so in England. The H7 breakout also drew his attention to failures in intelligence, vigilance and application of existing security protocols. Hennessy deemed it pertinent that 'too many staff had been lulled into a sense of complacency' in the H-Blocks.[467]

The *Hennessy Report* was debated all day in the House of Commons on 9 February 1984, providing MPs with opportunities to address the wider context of IRA and general political prisoners.[468] Among the most radical proposals, advanced by Brighton MP Julian Amery, was that IRA prisoners could be subdivided and transferred to England 'where their access to visitors would not be so easy, and where they would not have the opportunity to conspire with one another'.[469] Amery believed that visitors to the H-Blocks were complicit in the targeting of staff killed by the IRA. This elicited a sharp retort from Stephen Ross MP who queried if Amery was aware that 'six IRA men in the prison at Albany, admittedly they were sentenced in this country, [in May 1983] caused about 4 million worth of damage?' Ross claimed that contacts in the Prison Officers Association would confirm that 'the internal information among members of the IRA is extremely good, both in this country and in Northern Ireland .... If they were put in all our prisons in this country it would be a very costly exercise'.[470] In the short term, the drama and scale of the extraordinary overwhelmed international media reports of IRA prisoners anywhere outside the Six Counties. Within a few years, efforts to extradite the 'H-Block Four' from California prolonged the story and intersected with efforts to send untried republican suspects from the US directly to Ireland and England.[471] Numerous additional related cases came before the Special Criminal Court in Dublin.[472]

On several occasion in 1982–83 Gardaí and Irish Army soldiers were obliged to enter the landings of Portlaoise to carry out essential duties left undone by striking prison officers.[473] As in England, industrial actions exacerbated existing tensions inside the prisons. Governor Willie O'Reilly had survived at least one presumed assassination bid by the IRA in 1976 and both the Gardaí and Prison Service strongly suspected that republicans had grievously wounded Brian Stack, Head of Security, on 25 March 1983. Stack was shot in the head as he departed a boxing event he had just refereed at the National Stadium, Dublin. He died eighteen months later. Although not claimed by the IRA, which would have breached General Order No. 8 (a) of its 'Green Book' constitution by commissioning such an act in the Twenty-Six County jurisdiction, Midlands Prison staff correctly held the organization responsible. It was speculated that he had been targeted for his 'role in preventing a break out'.[474] Stack, however, managed the day-to-day regime of aggressive and repeated strip-searching which republicans and other prisoners regarded as deeply objectionable. He was under threat from the Official IRA, INLA and Provisional IRA. Following an internal investigation the Republican Movement admitted in August 2013 that its members had been responsible but had acted without authorization.[475]

The Irish public became aware of wider 'friction within the prisons' in March 1983 when prison officers complained of service issues while those they guarded alleged deteriorating conditions. In the aftermath of the 1977 IRA hunger strike in Portlaoise, political prisoners received superior treatment to that extended to criminals. IRA and INLA men were excused work duties, had improved association term, could receive additional correspondence and had an extra half hour of cell lighting. Many non-political prisoners in Limerick and Mountjoy resented this imbalance.[476] Increased frequency of strip-searching in Portlaoise, however, renewed hostility with staff and the *Irish Times* reported that a 'stand off' had developed with 'strongly-motivated INLA and Provisional IRA' cadres. Staff, locked into a major dispute with the Department of Justice on overtime, complained of being 'subject to threats and intimidation in the course of their work'.[477] When IRA prisoners in Portlaoise believed that Governor O'Reilly had reneged on an agreement on the timing and frequency of strip searches on 30 October 1983, around 250 prison officers, supported by Gardaí, were deployed to enforce the crackdown. This incident contributed to the establishment in April 1984 of the Portlaoise Prisoners Relatives Action Committee.[478] The move was timely as on 3 May 1984 a misfired escape attempt by ten IRA and INLA prisoners resulted in a 'riot' by staff.[479]

Parkhurst, October 1983

On 2 October 1983 a demonstration was held outside Parkhurst to mark the third anniversary of the death of Sean O Conaill who had been imprisoned in the facility just prior to his demise. Sinn Féin, TOM and others participated. The gesture was appreciated by Hugh Doherty, Pat Hackett, Bernard McCafferty, Stevie Nordone, Ronnie MacCartney and Billy Armstrong. Punter Bennett and John McComb were also held around this time.[480] McComb was Armstrong's first cousin and his sentencing on 26 May 1983 was shortly followed by the jailing in Belfast of another close relative on arms charges.[481]

Armstrong had more stimulation than he had wished for on the evening of Sunday 30 October 1983, when he was suddenly transferred from Parkhurst to the punishment block in Albany. No explanation was given, although he received notification from the Governor in the course of the following afternoon that he was to be 'put in patches'. This indicated that he had been implicated in an escape plot, an allegation which Armstrong vehemently denied. Accordingly, the Belfast man refused to don the modified uniform issued to him and would not accept food from 31 October. Clarification of the situation came on 1 November when security prison officers arrived from Parkhurst and told him an informer had indeed named him as being involved in an escape. This was actually untrue but he was, nonetheless, shifted to Winchester once more for a twenty-eight day lie-down. It transpired that the Parkhurst authorities had taken the tip-off very seriously and that armed police guarded the perimeter of the prison over the weekend.[482] Much to his surprise, Armstrong was returned to Parkhurst after twenty-one days. This would not have happened if the prison authorities believed the *News of the World* account of an escape compact with a prisoner in C Wing.[483] In the meantime he had once again experienced the most concerted form of twenty-four hour surveillance the Dispersal System had devised.

The allocation of John McComb from Wormwood Scrubs transformed his prison experience:

> That was the first time I got in and met other IRA people and you could tell the respect they had in the jails. I found this out very quick. If there was a problem within the jail because of the struggles over the years before I got there and the IRA going to the fore and they had to go to the fore after making their mark … When I got there they were already established so when you got there into the prison proper you were looked on with a bit of respect because of what had happened before. Prisoners would come to you and say, 'we're having a bit of a problem here. What do you think?' They would ask the IRA because the IRA would always go to the front.[484]

Unaccustomed to republican jail practices in England, McComb diverged from the norm by demanding a *quid pro quo* from London gangsters when they approached him in company with McCartney seeking assistance in a protest over visiting conditions. The perplexed English men believed common cause was futile owing to Home Office directed interference in IRA visits but had expected solidarity nonetheless, as per the norm. McComb's Long Kesh and ASU background equally informed his attitude towards incidences of 'bickering' and 'in-fighting'. McCartney, the IRA O/C in Parkhurst shared his view that the republicans had to be 'bonded, have an umbrella around yourselves, protect yourselves because there was enough coming at you from the screws and prisoners and everything else without you turning inwards on yourself'. Minor quibbles within the group disappeared when the men were reminded that General Order No. 13 (b) of the IRA Constitution classed Volunteers who engaged in 'slander and denigration' of comrades as 'bringing the Army into disrepute'. Those held responsible faced the minimum penalty of 'Dismissal with ignominy'.[485]

Life sentences

The ascent of Leon Brittan to the office of Home Secretary brought a degree of clarity to sentencing culture that it had hitherto lacked. Brittan prepared to introduce an automatic minimum tariff of twenty years for persons sentenced to 'life' imprisonment for serious offences, despite the objections of Sir James Hennessy, Chief Inspector of Prisons.[486] Brittan had told the Conservative Party Conference in Blackpool on 11 October 1983 that amendments to the definition of life sentences and eligibility for parole was in the offing. Lord Harris of Greenwich, former Home Office Minister of State and Chairman of the Parole Board, subsequently described these as 'radical' until 1982. While Harris was a member of the SDP and, as such, a political rival of the Conservatives, he contended that the proposed reforms stemmed from the simple fact that Brittan 'had succeeded Lord Whitelaw as Home Secretary'. Harris argued that the news of impeding major changes had been notified to Prison Department employees with 'less than twenty-four hours notice' and that sudden movements of certain prisoners on 11 October 1983 from 'open' to 'closed' prisons were unjustified, risk - laden and inimical to the status of the Parole Board.[487]

Lord Elton, however, was regarded as being entirely in accord with the Home Secretary and sharing a hard-line attitude towards long-term prisoners and the IRA in particular. When addressing the Annual Conference of Board of Visitors in London on 24 October, Elton affirmed that the Government sought to increase its 'control' of prisoners and that inmates would experience a 'much more definite connection' between their behaviour and 'privileges'.[488] *Irish Times* coverage noted 'it is widely acknowledged that the 60 IRA men held in British jails are regarded as being amongst the most troublesome and disruptive prisoners in the British system'.[489] The fact that Paul Norney not only participated in the Albany protest but had taken legal action in relation to being held for nine months in a Durham 'strip cell' highlighted the logistic limitations of the Dispersal System. Elton averred that 'control' was undermined by holding such prisoners in locations unsuited for Category A men 'for anything other than short periods'. He promised the establishment of new units 'as quickly as possible' to rectify the dearth of appropriate facilities.[490] In correspondence with Tony Benn, Home Secretary Brittan improbably claimed that 'solitary confinement as such does not exist within the penal system' while noting that issues of punishment, security and shortage of suitable accommodation for Category A prisoners could entail 'segregation'.[491]

On 30 November 1983 the Commons reconsidered its attitude towards life-sentenced prisoners and those regarded as 'violent offenders', an issue which concerned the vast majority of IRA prisoners in England and raised the important questions on parole and tariff policies. Brittan announced that 'terrorist murderers' and those who killed policemen or prison officers would serve 'a minimum' of twenty years.[492] While comparatively few IRA members in England fell within such categories in the new hierarchy of victim-hood, a number had been sentenced for incidents in which soldiers and civilians had perished. Brittan's caveat that 'risk to the public is the pre-eminent consideration in deciding release' was clearly applicable to IRA prisoners jailed on conspiracy charges and non-fatal offences.[493] This preserved the central tenet of Mountbatten's committee in 1966. Lord Harris regarded the new rigour as potentially dangerous to staff, whose professional associations had not been consulted, and that 'anxieties' within the Dispersal System had been accentuated. In retrospect he claimed:

> The concern of prison staff is easy to understand. Violence is only held in check with difficulty in a number of our dispersal prisons. There is a dangerous mixture of IRA terrorist prisoners and others well aware that they are certain to remain in prison for many years ahead; in some cases a few believe, sometimes with justification, that they may never be released. Regular attempts are made by some of these prisoners to provoke incidents which will lead to widespread violence; and sometimes they have succeeded. There have, in recent years, been serious disturbances at Hull, Gartree, Parkhurst, Albany and Wormwood Scrubs.[494]

More generally, changes to parole culture ensured that persons sentenced for serious offenses would remain in the Dispersal System for longer periods than before. This may have appealed to the conservative vote base agitated by media representations of rising crime and social disorder, but had significant implications for prison building, renovation, staffing and security.[495] Simultaneous efforts to increase control were evidently deemed sufficient to counteract the threat of backlash from those most impacted. Politicized prisoners in Wakefield were astounded by the initial disinterest of their long - sentenced wing mates. Shujaa Moshesh failed to convince more than twelve of at least 160 prisoners to sign a petition of protest. It had been held that some persons convicted of criminal offences had interpreted the disproportionate prison militancy of the IRA with reference to their relative lack of parole opportunities. Yet the removal of once automatic pathways for the vast majority went virtually unnoticed. Brittan's indication that exceptional circumstances and good conduct in jail would enable selected individuals to progress unilaterally was in step with Thatcherite views on the non-existence of 'society'.[496]

Harrods bombing, 17 December 1983

It was widely assumed that the six deaths and ninety-one injuries inflicted by the IRA bombing near Harrods department store on 17 December 1983 were intentional, despite the acknowledgement that a coded warning was received by the Samaritans thirty-seven minutes prior to the 1.21 p.m. detonation. The Press Association also logged a coded message from the IRA. An explosive - laden Austin 1300 had been parked in Hans Crescent around 12.20 which, if not literally 'outside Harrods' as the warning apparently claimed, would have been well within a car bomb security exclusion radius in Belfast, Derry and Dublin.[497] Police were already on 'Bikini Black Amber' maximum alert owing to a series of munitions finds in preceding months and bombings in Woolwich and Kensington High Street on 10 and 13 December.[498] Three of those who died were Metropolitan Police officers responding to the IRA warnings as relayed by the local Chelsea station: Inspector Stephen Dodd, Noel Lane and Jane Arbuthnot. Philip Geddes, Caroline Kennedy and Kenneth Salvesden were civilians whose individual personal circumstances collectively heightened the political and public backlash against the IRA. Geddes was a social columnist with the *Daily Express* who moved in prominent circles arising from his journalism and numbered celebrity composer Andrew Lloyd Webber amongst his acquaintances. Kennedy was an assistant stockbroker on the verge of moving with her young family to Scotland and Salvesden was an American citizen working for an English company.[499] The populist media in Britain was typically severe in its commentary and Tony Clarke in Strangeways was mindful of the psychological importance of firmly demanding the daily newspaper to which he subscribed without giving an impression of callousness.[500]

The *Boston Globe*, criticised at times by pro-republicans for being obsequiously anglophile, lambasted those responsible for the 'Horror at Harrods', and Irish-American media noted the bitter denunciation of the bombing in the Commons by respected SDLP leader John Hume.[501] It was claimed that the IRA Army Council investigated the 'political disaster' in London which, according to one source, destroyed 'their newly acquired alliance with the British radical Left led by Ken Livingstone in the wake of the [June] 1983 General Election, when Sinn Féin President Gerry Adams won the West Belfast parliamentary seat'.[502] This was an exaggeration, although the pressurized Labour Committee on Ireland admitted that the bomb 'set back our shared goal of strengthening the Livingstone-type dialogue in order to build a withdrawal movement'.[503] Nat Vella, a Dublin IRA courier subsequently jailed for fifteen years in England, claimed that the Chief of Staff had sent him to Britain to recall the ASU responsible. The *Times* cited Vella as claiming: 'We didn't want all those people killed. We didn't know if they had given the general 45-minute warning ... it should not have been a target'.[504] In Paris, a person regarded as an 'IRA leader' told *Liberation*: 'Every unit knows it has automatic authority to attack British soldiers and men of the U[lster] D[efence] R[egiment] ... But in Britain targets are carefully selected and it had been decided, before Harrods, not to attack economic targets where civilians would be at risk'. He also claimed: 'Woolwich [Barracks] will occur again, not Harrods'.[505]

The incident was certainly an aberration and the first occasion in which a republican bomb had claimed life in England since the Hyde and Regent Parks attacks on military personnel in July 1982. None of the men and women detained in London, Birmingham and Manchester under the PTA were charged with any offences.[506] A Belfast couple arrested in Wales by Scotland Yard's C13 squad were also quickly cleared of any connection with illegal activity.[507] On 12 December 1983 Scotland Yard claimed to have anticipated IRA 'retaliation' for the transfer that week of Tommy Quigley from Belfast to London to face trial in connection with republican attacks which had taken place in the British capital between August and November 1981. The warning followed the 10 December 1983 bomb, which injured three soldiers at the guardhouse of the Royal Artillery HQ in Woolwich. The IRA were suspected of commencing a pre-Christmas 'offensive', despite an admission of responsibility from the Scottish National Liberation Army.[508]

If the IRA statement regarding the Harrods car bomb was recklessly vague, as Anti-Terrorist Squad Commander William Hucklesby asserted, the assumption that the republicans expected political capital from deliberately killing ordinary Britons and overseas shoppers was illogical given the inevitably negative consequences.[509] Secretary of State Jim Prior gave consideration to proscribing Sinn Féin, prompted in part by comments made by Garret FitzGerald in London, but such a major move was contingent on the Irish Government taking the lead.[510] Peter Robinson of the DUP was angered that it had taken 'an incident in London to raise the question'.[511] As had occurred in the 1970s, the IRA responded to a surge of media opprobrium on 25 December 1983 by detonating a further device in Oxford Street, which if small in construction, nonetheless injured two civilians.[512] The robust message conveyed was that their campaign would proceed in the commercial heart of England for the duration of the British Army's

'Operation Banner' in Ireland in the absence of final status negotiations. Part of the investigation was directed by Commander Gilbert Kelland, Assistant Commissioner (Crime) and, therefore, Scotland Yard's head of 3,500 Metropolitan Police detectives. Kelland was credited with developing the use of 'supergrass' informers in anti-gangland investigations but did not produce an IRA equivalent in England.[513]

The spate of attacks in England coincided with discussion in the House of Lords of the Second Reading of the Repatriation of Prisoners Bill. Lord Elton, Junior Home Office Minister, addressed the febrile and often artificially unarticulated IRA dimension to the affairs of the British capital on 21 December 1983. He assured the unelected peers, hereditary aristocrats and Anglican bishops that the British Government 'intend that the public interest shall always be the basis of our decision when it is a case of not returning a prisoner'. This implied that much vaunted and oft-cited *Prison Rules* were, contrary to the import of their title, entirely malleable. Elton further indicated that European Conventions, whether signed, shelved or repudiated, were non-binding on the UK in relation to repatriation and were, at the very least, subordinate to contemporary governmental opinion. He continued with an indirect reference to IRA bombings in England: 'In recent and horrific circumstances I think none of your Lordships can be in any doubt where the public interest lies'.[514] The Council of Europe had opened the Convention for signing on 21 March 1983 but both Britain and Ireland were notably slow in seeking ratification.[515] From 1980, Prisoners Abroad, formerly known as the British National Council for the Welfare of Prisoners Abroad, campaigned for UK accession. Ian Baker and other activists noted that the United States had comparable arrangements in place, had been operating efficiently since 1977 and that the UK faced statistically negligible net increases in prison population.[516]

Regardless of the devolved view of the Prison Department, Irish republicans in English jails were subject to considerations that superseded standard Category A prisoners arising from the nature and context of their offences. This was an important, apposite and deliberate clarification. Elton had all but confirmed what the Republican Movement had proclaimed to its international support base and potential allies for years: IRA prisoners in England possessed political strategic utility. Their currency recalled the experience of consultations between the Army Council and British Government representatives in the early to mid 1970s. Batches of those interned in the wired compounds of Long Kesh had been discharged during historic discussions, as if the phased emancipation of hundreds of untried men was unrelated. While the Republican Movement accepted that its endeavours to achieve a negotiated triumph might have been manipulated by its skilful enemy, the imminent military defeat of the IRA promised by Roy Mason *et al* had not materialized. By the early 1980s, the unparalleled and refined threat posed by the IRA's England Department to the British state had very probably augmented the political value of its existing prison losses. All protagonists of the Irish conflict appreciated that normal penal regulations, customs and practices simply did not pertain: there would be no settlement, interim or definitive, without a *de facto* amnesty for all IRA prisoners in Ireland and Britain.

It was impossible for contemporaries to assess the long term impact of Harrods and Woolwich type attacks on the commercial life and 'security' of London, but the consequences for the IRA prisoners and few ex-prisoners capable of living in England was often serious. Eddie O'Neill received 'a bit of a working over' in Brixton following the bombings which resulted in the reassignment of a staff member.[517] The attack on John McComb in Wormwood Scrubs was far more severe. On the morning after the Harrods bombing, staff resorted to the 'velvet key treatment' whereby they quietly unlocked his cell to permit three prisoners in to badly beat the sleeping Belfast man. While Kevin Dunphy had a similar experience in November 1976, such confrontational tactics were increasingly unusual in the 1980s.[518] McComb recalled: 'I got sent on, I was moved the same day it happened because if they moved the problem then the problem didn't exist ... ended up in Parkhurst'.[519]

Gerry Small, who in March 1979 had occupied the rooftop of Parkhurst for three days to protest conditions in the H-Blocks, felt on being released on 20 November 1982 that insufficient energy had been expended on the situation in English prisons. Peter Hayes of *AP/RN* claimed 'there should be few' who disagreed with this observation, particularly in view of the tangible improvements in Long Kesh between 1981 and 1983.[520] Small had been a member of the Manchester/Birmingham IRA from late 1970, following an extended visit to his native Belfast in the midst of chronic upheaval. At the time of his release in England in November 1982, he had served two-thirds of his twelve-year sentence, an indication of the minimum duration expected of IRA prisoners who had lost remission by virtue of taking part in escape attempts and protests. Unusually for a Category A republican, Small was not immediately excluded from the UK under the PTA. He had migrated to the English Midlands in 1966, which was insufficient to merit automatic immunity under the long-term residency clause.[521] The inscrutable logic of the Home Office could never be satisfactorily divined by Irish republicans, but as Small was not overtly pressurized to inform for the Special Branch or MI5, tolerance of his liberty in England may have been a ploy to serve other interests. Domicile in England, however, was entirely contingent on official demeanour. Accordingly, Small's employment as a double-glazing salesman in Salford came to an abrupt end on 21 December 1983 when he was arrested under the PTA in the days following Harrods. If neither were suspected nor accused of complicity in IRA activities after release, Small was, nonetheless, subject to an Exclusion Order which dictated his precipitate return to Belfast on 26 December.[522]

Ex-Birmingham IRA Volunteer Jimmy Ashe was also arrested under the PTA after Harrods; after seven days detention he was deported to Ireland. Born in Dublin, Ashe's long-term residency in England and Wales had hitherto provided a degree of protection. He later returned to Britain.[523] Kevin Dunphy, similarly, was deported to Ireland upon release in December 1983 to prevent him resuming his habitual residence in North London. This was undoubtedly prudent from a Home Office perspective: Dunphy's acumen as a Sinn Féin fundraiser in the early 1970s, if anything, exceeded his judicially established skill as an IRA Volunteer.[524] Ex-IRA prisoner Jerry Mealy, however, was impervious to the PTA legislation due to his long term residence in England where his republicanism commenced in the 1960s with Clann na hÉireann. On 30 July 1984 Mealy addressed a Sinn Féin meeting in the British capital, detailing his experiences in the Dispersal System.[525]

The unexpected quashing of a charge arising from the Hull Riot provided Ray McLaughlin with an advanced release date from April 1984 to 28 December 1983.[526] The news stimulated McLaughlin in Wakefield to remain 'conscious of the ones left behind' and on 18 October 1983 he returned to his correspondence with O'Neill on the appropriate relationship between the British far left and Irish republicanism. McLaughlin had, in a personal capacity, praised the solidarity work of the RCG - linked *Fight Racism! Fight Imperialism!* group which he realised would 'probably raise a few eyebrows'. He was, however, a supporter of a 'broad front' strategy in Britain and applied himself to the question of optimum tactics:

> The ultra left groups appear to have a penchant for remaining a small isolated elite, their so called purity and ultra-militancy usually excludes them from performing any effective political work … 'Self-Determination to the Irish People' is a clear and succinct statement for our demands and it is likely to appeal to people with the democratic instinct whereas slogans like 'Victory to the IRA' while meaning essentially the same as the first slogan would tend to frighten away potential support because only the minute section of the British people who possess a revolutionary consciousness could politically understand or be sympathetic.[528]

The radical McLaughlin was deported to Ireland in early December 1983, having served the same amount of time in solitary during his nine years and two months in English prisons.[529] Neighbours and supporters lit bonfires on the roadsides leading to McLaughlin's home in Buncrana, Donegal.[530] His wife Mary and son Padraig had relocated from Birmingham in July 1983 to prepare for his homecoming after nine years absence and the necessarily intermittent and stressful visiting room contact. He had sent correspondence, handmade gifts and suggested readings to his family. Once re-established in Donegal, McLaughlin rejoined Sinn Féin and the IRA having added rudimentary Spanish and Arabic to his language skill base during imprisonment in England. A return to activism would have been all but impossible if the family had been permitted to remain in Britain. Among the many visitors to Buncrana in 1984 was Gerry Adams who spent part of his recuperation in the environs following an assassination attempt in Belfast.[531]

NOTES

1. Eddie O'Neill, 1 February 2008.
2. Eddie O'Neill, 1 February 2008.
3. Eddie O'Neill, 1 February 2008.
4. Eddie O'Neill, 1 February 2008
5. *AP/RN*, 17 February 1983.
6. Sr. Clarke, 'Richard Glenholmes', Clarke Papers (COFLA).
7. Sr. Clarke, 'Eddie O'Neill', Clarke Papers (COFLA) and *FRFI*, March 1983, p. 13.
8. Eddie O'Neill, 1 February 2008.
9. Una Toal to Noel Gibson, Kevin Dunphy and Con McFadden, 10 March 1983, Private Collection (Dunphy). Rex Bloomstein produced a two hour documentary '*Lifers*' in 1983 for Thames Television. *Report on the work of the Prison Department, 1983*, p. 65. Footage included part of the Aural Hearing of Sean Campbell at the ECHR. Rex Bloomstein to Sean Campbell, 26 September 1983, Private Collection (Campbell).
10. Armstrong to Wilson, 10 March 1983, Private Collection (Wilson). For British prisoner views of Baker see Parker, *Complete Parkhurst Tales*, Chapter Twelve.
11. *Irish People*, 5 February 1983.
12. *Irish People*, 5 February 1983. See also Ibid., 2 April 1983.
13. Liam Baker to the Editor, *Irish People*, 19 February 1983.
14. Hugh Doherty, Joe O'Connell and Harry Duggan quoted in Brigid Finn to the Editor, *Irish People*, 5 March 1983.
15. Kevin [Dunphy] to Mary [Anon], *Irish People*, 21 May 1983. Dunphy gained regular correspondents in California, Mississippi, Illinois, Pennsylvania and New York. Ibid. Holmes was amazed to receive 'dozens of birthday cards from America'. Paul Holmes to [Anon], *Irish People*, 30 July 1983.
16. *FRFI*, January 1983, p. 1.
17. Adams, *Hope and History*, p. 15. See Flackes and Elliott (eds.) *Political Directory*, p. 369 and *FRFI*, December 1982, p. 1.
18. *HC Deb 9 December 1982 vol 33 cc576–7W*. The question of banning Adams from Britain under the PTA had arisen in the aftermath of the INLA's fatal Ballykelly bombing in County Derry. *Guardian*, 8 December 1982. The invitation to Sinn Féin had been extended for a 14 December 1982 meeting in the name of twenty-six Labour Councillors on the GLC. For this and Conservative Party backlash see *Irish People*, 11 and 18 December 1982. The GLC formed the London Strategic Policy Unit which, among other interests, monitored anti-Irish policing in Britain. See *Policing the Irish community*, p. 4. Morrison was a member of the Sheffield branch of the NUJ. *Irish News*, 28 December 2013.
19. Armstrong to Wilson, 5 February 1983, Private Collection (Wilson).
20. Bobby Campbell to Leo Wilson, 24 February 1983, Private Collection (Wilson).
21. Campbell to Wilson, 24 February 1983, Private Collection (Wilson).
22. Armstrong to Wilson, 10 March 1983, Private Collection (Wilson).
23. Campbell to Wilson, 24 February 1983, Private Collection (Wilson).
24. Armstrong to Wilson, 10 March 1983, Private Collection (Wilson). MacCartney was in Parkhurst in August 1983, as was Stephen Nordone. Armstrong to Wilson, 14 August 1983, Private Collection (Wilson).
25. Armstrong to Wilson, 24 April and 19 May 1983, Private Collection (Wilson).
26. Armstrong to Wilson, 7 August 1984, Private Collection (Wilson).
27. Martin Coughlan, 24 August 2006.
28. Bobby Campbell to the Editor, *AP/RN*, 24 March 1983.
29. *FRFI*, March 1983, p. 13. Paul 'Dingus' Magee was among those attacked in Portlaoise. Ibid.
30. Armstrong to Wilson, 3 June 1983, Private Collection (Wilson).

31. Armstrong to Wilson, 27 June 1983, Private Collection (Wilson). Walsh was transferred from Albany to Parkhurst on 23 March 1983 and moved the following day to Winchester under Rule 43 'Good Order and Discipline'. He returned to Parkhurst on 14 April prior to a further Rule 43 move to Canterbury. On 17 June Walsh was sent to Gartree. Roy Walsh to the Secretary of State, [nd, c. June 1983], Private Collection (Walsh).

32. Liam Baker, 3 March 2008.

33. *Irish News*, 21 January 1983.

34. *Times*, 17 March 1982. See also *Guardian*, 17 March 1982.

35. *Irish News*, 29 May 1984.

36. *Guardian*, 18 March and 17 July 1982. During remand proceedings defence lawyer Tony Browne denied his client had admitted guilt to the police and stated: 'Things are not as they seem and events at the end of the day will prove his innocence'. Ibid. Another defendant, Anthony Walsh, was reported as having 'helped to secure Littlejohn's early release from Mountjoy Prison, Dublin' in 1981. *Guardian*, 27 March 1982.

37. Dillon, *Dirty War*, p. 105.

38. Murray, *SAS in Ireland*, p. 87.

39. O'Riain, *Provos*, p. 53. On 3 January 1973 Sir Stewart Crawford, Chair of the Joint Intelligence Committee, privately but formally disclosed to the Irish ambassador in London, Donal O'Sullivan, that Ken Littlejohn was indeed working as an infiltrator. See Donal O'Sullivan to Hugh McCann, 3 January 1973 cited in Keogh, *Lynch*, pp. 382–3. Information provided by Crawford indicated that Ken Littlejohn had joined the Provisionals in November 1971, although his actual affiliation was with Official IRA members. Ibid.

40. Dillon, *Dirty War*, p. 112.

41. Hayes, *Breakout*, p. 168. Onslow's deceased husband had been the Conservative Party's Assistant Chief Whip in the House of Lords and the family had links with British Intelligence. She worked as an official in the MOD and had her ancestral home at Rath House near Drogheda where her brother, Viscount Dillon, lived in the 1970s. Dillon, *Dirty War*, p. 98. In late 1971 Ken Littlejohn (aka Austen) reputedly made an approach to Onslow from Ireland, where he was living under an assumed name on the run from a £38,000 bank robbery he committed near Birmingham in August 1970. It has been claimed that Onslow's contacts led to a meeting in England between 'Austen' and Geoffrey Johnson-Smith MP, the Conservative Minister of State at the MOD. A deal was brokered in which the fugitive would regain legal status in Britain in return for working with MI6 in Ireland. Lord Carrington, Defense Minister, and another Onslow intimate later admitted having sanctioned the arrangement. Littlejohn resettled in Ireland with at least two MI6 contacts, not least John Wyman (aka Douglas Smythe) and the name of an English Special Branch officer to contact in the event of being compromised. O'Riain, *Provos*, p. 51. Ken Littlejohn claimed that he and his brother had been delivered to the Irish authorities in a Cold War style spy 'swop' in 1973 in return for British agents John Wyman and Garda Patrick Crinnion. *Irish Times*, 19 September 1981. Lord Onslow of Woking, a relative of the Earl of Onslow, was an MI6 officer, Conservative Party MP and Minister for State at the Foreign Office in 1982–4. 'Lord Onslow of Woking', *Guardian*, 19 March 2001.

42. Dillon, *Dirty War*, pp. 112–3.

43. *Irish News*, 14 December 1974.

44. *Irish News*, 12 December 1974, Mullin, *Error of Judgment*, pp. 161–2 and *Republican News*, 23 August 1975. For Watt see Gibson, *Birmingham bombs*, p. 91.

45. Hill, *Forever lost*, pp. 120–121.

46. *Irish News*, 21 January 1983. See also *Irish Times*, 28 June 1984.

47. Hill, *Forever lost*, p. 199.

48. *Irish Times*, 10 February 1983. The ISM ran busses from London to picket Gartree on 10 June 1984. Other events of the 'Week of Action' included picketing the BBC in Portland Place to protest censorship on Ireland and a Hyde Park demonstration 'against Reagan'. ISM, 'Week of Action, 4–10 June 1984, For the right of repatriation for Irish Prisoners of War', Flyer, Private Collection (O Mathuna).

49. *The Irish Prisoner*, No. 5 [1986].

50. Alistair Logan to Eddie Caughey, 9 June 1983, Private Collection (Caughey).

51. Jonathan Wray to the Editor, *Irish People*, 31 May 1984. Kinsella was moved from Gartree to Albany on 15 December 1983 and then to Wormwood Scrubs on 8 March 1984. Margaret Dixon to the Editor, *Irish People*, 26 May 1984.

52. Sr. Clarke, 'Sean Kinsella', Clarke Papers (COFLA).

53. See *HL Deb 7 July 1982 vol 432 cc886*.

54. *Report of Her Majesty's Chief Inspector of Prisons, 1984*, p. 20.

55. *Report of Her Majesty's Chief Inspector of Prisons, 1984*, p. 20.

56. Moshesh in *FRFI*, January 1989, p. 8.

57. *Irish Times*, 27 June 1984.

58. *Irish Times*, 26 June 1984.
59. Liam Baker, 8 March 2008.
60. *Guardian*, 26 June 1984.
61. Ronnie McCartney, 12 April 2008
62. Liam Baker, 3 March 2008.
63. Sean Kinsella, 3 August 2007.
64. *Irish Times*, 26 June 1984.
65. *Irish Times*, 27 June 1984. *AP/RN* claimed that all the IRA men involved were sent to the Punishment Block and had acted when 'former British agent Kenneth Littlejohn … was trying to intimidate them with a gang he had formed'. *AP/RN*, 10 March 1983. Ray McLaughlin reported from Wakefield: 'Liam Baker arrived here from Gartree last week, it appears that all four of the lads connected with the Littlejohn affair have been moved out. I got a letter from John Hayes in Manchester and he says that Tipp [Guilfoyle] and Sean K[insella] are in Liverpool. Apparently they aren't officially on 10/74 but the end result is the same … They are charged under a Section 18 which carries a life [sentence]'. Ray McLaughlin to Eddie O'Neill, 21 December 1983, Private Collection (O'Neill). RCG member and journalist Terry O'Halloran covered the trial. Sean Hayes to 'Peter Flynn', 14 April 1990, Private Collection (O Mathuna).
66. Liam Baker, 3 March 2008.
67. Hill, *Forever lost*, p. 200.
68. *Irish Times*, 27 June 1984. Guilfoyle denied attacking the English man and claimed that his desire to receive a visit from an American relative and release date of October 1985 disposed him to avoid trouble. Ibid.
69. *Guardian*, 29 June 1984.
70. *FRFI*, March 1985, p. 14.
71. Sr. Clarke, 'Pat 'Tipp' Guilfoyle', Clarke Papers (COFLA).
72. Sr. Clarke, 'Sean Kinsella', Clarke Papers (COFLA).
73. *AP/RN*, 20 January 1983. Allegations of physical abuse in Portlaoise on 30 October 1983 were raised by the Prison Officers Association which contended that the Department of Justice was unwilling to investigate. *Irish Times*, 26 May 1984.
74. *AP/RN*, 10 February 1983.
75. *HL Deb 26 January 1983 vol 438 cc249–362*.
76. Elton was a former NIO Undersecretary who had clashed with Lord Longford in December 1980 regarding IRA hungerstrikers in Long Kesh. Longford had asserted that the IRA and INLA members were 'dying for a cause' and that there was 'an element of nobility in people who are ready to lay down their lives for a cause'. Elton countered that while 'one must accept the courage of somebody's convictions' under such circumstances, 'their aim is the destruction of the state and there is nothing worthy in that'. *Guardian*, 12 December 1980. Hylton also supported the repatriation of Shane Paul O'Doherty. *Irish Times*, 13 February 1984. See also Sr. Clarke, 'Paul Norney', Clarke Papers (COFLA).
77. *HL Deb 26 January 1983 vol 438 cc249–362*.
78. *HL Deb 26 January 1983 vol 438 cc249–362*.
79. *HL Deb 26 January 1983 vol 438 cc249–362*.
80. Lord Elton to Chris Smith, 13 February 1983, Private Collection (O'Mathuna). Political correspondence from Lord Elton addressed other factors; including a Home Office 'policy' agreed with the NIO under which 'permanent transfers' were only considered if a prisoner had 'has at least six months left to serve' unless other 'exceptional and compelling compassionate circumstances' pertained. The fact that this did not obviate repatriation for persons with much longer terms was addressed by indisposition to transfers persons 'who might be regarded as underserving of any degree of public sympathy … especially in a case where there seems little prospect of being granted parole here'. Ibid. See also Lord Elton to Gerry Bermingham, 12 January 1984, Ibid.
81. *AP/RN*, 10 February 1983.
82. Ronnie McCartney to the Editor, *AP/RN*, 17 February 1983.
83. Bobby Campbell to the Editor, *AP/RN*, 24 February 1983.
84. Campbell to the Editor, *AP/RN*, 24 February 1983.
85. Chrissie Keenan, Paddy Brady, Margaret Brady, Mary Walsh, Patricia 'Patsy' Armstrong and Lily Glenholmes sent a joint letter to *AP/RN* to follow up another written by Tony Harris on 24 March 1983. The families sought 'a clear statement from the leadership of the Republican Movement' as to whether it approved and would support a major campaign on repatriation from English jails. *AP/RN*, 26 May 1983.
86. *Irish News*, 8 June 1983.
87. See *AP/RN*, 30 June 1983. The second family group comprised Marie Byrne, Helen O'Brien and Mary McLaughlin, relatives of Eddie Byrne, John McCluskey and Ray McLaughlin. Ibid. Eddie Byrne, when

in Long Lartin, engaged in a correspondence debate on the social composition and objectives of the Republican Movement. See Eddie Byrne to the Editor, *AP/RN*, 29 November 1984.

88. Bobby Campbell to the Editor, *AP/RN*, 24 February 1983. He was moved to Hull in March 1983. See Sr. Clarke, 'Robert Campbell', Clarke Papers (COFLA).

89. *AP/RN*, 10 March 1983.

90. *AP/RN*, 10 March 1983. McFadden was the only prisoner in Winchester block when sent to the prison for fifty-six days from Wormwood Scrubs in October 1977. Sr. Clarke, 'Conn McFadden', Clarke Papers (COFLA). The Wormwood Scrubs incident arose from difficulty with a Welsh staff member whom McFadden assessed would have to be either violently attacked or tolerated. The BOV honoured a deal to move him to another prison if he agreed to return to D Wing for a week. Con McFadden, 4 November 2006.

91. *Guardian* and *Newsline*, 21 May 1983.

92. *AP/RN*, 10 March 1983. 'Guildford Four' prisoner Carole Richardson was in Styal in December 1984. *Irish People*, 8 December 1984.

93. Clarke, *No faith*, p. 119. The Prison Department provided 'specialist training' to chaplains. *Report on the work of the Prison Department, 1984/ 85*, p. 19.

94. *Catholic Herald*, 9 July 1982 and Clarke, *No faith*, p. 120.

95. *Derry Journal*, 23 July 1982. James Delaney, President of the Rand Development Corporation, wrote from San Antonio, Texas, to defend O Fiaich. James Delaney to the Editor, *Irish Times*, 7 May 1983.

96. *Irish Times*, 19 March 1986.

97. *Irish Times*, 8 April 1983. See also *Daily Telegraph*, 8 April 1983.

98. *Irish Times*, 8 April 1983.

99. *Irish Post*, 26 February 1983. Theresa Smyth generally traveled to London twice a year to visit her husband. Protests to the Irish Embassy and Relatives and Friends of Prisoners Committee may have inspired the Home Office to relent and return Sean Smyth to Wormwood Scrubs via Durham. It was speculated that the unscheduled visit to Durham, where Smyth was to meet his sister Anne Maguire, had been arranged to palliate the 'ghosting' from London of a man due for release in August 1983. Ibid. The Home Office announced her reclassification as Category B on 6 July 1983, partly, it was contended, to off set public unease at an April *Panorama* documentary on Giuseppe Conlon, casting doubt on the forensic evidence used at his trial. *Irish News*, 7 July 1983. See also Ibid., 18 August 1983. Irish journalist Seamus Brady petitioned the Procedures and Petitions Committee of the European Parliament in the hope of securing a resolution encouraging the British Home Office to re-open the case of the Birmingham Six. By a vote of six to one the bid was rejected by a Committee with no Irish membership. *Irish Post*, 4 June 1983.

100. *Irish Times*, 22 August 1983.

101. *Irish Times*, 9 April 1983.

102. See *Derry Journal*, 12 April 1983. The editorial described comments made by Mates as 'despicable' and 'insulting'. Ibid.

103. See Eddie Abrahams, 'Hunger strike threatened' in *FRFI*, April 1983, p. 16.

104. *Sunday Press*, 8 May 1983. See also Ibid., 10 April 1983. O hAodha (aka Hayes), organized a meeting in TCD on 27 January 1983 where Mrs Lilly Hill, mother of the wrongfully imprisoned Paul Hill, addressed the students and public. *AP/RN*, 21 January 1982 and Declan Hayes to the Editor, *Irish Times*, 26 January 1982.

105. *Irish News*, 18 April 1983. See also *Irish Post*, 21 May 1983.

106. Ann and Eileen Gillespie, 8 June 2008. Ann Gillespie became ill at the time: 'We were really in pain – physically and mentally. We thought he'd hang on. He badly wanted to hang on till we got home. That's all he lived for. It was a terrible time for my mother too'. Ibid.

107. *Guardian*, 18 April 1983 and *Irish Post*, 3 September 1983. See also Sr. Clarke, 'Anne and Eileen Gillespie', Clarke Papers (COFLA). The Gillespies were acknowledged as 'Republicans' in *Irish political prisoners in England, Special Category 'A'*, a pamphlet released by Sinn Féin's POW Department in April 1980.

108. AE Huckle to RA Neilson , 6 March 1978, NAE, FCO 87/ 762. Harte met the Home Secretary in London on 2 November 1978 with TG Field-Fisher QC in an effort to have the sisters, whom he believed to be innocent, either released or have their case referred to the Court of Appeal. A Cogbill, 'Note of a meeting held on Thursday, 2 November 1978', NAE, FCO 87/ 762. Harte had previously met the Home Secretary in October 1977 and June 1978. 'Note of a meeting held on 8 June 1978', Ibid.

109. *Irish Post*, 23 April 1983.

110. *Irish Post*, 23 April 1983. Owen Sharkey averred: 'If, for example, one or both of the Gillespie sisters had the good fortune to escape the clutches of their jailers and make their way back to their home in Donegal, they would be dragged before the Special Criminal Court … If, on the other hand, they had the misfortune to die in an English prison their bodies would in all probability be hijacked, as the

cortege made its way back to Donegal and their coffins entombed in tons of concrete, as was Frank Stagg's'. Ibid. See also *Andersonstown News*, 7 May 1983. The Irish Embassy in London was believed to have made representations 'at the highest level' in support of weekend parole. *Irish Post*, 23 April 1983. The sisters published an account of their story in Irish in 1985, *Girseacha I nGeibheann*, which was re-released in an English edition translated by Nollaig O Gadhra as *Sisters in cells* in 1987. *Irish Democrat*, May 1987, p. 7. O Gadhra had to be dissuaded from using the working title 'Sisters in Bondage'.

111. *Irish Times*, 30 August 1983.
112. *Irish Press*, 30 August 1983.
113. *Irish People*, 10 September 1983. They expressed their gratitude for American support through a regular correspondent. Mary Boyle to the Editor, *Irish People*, 5 February 1983. In October 1985 the sisters were nominated for a major award at the Oireachtas, an annual Irish language competition, for their joint biography. *Irish Post*, 26 October 1985.
114. O Fiaich to Eamonn [O'Doherty], 6 January 1984, Private Collection (O Mathuna).
115. 'Relatives veto call on prisoners', *Irish News*, 8 June 1983. The signatories numbered relatives of Billy Armstrong, Brian Keenan, Martin Brady, Dickie Glenholmes and Bobby Campbell. Ibid. The group noted an 'ambivalence' on the repatriation issue by some prisoners in England and contended that 'a clear statement from the leadership of the Republican Movement supporting such a campaign' was necessary and that it should be 'initiated and led by the Republican Movement itself'. AP/RN, 24 May 1983. The May letter was signed by Patsy Armstrong, Chrissie Keenan, Paddy Brady, Margaret Brady, Mary Walsh and Lily Glenholmes. Ibid.
116. Richard Glenholmes to Editor, AP/RN, 30 June 1986.
117. Joseph and Samuel Glenholmes to the Editor, *Irish Post*, 21 May 1983. Republican sources noted that Glenholmes had been exchanged for Paul Holmes and that Young was due for release in a matter of months. Patrick Mulryan to [Anon], *Irish People*, 9 July 1983.
118. Colour section in Gerry Adams, *Before the Dawn, An autobiography* (Kerry, 1996). Maureen Maguire, formerly of the Belfast Ten Committee, went to Wormwood Scrubs for a demonstration ahead of a planned visit to IRA prisoners, including Glenholmes, who were inside: 'I ended up leaving in a package, a record player ... The authorities blew it up thinking it was a bomb'. Comment of Maureen Maguire, Dublin, RDS, 1 March 2008.
119. *Sunday Press*, 1 May 1983. See also Willie Kealy, 'Political prisoners for transfer home?', *Sunday Independent*, 24 April 1983.
120. *Sunday Press*, 1 May 1983.
121. Interview with Ursula Hayes by Eddie O'Neill, London, June 2008.
122. Ursula Hayes, June 2008.
123. HC Deb, 20 July 1984, vol. 64, cc 350–51.
124. *Irish Times*, 7 April 1983 and AP/RN, 9 June 2005. See also *Dáil Éireann*, Vol. 411, 22 October 1991. In 1977 Amnesty International Secretary General Martin Ennals wrote to Taoiseach Jack Lynch to note the 'consistency of the allegations' made in relation to the operation of the brutal Garda 'Heavy Gang'. See 'Lynch urged to act on Amnesty report into Garda 'Heavy gang', *Irish Times*, 31 December 1977.
125. *FRFI*, May 1983, p. 15.
126. *FRFI*, June/ July 1983, p. 13.
127. *Irish Times*, 6 May 1983.
128. *Irish Times*, 6 May 1983.
129. See 'Building an Irish Solidarity Movement', 12 March 1983, Poster, Private Collection (O Mathuna) and *FRFI*, November-December 1982, p. 2.
130. Irish Solidarity Movement, *Two years on from Albany*, pamphlet (1985), [p. 1]. See also Fight Racism! Fight Imperialism, *Building an Irish Solidarity Movement, Text of the speech given by David Reed*, Pamphlet, 1982.
131. See *The Red Mole*, 'Ireland Special', Broadsheet No. 3, July 1970.
132. *FRFI*, January 1983, pp. 8–9.
133. *FRFI*, April 1983, p. 12. ISC delegations from Edinburgh, Glasgow, Liverpool, Manchester, Bradford, Newcastle and London (North/ South/ East/West) attended. Contingents of socialists, communists and republicans arrived from 'Rochdale, Southampton, Hastings, Dundee, Farnham, Slough, Derbyshire, Watford and Nottingham'. Ibid. O'Halloran, as 'John Fitzgerald', edited *Hands off Ireland!* See David Reed, 'Terry O'Halloran, 1 May 1952–23 January 1989' in *FRFI*, February 1989.
134. *Two years on from Albany*, [p. 1].
135. *FRFI*, February 1985, p. 13.
136. Seamus O Mathuna to Ruan O'Donnell, 11 April 2012, Private Collection (O'Donnell).
137. John McCluskey quoted in 'Building an Irish Solidarity Movement', leaflet [1982], Private Collection (O Mahuna). The republican 'sponsors' were Gerry Mac Lochlainn, Eddie Byrne, Pat Hackett, Vince Donnelly, Ray McLaughlin, Jimmy Ashe, Andy Mulryan, Brendan Dowd, Kevin Dunphy, Sean

Hayes, Bobby Campbell, Roy Walsh, Liam Baker, Stevie Blake, John McCluskey, Tipp Guilfoyle, Con McFadden, Paddy Mulryan, Paul Norney and the innocent Paul Hill. Ibid. The RCG had a long public and private dialogue with ex-IRA Chief of Staff Sean Mac Stiofain from 1980. See Sean Mac Stoifain to the RCG in *FRFI*, May 1982, p. 11 and *FRFI*, January 1983, p. 12. McFadden, in Wormwood Scrubs, appreciated the necessity of educating 'the British working class as to what's really going on in Ireland'. Con McFadden to 'Friends', 17 November 1982, Private Collection (O Mathuna).

138. 'Republican POWs of Albany' [to the Liverpool Irish Solidarity Committee], 19 April 1983, *Two years on from Albany* [p. 14].

139. 'Republican POWs of Albany' [to the LISC], 19 April 1983, *Two years on from Albany* [p. 14]. For critiques of the CPGB and Connolly Association on the Irish Question see *Resistance*, No. 3, 1986 published by the Irish Republican Support Group (CPGB). See also 'Ten years of solidarity work – The Troops Out Movement' in Workers Power, *The British Left and the Irish War* (London, 1983), pp. 5–35. The RCG sent a delegation to the August 1983 Anti-Internment protest in Belfast and noted that the three black members were questioned by the RUC Special Branch in Larne. 'Peter Flynn' [Seamus O Mathuna] to Brian [Keenan], 25 August 1983, Private Collection (O Mathuna).

140. Noel Gibson to 'Peter' [Seamus O Mathuna], 30 May 1986, Private Collection (O Mathuna).

141. 'Republican POWs of Albany', 19 April 1983, *Two years on from Albany* [p. 14]. See also 'Dossier of police harassment of *Fight Racism! Fight Imperialism!* supporters in London', July 1982, Private Collection (O Mahuna).

142. 'Irish Solidarity Movement Formed', Leaflet [1983], Private Collection (O Mathuna).

143. 'Republican POWs of Albany', 19 April 1983, *Two years on from Albany*, [p. 14].

144. 'Republican POWs of Albany', 19 April 1983, *Two years on from Albany*, [p. 14].

145. Mathuna to O'Donnell, 14 April 2012, Private Collection (O'Donnell).

146. *Building an Irish Solidarity Movement! Newsletter*, No. 1, February 1983.

147. 'Republican POWs of Albany', 19 April 1983, *Two years on from Albany*, [p. 14]. See also *FRFI*, May 1983, p. 1.

148. 'Republican POWs of Albany', 19 April 1983, *Two years on from Albany*, [p. 14].

149. John McCluskey quoted in *Two years on from Albany*, [p. 2]. McCluskey was interviewed by *Fight Racism! Fight Imperialism!* after his release from prison in 1984. Ibid.

150. Ray McLaughlin to Eddie O'Neill, 23 November 1983, Private Collection (O'Neill). O'Neill initially contacted the RCG in March 1983 when returned to Albany following five weeks in solitary in Durham. Eddie O'Neill to 'Comrades', 10 March 1983, Private Collection (O Mathuna). O'Neill, McLaughlin and Tony Madigan met frequently to discuss the political situation and formulate documents for the IRA and Sinn Féin. Madigan recalled 'We would have had opinions about the [Armed] Struggle but you are inside and you are isolated and it's easy enough to have opinions but the reality doesn't impinge that much ... Lots of letters were sent out on various subjects ... They would go to the [Irish Republican] Army mainly, people who had connections'. Tony Madigan, 7 March 2008.

151. Mary Pearson, 'Draft of a letter to former Albany prisoners for discussion by TOM members only' in ISM, *Newsletter*, February 1984, p. 17.

152. Brian Keenan to 'Peter Flynn' (Seamus O Mathuna), 1 September 1983, Private Collection (O Mathuna).

153. Keenan to 'Flynn' (O Mathuna), 1 September 1983, Private Collection (O Mathuna). See also Keenan to 'Flynn' [O Mathuna], 2 August 1983, Private Collection (O Mathuna).

154. 'Republican POWs of Albany', 19 April 1983, *Two years on from Albany*, [p. 14].

155. Gerry McLaughlin [aka Mac Lochlainn] to Chris, 23 February 1983, Private Collection (O Mathuna).

156. Vince Donnelly to Alan, 21 February 1983, Private Collection (O Mathuna).

157. Bobby Campbell to 'Dear Comrades', 24 February 1983, Private Collection (O Mathuna).

158. Comment of Eddie O'Neill, Strabane, 2 August 2007. The Albany communication was sent to *AP/RN* by the ISC but not published. The West London ISC provided a copy for the St. James' Martyrs Sinn Féin Cumann in Belfast. P Bailey to Michael Doherty, 30 May 1983 and Niall Power to Editorial Board, *An Phoblacht/ Republican News*, 30 May 1983, Private Collection (O Mathuna). Doherty had expressed disappointment that the 12 March ISM/ RCG organized march in London competed with the TOM demonstration of 7 May and IFM/ RCP hunger strike commemoration on 8 May. Michael Doherty to the Editor, *AP/RN*, 10 March 1983. Sinn Féin had intended supporting the IFM event but due to anti-TOM sentiment of its hosts reverted to its own 1 May demonstration. See *FRFI*, April 1983, p. 13.

159. Martin Mansergh, 'The legacy of the Hunger Strikers', The Teacher's Club, Parnell Square, 23 June 2001 in Mansergh, *Legacy of History*, p. 405.

160. *Two years on from Albany*, [pp. 5–6].

161. *Guardian*, 20 February 1985.

162. *FRFI*, February 1985, p. 13.

163. Vince Donnelly to the Editor, *FRFI*, February 1985.

164. The launch copy claimed that the bulletin would 'be used to keep you updated with the plight of Irish republican POW's incarcerated in British jails, and any solidarity work done on their behalf in England, Wales and Scotland. *Sinn Féin Glasgow Republican Bulletin*, No. 1, November 1983. The newssheet was issued by the Francis Hughes Cumann, Glasgow and endorsed by Pat McAleer, Secretary of Sinn Féin, Glasgow.

165. *Sinn Féin Glasgow Republican Bulletin*, No. 1, November 1983.

166. *Sinn Féin Glasgow Republican Bulletin*, No. 3, January 1984.

167. *Sinn Féin Glasgow Republican Bulletin*, No. 1, November 1983. In 1989 group called An Cumann Cabhrach, Irish Republican Prisoners Welfare Group (Britain) was headquartered in Sparkhill, Birmingham. This worked 'under the direction of An Cumann Cabhrach's Central Committee (Ireland)'. *Tiocfaidh Ár Lá*, No. 7 [1989], p. 11.

168. *Troops Out*, Vol. 7, No. 10, August/ September 1984, p. 16.

169. *Times*, 26 January 1982.

170. *AP/RN*, 1 July 1993.

171. John McComb, 9 March 2008. McComb was held in solitary conferment in Wormwood Scrubs. *Irish News*, 12 January 1984.

172. *Irish News*, 29 January 1982. See also *Times*, 29 January 1982. See also *Irish News*, 26 January 1982, *Guardian*, 3 December 1982 and Sr. Clarke, 'John McComb', Clarke Papers (COFLA).

173. *FRFI*, September 1983.

174. John McComb, 9 March 2008.

175. John McComb, 9 March 2008.

176. John McComb, 9 March 2008.

177. Ray McLaughlin, 'One day in solitary' in *Irish Voices*, p. 159.

178. *Daily Telegraph*, 13 May 1983.

179. *Daily Telegraph*, 10 May 1983.

180. *Guardian*, 27 May 1983. See also *Times*, 27 June 1986 and *Captive Voice, An Glor Gafa*, Summer 1990, p. 30.

181. *FRFI*, June/ July 1983, p. 16 and August 1986, p. 12.

182. Ronnie McCartney to the Editor, *Irish People*, 14 May 1983. Gerry Adams equated the electoral success of Sinn Féin in the local government elections of 1985 with 'an achievement equal to MacSwiney's and MacCurtain's lord mayoralties of Cork city'. *Irish People*, 9 November 1985.

183. McCartney to the Editor, *Irish People*, 14 May 1983.

184. Ronnie McCartney, 12 April 2008.

185. TOM, *Close to home, Lessons from Ireland* (London [1983]), p. 35.

186. TOM, *Close to home, Lessons from Ireland* (London [1983]), p. 35.

187. *AP/RN*, 11 March 1982.

188. 'Roy Walsh', Clarke Papers (COFLA). See also McLaughlin, *Inside an English jail*, p. 79.

189. Paul Norney, 9 March 2008.

190. O'Donnell, *Special Category I*, pp. 485–7.

191. Eddie O'Neill, 10 February 2015.

192. Vince Donnelly, 27 July 2006.

193. Eddie O'Neill, 1 February 2008.

194. Vince Donnelly, 27 July 2006.

195. Vince Donnelly, 27 July 2006. The nail was secured to a makeshift wooden handle with tape. Having perforated the Governor once in the side of the neck, Donnelly handed the weapon to a senior Prison Officer; a factor of significance at his trial when a potentially major charge of attempted murder was reduced to mere aggravated assault. Ibid.

196. Hill, *Stolen years*, pp. 207–8.

197. Tony Clarke, 9 March 2008.

198. *Irish Times*, 22 August 1983. The release of Smyth inspired a long feature article by Annette Gartland who interviewed Sr. Sarah Clarke. She relayed the story of an Irish parent arriving into Wakefield to find that their son had been moved without notice in the middle of cleared, long planned visits. Another concerned the last minute shift of an elderly Dublin woman staying with relatives in Birmingham who received a 'last minute' phone call ahead of her traveling to Wormwood Scrubs with news that her son had just been moved to Canterbury. One male visitor, detained for nineteen hours under the PTA, was effectively deprived of availing of two of the approved four slots. A Prison Department spokesperson insisted that Irish Category A prisoners were not subject to additional shifts and were entitled to inform their relatives of moves after the fact with a first class letter. Ibid.

199. Sean Smyth, 2 June 2009.

200. Hill, *Stolen years*, p. 208. Prisoners in Wormwood Scrubs believed that breakfast comprised Grade A Canadian pig feed. Sr. Clarke, 'Wormwood Scrubs', Clarke Papers (COFLA). Prison authorities claimed 'with one exception, all the establishments inspected during the year [1983] provided meals of consistently high quality'. *Report of the Chief Inspector of Prisons, 1983*, p. 4. On 21 to 31 March 1983 Long Lartin was the sole Dispersal Prison given a 'full' inspection in the course of the year. Ibid., p. 21.
201. Hill, *Stolen years*, p. 208.
202. McLaughlin, *Inside an English jail*, p. 78.
203. McLaughlin, *Inside an English jail*, p. 79.
204. McLaughlin, *Inside an English jail*, p. 81.
205. McLaughlin, *Inside an English jail*, p. 80. The 'Spaghetti House Siege' prisoners were Frank Davies, Wesley Dick and Bonsu Monroe. McLaughlin recalled: 'These men were totally committed to the revolutionary struggle, and apart from our political relationship with them they were very interesting individuals'. Ibid. Dick had his dreadlocks torn from his scalp on a lie-down in Lincoln. Paul Norney, 9 March 2008.
206. McLaughlin, *Inside an English jail*, p. 80.
207. O'Neill 'Albany Document', p. 2.
208. 'Interview with Ray Mac Lochlainn' in *FRFI*, July/ August 1984, p. 8.
209. *Report of His Majesty's Chief Inspector of Prisons, 1983*, p. 6.
210. Moshesh, 'MUFTI riot' in *FRFI*, June 1982, p. 11.
211. McLaughlin, *Inside an English jail*, p. 81.
212. Vince Donnelly, 27 July 2006.
213. Eddie O'Neill, 1 February 2008.
214. See Eddie O'Neill, 'The English Penal System', MS [2006], Private Collection (O'Neill).
215. John McComb, 9 March 2008.
216. Vince Donnelly, 27 July 2006.
217. Martin Brady, 12 April 2008.
218. Eddie O'Neill, 1 February 2008. Prisoner repatriation was raised in an unusual context by *The News of the World* on 8 May 1983 when the paper reported that Britain's signing a Council of Europe agreement on transfers paved the ways for the return of 'hundreds of Britons held in European jails'. The populist newspaper had no comment on the controversial Irish implications or on a subsequent move within the National Association of Probation Officers to endorse the repatriation of republican prisoners held in England. See *Andersonstown News*, 15 October 1983. A resolution in favour of repatriation had been prepared for the NAPO AGM in Southport on 13 October but was not debated. Ibid.
219. *Daily Telegraph*, 25 May 1983.
220. *Guardian*, 21 May 1983.
221. *New Society*, 25 August 1983. In February 1984 James Prior, Secretary of State for Northern Ireland, confirmed to the House of Commons that IRA prisoners coming off protest in November 1982 had indeed received the restoration of 50 per cent remission by February 1983. *HC Deb 9 February 1984 vol 53 cc1044–45*.
222. *Newsline*, 26 May 1983. See also Geoff Coggan to the Editor, *Guardian*, 25 May 1983.
223. *Guardian*, 25 May 1983 and *FRFI*, June 1984, p. 12.
224. *FRFI*, April 1983, p. 6. The *Daily Telegraph* alleged that FRFI were the 'outside agitators' responsible for the actions, although the RCG editors of the paper claimed it had 'no need to "orchestrate" strikes and struggles. The prisoners themselves have organized and fought and will continue to fight'. Ibid. See also McLaughlin, *Inside an English jail*, p. 81.
225. An Albany staff member claimed the provision of such facilities as colour televisions to inmates made him 'wonder what the prisons are playing at'. *Daily Telegraph*, 25 May 1983.
226. *New Society*, 25 August 1983.
227. O'Neill 'Albany Document', 18 July [1983], Typescript, Private Collection (O'Neill), p. 1.
228. O'Neill 'Albany Document', p. 2.
229. *Session 1980–8 … 19 January 1981, HM Prison Brixton*, p. 85. The claim was made by Bernard McReynolds, Hospital Officer, POA, Brixton. Ibid. See also *Prior Report*, II, p. 16.
230. Jimmy Murphy to the Editor, *FRFI*, August 1983.
231. Jimmy Murphy to the Editor, *FRFI*, August 1983.
232. Robert McGhee to the Editor, *FRFI*, August 1983.
233. McLaughlin, *Inside an English jail*, p. 81.
234. Hill, *Stolen years*, p. 208.
235. *Report of Her Majesty's Chief Inspector of Prisons, 1983*, p. 1. See also *Report on the work of the Prison Department, 1983*, p. 32.
236. Hill, *Stolen years*, p. 208. Hill recalled: 'Sewing mailbags is deadening work. It is common in segregation blocks or in local prisons where most of the inmates are doing fairly short sentences. But

it was not intended for jails like Albany and was unsuitable for men serving long sentences. The news of the mailbag shop heightened tension at a time when there was already a great deal of ill-feeling'. Ibid.

237. Eddie O'Neill, 1 February 2008.
238. McLaughlin, *Inside an English jail*, p. 81.
239. McLaughlin, *Inside an English jail*, p. 82.
240. *Report on the work of the Prison Department, 1978*, p. 68. The Norfolk prison had an average population of fifty-three in 1978–79. Ibid. See also *Irish News*, 12 January 1984. Mary McLaughlin and her son Padraig visited Ray McLaughlin on 8 July 1983: 'I came home upset and I had to hide it because my young son was with me. We got to the prison at 1.20. We were kept waiting until 2.20 p.m. And no word of our visit. I had to go and ask. "He is a Category A prisoner – you have to wait until another Category A prisoner is having a visit" ... we were well out the gate by three o clock and this was our last visit until after Christmas this year'. Mary McLaughlin to Relatives and Friends of Prisoners Committee, 9 July 1983, Sr. Clarke Papers (COFLA).
241. Eddie O'Neill, 1 February 2008.
242. O'Neill 'Albany Document', p. 2.
243. O'Neill 'Albany Document', p. 2.
244. *Sunday Times*, 22 May 1983. This account claimed that fourteen men were fined for declining the mailbag sewing assignment. Ibid.
245. Hill, *Stolen years*, p. 208.
246. *Guardian*, 21 May 1983.
247. O'Neill 'Albany Document', pp. 2–3.
248. *Guardian*, 21 May 1983. See also *Newsline*, 21 May 1983.
249. Eddie O'Neill, 1 February 2008.
250. Hill, *Stolen years*, p. 209.
251. O'Neill 'Albany Document', p. 3.
252. Hill, *Stolen years*, p. 209.
253. O'Neill 'Albany Document', p. 3.
254. Hill, *Stolen years*, p. 209.
255. Tony Clark, 9 March 2008.
256. Hill, *Stolen years*, pp. 209–210.
257. O'Neill 'Albany Document', p. 3.
258. O'Neill 'Albany Document', p. 3.
259. *Daily Telegraph*, 21 May 1983.
260. Paul Norney, 9 March 2008.
261. Tony Clark, 9 March 2008.
262. Hill, *Stolen years*, p. 201. Clarke was amused by the sudden change in terminology: 'They used to call you, "Clarke" or "O'Neill" – now "Tony, stop this", first name came out'. Tony Clark, 9 March 2008.
263. McLaughlin, *Inside an English jail*, p. 83.
264. Eddie O'Neill, 1 February 2008.
265. *Guardian*, 23 May 1983 and *Irish Times*, 24 May 1983. The PFLP were regarded as allies of the INLA. See *Guardian*, 31 August 1982. Mihyi had been jailed for life arising from a 1979 attack on an El Al aircrew coach in Mayfair, London. *Times*, 24 May 1983. He was then 19 and had reputedly lost his 'entire family ... [to] Israeli forces in Jerusalem during the 1967 Six Day War'. *FRFI*, June/July 1991, p. 14. Sir Philip Goodhart, Conservative MP for Beckenham and a former NIO official, was personally acquainted with victims of republican and Arab militants. Airey Neave, killed in the House of Commons car park by the INLA in 1979, was an 'old friend' and he 'knew' Christopher Ewart-Biggs, British Ambassador to Ireland when killed by an IRA bomb in 1976. Goodhart also was an 'old friend' of Israeli Ambassador Shlomo Argov with whom he had discussed personal security on the day prior to his being seriously wounded by Palestinians in London. *HC Deb 7 March 1983 vol 38 cc76–77*. See also *Chicago Tribune*, 4 June 1982. IRA prisoners appreciated that the Palestinian activists in England were factionalized and that most had rejected PLO (Fatah) leader Yassir Arafat arising from his 'close ties with pro-American states such as Egypt'. John McCluskey to 'Peter' [Seamus O Mathuna], 19 March 1984, Private Collection (O Mathuna).
266. Paul Norney, 8 March 2008.
267. Bronson, *Bronson 2*, p. 238. The popular McGhee served ten years in prison and was fatally shot in the back of the head in a London pub after release. Eddie O'Neill, 10 February 2015. McLaughlin learned that the PO who had tried to intimidate the sewing shop strikers was involved in 'severe hammerings' meted out to McG[h]ee, Mohan, Bob Davies and another prisoner when they were in the Punishment Block. McLaughlin, *Inside an English jail*, p. 82. Hill evidently persuaded the men to target the workshop roof in preference to an office used by staff. He argued that anonymity provided by masks and back-up in the yard would safeguard their remission. Hill, *Stolen years*, pp. 208–209.

The feature film *Bronson*, directed by Nicolas Winding Refn and starring Tom Hardy, was released in England in March 2009. *Independent*, 13 March 2009.

268. Cited in *FRFI*, June/ July 1983, p. 10.
269. Paul Norney, 8 March 2008. See also *Times*, 26 May 1983.
270. *Evening Standard*, 25 May 1983.
271. Tony Clarke, 9 March 2008.
272. Eddie O'Neill, 1 February 2008.
273. Tony Clarke, 9 March 2008.
274. Paul Norney, 8 March 2008. Clarke recalled: 'When we seen the helicopters it hit every one of our heads right away … [They were going] to take a shot at us. And Maggie Thatcher going for this. That was in our heads too. She would do this. We knew she'd send the SAS in … "You better be ready here boys, something is going to happen"'. Tony Clarke, 9 March 2008.
275. Eddie O'Neill, 10 February 2015.
276. *Daily Telegraph*, 21 May 1983. In 1982–83 prison protesters sought the abolition of parole for fixed-term men and modification for those serving life sentences. This was described as an attempt to counteract the use of parole as 'a control mechanism'. *New Society*, 25 August 1983.
277. See *FRFI*, August 1983.
278. *Daily Telegraph*, 21 May 1983.
279. *Daily Telegraph*, 25 May 1983.
280. *Daily Telegraph*, 21 May 1983.
281. *Daily Telegraph*, 21 May 1983.
282. Hill, *Stolen years*, p. 210. Hill sensed danger the following day when taken to Reception for transfer with other prisoners, including his old associate Graham Little: 'The atmosphere was tense. I knew that a single word or gesture would set them off, so I avoided eye contact and willed the van driver to hurry up … three of us were hand-cuffed and put into the van'. Hill was left in Strangeways: 'One of the worst prisons in the system, its block one of the most feared … At the entrance to the block, the screws had fastened a sign: "Don't complain, you volunteered"'. Hill, *Stolen years*, p. 211.
283. O'Neill, 1 February 2008. McLaughlin, then in Bristol, was later told by Albany veterans that the MUFTI had 'batoned, kicked and elbowed every prisoner who happened to be in their way. Initially this onslaught led to prisoners on the second and third landings taking defensive measures. They barricaded the stairway from the first to the second floor … It was decided to go on the offensive and that meant wrecking everything around them in revenge for the injuries inflicted on their innocent fellow prisoners by the Mufties [sic]'. McLaughlin, *Inside an English jail*, p. 82.
284. *Times*, 23 May 1983 and *Irish Times*, 24 May 1983.
285. *Report on the work of the Prison Department, 1983* (London, 1984), p. 5.
286. *Report on the work of the Prison Department, 1983*, pp. 31–2.
287. *Irish Times*, 23 May 1983.
288. *Sunday Times*, 22 May 1983. Sr. Clarke understood that Walsh had been 'moved out to Parkhurst [a] week before the Albany Riot' and then via Canterbury to Gartree. Sr. Clarke, 'Roy Walsh', Clarke Papers (COFLA).
289. *Daily Telegraph*, 25 May 1983.
290. See David Beresford, 'Original goal for the Irish' in *Guardian*, 25 May 1983.
291. *Guardian*, 25 May 1983.
292. O'Neill 'Albany Document', p. 8. The RCG picketed the Home Office during the protest. O Mathuna to O'Donnell, 14 April 2012, Private Collection (O'Donnell).
293. O'Neill 'Albany Document', p. 8.
294. O'Neill 'Albany Document', p. 4.
295. Eddie O'Neill, 1 February 2008.
296. *Newsline*, 25 May 1983.
297. O'Neill 'Albany Document', p. 4.
298. *Irish Times*, 23 May 1983.
299. O'Neill 'Albany Document', p. 4.
300. *Guardian*, 23 May 1983.
301. O'Neill 'Albany Document', p. 5.
302. O'Neill 'Albany Document', p. 5. Maynard had recently visited Judith Ward and Anne Maguire in Durham prison. *Irish Post*, 21 May 1983.
303. O'Neill 'Albany Document', p. 5. One Principal Officer, 'deeply involved in the beating in 1976', had a narrow escape when spotted exiting a gate below the prisoners. A substantial concrete fixture was balanced above the route he used: 'He came out this night – he sneaked out the door – probably for his friends benefit. And the boys shouted down "My advice is not to come out that door again". And he looked up and he saw and someone said to him, "That will be revenge for [19]76" and he never came out again'. Ibid.

304. O'Neill 'Albany Document', p. 5.
305. Eddie O'Neill, 1 February 2008. The Home Office denied that an SAS unit was 'on standby to end the demonstration'. *Guardian*, 26 May 1983. In April 1990 participants in the Strangeways Riot were threatened: 'You come out now or you will be brought out eventually, if not by us then by the SAS'. Quoted in Jameson and Allison, *Strangeways*, p. 51.
306. O'Neill 'Albany Document', pp. 5–6.
307. *Newsline*, 26 May 1983. See also *Irish Times*, 25 May 1983.
308. *Guardian*, 25 May 1983. Contrary to published reports, Carron had, in fact, visited Albany in 1982 and was not impeded by industrial action by staff. Ibid.
309. O'Neill 'Albany Document', p. 6.
310. *Times*, 25 May 1983.
311. *Times*, 25 May 1983.
312. Tony Clarke, 9 March 2008.
313. Eddie O'Neill, 1 February 2008.
314. *FRFI*, June/ July 1985, p. 7.
315. McLaughlin, *Inside an English jail*, p. 83. McLaughlin described Gasmi as being 'immensely popular'. He also knew Hassan Masri, another Libyan, whose conduct impressed the IRA members. McLaughlin recalled: 'I felt a great empathy with both of them and I was highly impressed by their sincerity and commitment to the Libyan revolution. Normally Irish POWs would be very skeptical about becoming too closely allied to any other section of prisoners, but the Libyans were accepted immediately'. Ibid. McLaughlin exchanged language lessons with Gasmi. Information of Roy Walsh and Jimmy Ashe, Armagh, 20 June 2009. When required to sign for packages sent by the Libyan Embassy Gasmi wrote 'Long live Ghadaffi' in Arabic. Tony Madigan, 7 March 2008.
316. Tony Madigan, 7 March 2008.
317. *FRFI*, June/ July 1983, p. 10.
318. *Daily Telegraph*, 25 May 1983.
319. *Daily Telegraph*, 25 May 1983. Steel, when visiting Armagh for the funeral of Pat Kerr, expressed his opposition to a 1982 NIO out of court settlement with Loyalist prisoners who claimed to have been beaten by the deceased. The IRA shot Kerr, who had Catholic heritage, on 17 February 1985. *Irish Times*, 20 February 1985. See also *Lost Lives*, pp. 1008–1009.
320. *Times*, 25 May 1983.
321. *Guardian*, 25 May 1983.
322. *Irish Times*, 31 October 1983. The IRA mounted mass breakout attempts on 19 August 1974 and 17 March 1975, as well as numerous riots and protests. Ibid.
323. *Daily Telegraph*, 25 May 1983.
324. *FRFI*, June/ July 1983, p. 10.
325. *Daily Telegraph*, 25 May 1983.
326. See Sarah Nelson, 'Prisoners who hit the roof in protest over conditions' in *The Scotsman*, 2 June 1983.
327. Hill, *Stolen years*, p. 210. The threat was made as he was being placed in a Parkhurst cell: 'Before they closed the door one of them showed me a syringe with a long, vicious needle. "If there is any trouble out of you", he said, "you'll get some of this". The liquid cosh, it is called, and it holds more terror than the worst of beatings. We were next to one of the most feared wings in the British prison system – Dr. Cooper's F2, into which they dragged screaming men to turn into zombies'. Ibid., pp. 210–11. The press understood Hill had been held naked overnight in a 'strongbox' cell. He was moved to Manchester and then to Wormwood Scrubs. Hill was returned to Manchester to prevent him receiving a visit from his brother, Patrick Hill, who had traveled to London from Belfast. *Irish Times*, 22 August 1983
328. O'Neill 'Albany Document', Private Collection (O'Neill), p. 1.
329. *Guardian*, 25 May 1983.
330. Cited in *FRFI*, June/ July 1983, p. 10.
331. O'Neill 'Albany Document', p. 6.
332. O'Neill 'Albany Document', p. 6.
333. O'Neill 'Albany Document', p. 6.
334. Paul Norney, 8 March 2008.
335. O'Neill 'Albany Document', p. 6.
336. O'Neill 'Albany Document', p. 7.
337. O'Neill 'Albany Document', p. 7. In a communication with the South London Irish Solidarity Committee, O'Neill specified that 'by 11.40 p.m. Tuesday 24 May the Home Office *knew* that the protest would end at noon the following day'. Quoted in *FRFI*, August 1983, p. 1.
338. *Newsline*, 26 May 1983.
339. *Evening Standard*, 25 May 1983.

340. *Evening Standard*, 25 May 1983.
341. *Newsline*, 26 May 1983 and O'Neill 'Albany Document', p. 7. Early reports of the incident inspired an 'Irish prisoners in England' editorial in *Irish People*. See *Irish People*, 28 May 1983.
342. Tony Clarke, 9 March 2008.
343. O'Neill 'Albany Document', p. 7. Davies confirmed that he did not receive the document in an article entitled 'Prison protesters say authorities reneged on deal'. He understood the protesters 'agreed to abandon their protest peacefully after they had been assured that a list of their grievances would be passed to the *Guardian*. This was not done'. On questioning staff on this point Davies was told '"your name was mentioned. But it was not part of the agreement. No prison governor is going to agree to be the PRO for a group of prisoners who have misbehaved"'. *Guardian*, 18 June 1983.
344. *Irish Times*, 27 May 1983. John Sandy, Regional Director of the Prison Service, claimed on 25 May that the protest had been 'orchestrated, sponsored and controlled by the IRA'. An ex-prisoner at Albany expressed a more qualified view: 'Once it got under way they would put themselves in the forefront, but they generally keep themselves to themselves'. *Guardian*, 26 May 1983.
345. *Report on the work of the Prison Department, 1984/ 85*, p. 5.
346. *Newsline*, 3 June 1983.
347. *Andersonstown News*, 11 June 1983.
348. *Guardian*, 18 June 1983.
349. ISM, Press Statement, 17 May 1984, Private Collection (O Mahuna).
350. ISM, Press Statement, 17 May 1984, Private Collection (O Mahuna).
351. ISM, Press Statement, 17 May 1984, Private Collection (O Mahuna).
352. See *FRFI*, October 1984.
353. *Report on the work of the Prison Department, 1984/ 85*, p. 5.
354. *Report on the work of the Prison Department, 1984/ 85*, p. 42.
355. Cited in *FRFI*, April 1985, p. 14.
356. Mary Walsh noted the particular 'hostility' on arrival in Gartree from Ireland on 7 July 1983: 'We were taken into a small room no bigger than my bathroom with a door leading in and an exit door. I thought to myself that this surely could not be the visiting room but it was. Two screws stood at both doors and an extra chair was placed beside us for another screw to sit beside us. I was stunned because this had never happened before. They normally just sit at the door ... The screw put his hand on Roy to stop him [moving the extra chair] and Roy tried to defend himself and hit out at the screw who fell to the ground. Pandemonium broke out then with whistles blowing, doors being locked. The assistant governor and security officer came into the room. We were allowed to go on with the visit after all the screws left the room but the visit was cut short'. Mary Walsh to the Editor, *Andersonstown News*, 30 July 1983.
357. *Irish Times*, 22 August 1983.
358. Ronnie McCartney, 12 April 2008.
359. Sr. Clarke, 'Roy Walsh', Clarke Papers (COFLA).
360. Ronnie McCartney, 12 April 2008.
361. Walsh-BOV Adjudications' in A Aylett [For the Treasury Solicitor] to BM Birnberg & Co, 28 September 1990, Private Collection (Walsh).
362. Roy Walsh, MS Notes, [nd, c. December 1983], Private Collection (Walsh).
363. *Irish Post*, 22 October 1983.
364. Sr. Clarke, 'Roy Walsh', Clarke Papers (COFLA).
365. *New Statesman*, 26 August 1983.
366. *FRFI*, March 1984, p. 12.
367. *Andersonstown News*, 11 June 1983.
368. *Irish Post*, 9 July 1983. See also *Irish People*, 16 July 1983.
369. *Andersonstown News*, 11 June 1983. Hugh Feeney, who had been jailed in England in 1973 and moved to the H-Blocks in April 1975 recalled similar nights in solitary: 'You always know when it is nightfall because they switch off the white light and turn on the red one that you never get used to. Throughout the night you hear the spy-hole being lifted and dropped as the night-Screw makes his rounds'. Feeney, *Her Majesty's Prisons*, pp. 6–7
370. *Guardian*, 9 April 1984. Davis learned that the 1980 Circular Instruction was 'made available to MPs' but that the change 'had not been made public'. This followed his query as to why persons accused of assassinating Indian diplomat Ravindra Mhatre in Birmingham were being denied visitors. Ibid.
371. 'Disciplinary Charges arising from the disturbance at Albany Prison, 19–25 May 1983', 4 December 1983, NAE, HO 318/ 137. Baldock, Bennett, Blake, Browne, Clarke, McGee, Mihyi, Mohan, Norney and Sanchez were all found guilty. McGhee was acquitted on 20 July 1983 and Hill, Jamieson, Knight and O'Neill were not immediately adjudicated due to the Home Office moratorium. Ibid.
372. *Andersonstown News*, 11 June 1983.
373. *FRFI*, August 1983, p. 1.

374. *Guardian*, 9 November 1983.

375. *Irish News*, 18 August 1983. See also *Guardian*, 9 July 1983.

376. Plotnikoff, *Prison Rules*, p. 88.

377. *Irish News*, 18 August 1983 and Sr. Clarke, 'Anthony Clarke', Clarke Papers (COFLA). Blake was released on 29 July 1985. *Irish People*, 5 October 1985.

378. *FRFI*, September 1983, p. 2.

379. McLaughlin, *Inside an English jail*, p. 84. For overcrowding in Manchester see *HC Deb 30 October 1980 vol 991 c333W*.

380. *Irish News*, 12 January 1984.

381. *Andersonstown News*, 11 June 1983.

382. O'Neill 'Albany Document', p. 7.

383. Ray McLaughlin to Eamonn Og O'Neill, 18 October 1983, Private Collection (O'Neill).

384. Hill, *Stolen years*, p. 213.

385. Hill, *Stolen years*, p. 214.

386. Hill, *Stolen years*, p. 215.

387. Hill, *Stolen years*, p. 216.

388. *Times*, 12 August 1983.

389. *Times*, 9 November 1983.

390. See 'Prisoners force Home Office retreat' in *FRFI*, September 1983, p. 2.

391. 'Department Committee on the Prison Disciplinary System visit to Albany, Camp Hill and Parkhurst', 4 July 1984, NAE, HO 318/162.

392. *Irish News*, 18 August 1983.

393. *New Society*, 25 August 1983..

394. 'Home Office retreat' in *FRFI*, September 1983, p. 2.

395. *New Society*, 25 August 1983.

396. Jimmy Anderson quoted in *FRFI*, August 1983.

397. Jimmy Anderson quoted in *FRFI*, August 1983.

398. Jimmy Anderson quoted in *FRFI*, August 1983.

399. *New Statesman*, 26 August 1983.

400. *Report on the work of the Prison Department, 1983*, p. 31.

401. *Report on the work of the Prison Department, 1983*, p. 5.

402. *FRFI*, August 1983.

403. *New Statesman*, 26 August 1983. The Wormwood Scrubs protesters were Larry Delaney, Jimmy Anderson, John Mogridge, Chris Clarke, Wayne Smith, Alan Hirst, Neil Wallace and Tommy Tangney. Ibid. Kevin Dunphy regarded Wormwood Scrubs as 'the worst' of five prisons he had been held in since 1974: 'The Victorian conditions allow us an hour's exercise per day (if the weather permits). For four hours a day we go into workshops, doing tailoring, laundry or light engineering work'. Caoimhin [Kevin Dunphy] to [Anon], *Irish People*, 30 July 1983.

404. *FRFI*, October 1983, p. 12.

405. See 'Albany Disturbance, 19–25 May 1983: Disciplinary Proceedings', 4 December 1984, NAE, HO 318/ 137.

406. See 'Law Report November 9 1983 Divisional Court' in *Times*, 9 November 1983. The solicitors involved in the cases included BM Birnberg & Co as well as George E. Baker & Co which had extensive experience of Irish political trials. Stephen Sedley QC appeared for Anderson, Clark and Tangney. Ibid. Sedley had represented Billy Armstrong at trial in Winchester in 1973. O'Donnell, *Special Category*, I, p. 98.

407. *Times*, 9 November 1983.

408. *Guardian*, 9 November 1983.

409. *Prior Report*, II, p. 13.

410. *Report on the work of the Prison Department, 1984/ 85*, p. 31.

411. *Prior Report*, II, p. 29. The 'Webster criteria' issued for the deliberation of BOVs when assessing the propriety of permitting legal representation at adjudications were as follows: '(1) the seriousness of the charge and of the punishment which the inmate might incur; (2) whether any points of law were likely to arise (eg he considered that the definition of "mutiny" was likely to raise such points); (3) the capacity of the accused to present his own case (the judge quoted from a study of board of visitors' adjudications, *Home Office Research Unit Paper 3, 1981*, which had referred to poor education; poor English, low intelligence and psychiatric problems as factors likely to impair an inmate's defence; and he commented that the help of the panel chairman would often, but not always, suffice to ensure a fair hearing); (4) procedural difficulties (eg) lack of opportunity for the accused to interview potential witnesses before the hearing or the need for him to cross-examine witnesses without having had advance notice of their evidence); (5) the need to complete the adjudication with reasonable speed; (6)

the need for fairness between inmates and prison officers'. Ibid. Individual members of the Wormwood Scrubs BOV who met in the prison on 23 November 1984 already favoured a 'total judicial approach' to disciplinary affairs but this was neither unanimous nor in keeping with Prison Department practices. See 'Departmental Committee on the Prison Disciplinary System, Oral Evidence from the Board of Visitors Wormwood Scrubs Prison, Note by the Secretariat, 4 December 1984, NAE, HO 318/ 137.

412.   *HC Deb 29 November 1983 vol 49 c437W.*

413.   *Report on the work of the Prison Department, 1984/ 85*, p. 32.

414.   [Alastair Logan], 'Judicial Review, Re: Albany Board of Visitors Adjudication', Private Collection (Walsh).

415.   [Stevie] Blake to Eddie [O'Neill], 29 November 1983, Private Collection (O'Neill).

416.   See Tim Owen, 'Prison Law: 1' in *Legal Action*, January 1987, pp. 10–11. See also Joyce Plotnikoff, *Prison Rules, A working guide*, Revised Edition (London, 1988), pp. 74–5 and NIACRO, *Report on the Transfer of Prisoners Seminar held at ATGWU Hall Dublin February 8 1989*, p. 14.

417.   Alastair Logan to Roy Walsh, 29 February 1984, Private Collection (Walsh).

418.   *AP/RN*, 13 December 1984.

419.   *Irish News*, 24 November 1983 and *Prior Report*, II, p. 22.

420.   *Irish News*, 24 November 1983.

421.   *Guardian*, 29 June 1984.

422.   Quoted in *AP/RN*, 13 December 1984.

423.   *AP/RN*, 13 December 1984. The humanitarian Lord Hylton, whom Paul Hill had contacted to assist in securing repatriation, received an important response from Lord Elton on the post-Albany views of the NIO. Elton was informed that the NIO was 'unwilling to take any prisoner who is not cooperating with the prison regime in this country'. Hill, *Stolen years*, p. 217. See also *Sunday Press*, 26 January 1984. Hill had correctly predicted that 'many prisoners, especially the Irish POWs are going to be kept in isolation for as long as possible'. Paul Hill to the Editor, *FRFI*, October 1983, p.12.

424.   *Times*, 26 March 1983.

425.   *Times*, 22 December 1983.

426.   *Report on the work of the Prison Department, 1983*, p. 26.

427.   *Times*, 22 December 1983.

428.   *Irish News*, 24 November 1983.

429.   *Irish People*, 19 November 1983. In January 1983 Armstrong tried to send a decorated cloth out of the prison with the wife of a fellow republican. This was prevented when the authorities averred the design was produced on prison property. Armstrong to Wilson, 13 January 1983, Private Collection (Wilson).

430.   *Times*, 2 August 1983.

431.   *Times*, 2 August 1983. An 'unrepentant' Abse claimed in 1983 to have received the tacit support of his Advisory Council colleagues in the undermining of Mountbatten: 'To shift attention from the real issue of dispersal or concentration to another issue which would arouse the hostility of all the liberals, and place one on the side of the devils. It would provoke great controversy, and, by riveting attention upon an irrelevancy, enable our sabotage to go unnoticed amid the clamour. I put to my committee colleagues that perimeter security should be reinforced by the use of guns'. Ibid. Abse marched in London in August 1979 in support of British withdrawal from Ireland yet also supported the 'Peace People' who sought a unilateral cessation of the IRA campaign. *FRFI*, September 1982, p. 11.

432.   *Times*, 2 August 1983.

433.   *Irish Times*, 22 August 1983.

434.   Adams, who had been returned for the October 1982 Assembly election, garnered 16,379 votes compared with 10,934 won by SDLP candidate Joe Hendron and 10,326 won by the then 'Independent' Gerry Fitt. Worker's Party candidate, Mary McMahon, received 1,893. Flackes and Elliott (eds.), *Political Directory*, p. 394. Danny Morrison came within twenty-eight voles of being elected MP for Mid-Ulster in June 1983. *FRFI*, June/ July 1983, p. 1. By early 1985 Sinn Féin operated twenty-eight 'advice centres' in the North of Ireland. *Guardian*, 21 February 1985. See also Adams, *Hope and History*, pp. 17–18.

435.   G[erry] Adams to Leon Brittan quoted in *Irish News*, 28 December 2013.

436.   *HC 7 March 1983 vol 38 cc595.*

437.   David Hill (NIO), Memo, 1 August 1983 quoted in *Irish News*, 28 December 2013.

438.   *Andersonstown News*, 11 June 1983.

439.   *Andersonstown News*, 11 June 1983.

440.   *Guardian*, 28 July 1983.

441.   Carron had taken the seat in the 20 August 1981 by-election occasioned by the death of Bobby Sands on hunger strike in Long Kesh. He secured 20,954 votes in 1983 but required most of the 9,923 votes received in the same constituency by Mrs R. Flanagan of the SDLP. The SDLP decision to compete

for a seat it could not win gifted the prize to a hardline Unionist in a Nationalist majority sector. See Flackes and Elliott (eds.) *Political Directory*, p. 395. For SDLP opposition to 'unity' candidates during and after 1981 see Gerard Murray, *John Hume and the SDLP* (Dublin, 1998), pp. 108–109.

442. *Guardian*, 28 July 1983.
443. *Irish Times*, 29 July 1983.
444. *New York Times*, 29 July 1983. See also *Irish World*, 6 August 1983.
445. *Guardian*, 29 July 1983.
446. *Irish Times*, 29 July 1983.
447. *Irish Post*, 27 August 1983.
448. *Irish World*, 13 August 1983.
449. *Irish World*, 13 August 1983. 'Supergrass' Christopher Black had aided in the prosecution of thirty-five people linked to the Provisionals in Belfast Crown Court the previous week. Ibid. INA and Clan na Gael claimed that in May 1981 INS agents had 'harassed an immigration judge [Ernest Hupp] off of the O'Rourke case by tailing him like a couple of hitmen'. *Irish World*, 24 September 1983. See also Ibid., 15 October 1983. For evidence given by Harry Kirkpatrick against twenty-seven alleged INLA members see *Guardian*, 23 April 1985.
450. TOM, *Close to home, Lessons from Ireland* (London [1983]), p. 43. In June 1981 Pearson was part of a TOM delegation to the H-Blocks that met the first 'Blanketman' of the campaign, Kieran Nugent. Mary Pearson to the Editor, *AP/RN* in 18 May 2000.
451. TOM, *Close to home, Lessons from Ireland* (London [1983]), p. 34. See also *FRFI*, November-December 1982, p. 11.
452. See 'Prevention of Terrorism (Temporary Provisions) Act 1976, *HC 7 March 1983 vol 38 cc545–688*. See also *FRFI*, March 1983, pp. 1, 16.
453. TOM, *Lessons from Ireland*, p. 27. See also *Irish Democrat*, April 1983.
454. *HC 7 March 1983 vol 38 cc599–600*. Pitt, whose father was from Belfast and mother's family hailed from Kerry, described himself as 'a firm and long term believer in a united Ireland'. Ibid.
455. 'Earl Jellico', *Guardian*, 26 February 2007.
456. *Independent*, 8 July 1991.
457. *Irish Times*, 10 January 1989. See also *Irish Echo*, 11 February 1984.
458. Armstrong to Wilson, 2 October 1983, Private Collection (Wilson). See also *Irish News*, 27 December 2013.
459. Moloney, *Voices from the grave*, p. 145.
460. *Guardian*, 30 December 1983. MacFarlane was accused of playing a lead role in the abduction of businessman Don Tidey. The businessman was taken from his Dublin home on 24 November 1983 and recovered on 16 December following a violent incident near Ballinamore, Leitrim, in which a Garda and an Irish soldier were killed. No IRA men were detained at the scene or subsequently charged in relation to the deaths. Ibid. £5 million had been demanded for Tidey's release. *Irish Times*, 20 February 1985, *FRFI*, January 1984, p. 16 and *Irish Independent*, 14 January 1998.
461. *Irish Times*, 13 June 1986.
462. See *Labour and Ireland, A message to all trade unionists*, No. 12, [London], July-September 1986, p. 6. Edited by Martin Collins, the journal's advisors included Ken Livingstone, Richard Balfe MEP, Sheila Healy, Steve Bundred, Liz Curtis, Rosemary Sales, Aly Renwick, Mary Pearson, Desmond Greaves and Don Flynn. Ibid., p. 2.
463. *Guardian*, 13 January 1984. Kerry man Sean Kavanagh, who died in Dublin on 4 September 1984, had been jailed during the revolutionary period for being an IRA man involved in the counter-intelligence unit run by Michael Collins. After the Treaty he was variously Governor of Mountjoy and Limerick Prisons. *Irish Times*, 5 September 1984.
464. *Report of Her Majesty's Chief Inspector of Prisons, 1983* (London, 1984), p. 1. See also *Report of an Inquiry by HM Chief Inspector of Prisons into the Security arrangements at HM Prison, Maze, relevant to the escape on Sunday 25 September 1983 including the relevant recommendations for the improvement of security at HM Prison, Maze* (London, 1984).
465. *Economist*, 7 February 1981.
466. *Irish News*, 27 December 2013.
467. *Report of His Majesty's Chief Inspector of Prisons, 1983*, p. 12. See also *HC Deb 26 January 1984 vol 52 c627W*.
468. *HC Deb 9 February 1984 vol 53 cc1041–1111*.
469. *HC Deb 9 February 1984 vol 53 c1075*.
470. *HC Deb 9 February 1984 vol 53 c1076*.
471. See *Irish World*, 1 October 1983. Readers of the CNG weekly could not have anticipated that four persons discussed on the front page of the post-escape issue soon resided in their midst on the West Coast. *Irish World*, 8 October 1983. See also *Guardian*, 6 June 1992.

472. For Dublin extradition proceedings against 1983 H-Block escapers Robert 'Goose' Russell and Paul Kane see *Irish Times*, 10 January and 14 April 1989.

473. *Irish Times*, 26 March 1983.

474. *Sunday Independent*, 28 April 2013. Reilly was obliged to move home in 1976 when informed by Gardaí of a threat to his life and that of another senior staff member. *Irish Times*, 28 February 1987. An off-duty Prison Officer was assaulted when jogging in the Phoenix Park, Dublin, on Sunday before 1 April 1986. *Irish Times*, 1 April 1986. For IRA Constitution see O'Brien, *Long War*, p. 294.

475. *Irish Times*, 10 August 2013.

476. *Irish Times*, 30 March 1983.

477. *Irish Times*, 30 March 1983. In March 1983 Portlaoise contained 220 prisoners guarded by 360 prison officers with permanent onsite assistance from the Gardaí and Irish Army who controlled the outer perimeter. An average of £5,000 overtime was paid to every prison officer per annum. *Irish Times*, 30 March 1983. With 1,500 prison officers to 1,200 prisoners, the Twenty-Six Counties had one of the highest such ratios in Europe. Minister Noonan noted that there had been a 400 per cent increase in staff levels since 1973 despite a static prison population. *Irish Times*, 26 March 1983.

478. *The Irish Prisoner*, No. 1 [1985].

479. *FRFI*, June 1984, p. 16.

480. *Irish People*, 19 November 1983 and Armstrong to Wilson, 2 October 1983, Private Collection (Wilson).

481. Armstrong to Wilson, 3 June and 14 August 1983, Private Collection (Wilson).

482. Armstrong to Wilson, 2 November 1983, Private Collection (Wilson).

483. Armstrong to Wilson, 22 November 1983, Private Collection (Wilson). He was also aggrieved by a story in the *Daily Telegraph* which repeated the canard that a man had died during the bombing of the Old Bailey in March 1973. Wilson was asked to approach Dolours Price, then at liberty in Ireland, to see if she would initiate a libel action. Ibid.

484. John McComb, 9 March 2008.

485. Cited in O'Brien, *Long War*, p. 296.

486. *Guardian*, 11 August 1983.

487. Lord Harris, 'The error in Mr. Brittan's new parole system' in *Guardian*, 9 January 1984.

488. *Irish Times*, 2 October 1984. See also *FRFI*, March 1985, pp. 8–9.

489. *Irish Times*, 2 October 1984.

490. *Irish Times*, 2 October 1984.

491. Leon Brittan to Tony Benn, 4 June 1984, Private Collection (O Mathuna).

492. *Report on the work of the Prison Department, 1983*, p. 23. See also *Report on the work of the Prison Department, 1984/ 85*, p. 35.

493. HC Deb 14 November 1983 vol 48 c281W.

494. Harris, 'Brittan's new parole system', in *Guardian*, 9 January 1984. The Parole Board was also undermined, according to Harris, by certain new stipulation introduced by the Home Office. He objected to the rule that 'anyone' involved in robbery in which a person is killed by a firearm would face a minimum twenty years whereas a person who deliberately beat a victim to death faced no such tariff. Ibid.

495. See *Report on the work of the Prison Department, 1983*, pp. 22–3.

496. Moshesh, *FRFI*, January 1989, p. 9.

497. *Guardian*, 19 December 1983.

498. *Guardian*, 19 December 1983.

499. *Lost Lives*, pp. 970–71. The death of Geddes influenced the composition of Lloyd Webber's 'Requiem'. See Michael Walsh, *Andrew Lloyd Webber, His life and works, a critical biography* (London, 1989). Geddes, the son of a Polish wartime refugee, had danced with Princess Margaret when at Oxford. See Kevin Toolis, *Rebel Hearts, Journeys within the IRA's soul* (London, 1995), p. 279–81 and *Guardian*, 24 December 1983. Harrods was not 'a no warning' attack as has been claimed. For analysis see Thomas Hennessey, *The Northern Ireland Peace Process, Ending the Troubles?* (Dublin, 2000), p. 34. During a controversial appearance on TV-AM *Good Morning Britain* programme, Adams claimed, when defending the Harrods bombing: 'I would have considered it an honour to have been in the IRA'. *Irish World*, 21 January 1984.

500. Tony Clarke, 9 March 2008.

501. *Boston Globe*, 20 December 1983. See also *Irish Echo*, 7 January 1984. For Irish-American comment on US reportage see Paul O'Dwyer, 'England's Old Game' in *Irish World*, 6 August 1983, Marie E. Howe and Charles R Doyle to the Editor, *Irish People*, 4 February 1984 and *Irish World*, 24 December 1983.

502. Toolis, *Rebel Hearts*, p. 281.

503. Cited in *FRFI*, February 1984, p. 16.

504. *Times*, 8 March 1985.

505. *Liberation*, 29 December 1983 cited in *Irish Echo*, 7 January 1984. See also 'P O'Neill [IRA Army Council]' quoted in *Irish World*, 24 December 1983. For INA response see *Irish People*, 24 December 1983.

506. *Guardian*, 23 December 1983. Crossmaglen native Martin McAllister, an ex-IRA prisoner and member of Sinn Féin Ard Chomairle, was detained at Birmingham Airport on 15 December. Ibid. Official figures claimed 191 persons were detained under the PTA in 1983 compared with 220 in 1982, 274 in 1981and 1,067 in 1975. *Irish Echo*, 18 February 1984.

507. *Irish Echo*, 28 January 1984.

508. *Guardian*, 12 December 1983. The SNLA were blamed for posting incendiaries to the offices of Scottish Secretary George Younger and Employment Secretary Norman Tebbit in September 1983. The Woolwich attack involved a 20lb device which blew a twenty foot hole in the wall of the guardhouse. Ibid. The claim that the IRA ASU which bombed Harrods was 'led by Thomas Quigley and Paul Kavanagh' is incorrect. Quigley was then in Brixton Prison. Toolis, *Rebel Hearts*, p. 279. See also *Irish Times*, 12 December 1983. An IRA bomb exploded at Woolwich Barracks on 23 November 1981 when a dog triggered an anti-handling charge. *Irish People*, 28 November and 5 December 1981.

509. *Guardian*, 19 December 1983.

510. *Irish News*, 27 December 2013.

511. Cited in *Irish Times*, 28 December 2013.

512. McGladdery, *Provisional IRA in England*, p. 244.

513. See 'Commander Gilbert Kelland, Integrity at the Met' in *Guardian*, 2 September 1997, p. 2.

514. *Guardian*, 22 December 1983.

515. *Irish Post*, 30 August 1986.

516. NIACRO Information Unit Production, *Report on the Transfer of Prisoners Seminar held at ATGWU Hall Dublin February 8 1989* (Belfast, 1989), pp. 10–11.

517. Eddie O'Neill, 2 February 2008.

518. 'We demand the transfer of Irish political prisoners to jails in Ireland' advertisement in *Hibernia*, 18 February 1977.

519. John McComb, 9 March 2008. McComb recalled: 'There's me on my way to the Isle of Wight and I'm thinking ... Should I hope for Parkhurst where the guy [Felix McGee] had got stabbed or should I hope for Albany where our people had been slaughtered ... but when I got there I seen some of the English prisoners who I had met on remand and there was a completely different atmosphere from Brixton and from Wormwood Scrubs. And then I seen me cousin, Billy Armstrong ... Billy and Tony Clark ... Ronnie McCartney [and] Steven Nordone'. John McComb, 5 August 2008.

520. *AP/RN*, 20 January 1983. Diarmuid Breatnach, a London based Irish anarchist jailed for his part in a confrontation with National Front members, attempted to raise consciousness of anti-Irish racism in Britain following release. See Diarmuid Breanach to the Editor, *Irish Post*, 27 August 1977 and Liz Curtis, *Nothing but the same old story, The roots of anti-Irish racism* (London, 1984), p. 91. Curtis was married to TOM founder Aly Renwick.

521. *AP/RN*, 20 January 1983.

522. *Irish Press*, 30 December 1983 and ISM, *Newsletter*, February 1984, p. 27.

523. Sr. Clarke, 'Jimmy Ashe', Clarke Papers (OFSA).

524. Sr. Clarke, 'Kevin Dunphy', Clarke Papers (COFLA).

525. [Seamus O Mathuna] to Joe [O'Connell], 15 August 1984, Private Collection (O Mathuna).

526. Sr. Clarke, 'Ray McLaughlin', Clarke Papers, COFLA.[1,2,3]

527. Ray McLaughlin to Eddie O'Neill, 18 October 1983, Private Collection (O'Neill). The RCG/ISM noted that 'Eddie O'Neill gave his full support to SLISC's [South London Irish Solidarity Committee] picket of Brixton prison' on 18 February 1984. ISM, *Newsletter*, February 1984, p. 3.

528. *AP/RN*, 13 December 1984. See also *Irish Press*, 30 December 1983.

529. Mary McLaughlin, 'Long and painful road', Cunamh website, 20 January 2012.

530. Padraig Mac Lochlainn, 8 June 2008.

CHAPTER 8

Prisoners and the Law

British prisoners in London, including men who had taken part in actions in Albany, Winson Green and Parkhurst, commenced January 1984 with a series of peaceful protests which excited vigorous staff opposition in Wormwood Scrubs and Wandsworth on 7–8 January. The initiatives included protracted 'no wash' protests and fasting, which were met with 'strong box' punishment and riot squads.[1] Six prisoners in the Segregation Unit of Wormwood Scrubs then took part in a 'no wash' demonstration, one of whom persevered with single-minded tenacity into March. A food strike by prisoners in D Wing, Long Lartin, began on 9 January, and although quickly diminishing in scale to just two men on 19 January, one persisted until 25 January. By then eight cells had been 'smashed up' in the Segregation Unit after 'considerable damage' had been inflicted. Trouble flared in Gartree on 3–7 February which, following the Long Lartin pattern, spread from A Wing into the Segregation Unit. Ten activists were 'ghosted' in consequence.[2]

If reminiscent of recently jettisoned IRA modes of prison resistance, the organization was accused of promoting jail violence by *The News of the World* on 8 January 1984. Following a dramatic headline of 'IRA BOMB CLASSES IN PRISON' readers were informed of how 'IRA thugs' were 'teaching "hard case" prisoners how to make bombs'. A veteran of Wormwood Scrubs Segregation Block was quoted as saying 'The Irish regard themselves as prisoners of war'. The main difference between the revived story and earlier articles citing anonymous sources on the subject was the contention that IRA prisoners were not only tutoring suitable criminal acquaintances but were supplying logistic support to those who had been released. A press 'investigator' claimed to have interviewed a young black man who served a six-year sentence for robbery in Parkhurst and was reputedly expected to 'act for' his IRA mentor on the outside. Another Parkhurst prisoner allegedly claimed: 'Nobody really knows what's going on in here. The IRA pick on militants, many of them black, and tell them how to use explosives. They tell us how to place bombs and how to create diversions and disappear into crowds. These people are terrorists 24 hours a day. They talk of nothing else'.[3]

The report compiled by Iain MacAskill averred that one of those released was given a phone number for a weapons supplier. A journalist, it was claimed, met 'a mystery Irishman' outside the Brook Green Hotel in Hammersmith, who then handed over ten rounds of .303 ammunition for £20. This was an expensive exchange given that the obsolete Lee Enfield rifle calibre was widely available in England. More seriously, the man offered a Sten 9mm sub-machine gun for £250. Conservative MP John Wheeler, former Assistant-Governor of Brixton and Wandsworth, told *NOTW*: 'Terrorists are bound to talk about their own interests'.[4] This was self-evident for advanced practitioners of guerrilla warfare, and while IRA prisoners constantly strove to forge alliances in the Dispersal Prison, and at times disseminated illegal technology to associates, it was inherently unlikely that anyone other than opportunist criminals would have sold weapons and munitions to ex-prisoners in London. In the early 1970s the IRA utilized Britain's criminal underworld to acquire emergency stocks of war material, but the steady stream of higher quality items from North America, North Africa and the European continent quickly lessened the importance of such sources.[5] Several IRA prisoners, including Noel Gibson, Ray McLaughlin and Andy Mulryan, had actively encouraged the politicization of black prisoners, whom they regarded as racially oppressed, but direct collusion with non-IRA members and enlistment of proxies did not feature among standard republican methods. The January 1984 argument was the inverse of that used by the Prison Department in February 1982 when accounting for unrest in Wormwood Scrubs. At no time during the Long War was credible evidence presented to suggest that the IRA exploited black prisoners. The fact that republicans were deemed capable of subverting a prison demographic both inside and beyond the walls of Category A institutions was, however, a significant example of their imagined potency.[6]

One of the most high profile IRA prisoners in England, Shane Paul O'Doherty, had experienced a drastic diminution in treatment following his attempt to shield a black prisoner from staff abuse in Long Lartin on 18 November 1983. O'Doherty responded to an incident in the Segregation Unit during which the man was allegedly severely beaten by warders. When the Derry man and others verbally protested the situation escalated to the point that cell furniture was vandalized. This breach of Prison Rule 47 (11) resulted in a twenty-eight day transfer to Winson Green Prison, Birmingham. On his return to Long Lartin matters deteriorated for O'Doherty as he was confined for four days without being permitted to 'slop-out' his chamber pot. By 22 December 1983 the all but inevitable spillage was inaccurately characterized by the prison staff responsible as a 'dirty protest [sic]' for which he was 'shanghied' to Bristol the following day.[7] Cardinal O Fiaich followed his case with dedication and not only lobbied Leon Brittan but pressed a Bristol based priest from Monaghan to establish contact.[8]

Within a few weeks of arrival in Bristol O'Doherty once again ran foul of the authorities due to an apparent misunderstanding regarding his possession of a blade without the permission of the Principal Officer. He claimed that he requested segregation to protest being harassed by warders demanding the surrender of the implement and that he was instructed to bang his cell door to provide the pretext for the move. This occurred on 26 January 1984 when he was shifted into an unheated cell with broken windows which he was falsely accused of smashing. On 14 February 1984, the day of a planned legal visit, O'Doherty was transferred to Wakefield's F Wing where he endured 'the worst treatment' of his long imprisonment in England.[9] He defied orders not to speak audibly by shouting out the window to militant Donegal republican Stevie Blake. He also conversed with Shujaa Moshesh, a black political prisoner jailed for the 'Spaghetti House Siege'.[10]O'Doherty claimed: 'In nine years I've never met any of these rules. These are control unit rules and they are designed to break prisoners. I think they are doing this to me because I have achieved a lot of publicity and they are annoyed with the European Court action I am taking'.[11] The shift from Bristol occurred on the day following the publication of a major *Irish Times* feature which identified the Derry man's numerous clerical and political advocates.[12]

The substance of O'Doherty's complaints were refuted by the Home Office, who insisted that he was being held in standard segregation and that England operated 'cellular' rather than 'solitary' confinement.[13] Many influential persons, however, suspected his allegations of isolation, unusual prison uniform regulations and low-level sensory deprivation were genuine. The move to Wakefield prevented his consultation in Bristol with solicitor Gareth Pierce, who had the foresight gained from prior bad experiences of prison visits to check his whereabouts with Paddington Station.[14] The Home Office was not unmindful of the serious legal and procedural questions surrounding prison adjudications; Peter J Prior, chair of the committee announced in October 1983 to examine the prison disciplinary system, got to work in March 1984. Its membership was confirmed in the Commons on 8 March 1984 and their expansive *Prior Report* was delivered in two volumes on 3 October 1985. The intervening impact of the 'landmark' *Tarrant* judgement greatly increased its relevancy.[15]

On 21 March 1984, Andrew Bennett MP (Denton and Reddish) received a written reply in the House of Commons from Douglas Hurd on the nine charges levelled against O'Doherty between November 1983 and March 1984. This had been requested by O'Doherty's brother, Eamonn, a teacher in Peterborough, who lobbied for assistance through his local MP. Belfast-born Conservative Brian Mawhinney responded to the overture.[16] Labour Party member Bennett was one of five MPs who believed O'Doherty should be sent back to Ireland where, if subsequently paroled, he would constitute a positive force in achieving a more irenic environment in Derry. Bishop Daly publicly anticipated this rare prisoner - related dividend.[17] The deal implied a boon for Britain in Ireland, despite William Whitelaw's clear articulation of the importance of deterring costly and politically embarrassing IRA operations in England. Lord Elton, representing the Home Office perspective, subtly indicated a possible line of compromise when stating that there had been 'no convincing evidence to suggest that he has broken his links with the terrorist organisation'.[18] Elton referenced one of the points made by then Home Secretary Whitelaw in April 1982 when outlining basic working criteria for permitting repatriation of Irish republicans. The March 1984 suggestion that it might be the paramount concern, *vis à vis* O'Doherty if not also others, was novel.[19]

Rewarding conformity was by no means alien to Prison Department norms, although extending benefit in the form of repatriation was of a much higher order than typical. Recipients would become immediately entitled to 50 per cent remission of sentence in the Six Counties rather than 33 per cent in England.[20] This countered the logic of the Home Office under the rightist leaning tenure of Leon Brittan. A statement by Brittan was interpreted by the Republican Movement in January 1984 as a declaration that 'life would mean life' in England and Wales. Hitherto, the only certainty surrounding the matter pertained to men such as Paul Hill, who had been sentenced to 'natural life' following wrongful conviction. Hill was expected to die in prison. If, as Brittan clearly intended, 'life' entailed exceptionally long as well as permanent incarceration, the question of repatriating the IRA cohort was all the more pressing as they were certain to receive minimum consideration in England.[21] When critiquing the Home Office - sponsored reforms on 9 January 1984, Lord Harris had specifically referenced the applicability to the IRA prisoners in the Dispersal System.[22] There were an estimated fifty-five such persons in England in February 1984, of whom twenty-five were serving life sentences and twelve terms of twenty years. All but two were Category A and six IRA men occupied 50 per cent of all Special Security Unit accommodation available in England. An estimated eight to twelve IRA men were contemporaneously undergoing solitary confinement.[23]

Brittan's comments formed part of a series of official statements from politicians and civil servants which collectively signalled a hardening of attitudes towards the prison population. When the Chief Inspector of Prisons described Brixton in March 1983 as holding men in 'cramped and deplorable' conditions, it was on the simple basis that 770 were being locked into cells designated for a maximum occupancy of 482. Reducing numbers remanded by the courts by such means as alternatives to imprisonment, however, was not envisaged in Whitehall. Instead, proposals were made to construct a major new London prison.[24] Urgency was added in September 1983 when the higher tempo of clashes between staff and maximum-security inmates injured fifteen employees in a single disturbance.[25] Brittan gratified conservatives in December 1983 by confirming that £262 million had been earmarked for prison building to be completed by 1991. This included £35 million for a 770-cell facility in Woolwich, London, which was envisaged to either replace or downgrade Brixton in 1987. In all, 5,000 additional prison officers were to be recruited by 1988 to enable the efficient administration of a projected 10,600 extra prisoners.[26] New facilities were constructed under the aegis of the state's Property Services Agency, which acted for the Home Office in such circumstances, whereas renovations of existing sites was the remit of the Directorate of Works.[27]

Modernization was a non-contentious justification for financing what amounted to a more extensive prison regime where, despite objections by British liberals, select prisoners would be held for longer terms. In August 1985, the revised estimate for Brittan's plans predicted £350 million being incurred in capital costs on sixteen projects. The expense of holding one man in maximum security was £24,856 per annum. This did not take into account the additional full economic costing pertaining to guarding the manpower intensive Category A quotient. Female prisoners required expenditure of £17,160 in comparison in 1985, with £12,428 needed for men in Category B prisons.[28] Such anomalies were raised in the House of Lords on 21 March 1984 by Lord Longford, who referenced the three presumed IRA women held in H-Wing, Durham: '[They] it was thought, required very secure conditions, and 33 women prisoners of other categories who did not. Therefore, for the sake of making sure that the three Category A women did not escape, these conditions, condemned by every kind of inquiry and investigator, were imposed on all 36'.[29] Longford's compassionate concerns gained no purchase in the Commons where, on 6 March 1984, Douglas Hurd had assured a doubting Jo Richardson 'we are satisfied that conditions in H wing are humane'.[30] By September 1993 approximately £4 million had been expended upgrading security deemed necessary to hold two IRA women in Durham's 'she-wing'.[31] Bishop Daly of Derry, who had visited the Gillespie sisters in Durham, spoke in favour of repatriation in 1984. Fr. Piaras O Duill reinforced this initiative in a letter carried by the *Sunday Press* and *Irish Times*. He argued: 'It might surprise some that almost half of the Irish prisoners in Britain come from the twenty-six county jurisdiction … Surely this should be of deep concern to an Irish Government'. However, 'the government is over sensitive to the fact that its own house is far from being ordered'.[32]

In January 1984 the annual 'Bloody Sunday' march was banned in London for the first time since 1972, a move described by the RCG as a 'serious setback to Irish solidarity in Britain'. TOM, generally opposed to participating in illegal marches, declined to press the matter with the RCG - organized Irish Solidarity Movement. This divergence deepened the mutual estrangement of left groupings linked to Sinn Féin which, meanwhile, recommitted itself to a campaign for repatriation.[33] An 8 February 1984 press conference in Conway Hall was held under the banner of the Irish

Republican Prisoners of War Campaign Committee. Gerry Mac Lochlainn, freed from Maidstone on 9 November 1983, announced the renewed call alongside North Belfast Sinn Féin Councillor Alex Maskey, Eddie Caughey and Oliver Bruen.[34] The Derry man, who had served two years and eight months of a four year sentence for conspiracy to cause explosions, claimed that the Prison Department operated a discriminatory policy in which Irish republicans in English prisons received disproportionate terms of solitary confinement.[35] He had immediately re-engaged with political work following release and on 27 November 1983 appeared alongside Sinn Féin's Jim McAllister during the annual Manchester Martyrs commemoration.[36] The 'five demands' variant promoted in England called for repatriation on demand, emancipation of all those 'framed by the British state', liberation of all from solitary confinement and SSUs, release of Pat Hackett on medical grounds and the abolition of the PTA.[37] A sixteen page booklet entitled *Irish Republican POW Campaign, Britain* detailed the arguments underpinning the issues in focus. RCG/ ISM allies held a 'week of action' on 12–18 March 1984, during which five prisons were picketed and marches held in Manchester, London and Dundee. Other left wing, liberal and student organizations participated, including contingents of TOM in Bristol and Leicester, which otherwise remained detached.[38] A further 'week of action' was held outside Gartree on 4–10 June 1984 to assert the 'right of repatriation for Irish Prisoners of War'.[39]

Efforts to compile full, updated and accurate files on the prisoners in England was complicated by the multiplicity of agencies and individuals attempting to assist. The POW Department, where such tasks would ideally be centralized, lacked the personnel, premises, financial resources and logistics to adequately manage the vast legal, welfare and political areas within their theoretical remit. Martin Brady appreciated that the ultimate aim of presenting a case to the ECHR on repatriation was extremely important, if exasperated by what appeared to be the repeated invitations to furnish identical information. By 1984 the stress of repetition, exacerbated by the constant raising and dashing of expectations, moved him to decline cooperation until Birmingham based Eddie Caughey persuaded him to persist.[40] After a decade in prison, day-to-day life remained hard for other members of the 'Belfast Ten'. Roy Walsh, one of the first IRA prisoners sentenced to life in England, was on 20 January 1984 given thirty-six days solitary confinement for smashing D3 Recess on 4 December 1983.[41] Sr. Clarke heard he was punished with fifty-six days in solitary for 'going late to football' following twenty days in solitary in the lead up to Christmas. Efforts by Sr. Clarke to send a solicitor to the Board of Visitors proceedings were prevented by the Home Office. Having been 'ghosted' twelve times in twelve months, Walsh was shifted to Armley, Strangeways, Wormwood Scrubs and Norwich by early September 1985.[42]

Gartree, early 1984

Gartree was disrupted on 7 February 1984 when approximately sixty prisoners refused to attend work assignments until they were satisfied that one of their associates had not been injured by staff. The incident ended without severe consequences, although John McCluskey, who had acted as 'spokesman for the prisoners', was promptly moved to Liverpool for so doing.[43] In a long - anticipated development, Billy Armstrong was sent from Parkhurst to Gartree on 27 February 1984. Tony Clarke and Tipp Guilfoyle were 'swopped' for him and arrived the same day in Parkhurst. This, however, posed a significant problem for Armstrong as the ill-treatment of his family on visits to Gartree in 1976 had obliged his wife Patsy to rule out further trips to the rural Market Harborough area. Given that Armstrong could well have spent a number of years at Gartree with exceptionally negative consequences for the well being of his family, he lost no time in applying for a transfer. He 'explained all this to one of the Gov[ernor]s here and have advised him it would be in his and his officers interests to move me as soon as possible'.[44] 'Ghosting' Liam Baker to solitary confinement in Wakefield struck his Gartree comrades as strange and elicited a call from a correspondent, Maria Kane, for the Irish-American community to intervene in the form of sending messages of support directly to the Yorkshire prison.[45] Republicans inferred that Baker was being isolated in order to disorientate him ahead of the scheduled June 1984 trial for the premeditated IRA attack on Ken Littlejohn. This tactic, they believed, had been used against Brendan Dowd in October 1977 when he attempted to clear the 'Guildford Four' during their unsuccessful bid at the Court of Appeal.[46]

Gartree was a prison where the high numbers of long-term prisoners ensured that concerted action was eminently possible. At the time of Armstrong's arrival in February 1984, Noel Gibson was on the same wing, a man he had last seen in Parkhurst in August 1977. He had become embroiled in further disputes over 'closed' visits and was obliged to send his sisters home without direct contact when brought to 'a small room with heavy security'.[47] Such treatment was unlikely to improve for republicans given that the Chief Inspector of Prisons had recommended in January 1984 that 'closed visits should continue to be the normal practise where there is evidence to show that a prisoner or his visitor cannot be trusted in open conditions', albeit with specific reference to the IRA in the H-Blocks.[48] The IRA contingent on other Gartree wings numbered Vince Donnelly and Con McFadden, who were on good terms with the capable Paul Hill and Paddy Armstrong of the 'Guildford Four'.[49] Donnelly had spent almost a year in segregation in Norwich.[50]

The regime in Gartree proved particularly irritating to Armstrong who resented the heavy-handed cell 'spins' and strip-searches, and tended to avoid conversation with the staff. This disdain had repercussions on 29 March 1984 when the Belfast man's refusal to confirm his name on entering a workshop led to an appearance at an adjudication and a small fine.[51] His transfer request was formally turned down on 4 June 1984 and a counteroffer for him to petition in order to obtain accumulated visits in a 'local prison' was solicited, an option with inevitably entailed further delays in communication.[52] A protest was in the offing and took the form of the destruction of another two colour televisions, a reprise of his action in the summer of 1983. On this occasion, Armstrong was sent on a lie-down to Winson Green, Birmingham, where he arrived on 23 June 1984 for the standard twenty-eight days.[53] On returning to Gartree he found that Gibson had been sent to Albany and McFadden to Wakefield.[54] Gibson had by then decided to seek the assistance of solicitor Gareth Pierce in the legal assertion of what he regarded as basic rights.[55] Donnelly was dispatched to Winson Green on 13 June under Rule 43 for reasons, the Home Office declared, that 'had nothing to do with Mr. Donnelly's nationality or the offence for which he is in prison'.[56] The IRA regarded Gartree as a place where a 'tougher regime has been established' and noted that six members of the MUFTI squad, which had attacked prisoners in Wormwood Scrubs in August 1979, had been added to the staff.[57]

Although no longer facing 'mutiny' charges, former Albany rooftop protesters were alleged by republicans to be receiving unusually harsh treatment in March 1984. Ray McLaughlin told *AP/RN* that Paul Norney was 'in a converted strip cell', Stevie Blake in Wakefield's F Wing, Tony Clarke was held in Manchester while Eddie O'Neill occupied 'a dungeon in Brixton'. Vince Donnelly's captors during his stint in Norwich were apparently 'so paranoid' that three prisoners who dared to speak to him were promptly transferred.[58] O'Neill's elderly parents, Patrick and Josephine, travelled from east Tyrone to see him in London with the requisite documentation to permit four 'accumulated' visits starting 28 March. The second visit was terminated after twelve minutes whereupon O'Neill was 'ghosted', as they later discovered, to Wakefield in the north of England. He informed a RCG contact: 'Such an action shattered my parents ... the H[ome] O[ffice] will no doubt claim my move was not designed to disrupt my visits'.[59] The sudden shift added expense, inconvenience and tension to the trip. A lesser quality experience for the remaining slots had been engineered and the couple found on arrival in the Yorkshire prison that two tables had been positioned to prevent physical contact.[60] O'Neill credited Sr. Clarke with helping his parents cope with such reverses. He did not then realize that his mother had sustained a serious knee injury in the course of her travels.[61]

The O'Neills were soon followed to Wakefield by Derry Independent Councillor Liam Bradley, who first visited Johnny Walker of the 'Birmingham Six' in Long Lartin. Walker's demeanour and that of prison staff towards him convinced Bradley that nobody in direct contact with the Derry man believed him to be guilty of the offences for which he was jailed. He proceeded to Wakefield where he found Shane Paul O'Doherty flanked during the visit by two staff members. Both Irish men supposedly posed an equal security threat rated Category A, but the reality was quite different. As before, O'Doherty attempted to situate his personal demand for repatriation to Ireland within the overall republican prisoner experience in England: 'He told me that the Irish prisoners felt let down by a lack of action on the part of the Irish Government'.[62] Bradley agreed to raise the matter with Charles Haughey, who was in the midst of a General Election campaign in the Twenty-Six Counties.[63] The election also spurred the Repatriation Committee of Republican Prisoners held in England to solicit intervention from the main political parties.[64]

Between 12 and 18 March 1984 various branches of the RCG-backed Irish Solidarity Movement organized meetings and demonstrations in six London locations in support of IRA prisoners. A hardcore if numerically modest crowd of twenty picketed Durham on 11 March; and sixteen people convened outside Albany and Parkhurst on 24 March in actions arranged by Southampton ISM and associates in Bristol TOM and South London Irish Solidarity Committee. In Gartree, ISM advocate Vince Donnelly was unconvinced that regular small demonstrations were effective in lieu of occasional, larger gatherings. Those assembled by Sinn Féin had 'started well' in the 1970s but falling numbers of attendees threatened to bolster the morale of the staff rather than prisoners. As a backer of the IRA 'Albany letter' position on maximizing unity and affinity across solidarity groups, Donnelly possessed a high degree of individual authority. He reported to the ISM:

> You will be pleased to know that your hard work is achieving results inside, such that where previously the POWs could safely be blamed for all 'subversion' in the prisons this is no longer the case. The 'natives' are now well and truly wised up and achieving reform in their own right, which is very encouraging to us all. Repression always breeds resistance and at the end of the day any system can only operate satisfactorily when there is a modicum of respect and tolerance between both sides of the divide. The increasing resistance of British prisoners to the politically orientated Prison Dep[artmen]t is a natural response to the intolerant attitudes directed against those who question the status quo. Through these prisoners we POWs feel a much stronger link than in the past with the underprivileged and oppressed on the outside of the wall.[65]

Advance news of the ISM's Parkhurst demonstration also spurred Joe O'Connell to write from the SSU to Southampton based organizer, Tania Johnson. He urged a primary focus on repatriation:

> It would be the biggest lift to morale that the harassed people of West Belfast, Derry and other areas could be given to something like this achieved by those who

favour British withdrawal in Britain … support for British withdrawal is becoming harder to ignore by Socialists in this county, if only for the reason that as things stand it makes it all the easier for Thatcher and Company to maintain and build up their repressive laws as long as they maintain their presence in Ireland.[66]

Such was O'Connell's physical isolation in Parkhurst's SSU that he was obliged to await delivery of *AP/RN* and *FRFI* to access detailed reports of the June 1984 Michael Gaughan anniversary commemoration held outside the prison.[67] He did not realize that other IRA men in Parkhurst had interpreted the Southampton ISM overture in a different manner.

Ronnie McCartney, located on the wings of Parkhurst, queried if the bypassing of Sinn Féin (Britain) and direct personal appeal to him from Johnson in a letter of 9 March 1984 seeking his 'permission for this proposed action', was politically prudent.[68] When raising the matter with Sinn Féin in Dublin he asked:

> We would appreciate it if the Ard Comhairle would consider the possibility of instructing Sinn Féin Britain to contact these groups and inform them of the … [Head Office] position in regards prisoners' support … If they are asking for guidance or support I see no reason why they should not contact the Republican Movement. As members of the Movement, we are being put in a Catch-22 position by these groups. We would, therefore, be appreciative if these groups could be made aware of the situation.[69]

Sinn Féin General Secretary Denise Cregan responded on 10 April 1984, clarifying: 'In relation to groups such as ISM and their correspondence to prisoners, the Coiste Seasta has ruled that in future all requests from other groups should be referred to Head Office in Dublin'.[70] The merit of Sinn Féin's interest in promoting the TOM as its principal ally in Britain, described by Gerry Cunningham in Parkhurst as 'continued infatuation', was separately queried. He argued TOM had failed to 'make any impression on the British people' if equally cautious of Sinn Féin investing faith in the capacity of the RCG and ISM to deliver concrete benefits.[71] The apparently 'instrumental' impact of the 'Albany letter' in 'bringing about a fundamental change in our relationship with TOM' was noted in Long Lartin, although Cunningham in May 1984 remained ambivalent about the alternative position of the newer far left bodies being uncertain of their 'composition'. Sinn Féin (Britain), however, was heavily criticized: 'Its Easter commemoration in London was a disgrace and reflected the disorganized character of SF England … it is tied in with SF policy in England which amounts to the [TOM strategy of] building up of an anti-war movement. This policy was challenged at the last Ard Fheis [in Dublin] but was retained'.[72]

Extradition, early 1984

The early months of 1984 witnessed a sea change in international attitudes towards the extradition of IRA suspects both into and out of Ireland. This had major implications regarding the location of persons on the run (aka 'OTRs') and, in the event of prosecution, place of trial and incarceration. Given the faltering operation of the Criminal Jurisdiction Act in the Twenty-Six Counties, which had singularly failed to imprison significant numbers of IRA personnel who had operated in England, it was conceivable that numerous persons named by Scotland Yard in connection with such activities could have been extradited to the Old Bailey for trial. The DUP estimated that there were 600 republicans wanted by the RUC living in the Twenty-Six Counties, a total with the potential to augment their presence in the Dispersal System if the Home Office expressed an interest in the quotient known to have been active in Britain.[73]

This pertained equally in principle, if not numbers, to the USA where American Liam Quinn resettled after a period of engagement with the Republican Movement. Quinn allegedly joined the IRA in Ireland in September 1971 and in April 1975 was sentenced to a year in Portlaoise for membership of the organization.[74] On 18 May 1975 a London Special Branch officer identified the Irish-American as a suspect in the fatal shooting of PC Stephen Tibble in London on 27 February 1975, when the 'Balcombe Street' group were causing huge disruption in the Home Counties.[75] Having lived openly in Dublin, Quinn returned to his family home in the Sunset District of San Francisco in 1979. The FBI arrested him in Daly City on his way to work in his uncle's stationary shop on 30 September 1981. This set in motion a legal battle notable for his being denied bail. It transpired the arrest was on foot of a British request, represented by Assistant US Attorney Mark Zanides, and that he was not accused of any offence in his native country.[76] Federal Prosecutor F Steele Langford outlined the case against Quinn in October 1981, but delays in bringing him to trial in the US or extraditing him to Britain dragged on for years. Langford had prosecuted heiress turned revolutionary Patti Hearst and it was speculated that 'legal precedence' was unfavourable in sending Quinn to Britain. His reception in a London court was open to question, particularly in view of British press accounts which referred to him in prejudicial terms as a 'suspected IRA murderer'.[77] Peter Murphy represented the British Government in San Francisco where he described the lack of progress achieved in six hearings over an eight-month period as 'outrageous'.[78] Writers J Bowyer Bell and Jack Holland testified on the origins and nature of the Irish conflict and bluntly countered the version propagated by pro-British agencies.[79]

After almost five months of private deliberation, Langford rejected the plea against extradition on 29 September 1982 on the grounds that the precedent of shielding alleged IRA member Dessie Mackin from deportation to Ireland was immaterial owing to the location of Quinn's cited offences in England. This was immediately appealed to the District Court for Northern California.[80] The tendentious Mackin case had grouped a talented new generation of Irish-American lawyers, several with Irish Northern Aid associations from the early 1970s, under the expert tutelage of Paul O'Dwyer and Frank Durkan.[81] In October 1983 Judge Robert Aguilar blocked Quinn's extradition to the UK when he ruled that US citizens accused of political offences could not be sent for trial overseas. This effectively extended the Mackin precedent to IRA attacks in England. However, the two-judge panel of the Ninth Federal Circuit Court of Appeals challenged the decision and retained Quinn inside the maximum-security wing of San Francisco County Jail. He was not welcomed by Sheriff Mike Hennessy, who dispatched a delegate to a June 1984 rally organized by the Committee to Free Bill Quinn and INA.[82] Support was also extended to Quinn on the East Coast by a joint Clann na Gael and INA backed venture which raised funds for the legal defence of Dessie Ellis, Michael 'Mick' O'Rourke and Gabriel 'Gabe' Megahey.[83] Dublin IRA engineer Ellis had vainly sought asylum in the US following his arrest with four Belfast men at a border crossing on the Ontario/New York border.[84]

While domestic US legal issues and traditions strongly applied to trans-Atlantic extradition, the movement of persons between the UK and Ireland came under the nominal remit of the 1977 European Convention of the Suppression of Terrorism.[85] Ireland, one of seventeen members of the Council of Europe to sign the Convention, was reticent in applying its protocols. The key fault line from the perspective of the Irish Government was a standard interpretation of Article 29.3 of *Bunreacht Na hÉireann, Constitution of Ireland,* which indisposed Irish courts to transfer citizens into UK jurisdictions for trial for political offences. Sections 44 (2) and 50 (2) of the Extradition Act 1965 stipulated that warrants should be declined if they related to 'a political offence or an offence connected with a political offence'.[86] From 1976, the Criminal Jurisdiction Act (CJA) remnant from the disastrous Sunningdale Agreement of 1974 made provision for the trial of persons for certain classes of political offences committed in the separate jurisdictions of the UK and Ireland. Brixton escaper Gerry Tuite became the sole example of its successful application regarding IRA actions in England on 13 July 1982. He was jailed in Portlaoise.[87]

On 7 December 1982, however, the Supreme Court in Dublin established a new precedent in ruling that INLA leader Dominic McGlinchey could be transferred into the Six County zone, arising from an incident which Chief Justice Tom O'Higgins claimed 'could not be said to be either a political offence or an offence connected with a political offence'.[88] O'Higgins, ex-Fine Gael Cabinet Minister and the grandnephew of Minister for Home

Affairs Kevin O'Higgins, assassinated by the IRA in Dublin in July 1927 to avenge his agency in the execution of seventy-seven republicans during the Civil War, represented a distinctly conservative voice on the Supreme Court.[89] The extradition judgement was announced on the day following the INLA bombing of the 'Droppin Well' club in Ballykelly, County Derry, in which eleven British soldiers and six civilians were killed.[90] However, McGlinchey, frequently referred to by the pejorative sobriquet 'Mad Dog', was at liberty and unavailable for delivery into the hands of the RUC. When captured in Clare on 17 March 1984, Attorney General Peter Sutherland and an unprecedented Bank Holiday night sitting of the Supreme Court ensured that he was delivered to the RUC in less than twenty-four hours.[91] Unfortunately for those wishing to uphold the integrity of such interactions, evidence produced in the juryless Diplock court against McGlinchey on 24 December 1984 was insufficient to maintain his conviction in the light of an appeal. He was returned to the Gardaí in what amounted to a humiliating reverse for the authorities on 11 October 1985. A 'score' of Special Branchmen brandishing Uzi machine pistols retrieved him from the RUC at the frequently razed Killeen border crossing.[92] Yet, in January 1984, the High Court cited the vitiated McGlinchey judgement to transfer Seamus Shannon, the Derry man's brother-in-law, over the border in relation to a major IRA attack in January 1981 in which he denied involvement and was never convicted.[93] This did not occur until 31 July 1984, when angry crowds thronged the Dundalk to Newry road spanning the border. Incredibly, the charges against Shannon also collapsed upon appeal and the tactical use of two 'hard cases' to implement unpopular policy spectacularly backfired.[94]

Justice Williams had claimed to see 'no difference' in the nature of the offences given that both involved elderly non-combatants. In rejecting allegations that Six County courts did not offer adequate protection to suspects, Williams advanced the process of inuring the population of the Twenty-Six Counties to hitherto controversial interactions between the two Irish jurisdictions.[95] The widespread belief that the RUC and British Army were pursuing a 'shoot to kill' policy in which suspected republicans were ambushed and fatally shot rather than arrested, coupled with insensitive remarks by Justice Maurice Gibson, created a temporary 'rift' in June 1984.[96] On 26 June 1984 the Supreme Court cited Article 40 of the Constitution to prevent the extradition of a former IRA member who had escaped from Newry Courthouse on 10 March 1975.[97] This blockage was cleared by the fractious Shannon extradition, which ended in yet another failed prosecution.[98]

In America, where the 'political exception' clause restated by the McMullen judgement in May 1979 had barred the transfer of IRA Volunteers wanted in Ireland and Britain, the complicated and protracted case of Mick O'Rourke (aka 'Patrick Mannion') resulted in a decision favourable to Dublin. An admitted IRA member since 1971, O'Rourke had escaped from custody during his trial on 15 July 1976 and was permitted by the US Court of Appeals to take his claim for political asylum in America to the New York Supreme Court on 22 February 1984. The Manhattan court then noted that 'fear of prosecution alone will not make an applicant a political refugee'.[99] An extradition warrant had been issued in Dublin on 7 November 1979, shortly following his arrest in Philadelphia arising from passport irregularities. He was not, however, deported to Ireland until 20 June 1984, when he appeared in the same Special Criminal Court in Green Street, from which he was one of five IRA men who had blasted their way to temporary freedom.[100] Deportation by the Immigration and Naturalisation Service was the only option available to the US authorities as no extradition treaty was in place with the Republic of Ireland.[101] His long stay in the Manhattan Correctional Center and decision to abandon his legal challenge to deportation presaged the even more contentious imprisonment of Crumlin Road prison escaper Joe Doherty.[102]

Doherty was arrested in New York in June 1983 on the ostensible basis of visa irregularities but actually due to his June 1981 conviction *in absentia* for taking part in the lethal shooting of SAS Captain Westmacott in Belfast. Britain had sought his extradition. Doherty had escaped from Crumlin Road prison prior to sentencing and commenced a new life in the United States where he worked under an assumed name for prominent Irish Northern Aid bar owner Alan Clancy senior.[103] The fact that he was a jail escaper, as with Tuite and O'Rourke, may have increased his perceived utility as a test case in view of the obvious fact that he had not only committed illegal acts but also re-offended in order to circumvent state proceedings. In a naked act of political interference, Judge John Sprizzo of the Southern District of New York was warned by the State Department of the possible 'damage in relations between Great Britain and the United States' if the 'political offence doctrine' prevented extradition.[104] Hardline Unionist politician Robert McCartney appeared to support the proposed extradition and was countered by Nobel 'Peace Prize' winner Sean MacBride, Bernadette McAliskey and Tim Pat Coogan.[105] Undeterred, Judge John E Sprizzo found in December 1984 that Doherty's case comprised the 'political offence exception in its most classic form'.[106] Stephen Trott, head of the Justice Department's Criminal Division, described the decision as 'outrageous' and the 'political exception' concept as 'nonsense among free, friendly nations'.[107] A new extradition treaty between Ireland and the US was inaugurated in Dublin on 17 December 1984, mere days after Sprizzo's surprise decision undermined its rationale. Although apparently arranged in relation to three separate and expressly criminal cases, the timing of the reform strongly indicated behind the scenes manoeuvring to create a trans-Atlantic legal framework favourable to counterinsurgency.[108] Trott boldly claimed on 19 December in relation to the Doherty judgement that the Justice Department was going to 'have to attack this treaty by treaty and redo the extradition language'.[109] Similarly, the *Chicago Tribune* called for 'congressional action' to correct Judge Sprizzo's alleged violation of 'the clear rules of common sense'.[110]

The O'Rourke decision in New York had implications for the case of San Francisco ex-IRA member Liam Quinn who was still fighting extradition to Britain with the added protection of American citizenship. Other Irish republicans, including Joe Cahill and Jimmy Drumm, faced less serious deportation proceedings for passport offences in New York in May 1984.[111] Cahill had made numerous illegal trips to North America to raise money for the Republican Movement and advised on gunrunning operations. O'Rourke, ironically, had been appointed Honorary Grand Marshall of Philadelphia's huge St. Patrick's Day parade in March 1983. It was reported in the US media that he was to be questioned in relation to the assassination of British Ambassador Christopher Ewart Biggs in County Dublin on 21 July 1976, a globally reported incident for which he was never charged and had no role.[112] Joseph A Roche, National President of the Ancient Order of Hibernians, urged Irish-Americans to lobby their Congressmen in order to secure O'Rourke's asylum.[113]

The confidence expressed by the Irish High Court and Supreme Court in the integrity of British law was called into question in London on 16 April 1984 when Paddy Maguire spoke to the press about his still unrecognized wrongful imprisonment in Wakefield. No IRA member imprisoned in England had made comparable claims upon release and the tone of the mainstream feature strongly implied assumption of its veracity. He imparted to journalists details of his arrest that many would have dismissed out of hand when they originally occurred: 'They punched me and said they would throw me down the stairs. But the advice of counsel was not to mention that at the trial – it's very hard to prove police brutality'. Jailed for fourteen years in February 1976 on what the *Irish Times* described diplomatically as 'controversial forensic tests', the innocent Maguire 'every day ... waited for someone to come along and say, "yes, we have looked into your case, we were wrong".'[114] Anne Maguire, his innocent wife and fellow member of Paddington Conservative Club prior to her arrest, remained in H Wing, Durham. Fr. Denis Faul, who had been bitterly estranged from republicans in the summer of 1981 due to profound disagreements on the protests of Long Kesh prisoners, criticized the Home Office in August 1984 when Anne Maguire was refused permission to visit her terminally ill father in Belfast. He claimed: 'Britain just doesn't understand how to deal with Irish prisoners in their own jails. They think when they are down they can sit on them ... They are alienating the Catholic community'.[115]

The Home Office had acknowledged its reclassification of Maguire to Category B on 6 July 1983, at which time there was optimism this 'change of heart' entailed improved conditions.[116] Maguire was granted weekend parole in the advent of Christmas 1984 when her release was anticipated, a concession which no actual IRA prisoner in England had ever received.[117] She was freed from Cookham Wood Prison, Rochester, Kent, on 22 February 1985, proclaiming to be 'as innocent today as I was ten years ago'.[118] Her quest for vindication was observed from Parkhurst by Joe O'Connell, who had attempted to assist the exoneration of the 'Maguire Seven' and 'Guildford Four' by repeatedly claiming responsibility for incidents wrongly attributed to the eleven.[119]

Non-judicial matters also pertained. The Department of Foreign Affairs in Dublin had to contend with competing diplomatic interests, which the vagaries of the Irish conflict continually disrupted and complicated. Whereas the State Department's 1983 report on human rights noted the unease caused by 'supergrass' trials in the Six Counties, a concern amplified by the pro-Irish Democratic Party Congressman Mario Biaggi (New York), the Twenty-Six Counties simultaneously overtook West Germany as the preferred location of US electronic industry Foreign Direct Investment.[120] Scope for significant lobbying in the US on behalf of Irish citizens facing alleged persecution from America's most significant NATO ally in Germany was limited. Meanwhile, the sympathetic Irish-American media, availed of by Biaggi and many powerful East Coast US politicians, disseminated news that Cardinal O Fiaich had, on 26 April 1984, gone much further that Bishop Daly in condemning 'degrading' strip-searching in Armagh, 'supergrass' utilization and the 'stone wall' encountered by Churchmen when advocating the repatriation of prisoners from England. O Fiaich's unambiguous comments were made during an Easter Chaplaincy event in the presence of Cardinal Basil Hume of Westminster and Ireland's London Ambassador Noel Dorr.[121] Publicity and celebrity lobbying, coupled with the potent image of religious reflection, contributed to the promotion of Shane Paul O'Doherty's case in the US. In March 1984 Gerdi Lipshute, Democratic member for Queens in the New York State Assembly, announced the passage of a resolution urging the British Government to transfer the Derry man to Ireland.[122]

On 16 March 1984, two days prior to the sensational handover of INLA leader Dominic McGlinchey to the RUC, Paul Kavanagh was arrested in his Belfast home. Kavanagh's address and jurisdiction rendered him vulnerable to legally uncomplicated removal to England. He was flown to Paddington Green Station in London where Alastair Logan was secured to provide legal assistance. Kavanagh was charged on 22 March with numerous counts of causing and conspiracy to cause explosions in England between 7 August and 13 November 1981. Charges included bombing Chelsea Barracks, killing bomb disposal officer Kenneth Howarth and grievously wounding General Sir Steuart Pringle. Kavanagh's 'Provisional' Category A rating in

Wormwood Scrubs and Prison Department policy delayed the provision of necessary surgery. Parkhurst Prison Hospital declined to facilitate a remand prisoner and Brixton staff, by whom Kavanagh was held for a week of medical observation, would not use their prerogative to release him to a general hospital in London.[123]

Irish-Italian Natalino 'Nat' Vella, from the west Dublin suburb of Tallaght, was arrested in Heathrow on 18 June 1984 on charges connected to Paul Kavanagh. He appeared seven days later in Lambeth Magistrates Court where he was accused of conspiring to cause explosions with Kavanagh between 6 October 1983 and 25 January 1984. Vella was further charged with possession of firearms and munitions found in Salcey Forest, Northamptonshire.[124] The Dubliner was described in legally damaging and inflated terms as an IRA Quartermaster after pleading guilty in March 1985 to 'possessing arms and explosives'. It was claimed he had been dispatched to England by the Chief of Staff to ascertain why events had gone 'badly wrong' during the December 1983 Harrods bombing.[125] It transpired that the Special Branch had been tracking an 'IRA cell' when members of the ASU visited the staked out 'buried hoard' in January 1984. Occupants of the car being followed had then 'slipped through their fingers'.[126] Following the conviction of Kavanagh and Vella, it was claimed that the man 'most' wanted for the Harrods blast had been photographed in their company by undercover police in Northampton railway station during the Salcey surveillance, but that the Anti-Terrorist Squad had not been informed of the concurrent Special Branch operation.[127]

A primed bomb detonated by controlled explosion in Phillimore Gardens, west London, on 13 December 1983, contained forensic features linked to the forest find and another in Pangbourne, Berkshire, in October 1983.[128] Tommy Quigley, tried with Paul Kavanagh, had been seized alighting from a taxi in Belfast on 2 December 1983. Although taken to Castlereagh Interrogation Centre for initial questioning, Quigley was sent to Paddington Green Station and charged on 7 December with conspiracy to cause explosions in England.[129] For five nights supporters of the RCG - linked South London Irish Solidarity Committee picketed the station despite believing the Irishman's location in the building would render him oblivious to the gesture. Quigley had completed three years in Long Kesh and was mentally prepared for the ordeal in England. A weak attempt at intimidation by a National Front skinhead counter demonstration backfired when two protesters felt obliged to make a hasty retreat. The SLISC mounted a further picket on Brixton on 12 May 1984 to protest the wider issue of what they termed the 'conveyor belt of British injustice'.[130]

The experiences of Geraldine Bailey were exceptionally trying for the Belfast woman visiting her partner, Tommy Quigley, in English jails in the 1980s. Financial constraints necessitated her relocation with two children,

Seaneen and Danielle, into her sister-in-law's home over the winter to fund visits to Brixton.[131] One journey to London was reported in the Irish press on 27 May 1984 due to the concentrated advocacy of Sr. Sarah Clarke. Bailey was detained under the PTA outside Victoria Station after a short visit to her fiancé. She was held overnight in Paddington Green Police Station, during which time she was callously strip-searched on three occasions. Sr. Clarke commented: 'Families are being treated like terrorists' and criticised the apparent disinterest shown by the Irish Embassy.[132] Bailey recalled: 'They were saying all these threats: "You are never going to go back to your kids. Who is minding them now?"' There was incomprehension when she replied that her sister, who was married to a British soldier and normally resided in England, was looking after the two children in Belfast.[133] Bailey regarded her maltreatment as 'pure harassment, just to frighten me'.[134] Sr. Clarke had spent weeks helping to arrange visits by the Irish families of IRA prisoners, innately humanitarian as well as political solidarity work, for which the *Irish Post* gave her an award in June.[135] In late April 1984 her close associate Cardinal O Fiaich reiterated his call for the transfer of all Irish prisoners held in Britain to their native country.[136] Sr. Clarke's personal difficulties increased, however, when she was required to leave the Highgate convent where she had, on occasion, illicitly accommodated unapproved visitors from Ireland. Moving into a private flat diminished her access to subsidized resources but did not prevent further progressive work. A hit and run incident in which she sustained a broken leg from a speeding car was interpreted by many in the London Irish community as an attempt on her life.[137]

The IRA in Gartree issued a statement carried by the *Irish News* on 28 May 1984 in which staff were accused of behaving in a 'provocative' manner. They noted: 'A tougher regime has been established, a regime designed, we believe, to either "break" prisoners, or in failing on this aim, to create enough tension within the prison that anther riot becomes inevitable and the opportunity is thus presented for the MUFTI ... strengthened by "experienced" members, to physically "break" prisoners'.[138] They speculated that the Home Office wished to gloss over endemic problems within the crumbling Victorian prisons by highlighting and exaggerating the role of the IRA contingent. All Gartree prisoners were coping with a system that had reduced exercise time from sixty to thirty-five minutes per day, with limits on the number of wings unlocked for the purpose. Evening 'association' had been reduced from three to two hours and, they claimed, £250,000 expended on a 'special control unit' for punishment of infractions.[139] The IRA men alleged that non-political prisoners were informed that the new stringency was attributable to the republican presence in their midst, an explanation which tallied with POA aspirations to concentrate them in control units.[140] POA members who had served secondments in the Six

Counties in the 1970s must have reflected on the fate of H-Block Assistant Prison Governor William McConnell, who was killed by the IRA in Belfast on 5 March 1984.[141]

Sinn Féin (Britain) organized a protest meeting at Wakefield on 15 July 1984 to support IRA prisoners. TOM delegations from Leeds and Sheffield attended, as did the Nottingham Irish Solidarity Group and Irish Solidarity Movement.[142] Sinn Féin had a cumman in Nottingham and Angela O'Dwyer, a friend of Helen O'Brien, frequently accommodated the families of prisoners visiting from Ireland.[143] Eddie O'Neill was placed on a wing where conditions remained so poor that he refused visits. Two of the more unusual Category A prisoners present on arrival from Brixton had been sentenced to life for killings committed when on active duty with the military in Fermanagh in 1981. While the pair allegedly received 'VIP treatment', unrelated friction with another ex-soldier jailed for killing a woman in Britain proved intolerable. O'Neill surmised from events that staff were seeking pretexts to assault him in order to avenge his leading role in the Albany riot. It appeared as if the well-built ex-soldier was a vehicle for their ambition as, notwithstanding his centrality to running protection rackets, he ignored the nearby presence of staff when making verbal threats against the IRA. Denied access to the workshops and unlocked at a different time and location than the provocateur, O'Neill felt obliged to engineer a confrontation when his antagonist appeared to seek jailhouse ascendancy by goading him openly in the food queue.[144]

A warning that his detractor had obtained a knife spurred the Tyrone man into pre-emptive action. Having noted that the man obsessively showered during the evening, O'Neill invited an inexperienced prison officer to unlock him in order to go to the shared ablutions block. This provided access to his quarry. When challenged one-on-one the surprised ex-soldier bolted towards his radio where he had stashed a blade. He did not acquire the weapon in time and was badly beaten in an audible manner that brought the staff team on 'bars and bolts' duty running to the scene. One pinioned the victorious O'Neill against the wall. He was obliged to react, however, when his defeated foe rose to his feet and ran at him screaming while attempting to punch his face. Although still under the physical restraint of trained personnel, O'Neill dodged a misdirected fist and landed an effective counterpunch which shattered the nose of his attacker. Prisoners saw an iron bar brandished by staff as they escorted the men singly from the shower block and wrongly deduced that O'Neill had used it as a weapon. Expecting a hostile reaction from the wing ODCs, he was clapped and cheered by the men whom his imposing foe had been persecuting. Both fighters were sent to the Segregation Block, and on the eve of the expiration of their fourteen-day punishment, the hitherto quiescent ex-soldier started shouting threats from the safety of his cell. O'Neill assumed he wished to avoid being rehoused on the same wing. In the event it was the Irish man who departed on a 'lie down' to Strangeways. Other than a token twelve-hour stint, he was not held on the wings of the Yorkshire prison once returned. Con McFadden was less than twenty-four hours in Wakefield when the formerly hostile prisoner at the centre of the dispute passed him a message expressing regret for challenging 'IRA people'. Following the 'usual run in with National Front screws' in Manchester, O'Neill was transferred to F Wing where he and others 'were nicked virtually every day for talking'.[145]

While the general operation of F Wing changed little in the course of the decade in which IRA prisoners were confined within its walls, the circumstances of its utilization alerted republicans to policy changes at the Prison Department: 'It was ongoing ... they were keeping the IRA prisoners in general in F Wing conditions – in punishment conditions. A thing that had been outlawed; sensory deprivation. So we decided we'd smash up as best we could ... We'd get beaten but at least it would come to public attention'.[146] Their options were strictly limited. As before, prisoners were given exercise singly in a small enclosure bounded by walls decorated with strange quasi-psychedelic paint patterns. They were forbidden to converse under pain of further loss of privileges, namely exercise, and were obliged to shower in an open setting in view of glaring staff. Communication was by 'talking' through heating pipes, illicit snatched words from those on the yard and by a complicated process of messaging through intermediaries.[147] O'Neill was held with Stevie Blake, ex-Loyalist and British military agent Albert Baker, Shujaa Moshesh and, theoretically, with Shane Paul O'Doherty, who generally kept his own counsel and was physically distanced by cell location.[148] Baker had written to an MP regarding the disputed existence of the silent regime in Wakefield, and it was deemed likely that Lord Alport would represent the prisoner's perspective in the House of Lords if a major stunt could be carried out to render the wing unusable.[149]

Lacking wooden furniture, removable metal fittings, radios, unmeshed paned windows and porcelain facilities, cell wrecking in F Wing represented a challenge. Several men decided to attempt to dislodge the bed units which were concreted to the floor by means of exhausting physical pressure over a period of time. In the event of cracking the slabs away from the floor, the men planned to wedge the cell doors during the evening shift when fewer staff were on duty and, with the time obtained in consequence, use the beds to smash cavities into the walls. After weeks of quiet work, a number of the men succeeded in crumbling their fused bed bases. As a joint enterprise was initiated until all were equally ready. Just prior to the allotted time for action, the authorities moved and all those involved were moved out. This was regarded as a positive return on the strategy. O'Neill was once again driven to Strangeways for indefinite solitary confinement given the revelation of a very senior staff member that 'we can't get you allocated anywhere' in the Dispersal System. As the year drew to a close, he was moved after another 'lie down' in Durham to the 'brand new' Frankland which had held no IRA and only low numbers of Category A prisoners from November 1983.[150]

Victory in Strasbourg, 28 June 1984

The November 1982 decision of the European Commission of Human Rights in Strasbourg to refer the case taken against Sean Campbell and Fr. Pat Fell to the European Court of Human Rights amounted to a major victory for the IRA prisoners. This signalled that the ECHR accepted contentions that Article 6 of the Human Rights Convention may well have been breached by the authorities which imposed penalties on the two IRA men in the aftermath of the Albany 'riot' of September 1976.[151] Campbell had spent ninety days in solitary confinement and lost 690 days remission arising from disciplinary proceedings in which he was denied legal assistance and did not attend. Fr. Fell had additionally complained that restrictions placed on his correspondence were detrimental to his best interests, an argument which the Home Office had effectively already conceded by liberalizing its regulations.[152] The planned ECHR hearing in Strasbourg on 20 September 1983 was expected to result in a negative decision against Britain. Fr. Fell's complaint centred on his claim that interference with his mail with legal representation infringed Article 8 of the European Convention received a boost when the European Commission accepted the argument. Campbell's claim that Article 6 had been breached by the operation of closed hearings by Boards of Visitors was potentially even more significant in that it threatened to undermine the culture of secrecy cultivated by the Home Office.[153] British penal reformers, not least the distinguished Howard League, had long claimed that BOVs neglected to utilize potentially powerful privileges in relation to assessing the accountability of prison staff.[154]

A British former President of the European Commission of Human Rights, Sir James Fawcett, cited the *Campbell and Fell* case as an example of inordinate bureaucracy. Applications had been received by the Commission in March 1977 regarding an incident which had occurred in September 1976. Their report was not adopted until May 1982 and the judgement of the Court was published in June 1984.[155] On 28 June 1984 Fr. Fell and Campbell won their case on the right to legal representation at disciplinary hearings. The ruling addressed related issues such as the right to legal assistance in cases taken against prison staff and egregious censorship of letters.[156] The IRA men were awarded their costs of £13,000 but claims for damages were rejected.[157] The British Government was not directed to open Board of Visitors proceedings to the press and public and had, arising from a separate case involving IRA prisoners heard by the High Court in November 1983, permitted jailed defendants to receive legal advice.[158] The Home Office, in order to 'give effect' to the ruling in the UK as required by states that were 'party' to the Convention but had not adopted it into national law, directed that BOVs tasked with adjudicating charges of 'mutiny' and 'incitement to mutiny and doing gross personal violence to an officer' should: '(i) ... invariably accede to a request by an accused prisoner to be legally represented; and (ii) they should publicise the outcome of such cases in the form of a letter to the local press'.[159]

From his Gartree cell, Dickie Glenholmes noted that whereas Fr. Fell and Campbell were at liberty due to the expiration of their sentences, other IRA men attacked in Albany in the same incident were serving terms which had been effectively extended due to loss of remission by the BOV proceedings faulted in the ECHR ruling.[160] Eddie Byrne, one of those personally concerned, issued a public call for the restoration of 690 days of forfeited remission as no provision had been made to redress the situation.[161] He believed Britain would have been liable for full legal costs and expenses if the two principal complainants had not been freed.[162] The IRA in Parkhurst SSU, Joe O'Connell, Harry Duggan and Hugh Doherty, hailed the belated decision as 'an important verdict at least against the Brit[ish] prison system, or rather a crack has been exposed in it'.[163]

The 'five demands' campaign appealed to a spectrum of Irish support groups and an early demonstration on the issue was held in Sheffield on 5 August 1984 under the auspices of TOM. On 8 and 18 August 1984, the RCG participated in Sinn Féin events in London, leading to assertions that other pro-Irish elements had allowed 'their own sectarian interests outweigh ... those of the Irish people and their POWs'.[164] Pro-IRA slogans antagonized the Metropolitan Police who, according to media reports monitored in Parkhurst, threatened to arrest Jeremy Corbyn MP. On 29 September 1984 the Irish in Britain Representation Group, Labour Committee on Ireland, Sinn Féin and TOM jointly organized a meeting in Digbeth Civic Hall, Birmingham, to publicize the issues.[165] The thrust of the campaign was that it was unfair, if not illegal, for the British government to transfer eighty British soldiers convicted of crimes in Ireland to jails in England whilst disregarding Prison Rule 31 in every case regarding Irish republicans. The use of Rule 43 to keep Mick Murray in solitary confinement for five years was highlighted as anomalous, as was the denial of specialist medical treatment to the badly injured Pat Hackett. In 1984 informed republicans in Britain acknowledged forty-one imprisoned comrades and twelve other innocents who had been 'sentenced in "show trials" to placate public opinion'.[166]

On 12 August 1984 violence erupted at the annual Anti-Internment rally in Andersonstown, West Belfast, when the RUC moved into a large crowd firing plastic bullets. Local man Sean Downes, who had a 1977 conviction for IRA membership, died when shot in the stomach at point-blank range by an RUC man.[167] Attempts by RUC Chief Constable Sir John Hermon to contextualize the incident met with vigorous contradiction by journalists who had witnessed events.[168] Writing in the *New Statesman*, reporter and witness Terry O'Halloran described what he had seen as 'state terrorism'.[169] Downes was not regarded as an IRA Volunteer in 1984 and was unarmed at the time of his death. The fact that the incident had been captured on film added to its political impact.[170] Irish Northern Aid leader Martin Galvin was present in calculated defiance of the 29 July ban on his admission to the Six Counties. This encouraged speculation that the RUC were under pressure to effect Galvin's deportation from Northern Secretary James Prior. The incident was cited by Congressman Mario Biaggi during successful attempts to press President Ronald Reagan to retain the 1979 embargo on US arms exports for the use of the RUC.[171] Forty members of Congress additionally urged Thatcher to address the 'indiscriminate use of plastic bullets by the British Army and other security forces in the North of Ireland' when visiting them on 20 February 1985.[172]

British group 'Justice' examined the use of fingerprint evidence at the 'Uxbridge Eight' trial in January 1975. Gerry Cunningham, one of the 'Uxbridge Eight', persisted in protesting that his fingerprint had not been found on an IRA timing device, as the jury was informed, and must have been planted by police or others. 'Planting prints' was facilitated by the technique of using an adhesive strip to 'lift' prints from evidence once the 'dusting' method was abandoned by police in 1973.[173] Ex-Scotland Yard Chief Superintendent Harold Squires disbelieved the claims of criminals who claimed to have been framed by police but admitted that transferring a lifted fingerprint to a new location was 'almost impossible but it can be done'.[174] Whereas Cunningham expressed no regret for his IRA background, vindication was an essential objective of Paddy Joe Hill of the innocent 'Birmingham Six'. Hill's letter, carried by the *Irish Post* on 15 September 1984, was reprinted by TOM using the 'Information on Ireland' imprint developed by Aly Renwick and Liz Curtis.[175] Writing from Gartree, Hill urged supporters and 'all Irish organizations in Britain' to 'do what they can to seek justice for us'. TOM recommended writing to Home Secretary Douglas Hurd and Irish Ambassador Noel Dorr, in addition to forwarding resolutions of support through the trade unions and political parties.[176] Hurd was appointed Secretary of State for Northern Ireland in September 1984. This was negatively interpreted in Long Lartin where Gerry Cunningham opined: 'The appointment of Douglas Hurd ... and the prospect of repatriation as expressed in the "Joint Authority" option put forth by the "Forum" are also reasons why we should go into the Dáil'.[177] As Home Secretary on 15 May 1984, Hurd had countered Jeremy Corbyn's request in the Commons for Home Office approval of repatriation by the mantric phrase 'applications for transfer to Northern Ireland under the Criminal Justice Act 1961 will continue to be considered on their merits, in the light of the Government's policy on such transfers'.[178]

The 29 September 1984 interception of the *Marita Ann* off the Kerry coast created a sensation in Ireland. The trawler was carrying seven tons of American, German and Russian weaponry and munitions transhipped in the Atlantic from the Gloucester, Massachusetts - based *Valhalla*. This confirmed that the 'American Connection' was not, at the very least, eradicated by the conservative tendencies of the Reagan administration.[179] The presence on board the *Marita Ann* of John 'Sean' Crawley, a former member of the elite US Marine Corps Force Recon and originally from Celbridge, Co. Kildare, signalled direct input from American based groupings.[180] The other men seized on the *Marita Ann* included Martin Ferris of Ardfert, Kerry and Michael Browne.[181] Crawley received a ten year sentence for his participation and was subsequently arrested with an IRA ASU in England in July 1996.[182]

Those within the Dispersal System had been advantaged by Strasbourg rulings which disposed the Home Office to liberalize correspondence between prisoners and solicitors, access to legal aid and reduced censorship, although this was balanced by Lord Elton's October 1983 announcement that 'new special units for disruptive prisoners' were planned.[183] Although clearly informed by local considerations in which the IRA were one of a number of elements, the long term recommitment to SSUs may have been affected by a disturbing report from Belfast. On 13 September 1984 Director of Prison Operations William Kerr apprised Douglas Hurd that a 'major PIRA escape plan' from the H-Blocks involving at least one staff collaborator had been averted when he was observed in the company of two republican acquaintances in Lurgan, Armagh. When confronted, the man admitted that provision of a key impression and direct assistance on a planned night and early morning breakout involving the additional help of a 'suborned' colleague were among the services originally under discussion. Coming just over a year after thirty-eight IRA men had exited H7, the political ramifications of a possible repeat were considerable.[184]

Life-sentenced Gartree IRA prisoners Ronnie McCartney and Paul Norney wrote to the *Andersonstown News* in a letter carried on 20 October 1984, setting out their views on the major issues of the prison struggle in England. They objected to the prevalent humanitarian argument being advanced in support of the repatriation of IRA prisoners on the grounds that it rested on a misinterpretation of the core question. Having cited their personal 'ideological commitment to socialism', a term which many but not all IRA prisoners in Ireland would have accepted, the pair characterized their enemy as 'imperialists' in league with 'colonialist, and neo-colonialist forces'. Irish 'POWs', therefore, should never petition captors for 'gestures' even if they believed those 'who lack humanity' were likely to acquiesce.

They implied that the objective of a 'free, United and Socialist Ireland' was paramount and that none should invite 'discredit' or 'enhance the status' of the enemy by seeking humanitarian intervention.[185] McCartney also privately corresponded with Sinn Féin Head Office in Dublin on general political development themes, including youth organization.[186]

Having clashed repeatedly with Gartree staff arising from family visits, Billy Armstrong applied during the summer months to receive accumulated sessions in Wormwood Scrubs. Instead, he was offered a temporary transfer to Wandsworth where, in early September, he spent two weeks under virtual punishment conditions. Wandsworth did not normally accommodate convicted Category A men, other than those admitted to segregation under Rule 43, and the Belfast man was deprived of exercise when awaiting the arrival of his family from Ireland. On a more petty level, Armstrong was prevented from having his broken radio repaired.[187] There may have been a degree of black humour intended given his track record of destroying prison communications. Ironically, Armstrong was finally adjusting to the Gartree regime when moved to Hull on 24 October 1984. The move came less than two weeks after the 'Brighton Bombing', which raised the spectre of increased coercion.[188]

Brighton, 12 October 1984

On 12 October 1984 the IRA mounted a devastating attack on the Grand Hotel, Brighton, as the Conservative Party held its annual convention. The device exploded in the *en suite* bathroom of room 629 at 2.54 a.m., blasting through the partition wall into 628 and causing the collapse of rooms in a vertical column below. Foreign Secretary and Thatcher confidant Sir Geoffrey Howe probably survived death or serious injury by the good fortune of being absent from the lowest level room, 128. Roberta Wakeham, wife of Government Chief Whip Robert Wakeham, was killed as the centre of the hotel imploded, as was Jeanne Shattock. Secretary of State for Trade and Industry Norman Tebbit and his wife Margaret were seriously injured. Sir Anthony Berry MP (Enfield-Southgate) and Eric Taylor died from traumatic asphyxia. Mrs Muriel MacLean, wife of leading Scottish Conservative David MacLean, was fatally wounded.[189] Roy Bradford, described as a veteran of 'several perilous Northern Ireland governments', was reputedly 'saved by a couple of walls'.[190]

The bedroom occupied by the Prime Minster was badly damaged and the *Irish Press* conceded that the IRA had 'almost assassinated Mrs Thatcher'.[191] The trenchant IRA admission of responsibility claimed: 'Mrs Thatcher will now realise that Britain cannot occupy our country and torture our prisoners and shoot our people in their own streets and get away with it ... we only have to be lucky once – you will have to be lucky always'.[192] Republicans subsequently claimed to have planted 160lbs of gelignite in an operation which 'smashed the myth that the British government was impregnable', although other forms of explosives may well have been used.[193] Commander Hucklesby of Scotland Yard's Anti-Terrorist Branch warned of further attacks.[194] Home Secretary Brittan claimed in the Commons on 22 October that 228 police officers were engaged in sifting through the debris of the hotel while in excess of 200 more pursued those responsible.[195] Thatcher was visibly shaken when filmed addressing the conference the following day, although her projection of 'manifest courage and impertubility … after her narrow escape' impressed Tory supporters.[196] She believed the hall was 'half full … because the rigorous security checks held up the crowds trying to get in … The bomb attack … was an attempt not only to disrupt and terminate our conference. It was an attempt to cripple Her Majesty's democratically elected government'.[197]

Rumours abounded as to how such a potent onslaught had been carried out. On 15 October 1984 the *Irish Press* repeated stories that the IRA possessed a team of four to five 'English volunteers' and wildly speculated that the operation had been postponed from the previous year owing to the infiltration of 'British based cells'.[198] The only man convicted of direct involvement in the attack was the experienced north Belfast IRA Volunteer Pat Magee. Evidence heard at trial in June 1986 asserted that another man identified as 'the Pope' had been present in Room 629 when the bomb was emplaced. Weak forensic evidence suggested that Magee had used the name 'Roy Walsh' when booking into the Grand Hotel on 15 September 1984.[199] It was claimed that Magee and 'the Pope' had been observed by British agents in the summer of 1983 when they allegedly reconnoitred a 'soldiers' pub' in Blackpool, Lancashire.[200] Yet the trail did not lead to Brighton where the IRA came close to wiping out the British Cabinet the following year. English police apparently knew that 'Walsh' was actually Magee in January 1985.[201] The actual Roy Walsh was moved from Albany to a lie-down in Wandsworth when his name was broadcast as a person of interest to Scotland Yard.[202]

Pat Magee had been arrested at the request of Scotland Yard in Venray, Holland, in September 1980 and held in custody until 8 January 1981, despite his possession of valid work and settlement papers. There was no suggestion, let alone formal legal accusation, of improper conduct on his part in the Netherlands. Indeed, the net effect of rousting Magee from his Continental retirement appears to have been his leading role in the attempt on the life of the British Prime Minister in 1984. His extradition case was heard on 20 January 1980 in the Den Bosch Court of Justice, an austere forum comprising a panel of three judges. When awaiting the decision of the Court in Nijmegan, Magee optimistically declared: 'I do not think I will suffer in future from the British accusations against me'.[203] Dutch authorities centred their objections to deportation to England on the lack of evidence against Magee and, the words of Public Prosecutor Mr. W Moors, their rejection of 'conspiracy as defined under British law'.[204] A request of political asylum was abandoned in February 1980 when he travelled to Dublin from Amsterdam with an Irish friend. He was shot and wounded in the Irish capital on 25 November 1981 during a UDA/ UFF attack on the Parnell Square offices of *AP/RN*. Scotland Yard alleged Magee subsequently moved between Ireland, England, Wales and France in 1982–83 prior to checking into the Grand Hotel.[205]

Emotions ran high at the Kilfeacle gravesite of IRA Third Tipperary Brigade War of Independence hero Sean Treacy when ex-Fianna Fáil Taoiseach Jack Lynch described the Brighton bombing as 'an atrocity'. He was heckled by elements of the crowd who belonged to the mainstream party and believed otherwise. Gerry Adams entered the cemetery later that day with the distinct Sinn Féin contingent and in his oration promised that 'the work left unfinished by Sean Treacy' in the 1920s would be pursued.[206] Treacy had been killed on 14 October 1920 in a shootout with plainclothes British Intelligence operatives in Dublin.[207] Adams was recovering from multiple gunshots received in an assassination bid in Belfast on 14 March 1984, mounted by British backed Loyalists.[208] Manus Canning, former Derry IRA prisoner in Wormwood Scrubs and Wakefield in the 1950s, wrote from his New York home to the editor of the *Irish Echo* in April 1984 to commend the tactic of striking Britain's political elite.[209] The perceived significance of a pro-republican Irish-American lobby was reflected in calls for the proscription of Irish Northern Aid, although the US Ambassador to London, Charles Price, noted that such a move 'might very well under our constitution run into constitutional problems'.[210]

In retrospect Pat Magee theorized: 'The [1981] Hunger Strike destroyed the notion of criminalisation and the Brighton bombing destroyed the notion of containment ...Until Brighton we were not being taken seriously by the British political establishment ... After Brighton, anything was possible ... even the IRA ... began to fully accept the priority of the campaign in England'.[211] The attack had an invisible secondary effect of postponing a joint British/Irish Government effort to curtail the growth of Sinn Féin while situating the SDLP in a Belfast forum alongside the more amenable wing of Unionism. The Armstrong/Nally dialogue, privately endorsed in June 1984 by Thatcher, was advanced in October when the Prime Minster was informed of proposals to 'introduce a system of devolved government into Northern Ireland'.[212] Garret FitzGerald manoeuvred to counteract the IRA by announcing that considerable progress had been made on security cooperation in DFA/FCO discussions. This, however, was primarily assessed in London through the selfish prism of the UK gaining assistance in the face of the enhanced lethality of the Republican Movement. The Irish Government had, in May 1984, published the *New Ireland Forum* in conjunction with the SDLP, yet devoid of republican input. Exclusion repeated the critical error of Sunningdale. Gerry Adams perceived the format as an attempt to provide a 'lifeline' for the SDLP and described the exclusion of his party as 'stupid, counter-productive and short-sighted'.[213] Yet Thatcher's cool reception of the moderate document injected uncertainty as to the willingness of London to work with Dublin in efforts to bring the conflict to a close. On 19 October 1984 the mood was different in 10 Downing Street and Charles Powell briefed the FCO: 'The prime minister commented that the terrorist bomb in Brighton has slowed these confidential talks down and may, if it turns out to be the first in a series, kill the initiative altogether'.[214] Thatcher stated: 'Events of Thursday night in Brighton mean that we must go very slowly on these talks if not stop them. It could look as if we were bombed into making concessions to the Republic'.[215]

The Chequers meeting of Garret FitzGerald and Margaret Thatcher on 18–19 November 1984, relocated from Dublin owing to British security fears post-Brighton, proved even more disastrous than predicted. The total, vitriolic rejection of the all-Ireland constitutional nationalist analysis of the conflict by the British Prime Minister humiliated the mild mannered and seemingly weak Taoiseach. In playing to a Conservative and Unionist gallery in such an irrational fashion, Thatcher had also badly damaged the credibility of the SDLP and their influential supporters in the Twenty-Six Counties.[216] Many within Sinn Féin, however, appreciated that the Irish Government's alliance with the SDLP threatened to widen their party's estrangement from mainstream politics. The November 1984 Sinn Féin Ard Fheis in Dublin returned Gerry Adams to the Presidency of the party, with John Joe McGirl as Vice-President. Joint Treasurer Seamus McGarrigle, one of the first IRA prisoners jailed in England in 1970, partnered Joe Cahill. Pat Doherty, Alex Maskey and Owen Carron were among the incoming Ard Chomhairle with direct involvement in the prisons issue.[217] Doherty, a Donegal-Glaswegian, was brother of 'Balcombe Street' prisoner Hugh Doherty, then in Parkhurst SSU.[218] Adams had been the natural successor to Ruairi O'Bradaigh at the political helm in November 1983 when the former IRA Chief of Staff resigned his party position, citing the discarding of the federalist 'Eire Nua' strategy as a major concern. O'Bradaigh remained a personal force within Sinn Féin and retained the allegiance of leading supporters on the IRA's Army Executive, who opposed the new mode of electoral engagement. Early signs of ballot box success at local level, however, consolidated the position of Gerry Adams and Martin McGuinness.[219]

Contesting elections stimulated the steady expansion of Sinn Féin's voting base which, in turn, inspired a change in tactics by Loyalist elements receiving intelligence, direction, armament and active support from official British counterinsurgents. Elected councillors, party activists and families with republican connections were targeted as never before in a presumed effort to dissuade people from either joining or assisting Sinn Féin. Diverting the IRA from its more refined campaign against the British military and state into retaliatory action against Loyalists was probably an additional factor. On 14 March 1984 Adams narrowly avoided assassination when shot five times by Loyalists taking advantage of his scheduled court appearance in Belfast city centre.[220] He contended that authorities had deployed an SAS team to shadow the car in which he travelled. Elite British soldiers played no role in either intercepting the attack or detaining those responsible, although other military personnel subsequently made arrests.[221]

Adams recuperated in the Buncrana district of Donegal where Ray McLaughlin, recently released from jail in England, provided accommodation. Local Sinn Féin Councillor Eddie Fullerton, among the first party members elected in the Twenty-Six Counties under the new political direction, had lived for many years in Birmingham's substantial Irish community.[222] McLaughlin was one former IRA prisoner in England who rejoined the Republican Movement and went on the run in the Twenty-Six Counties following the discovery of ammunition in a car he was using.[223] He died in a swimming pool accident in Shannon, County Clare, on 9 September 1985 in the presence of his wife Mary and 11-year-old son Padraig, future Sinn Féin TD for Donegal. The tragedy occurred during a rare holiday reunion. For years Ray McLaughlin had sent Padraig letters from prison which required him to research Irish words in dictionaries. This encouragement was a means of strengthening a parental bond which occasional and often traumatic prison visits could not fulfil.[224] He was listed on the 'Republican roll of honour, Tir Chonaill Command', as was his mentor Eddie Fullerton following his assassination in Donegal in 1991.[225]

The release of John McCluskey from Parkhurst on 10 October 1984 attracted disproportionate public and private commentary. When nearing the date, McCluskey received what Clare Short MP termed 'the inevitable reply' from the Home Secretary in relation to his application for permission to attend his father's funeral in September 1983.[226] Such were the vagaries of the system that his IRA comrades in Leicester, where McCluskey spent a 'lie-down' in the summer of 1983, incorrectly believed he would be 'out soon'.[227] He spent four and a half years of his ten-year sentence in solitary, having lost all remission for numerous protest actions.[228] Jim McDonald, Helen O'Brien and Jan Taylor waited patiently for McCluskey to emerge from the prison but staff were precise in ensuring he served literally every minute of his term: 'They kept him three hours. He was released at 10.00 a.m.'.[229] McCluskey, as with Roy Walsh and others, persisted with legal cases taken to the European Commission of Human Rights in pursuit of the right of repatriation. Plans by the London Irish Freedom Movement to celebrate McCluskey's release by 'rocking the Tory party conference at Brighton' were criticized by the DUP in the aftermath of the IRA bombing of the gathering. Mick Hume of the IFM explained that 'rocking' comprised a street demonstration which occurred as planned to show their opposition to the PTA and support for 'political status for Irish Republican prisoners in British jails'.[230]

McCluskey had attempted to discover whether the Home Office would seek to have him excluded from the UK under the PTA, but in correspondence requesting clarification, he insisted that he would not 'see or be interviewed' by officials unless permitted to have 'an Irish political prisoner' witness. No Exclusion Order was served and on deciding to reside with family members in London for two weeks, McCluskey was in a position to accept requests for appearances from left wing organizations, including the IFM linked WRP. This had been long planned and the Irish man in May 1984 praised the engagement of Gerry Mac Lochlainn in similar events: 'It's wonderful to see S[inn] F[ein] coming out & speaking at all these meetings, it's just a tragedy that they hadn't been doing this over the years … The Miners are now witnessing the brutal arm of the State. Lets hope they learn something from this'.[231] His desire to participate in left politics in England did not accord with Sinn Féin political strategy. McCluskey appeared as a guest of the WRP despite a hand delivered instruction from a senior Sinn Féin figure in Belfast that he should not share the platform with an ultra-leftist group which had been openly critical of the Armed Struggle.[232] A defiant McCluskey also spoke in public on Sunday 14 October when he clasped hands with Malcolm Pitt, President of the Kent Area National Union of Miners, during an ISM sponsored conference in Claxton House, St. John's Way, Archway.[233] Pitt attended in a personal capacity and had previously addressed pro-Irish gatherings in London during which he emphasised the sense of common cause between persons united by a common Thatcherite enemy.[234] In Archway Pitt railed against the sections of the labour movement in Britain which questioned the democratic basis of the strike: 'These are the people who have denied the Irish people the right to unity and nationhood. These are the people who for years played the Orange card and gerrymandered the constituencies of Derry and Belfast'.[235]

This militant labour/republican nexus was hailed by Tommy Quigley in A Wing of Brixton as 'very significant' and a 'step forward'.[236] Endorsement also came from H5 of Long Kesh when Laurence 'Lorny' McKeown, who narrowly survived the 1981 hunger strike, offered 'the hand of revolutionary solidarity and comradeship' to the miners and their families.[237] McKeown identified with the sense of 'treachery and loneliness' experienced by strikers when censored in expressing their perspectives and facing a barrage of criticism from the mainstream Labour Party and Trade Union Congress.[238] McCluskey's personal interaction in London, however, created a sense of immediacy. As such, his trenchant backing of the NUM obviously heartened those in attendance and enabled him to offer a challenge to its leadership to formulate 'their position in relation to their imprisoned comrades'. With considerable understatement borne of a personal sense of identification he queried:

> Will they be forgotten about or is it just a memory, a demonstration outside the prisons now and again? … If they are political prisoners obviously they must fight for political status within the prison … We had to fight for political status and political prisoners in this country, although they are not recognised as political prisoners, have nevertheless achieved quite a lot over the last ten years … struggling on different fronts, trying to educate different prisoners around us, struggling against horrible conditions and paying a fairly heavy penalty for that struggle.[239]

When expressing solidarity with McCluskey, Pitt was in the company of David Yaffe of the ISM and Liz Hill, mother of Paul Hill, for whom she campaigned. Yaffe, an Economics academic and lecturer also known by his *nom de plume* 'Reed', authored *Ireland: Key to the British Revolution* in 1984, and was a key ideologue in RCG/ISM politics.[240] Labour MEPs Richard Balfe and Christine Crawley supported the weekend, as did a broad sweep of opinion encompassing Young Liberals, IBRG, Manchester Area National Union of Students and Scottish republican bands.[241] Alf Lomas, MEP for London North East, backed the endeavour having raised the question of repatriation in the European Parliament.[242] The convergence of Irish and British radicals drew the negative attention of Sir Alfred Sherman, an adviser to the Prime Minister, who alluded to it during a BBC Radio One interview.[243] In a similar vein, Thatcher envisaged a multifaceted domestic threat comprising 'the most testing crisis of our time – the battle between the extremists and the rest'.[244] Undeterred, McCluskey addressed a November 1984 public meeting at the Asian Centre in Hackney, London, where the Asian Collective of East London and the Black People's Socialist League hosted him together with ex-Armagh Prison republican Linda Quigley. He appeared alongside Molefe Pheto and Johnson Mlambo, who had been jailed in Robben Island, South Africa with other African National Congress members and the famed Nelson Mandela.[245] The ANC were annual guests at Sinn Féin Ard Fheiseana and the full extent of connections between the IRA and MK spanned many years in several countries. The public affiliation of the Sinn Féin with the Irish Anti-Apartheid Movement, a body organized under the ANC, prompted Garret FitzGerald and Minister for Health Barry Desmond to resign.[246]

Sinn Féin (Britain)

The pragmatism of Sinn Féin on the prison issue in England was illustrated by the fact that John McCluskey was provided a platform at the November 1984 Ard Fheis in Dublin within weeks of defying party instructions in London. McCluskey reminded delegates of the difference between incarceration in England and Ireland.[247] It may not have been coincidental that he and Ray McLaughlin were reputedly 'strongly in favour' of the major decision to stand down but not abolish Sinn Féin (Britain). While full details of the development could not be ascertained in Parkhurst SSU, Joe O'Connell ascertained that 'serious internal disputes' in England were causative factors. Writing on 15 November 1984, a forum subject to censor's interdiction, O'Connell represented himself as patiently 'waiting to see what way the new arrangements work out'.[248] For a variety of reasons, Gerry Cunningham was much less satisfied in Long Lartin and moved to reassure the aggrieved Eddie Caughey that 'the disbandment of SF in Britain came [as] somewhat [sic] of a shock for me at least. Were I to have been consulted I would have vigorously opposed such a motion'.[249]

Writing from his well spied on and frequently attacked Birmingham home, Caughey was utterly dismayed by the turn of events. Once the initial shock of being effectively disowned by Sinn Féin Headquarters hit home, a major issue for a man who had braved death threats, domestic harassment, imprisonment and sectarian hostility for advocating the progressive political doctrines of the pluralist United Irishmen, he was additionally frustrated that the additional mooted 'discussions about disbandment … never took place'. Acknowledging that the Ard Chomhairle was justified in divining major 'problems' with the functionality of the party's satellite presence in Britain, the Belfast man defiantly opposed the decision to 'shut shop' on the ambitious project he had invested more than most in Britain.[250] The one day warning of the proposal at the Dublin conference did not permit sufficient time to table countervailing motions from numerous allied English and Scottish cummain. In private correspondence Caughey confirmed his faith in the upper leadership while inferring that their perspective on the potential of UK solidarity had been influenced by hostility towards Sinn Féin (Britain) from 'Labour Party, TOM and LCI' quarters.[251] Caughey insisted that he welcomed political assistance from 'genuine groups and people who recognise our just struggle' but argued 'at the end of the day that it will be as a result of our own efforts that our own movement will win and obtain the mandate of the Irish people for the introduction of a thirty-two county socialist republic'.[252]

Such articulate, politicized and credible ex-IRA prisoners who had served sentences in England as McCluskey and McLaughlin could not be outdebated by the lone voice of Caughey. With three minutes allotted for his rebuttal of the most propitious motion aired on the UK scenario since 1968, procedural protocols and timetabling did not favour the generally acclaimed stalwart of An Cumman Cabhrah in England. He rejected implications tending to aver that insufficient effort had been expended by Sinn Féin in England to aid Dispersal System prisoners. When defeated on the motion, a magnanimous

Caughey emphasised that he would continue to advance the 'POW Campaign and the welfare of all our POWs in Britain'.[253] Those in Long Lartin, at least, had a minor grievance in that a motion on abstentionism, channelled through Caughey to Head Office, had been omitted from the Clar. Upon investigating its exclusion with Joe Cahill and Denise Cregan, Caughey, was informed that the Ard Chomhairle regarded it as 'too contentious'.[254] After years of behind doors debate between 1962–68, abstentionism had been a catalyst in the major split the Republican Movement, which resulted in the creation of the Provisional IRA in December 1969. Freethinking and semi-independent groups of IRA prisoners in England in the mid-1980s produced draft documents and Sinn Féin motions with potential to disrupt an expanding party taking steps towards some 'broad front'; and electoral participation modes were being outlined in Long Lartin and Parkhurst. In November 1984 Gerry Cunningham was placated to find that while the drive to promote repatriation 'in this country seems to have run its course … the number of resolutions on the Clar relating to it was quite heartening'.[255]

Events in Dublin, as per the norm, had repercussions in republican Britain. In West London, the Terence MacSwiney Cumman of Sinn Féin was disconcerted by the news as reported by their delegate Jan Taylor.[256] No administrative re-configuration was immediately required in England, although the situation in Scotland proved more complicated. The Glasgow Irish Republican POW Committee was formed in November 1984 to agitate for the five demands of IRA prisoners. This focused the energies of the existing *Republican Bulletin* grouping and a new title, *The Irish Prisoner*, was launched in 1985 as an enhanced, higher quality successor.[257] This endeavour was necessary as the 1984 Dublin Ard Fheis, which endorsed the demands, effectively disbanded Glasgow Sinn Féin. The re-coalescence of Tony O'Mara *et al* around the POW Committee provided the editorial continuity and administration necessary for success.[258] Once established, the paper attracted comments from Gerry Cunningham, Brendan Dowd, Gerry McDonnell and other IRA prisoners in England in the late 1980s.[259] Typically, in view of his militancy, Dowd strongly opposed efforts to create a pro-Irish campaign in Britain on the basis of humanitarian arguments.[260] The magnitude of any prisoner - centred endeavour was indicated by a *Sunday Mirror* feature on Parkhurst headed 'Evil ghosts that stalk a jail'. The three IRA men in the SSU were described as 'terrorists' whose demands for political status stemmed from mere 'fanaticism'.[261] The chances of influencing a generally misinformed British public opinion remained as remote as ever.

Paddy Brady, brother of IRA prisoner Martin Brady, was shot dead on his South Belfast milk round by the UDA on 16 November 1984. As a Sinn Féin member he had attended the recent Ard Fheis in the capital.[262] Loyalist and presumed British agent Michael Stone was convicted of the killing following his rescue from unarmed republicans who halted his 16 March 1988 grenade and pistol attack on mourners in Milltown Cemetery, Belfast. Stone told RUC interrogators that he had consulted Brady's file, as compiled by the 'security forces', and regarded him on that basis as 'a legitimate target'.[263] He claimed to have utilized a technique favoured by the British military's 14th Intelligence Company, successor to similar SAS linked undercover units which employed illegal tactics.[264] As many IRA prisoners in England were aware, Brady had assisted families in their efforts to elevate the repatriation problem and worked with the POW Department. Sinn Féin denounced the predictable Home Office decision to deny Martin Brady compassionate parole from Long Lartin. IRA prisoners in Hull placed condolences in republican newspapers.[265] Martin Brady was prevented from visiting the cemetery until freed from Maghaberry: 'It wasn't till I got out of prison that I went to the graveyard ... [and] I actually buried my brother'.[266]

IRA and Sinn Féin personnel knew that elements of British Intelligence interacted with select Loyalist proxies who seemed immune from prosecution, as well as conducting various forms of lethal 'dirty tricks'. It was held that Michael Bettaney, an MI5 officer who ran agents in the North of Ireland in 1979–81, sought contact with the IRA in English jails once exposed as a putative Warsaw Pact agent.[267] Hailing from Stoke-on-Trent, Bettaney, an Oxford English literature graduate, joined K Branch of MI5 at a time when it specialised in countering Soviet espionage in Britain.[268] Colleagues included masterspy John Deverell and future MI5 supremo in 2002–2007 Eliza Manningham-Buller, who, among a highly elite few, appreciated that senior KGB member, Oleg Gordievsy, was a prized MI6 asset.[269] Gordievsy apparently informed MI6 that Bettaney, described as a 'middle ranking officer in MI5', had violated Section 1 of the Official Secrets Act (1911) and Section 7 of the OSA (1920) by passing documentation to Soviet agents in Britain in 1983.[270] He was remanded in custody to Brixton from Horseferry Road Magistrates Court on 19 September 1983.[271]

Press accounts portrayed Bettaney as an eccentric right wing Catholic and inept radical who had treasonously approached Arkady Gouk, a Soviet diplomat and suspected high ranking KGB officer he was responsible for monitoring in the UK. Details of the English man's years 'working in Northern Ireland', however, were not imparted and on 16 February 1984 a ruling by Lord Chief Justice Lane ensured that all but thirty-five minutes of the five-day trial in the Old Bailey was held in camera.[272] Attorney General Sir Michael Havers, a prime and confirmed IRA target, opened proceedings in the Old Bailey where, on 16 April 1984, Bettaney received a heavy sentence of twenty-three years after trial for non-fatal offences.[273] Following conviction, a statement released through his solicitor asserted: 'In pursuing its domestic security policy, the [British] Government relies on the aid of a security service which cynically manipulates the definition of subversion and thus abuses its charter so as to investigate and interfere in the activities of legitimate political parties, the Trade Union Movement and other progressive organisations'.[274] This cry from the heart, so clearly laden with personal experience, had obvious applicability to Whitehall's bitter war in Ireland. Bettaney was immediately sent to 'special secure accommodation' at Coldingley prison in affluent Home County Surrey with the express purpose of keeping him isolated from 'other high security prisoners'. This extended to the unreferenced IRA in the mainstream SSUs where apprehended spies were theoretically destined as special 'Category A'. A Home Office functionary acknowledged that this unusual and possibly unprecedented step was predicated on Bettaney's possession of 'highly sensitive knowledge'. This, given the absence of the KGB, GRU and Stasi from England's many maximum prisons, indicated the salient Irish dimension.[275]

It was not widely revealed that Bettaney had already established contact with the IRA in Wormwood Scrubs just after conviction. He arranged a short meeting with 'Belfast Ten' IRA man Paul Holmes in the chapel by simply enquiring from other prisoners 'is there any republicans here?' A curious Holmes responded to the entreaty but owing to the fact that he 'wasn't one for going to chapel', vigilant staff rapidly terminated a potentially extraordinary interaction. The toxic English man was quickly relocated to Coldingley from which republicans were routinely excluded.[276] Another 'Belfast Ten' prisoner, Billy Armstrong, following the sensational public disclosures made by 'the spy Colin Wallace' in 1987, was more relieved than vindicated when his original plans to 'do him in the Scrubs' had not come to fruition.[277] Wallace had been interviewed by the RUC in Parkhurst in 1984 in relation to his insights and morally informed objections regarding the role of the British Intelligence Services in the Kincora Boys Home 'honeypot' sexual abuse scandal.[278] Formerly head of the British Army's Information Policy Unit, a shadowy formation engaged in black propaganda and with links to the Foreign Office's Information Research Department, Wallace was indisputably a counterinsurgent of distinction.[279] Irish republicans tended to seek political dividends from such bizarre scenarios and both Wallace and Holroyd received invitations to speak publicly in the USA.[280]

A *Sunday Times* report which named Evelyn Glenholmes as a Scotland Yard suspect in relation to five IRA attacks in England in 1981 created a furore in November 1984 when it pre-empted the issuing of an extradition application. The first warrant delivered to Dublin was necessarily voided on the grounds that it listed the wrong name and age of the person sought. British detectives were obliged to return to London to obtain accurate documentation. Far from 'stalling' on the matter, Irish officials were astounded by the ineptitude displayed by their counterparts, whom they clearly wished to assist, and incredulous that a weekend newspaper subsequently printed 'scandalous' information on a woman who had not been charged in any jurisdiction.[281] A catalogue of serious incidents listed in the *Sunday Times*, including the Chelsea Barracks bombing in which two people were killed and an attack on the Wimbledon home of Sir Michael Havers in November 1981. Glenholmes was also speculatively if not maliciously linked to the Brighton bombing, for which she was never charged. Newspapers commented on the judicially irrelevant presence in Long Lartin of her father, leading Belfast republican Dickie Glenholmes.[282] On the basis of such information British tabloid media created the persona of 'The Blonde Bomber'.[283]

Evelyn Glenholmes lived in the Muirhevinmore estate in the Twenty-Six County border town of Dundalk, Louth, and her planned deportation to England consequently created problems for the Irish authorities at a time when public tolerance of a measure backed by Dublin courts was in the balance.[284] This factor differentiated controversy surrounding the incident from earlier instances when Margaret McKearney, Marian Coyle, Brendan Swords, John Downey and others had been named in England in the absence of detention, extradition proceedings, preferment of charges or attempted Criminal Law Jurisdiction prosecution. In September 1983 Glenholmes appeared in a Belfast court charged with membership of Cumann na mBan, the 'Women's IRA', on the basis of information passed to the RUC by IRA informer Bobby Lean. She spent a month remanded in custody which ended when the putative 'supergrass', a former aide to Gerry Adams, recanted his apparently coerced statements.[285] The RUC clarified that contrary to defamatory media reports she was not 'wanted' in the Six Counties.[286]

Ireland's Attorney General Peter Sutherland contacted Britain's Sir Michael Havers directly and Taoiseach Garret FitzGerald called in British Ambassador Alan Goodison on 11 November 1984. In a placatory move Havers repudiated *Sunday Times* allegations that the Irish Government was impeding extradition while the newspaper's editor, Andrew Neill, stood over claims that the British Government were aware that the story was going to run.[287] Regardless of the factual status and true purpose of the leaks, members of the Special Task Force in Dublin were irritated that the request to detain Glenholmes for questioning about IRA activities in England had been made public. They were also embarrassed by their failure to locate her after the premature publicity. As was possibly intended, attention was drawn to Irish extradition legislation which did not permit the transfer of a person to simply answer questions in a foreign jurisdiction.[288] The revelation that a serving member of the British Army had been granted a 'secret transfer' to an English prison following conviction for murder in Ireland disposed the moderate pro-SDLP *Irish News* to allege a 'double deal' under which Irish political prisoners in England were being aggrieved.[289] Moving convicted persons in the pay of the state had never been a major issue for the British Government. Private Ian Thain, 1st Battalion, Light Infantry, was sentenced to life imprisonment on 14 December 1984 for the fatal shooting of Thomas 'Kidso' Reilly in Belfast on 9 August 1983. Reilly was shot through the heart as he ran away from the scene of a fracas between patrolling soldiers and local youths. Thain was the first soldier convicted of murder when on duty and his transfer to an English prison near his Doncaster home and ahead of early release created controversy.[290] The RCG in London described Reilly's death as an example of 'British Terror'.[291]

With 15–22 December 1984 designated 'Prisoners' Week' in accordance with the resolution of the Ard Fheis, the POW Department enumerated its remit as containing 'over 1,000' men and women. The smaller totals included the twenty-eight women held in Armagh Jail and Limerick Prison and seven men detained in the United States. In England only forty of the fifty-three people held in eleven prisons on republican charges were recognized by the Republican Movement, arising from the prevalence of wrongful conviction.[292] Groundwork for this minority element had been laid by the Ard Chomhairle on 14 December 1984, which, on the eve of the Sinn Féin conference 'endorsed the extension of the sub-committee for Britain to include prisoners in the 26 Counties'. They appointed ex-IRA prisoner in England John McCloskey, then resettled in Convoy, Donegal, to 'cover' this duty and notified Marie Moore of the POW Department office in Belfast of the development. A disproportionate number of those jailed in England were from the 'south' of Ireland.[293]

Issues of propriety and parliamentary security in the light of the Brighton attack were raised in late December 1984. Jeremy Corbyn, Labour MP for Islington North and member of the Labour Committee of Ireland, was rebuked during a meeting with Opposition Chief Whip Michael Cocks on 17 December 1984 for having invited two presumed ex-IRA prisoners to the Commons to meet members of the LCI. Corbyn, who had no compunction in criticizing the Brighton bombing, extended the invitation to Gerry Mac Lochlainn, released from Maidstone prison in November 1983, and Linda Quigley, who had served two terms in Armagh Gaol for republican activities in the Six Counties.[294] Deirdre Whelan, Secretary of the Portlaoise Prisoners Relatives Action Committee and Joe McDonagh of the Dublin Sinn Féin POW Department assisted the organization of protests in the Twenty-Six Counties.[295]

Gerry Adams observed that an Irish Government which persisted with efforts to extradite republicans despite knowledge of 'show trials' in the Six Counties might well resort to 'immense repression'.[296] Pro-Irish groups in the UK were targeted during a crackdown under the PTA in December 1984. Home Secretary Brittan's 29 January banning of the annual Sinn Féin 'Bloody Sunday' march due to take place in Sheffield, Yorkshire, had alerted the RCG and others to the threat of renewed repression at a time when the Miners' Strike and disturbances surrounding NATO nuclear weapons being stored at Greenham Common were being met with plastic bullets, military backed riot squads, road blocks, strip-searching and various forms of counter-demonstration legislation resonant of Irish prototypes. A peak in PTA legitimised harassment occurred in December 1984, leading the RCG to encourage joint action by TOM, IBRG and all those who campaigned on the Irish conflict and prisoner issues. RCG under their ISM banner picketed the Home Office on 31 December 1984 and in February 1985 assembled 200 persons opposed to the flagrant misapplication of the PTA.[297] The specific question of repatriation, however, encouraged second generation Irish IBRG veterans Tom Barron and Mairin Higgins to found the dedicated Irish Republican Support Group in London in 1985.[298]

Parallel political and legal developments in London, Dublin and Strasbourg altered the manner in which Irish republican prisoners were treated and perceived in Britain in the eventful period 1978 to 1985. As the 'Long War' gradually generated political growth for Sinn Féin in the aftermath of the 1981 Hunger Strike breakthrough, IRA prisoners in England were, paradoxically, overshadowed in the public eye while retaining their anomalous 'special' designation among their captors. Events in Albany and Wormwood Scrubs typified this mutually maintained exceptionalism. In the final phase of the IRA's intergenerational conflict with the British State, major targets in England received unprecedented attention from the leadership of the Republican Movement. Any question as to whether the Category A men and women held in Britain constituted 'strategic' prisoners was answered by the evolution of the 'end game' period and manifested in the text of the Good Friday Agreement of 1998. While no additional republican prisoners perished in the Dispersal System in the advent of the historic compromise, the various departures in tactics, organization and mentality in England were critical to the fortunes of the nascent Peace Process.

NOTES

1. *FRFI*, March 1984, p. 12.
2. *Report on the work of the Prison Department, 1984/ 85*, p. 39.
3. *News of the World*, 8 January 1984.
4. *News of the World*, 8 January 1984.
5. See O'Donnell, *Special Category*, I, Chapter One.
6. See Nordone to the Editor, *AP/RN*, 1 April 1982 and *Guardian*, 25 February 1982.
7. *The Irish Prisoner*, No. 11 [1987], p. 10.
8. Cardinal Tomas O Fiaich to Eamonn [O'Doherty], 6 January 1984, Private Collection (O Mathuna).
9. O'Doherty, *Volunteer*, p. 222.
10. *The Irish Prisoner*, No. 11 [1987], p. 12. See also O'Doherty, *Volunteer*, pp. 220–24, *Irish Post*, 28 January 1984 and Sr. Clarke, 'Wakefield', Clarke Papers, (COFLA). Blake was moved to Strangeways and on to Hull prior to release. Sr. Clarke, 'Stephen Blake', Clarke Papers (COFLA). Moshesh was sent to Hull on 10 July 1984 after almost ten months in F Wing. *FRFI*, July/ August 1984, p. 12.
11. Shane Paul O'Doherty to Eamonn O'Doherty quoted in *Irish News*, 24 February 1984. Eamonn O'Doherty was deeply involved in the campaign to secure the repatriation of his brother and other IRA prisoners. Ibid.
12. *Irish Times*, 13 February 1984.

13. *Irish Times*, 13 February 1984. 'Cellular confinement' was defined by the Home Office spokesman as holding a prisoner where 'he would normally be able to converse with prison staff, and have exercise periods ... He would not be able to associate with other prisoners but ... his cell would not differ from those of other inmates'. Ibid.

14. *Irish News*, 24 February 1984.

15. *Prior Report*, I, p. 3. See also *Report on the work of the Prison Department, 1984/ 85*, p. 31.

16. See 'An Irish prisoner and Home Office lies' in *The Irish Prisoner*, No. 11 [1987], pp. 10–11 and *Irish Times*, 6 September 1985.

17. *Irish Times*, 2 March 1984.

18. *Irish Times*, 13 February 1984. Bishop Daly of Derry visited O'Doherty in Wakefield in late February 1984 after which he claimed: 'I feel it is time that the British Government should show a little compassion for Shane O'Doherty and some of the other prisoners from here who have served many years in English prisons and who wish to be transferred to prisons here to be closer to their families ... There are serious doubts in my mind as regards the guilt of several of the Irish prisoners held in English prisons'. Quoted in *Irish Echo*, 17 March 1984. See also *Irish Times*, 2 March 1984.

19. *Guardian*, 2 April 1982.

20. *Irish Times*, 30 March 1983.

21. *AP/RN*, 26 January 1984.

22. Harris, 'Brittan's new parole system' in *Guardian*, 9 January 1984.

23. *FRFI*, March 1984, p. 16.

24. *Times*, 17 March 1983.

25. *Times*, 21 September 1983.

26. *FRFI*, January 1984, p. 12.

27. *Twenty-Fifth report from the Committee of Public Accounts, Session 1985–86, Prison Building Programme, Home Office Property Services Agency* (London, 1986), p. 5.

28. See Terry O'Halloran, 'Fighting Brittan's prisons' in *FRFI*, September 1985, p. 14.

29. *HL Deb 21 March 1984 vol 449 c1337.*

30. *HC Deb 6 March 1984 vol 55 c541.*

31. *Guardian*, 29 December 1993.

32. Fr. Piaras O Duill to the *Sunday Press*, 11 March 1984.

33. Joe O'Connell to 'Peter' (Seamus O Mathuna), 19 August 1984, Private Collection (O Mathuna).

34. *Irish People*, 25 February 1984. See also P[adraic] Wilson to the Editor, *Irish People*, 20 October 1984. Mark Barnsley, an Anarchist prisoner jailed for importing plastic explosives, was released from Maidstone in 1982. He recalled: 'Revolutionaries behind bars also have a duty, a duty to behave with integrity, and in line with the principles we claim to hold dear. Few of the Irish Republican prisoners ever needed to be reminded of this duty, nor did the Angry Brigade prisoners'. Mark Barnsley, 'Anarchist Prisoners-Taking the fight inside', April 2002, http://leedsabc.org/publications/mark-barnsley.

35. *Guardian*, 9 February 1984. See also *Times*, 23 January 1985.

36. *FRFI*, January 1984, p. 13.

37. *FRFI*, March 1984, p. 16. Gerry Cunningham, who had compiled information on repatriation since 1981, was displeased that the research material furnished to Eddie Caughey in 1983 was not fully 'reflected' in the new pamphlet. Gerry Cunningham to Jim McDonald, 10 July 1983, Private Collection (McDonald). Cunningham was kept abreast of prisoner related news by Maureen Maguire, former mainstay of welfare activities in London, who had relocated to Dublin. Maureen Maguire to Gerry Cunningham, 15 October 1988, Private Collection (Cunningham).

38. *FRFI*, April 1984, p. 16.

39. *Irish Solidarity Movement, Week of Action, 4–10 June 1984*, Flyer.

40. Martin Brady, 12 April 2008.

41. 'Walsh-BOV Adjudications' in A Aylett [For the Treasury Solicitor] to BM Birnberg & Co, 28 September 1990, Private Collection (Walsh).

42. Sr. Sarah Clarke, 'Roy Walsh', Clarke Papers (COFLA). Paul Holmes was evidently moved out of Hull to make room for Walsh. On arriving into Armley he re-encountered Fr. Lawn, ex-Catholic Chaplain in Brixton during the 1973–1974 hunger strike. Holmes informed Sr. Clarke that Fr. Lawn 'got older but [was] unchanged'. Sr. Clarke, 'Paul Holmes', Clarke Papers (COFLA).

43. John McCluskey to 'Peter' [Seamus O Mathuna], 19 March 1984, Private Collection (O Mathuna).

44. Armstrong to Wilson, 27 February 1984, Private Collection (Wilson).

45. Maria Kane to the Editor, *Irish People*, 4 February 1984. Kane described herself as the 'special friend' of Billy Armstrong in Parkhurst where Bennett, McComb, McCartney, Nordone and Hackett were then located. Ibid. She was Secretary of the Saor Eire Unit, INA, Oswego County, New York. *Irish People*, 11 August 1984.

46. Wray to the Editor, *Irish People*, 31 May 1984 and O'Donnell, *Special Category*, I, pp. 490–92.

47. Sr. Clarke, 'Noel Gibson', Clarke Papers (COFLA). Gibson was moved between Wormwood Scrubs, Gartree and Albany between January 1983 and August 1984. Registered letters to Albany were ignored and two of his sisters were informed they would need to re-apply for clearance to visit the new location. Maureen Lyons and Ann Woods, Gibson's Dublin based sisters, visited him in Gartree on 13–14 August 1983. Ann Woods and Aileen Gibson did so on 14–15 April 1983. Enquiries by Alastair Logan, assisted by Eddie Caughey, ascertained that the Home Office was 'unable to determine whether or not they have in fact granted consent to Miss Gibson because he has a number of sisters and until they know the Christian name they cannot be certain'. Alastair Logan to Eddie Caughey, 19 October 1984, Coiste Archive (Dublin).

48. *Report of an Inquiry … HM Prison, Maze*, p. 67.

49. Armstrong to Wilson, 27 February 1984, Private Collection (Wilson).

50. Vince Donnelly, 27 July 2006.

51. Armstrong to Wilson, 29 March 1984, Private Collection (Wilson).

52. Armstrong to Wilson, 4 June 1984, Private Collection (Wilson).

53. Armstrong to Wilson, 8 July 1984, Private Collection (Wilson).

54. Armstrong to Wilson 20 September 1984, Private Collection (Wilson).

55. Sr. Clarke, 'Noel Gibson', Clarke Papers (COFLA).

56. Lord Elton to Clare Short, 2 August 1984, Private Collection (O Mathuna).

57. 'Message from Gartree Prison', [c. March 1984] in ISM, *Newsletter*, May 1984, p. 13.

58. *AP/RN*, 29 March 1984.

59. Eddie O'Neill to Pauline [Sellars], April 1984 in ISM, *Newsletter*, May 1984, p. 10. The official view counted legal conferrals as 'visits' and held: 'Whilst at Brixton, Mr. O'Neill had from the end of May [1983] 15 visits in 1983 and six up to 8 March [1984] … He was able to converse daily with staff and enjoyed limited association with other prisoners during exercise periods'. Leon Brittan to Tony Benn, 4 June 1984, Private Collection (O Mathuna). The Governor of Brixton informed Ted Knight, Leader of Lambeth Council: 'So far as opportunities for activities within the prison are concerned Mr. O'Neill has taken daily outdoor exercise with other prisoners, has been able to attend Chapel on Sundays and has done so on the last two Sundays. He has also for the past few weeks been able to associate with other prisoners in his or their cell during the morning and afternoon'. Ted Knight to 'Peter Flynn', 15 March 1984, Private Collection (O Mathuna).

60. *Irish Post*, 7 April 1984. Supporters who were in direct contact closely followed movements of the Albany protesters. See Maryellen Cantlin to the Editor, *Irish People*, 24 March 1984. In December 1984 it was observed that Eddie O'Neill, then Frankland, 'has been in solitary almost continually since May 1983'. *Irish People*, 8 December 1984. IRA comrades were aware that he had 'been down the block a few times since going to W[akefield]' and had been returned to Manchester prior to being sent to Frankland. Joe O'Connell to 'Peter' (Seamus O Mathuna), 11 July 1984, Private Collection (O Mathuna). He had been shifted on a 'lie down' from Wakefield to Durham on 25 July 1984. *FRFI*, October 1984.

61. Eddie O'Neill, 1 February 2008.

62. *Irish News*, 18 April 1984.

63. *Irish News*, 18 April 1984.

64. *Irish News*, 10 April 1984.

65. Vince Donnelly [March 1984] to Dale in ISM, *Newsletter*, May 1984, p. 9. Donnelly was moved under Rule 43 to Winson Green on 13 June. Lord Elton to Claire Short, 2 August 1984, Private Collection (O Mathuna).

66. Joe O'Connell to Tania [Johnson], [March 1984] in ISM, *Newsletter*, May 1984, p. 8.

67. Joe O'Connell to 'Peter' (Seamus O Mathuna), 5 June 1984, Private Collection (O Mathuna). *FRFI* was withheld from Parkhurst prisoners for a period in the late summer of 1984. *FRFI*, September 1984, p. 5.

68. Tania Johnson to Ronnie McCartney, 9 March 1984, Coiste Archive (Dublin).

69. Ronnie McCartney to Denise Cregan and Brendan [Golden], 10 March 1984, Coiste Archive (Dublin).

70. Denise Cregan to Ronnie McCartney, 10 April 1984, Coiste Archive (Dublin).

71. Gerry Cunningham to Jim McDonald, 2 January 1984, Private Collection (McDonald). Cunnigham recognized that the ISM 'seems to be doing a lot of work on the prisoners transfer and on the "Irish" question/ answer in general. What's their strength'.

72. Gerry Cunningham to Jim McDonald, 23 May 1984, Private Collection (McDonald).

73. *Irish Times*, 19 March 1984.

74. *Irish People*, 9 and 16 October and 18 December 1982. In March 1975 a British journalist leaked Quinn's name as a suspect to Unionist politician Lord Brookeborough. The Fermanagh magnate publicly asserted that Quinn had been arrested in 'the Irish Republic' and that Scotland Yard had not disputed his identification. See *Guardian*, 10 March 1975.

75. *Irish People*, 8 October 1983. See also *Guardian*, 10 March 1975, Huntley, *Bomb Squad*, p. 185 and *Lost Lives*, p. 521.

76. 'Stop Extradition of William Quinn!' in *Irish People*, 28 November 1981 and *Irish People*, 14 April 1984. See also Liam Quinn to the Editor, *Irish People*, 28 April 1984.

77. *Guardian*, 1 September 1982.

78. *Guardian*, 1 September 1982.

79. *FRFI*, April 1982, p. 16.

80. Farrell, *Sheltering the fugitive?*, p. 88.

81. Jim Cullen, 30 March 2015.

82. *Irish People*, 8 October 1983, *Irish Echo*, 23 June 1984 and *Chicago Tribune*, 21 October 1986. Seamus Gibney of INA opened the rally at the United Irish Cultural Center after music from the Pearse and Connolly Fife and Drum Band. The Free Bill Quinn Committee was chaired by Connie Malone. Fr. Paul Devine of the San Francisco Apostolate of the Sea attended. Ibid. Sheriff Hennessy was described as 'the reluctant keeper' of Quinn. *Irish Echo*, 23 June 1984.

83. See 'Harrison-Falvey Defense Committee Fund Raising Dance for the Legal Expenses of Those Who Are Accused of Attempting to Assist Ireland's Freedom Fighters' in *Irish World*, 23 October 1982. The Committee was named in honour of George Harrison and Tom Falvey, two of the 'Brooklyn Five' (aka 'IRA Five') acquitted of gunrunning in November 1982. *Irish World*, 23 and 30 October 1982. The 1981 arrest of Megahey on suspicion of attempting to procure 'Redeye' surface-to-air missiles, evidently spurred a crackdown in the radical Irish community in Southampton, England, where the Belfast man had resided until subjected to an Exclusion Order. *Irish People*, 18 September 1982.

84. *Irish News*, 2 March 1982.

85. *Irish Times*, 19 March 1984.

86. Cited in Kevin Burke, 'Extradition, The ultimate collaboration' in *Irish People*, 21 January 1984. Burke was the nom de plume of *AP/RN* editor and Sinn Féin Ard Comhairle member Mick Timothy. Born in Manchester, Timothy had IRA experience and died in Kildare on 26 January 1985. *FRFI*, March 1985, p. 13 and *Tírghrá*, p. 269.

87. *Irish Times*, 19 March 1984 and *FRFI*, September 1982, p. 13.

88. Cited in *Irish Times*, 19 March 1984. The RUC claimed that McGlinchey was present when Hester McMullen died during a 28 March 1977 IRA attack on her RUC Reserve son in Toomebridge, Antrim. The Derry man was then in the IRA. Ibid and *Lost Lives*, p. 712. See also Joe Joyce and Peter Murtagh, *The Boss, Charles J Haughey in Government* (Dublin, 1983), pp. 204–5.

89. Farrell, *Sheltering the fugitive?* , p. 94 and *Guardian*, 11 February 1994.

90. Holland and McDonald, *Deadly Divisions*, pp. 215–16. The authors linked McGlinchey's increased notoriety to the controversial 'shoot to kill' deaths of INLA men Seamus Grew and Roddy Carroll on 12 December 1984 when ambushed by the RUC's elite Headquarters Mobile Support Unit and E4A in Killylea Road, Armagh. An informer had stated that McGlinchey was traveling in their company. Ibid., p. 217 and *Lost Lives*, p. 929. McGlinchey admitted indirect involvement in the Ballykelly incident. *Sunday Tribune*, 27 November 1983. The INLA was banned in the Twenty-Six Counties on 5 January 1983. *Guardian*, 6 January 1983.

91. Farrell, *Sheltering the fugitive?*, pp. 99–100.

92. *Irish Times*, 12 October 1985.

93. *Irish Times*, 1 August 1984 and *Chicago Tribune*, 25 December 1984.

94. *Irish Times*, 1 August 1984 and *Guardian*, 6 August 1984. .

95. *Irish Times*, 19 March 1984. Shannon was accused of involvement in the IRA shooting of Sir Norman Stronge and James Stronge at Tynan Abbey, Armagh, on 21 January 1981. Norman Stronge had been a Stormont Unionist MP for Mid-Ulster from 1938–69 and Speaker of the body for many years. He headed the quasi-Masonic Royal Black Institution. James Stronge was an ex-captain in the Grenadier Guards, Orangeman and member of the RUC Reserve. The IRA attacked five days after Bernadette Devlin-McAliskey and her husband Michael McAliskey were shot during an assassination attempt in their Tyrone home. *Lost Lives*, pp. 849–50. See also *FRFI*, March/ April 1981, p. 14.

96. *Irish Times*, 11 June 1984. Justice Gibson had claimed that the RUC men who shot three IRA suspects on 11 November 1982 should be commended for bringing the deceased to 'the final court of justice'. British Ambassador Alan Goodison was 'called in' over the remarks by Minister for Foreign Affairs Peter Barry. Ibid. See also Stalker, *Stalker Affair*, pp. 38–9 and *Guardian*, 6 August 1984. Gibson was killed by the IRA on 25 April 1987. *Lost Lives*, p. 1075. Gibson dismissed the 'supergrass' evidence of Jackie Grimley against twenty-one alleged INLA members. *Irish Echo*, 28 January 1984. For overview see *Irish Times*, 26 April 1987.

97. *Irish Times*, 27 June 1984.

98. In Parkhurst SSU the IRA prisoners interpreted the Gibson judgment as an imprimatur for 'killing nationalists'. Joe O'Connell argued that the ruling undermined the SDLP support for a phased

rather than immediate British withdrawal by illustrating 'what continued British rule means for the Nationalist community'. Joe O'Connell to 'Peter' (Seamus O Mathuna), 5 June 1984, Private Collection (O Mathuna).

99. *Irish Times*, 23 February 1984.
100. *Irish Times*, 21 June 1984. O'Rourke had been arrested in relation the possession of explosives at a 'bomb factory' in Donabate, Dublin, on 28 April 1975. *Irish Times*, 17 October 1984. Jim Monaghan, a former IRA prisoner in England, was recaptured outside the courthouse during the incident in which O'Rourke escaped. See *Irish World*, 5 February 1983, *Irish People*, 24 July 1982 and Professor Charles E Rice to Senator Strom Thurmond in *Irish World*, 15 October 1983. Rice, a Law professor at Notre Dame University, Indiana, supported the asylum for both O'Rourke and Doherty. Charles E Rice to Ian Martin, Secretary General, International Secretariat, Amnesty International, 11 October 1990, Private Collection (O'Donnell).
101. Farrell, *Sheltering the fugitive?*, p. 91.
102. For engagement of the Irish American Defense Fund on behalf of O'Rourke, Liam Quinn and Colm Murphy see *Irish Echo*, 25 February 1984. Belfast solicitor Pat Finucane was the guest speaker at the 11 May 1984 annual fundraiser. See *Irish World*, 5 and 12 May 1984. For visiting conditions in MCC in late 1982 see *Irish People*, 18 December 1982.
103. See Martin Dillon, *Killer in Clowntown, Joe Doherty, the IRA and the Special Relationship* (London, 1992).
104. Cited in Farrell, *Sheltering the fugitive?*, p. 113. See also Holland, *American Connection*, pp. 173–6.
105. *Irish People*, 7 April 1984.
106. Cited in Farrell, *Sheltering the fugitive?*, p. 115.
107. Quoted in *Irish Times*, 29 December 1984. The *New York Times* and *Wall Street Journal* also rebuked Judge John E. Sprizzo. Ibid.
108. *Irish Times*, 16 January 1985.
109. *Irish Times*, 20 December 1984.
110. *Chicago Tribune*, 12 January 1985.
111. *Irish Times*, 19 May 1984. See also *Irish World*, 9 June 1984.
112. *Chicago Tribune*, 21 June 1984. See also *Irish Echo*, 28 January 1984, *Irish World*, 26 February 1983 and *New York Times*, 13 February 1983. Acquitted 'Brooklyn Five' gunrunner Michael Flannery, head of the GAA in America and veteran of the Tipperary No. 1 Brigade in the War of Independence, was Grand Marshal in 1983. He was succeeded in an Honorary capacity in March 1984 by the still jailed O'Rourke. *Irish World*, 19 February 1983 and 25 February 1984. The Irish Government was perturbed as it had lifted the ban on official state representation at the parade which they imposed to isolate Flannery. *Irish Times*, 17 October 1984.
113. *Irish World*, 5 February 1983.
114. *Irish Times*, 17 April 1984. See also *Irish Echo*, 5 May 1984.
115. *Sunday Press*, 26 August 1984. Reports of the reclassification of Anne Maguire as Category B in July 1983 were related to the 'Panorama' documentary on Giuseppe Conlon. As normal, the Home Office declined to comment on its reasoning. *Irish News*, 7 July 1983.
116. *Irish News*, 7 July 1983.
117. AP/RN, 13 December 1984.
118. *Irish Times*, 23 February 1985. Anne Maguire claimed: 'I lost a terrible lot. I have suffered, losing my children, my boys. My little girl was only 9. She is 19 now. As any mother I used to dream about the future for my children – what they would be. They took all that away'. Ibid.
119. Joe O'Connell to 'Peter' (Seamus O Mathuna), 28 February [1985], Private Collection (O Mathuna).
120. See *Irish Echo*, 17 March and 28 April 1984. Biaggi chaired the Ad Hoc Congressional Committee for Irish Affairs which united 102 members on a bi-partisan basis. He claimed to have 'worked to elevate the Irish issue as both a political and a foreign policy issue'. See Mario Biaggi to the Editor, *Irish World*, 21 January 1984. He was an early advocate of a US visa for Gerry Adams. *Irish World*, 23 June 1984. Judge Basil Kelly, an ex-Unionist MP presiding over a juryless Diplock court in Belfast, sentenced thirty-eight people to jail terms for IRA activities on the evidence of informer Christopher Black. *FRFI*, September 1983.
121. *Irish Times*, 27 April 1984. See also *Irish Echo*, 5 May 1984.
122. *Irish World*, 24 March 1984.
123. Sr. Clarke, 'Paul Kavanagh', Clarke Papers (COFLA).
124. *Daily Telegraph*, 25 June 1984.
125. *Times*, 8 March 1985.
126. Channel Four, 'Trial and Error' (Danny McNamee).
127. *Times*, 11 March 1985.
128. Channel Four, 'Trial and Error' (Danny McNamee).
129. Tommy Quigley, 14 April 2008 and Sr. Clarke, 'Tommy Quigley', Clarke Papers (COFLA).

130. 'Prison Picket', May 1984 Flyer, Private Collection (O'Mathuna). See also ISM, *Newsletter*, February 1984, p. 27.
131. Geraldine Bailey, 14 April 2008.
132. *Sunday Tribune*, 27 May 1984.
133. Geraldine Bailey, 14 April 2008.
134. Geraldine Bailey quoted in *FRFI*, October 1987, p. 13.
135. *Sunday Tribune*, 27 May 1984. See also *Troops Out*, Vol. 7, No. 10, August/ September 1984, p. 6 and Clarke, *No faith*, pp. 100–101. Sean Bailey, first husband of Geraldine Bailey (nee McGranaghan), had been mortally wounded on Nansen Street on 12 February 1976 in a premature explosion. The operation was one of several planned to mark the death on hunger strike of Frank Stagg in Wakefield Prison. He lived at Earlscourt Street and was a member of the 2nd Battalion, Belfast Brigade, IRA. The couple married on 10 March 1973 and he was twenty-three at the time of his death. *Belfast Graves*, p. 139 and *Lost Lives*, p. 625. South London Irish Solidarity Committee picketed Brixton on 12 May 1984 when police reconsidered making arrests for 'obstruction'. Pauline Sellars to Tommy Quigley, 22 May 1984, Private Collection (O Mathuna).
136. *Irish Echo*, 5 May 1984.
137. Ursula Hayes, June 2008.
138. *Irish News*, 28 May 1984.
139. *Irish News*, 28 May 1984. See also *FRFI*, June 1984, p. 16.
140. *Irish News*, 28 May 1984. A letter from Paul Norney was widely published in May 1984. According to Billy Armstrong: 'every paper put Paul N[orney's] letter in their editions except "our own" and we are not pleased!' Armstrong to Wilson, 4 June 1984, Private Collection (Wilson). Another letter appeared in late October 1984 in *AP/RN*. Armstrong to Wilson, 14 February 1985, Private Collection (Wilson).
141. Simpson, *Murder madness*, p. 215.
142. *Troops Out*, Vol. 7, No. 10, August/ September 1984, p. 12.
143. Michael Holden, 23 June 2008.
144. Eddie O'Neill, 2 February 2008.
145. Eddie O'Neill, 2 February 2008.
146. Eddie O'Neill, 2 February 2008.
147. Eddie O'Neill, 7 March 2008.
148. Eddie O'Neill, 2 February 2008.
149. Eddie O'Neill, 7 March 2008.
150. Eddie O'Neill, 2 February 2008. See also *Report on the work of the Prison Department, 1983*, p. 21.
151. *Daily Telegraph*, 10 November 1982. The Home Office has resiled from a 1982 commitment to overhaul the *Prison Rules* in a systematic and comprehensive fashion citing resource problems within the Prisons Department. Reformers suspected that the main problem was 'a reluctance to open up the debate on minimum standards and legally enforceable rights for prisoners'. Plotnikoff, *Prison Rules*, p. 7. For legal analysis of *Campbell and Fell* see *Prior Report*, II, Appendix 15, pp. 133–6.
152. *Irish Times*, 29 June 1984.
153. *Irish Post*, 3 September 1983.
154. See Louis Blom-Cooper to the Editor, *Times*, 21 October 1981.
155. Cited in Plotnikoff, *Prison Rules*, p. 13.
156. *Troops Out*, Vol. 7, No. 10, August/ September 1984, p. 15.
157. *Irish Times*, 29 June 1984.
158. *Guardian*, 29 June 1984. Fr. Ray Murray, who had co-authored a pamphlet on the case with Fr. Denis Faul, commented that the highlighting of prisoners rights applied 'to Portlaoise as much as anywhere else'. *Irish Press*, 29 June 1984.
159. Cited in *Prior Report*, II, p. 137.
160. R[ichard] Glenholmes to the Editor, *Irish Post*, 25 August 1984. See also *Irish Post*, 7 and 14 July 1984.
161. Eddie Byrne to the Editor, *Irish People*, 28 July 1984.
162. Eddie Byrne to 'To whom it may concern', 21 July 1984, Private Collection (O Mahuna).
163. Joe O'Connell to 'Peter' (Seamus O Mathuna), 19 August 1984, Private Collection (O Mathuna). In May 1984 the main prison held John McCluskey, Pat 'Tipp' Guilfoyle, Stevie Nordone, Tony Clark, James 'Punter' Bennett and John McComb. John McCluskey to Jim McDonald, 30 May 1984, Private Collection (McDonald).
164. *Two years on from Albany*, [pp. 6].
165. 'Irish Political Prisoners in Britain', flyer, Private Collection (McDonnell).
166. 'Irish Political Prisoners in Britain', flyer, Private Collection (McDonnell). Five Ulster-born soldiers of the total eighty declined to be moved to England to serve their terms of imprisonment. *The Irish Prisoner*, No. 4 [1985].
167. *Lost Lives*, p. 993.

168. *Guardian*, 14 August 1984.
169. Cited in London Strategic Policy Unit, *Police monitoring and research group, Briefing paper no. 5, Policing the Irish community*, pamphlet (London, 1988), p. 13. The South London Irish Solidarity Movement/ RCG sent a delegation to the Anti-Internment weekend in Belfast. [Seamus O Mathuna] to Joe [O'Connell], 15 August 1984, Private Collection (O Mathuna).
170. *AP/RN*, 25 August 1988.
171. *Irish World*, 29 September 1984. See also *Irish People*, 27 July 1985.
172. *Irish Times*, 20 February 1985. Thatcher had signaled her intention to criticize INA and similar bodies which the British Government contended had channeled over $4 million to Irish republicans. This stance was supported by Labour Opposition leader Neil Kinnock. Ibid. Vince Donnelly regarded the Labour Party as 'neo-Tory' in character. Vince Donnelly to Terry, 27 September 1984, Private Collection (O Mathuna).
173. *Sunday Press*, 26 August 1984. See also O'Donnell, *Special Category*, I, pp. 304–6.
174. *Daily Telegraph*, 22 August 1984.
175. Renwick, 16 November 2007.
176. *The case of the Birmingham 6*, TOM poster magazine (London, 1986). Frank Johnson, an Irish man jailed for life in 1976 for murdering John Sheridan, was regarded as innocent by many IRA prisoners. Sheridan was killed in his East End, London shop, where Johnson worked. Ex-solider David Smart, who admitted throwing petrol on Sheridan, and police agent Jack Tierney, implicated Johnson. Tierney was a known agent provocateur who had attempted to prosecute Angry Brigade members in the early 1970s. Press created stories of an 'IRA angle' apparently stemmed from the Irish background of most of those concerned, although this was illusory. A Free Frank Johnson Campaign was supported by the RCG. *FRFI*, April/ May 1993, p. 13.
177. Gerry Cunningham to Jim McDonald, 13 September 1984, Private Collection (McDonald).
178. *HC Deb 15 May 1984, vol. 60, cc 216.*
179. *Irish World*, 6 October 1984.
180. *Irish World*, 6 October 1984. The bi-partisan nature of pro-IRA support in America was signaled in October 1984 when New York Longshoreman union leader Teddy Gleason, who had played a role in obtaining the Cypriot arms ship *Claudia* for the IRA in 1974, backed the Reagan Presidency. *Irish World*, 13 October 1984. RUC claims that they had captured 'the IRA's last Soviet-made rocket launcher [i.e. RPG7]' in May 1981 appeared premature. *Chicago Tribune*, 27 May 1981. It was later claimed that the IRA retained one damaged RPG and 'an M60 machinegun'. *Guardian*, 21 February 1985.
181. The men tried in connection with the *Marita Ann* were Martin Ferris, John Crawley, Gavin Mortimer, John McCarthy and Michael Browne. *Irish Times*, 1 July 1987 and *Chicago Tribune*, 1 October 1983. The irony that the Tanaiste had just unveiled a new memorial to 1916 republican gunrunner Roger Casement near Banna Strand, Kerry, inspired a bitter anti-IRA editorial in Ireland's paper of record. *Irish Times*, 1 October 1984. Oisin Kelly's statue had been completed in 1971 and stored by the Office of Public Works for thirteen years until it was deemed politically appropriate to have it dedicated. *Irish Times*, 29 December 2007. For US indictments of *Valhalla* grouping see *Irish Times*, 18 April 1986. On 30 June 1987 Judge Joseph Tauro sentenced Joseph Murray to ten years and both Robert Anderson and Pat Nee to four years. *Irish Times*, 1 July 1987.
182. *Sunday Times*, 21 July 1996.
183. Cited in *AP/RN*, 13 December 1984. Elton was addressing the AGM of the Boards of Visitors. Ibid. For prison correspondence censorship debate see *Guardian*, 23 September 1982.
184. William Kerr to Douglas Hurd, 13 September 1984 in *Irish News*, 29 August 2014.
185. Paul Norney and Ronnie McCartney to the Editor, *Andersonstown News*, 20 October 1984.
186. Ronnie McCartney to Denise Cregan and Brendan [Golden], 10 March 1984, Coiste Archive (Dublin).
187. Armstrong to Wilson 20 September 1984, Private Collection (Wilson).
188. Armstrong to Wilson, 24 October 1984, Private Collection (Wilson).
189. *Times*, 11 June 1986.
190. *Observer*, 14 October 1984.
191. *Irish Press*, 15 October 1984.
192. Cited in Adams, *Hope and History*, p. 32. Adams recalled: 'Given the consequences of Mrs Thatcher's policy in Ireland, the Brighton operation was enormously popular among Irish nationalists and republicans'. Ibid. For security responses see Fleming and Miller, *Scotland Yard*, pp. 145–7.
193. *AP/RN*, 11 October 2001.
194. *Irish Press*, 15 October 1984.
195. *HC Deb 22 October 1984 vol 65 cc440.*
196. Ian Gilmour, *Dancing with Dogma, Britain Under Thatcher* (London, 1992), p. 256.
197. Margaret Thatcher, *The Downing Street Years* (New York, 1993), p. 382.
198. *Irish Press*, 15 October 1984. The Blackpool Conservative Party convention of 1983 was not, in any event, attacked by the IRA. See *Irish Echo*, 20 October 1984.

199. *Times*, 11 June 1986.

200. *Times*, 27 June 1986. Police claimed that Magee had used the name 'Roy Walsh' in 1983, sixteen months before the Brighton attack. Ibid. The high level of cooperation between the Gardai and Scotland Yard was indicated when a British police source claimed in the aftermath of Brighton that the timing devices used in England were 'identical' in design to a cache found in Lusk, Dublin, in late September. *Irish Press*, 15 October 1984. The 'Pope' and other IRA men active in England in the 1970s and 1980s were named in the World in Action *Who bombed Birmingham?* documentary broadcast on Granada TV on 28 March 1990. See *Guardian*, 29 March 1990. Dick Timmins, a leading IRA activist in England during the 'S-Plan' bombing campaign of 1939–40 was convicted at his Swansea trial as 'Richard Cohen' aka 'Michael Farrell'. Timmins was the IRA's London O/C and escaped from Leyhill Prison in March 1947. *The People*, 14 September and 26 October 1952. See also *Gaelic American*, 18 January and 7 June 1947. When discussing the professional attributes of the twenty-five top counter insurgents and four Special Forces aircrew killed on 2 June 1994 in a Chinook helicopter crash at Mull of Kintyre, only Assistant Chief Constable Brian Fitzsimmons received a specific accolade. As head of the RUC Special Branch, Fitzsimmons was credited with being 'responsible for tracking down the Brighton bomber Patrick Magee'. Steuart Campbell, *Chinook crash, The crash of RAF Chinook helicopter ZD576 on the Mull of Kintyre* (Barnsley, 2004), pp. 1–2.

201. Bishop and Mallie, *Provisional IRA*, p. 340.

202. Roy Walsh, 9 March 2008.

203. *Guardian*, 11 January 1981.

204. *Guardian*, 10 January 1981.

205. *Guardian*, 12 June 1986. Magee lost most of his right index finger during the gun attack. The UDA made an unrealistic claim that the intended target was Sinn Féin President Ruairi O'Bradaigh. *Irish Times*, 13 June 1986 and *FRFI*, January 1982.

206. *Irish Press*, 15 October 1984.

207. *Last Post*, p. 44.

208. See *Irish News*, 27 December 2013.

209. Manus Canning to the Editor, *Irish Echo*, 10 April 1984. Canning was related by marriage to Martin McGuinness.

210. *Irish Press*, 15 October 1984.

211. *Irish News*, 31 August 2000.

212. Sir Robert Armstrong quoted in BBC News Northern Ireland website, 3 January 2014.

213. Adams, *Hope and History*, p. 31.

214. Charles Powell quoted in BBC News Northern Ireland website, 3 January 2014.

215. Margaret Thatcher quoted in BBC News Northern Ireland website, 3 January 2014.

216. *Irish Press*, 20 November 1984. See also *AP/RN*, 22 November 1984.

217. *Irish People*, 17 November 1984. Carron adopted a much lower profile following his 19 December 1985 arrest in relation to arms charges near Belcoo, Fermanagh. *Irish Times*, 1 and 7 January 1986. He was bailed from Crumlin Road Prison after twenty-seven days in custody and was reported to be 'on the run' on 26 January 1986. *Guardian*, 27 January 1986.

218. *Irish People*, 8 December 1984.

219. Adams, *Hope and History*, p. 19.

220. Adams, *Hope and History*, pp. 21–22.

221. Adams, *Hope and History*, p. 24.

222. Adams, *Hope and History*, p. 26.

223. *Tirghra*, p. 275.

224. Mary McLaughlin, 'A long and painful road', Cunamh Website, 20 January 2013.

225. See *The Rosses Martyrs*, pamphlet, new edition (2006).

226. Clare Short to Eddie Caughey, 30 December 1983, Private Collection (Caughey). See also *FRFI*, September 1983, p. 14.

227. Brian Keenan to 'Peter Flynn' (Seamus O Mathuna), 1 September 1983, Private Collection (O Mathuna).

228. *AP/RN*, 13 December 1984. Practices concerning the restoration to a prisoner of lost remission, formerly guided by CI 23/1974 were 'cancelled' once superseded in 1976 by CI 58/ 1976. Once a prisoner had enjoyed a period of at least nine months without committing an offence 'for which forfeiture of remission was awarded', they could apply for its restoration. The many caveats dictated that the prisoner's 'recent institutional behaviour has shown a significant improvement, indicative of a genuine change of attitude' and that its restoration would not 'be prejudicial to discipline in the prison'. Those punished for 'mutiny or assault on staff' were deemed to require 'especially good reasons for restoration' which included consideration of whether there was a 'serious risk of deterioration if improvement is not recognised'. *Prior Report*, II, p. 138.

229. Jim McDonald, 2 July 2008.
230. *Irish Times*, 18 October 1984.
231. John McCluskey to Jim McDonald, 30 May 1984, Private Collection (McDonald).
232. John McCluskey, 3 August 2007.
233. *Two years on from Albany*, p. 13.
234. Tony Sheridan to 'Dear comrades', n.d. [October 1984], Private Collection (O Mathuna). See also *The Miner*, 31 August 1984. The ISM noted that former RUC Chief Constable Sir Kenneth Newman, 1976–1979, was head of the Metropolitan Police since October 1982. ISM, 'Irish Solidarity Weekend', 13–14 October 1984, Flyer.
235. Malcolm Pitt cited in David Reed and Olivia Adamson, *Miners Strike, 1984–1985, People versus the state* (London, 1985), p. 65. See also *FRFI*, 'Special Pullout', December 1984.
236. Tommy Quigley to Aine [Fury], 'Saturday' [c. October 1984], Private Collection (O Mathuna).
237. See Laurence McKeown, 'H-Block solidarity with the miners' in Reed and Adamson, *Miners Strike*, p. 121. See also Ibid., pp. 117–121.
238. McKeown, 'H-Block solidarity' in Reed and Adamson, *Miners Strike*, p. 118.
239. John McCluskey cited in Reed and Adamson, *Miners Strike*, p. 62.
240. David Reed, *Ireland: The key to the British Revolution* (London, 1984). Joe O'Connell and other IRA prisoners in Parkhurst regarded Yaffe's book as 'very good'. Joe O'Connell to [Seamus O Mathuna], 5 June 1984, Private Collection (O Mathuna). See also *IRIS*, No 10, July 1985 and David Reed to the Editor, 22 July 1985 in *FRFI*, September 1985.
241. Irish Solidarity Movement, Press Statement, 13–14 October [1984], Private Collection (O Mathuna).
242. Alf Lomas to Gerald Johnson, 24 September 1984, Private Collection (O Mathuna).
243. O Mathuna to O'Donnell, 14 April 2014, Private Collection (O'Donnell).
244. Margaret Thatcher cited in Reed and Adamson, *Miners Strike*, p. 66.
245. *AP/RN*, 13 December 1984. The IRA PRO in Wormwood Scrubs wrote from solitary confinement to encourage pro-ANC pickets in London. See *FRFI*, November-December 1982, p. 3. For Quigley in London see *FRFI*, November/ December 1984, p. 16. Pheto belonged to the Black Consciousness Movement of Azania and contributed to the 5 October 1985 'Freedom for the Irish! Freedom for us all!' themed conference in Conway Hall, London. See *FRFI*, October/ November 1985, p. 16.
246. *FRFI*, November/ December 1984, p. 4.
247. *AP/RN*, 13 December 1984. See also Sr. Clarke, 'John McCluskey', Clarke Papers (COFLA).
248. Joe O'Connell to 'Peter' (Seamus O Mathuna), 15 November 1984, Private Collection (O Mathuna).
249. Gerry Cunningham to Eddie Caughey, 20 November 1984, Private Collection (Siobhan Maguire).
250. Eddie Caughey, 16 September 2008.
251. Eddie Caughey to Gerry Cunningham, 26 November 1984, Private Collection (Siobhan Maguire).
252. Caughey to Cunningham, 26 November 1984, Private Collection (Siobhan Maguire).
253. Caughey to Cunningham, 26 November 1984, Private Collection (Siobhan Maguire). Eddie and Rosie Caughey were the 'International Nominees' honoured by Sinn Féin in 2009. See *Le Cheile, Testimonial Dinner, Saturday 21ˢᵗ February 2009*, Booklet, Dublin.
254. Eddie Caughey to Gerry Cunningham, 26 November 1984, Private Collection (Siobhan Maguire).
255. Cunningham to Caughey, 20 November 1984, Private Collection (Siobhan Maguire).
256. Information of Jim MacDonald, 14 December 2014.
257. See *The Irish Prisoner*, No. 4 [1985].
258. *The Irish Prisoner*, No. 1 [1985].
259. *The Irish Prisoner*, No. 8 [1986]. Cunningham, when in Long Lartin in 1986, wrote to encourage the use of the Irish language. Ibid.
260. Brendan Dowd to the Editor, *AP/RN*, 7 October 1984.
261. *Sunday Mirror*, 18 November 1984.
262. *Lost Lives*, p. 1000 and *FRFI*, January 1985, p. 16.
263. Cited in Dillon, *Stone Cold*, p. 184. See also Ibid., Chapter Seven and Michael Stone, *None shall divide us* (Wales, 2003), pp. 66–70.
264. Colin Crawford, *Inside the UDA, Volunteers and violence* (London, 2003), p. 147.
265. Armstrong to Wilson, 28 November 1984, Private Collection (Wilson) and 'Sinn Féin, Roll of Honour, 1969–2012' in Sinn Féin, *Peter Corrigan, 1935–1982*, pamphlet (2012). It was noted that 'Sinn Féin criticized a government decision not to allow compassionate parole to a close relative [Martin Brady], said to have spent 11 years in English jails, to attend the funeral'. *Lost Lives*, p. 1000. From Long Lartin Martin Brady acknowledged sympathy cards from overseas well-wishers in correspondence with a Canadian namesake. See John Brady to the Editor, *Irish People*, 23 March 1985.
266. Martin Brady, 10 April 2008.
267. See *Guardian*, 5 June 1995, Nicholas Davies, *Ten Thirty-Three*, p. 63 and Mansfield, *Memoirs*, pp. 68–9.

268. *Times*, 4 June 1994.
269. *Times*, 4 June 1994.
270. *Times*, 20 September 1983.
271. *Times*, 20 September 1983.
272. *Times*, 8 November 1983. See also *Times*, 17 February 1984.
273. *Times*, 17 April 1984.
274. Cited in *Times*, 17 April 1984.
275. *Times*, 17 April 1984. It was apparently planned that Bettaney would spend five years in isolation but this was rescinded by May 1985. The official explanation linked the liberalization of his regime to pay related labour disputes, although it occurred shortly following his alleged interaction with the Security Commission investigating the security services. *Times*, 22 January and 22 May 1985. He was released from Swaleside Prison, Kent, in May 1998. *Times*, 14 May 1998. See also *Spartacist*, June 1984, pp. 2, 10.
276. Paul Holmes, April 2011.
277. Armstrong to Wilson, 1 April 1987, Private Collection (Wilson).
278. See Wallace Papers, Private Collection (Wallace).
279. Paul Foot, *Who framed Colin Wallace?* (London, 1989), pp. 20–22.
280. Owen Rodgers, 30 March 2015.
281. *Guardian*, 12 November 1984.
282. *Guardian*, 13 November 1984.
283. *Daily Mirror*, 12 December 1984.
284. *Irish Times*, 12 November 1984.
285. *Guardian*, 13 November 1984. See also *FRFI*, January 1985, p. 16.
286. *Irish Times*, 12 November 1984.
287. *Irish Echo*, 17 November 1984.
288. *Irish Echo*, 17 November 1984. See also 'The sisters of hate' in *Daily Mirror*, 12 December 1984.
289. *Irish News*, 22 December 1984.
290. *Irish Times*, 15 December 1984 and *FRFI*, February 1985, p. 13.
291. *South London Irish Solidarity Committee*, Newsletter, No. 5 [1983].
292. *AP/RN*, 13 December 1984. Male republican prisoners were being held in Long Kesh (H-Block and 'cages'), Magilligan and Portlaoise. In the USA seven men were held in Oxford, Wisconsin (Gabe Megahey); Lake Placid, New York (Eamonn Meehan); Danbury Correctional Centre, Connecticut (Colm Meehan, Andy Duggan and Barney McKeown); San Francisco (Liam Quinn) and Manhattan Correction Centre (Joe Doherty). Ibid.
293. Denise Cregan and Tom Hartley to Marie Moore, 19 December 1984, Coiste Archives (Dublin).
294. *Irish Times*, 17 and 18 December 1984. The *Irish Times* was incorrect in stating 'MPs met two convicted bombers'. Mac Lochlainn was neither charged nor convicted of carrying out bombings. *Irish Times*, 17 December 1984.
295. *AP/RN*, 13 December 1984.
296. *Irish Times*, 15 October 1984. Adams noted that persons, such as he, might be jailed or targeted for assassination arising from the Brighton attack. Ibid.
297. *Two years on from Albany*, [p. 7.] and *FRFI*, June 1984, p. 13.
298. Interview of Mairin Higgins by Siobhan Maguire, London, 20 April 2011.

Bibliography

Interviews

Armstrong, Billy, Belfast, 13 October 2007 and 13 April 2008
Armstrong, Patsy, Belfast, 14 April 2008
Ashe, Jimmy, London, 2 July 2008
Baker, Liam, Belfast, 8 March 2008
Brady, Martin, Belfast, 12 April 2008
Breathnach, Diarmuid, Dublin, 6 September 2008[1]
Butler, Eddie, Limerick, 21 December 2007
Campbell, Mary and Terry, Tyrone, 2008[2]
Caughey, Eddie, Birmingham, 16 September 2008[3]
Clarke, Tony, Belfast, 9 March 2008
Coughlan, Martin, Dublin 24 August 2006
Cunningham, Gerry, Dublin, 25 September 2007
Cunningham, Michael, Strabane, 2 August 2007
Cunningham, Busty, Strabane, 2 August 2007
Doherty, Winnie, Donegal, 7 June 2008
Doherty, Hugh, Donegal, 23 June 2006 and 7 June 2008
Donnelly, Vince, Dublin, 27 July 2006
George, Patricia, Belfast, 15 May 2009
Gibson, Noel, Dublin, 24 August 2006 and Limerick, 22 August 2008
Gillespie, Ann and Eileen, Donegal, 7 June 2008
Grealy, Aine, New York, 13 November 2005
Hackett, Pat, Limerick, 21 December 2007
Harrison, George, New York, 12 June 2001
Hayes, Ursula, London, June 2008[4]
Higgins, Mairin, London, 20 April 2011[5]
Holden, Michael, Luton, 23 June 2008[6] and 14 March 2009
Kaye, Jackie, London, 16 November 2007
Kelly, Jimmy, Belfast, 13 October 2007
Kilroy, Jack, Cleveland, 3 July 2014
Kinsella, Sean, Clones, 3 August 2007
Keenan, Brian, Louth, 26 May 2007
Lawless, Gerry, London, 1 July 2008
Madigan, Tony, Dublin, 7 March 2008

Maguire, Maureen, Dublin, 19 July 2007 and 1 March 2008
Maguire, Chris, London, 6 July 2008
Mac Lochlainn, Padraig, Donegal, 8 June 2008
McCartney, Ronnie, Belfast, 12 April 2008
McCluskey, John, Donegal, 2 August 2007
McComb, John, Belfast, 9 March 2008 and 5 August 2008
McDonald, Jim, London, 2 July 2008
McFadden, Con, Dublin, 4 November 2006
Mealy, Jerry, Luton, 14 March 2009
Monaghan, Jim, Dublin, 22 September 2006
Mulryan, Andy, Dublin, 17 November 2008
Mullen, Nick, London, 11 March 2012
Murphy, Seamus, Wicklow, 8 January 2005
Norney, Paul, Belfast, 9 March 2008
O'Connell, Joe, Donegal, 7 June 2008
O'Donnell, Joe, Belfast, 15 May 2009
O'Donnell, Pat, Tipperary, 3 March 2009
O Duil, Piaras, Dublin, 20 July 2007 and 6 July 2011
O'Dwyer, Ella, Dublin, 22 September 2006
O'Neill, Eddie, Dublin, 23 June 2006 and 19 July 2007; Clones, 3 August
2007; Belfast, 8 March 2008
O'Riordain, Enda, Tipperary, 5 February 2008
O'Shea, Deirdre, Dublin, 2 October 2008
Panaro, Jim, Florida, 11 November 2009
Payne, Jenny, London, 2 July 2008
Pierce, Gareth, London, 2 July 2008
Regan, Matt, Philadelphia, 19 June 2014
Renwick, Aly, London, 16 November 2007
Ryan, Mick, Dublin, 23 July 2007
Ryan, Paddy, Dublin, 26 August 2009
Smyth, Sean, Belfast, 2 June 2009
Tuite, Gerry, Dublin, 11 September 2009
Walker, Johnny, Donegal, 7 June 2008
Walsh, Mary, Belfast, 9 March 2008
Walsh, Roy, Belfast 9 March 2008
Young, Gerry, Belfast, 8 March 2008

NOTES

[1] Interviewed by Siobhan Maguire.
[2] Interviewed by Eddie O'Neill.
[3] Interviewed by Siobhan Maguire.
[4] Interviewed by Eddie O'Neill
[5] Interviewed by Siobhan Maguire
[6] Interviewed by Eddie O'Neill.

Newspapers and periodicals

An Phoblacht
An Phoblacht/ Republican News
Belfast Bulletin
Belfast Telegraph
British Medical Journal
Camden New Journal
Captive Voice, An Glor Gafa
Chicago Tribune
Daily Telegraph
Derry Journal
Fight Imperialism! Fight Racism!
Free Ireland, Newspaper of the Anti-Internment League
Gaelic American
Guardian
Hands off Ireland!
Hibernia
Irish Democrat
Irish Echo
Irish Examiner
Irish Independent
Irish News
Irish People
Irish Political Review
Irish Post
Irish Press
IRIS
Irish Republican Information Service
Irish Times
Irish Warrior, The Republican Voice of Freedom
Irish Voice
Irish World
Left Republican Review

Legal Action
Longford Leader
Mail on Sunday
Newsline
New Society
New Statesman
New York Times
PAC Bulletin
PAC News
Red Weekly
Republican News
Rosc Catha
Saoirse
Sinn Féin Glasgow Republican News
Socialist Challenge
Socialist Worker
Spartacist
Sun
Sunday Times
Teoiric, Theoretical & Discussion Journal of Sinn Féin the Worker's Party
The Irish Prisoner
The Irish Worker, Bulletin of Clann na hÉireann
The Leveller
The Observer
Times
Troops Out
United Irishman
Western People
Wolfe Tone Annual
Yorkshire Post

Media

Heist, part three, RTE 2, 29 July 2008
Remember our Volunteers Committee 2008, DVD, (Belfast, 2008)
Fullerton, documentary, TG4, 5 January 2010
Trial and Error (Danny McNamee), Channel Four, 1997

Archives and Libraries

Cardinal O Fiaich Library, Armagh
Hesburgh Library, University of Notre Dame, Indiana
Linen Hall Library, Belfast
National Archives, Dublin
National Archives, London
National Library of Ireland, Dublin
Public Record Office of Northern Ireland, Belfast
Tamiment Library, New York University
University of Limerick Library, Limerick
Sinn Féin/ Coiste na Iarchimini Archive, Dublin

Printed works

Adams, Gerry, *Peace in Ireland? A broad analysis of the present situation* (Belfast, 1976)
Adams, Gerry, *Before the Dawn, An autobiography* (Kerry, 1996)
Adams, James, *The financing of terror*, (New York, 1986)
A dossier concerning the treatment of prisoners during and after the disturbance at Albany prison in September 1976 (London, [1977])
Amphlett Micklewright, FH 'The quality of mercy' in *Labour Monthly*, August 1976, pp. 362–6.
Ardoyne Commemoration Project, *Ardoyne: The untold truth* (Belfast, 2002)
Ballymacarrett Research Group, *Lagan Enclave, A history of conflict in the Short Strand, 1886–1997* (Belfast, 1997)
Barker, John, *Bending the Bars* (2002)
Behan, Brendan, *Confessions of an Irish rebel* (London, 1965)
Belfast Graves (Dublin, 1985)
Bell, Geoffrey, *Troublesome Business, The Labour Party and the Irish Question* (London, 1982)
Bell, Geoffrey, *British Labour and Ireland: 1969–97*, pamphlet (London, 1979)
Benn, Tony, *The Benn Diaries* (London, 1995)
Beresford, David, *Ten Men Dead, The story of the 1981 Irish hunger strike*, American Edition (New York, 1987)
Birchall, Peter, *The longest walk, The world of bomb disposal* (London, 1997)
Boda, Shari-Jayne, *Real crime, four crimes that shocked a nation* (London, 2003)
Bowyer Bell, J, *The secret army*, 3rd edition (Dublin, 1989)
Bowyer Bell, J, *IRA tactics and targets, An analysis of Tactical Aspects of the Armed Struggle, 1969–1989* (Dublin, 1990)
Boyd, Andrew, *The informers, A chilling account of the Supergrasses in Northern Ireland* (Dublin, 1984)

Boyne, Sean, *Gunrunners, The covert arms trail to Ireland* (Dublin, 2006)

Bradley, Anthony, *Requiem for a spy, The killing of Robert Nairac* (Cork, 1993)

Bradley, Gerry with Feeney, Brian, *Insider, Gerry Bradley's life in the IRA* (Dublin, 2009)

Broderick, Francie, Coleman, Gerry and Kilroy, Jack (eds.) *Where is liberty? The prosecution of Irish Republicans in the United States* (Ohio, 1995)

Bronson, Charles, *Bronson 2, More porridge than Goldilocks* (London, 2009)

Bronson, Charlie (with Steven Richards), *The Good Prison Guide* (London, 2007)

Burns, Paul, *A fighting spirit* (London, 2010)

Cadwallader, Anne, *Lethal Allies, British collusion in Ireland* (Dublin, 2013)

Callaghan, Hugh, *Cruel Fate, One man's triumph over injustice* (Dublin, 1993)

Callan, Dick, *Gartree, The story of a prison* (Leyhill, 2005)

Campbell, Brian, McKeown, Laurence and O'Hagan, Felim, *Nor meekly serve my time, The H-Block struggle, 1976–1981* (Belfast, 1994)

Campbell, Julieann, *Setting the truth free, The inside story of the Bloody Sunday Justice Campaign* (Dublin, 2012)

Campbell, Steuart, *Chinook crash, The crash of RAF Chinook helicopter ZD576 on the Mull of Kintyre* (Barnsley, 2004)

Carlen, P. and Collision, M., *Radical issues in Criminology* (London, 1980)

Christie, Stuart, *Granny made me an anarchist, General Franco, The Angry Brigade and me* (London, 2004)

Clann na hÉireann, Where we stand [c. 1975]

Clark, Alan, Diaries, *Intopolitics* (London, 2000)

Clarke, George, *Border Crossing, True stories of the RUC Special Branch, The Garda Special Branch and the IRA moles* (Dublin, 2009)

Clarke, Sr. Sarah, *No faith in the system* (Dublin, 1995)

Clarkson, Wensley, *Moody, The life and times of Britain's most notorious hitman* (Edinburgh, 2004)

Clarkson, Wensley, *Gangs of Britain* (London, 2008)

Clifford, Angela, *Military aspects of Ireland's Arms Crisis of 1969–70* (Belfast, 2009)

Clifford, Angela, 'Arms Crisis Misconceptions' in *Irish Political Review*, December 2009, pp. 17–18

Cronin, Sean, *Irish Nationalism, A history of its roots and ideology* (New York, 1980)

Committee of Public Accounts, Interim and final reports (order of the Dail of 1 December 1970) (Dublin, 1970 and 1972)

[Edmund Compton] *Report of the enquiry into allegations against the security forces of physical brutality in Northern Ireland arising out of events on the 9th August, 1971* (London, 1971)

Conlon, Gerry, *Proved Innocent, The story of Gerry Conlon and the Guildford Four* (London, 1990)

Coogan, Tim Pat, *The IRA*, new edition (London, 1995)

Coogan, Tim Pat, *On the blanket, The inside story of the IRA prisoners' "Dirty" protest* (Dublin, 1980)

Cox, Tom, *The trial of the IRA five* (Florida, 1992)

Craig, Anthony, *Crisis of confidence, Anglo-Irish relations in the Early Troubles* (Dublin, 2010)

Crawford, Colin, *Inside the UDA, Volunteers and Violence* (London, 2003)

Cronin, Sean, *The McGarrity Papers, Revelations of the Irish revolutionary movement in Ireland and America 1900–1940*, American Edition (New York, 1992)

Cronin, Sean, *Irish Nationalism, A history of its roots and ideology* (New York, 1980)

Curtis, Liz, *Ireland and the propaganda war, The British media and the 'battle of hearts and minds'* (London, 1984)

Curtis, Liz, *Nothing but the same old story, The roots of anti-Irish racism* (London, 1984)

Cunningham, Michael, *Monaghan: County of Intrigue* (Cavan, 1979)

Darragh, Sile, *'John Lennon's Dead', Stories of protest, hunger strikes & resistance* (Belfast, 2011)

De Baroid, Ciaran, *Ballymurphy and the Irish war*, revised edition (London, 2000)

Dewar, Michael, *The British Army in Northern Ireland* (London, 1985)

Dillon, Martin, *Killer in Clowntown, Joe Doherty, the IRA and the Special Relationship* (London, 1992)

Dillon, Martin, *The enemy within, The IRA's war against the British* (London, 1994)

Doherty, Joe, *Standing proud, writings from prison and the story of his struggle for freedom* (New York, [1991])

Donnelly, Donal, *Prisoner 1082, Escape from Crumlin Road, Europe's Alcatraz* (Cork, 2010)

Donoughue, Laura K, *Counter-Terrorist Law and Emergency Powers in the United Kingdom, 1922–2000* (Dublin, 2001)

Dunne, Derek and Kerrigan, Gene, *Round up the usual suspects, The Cosgrave Coalition and Nicky Kelly* (Dublin, 1984)

Edmonds, Sean, *The gun the law and the Irish people* (Kerry, 1971)

Egan, Bowes and McCormack, Vincent, *Burntollet* (London, 1969)

Ewart-Biggs, Jane, *Pay, pack and follow, Memoirs* (London, 1984)

Faul, Denis and Murray, Fr. Raymond, *Ballykelly, RUC Special Branch Interrogation Centre*, pamphlet ([1973]).

Faul, Denis and Murray, Raymond, *Long Kesh, The iniquity of internment*, pamphlet (1974)

Faul, Denis and Murray, Raymond, *The Flames of Long Kesh/ The murder of Hugh Gerard Coney, Internee*, pamphlet (Cavan, 1974)

Faul, Denis and Murray, Raymond, *The shame of Merlyn Rees, 4th year of internment in Ireland, Long Kesh, 1974–1975*, pamphlet (Cavan, 1975)

Faul, Denis and Murray, Raymond, *The British dimension, brutality, murder and legal duplicity in N. Ireland*, pamphlet (np, 1980)

Feeney, Hugh, *In the care of Her Majesty's prisons, Irish P.O.W.s in England* (Belfast, [1976])

Fianna Fáil and the IRA ([Dublin, c. 1972])

Fitzgerald, Mike, *Prisoners in revolts* (Middlesex, 1977)

Fitzgerald, Garret, *All in a life, an autobiography* (Dublin, 1991)

Flackes, W.D., and Elliott, Sydney, *Northern Ireland, A political directory, 1968–1993*, Revised edition (Belfast, 1994)

Fleming, Robert with Miller, Hugh, *Scotland Yard* (London)

Flynn, Barry, *Pawns in the game, Irish hunger strikes 1912–1981* (Cork, 2011)

Foot, Paul, *Who framed Colin Wallace?* (London, 1989)

George Plant, Irish Republican Army, Executed by firing squad in Portlaoise Prison, March 5th, 1942 (Tipperary, 1992)

Gibson, Brian, *The Birmingham bombs* (London, 1976)

Gilmour, Ian, *Dancing with Dogma, Britain under Thatcher* (London, 1992)

Hamill, Desmond, *Pig in the Middle, The Army in Northern Ireland, 1969–1984* (London, 1985)

Hanley, Brian and Millar, Scott, *The Lost revolution, The story of the Official IRA and The Workers' Party* (Dublin, 2009)

Hannigan, Dave, *Terence MacSwiney, The hunger strike that rocked an empire* (Dublin, 2010)

Harnden, Toby, *'Bandit Country', The IRA & South Armagh* (London, 1999)

Hart, Mathew, *The Irish game, A true story of crime and art* (London, 2004)

Hattersley, Roy, *Fifty Years On, A prejudiced history of Britain since the War* (London, 1997)

Hayes, Declan (ed.) *Irish political prisoners, In prison in England* (Dublin, 1981)

Hennessey, Thomas, *Hunger Strike: Margaret Thatcher's battle with the IRA 1980–1981* (Dublin, 2014)

Herbert, Michael, *The wearing of the green, A political history of the Irish in Manchester* (London, 2001)

[Higgins, John et al], *Irish political prisoners in England, Special Category 'A', An account of prison life in England based on the experiences of Irish Republican John Higgins imprisoned between 1976 and 1979* (Dublin, 1980)

Hill, Paddy Joe (and Gerard Hunt), *Forever lost, forever gone* (London, 1995)

Hill, Paul (with Ronan Bennett), *Stolen Years, Before and after Guildford* (London, 1990)

Hillyard, Paddy, *Suspect Community, People's experience of the Prevention of Terrorism Act in Britain* (London, 1993)

Holland, Jack and McDonald, Henry, *INLA, Deadly divisions* (Dublin, 1994)

Home Office Statement on the Background, Circumstances and Action Subsequently Taken relative to the Disturbance in D Wing at HM Prison Wormwood Scrubs on 31ˢᵗ August 1979; Together with the Report of an Inquiry by the Regional Director of South East Region of the Prison Department (London, 1982)

Home Office, *Twenty-Fifth report from the Committee of Public Accounts, Session 1985–86, Prison Building Programme, Home Office Property Services Agency* (London, 1986)

Huntley, Bob, *Bomb Squad, My war against the terrorists* (London, 1977)

Irish voices from English jails, writings of Irish political prisoners in English prisons (London, 1979)

IRSP, *Republican Socialist Programme for Ireland*, pamphlet

Interim Report on the Report of the Independent Commission of Inquiry into the Dublin and Monaghan Bombings (Dublin, 2003)

Jameson, Nicki and Allison, Eric, *Strangeways, 1990, A serious disturbance* (London, 1995)

Johnston, Roy H.W., *Century of Endeavour, A biographical autobiographical view of the Twentieth century in Ireland* (Dublin, 2003)

Jordan, Hugh, *Milestones in murder, Defining moments in Ulster's terror war* (Edinburgh, 2002)

Joyce, Joe and Murtagh, Peter, *The Boss, Charles J Haughey in Government* (Dublin, 1983)

Kee, Robert, *The Green Flag* (London, 1972)

Kee, Robert, *Trial and Error, The Maguires, the Guildford Pub Bombings and British Justice* (London, 1986)

Keenan-Thompson, Tara, *Irish women and street politics, 1956–1973* (Dublin, 2010)

Kennedy-Pipe, Caroline, *The origins of the present Troubles in Northern Ireland* (London, 1997)

Kelleher, Derry, *An open letter to Ian Paisley, demythologizing history* (Wicklow, 1991)

Kelly, Gerry, *The Escape, The inside story of the 1983 escape from Long Kesh prison* ([Belfast], 2013)

Kelly, Paddy, 'No peace without justice' in *Irish Reporter*, No. 21, February 1996, pp. 5–12.

Keogh, Dermot, *Jack Lynch, A biography* (Dublin, 2008)

Kerr, Robert, *Republican Belfast, A political tourists guide* (Belfast, 2008)

Kerr, Michael, *The Destructors, The story of Northern Ireland's lost peace process* (Dublin, 2011)

Kerry, Robert, *Three Gaols, Images of Crumlin Road, Long Kesh and Armagh Prison* (Belfast, 2011)

Kerrigan, Gene, *Hard cases, True stories of Irish crime* (Dublin, 1996)

Kilmichael and Crossbarry Commemoration Committee, *The wild heather glen, The Kilmichael story of grief and glory*, New edition (Cork, 2005)

King, Roy D. and Elliott, Kenneth W., *Albany: birth of a prison-end of an era* (London, 1977)

King, Roy D. and Resondihardjo, Sandra L., 'To max or not to max: Dealing with high risk prisoners in the Netherlands and England and Wales' in *Punishment and Society*, 2010, Vol. 12, p. 69

Larkin, Paul, *A very British jihad, Collusion, conspiracy and cover-up in Northern Ireland* (Belfast, 2004)

Lawlor, Catriona (ed), *Sean MacBride, That day's struggle, A memoir 1904–1951* (Dublin, 2005)

Liebling, Alison, 'Prison Officers, Policing and the Use of Discretion' in *Theoretical Criminology*, 2000, Vol. 4, p. 341.

Louis Leonard Sinn Féin Cumann, *The 'Pitchfork' murders, Uncovering the cover-up* (Fermanagh, 2012)

Livadas, Vias, *Cypriot and Irish political prisoners held in British prisons, 1956–1959* (Nicosia, 2008)

Mac Eoin, Uinseann, *Harry, The story of Harry White* (Dublin, 1985)

Mac Eoin, Uinseann, *The IRA in the twilight years, 1923–1948* (Dublin, 1997)

McElrath, Karen, *Unsafe haven, The United States, the IRA and political prisoners* (London, 2000)

McGeough, Gerry, *The ambush and other stories, A selection of prison writing by Irish Republican Gerry McGeough* (USA, 1996)

McManus, Sean Fr, *My American Struggle for justice in Northern Ireland* (Cork, 2011)

MacSwiney Brugha, Maire, *History's daughter, A memoir from the only child of Terence MacSwiney* (Dublin, 2005)

Maguire, Ann (with Jim Gallagher), *Why my? One woman's fight for justice and dignity* (London, 1994)

Maguire, John, *IRA internments and the Irish government, subversives and the state, 1939–1962* (Dublin, 2008)

Maguire, Mike et al (eds.) *Accountability and prisons: opening up a closed world* (London, 1985)

Martin, David, *The Case of the Belfast Ten,* (London, 1973)

Mahon, Tom and Gillogly, James J, *Decoding the IRA* (Cork, 2008)

Mansfield, Michael, *Presumed Guilty, the British legal system exposed* (London, 1993)

Mansfield, Michael, *Memoirs of a radical lawyer* (London, 2009)

Martin, David, *The case of the Belfast Ten, A Free Ireland pamphlet* (London, 1973)

Martin, David and Rose-Smith, Brian *The case of the Irish political hostages* (London, 1974)

Mason O'Connor, Kristine, *Joan Maynard, Passionate Socialist* (London, 2003)

McIntyre, Ben, *Agent Zigzag, A true story of Nazi espionage, love, and betrayal*, American Edition (New York, 2007)

McLaughlin, Raymond, *Inside and English jail, The prison diary of the IRA Volunteer Raymond MacLaughlin* (Dublin, 1987

McEvoy, Kieran, *Paramilitary imprisonment in Northern Ireland, Resistance, management and release* (Oxford, 2001)

McGarry, Patsy, *While justice slept, The true story of Nicky Kelly and the Sallins train robbery* (Dublin, 2006)

McGladdery, Gary, *The Provisional IRA in England, The bombing campaign 1973–1997* (Dublin, 2006)

McGuffin, John, *The Guineapigs* (London, 1974)

McIlkenny, Richard *Behind the bars I have learned again to pray* (Dublin, 1990)

McKeown, Laurence, *Out of Time, Irish Republican Prisoners, Long Kesh, 1972–2000* (Belfast, 2001)

McManus, Fr. Sean, *My American struggle for justice in Northern Ireland* (Cork, 2011)

McVeigh, Jim, *Tom Williams and the IRA* (Belfast, 1999)

Michael Gaughan, prepared to fight or die (Dublin, 2009)

Monaghan, James, *Colombia Jail Journal, The compelling, exclusive inside story of the Colombia Three* (Dublin, 2007)

Montgomery Hyde, H, *George Blake, Superspy* (London, 1987)

Morrison, Danny, *All the dead voices* (Cork, 2002)

Mountbatten, Earl, *Report of the Inquiry into prison escapes and security* (London, 1966)

Moysey, Stephen, *The road to Balcombe Street, The IRA reign of terror in London* (London, 2007)

Mullan, Don, *The Dublin & Monaghan bombings, The truth, The questions and the victims stories* (Dublin, 2000)

Murphy, Brendan and Kelters, Seamus, *Eyewitness, Four decades of Northern life* (Dublin, 2003)

Murray, Raymond, *The SAS in Ireland* (Dublin, 1990)

Murray, Raymond, *Hard time, Armagh Gaol 1971–1986* (Cork, 1998)

Murray, Raymond, *State violence, Northern Ireland, 1969–1997* (Dublin, 1998)

O'Bradaigh, Ruairi, *Our people, our future, what Eire Nua means* (Dublin, 1973)

O'Brien, Brendan, *The long war, The IRA and Sinn Féin, 1985 to today* (Dublin, 1993)

O'Brien, Justin, *Killing Finucane, Murder in the defence of the realm* (Dublin, 2005)

O'Brien, Justin, *The Arms Trial* (Dublin, 2000)

O'Connor, Kevin, *Blake and Bourke & The end of empires* (London, 2003)

O'Doherty, Malachi, *The telling year, Belfast 1972* (Dublin, 2007)

O'Doherty, Shane, *The Volunteer, A former IRA man's true story* (London, 1993)

O'Donnell, Ruan, *Special Category, The IRA in English prisons*, Volume One (Dublin and Portland, 2012)

O'Dowd, Niall, *An Irish Voice* (Dublin, 2010)

O'Dwyer, Paul, *Counsel for the Defense, The autobiography of Paul O'Dwyer* (New York, 1979)

O Fearghaill, Sean Og, *Law (?) and Orders, The Belfast 'Curfew' of 3–5 July 1970* (Dundalk, 1970).

O'Hagan, Des, *Letters from Long Kesh* (Dublin, 2012)

[Official] Sinn Féin Ard Fheis Report, 1973 (Dublin, 1973)

O'Hearn, Denis, *Nothing but an unfinished story, Bobby Sands, The Irish hunger striker who ignited a generation* (New York, 2006)

O'Mahoney, Brendan with McGovern, Mick, *Soldier of the Queen* (Kerry, 2000)

O'Mahoney, Sean, *Frongoch, University of Revolution*, (Dublin, 1987)

O'Malley, Padraig, *Biting at the grave, The Irish hunger strikes and the politics of despair* (Boston, 1990)

Oppenheimer, A. R., *IRA, The bombs and the bullets, A history of deadly ingenuity* (Dublin, 2009)

O'Reilly (ed), Dermot, *Accepting the challenge, The memoirs of Michael Flannery* (Dublin, 2001)

O Suilleabhain, Diarmaid, *Towards Ireland Britless, A personal view* (Dublin, 1978)

Owen, Tim, 'Prison Law: 1' in *Legal Action*, January 1987, pp. 10–11.

Parker, John, *Death of a hero, Captain Robert Nairac, GC and the undercover war in Northern Ireland* (London, 1999)

Parker, Norman, *The complete Parkhurst tales* (London, 2006)

Pilmot, Ben, *Harold Wilson* (London, 1992)

Plotnikoff, Joyce, *Prison Rules, A working guide*, Revised edition (London, 1988)

PROP, *Don't mark his face: Hull prison riot 1976* (London, 1979)

Prisoners of Partition, H-Block/ Armagh, A Peoples Democracy pamphlet ([Belfast], nd)

Quinn, Raymond, *The Rising of the Phoenix, The creation of the Provisional IRA, The historic battle of St. Matthew's, The Falls Road curfew*, 2nd edition (Belfast, 2007)

Reed, David and Adamson, Olivia, *Miners Strike, 1984–1985, People versus the state* (London, 1985)

Reed, David, *Ireland: The key to the British Revolution* (London, 1984)

Relatives for Justice, *New Lodge Killings, 40th year anniversary*, pamphlet (Belfast, 2013)

Report of an Inquiry by the Chief Inspector of the Prison Service into the cause and circumstances of the events at H.M. Prison Hull during the period 31st August to 3rd September 1976 (London, 1977)

Report of the Independent Public Inquiry into Abuse and Torture of Irish Prisoners, pamphlet (Dublin, 1978)

Report of the Commissioner of Police of the Metropolis for the year 1978 (London, 1979)

Report of the work of the Prison Department, 1978 (London, 1979)

Report on the work of the Prison Department, 1980 (London, 1981)

Report on the administration of the Prison Service, 1980 (London, 1981)

Report of Her Majesty's Chief Inspector of Prisons for England and Wales, 1981 (London, 1982)

Report of Her Majesty's Chief Inspector of Prisons, 1983 (London, 1984)

Report on the work of the Prison Department, 1984/85 (London, 1985)

Report of the Committee on the Prison Disciplinary System, 2 vols (London, 1985)

Rees, Merlyn, *Northern Ireland, A personal perspective* (London, 1985)

Renwick, Aly, *Hidden wounds, The problems of Northern Ireland veterans in civvy street* (London, 1999)

Revolutionary Communist Group, *The road to communism in Britain, Manifesto of the Revolutionary Communist Group* (London, 1984)

Richardson, Eddie, *The last word, my life as a gangster boss* (London, 2005)

Rolston, Bill and Miller, David (eds.) *War and words, The Northern Ireland media reader*, (Belfast, 1996)

Ryan, Meda, *Tom Barry, IRA freedom fighter* (Cork, 2003)

Ryan, Mick, *The politics of penal reform* (London, 1983)

Ryder, Chris, *Fighting Fitt* (Dublin, 2006)

Ryder, Chris, *Inside the Maze, The untold story of the Northern Ireland Prison Service* (London, 2000)

Sands, Bobby, *Skylark sing your lonely song, An anthology of the writings of Bobby Sands* (Dublin and Cork, 1982)

Scott, GD and Gendreau, Paul, 'Psychiatric implications of sensory deprivation in a maximum security prison' in *Canadian Psychiatric Association Journal*, Vol. 14, no. 4, pp. 330–38.

Seamus Costello, 1939–1977, Irish Republican Socialist (Dublin, [1979])

Shaw, Roy (with Kate Kray), *Prettyboy* (London, 1999)

Sheehy, Kevin, *More questions than answers, Reflections on a life in the RUC* (Dublin, 2008)

Sim, Joe, *Medical power in prisons-The Prison Medical Service in England* (London, 1990)

Simpson, Alan, *Murder madness, True crimes of the Troubles* (Dublin, 1999)

Sinn Féin, *'"We live in our areas, our people know us", Interviews with Provisional Sinn Féin'*, pamphlet (London, 1981)

Sinn Féin, *This baby is being body-searched in Armagh …*, pamphlet ([1984])

Sinn Féin, *2014 Le Cheile*, programme (Dublin, 2014)

Sorohan, Sean, *Irish London during the Troubles* (Dublin, 2012)

Smith, Richard, 'Deaths in prison' in *British Medical Journal*, vol. 288, January 1984

Smullen, Eamonn, 'Peace' in *Teoiric, Theoretical & Discussion Journal of Sinn Féin the Worker's Party*, Winter 1977–78, pp. 19–29.

Statement from the Relatives of the Nine Irish Men and Women Seeking Political Status and Transfer to Prisons in Northern Ireland, 27 November 1973

Swan, Sean, *Official Irish republicanism, 1962 to 1972* (USA, 2007)

Sweetman, Rosita, *On our knees, Ireland 1972* (London, 1972)

Taylor, Maxwell and Quayle, Ethel, *Terrorist lives* (London, 1994)

Thatcher, Margaret, *The Downing Street years* (London, 1993)

The Last Post, New edition (New York, 1986)

Tirghra, Ireland's patriot dead (2002)

Tomlinson, Ricky, *Ricky* (London, 2004)

Toolis, Kevin, *Rebel Hearts, Journeys within the IRA's soul* (London, 1995)

Treacy, Matt, *The Communist Party of Ireland, 1921–2011, Volume 1: 1921–1969* (Dublin, 2012)

Trials by ordeal, Irish political prisoners and English law (London, [1994])

Troops Out Movement, *The British media and Ireland, Truth: The first casualty*, pamphlet ([London, 1979])

Thomas, JE and Pooley, R., *The exploding prison* (London, 1980)

Thompson, Tony, *Gangs, A journey into the heart of the British underworld* (London, 2004)

Van Der Bijl, *Operation Banner, The British Army in Northern Ireland* (Barnsley, 2009)

Wakefield, Doug, *A thousand days in solitary* (London, 1990)

Walker, RK, *The Hunger Strikers* (Belfast, 2006)

Walmsley, Roy, *Special Security Units, Home Office Research Study 109* (London, 1989)

Walsh, Dermot, *Bloody Sunday and the rule of law in Northern Ireland* (Dublin, 2000)

Walsh, Pat, *Irish Republicanism and Socialism, The politics of the Republican Movement 1905 to 1994* (Belfast, 1994)

Walsh, Liz, *The final beat, Gardai killed in the line of duty* (Dublin, 2001)

White, Robert W., *Ruairi O'Bradaigh, The life and politics of an Irish Revolutionary* (Indiana, 2006)

White-Spunner, Barney, *Horse Guards* (London, 2006)

Wilson, Edward, *Sociobiology: The New Synthesis* (New York, 1975)

Workers Power, *The British Left and the Irish War* (London, 1983)

Wright, Martin, *Making Good: prisons, punishment and beyond* (London, 1982)

Zeeman, EC, 'Catastrophe Theory' in *Scientific American*, April 1976, pp. 65–83

Zellick, Graham, 'The Hull prison riot' in *British journal of criminology*, Vol. 18, No. 1, January 1978

Index